Mastering Turbo Debugger®

Mastering Turbo Debugger®

Tom Swan

HAYDEN BOOKS

A Division of Macmillan Computer Publishing

11711 North College, Carmel, Indiana 46032 USA

International Standard Book Number: 0-672-48454-4
Library of Congress Catalog Card Number: 90-61921

Acquisitions Editor: *Linda Sanning*
Manuscript Editor: *Sara Black*
Production Editor: *Kathy Grider-Carlyle*
Production Coordinator: *Steve Noe*
Cover Concept and Art Direction: *Dan Armstrong*
Compositor: *Cromer Graphics*
Illustrator: *Don Clemons*
Production Assistance: *T. R. Emrick, Tami Hughes, Bill Hurley, Chuck Hutchinson, Betty Kish, Bob LaRoche, Diana Moore, Bruce Steed, Mary Beth Wakefield*
Indexer: *Sharon Hilgenberg*
Technical Reviewer: *Rick Naro*

Printed in the United States of America

To my mother Mary P. Swan and my father Reyer O. Swan,
the beekeepers!

To my mother Mary P. Swan and my father Reyer O. Swan,
the beekeepers!

Overview

Contents

4   Windows, Menus, and Hot Keys   *71*

6   Using TD's Utility Programs   *177*

9   Evaluating Expressions

10   Common C Bugs

11   Hands-On Debugging for C   *279*

12 Common Pascal Bugs

13   Hands-On Debugging for Pascal   *345*

14 Common Assembly Language Bugs   377

19   Debugging Resident Programs   *483*

Part 4 Data-Structure Guides

20 C and C++ Data Structures

Bibliography   585

Index   587

Preface

ALL PROGRAMS have bugs. You've heard it said, but is it true? Maybe not, although it does seem that few programmers write bug-free code on the first try. Any sizable program is bound to catch a few snags at some stage in its development.

The trick, of course, is to find and fix the bugs before others see them. But, despite what you may have heard or read elsewhere, debugging is not an obscure ritual that only programming wizards can possibly master. Debugging is a skill—one that all programmers can learn how to perform successfully and with a minimum of fuss and frustration.

With that thought in mind, over a year ago, I began writing *Mastering Turbo Debugger*. Originally, I meant to focus on two themes: First, how to use *Turbo Debugger* to debug MS-DOS programs in C, Pascal, and assembly language; and, second, how to combine that practical knowledge with the elements of a good debugging style.

While researching that second theme, however, I ran into an unexpected stumbling block. To my surprise, I found that very little had been written about how to acquire useful debugging skills, or even about what those skills are. Of the few books and articles that mention debugging, most do so only in passing. ("While debugging, watch out for uninitialized pointers. They can bite."). I knew that already—I wanted to learn how to bite back!

Resigned to getting little help from currently published material, I discarded two earlier rough-draft manuscripts and started over from scratch. Little by little, ideas took form and the chapters fell into place. By drawing on my own experiences with debugging and programming, by reading between the lines in the very few references that treat debugging seriously, and by sharing ideas with friends and colleagues, I was able to assemble a collection of practical advice about debugging that I hope will make it easier for others to identify and stamp out bugs.

Now that the book is done, and I'm finally typing these last few words, I can say truthfully that writing *Mastering Turbo Debugger* has been a remarkable learning experience for me. When I began writing the book, I thought that I knew what debugging was "all about." But I soon discovered that what I *didn't* know could, well, fill a book. So, here is that book. May it serve your own debugging efforts well.

TOM SWAN

Note: The complete *Turbo Debugger and Tools* package from Borland includes three products: *Turbo Debugger 2.0*, *Turbo Assembler 2.0*, and *Turbo Profiler 1.0*. This book covers *Turbo Debugger 2.0*. For an assembly language tutorial, see my book *Mastering Turbo Assembler*, Howard W. Sams, 1989. *Mastering Turbo Debugger* does not cover *Turbo Profiler*. Profiling is a subject that demands more than a glossing over in a chapter or two—and for that reason, this book concentrates on its defined goal: explaining how to use *Turbo Debugger* as a tool for developing useful debugging strategies. Will there be a *Mastering Turbo Profiler*? Let me turn the question back to you. Would you find such a book to be useful? If so, let me know by writing to me in care of Howard W. Sams, 11711 N. College Ave., Carmel, IN 46032.

Acknowledgments

THIS BOOK would not exist without the efforts of the following people. To all of you: Please accept my sincere thanks and appreciation for your time, your patience, and your expertise.

To everyone at Howard W. Sams, especially Sara Black, Kathy Grider-Carlyle, Chuck Hutchinson, Betty Kish, Jennifer Matthews, San Dee Phillips, Glen Santner, Linda Sanning, Richard Swadley, Ann Taylor, and others who edited and "debugged" the text: Thanks for your painstaking attention to countless details. To Rick Naro at Paradigm Systems, who read the manuscript for technical accuracy: Thank you for your many helpful suggestions. To the Turbo Debugger development team and supporting players at Borland International, including Nan Borreson, Chuck Jazdzewski, Matt Pietrek, Steve Sheridan, Eugene Wang, and Tom Wu: Thank you for answering my questions and for supplying the prerelease software that made it possible for me to write this book. To Turbo Debugger's developers at Purart, especially Chris Williams: Thanks for an excellent debugger. To my correspondents on Borland's Compuserve forums: Thank you for many hours of engaging, informative, and always entertaining conversation. To my friend Ron Borthwick, who knows PC hardware inside and out, thanks for helping more than you realize. And, to my wife and assistant Anne: A special thank you not only for helping with this book, but for being there always.

Trademarks

All terms mentioned in this book that are known to be trademarks or service marks are listed below. In addition, terms suspected of being trademarks or service marks have been appropriately capitalized. SAMS cannot attest to the accuracy of this information. Use of a term in this book should not be regarded as affecting the validity of any trademark or service mark.

386-MAX™ is a trademark of Qualitas, Inc.

BRIEF™ is a trademark of Solutions Systems Company.

DESQview™ is a trademark of Quarterdeck Office Systems.

IBM® PC is a registered trademark of International Business Machines Corporation.

Microsoft® C is a registered trademark of Microsoft Corporation.

Microsoft® Macro Assembler is a registered trademark of Microsoft Corporation.

Microsoft® Windows™ is a registered trademark of Microsoft Corporation.

Microsoft® Windows™/386 is a registered trademark of Microsoft Corporation.

MS-DOS® is a registered trademark of Microsoft Corporation.

Periscope™ II-X is a trademark of The Periscope Co., Inc.

PC-Kwik™ is a trademark of Multisoft Corporation.

PS/2™ is a trademark of International Business Machines Corporation.

SideKick® is a registered trademark of Borland International, Inc.

VEDIT® is a registered trademark of CompuView Products, Inc.

WordStar® is a registered trademark of WordStar International Incorporated.

Part One

Guide and Reference

Chapter 1

Introduction

Most Programmers view debugging as all work and no fun. But that's understandable—instead of finding and fixing bugs, who wouldn't prefer to write new code? Nothing ruins the day like a nasty bug that pops up out of nowhere in a program that seemed to work just fine. Programming is often enjoyable. Debugging is always a grind.

So, I won't promise to make debugging fun. Nobody can do that. Instead, with the help of Borland International's *Turbo Debugger* (TD) 2.0, I aim to demonstrate in this book how you can master the art of debugging, not as a tedious, distasteful chore, but as an interesting challenge, just another part of your normal programming activities. Debugging won't ever be fun. But it can be rewarding when accomplished with patience and skill.

Like all skills, however, improving your ability to find and fix bugs in code will take time. And that's where this book and TD 2.0 come in. In the following chapters, you'll meet every TD command and feature. You'll learn ways to develop useful debugging strategies using TD to find out quickly what's causing your program to misbehave. And, you'll investigate many common bugs in C, Pascal, and assembly language, which will help you to avoid making these same mistakes in your own programs.

In researching the material for this book, I combed language tutorials for debugging tips, I monitored Borland's Compuserve forums, and I took thousands of notes about my own debugging experiences with TD. I spent countless hours using TD 2.0, from its early "alpha" and "beta" tests, to the production version you can purchase today. Along the way, I nearly became bug-eyed looking at buggy code—but I also discovered there was more to the art of debugging than I ever expected to learn.

The result of those efforts is *Mastering Turbo Debugger,* a guide to the art of debugging in C, Pascal, and assembly language and a complete reference to TD's windows, commands, and hot keys. This chapter introduces the book and explains how to get the most from its four parts:

- Part 1 is a *Guide and Reference* to installing and using TD. Read these chapters quickly your first time through for an overview of TD's commands.

- Part 2 explores *The Art of Debugging* from a language point of view. In this part, you'll learn how to develop successful debugging strategies. You'll also follow hands-on demonstrations in C, Pascal, and assembly language to see TD in action as you find and fix several dastardly bugs.

- Part 3 covers *Advanced Debugging Topics,* including macros, keystroke recording, remote and dual-monitor debugging, hardware debugging, TSRs, and device drivers.

- Part 4 closes the book with detailed *Data-Structure Guides,* which show how to use TD to examine simple and complex data structures in C, Pascal, and assembly language. Use this section as a reference for investigating variables in your programs.

You'll also want to cut out one of the keyboard overlays inside the book's back cover. Place the appropriate template on your keyboard for a handy reference to TD's function keys.

Requirements

The following sections list required and optional hardware and software items that you'll need to use the information in this book.

Required Hardware

- Any IBM PC, PS/2, or compatible computer.
- At least 384K of RAM available *after* booting.
- One hard drive or a high-density diskette drive. (A hard drive is recommended—TD 2.0 will not work with standard 360K drives.) Note: You may not be able to run the automated INSTALL program to install TD on a high-density floppy. In that case, you'll have to run the UNZIP utility manually (see chapter 6) to extract files from the .ZIP archives on TD's master diskettes.
- Color or monochrome display.
- Keyboard.

Required Software

- *Turbo Debugger* 2.0. You may be able to get by with an earlier version, but most of the information in this book requires TD version 2.0.

- DOS 2.0 or a later version.

- For Pascal: *Turbo Pascal* (TP) 5.0 or later versions. TP 5.5 or later is required for object-oriented examples. It's possible to debug TP 4.0 programs with TD (see chapter 2), but versions 5.0 or later give better results.

- For C: *Turbo C* (TC) 2.0 or later versions. TC++ 1.0 is required for object-oriented C++ examples.

- For assembly language: *Turbo Assembler* (TASM) 2.0, supplied with TD. To enter programs, you'll also need a programmer's text editor such as *Brief, Multi-Edit, Epsilon, VEdit,* or Borland's *Sidekick.* Or, you can use any word processor that can save files in plain ASCII format.

- You may also use *Microsoft C* (MSC), *Microsoft Macro Assembler* (MASM), and other languages as explained in chapter 2. However, you will have to modify some of the program listings before they will compile or assemble with non-Borland language products.

Required Knowledge

- You'll need a fundamental knowledge of C, Pascal, or assembly language programming. The more you know about one or more of these languages, the better you'll be able to use TD and the information in this book.

- You'll also need a working knowledge of DOS commands, batch files, and related topics. A good DOS reference (see Bibliography) is a practical necessity.

Optional Hardware

- An 80286-based PC and at least 640K of extended memory for debugging in protected mode with the alternate TD286 debugger.

- Or, an 80386- or 80486-based computer for installing the TDH386.SYS device driver, which lets TD use special debugging features available on these processors.

- On 80386- and 80486-based systems, at least 640K of extended memory to use the optional TD386 supervisor for debugging programs and running TD in virtual 8086 machines. (The TDH386.SYS device driver must also be installed.)

- Printer.

- Mouse input device.
- 8087, 80287, or 80387 numeric data processor (NDP).
- Additional expanded memory for large-program debugging.
- EGA or VGA display capable of showing 43 or 50 lines.
- Second PC or compatible computer attached to a host system with a serial cable for remote debugging. Or, separate monochrome and color display adapters for dual-monitor debugging. (See chapter 17.)
- Trapper debugger board for using TD's hardware-breakpoint features (see chapter 18 and Bibliography).

How to Use This Book

If you've never used TD before, it's probably best to read this book from cover to cover. I organized the chapters to introduce debugging concepts and to serve as a reference to TD's commands. If you read the chapters in order, you'll never meet an unexplained term, although, from time to time, I may refer you to other chapters where you can find more information about a topic.

If you're familiar with any version of TD, you may be able to skip the rest of part 1 and start with part 2's discussion of debugging strategies. TD 1.x users should at least skim chapters 4 and 5 in part 1 for descriptions of new features in TD 2.0. Everyone should read chapter 2's instructions about preparing programs for debugging, using a variety of compilers and assemblers.

Chapters 10–15 and 20–22 are devoted to C, Pascal, and assembly language (three chapters each). You can read only the chapters that apply to your favorite language, but you might want to browse through the others for additional debugging tips. Some of the material in these chapters is duplicated, but to avoid too much redundancy, I've tried to concentrate on tips that apply uniquely to each language.

Scan the following chapter summaries for a closer look at the book's contents. If you don't want to read these descriptions now, turn to the next section, "Listings," and read the remainder of this chapter for several important details that will help you to get the most from this book.

About the Chapters

The following brief descriptions explain the contents of *Mastering Turbo Debugger*'s chapters. Read this information for an overview of the book's contents.

Part 1: Guide and Reference

- Chapter 1, "Introduction," lists requirements and explains how to use this book effectively.

- Chapter 2, "Preparing Programs for Debugging," details how to prepare C, Pascal, and assembly language programs for debugging, using a variety of language products.

- Chapter 3, "Getting Turbo Debugger Up and Running," shows how to install, configure, and run TD. The chapter also covers TD's command-line options.

- Chapter 4, "Windows, Menus, and Hot Keys," is a guide to most of TD's commands and keys. Read this chapter for general information about using windows, dialog boxes, the keyboard, and a mouse.

- Chapter 5, "Views and Local Commands," covers the commands in TD's **View** menu. The chapter is a reference to TD's main features—those you will use most frequently during debugging sessions.

- Chapter 6, "Using TD's Utility Programs," describes miscellaneous utilities such as TDMAP and TDSTRIP, which are supplied with TD. Just browse through this chapter at first so you'll know where to find specific facts as you need them.

Part 2: The Art of Debugging

- Chapter 7, "Developing a Debugging Strategy," discusses approaches to debugging, using TD as the primary weapon in your arsenal. Read this chapter for tips about developing a good debugging style.

- Chapter 8, "Breakpoints and Code Tracing," details the finer points of these powerful debugging tools, two of TD's most important features.

- Chapter 9, "Evaluating Expressions," documents TD's expression-handling abilities in C, Pascal, and assembly language. Read this chapter for tips on entering expressions and to learn how to use expression side effects to call C and Pascal routines out of context from the rest of a program loaded into TD.

- Chapter 10, "Common C Bugs," lists bugs that often plague C code. Use this chapter as a guide to avoid making typical errors in your C programs.

- Chapter 11, "Hands-On Debugging for C," is the first of three chapters that include a medium-size program with several documented bugs. Step-by-step, hands-on demonstrations show TD in action as you enter commands to track down bugs in a *Turbo C* program. You can also use this chapter and the similar chapters 13 and 15 for Pascal and assembly language as self tests of your debugging skills.

- Chapter 12, "Common Pascal Bugs," lists bugs that typically appear in Pascal programs.

- Chapter 13, "Hands-On Debugging for Pascal," is similar to chapter 11 but contains information for *Turbo Pascal* programmers. Despite the similarities, however, the program listing and bugs in this chapter are different from those in chapter 11; therefore, you can read either chapter without spoiling the plot in the other.

- Chapter 14, "Common Assembly Language Bugs," lists bugs that are both common and unique to assembly language.

- Chapter 15, "Hands-On Debugging for Assembly Language," is similar to chapters 11 and 13 but contains information for *Turbo Assembler* programmers. As in chapter 13, the program listing and bugs in this chapter are different from the ones in the other two. You can follow the hands-on debugging demonstrations in this chapter and take the self tests even after you've solved the other chapters' "whodunits."

Part 3: Advanced Debugging Topics

- Chapter 16, "Macros and Keystroke Recording," shows how to use these advanced TD features to create your own commands, to automate parts of a debugging session, and to replay recorded keystrokes, useful for designing repeatable test procedures. Several sample macros are listed for C, Pascal, and assembly language.

- Chapter 17, "Remote and Dual-Monitor Debugging," explains how to take advantage of two computers connected with a serial cable or two display adapters in one system. With these setups, output from TD and the target program appear on separate monitors, simplifying debugging of graphics applications and other display-oriented programs.

- Chapter 18, "Hardware-Assisted Debugging," discusses in detail extra features available for 80386- and 80486-based systems. The chapter shows how to install and use a Trapper debugging board to take advantage of TD's advanced hardware-breakpoint abilities.

- Chapter 19, "Debugging Resident Programs," tours the byways of TSR and device-driver debugging, using TD's new resident commands.

Part 4: Data-Structure Guides

- Chapter 20, "C and C++ Data Structures," lists common C data types and shows how to use TD to inspect them. Use this and the next two chapters as guides for examining variables in your own programs.

- Chapter 21, "Pascal Data Structures," lists common Pascal data types and shows how to use TD to inspect them.
- Chapter 22, "Assembly Language Data Structures," lists common assembly language data types and shows how to use TD to inspect them.

Listings

Many of the C, Pascal, and assembly language listings in this book are printed with line numbers for reference. When entering the listings into your editor, type only the text that follows the reference numbers and colons along the left border.

Unlike many of my books, this one does *not* include an offer to sell the program listings on disk. There are several reasons for this. For one, many of the programs in this book have bugs, and I'm reluctant to offer for sale programs that don't work! For another, this book does not teach you how to program, and, therefore, most of the program listings are short fragments that illustrate various principles. You can understand most of these examples just by reading them.

However, the hands-on demonstrations in chapters 11, 13, and 15, do require you to enter three sizeable programs (about 400 lines each). I suggest you bite the bullet and type them into your editor. But if you don't have time to do that, you can download the listings from Borland's Compuserve forum. To join, type **GO BOR** at any Compuserve main prompt and follow directions. Then, search the Turbo Debugger section library for the keyword MTD (for *Mastering Turbo Debugger*). You may also find these same listings on an electronic bulletin board. (If you manage a BBS, feel free to place the files on your service—with the bugs intact, please.)

Keyboard Keys

Angle brackets surround references to named keys—for example, ⟨F1⟩, ⟨Ctrl⟩, and ⟨Alt⟩. F1 without brackets means to type an F followed by 1. With the brackets, ⟨F1⟩ means to press the function key labeled "F1." (By the way, this is the same style used by *PC World* magazine.)

A dash between keys or characters means you should press the first key and hold it down while you press the second. For example, ⟨Alt⟩-⟨F5⟩ means to press ⟨Alt⟩, hold it down, and press ⟨F5⟩. ⟨Ctrl⟩-C means to press and hold ⟨Ctrl⟩ while you press C. (Even though character keys are printed in uppercase, you don't have to press ⟨Shift⟩ unless instructed to do so.) When two keys are printed together without a dash as in ⟨Esc⟩X, this means to press and *release* ⟨Esc⟩, and then to press X.

The two forms are often combined. For example, ⟨Alt⟩-XC means to press and hold ⟨Alt⟩, press X, release those two keys, and then press C. The familiar "reboot" sequence ⟨Ctrl⟩-⟨Alt⟩-⟨Del⟩ means to press and hold ⟨Ctrl⟩, press and hold ⟨Alt⟩, press ⟨Del⟩, and then release all three keys.

Cursor keys are named ⟨Cursor Up⟩, ⟨Cursor Down⟩, ⟨Cursor Left⟩, and ⟨Cursor Right⟩. Other keys such as ⟨Page Up⟩ and ⟨Insert⟩ are spelled as they appear on most extended keyboards (the ones with function keys along the top row). On other keyboards, these keys may be abbreviated, for example, as ⟨PgUp⟩ and ⟨Ins⟩.

Text Styles

Many computer books adopt a gaggle of text styles: one for key words, one for input, one for output, one for listings, and so on. This book follows a simpler (and, I think, less confusing) three-way design:

- Language key words, listings, and items such as menu names and option settings that you see on screen are printed in `monospace`. Text that you enter at the DOS prompt to compile, link, and run various utility programs is printed in this same style, matching the way these lines appear on your display.

- In paragraphs, keys that you are to press and entries that you are to make are printed in **bold**.

- Important passages, new terms, plus book, product, and other titles are printed in attention-getting *italic*. Program abbreviations such as TD, TP, and MSC are not italicized.

Colons (:) separate multiple commands. To save space, command names followed by a three-dot ellipsis on screen do not include that symbol, which indicates that choosing the command opens a dialog window for selecting options (see chapter 4). For instance, the `Module...` command in the `View` menu is printed here as `View:Module`.

You may enter DOS and most other commands in upper- or lowercase as you prefer. However, be aware that some option letters for selecting various program features may be case-sensitive—for example, -s and -S might have different meanings. Commands are printed in this book in lowercase except when uppercase is significant.

File Names

Casual references to file names and DOS commands are in uppercase—for example, DIR and TD.EXE. When they refer to something you should enter, these same names are in lowercase (because that's how you'll type them) and are printed in bold. For example, you may see a sentence such as: "Enter **cd \ td** to switch to the \ TD directory, using the DOS CD command."

Program names include the file-name extension only when they refer to that file as listed in a DOS directory. For example, TDMAP.EXE is the *file name* for the TDMAP *program.* I may also tell you to enter the **tdmap** *command* at the DOS prompt to run TDMAP. The lowercase and bold **tdmap** indicates that this is something you can enter.

Where to Go from Here

Read chapter 2 next for instructions about preparing programs for debugging. If you already know how to do that, turn to chapter 3 to get TD up and running.

Summary

Debugging is no fun, but it can be challenging, as this book attempts to show. If you're new to TD, read all chapters from cover to cover. Or, if you have some debugging experience, start with part 2 and turn to the other chapters as you need them.

This introduction to *Mastering Turbo Debugger* explains several important details that will help you to get the most from the book. It also lists required hardware and software that you'll need in order to use the information that follows.

Chapter 2

Preparing Programs for Debugging

A SENSE OF DIRECTION isn't one of my better skills—when traveling without a map, I'm lucky to find my way home. To find its way around programs, TD needs a different sort of map, one that charts the symbols, line numbers, and other landmarks in compiled code. Collectively known as the *symbol table,* this detailed mapping of a program's parts and pieces lets TD relate machine-code instructions and raw binary data to source-code lines, variables, and other structures in the program's high-level language (HLL), usually, C, Pascal, or assembly.

The symbol table in a compiled or assembled program makes it possible for TD to execute binary code while displaying statements and data structures from the program's text. Rather than forcing you to pick apart machine-code instructions and hunt through data segments looking for variables—as you must, for example, with DOS DEBUG—the symbol table simplifies debugging by letting you focus on data structures and statements in their more familiar (and more readable) source-code forms. This is why TD is known as a *symbolic debugger.* It uses symbolic information in compiled code to let you debug programs on the source-code level.

But compiled code straight from the compiler lacks the symbolic information that TD requires. So, the first step in preparing programs for debugging is to give the compiler and linker special commands that add symbols and line numbers to the program's compiled result. This chapter explains how to do that for several different compilers and assemblers. It's possible to use TD to examine code that doesn't have a symbol table, but in that event, you'll see only the disassembled machine code. You won't be able to view variables by name or trace C, Pascal, and assembly language statements.

That same rule applies to all programs, whether composed of one or several modules. In every case, before using TD to debug the code, you must compile or assemble the program with the correct commands to add symbolic information to all the program's parts and pieces. If you don't, TD will show statements and data structures for only the parts that have symbol tables attached. For that reason, when developing new software, it's usually best to add a symbol table every time you compile. This will lengthen compile times somewhat, but when a bug surfaces (and it will, it will), you can then load the program immediately into TD for debugging.

Also, be sure to store the program's original source-code text files in a directory where TD can find them—usually in the current directory or in a path specified with `Options:Path for source`. TD displays the program's lines and data structures directly from these files—the lines you see on TD's display are the same lines you wrote into the program's text.

> In C and Pascal, one line may contain two or more statements. However, because TD is line-oriented, not statement-oriented, many debugger commands work best when there is only one statement per line. Try to follow this one-statement-per-line design rule in your own programs. You'll find TD easier to use, and you may also discover that your program's logic is clearer and, therefore, easier to debug.

When TD searches for source-code files, it looks in various directories in this order:

- The directory from which the compiler or assembler reads the original source-code files.
- One or more directory path names listed in `Options:Path for source` or specified with the -sd option (see chapter 3).
- The current directory.
- The same directory where the .EXE, .COM, or other file loaded into TD is located.

How To Use This Chapter

The information in this chapter will help you to determine the proper commands to use with your compiler and assembler to add symbol tables to compiled and assembled code. Three main sections—one each for C, Pascal, and assembly language—include detailed instructions for building programs with various languages listed alphabetically by product (not company) name. As these instructions demonstrate, you can use TD to debug programs written with just about any language that can generate Microsoft *CodeView* symbols or a .MAP text file. You don't have to use a Borland language to take advantage of TD's features.

Each main section in this chapter also includes a small sample program that you can use to test your compiler and linker. After reading the section that applies to your language, enter the sample program and try out the instructions for compiling and loading the result into TD. Then turn to chapter 3, "Getting Turbo Debugger Up and Running," to begin learning your way around TD's windows and commands.

The Design-Compile-Debug Cycle

Many programmers use a debugger as a last-ditch attempt to investigate why a program isn't working as expected. In fact, until I became more familiar with TD, I was a proud member of the I-hate-to-debug club. But now I use TD as an everyday programming tool to examine the inner secrets of my code—not just to track down bugs.

After a year or so of working with TD, my programming habits have settled into a design, compile, and debug cycle, illustrated in Figure 2.1. Use the diagram as a guide to the steps required to compile and link programs for debugging. As the figure shows, although there are many ways to prepare programs for TD, the goal is always the same: to transfer a symbol table (represented by a boxed-in S) from the compiler's output to the executable code file or to store the symbols separately in a .TDS (*Turbo Debugger Symbol*) file. Either way, TD can then load the program and use the symbols for debugging on the source-code level. Figure 2.1 also lists typical files identified by file-name extensions such as .PAS, .C, and .OBJ, generated at each stage in the process of preparing programs for debugging. Chapter 6 describes how to use the utility programs, such as TDMAP and TDSTRIP, mentioned in Figure 2.1.

Compiler Updates

Sometimes it seems that software manufacturers release new compiler versions faster than rabbits make bunnies. Although I've used the most recent versions of compilers available to me, in a few months after this book is printed, some of the information here may become obsolete. If your compiler or assembler isn't listed, or if the instructions in this chapter don't work for other versions, try these suggestions:

- Use the commands for the previous release. If they don't work, you may find a note in your language manuals that explains a change to a command-line option used here.

- Read the instructions for a similar product (e.g., another C compiler). This may give you enough hints to get started.

- Look in your manuals for information about how to add *CodeView* debugging information to compiled and assembled code. Also read the notes in

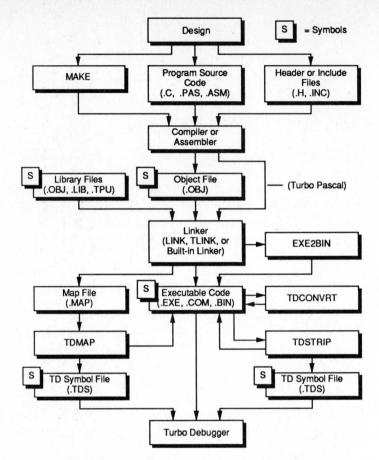

Figure 2.1.   Preparing programs for debugging.

this chapter for compiling *Microsoft C* programs and converting their *CodeView* symbol tables to TD's format by running the TD utility program TDCONVRT (see chapter 6).

• Read "Compiling Other Programs for Debugging" near the end of this chapter. If your language can create a standard .MAP file, you can debug the code with TD, but with some limitations—for example, all data structures will be represented as arrays of bytes or words.

> The following sections assume that you've installed your compiler or assembler according to the manufacturer's instructions, set required environment variables, and included necessary directories in a DOS PATH statement. Before trying out the commands in this chapter, be sure that you can compile, link, and run a small test program.

Managing Object Libraries with TLIB

Be sure to use the TLIB program that comes with TD (on one of the *Turbo Assembler* disks) to add object-code files to library files. Older versions of TLIB strip symbol tables from .OBJ files, making it impossible to view the source-code for those files in TD's Module window.

Before debugging programs linked to files in libraries, you may have to recompile each object-code file and rebuild the library files with the new TLIB.

Compiling C and C++ Programs for Debugging

C programmers all have their favorite MS-DOS compilers, and there are so many good C-language products to choose from, it's impossible to cover them all here. For this section, therefore, I've tried to select compilers from the mainstream—the ones against which most others compete. Even if your compiler isn't listed, you may be able to use commands similar to those in this section.

Sample C Program

Listing 2.1, SAMPLE.C, is a short C program that you can use to test the commands in this section. The program displays command-line arguments in reverse order. For example, after compiling and linking SAMPLE, typing **sample arg1 arg2 arg3** from DOS displays:

```
Argument #3 : arg3
Argument #2 : arg2
Argument #1 : arg1
```

Listing 2.1.   SAMPLE.C.

```
 1:  /*
 2:  **     Test C program
 3:  */
 4:
 5:  #include <stdio.h>
 6:
 7:  main(int argc, char *argv[])
 8:  {
 9:     while (--argc > 0)
10:        printf("Argument #%d : %s\n", argc, argv[argc]);
11:     exit(0);
12:  }
```

Some compilers do not allow typed parameters in function declarations, as used here in Listing 2.1 at line 7. In that case, try the alternative old-style program in Listing 2.2, SAMPLE2.C, and substitute SAMPLE2 for SAMPLE elsewhere in this chapter.

Listing 2.2.   SAMPLE2.C.

```
 1:  /*
 2:  **      Test C program (old-style)
 3:  */
 4:
 5:  #include <stdio.h>
 6:
 7:  main(argc,argv,envp)
 8:  int argc;
 9:  char *argv[];
10:  char *envp[];
11:  {
12:      while (--argc > 0)
13:          printf("Argument #%d : %s\n", argc, argv[argc]);
14:      exit(0);
15:  }
```

Lattice C 3.3

Lattice C (LC) represents the "unusual" category of C compilers in this chapter. That's not to detract from the quality of this product—LC is a very capable compiler for MS-DOS and OS/2 programming, and it's well regarded among programmers. But the steps required to prepare LC programs for debugging with TD require the most finagling, and similar steps may be necessary for other non-Microsoft and non-Borland compilers. So, if you can't get TD to recognize your code, these tips may help.

First, you must compile and link your program modules separately. LC 3.3 uses the *Microsoft Overlay Linker* version 3.64, but it can't give the necessary commands to create a .MAP file in the form that TD requires. Luckily, though, it can put basic debugging information in the .OBJ file, so that's the first step. For example, to compile SAMPLE.C to SAMPLE.OBJ, use the command:

```
lc -d sample
```

The -d option inserts line number information into SAMPLE.OBJ. (You might also try -d1 or -d2, which are supposed to insert other symbols and data-type information as well as line numbers. But my tests indicate these alternate options do not affect TD's ability to view LC source code.)

Next, link the .OBJ file to the appropriate LC libraries. The key here is to give the commands needed to create a .MAP file with line numbers and other symbols intact. For the small memory model, this command is:

```
link /NOIGNORECASE /LINENUMBERS /MAP
c:\lc\s\c.obj+sample.obj,sample,sample/M,
c:\lc\s\lc+c:\lc\lapi.lib;
```

Type all of that on one line, or better, insert it into a batch file named
LCL.BAT (or another name), and then type **lcl** to link. You may have to use the
correct path names for your libraries in place of the names listed here. But, to
avoid hunting through manuals looking for those and other details, you can use
the compiler to generate the correct information. For example, enter **lc -L
sample**. Then, use the text in the resulting SAMPLE.LNK file to create LCL.BAT.
(Before debugging, be sure to recompile the program as explained earlier.)

After compiling and linking, you'll have on disk a file named SAMPLE.MAP,
which TDMAP can use to add TD-format symbols to SAMPLE.EXE. The final
step is to process that file and load the code into TD. To do that, enter the two
commands:

```
tdmap sample.map
td sample
```

That converts and loads SAMPLE.EXE into TD. If you see the `CPU` window
instead of the expected source-code view, choose TD's `View:Module` command,
highlight one of the listed module names, and press ⟨**Enter**⟩. (If the entire
program is in one source-code file, there will be only one name.) After that,
press ⟨**F2**⟩ to set a breakpoint at the first executable statement in the code, then
press ⟨**F9**⟩⟨**F2**⟩ to run the program to that stopping place and remove the
breakpoint. This positions the cursor on the first executable source-code statement and initializes data segment registers so you can view variables in memory. (Later chapters explain more about breakpoints and using TD commands—
these keystrokes will let you begin using TD while you learn about these and
other commands.)

Microsoft C 5.1

To compile a *Microsoft C* (MSC) program contained in a single text file, run the
CL Compiler-Linker executive program with the /Zi option. This adds
CodeView debugging information to the compiled .OBJ code file and automatically runs the linker. Also specify the /Od option to disable optimizations,
which can affect TD's ability to relate source and binary machine code:

```
cl /Zi /Od sample.c
```

The .C file-name extension is required, and the two options /Zi and /Od are
case-sensitive—/zi and /od won't work. The command first compiles SAMPLE.C
to SAMPLE.OBJ and then runs the linker, giving the necessary commands
to link in library modules and transfer *CodeView* debugging information to

SAMPLE.EXE. You can then convert the finished code and load the result into TD by typing:

```
tdconvrt sample.exe
td sample
```

Compiling multimodule programs is equally simple—just give CL all of the program's .C files. Specify the main module first. For example, to compile MAIN.C with submodules SUB1.C and SUB2.C, use the command:

```
cl /Zi /Od main.c sub1.c sub2.c
```

You can then run TDCONVRT on MAIN.EXE as before to convert the *CodeView* information for debugging with TD.

Microsoft C 6.0

Follow the instructions for Microsoft C 5.1 in the previous section. The commands for preparing code are the same for MSC versions 5.1 and 6.0.

QuickC 2.01

The steps to use the Microsoft *QuickC* (QC) command-line compiler for C programs are the same as they are for the compiler's built-in assembler (see "QuickAssembler 2.01" later in this chapter). To compile SAMPLE.C and load the finished code into TD, use the /Zi *CodeView* debugging option (the Z must be in uppercase) and convert the symbols in SAMPLE.EXE to TD's format with TDCONVRT:

```
qcl /Zi sample.c
tdconvrt sample.exe
td sample
```

Be sure to specify the .C and .EXE file-name extensions as shown here. To compile a multimodule program, feed the individual source-code modules to QCL:

```
qcl /Zi main.c sub1.c sub2.c
tdconvrt main.exe
td main
```

Or, you can compile the submodules separately with the /c ("compile-only") and /Zi options and then compile and link the separate .OBJ code modules to the main code file before converting the result with TDCONVRT and loading into TD:

```
qcl /c /Zi sub1.c
qcl /c /Zi sub2.c
qcl /Zi main.c sub1.obj sub2.obj
tdconvrt main.exe
td main
```

Turbo C 2.0 Integrated Environment

Turbo C 2.0's (TC2) integrated environment combines a text editor, C compiler, and a drastically stripped-down version of TD for a complete development system in one package. Although TC2's Integrated Development Environment (IDE) is convenient for entering, compiling, and testing small programs, you'll want to take advantage of features in the stand-alone TD for serious debugging work. This can also free extra memory for debugging large programs.

To continue using the IDE for editing and compiling, but to prepare code for debugging with TD, you'll need to change a few IDE settings. After starting TC2, select Options:Compiler:Code generation. Highlight OBJ debug information and press 〈**Enter**〉 to change this setting to On. Press 〈**Esc**〉, select Optimization, and set Jump optimization to Off. If you don't do this, TD may not be able to relate optimized machine code to the appropriate C statements. Next, open the Debug menu, and change Source debugging to Standalone. When you compile a program, this adds symbolic debugging information to the finished .EXE disk file, preparing the code for loading into TD.

You may want to save these settings in a configuration file. That way, you won't have to make the same modifications every time you start TC2. To do this, select Options:Save options and specify a file name, or press 〈**Enter**〉 to accept the default TCCONFIG.TC.

After setting TC2's options, either manually or by loading a configuration file, you're ready to compile and debug programs. First, load or enter the program text (SAMPLE.C, for example) into TC2's editor and use Compile:Make EXE file to compile the source code to disk. You can also specify a project file according to directions in the *Turbo C User's Guide* for compiling multimodule programs.

If you haven't made any changes to the program recently, instead of compiling, you may see a message that your file "is up to date." In that case, because the compiler skips re-creating the .EXE disk file, it also skips adding debugging information to code that you compiled before under different settings. If that happens, you have several options:

- Delete the program's .EXE and .OBJ files and recompile.
- Make an unimportant change to the source text.
- Use the Compile and Build all commands.

Whatever approach you decide to use, the result is to create an .EXE disk file with the necessary information required to load the program into TD. After compiling, be sure that all .C source files are available to TD. Then, quit TC2 and type **td sample** to begin debugging.

Turbo C 2.0 Command-Line Compiler

Many professional C programmers prefer to use TC2's command-line compiler (TCC) along with a separate text editor for entering and modifying source code. This arrangement frees extra memory for compiling large programs, and it also lets you take advantage of various options and in-line assembly language—features that are not available in the IDE. To compile SAMPLE, use TCC's -v option and load the finished code file into TD:

```
tcc -v sample
td sample
```

Compiling programs stored in multiple source code files is equally simple. For example, if your main program text is stored in MAIN.C, which calls functions in submodules SUB1.C and SUB2.C, create and load MAIN.EXE into TD with the commands:

```
tcc -v main sub1 sub2
td main
```

Another way to handle multimodule programs is to compile individual modules separately with the -c ("compile-only") option, and then use TCC to link the .OBJ files to the finished main code file. Just remember to use the -v option for all steps. Also, be sure to specify the .OBJ file-name extension for SUB1.OBJ and SUB2.OBJ (on the third line below) to avoid recompiling those modules:

```
tcc -v -c sub1.c
tcc -v -c sub2.c
tcc -v main sub1.obj sub2.obj
td main
```

If you store various options in a TURBOC.CFG configuration file, and if one of those options is -O (Optimize jumps), add the option **-o-** to TCC to disable optimizing in all of the previous commands. This will keep the debugger in sync with the `Module` window's source-code display.

Turbo C++ 1.0 Programmer's Platform

The newest version of Borland's *Turbo C* compiler adds C++ object-oriented features, ANSI standard compatibility, and a vastly improved IDE—now named the *Programmer's Platform*. (I'll refer to this version as TC++.) The new IDE includes a stripped version of TD that's suitable for examining small programs and tests. But for debugging larger programs and for finding elusive mistakes, you'll still want to use the full TD 2.0.

As already explained, to use previous TC and TD versions together, you would have to compile a program, quit to DOS, load the result into TD, debug, quit TD, reload TC2's editor, and so on. TC++ changes that endless runaround by letting you transfer control from the IDE to another program, usually TASM or TD. To start debugging after compiling a program, you simply transfer control directly to TD without quitting to DOS. Then, to return to TC++ after debugging, quit TD by pressing ⟨**Alt**⟩-**X**.

Your TC++ installation may already be configured to call TD. To find out if it is, start TC++ (enter **tc** at the DOS prompt) and press ⟨**Alt**⟩-⟨**Space**⟩ (or ⟨**Alt**⟩-**F**⟨**Cursor left**⟩ under Microsoft Windows). If "Turbo Debugger" is listed as a command in TC++'s System menu, your system is configured. Otherwise, follow these steps to transfer to TD for debugging. You can also repeat the same steps to modify the transfer configuration:

1. With TC++ running, press ⟨**Alt**⟩-**OT** and move the highlight bar to a blank line or to an existing transfer-command name that you want to modify. Then, press **E** or click the Edit button to add or change the entry.

2. Enter **Turbo ~Debugger** as the Program Title. The tilde (~) is optional— it enables the following character (D in this case) as the hot key that you can press when the System menu is visible. If you don't want to assign a hot key, don't enter the tilde.

3. In Program Path, enter **td**. This assumes that TD's directory is listed in a PATH statement. If it isn't listed, enter the full path name, for example, **c:\ td**.

4. In Command Line, enter **$EXENAME** to pass the name of the current program to TD for debugging. You can also add additional command-line options such as -k, -r, or -vg (see chapter 3). To have TC++ prompt you for additional arguments before transferring to TD, append **$PROMPT** to the end of the line.

5. Next, select an optional Hot Key assignment from the list at the right of the Modify/New Transfer Item dialog box. You can then press ⟨**Shift**⟩ plus the selected function key to transfer to TD.

6. When you've prepared TC++, select the New or Modify buttons and press **K** (or click the mouse cursor on Ok) to erase the Transfer dialog and accept your changes. Use the Options:Save command to save the configuration for the next time you run TC++.

After following those steps to prepare TC++, you're ready to transfer control directly to TD by pressing the programmed hot keys or by selecting Turbo Debugger from the System menu. Make sure that debugging information is added to the compiled code (press ⟨**Alt**⟩-**OB** and verify that `Source Debugging is On`). Use the `Compile` menu's `Make EXE file` or `Build all` commands to compile and link the program. Then, transfer to TD for debugging.

Turbo C++ 3.0 Command-Line Compiler

See "Turbo C 2.0 Command-Line Compiler." The instructions for compiling and linking C programs are identical for the command-line TC compiler versions 2.0 and TC++ 1.0.

To compile C++ programs, unless you've configured the compiler to always recognize C++ code, you may have to specify the file-name extension .CPP. For example, to compile and debug SAMPLE.CPP (not shown here), enter the command:

```
tcc -v sample.cpp
td sample
```

If you don't supply the .CPP extension, TCC++ looks for the file SAMPLE.C by default, not SAMPLE.CPP. Except for this difference, the other commands should work as they do for TCC 2.0.

Zortech C++ 1.07

Zortech C (ZTC) can compile programs written in C and C++. But because the compiler outputs *CodeView*-compatible debugging information and because *CodeView* cannot understand elements that are unique to C++, objects and methods (among other things) are translated into C equivalents for debugging. In other words, you can load a C++ program into TD, but you may not be able to view your program's structures in every detail. Also, variables loaded into registers may display as four question marks (????)—TD's "value unknown" symbol.

There are several ways to compile programs with Zortech C++. The simplest plan is to use the ZTC compiler control program. Specify the -g option to add line numbers and symbols to .OBJ code files; insert a -co option to call the *Microsoft Overlay Linker* and to add *CodeView* debugging information to the finished code. To save a small amount of memory, you can also use -gl (line numbers only) or -gs (symbols only), although the results aren't as good. Zortech also recommends using the -S stack-frame option. After compiling and linking, process the result with TDCONVRT and load into TD. For example, these commands compile and load the SAMPLE program:

```
ztc -g -S -co sample.c
tdconvrt sample.exe
td sample
```

To compile a multimodule program with a main module MAIN.C and two submodules SUB1.C and SUB2.C, just list all submodules after the main one:

```
ztc -g -S -co main.c sub1.c sub2.c
tdconvrt main.exe
td main
```

Or, you can compile the submodules separately with the -c ("compile-only") option, and then let ZTC link the individual .OBJ files to the finished .EXE code file. In this case, specify the -co *CodeView* option only in the last ZTC command:

```
ztc -c -g -S sub1.c
ztc -c -g -S sub2.c
ztc -g -S -co main.c sub1.obj sub2.obj
tdconvrt main.exe
td main
```

Zortech C++ 2.0

See "Zortech C++ 1.07." The commands to prepare programs for versions 1.07 and 2.0 of the Zortech compiler are identical.

Compiling Pascal Programs for Debugging

Because there aren't as many MS-DOS compilers for Pascal as there are for C programmers, most people use *Turbo Pascal* (TP). That's just as well because TD can't load *Microsoft QuickPascal* (QP) programs, even though QP is largely compatible with TP on the source-code level. Even so, TD can debug Microsoft Pascal 4.0 code, as explained in the next section.

Sample Pascal Program

Listing 2.3, SAMPLE.PAS, is a short Pascal program that you can use to test the instructions in this section. The program displays command-line arguments in reverse order. For example, after compiling and linking SAMPLE, typing **sample arg1 arg2 arg3** displays:

```
Argument #3 : arg3
Argument #2 : arg2
Argument #1 : arg1
```

Listing 2.3.   SAMPLE.PAS.

```
 1: (*
 2: **      Sample Pascal program
 3: *)
 4:
 5: program Sample;
 6: var i : integer;
 7: begin
 8:    for i := paramCount downto 1 do
 9:        writeln( 'Argument #', i, ' : ', paramStr( i ) );
10: end.
```

Microsoft Pascal 4.0

Although it can generate *CodeView* debugging information, *Microsoft Pascal* 4.0 (MSP4) is not compatible with Microsoft's *QuickPascal* or *Turbo Pascal*. For this reason, MSP4 can't compile SAMPLE.PAS (Listing 2.3). Instead, use MSPSAMP.PAS in Listing 2.4. The program prompts for up to eight arguments, stored in an array of Lstring. When you press ⟨**Enter**⟩ to return to DOS, the program displays these pseudo "arguments" in reverse order.

Listing 2.4.   MSPSAMP.PAS.

```
 1: (*
 2: **      Sample Microsoft Pascal 4.0 program
 3: *)
 4:
 5: program Sample( input, output );
 6: var
 7:    i, paramCount : integer;
 8:    paramStr : array[ 1 .. 8 ] of Lstring(80);
 9:    done : Boolean;
10: begin
11:    done := false;
12:    paramCount := 0;
13:    while (not done) and (paramCount < 8) do
14:    begin
15:       paramCount := paramCount + 1;
16:       write( output, 'Argument? ' );
17:       readln( input, paramStr[ paramCount ] );
18:       done := paramStr[paramCount][0] = chr(0)   { len = 0 }
19:    end;
20:    paramCount := paramCount - 1;
21:    for i := paramCount downto 1 do
22:        writeln( output, 'Argument #', i:1, ' : ', paramStr[ i ]
);
23: end.
```

To compile MSP4 programs for running in TD, use the PL.EXE Pascal/Link driver program with the /Zi option and convert the *CodeView* symbols in the finished code file with TDCONVRT. The /Zi option is case-sensitive: Z must be uppercase and i, lowercase. Also use the -sc option when starting TD to ignore case for symbols—if you don't specify this option, you'll have to use `View:Variables` to select variables for watching and inspecting (subjects covered later in this book). For example, to compile, link, and load MSPSAMP into TD, use the commands:

```
pl /Zi mspsamp.pas
tdconvrt mspsamp.exe
td -sc mspsamp
```

If the `CPU` window appears when TD starts, use `View:Module` to select the MSPSAMP source module. When the `Module` window opens, press ⟨**F5**⟩ to zoom the window to full screen. Then, press ⟨**F2**⟩ to set a breakpoint on the program's first statement. You don't have to highlight that statement, just press ⟨**F2**⟩—TD will set the breakpoint at the first executable statement it finds. After this, press ⟨**F9**⟩⟨**F2**⟩ to run past the program's startup code and remove the temporary breakpoint. This positions the cursor on the program's first line— similar to the display that comes up for Turbo Pascal programs. (See chapters 4 and 5 for full descriptions of these commands.)

> You might want to enter the keypresses in the previous paragraph as a macro. Then you can press the macro's assigned key every time you need to issue these same commands. Chapter 16 explains how to enter macros.

To compile multimodule programs, give PL all the program's module names, some of which might be MSP4 *modules* and others might be *units* (two different methods for breaking an MSP4 program into pieces). For a main program MAIN.PAS that uses a unit UNIT.PAS and module MOD.PAS, compile, link, and load the program into TD with the command:

```
pl /Zi main.pas unit.pas mod.pas
tdconvrt main.exe
td -sc main
```

Use the `View:Module` command to view the program's source code in TD. Then, press ⟨**F8**⟩ to execute the program's startup code and position the cursor on the first program statement.

You can also compile modules and units separately. To do this, add the /c ("compile only") switch to /Zi for the separate modules, then use PL to compile and link the pieces:

```
pl /Zi /c unit.pas
pl /Zi /c mod.pas
pl /Zi main.pas unit.obj mod.obj
```

```
tdconvrt main.exe
td -sc main
```

When debugging MSP4 programs, you may have to set `Options:Language` to `Pascal`. (Save a TDCONFIG.TD configuration file in the current directory to avoid having to change this setting for each debugging session.)

QuickPascal 1.0

It's not possible to use TD to debug programs compiled with Microsoft's *QuickPascal* 1.0. The QP compiler has its own built-in debugger, which can't generate *CodeView* information or a .MAP file. The command-line QP compiler QPL.COM isn't any help either. So if you have hopes of using TD together with QP and QPL, you're out of luck.

Perhaps a future QP version will generate *CodeView* debugging information, or at least a .MAP file. In that case, you might be able to use TDCONVRT and TDMAP to translate that information to TD's required format.

Turbo Pascal 4.0

Contrary to what you may have heard or read elsewhere, you can debug *Turbo Pascal* 4.0 (TP4) programs with TD. Of course, you'll get better results with TP versions 5.0 or 5.5 (collectively known as version 5.x), which can generate TD symbols directly. But, by creating an intermediate .MAP file with the TP4 compiler, you can view symbolic information in TD, set breakpoints, and trace through a program's statements—even those in multiple units. You won't be able to examine data structures with as much detail as you can by compiling with later TP versions. But until you can upgrade your compiler, at least you're not stuck out on a limb without a ladder.

To prepare TP4 programs for debugging, you can use the TP4 integrated development environment (IDE) or the command-line compiler. If you are using the IDE, open the `Options:Compiler` menu and set `Turbo pascal map file` and `Debug information` to `On`. You must turn on this second setting to transfer the necessary symbolic information and line numbers to the compiled code. Unfortunately, those symbols are not in TD's format but are instead intended for use with Microsoft's SYMDEB debugger, which isn't compatible with *CodeView* or TD. For that reason, it's also necessary to create a .TPM (Turbo Pascal Map) file of the same symbols, which can then be translated by other utilities into TD's required format.

To compile with the command-line compiler, use the /$T + option to create the .TPM map file. After that, or after compiling from inside the IDE and quitting to DOS, convert the .TPM file to a .MAP text file with the TP4 utility TPMAP. Then, process that file with TD's TDMAP program to write the symbols back to the .EXE file in TD's format. For example, use these commands to compile SAMPLE and load the result into TD:

```
tpc /$T+ sample
tpmap sample
tdmap sample.map
td sample
```

Notice that the second line runs T*P*MAP; the third runs T*D*MAP—two different programs. For multimodule programs, add the /M ("make") or /B ("build") options to the TPC command. This will compile individual units and include their symbols in the .TPM map file. Use TD's `View:Module` command to select among various source-code modules.

Turbo Pascal 5.x Integrated Environment

Turbo Pascal 5.0 and 5.5 (I'll refer to them both as TP5) come supplied with an IDE that includes the compiler, editor, and stripped-down debugger in the file TURBO.EXE. Although useful for examining small programs and tests, TP5's built-in debugger lacks the features and memory capacity of the full-powered TD. To take advantage of those features, but still be able to edit and compile programs in the IDE, you'll need to set various switches to add symbols and line numbers to compiled Pascal programs. You can then load the .EXE file into TD.

To prepare programs for debugging, start TP5 and set `Debug:Standalone debugging` to `On`. You can also change `Integrated Debugging` to `Off`, although this is not required. If you want to view local variables declared in procedures and functions, use `Options:Compiler` to change `Local symbols` to `On`. Turning this option off might save a little memory, but then you won't be able to view local variables in TD. (Alternately, you can insert a `{$L+}` option in the source code to enable local symbols.)

Also change `Debug information` to `On`. If this option is off, no symbols will be written to the compiled code file, regardless of the other switch settings. (This makes the `Debug information` command handy for turning symbol generation on and off quickly without changing other settings.) In addition to these settings, change `Compile:Destination` to `Disk`; otherwise, TP5 compiles to memory, making the result inaccessible to TD. You must compile your program to a disk .EXE file before you can load the code into the debugger.

After making these changes, you may want to use `Options:Save options` to save the new configuration in a TURBO.TP file, which TP5 will read from the current directory the next time you start the IDE. Or, specify a different file name (perhaps TD.TP), which you can load with `Options:Retrieve options` to configure the IDE for debugging.

With all the proper switches set, compile your program with one of TP5's three `Compile`-menu commands—`Compile`, `Make`, or `Build`. For simple programs like SAMPLE, load the text into the editor and select `Compile.` For programs that use custom units, use `Make` to compile only those modules that have changed since the previous compilation. Use `Build` to compile all modules.

After a successful compilation, press ⟨**Alt**⟩-**X** to quit TP5. Then, type **td sample** to load SAMPLE.EXE into TD for debugging.

Turbo Pascal 5.x Command-Line Compiler

Many professional Pascal programmers prefer to use Turbo Pascal's command-line compiler (TPC) along with a separate text editor for entering and modifying source code. This arrangement can also free extra memory for compiling large programs with many symbols.

To use TPC to compile SAMPLE, specify the /v option, which adds symbols and line numbers to the finished .EXE code file in TD's required format. You can then load that file into TD using the commands:

```
tpc /v sample
td sample
```

When compiling programs that use units, also specify /m ("make") or /b ("build") options to compile out-of-date modules. For example, to compile a program file MAIN.PAS that uses two units in UNIT1.PAS and UNIT2.PAS, and then load MAIN.EXE into TD, use the commands:

```
tpc /v /b main
td sample
```

Replace /b with /m to compile only the minimum number of modules to bring the entire program up to date. (If TD doesn't display source code for some modules, use /b the first time you compile. Use /m from then on. This ensures that all .TPU [Turbo Pascal Unit] files have symbolic debugging information.)

You can also compile units separately if you prefer, although this isn't necessary for most programs. The following commands are equivalent to the previous two:

```
tpc /v unit1
tpc /v unit2
tpc /v main
td main
```

To conserve memory, you can specify the option /$D- for tpc in addition to those listed here. This disables local-symbol generation, adding only global symbols for debugging.

Preparing Assembly Language Programs for Debugging

It's probably true that most people think a symbolic debugger like TD is most useful for debugging C and Pascal code. But even though assembly language symbols have a direct relationship to the finished machine code, and, therefore, you might think a nonsymbolic debugger like DEBUG would be adequate for investigating problems, there are many advantages to symbolic versus machine-code assembly language debugging.

For one, TD's main **Module** window displays the program's source-code lines and comments from the original text files. You see your program in the debugger exactly as it appears in the editor. Other TD windows can display variables, evaluate expressions, and set breakpoints to enhance your ability to comprehend just what your exquisitely written (but unfortunately buggy) machine code is doing. The alternative—and I'm always amazed to discover programmers still doing this—is to pick apart a DEBUG hex dump and hunt through a disassembly of the program's instructions to rout out the bugs.

There are times, though, when looking deep inside a program's executable machine code is useful—for example, when you want to try a temporary optimization or if you suspect that the compiler's or assembler's output is faulty (unlikely, but possible). At such times, when you do need to see the assembled machine code, you can open TD's **CPU** window by pressing ⟨**Alt**⟩-**VC**. Then, to switch back to the source-code **Module** window, press ⟨**F6**⟩. (See chapters 3–5 for more details about these and other TD commands.)

Sample Assembly Language Program

Listing 2.5, SAMPLE.ASM, is a short assembly language program in standard *Microsoft Macro Assembler* (MASM) syntax that you can use to test the assembly language instructions in this chapter. The program displays a short message and then ends. You might want to verify that the code assembles and runs correctly before trying to load the result into TD. To do that with *Turbo Assembler,* enter the commands:

```
tasm sample
tlink sample
sample
```

Listing 2.5.   SAMPLE.ASM.

```
1:          TITLE    Test Assembly Language Program (MASM syntax)
2:
3:          DOSSEG
4:          .MODEL   SMALL
5:          .STACK   100h
6:
7:          .DATA
```

Listing 2.5. *(cont.)*

```
 8:
 9: string  db      "Test Program",13,10
10: len     equ     $ - string
11:
12:         PUBLIC  string
13:
14:         .CODE
15:
16: start:  mov     ax, @DATA         ; Assign address of data
17:         mov     ds, ax            ;  segment to ds
18:         mov     bx, 1             ; Select standard out
19:         mov     cx, len           ; Set cx = string length
20:         mov     dx, OFFSET string ; Address string with dx
21:         mov     ah, 40h           ; Select DOS write function
22:         int     21h               ; Display string
23:         mov     ax, 4C00h         ; Select DOS exit function
24:         int     21h               ; Exit program
25:
26:         END     start
```

Microsoft Macro Assembler 5.1

This version of the *Microsoft Macro Assembler*—better known as MASM—can generate *CodeView* symbol tables directly. After assembling and linking (I used version 3.64 of the *Microsoft Overlay Linker* to test these commands, although other versions probably will work), run the TD utility program TDCONVRT to translate the *CodeView* symbols in the finished .EXE file to TD's format. For example, to assemble, link, and debug SAMPLE, enter:

```
masm /zi sample;
link /CO sample;
tdconvrt sample.exe
td sample
```

The semicolons are optional, but if you leave them out, MASM and LINK will prompt you for various file names. Be sure to supply the entire file name (SAMPLE.EXE here) to TDCONVRT. Some versions of this utility create spurious files (such as AA.AAA) if you don't specify the full file name with its extension.

The /zi option tells MASM to include *CodeView* debugging information in the output file, SAMPLE.OBJ in this example. The /CO option tells LINK to copy that information to SAMPLE.EXE, preparing the code for loading into TD. You can also replace /zi with /zd, which adds only line number information to the .OBJ output file. But you can then view only source-code lines in TD, not other symbols. Usually, there's no reason to use this option except, perhaps, to conserve a little memory for debugging large programs.

To link multiple object files for debugging, first assemble each source-code file with the /zi or /zd options. Then link with a command such as:

```
link /CO main+sub1+sub2
```

That links MAIN.OBJ, SUB1.OBJ, and SUB2.OBJ to produce MAIN.EXE. Other arrangements will also work as long as you include the /CO option. Consult MASM's manuals for LINK's complete syntax.

OptASM 1.5

OptASM from SLR Systems can insert debugging information into .OBJ output files, but because some versions of this popular assembler don't come with a linker, it may be necessary to create a .MAP file and then translate that information with the TDMAP utility. Using the MS-DOS 8086 Object Linker version 3.05 as supplied with MS-DOS 3.3 (other versions should work the same way), the steps to assemble, link, and debug SAMPLE are:

```
optasm /zi sample;
link /LINENUMBERS /MAP sample;
tdmap sample
td sample
```

You may also want to use the -B or -E options along with TDMAP. (See chapter 6.) Also, all symbols that you want to view in TD must be declared in **PUBLIC** statements. Local symbols are not transferred to the map file.

OptASM also has a /zt option, which is supposed to generate "Turbo" line numbers. I've had better luck using /zi, but check your manuals for details—perhaps newer assembler versions will generate TD-compatible symbols.

Link multiple modules as with MASM, or check your linker's manual for details. If your linker recognizes *CodeView* debugging, use that option and translate the result with TDCONVRT instead of TDMAP.

QuickAssembler 2.01

Microsoft's *QuickAssembler* 2.01 is built into the *QuickC* 2.01 compiler. Of course, most people use *QuickC* to compile C programs, but you can also use it for stand-alone assembly language work. For this purpose, it's probably easiest to run the command-line compiler QCL, although it is possible to assemble programs from inside the integrated editor. Here's how to use QCL to assemble SAMPLE and load the result into TD:

```
qcl /Zi sample.asm
tdconvrt sample.exe
td sample
```

The /Zi option is case-sensitive—the Z must be uppercase and the i, lower-case. Also, you must specify the .ASM and .EXE file-name extensions for the file-name arguments supplied to QCL and TDCONVRT.

There are two ways to compile a multimodule program. The first is easiest in most cases—just list the main module first, followed by others. For example, if the main module MAIN.ASM calls routines in a submodule SUB.ASM, assemble for debugging with the commands:

```
qcl /Zi main.asm sub.asm
tdconvrt main.exe
td main
```

Or, you can assemble the individual modules by first adding a /c option and then specifying the object files in the final QCL command. This will assemble the main module and link it to other object-code files assembled earlier:

```
qcl /c /Zi sub.asm
qcl /Zi main.asm sub.obj
tdconvrt main.exe
td main
```

Turbo Assembler 2.0

Borland's *Turbo Assembler* (TASM), which is supplied with the full *Turbo Debugger and Tools* package, can add TD symbolic information directly to the .OBJ output file. To assemble SAMPLE and load the finished code into TD, use these commands:

```
tasm /zi sample
tlink /v sample
td sample
```

The /zi option adds symbols and line numbers to SAMPLE.OBJ. You can replace /zi (line numbers and other symbols) with /zd (line numbers only) to conserve memory. If you do that, you can still view variables by name, but you won't see full data structures. For example, strings declared with DB display as word values, not as character arrays as they normally do when the code is assembled with the /zi option. The /v option for TLINK transfers the symbol table from SAMPLE.OBJ file to SAMPLE.EXE. You must remember to use both options. If you forget to insert /v during the link step, the symbol table will not be included in the result even if you assembled the source-code text with /zi.

To compile a multimodule program with a main module MAIN.ASM and a submodule SUB.ASM, assemble the parts separately and link them with TLINK as shown here:

```
tasm /vi main
tasm /vi sub
tlink /v main sub
td main
```

Preparing .COM Programs for Debugging

Not long ago, the preferred code-file format was a .COM (command) file, which normally limits programs to 64K of memory and stores the code, data, and stack in a single segment. Today, the issues that made .COM files popular in the past—faster loading, faster compilation, and simple organization—are no longer critical, and most programmers compile to .EXE code files instead.

Preparing .COM code files for debugging is less straightforward than preparing .EXE files because a .COM file reserves no space for a symbol table. The answer to this dilemma is to store symbols and line numbers in a separate .TDS file, which TD can read and overlay onto the code in memory, accomplishing the same effect as loading an .EXE file that contains all the information TD needs. The following sections explain how to do this in assembly language.

Sample .COM Program

Assemble Listing 2.6 to test the following instructions for debugging .COM code files. As written, the program assembles only with TASM. Delete line 4 and remove the first semicolon from line 5 for MASM.

Listing 2.6. COMPROG.ASM.

```
 1:              TITLE   Test Assembly Language .COM Program
 2:
 3:              DOSSEG
 4:              .MODEL  tiny            ; TASM
 5:  ;           .MODEL  small           ; MASM
 6:
 7:              .DATA
 8:
 9:  string  db      "Test .COM-style Program",13,10,'$'
10:
11:              .CODE
12:
13:              ORG     100h
14:
15:  Start:  mov     dx, offset string
```

Listing 2.6.   *(cont.)*

```
16:          mov      ah, 09h
17:          int      21h
18:   Exit:
19:          mov      ax, 4C00h
20:          int      21h
21:
22:          END      Start
```

Assembling .COM Programs

To assemble and link a .COM-style program with TASM and TLINK, use the /zi
option and link with /v. Don't use the /t option with TLINK as you normally do
to create .COM files—this option removes the symbol table from the object
code. Instead, process the .EXE file with TDSTRIP, using the -c option to create
the finished .COM file and -s to store the symbol table in a .TDS file. The
complete instructions for assembling, linking, and loading COMPROG.ASM into
TD are:

```
tasm /zi comprog
tlink /v comprog
tdstrip -c -s comprog
td comprog
```

Ignore the "no stack" warning from TLINK. Because this step creates
COMPROG.EXE, the linker warns about the missing stack segment, which isn't
needed for a .COM code file.

With a little more work, you can also assemble .COM code files with MASM
5.1. (Be sure to change **.MODEL** to `small`—MASM doesn't recognize TASM's `tiny`
memory model key word.) The trick this time is to generate *CodeView* symbols
in the .EXE file, use TDCONVRT to translate those symbols to TD format, and
then strip the symbols with TDSTRIP to create the finished .COM code file:

```
masm /Zi comprog;
link /CO comprog;
tdconvrt comprog.exe
tdstrip -c -s comprog
td -sc comprog
```

The -sc option tells TD to ignore symbol case. After TD starts, use
`View:Module` to open a source-code window, press ⟨**F2**⟩ to set a breakpoint on
the first source-code executable instruction, and then press ⟨**F9**⟩⟨**F2**⟩ to start
the program and halt at the first line. This simulates the conditions of a .COM
program loaded into memory just before the first instruction executes. (See
chapters 4 and 5 for more details about these and other TD commands.)

> If you follow these steps and still don't see your source code in TD, you may have to run the TOUCH utility to update file dates and times. Just enter **touch *.*** to update all files in the current directory, then try the TD command again. Also see chapter 6 and the notes near the end of this chapter for more information about TOUCH.

Compiling Other Programs for Debugging

In general, if your language can generate a .MAP file that lists public symbols and source-code line numbers, you can use TD to debug the code. This goes for *any* language, not only C, Pascal, and assembly. You won't be able to see every detail of exotic data structures in their original source-code forms, but you can still view their values as bytes and words in memory. What's more, you can use TD's code-tracing, breakpoint, and expression features to help find the bugs in your programs.

If you have trouble getting TD to recognize your language's .MAP file format, compare the sample .MAP file text in Figure 2.2 to the output from your compiler or linker. Perhaps you'll be able to convert a nonstandard format to match the one that TDMAP requires. To create this text, I entered the TASM commands **tasm /zi sample** and **tlink /m /l sample**.

```
Start  Stop   Length Name              Class
00000H 00016H 00017H _TEXT             CODE
00018H 00025H 0000EH _DATA             DATA
00030H 0012FH 00100H STACK             STACK

  Address         Publics by Name

0001:0008         STRING

  Address         Publics by Value

0001:0008         STRING

Line numbers for sample.obj(SAMPLE.ASM) segment _TEXT

    16 0000:0000    17 0000:0003    18 0000:0005    19 0000:0008
    20 0000:000B    21 0000:000E    22 0000:0010    23 0000:0012
    24 0000:0015

Program entry point at 0000:0000
```

Figure 2.2. Sample .MAP file contents.

After creating a standard .MAP file, use the command **tdmap file.map** to translate the map text information into a TD symbol table and write that data to FILE.EXE. If you are creating a .COM file, perform these steps before running TDSTRIP to store the symbol table in a .TDS file and create the .COM code file on disk, as explained earlier in "Assembling .COM Programs."

When using TDMAP, specify -C if your language's symbols are case-sensitive. Add the -B option if you want to view variables as bytes instead of as word values. Also add -Exxx where xxx is a file-name extension such as ASM or HCC for any files listed in the .MAP file without extensions. This will enable TD to load those files and relate the source-code lines to the compiled code.

Debugging Without the Source

Debugging is more complicated (to say the least) when you don't have the source code to a program. That's rare, but it happens. Perhaps you've lost a version of a program's source, or maybe you just want to dissect a commercial program, using TD as your scalpel to slice into the code and see what makes it tick. At such times, don't resort to using DOS DEBUG—you may still be able to debug the code at the source level with TD.

The first approach to debugging a sourceless program is simply to load the code as is into TD. When you do this, you'll see a machine-language disassembly of the program in TD's CPU window, similar in some ways to what DEBUG's "unassemble" command produces. You've got to be sharp to debug machine code this way—there are no landmarks to recognize and no comments or procedure headers to denote logical divisions in the program. Also, it's up to you to separate data from code. TD can't know which is which, and if you accidentally execute some data as instructions, the program may crash. Still, you can set breakpoints and use most other commands as described in later chapters. TD is far superior to DEBUG for examining programs in this rawest of low-level forms.

Another possibility is to disassemble the code with a program designed for this purpose. A capable disassembler can read a compiled .EXE, .COM, or device-driver file and create pseudo source-code assembly language text. You can then assemble the pseudo source code with TASM or MASM (or another assembler) according to instructions earlier in this chapter to add a symbol table to the result, which you can then load into TD for debugging at the source level—or as close as you're likely to get.

An excellent disassembler is *Sourcer* from V Communications, Inc. This program does an amazing job at identifying procedures and separating code from data. It also identifies DOS and BIOS function calls, locates external subroutine entry points, and inserts comments in the pseudo source code. (Some of the comments are a bit simple-minded, but even minimal comments are better than none at all.)

Be careful when running disassembled code files after reassembly. Usually, the pseudo source text will assemble without errors, but the result might not run correctly without further modifications. To disassemble and debug a large program is a major undertaking—but at least *Sourcer* and TD give you a flying start.

Using TOUCH to Update Files

On occasion, you may be unable to run TDSTRIP and other utilities on various files as described in this chapter. If you receive errors, and especially if that happens for commands that worked perfectly well before, try running the TOUCH utility on all or some files in the directory. To update all files in the current directory, enter **touch *.***.

That sets all file dates to the current date and time. Sometimes this is necessary to force a utility to process a set of files that, because of their differing dates and times, are incorrectly flagged by the utility as unrelated.

Summary

TD needs a map, called the symbol table, to find its way around a program's compiled code. This chapter explains how to add a symbol table to programs using a variety of C, Pascal, and assembly language compilers and assemblers.

Of course, Borland's own languages—*Turbo C, Turbo Pascal,* and *Turbo Assembler*—can generate TD symbol tables directly; therefore, these are the most convenient languages to use with TD. But if your language can add Microsoft *CodeView* debugging information to compiled code, or if it can at least create a standard .MAP text file, TD can help you to debug the program.

Because TD is line-oriented, not statement-oriented, some commands work best when each line contains only one statement. Following this one-statement-per-line design rule may also help to make your source code more readable and, therefore, easier to debug.

This chapter also explains how to debug .COM programs, how to translate a .MAP file to a TD symbol table, and how to use a source-code disassembler to debug programs for which the original source text is lost or unavailable.

Chapter 3

Getting Turbo Debugger
Up and Running

Installing TD is a simple process—just run the INSTALL program on TD's "Install" diskette and follow the instructions. Because these and other installation details are covered in the *Turbo Debugger User's Guide,* instead of duplicating that information, this chapter concentrates on tips for configuring TD, installing a mouse, saving disk space, using extended and expanded RAM, setting up TD to run a text editor, and using TD with multitasking software such as Microsoft *Windows.* The chapter ends with a complete reference to TD's command-line options.

It's probably best to skim this chapter (and the next two) to become familiar with the layouts. You can then refer back to these pages for help with specific commands and configurations as you need them.

Before running INSTALL, you may have to reboot to remove TSRs and, possibly, to disable a disk cache such as *PC-Kwik;* otherwise, INSTALL may hang while unpacking archived (compressed) files. The problem is caused by a conflict between some versions of the UNZIP utility and the cache software.

Configuration Tips

The tips in this section will help you to configure TD for peak performance. On my system, I keep two configurations—one for 80386 virtual debugging and another for DOS and *Windows.* I run a simple batch file to copy the appropriate AUTOEXEC.BAT and CONFIG.SYS files to my C:\ root directory so I can quickly switch from one setup to another.

I also keep several "local" configurations in my project directories by saving TDCONFIG.TD files with TD's `Options:Save options` command. This records the options I use to debug various programs, saving me the trouble of resetting those same options the next time a bug surfaces in the code.

When configuring TD for your system, don't aim for perfection. Each buggy program will pose unique problems to solve, and you'll probably have to reconfigure TD frequently to find different kinds of bugs. Use the information in this chapter to find a "happy medium" that works for most programs. You can always create configuration files to fine-tune TD if necessary.

Black-and-White Graphics

Most CGA, EGA, and VGA video displays are color, but if yours is in black and white (or green, amber, or even shocking monochromatic pink), you might not be able to read INSTALL's messages. In that case, press **q** to quit to DOS and restart with the command **install /b** to fix the problem. You'll also want to configure TD to use black-and-white "colors." See "Custom Setups" later in this chapter.

Setting Up Directories

Most people install TD—plus the other two programs in the *Turbo Debugger and Tools* package, TASM and *Turbo Profiler* (TPROF)—on a hard drive in the subdirectories C:\TD, C:\TASM, and C:\TPROF. If you are using floppy diskettes, you'll need at least one high-density 5.25-inch 1.2-megabyte, or one 3.5-inch 720K or better, drive. TD's code file TD.EXE is too large to fit on a standard 360K floppy diskette. (Unfortunately, you can't use INSTALL to install TD on high-density floppies. To do that, you must unpack the .ZIP archive files manually with the UNZIP utility. See chapter 6.)

Whatever directory names you decide to use, be sure to add a command such as **path = c:\dos;c:\td** to your AUTOEXEC.BAT file. This will let you switch to your working directories and run the debugger by typing **td** plus a program name. If you are using two high-density disk drives instead of a hard drive, insert the command **path = a:\;b:** in AUTOEXEC.BAT so you can run TD in one drive while the other is current.

Some programmers prefer to store all TD files along with TASM and TPROF in a common directory, typically named C:\UTIL or C:\BIN. You might also store your compiler's executable files there plus other utility programs. This arrangement offers three advantages over using the stock setup's multiple subdirectories:

- The PATH environment variable is kept short.

- Programs start more quickly (on the average) because COMMAND.COM needs to search only two directories for executable files—the current directory and the one listed in PATH.

• The newest versions of utilities such as README, GREP, and MAKE automatically replace old files of the same names. This also prevents wasteful
duplicate files in multiple directories.

A disadvantage of this technique is that some programs may start more
slowly if C:\BIN becomes very full. Also, to uninstall programs and to upgrade
to future versions requires manually deleting old files, which can be tedious.

System RAM

TD can use three kinds of memory: *system, expanded* (EMS), and *extended*
(XMS). Normally, the debugger shares system RAM with the code that you want
to examine, an arrangement that works surprisingly well even for medium-size
programs. You'll need a minimum of 384K available in addition to DOS and any
resident programs, but the more memory you have, the better. Figure 3.1
illustrates this common configuration and lists rough sizes for each component
in RAM. (Exact sizes will vary from one installation to another.)

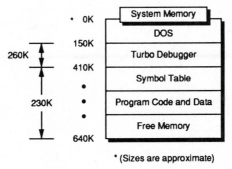

Figure 3.1.   System-memory map.

Expanded RAM (EMS)

If your system has an expanded memory card installed, TD can store its overlays
and program symbols there to free some system RAM for the debugger and the
program's code. For debugging medium- to large-size programs, if you run out
of room in system RAM, increasing your system's EMS capacity may be the least
costly solution. Figure 3.2 illustrates how TD uses EMS RAM to store symbol
tables, plus a few other items you'll meet later.

Other programs may compete with TD for EMS RAM. For example, you
may install a large RAM drive at boot time. In that case, be sure to reserve some
EMS for TD. The exact amount depends entirely on the size of your program's

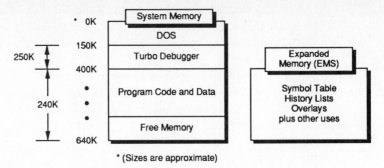

Figure 3.2.   Expanded-memory (EMS) map.

code and how many public symbols it defines, so it's impossible to calculate how much EMS RAM you need. Experiment until you find a setting that works.

Extended RAM (XMS)

Extended RAM is found only on 80286-, 80386-, and 80486-based systems; therefore, if you have an XT-style PC, skip to "Remote and Dual-Monitor Installation." Only AT-class machines can use extended RAM, which *extends* the computer's address space above a standard PC's 1-megabyte high-water mark. Figure 3.3 illustrates TD's use of extended RAM.

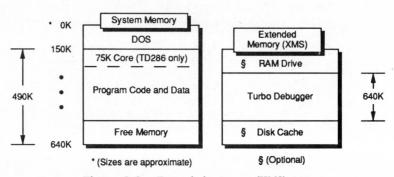

Figure 3.3.   Extended-memory (XMS) map.

Many AT-class systems come with extended RAM installed on the motherboard. Others have XMS cards that you can configure to EMS or XMS specifications (or both). These tips and the notes that follow for 80286-, 80386-, and 80486-based PCs will help you to choose the best arrangement for your system:

- 80286 and 80386 systems need about 640K extended RAM. (In past TD versions, the recommended extended RAM minimum for TD386 was 700K.

Actually, that figure is approximate, and a smaller value might work equally well, especially if you also have EMS for TD to store symbol tables. See the -f option later in this chapter.) If you have less than 640K extended RAM, you may not be able to run TD286 or TD386.

- If you have a large amount of extended RAM (at least 1 megabyte), configure about 700K as extended and, if possible, the rest as expanded RAM. You can then run TD, TD286, or TD386 to debug very large programs.

- If you are using other programs such as a disk cache or RAM drive that compete with TD for extended RAM, be careful not to allocate the same RAM for more than one use. See Figure 3.3 for help in planning your extended RAM usage.

One way to prevent conflicts when multiple programs share extended memory is to install an extended-memory manager and, possibly, Microsoft's XMS HIMEM.SYS driver, supplied with Microsoft *Windows*. This driver makes a 64K *High Memory Area* (HMA) available starting at the base of extended RAM.

If you aren't using *Windows,* you can get a free copy of the XMS software and documentation by calling the Microsoft Information Center (MIC) toll free at 800-426-9400. When you hear the recording, follow instructions to connect to the MIC and ask for the "XMS documentation and driver source code for the Extended Memory Specification."

TD286 also respects the VCPI *(Virtual Control Program Interface)* specification, available at no charge from Phar Lap Software, Inc., 60 Aberdeen Ave., Cambridge, MA 02138. Their phone number is 617-661-1510. (This is *not* a toll-free call.) Programs that are VCPI-aware can share extended RAM without conflicts.

Neither of these solutions is perfect, however, and they do *not* permit TD386 to run along with other protected-mode software such as *Windows/386* and *DesqView.* Also, all programs and TSRs must recognize the existence of an extended-memory driver—this isn't automatic.

Converting Extended to Expanded RAM

There are public domain drivers available such as EMS40.SYS published by *PC Magazine* (Vol 8, No. 12) that use an 80386 or 80486 processor's paging abilities to convert extended memory to EMS. Unfortunately, because these drivers switch in and out of protected mode to perform a copy subroutine for each access to a new memory page, they can cause TD's performance to drop through the bottom of the barrel.

For this reason, if you want to convert extended RAM to EMS for storing symbol tables, one of these drivers may not be the best choice. Instead, try these suggestions:

- Use the -f switch with TD386 to convert additional extended RAM to EMS for TD's use. (This RAM is not available to your program. It's strictly for TD's private consumption.)

- Purchase an expanded memory card. You can install extended and expanded RAM in the same computer, and TD can use both kinds of memory simultaneously.

- Run TD or TD286 (not TD386) under *Windows/386* or *Windows 3.0* with the HIMEM.SYS XMS driver installed according to directions. Depending on the total amount of extended RAM in your system, *Windows* will automatically convert extended RAM to EMS, which TD will use. Under *Windows 3.0* on an 80386- or 80486-based system, you can also install the supplied EMM386.SYS device driver to convert a portion of extended RAM to EMS.

- Some people with 80386 systems recommend running TD and *Windows/286* or *Windows 3.0* in real mode with *386-Max* from Qualitas to manage extended memory. (See Bibliography.) However, you must run TD or TD286, not TD386, under this configuration.

80286 Installation

AT-class PCs with 80286 processors and at least 640K of extended RAM can run TD 2.0 in protected mode. With this configuration, the TD286 debugger loads all but a small portion of itself into extended RAM. Only a small core of about 75K remains behind in system memory, freeing the rest of RAM to hold a target program's executable code and data. (See Figure 3.3.) According to Borland, because TD286 recognizes the VCPI specification, you may also be able to use TD286 with a VCPI-aware extended memory manager.

Because all 80286-based systems are not equal, before running TD in protected mode, change to TD's directory and execute TD286INS to configure TD286 for your hardware. The *Turbo Debugger User's Guide* implies that, in some cases, this may hang your computer, forcing you to reboot. If that happens, the guide suggests restarting the program to continue configuring. I'd also suggest removing all TSRs and device drivers before running TD286INS for the first time. That may not be necessary, but experience teaches that limiting the number of variables while configuring software is often a good idea.

After configuring TD286, you're ready to run TD in protected mode. Turn to "Running TD" later in this chapter for details.

> You can't use TD286 and another protected-mode program such as a DOS extender at the same time. Also, if you have an 80386- or 80486-based system, you may run TD286, but usually, you'll want to use TD386 instead, as the next section explains.

80386 Installation

If you're fortunate to have an 80386- or 80486-based system, you can install the TDH386.SYS device driver to take advantage of special debugging registers on these processors. Patterned after ICE hardware—the vastly more expensive *In-Circuit Emulators* hardware used by system designers—these features let you set breakpoints (instructions to halt a program based on certain conditions) to monitor bytes in memory without slowing TD's performance. You can set similar breakpoints on systems with 8088, 8086, and 80286 processors. But, without hardware debugging abilities, TD has to monitor memory locations by brute force, which can drastically reduce runtime speed. (Chapter 8 covers breakpoints in more detail. Also see chapter 18.)

To install the TDH386 device driver, add the following line to your CONFIG.SYS configuration file in your boot drive's root directory:

```
DEVICE=C:\TD\TDH386.SYS
```

This assumes that TD is installed in C: \ TD. After rebooting, when you next run TD, the device driver gives the debugger access to debugging registers on 80386 and 80486 processors.

If you also have at least 640K of extended memory available, after booting to install TDH386.SYS, you can run the TD386 protected-mode supervisor. This runs the target program and TD in two 8086 *virtual machines,* replicating the runtime conditions that exist during normal operation of a buggy program under DOS. (See "Running TD" later in this chapter for more information about running TD386.)

Among the many advantages of running TD386 in protected mode on 80386 systems, these head the list:

- All available system memory is allocated to your program. TD and the symbol table no longer have to share memory with the program's code. Provided you have enough RAM, this should make it possible to debug programs of *any* size. (See also the -f switch, which lets TD386 use some extended RAM as EMS for storing large symbol tables.)

- The buggy code runs under conditions that are identical to normal DOS operation. TD386 can help pinpoint positional bugs that appear when the code runs from DOS, but disappear when the program runs under control of the debugger—an exasperating experience, as anyone who's faced this kind of bug can verify.

- The debugger and program symbols are protected from wayward statements, pointers, and array index faults (among other problems) that overwrite RAM allocated to TD. All memory outside of the program's virtual machine is protected from unauthorized changes. (But see "Exceptions" later.)

• Conflicts between the debugger and program code are eliminated. All system resources (disk drives, keyboards, video displays, and so on) are available to the program.

There are still a few restrictions when using TD386: you can't debug protected-mode programs, you can't access memory above the lower 1-megabyte address space, and you can't execute privileged instructions. Also, only one program at a time may serve as the protected-mode supervisor; therefore, you can't run TD386 along with other multitasking software such as *Windows/386, Windows 3.0* in 386 enhanced mode*, QEMM, 386-Max* and *DesqView.* You can run only plain TD and TD286 when using those and similar programs.

Even so, when running one of those multitaskers, or if you don't have 640K of extended RAM available for TD386 or TD286, you can still install the TDH386.SYS device driver on 80386 and 80486 systems. This lets TD take advantage of hardware debugging registers on the processor. You don't have to run TD386 to enable hardware breakpoints.

Exceptions

Even with TD386, it's still possible for an exception violation to occur when TD386 intercepts an unexpected critical interrupt. Typical exception values are 0 (divide error), 6 (illegal machine code), 13 (general protection exception), and 14 (page fault). Some network cards cause TD386 to fail with exception 13. Code that was trashed by a bad pointer often leads to exception 6. Some TSRs are also known to cause similar headaches.

The only solution to these problems is to remove the card or software that's at fault. In the case of exception 6, the error is probably in the target program (but remove all TSRs just to be safe). Unfortunately, when the problem is caused by conflicting hardware, there aren't any easy answers. Complain loudly to manufacturers, stressing that they should document the interrupts used in their peripherals.

Reserving Environment Variable Space

When TD386 creates the virtual machine under which a target program's code runs, it allocates 256 bytes for environment variables. If your program needs more or less than this default amount, specify the space you need with the device-driver's -e option in CONFIG.SYS. For example, this line reserves 800 bytes for environment variables:

```
DEVICE=C:\TD\TDH386.SYS -e800
```

This option affects *only* the amount of system RAM reserved for environment variables that your program code requires. It does *not* affect how TD386 loads TD into extended RAM—a common misconception. (The option is equivalent to COMMAND.COM's /e switch.) For other memory options, see "Running TD" later in this chapter.

Remote and Dual-Monitor Installation

Chapter 17 explains how to link two systems for remote debugging, and it shows how to install TD for use with two monitors connected to one computer. These configurations make it possible to view TD's screen while seeing your program's display at the same time. A remote link is the safest possible setup—it completely isolates the development system from harm caused by bugs. Even the TD386 virtual debugger can't prevent a bug from erasing source code and other files on your disk drive!

If you have two PCs, or if you have two video adapters in your computer, you might want to read chapter 17 now to learn how to prepare TD for remote or dual-monitor debugging. You can then use this configuration along with most of the other information in this book. (You can't debug remotely while running TD286 and TD386, though.)

Installing a Mouse

You don't have to take any special actions for TD to recognize most popular brands of mouse input devices. I use a Microsoft "Bus" mouse, but those from other manufacturers (e.g., Logitech) should work equally well. If you have a Microsoft mouse, there are two ways to install the required device driver:

- Insert the command DEVICE = d: \ dir \ MOUSE.SYS in your CONFIG.SYS file, where d: \ dir \ is the optional drive and directory that contains the MOUSE.SYS file.
- Or, insert the command d: \ dir \ MOUSE into AUTOEXEC.BAT to install the MOUSE.COM program stored in d: \ dir \.

Installing MOUSE.SYS may save a little RAM by avoiding unnecessary duplication of environment variables attached to every TSR that you load. But only the MOUSE.COM method lets you run the Microsoft CPANEL Control Panel program to adjust mouse sensitivity. Also, you can enter the command MOUSE OFF to remove the TSR mouse driver from RAM without rebooting. If you use a

mouse only with TD, you can save about 15K of RAM for compiling and editing
by starting the debugger with the batch file in Listing 3.1, TDM.BAT.

Listing 3.1.   TDM.BAT.

```
mouse
td %1 %2 %3 %4 %5 %6 %7 %8 %9
mouse off
```

Replace **td** with **td286** or **td386** if you have the appropriate hardware. Use
the command **mouse /Sn** where *n* is a number between 0 and 100 to adjust
sensitivity—that is, the speed of the mouse pointer relative to how much you
move the mouse device. Store TDM.BAT, MOUSE.COM, and TD.EXE in directories listed in a PATH statement. From then on, enter TDM instead of TD to
start the debugger and enable the mouse. When you quit TD, the final command removes the mouse driver from memory, freeing about 15K.

Using a Mouse with Microsoft Windows

Even though Microsoft *Windows* has its own mouse driver, you still have to
install MOUSE.SYS or MOUSE.COM to use a mouse with TD. When running
under *Windows*, TD's mouse cursor appears only in a full-screen text window.
When running the debugger in a graphics window, you can't use the mouse to
pull down TD menus and select commands. To do that, you must switch to text
mode (usually by pressing ⟨**Alt**⟩-⟨**Tab**⟩) before TD will recognize and use the
mouse driver you installed at boot time. This is a limitation that *Windows* places
on *all* DOS applications.

Minimum Configurations

If you're short on disk space, consult Table 3.1 for the minimum number of files
required to run TD, TD286, and TD386. Also listed are the files required for
remote debugging with two computers (see chapter 17).

As the table shows, the only required file for all systems is TD.EXE. When
debugging in remote mode, the remote system needs only the
TDREMOTE.EXE file.

If you can spare the room, you should also keep TDHELP.TDH in TD's
directory. This file stores the text for TD's extensive on-line help—if the file is
missing, you'll see the message "Help file tdhelp.tdh not found" when you press
⟨**F1**⟩. You may also want to keep various TD utilities on disk. See chapters 2 and
6 for hints about selecting which utilities you need.

Table 3.1. Minimum files required for debugging.

System	Required Files
All	TD.EXE
80286	TD.EXE
	TD286.EXE*
80386	TD.EXE
	TDH386.SYS
	TD386.EXE*
Remote	TD.EXE
	TDREMOTE.EXE
	TDRF.EXE

*Required only for protected-mode operation.

Custom Setups

After installing TD's files, run the configuration program TDINST to select various settings and options. Don't put this job off until later—some of the settings can drastically affect TD's performance; therefore, selecting the right options for your hardware can improve TD's ability to help you find bugs quickly.

Some TDINST commands require you to enter text, others let you select one or more options, and still others are enabled or disabled by a check box. Many settings are grouped in a *dialog box*. To select these options, press ⟨**Tab**⟩ to move among option groups and ⟨**Shift**⟩-⟨**Tab**⟩ to move in the opposite direction. Or, point the mouse cursor at an item to change and click the left button. Enable *check boxes* [X] by pressing ⟨**Space**⟩ or clicking the mouse. Use ⟨**Cursor Up**⟩ and ⟨**Cursor Down**⟩ to select settings marked with a round dot (called *radio buttons* because they resemble the buttons on a car radio). When you're done making changes in a dialog box, press ⟨**Enter**⟩ or click Ok to accept the settings, or press ⟨**Esc**⟩ or click Cancel to restore the previous values. (Also see chapter 4 for a more complete description about using dialog boxes.)

When you have configured TD, use TDINST's Save command to store your settings directly in TD.EXE or in a configuration file, usually named TDCONFIG.TD. The next time you start TD, it will read TDCONFIG.TD from the current directory, in the "Turbo" directory specified with TDINST, or in the same directory where TD.EXE is located. If it doesn't find a TDCONFIG.TD file in one of those locations, TD uses the default configuration stored in TD.EXE.

> Some people report problems seeing TDINST and TD's displays and cursors, which can happen on systems that don't support multiple video pages or that install a single-page ANSI.SYS device driver. Follow these steps to cure the problem. Run TDINST (even though you can't see its output) and enter **dw⟨Enter⟩s⟨Enter⟩⟨Enter⟩q**. This creates a TDCONFIG.TD file with User screen updating set to Swap, preventing TD from using multiple video pages. You can also specify the -ds option for TD as explained later in this chapter.

Editing Configuration Files

In time, you'll probably collect many TDCONFIG.TD files in various directories with custom settings for different projects. If you need to store more than one configuration file in the same directory, use the DOS RENAME command to change TDCONFIG.TD to any name you like. You can then pass the file to TD to select that configuration (see the -c switch later on in this chapter).

For example, to debug a program named PROG.EXE and use a configuration named NEW.TD, enter **td -cnew.td prog** with no space between the c and the first letter of the file name. You can also use a similar command with TDINST to edit a custom configuration. To do that for NEW.TD, enter **tdinst -cnew.td**.

Restoring Original Settings

Enter the command **tdinst -c** with no file name to load a fresh copy of TD's original unchanged settings. You can then save those changes back to TD.EXE to restore the program to its virgin state as it existed just after installation. You can also use this trick to create a TDCONFIG.TD file with the original settings. Start TDINST with the nameless -c option, then save the configuration in TDCONFIG.TD.

> I discovered the nameless -c trick by accident—this is not a documented feature, so it may or may not work in the future. Borland recommends recopying the TD.EXE file from its master disk if you need to install a fresh copy of the debugger. Actually, that won't work either because the TD.EXE file is compressed, and you'll either have to rerun INSTALL or use the UNPACK utility (see chapter 6) to extract the file from the archive. Try **tdinst -c** first. It's much easier than those alternatives.

TDINST Commands

Most of TDINST's commands follow, with additional hints for creating custom configurations. To save space, a few commands that have obvious purposes and that are covered in the *Turbo Debugger User's Guide* are not listed. Most of the tips here are not in the TD guide.

Colors

The following hints are for using the two TDINST `Colors` subcommands.

Customize

Select this command to customize display colors. Choose `Windows`, `Dialogs`, `Menus`, or `Screen` and use the resulting menus to make your changes. Sample windows show the results of new settings. Hint: If you press ⟨**Print Screen**⟩ frequently to print copies of TD's display, set `Screen:Pattern for background` to `Blank` to reduce printing time.

Default color set

Choose this command, press ⟨**Tab**⟩ twice to select `View colors`, and then press ⟨**Cursor Up**⟩ and ⟨**Cursor Down**⟩ to review colors for various display samples.

Display

Selecting the `Display` command in TDINST's main menu brings up the `Display options` dialog box with the following options.

Display swapping

Set to `None` for debugging programs with no display output. Set to `Smart` to let TD decide when to switch from its own display to the program's. Set to `Always` to switch to the output display between every executed statement. The option has no effect when debugging in remote or dual-monitor modes. Hint: Use the `Smart` setting to reduce display "chatter."

Integer format

Most programmers prefer setting this to `Both`, which displays all integer values in hexadecimal and in decimal. Hint: Set to `Hex` or `Decimal` to reduce screen clutter, at the expense of not seeing both integer formats together.

Beginning display

Set to `Source` to view the `Module` window and your program's source code when TD starts. Set to `Assembler` to view the `CPU` window at startup instead. When set to `Source`, TD runs a compiled program's C or Pascal startup code automatically, pausing at the first source-code instruction. When set to `Assembler`, TD does not execute the startup code; therefore, it may not be able to find program variables until you run enough of the startup programming to initialize segment registers. Hint: Usually, set this option to `Source` unless you want to debug a compiled program's startup code, or if you prefer to have the `CPU` window open for assembly language debugging.

Screen lines

Use the `43/50` setting to display 43 (EGA) or 50 (VGA) lines. Use `25` for all other displays. Hint: To gain a little more memory for symbols, set to `25` and uncheck `Permit 43/50 lines`. Borland's documentation claims this can save 8K of RAM, but I've measured as much as 16K savings with some configurations.

Tab size

This option specifies the size of each tab column but has no effect on source code created with editors that insert spaces for tabs. Use this option to config-ure TD's display only if your editor inserts tab control codes in text. The maximum value is 32. (Do you know anyone who actually uses 32-character tabs?) Hint: Typical values are 3 or 4 for C and Pascal and 8 for assembly language. Set to 1 or 2 for heavily indented programs. This will pack more text horizontally in the `Module` window.

Max tiled watch

This value limits the automatic expansion of the `Watches` window. It doesn't affect the number of variables you can watch, only the number you see on screen at the same time. Hint: Set to 10 or a little higher if you've enabled 43/50 screen lines for EGA or VGA displays. This will still leave plenty of room to view source-code statements in the `Module` window.

Fast screen update

If you have a CGA display and if you see interference or "snow" on screen when TD writes to the display and when you press keys, uncheck this option. Normally, leave the option checked on. Hint: If you can live with the snow on a CGA display, check this option for faster displays. You may also want to change this setting when using dual monitors if one of the displays is attached to a CGA card (see chapter 17).

Permit 43/50 lines

Check this option to debug programs that display in EGA or VGA 43/50-line modes. Unchecking it forces TD to display 25 lines regardless of the Screen Lines setting, allowing the target program to display 43- or 50-line text screens. Hint: Uncheck to conserve up to 16K RAM.

Full graphics save

Check only if you will debug graphics programs. You might have to use this option to prevent conflicts between TD's text screen and the graphics display. Hint: Leave the option unchecked to conserve up to 8K RAM on some systems. Check it only if you experience problems with graphics output.

User screen updating

Toggle Other display if you have two display adapters (see chapter 17). The two circuits must use different video buffer addresses. Toggle Flip pages on if your display adapter supports multiple pages (most CGA, EGA, and VGA displays do). Set to Swap only if you experience problems when TD switches between its display and your program's. Hint: Swap uses extra memory (up to 16K) for display buffers. Don't enable this setting unless absolutely necessary.

Log list length

Sets the number of lines (from 4 to 200) held in the in-memory log. It has no effect on log information written to disk. Hint: Make sure this value is at least as large as the number of Screen Lines you specify so that you can use the Window:Dump pane to log command to log the contents of any window.

Floating precision

Normally set to 6, this value controls the maximum number of digits used to display floating point (real) values. You can specify from 1 to 32 digits. Hint: Higher values let TD display larger and smaller real numbers in decimal notation. For best results, choose a setting that matches the precision of the precision-point data type your programs use most often.

Range inspect

Change the default value of 5 to expand the number of elements TD shows for untyped arrays viewed in `Inspector` windows when you press ⟨**Ctrl**⟩**-R** to choose the `Range` command. (Chapter 4 introduces `Inspector` windows.) Hint: You need to change this value only if you always modify the default range when you choose that command. I change it to 10 so I can see more of my arrays in inspector windows without having to make adjustments.

Options

Selecting `Options` from TDINST's main menu brings up a submenu of four other commands.

Directories

Enter the full path name of your program editor in `Editor program name`. When TD's `Module` window is active, you can then press ⟨**Ctrl**⟩**-E** to run your editor—that is, if your system has enough memory. TD passes the name of the file displayed in the `Module` window to the program you specify. (For other ways to use this feature, see "Creating a Debugging Workstation" later in this chapter.) In `Source directories`, enter the directory names where you store source-code files. Enter TD's home directory name in `Turbo directory`. Hint: Change `Source directories` if you separate source and .OBJ files after compiling (e.g., after inserting compiled modules into .LIB files). Change `Turbo directory` if pressing TD's help key ⟨**F1**⟩ brings no help at all when TD's directory is not current. Otherwise, you can usually leave these two settings blank.

Input & prompting

Set `History list length` to the number of entries you want TD to save in prompt boxes. You can then select from the recorded histories to save retyping responses to most prompts. Hint: 10 is adequate; 15 is better.

Use `Interrupt Key` to change TD's break key—normally set to ⟨Ctrl⟩-⟨Break⟩. Selecting `Other` enables the `Set Key` button, which lets you program any key combination for breaking. You may have to change this setting to debug programs that need to use the break key. Some people also prefer to change the key to ⟨F12⟩ on extended keyboards with more than ten function keys. However, because some keyboards may not generate the expected break signal, after reprogramming this setting, load a test program that pauses for input (just execute a `readln` statement in Pascal, or a `scanf()` function in C, or call a DOS input function in assembly language), press **⟨F9⟩** to run the code, and try your new break key to be sure it works.

Always switch on **Mouse enabled** unless you are 100% positive you will not use a mouse. Leaving this option on has no effect even if you don't have a mouse, so the only reason to disable the switch is if you're debugging a custom mouse driver that you don't want TD to use.

Turn off **Beep on error** for silent running. That way, it will be easier to hear the bugs chewing up your code. (Just kidding.)

Toggle on **Keystroke recording** to use TD's ability to record every keystroke and then play that recording back. Hint: Turn this option off unless you always plan to use the -k option, explained later in this chapter. When this setting is on, TD will create a .TDK *(Turbo Debugger Keystroke)* file for every program you debug. Turn it off if these extra files become a problem—you can always enable keystroke recording with -k when needed.

Turn on **Control key shortcuts** to enable ⟨Ctrl⟩ hot keys, which you can press to issue local commands in windows (see chapter 5). Hint: Turn this one off only if you need additional keys to assign to macros or if you want to use WordStar-editing keys such as ⟨Ctrl⟩-C and ⟨Ctrl⟩-S, which conflict with those same hot keys in some windows. Because hot keys make TD much easier to use, usually, it's best to leave this option on.

Source debugging

Set **Language** to **Source module** to let TD choose expression and other data formats based on the source-code file name. Change to **C**, **Pascal**, or **Assembler** to force the debugger to use one of those formats at all times. Set **Ignore symbol case** on if TD doesn't recognize variable names embedded in source code, but does display those variables in uppercase in the **View:Variables** window—a sign that TD is treating the symbols as case-sensitive when they're not. Hint: C programmers who occasionally use Pascal may want to select the **C** source setting and then use C-style expressions while debugging Pascal code. Pascal fans who use C infrequently may want to select **Pascal**. You may also have to change this setting when debugging code from compilers that TD fails to recognize.

Miscellaneous

NMI intercept lets TD deal with *nonmaskable interrupts,* which have been put to all sorts of unwelcome uses in various PCs and peripherals. If TD hangs or if your system is connected to a network or if TD resets the system clock or if you experience other odd problems running the debugger (especially intermittent failures), try unchecking this option. Hint: On systems with multispeed (sometimes labeled "Turbo") switches, run TD, quit to DOS, and check that the speed didn't change. Some computers have lights to indicate the current speed; others don't. You may have to inspect the setting using a utility supplied with your system. Or, type **dir** at the DOS prompt before and after running TD to see if TD affects performance. If you notice a slowdown, toggle NMI intercept off.

Uncheck Use expanded memory to let your program (not TD) use EMS RAM for its own data. Hint: Whether or not your program uses EMS, normally leave this option checked on so TD can store symbols in EMS RAM. Check it off only if your code must have access to *all* available EMS space.

In most cases, leave Change process ID checked—it resolves potential conflicts between TD and your program's use of DOS function calls and file handles. Hint: Unchecking this option allows you to trace into DOS function calls. But if you do this, be prepared for system crashes and, possibly, a reduced number of file handles available to your code.

OS shell swap size (Kb) sets the amount of code TD swaps to disk when you choose the File:DOS shell command. The value is meaningless for virtual-mode debugging on 80386 or 80486 systems and for protected-mode operation on 80286 systems, which never swap program code to disk. Hint: Set to 0 to swap the entire program to disk.

Spare symbol memory (Kb) reserves room for symbol tables loaded with File:Symbol load. Hint: This option has no effect on TD's normal operation, but high values may waste memory when debugging small programs. For that reason, the default value of 0 is probably best—you can always use the -sm command-line option to select symbol-table size as needed.

Turn on Remote debugging only if you will always debug programs with two systems as chapter 17 explains. Because you can use the -r option to do this anyway, there's rarely a compelling reason to switch this option on. Leaving it off gives you the choice of running TD normally or via a remote link—it doesn't prohibit remote debugging.

Use Remote link port to select your serial I/O port, COM1 or COM2. Hint: Don't look for other choices; TD can't use COM3 or COM4 for remote debugging.

Set Link speed to the maximum I/O port speed. 40 stands for 38,400; 115 for 115,200 baud—the fastest setting. Always use the 115 Kbaud setting unless you experience I/O problems.

Mode for Display

Use this command to select among five display modes, Default, Color, Black and white, Monochrome, and LCD. Normally select Default to let TD detect and use a display mode that's appropriate for your system. Hint: If you have a CGA, EGA, or VGA display, but are using a black-and-white monitor, use the command MODE BW80 before starting TDINST and then select Black and white or LCD. Do this *before* using TDINST's Colors command to customize display colors. If you still have trouble seeing menus, you might have to type **tdinst /b** to run TDINST in black-and-white mode on monochrome displays that emulate CGA hardware.

Save

Select this TDINST main menu command to save a custom setup in one of the following two ways.

Save configuration file

Choose this subcommand to save all settings in a named file, usually TDCON-FIG.TD. Hint: This command overwrites existing files with no prior warning. Use extreme caution when changing the default file name.

Modify td.exe

Select this subcommand to save settings directly to TD.EXE. A TDCONFIG.TD file will override any settings in TD.EXE, so if your changes don't seem to take, you may also have to erase an old configuration file in the current directory or in TD's home directory.

Quit

Select Quit to return to DOS. If you made any changes to various settings, TDINST will warn you before quitting if you didn't save them.

Creating a Debugging Workstation

There's a simple reason that many programmers shy away from using debuggers—they take time to load and execute, and using them can increase compilation times. Even a few seconds added to the design-compile-debug cycle discussed in chapter 2 can lead to hours of wasted time over several months. It's also annoying to have to quit the editor, run the compiler, load the debugger, quit the debugger, reload the editor, and so on.

One answer is to create your own *debugging workstation*, using features in TD and other software to make your editor, compiler, and TD readily available.

This section discusses several approaches for preparing a comfortable working environment that can reduce design-compile-debug cycle times while filling in work-habit ruts you may have fallen into.

Running Editors and Other Programs

As explained previously, you can enter the path name of your editor with TDINST's `Options:Directories` command. Actually, that name can refer to any program—TD doesn't know MR-ED.EXE from a talking horse. TD passes the name of the current module displayed in the `Module` window to whatever program you choose to run by this method, a fact that may be useful for running other programs that accept a file name.

This suggests numerous ways to use this feature. For example, you might run a compiler and use a pop-up editor to enter program text from inside TD. That way, you need to load TD only once at the start of the day. Or, you might run another program to modify data files required by the program being debugged. This may be faster than quitting TD, entering new data, and then reloading the debugger to continue testing.

You can also run a batch file by entering its file name as the TD "editor." When the `Module` window is active in TD, you can then press ⟨**Ctrl**⟩-**E** to execute the batch file's commands, which can run utilities, erase temporary files, and perform other jobs.

Another possibility is to run your editor (or any other program) with TD's `File:Open` command. In other words, instead of shelling to DOS or installing the editor's file name with TDINST, load your editor's .EXE or .COM file as though you were going to debug it, and then press ⟨**F9**⟩ to run! When you quit your editor, you'll be back at TD's display. This trick is especially useful when running TD286 or TD386 (which frees all or most system RAM for running programs), and it's often much faster than quitting to DOS to run another program. You can even run the full TP or TC IDE editors and compilers under TD's control this way.

Shelling to DOS

Use TD's `File:DOS shell` command to suspend debugging temporarily and return to DOS. You can then run editors, compilers, and linkers to modify your program. When done, enter **exit** at the DOS command line to get back to TD.

> If you use this method to edit and recompile program source-code files, be sure to reload the compiled program with `File:Open`; otherwise, TD will use the old code that it previously swapped to disk.

You might have to use TDINST's `Options:Miscellaneous` command to increase the amount of memory reserved for `OS shell`, normally set to 128K. Some compilers and editors can run in that small amount of space, but most require more room. Remember, this setting has no effect when running TD286 and TD386, which disable swapping program code and data to disk when shelling to DOS.

Installing Language Help

TP and TC programmers may want to install the on-line help systems for those languages before running TD by changing to the TP or TC directory and entering **thelp** at the DOS prompt. Doing this loads the on-line help TSR into RAM. You can then press 〈**F1**〉 to use TD's on-line help system or press **5** on the numeric keypad to get help with Pascal or C. You can also move the cursor to any source-code statement in a TD window and press **5** to bring up documentation about that command, library function, or data structure.

Listing 3.2, TDH.BAT, shows how to enable language help temporarily during TP debugging sessions. Enter the batch file and then type a command such as **tdh prog** to debug a compiled program PROG.EXE and load TP's on-line help. (This assumes that TURBO.HLP is in the C: \ TP directory.) The third line removes the help program from RAM after you quit TD. TC users should change the help file's path name to C: \ TC \ TCHELP.TCH, assuming that TC is installed in C: \ TC. The batch file requires the TP or TC directory to be listed in the current PATH.

Listing 3.2. TDH.BAT.

```
thelp /Fc:\tp\turbo.hlp
td %1 %2 %3 %4 %5 %6 %7 %8 %9
thelp /U
```

Microsoft Windows

Probably the best all-around way to design a debugging workstation is to enhance DOS with a program switcher or multitasker such as Microsoft *Windows* or *DesqView*.

Whatever setup you choose, you can then run your editor, compiler, and TD in separate windows and use mouse or keyboard commands to switch between those and other tasks. For best results, a fast AT or 80386-based system and a high-quality color EGA and VGA display are practical necessities. You'll also need at least 2 megabytes of RAM—4 is better.

To run TD under *Windows,* you must create a .PIF (program information) file, and run that file to start TD. Or, you can open a COMMAND.COM window and then run TD and other DOS applications as you normally do from the DOS prompt. Several sample .PIF files are provided with *Windows* for this purpose. Use the supplied PIFEDIT program to create TD.PIF and store the file in TD's directory or with other PIF files. (This program is named *PIF Editor* under *Windows 3.0*.) When running PIFEDIT, set `Required` memory to 384; `Desired` to 512 or 640. Other settings are optional, and you'll have to experiment to achieve the best results for your system.

Running TD

With your code compiled and with TD installed and configured, you're ready to begin learning more about TD's many features. Starting TD is easy—just type **td** plus the name of a program to debug. If that program takes command-line parameters, add them after the program name. For example, to load a sorting program that operates on input and output files, enter a command similar to this:

```
td mysort input.txt output.txt
```

Enter **td286** instead of td if you've configured an 80286 system to run in protected mode. Or, enter **td386** instead of td for virtual debugging on 80386 systems. (This requires the TDH386.SYS driver to be installed in CONFIG.SYS as described earlier.)

To debug *filter* programs that process redirected input and, usually, write output to the standard DOS output file, enter a command such as:

```
td filter < infile.txt
```

You can also start TD with no parameters, in which case you'll see the `CPU` window instead of the usual source-code `Module` view. If you start TD this way under *Windows* or another multitasker, you can then use `File:Open` to load programs for debugging.

The complete syntax for running TD, TD286, and TD386 with optional elements in brackets, is:

```
td[286|386] [option...] [program [<] [arguments...]]
```

TD Command-Line Options

The following reference includes all TD command-line options. Because some of the features are covered in later chapters, you might want to skim this material now so you can look up specific details later. To view a list of TD options on screen, enter **td -h** or **td -?**. To print a reference copy, enter **td -h)prn**.

TD286 and TD386 options are also listed in this section. To view them on screen, use the -h or -? options. This works for TD386 only on 80286 or on 80386 systems with the TDH386.SYS driver installed in CONFIG.SYS. Also, you'll receive an error message if you try to run these programs while another protected-mode supervisor (such as *Windows* or *DesqView*) is in charge.

To enable an option, type a dash and the option letter in upper- or lower-case between TD and the optional program name. You can replace the dash with a forward slash (/) if you prefer. Follow the letter with a dash (representing minus) to disable an option. Follow it with a plus sign (+) to turn that option on. Separate multiple options with spaces. For example, to load MYPROG.EXE (or MYPROG.COM) and to disable 43/50-line mode and the mouse, you would enter:

```
td -vn -p- myprog
```

> All command-line options take precedence over settings in a TDCONFIG.TD configuration file and defaults stored directly in TD.EXE by TDINST.

The following TD command-line options are arranged alphabetically. A few related options are listed together—for example, -do, -dp, and -ds. Optional arguments are bracketed [like this]. The notation [+ | −] indicates you can type a plus to enable or a minus to disable this option. (The plus sign is the default— you never have to type it.) Where appropriate, the TDINST configuration command that's related to an option is also listed in this section.

-c[file]

This option loads a configuration file named *file*. There should not be any space between the c and the first letter of the file name. Normally, *file* is named TDCONFIG.TD, but you can use any other name. TDINST command: none. (Use the similar -c option with TDINST to edit a configuration file.)

-do, -dp, -ds

Use only one of these three options at a time: -do to enable a second display in a two-display system; -dp to select page flipping for multipage video display adapters (normally, the default setting); and -ds to cure problems when TD switches between its display and a program's. Use -ds if a program loaded into TD displays text on multiple pages, in which case you should *not* use -dp. (Your program or TD can flip pages, not both.) When debugging graphics programs, if you receive the message "Video mode switched while flipping pages," start TD with the -ds option and the problem should disappear. (See also the -vg option.) TDINST command: `Display:User screen updating:Other display` (-do), `Flip pages` (-dp), `Swap` (-ds).

-h, -?

Use either of these two commands to list TD's options to the standard output. The presence of either option prevents TD from running, even if you also specify additional options and a file name. TDINST command: none. (You can use these same command-line options to display TDINST's instructions.)

-i[+ | -]

Enables or disables process ID switching. Use -i- only if you want to trace into DOS routines. Use -i if you did *not* check the related TDINST option (thus allowing DOS tracing) and you *don't* want to trace into DOS routines for this debugging session.

Process ID switching allows TD and your program to call DOS functions and use file handles without conflicts. Disabling this feature with -i- allows you to trace into DOS, but it also causes your program to share file handles with TD. Because tracing DOS routines is dangerous and may cause DOS to become unstable, use -i- with extreme caution. TDINST command: `Options:Miscellaneous:Change process ID`.

-k[+ | -]

Enable or disable keystroke recording. When enabled (-k), all keystrokes are saved in a .TDK file, and you can use `View:Execution history` to replay all recorded activity to rerun various test sequences. Unlike simple macros, keystroke recording saves all input to TD and to the program being debugged; therefore, you can use this feature to repeat every command that you issue while debugging.

If you enabled this option with TDINST, you can temporarily disable it with -k- to avoid creating a .TDK file in the current directory. TDINST command: `Options:Input & prompting:Keystroke recording`.

-l

Enable this command to force TD to display the **CPU** window at startup, and not to run startup code added by the compiler before the first source-code statement in a target program. You can then press ⟨**F7**⟩ and ⟨**F8**⟩ and use other commands to trace the program's initializations. When you do that, you may have to step through code that initializes segment registers **ds** and **es** before TD will be able to locate variables in the data segment.

Another time when -l- is useful is to view the `Module` window when TD starts if you previously used TDINST to force the `CPU` window to come up by default. TDINST command: `Display:Beginning display`.

-m⟨#⟩

Use -m to set TD's heap size to #K. For example, -m12 allocates a 12K heap. Normally, TD sets aside 18K for its heap, in which it stores various dynamic items, including command histories and breakpoint information. Use -m0 to allocate a maximum 18K heap. In some cases, a slightly smaller heap will allow TD to function normally but will free enough room for a large symbol table. This won't always work, but it's worth a try. The smallest heap TD can use is 7K. TDINST command: none.

-p[+|-]

Unless you turned off mouse support with TDINST (which is rarely necessary), you'll never have to use this command. TD automatically recognizes and uses a mouse if you have one. But you can use -p- to disable mouse support temporarily if that ever becomes necessary, for example, to debug a custom mouse driver. TDINST command: `Options:Input & prompting:Mouse enabled`.

-r[+|-]

Start TD with -r to activate remote debugging. You'll also have to connect your two systems with a serial cable and start TDREMOTE on the remote computer. See chapter 17 for more information about debugging in remote mode. You can't use this option with TD286 or TD386. TDINST command: `Options:Miscellaneous:Remote debugging`.

-rp⟨#⟩

When using -r, you can also use -rp1 or -rp2 to select COM1 or COM2, the only two I/O ports that TD supports for remote debugging. Usually, you'll use -rp to test your remote hookup as chapter 17 explains, and then run TDINST to record the correct port in TD.EXE or in a configuration file.

You can't use this command without also using -r. TDINST command: `Options:Miscellaneous:Remote link port`.

-rs⟨#⟩

Similar to -rp, when using -r, you can also specify -rs1 (9600 baud), -rs2 (38.4 Kilobaud), or -rs3 (115.2 Kilobaud) to set I/O transfer speed. Usually, you'll use this command to test a remote hookup and then run TDINST to record the correct speed in TD.EXE or in a configuration file. Also, as with -rp, there's never any reason to use -rs without also using -r. TDINST command: `Options:Miscellaneous:Link speed`.

-sc[+ | -]

Enable the ignore-symbol-case option with -sc to treat upper- and lowercase symbols equally (the default). Disable with -sc- to make case significant so that `myVar` and `MyVAR` are considered to be different symbols. Either way, this option affects only programs that are compiled and linked with your language's case-sensitive switch on. Most C but not Pascal programs are case-sensitive. Assembly language programs are usually not case-sensitive unless linked to C code. TDINST command: `Options:Source debugging:Ignore symbol case`.

-sd⟨dir⟩

Use -sd to specify an alternate directory where you store your source-code files. To list more than one directory, enter multiple -sd commands such as **td -sd \ include -sdc: \ lib**. All specified directories are added to those listed in a configuration file. TDINST command: `Options:Directories:Source directories`.

-sm⟨#⟩

This option allocates from 0 to 256K of memory for a symbol table to be loaded by `File:Symbol load`, usually to debug resident device drivers and TSRs (see chapter 19). Before using this option, type **dir** to list the .TDS file name that contains the symbols stripped from a code file by TDSTRIP or prepared from a .MAP file by TDMAP. Then, use -sm to allocate about 1.5 to 2 times the size that DIR reports for the symbol-table file. For example, if DIR reports the .TDS file size to be 8750 bytes, use the command -sm13. If you receive an error when loading the symbol table, quit TD and increase the -sm value until you get a successful load.

Because the allocated space is added to TD's normal symbol-table room, there's no reason to use -sm except when loading a symbol-table file from a .TDS file. TDINST command: `Options:Miscellaneous:Spare symbol memory`.

-vg[+|-]

Specify -vg to debug graphics programs, especially if you receive error messages or experience problems when TD switches between its display and the program's. You might also need to use both -vg and -ds to debug graphics programs successfully. (Note: Debugging graphics programs is *much* easier with two computers or two monitors—see chapter 17 for details.) TDINST command: `Display:Full graphics save`.

-vn[+|-]

If you've enabled 43/50-line mode with TDINST for an EGA or VGA display, use -vn to temporarily `disable` the extra-length mode and display TD in 25 lines. The option has no effect if 43/50-line mode was disabled with TDINST. In other words, you can't use -vn- alone to switch on 43/50-line displays, you can use -vn only to switch them off. TDINST command: `Display:Screen lines.`

-vp[+|-]

Use -vp to enable EGA palette save mode. This option is necessary only if you experience problems with EGA colors. Normally, it's not needed. TDINST command: none.

-y⟨#⟩

This option can help strike a balance between performance and memory savings by adjusting the size of TD's overlay buffer from 20K (-y20) up to 200K (-y200). (The default value is 80K.) Smaller values cause TD to load overlays more frequently from disk, thus reducing performance while making more memory available for a program and its symbols. Larger values improve TD's performance but decrease the maximum size of a target program you can load. This option has no effect with TD286 or TD386, which do not use overlays. TDINST command: none.

-ye⟨#⟩

If expanded memory is available, TD will use up to 192K (twelve 16K pages) for its overlays. If that doesn't leave enough expanded memory for your program's own use, you can specify this option to limit how much RAM TD should use in 16K chunks. For example, -ye8 allocates eight 16K pages, or 128K. To debug programs that need access to all available EMS RAM, specify -ye0 to disable TD's use of EMS for overlays. Like -y, this option has no effect when used with TD286 or TD386. TDINST command: `Options:Miscellaneous:Use expanded memory`.

TD286 Command-Line Options

TD286 recognizes all of the same options available to TD except the overlay options -y and -ye (TD286 doesn't use overlays) and the remote-mode options -r, -rp, and -rs. To debug in remote mode, you must use TD.

TD386 Command-Line Options

The following options are available for TD386 in addition to those listed for TD (except where noted). Like TD286, TD386 does not recognize the -y, -ye, -r, -rp, and -rs options.

To use TD386, you must have an 80386- or 80486-based system, and you must install the TD386H.SYS device driver as explained under "80386 Installation" near the beginning of this chapter.

-b[+ | –]

Specify -b to allow ⟨Ctrl⟩-⟨Break⟩ to interrupt a hung program even when interrupts are disabled. This is so helpful, you may want to enable this option permanently. To do that, type **td386 -b -w** and press ⟨**Enter**⟩ to accept the default path name where TD386.EXE is located. Or, enter a different file name ending in .EXE to preserve the original file. Be careful when entering this command—the option overwrites any existing file of the name you specify without warning.

-e⟨#⟩

Use -e to specify an amount of extended memory in 1,024-byte increments that other programs use. Normally, TD386 loads TD into extended memory starting at the 1-megabyte address boundary. The -e option moves TD's load address higher to avoid overwriting another program in that same space. For example, if you are running a 250K RAM drive in extended memory, run TD386 with the option -e250.

Disk cache programs such as PC-KWIK load from the top of available extended RAM down; therefore, you don't have to use -e to reserve space for a cache—a common misconception. But you do have to tell the cache not to grow down past the 640K limit in order to reserve enough room to run TD286 in protected mode or for virtual debugging with TD386. To do this with PC-KWIK, use an option such as /E:1724 to reserve 700K in low extended RAM for TD386 to use. (Note: That's a PC-KWIK, not a TD, option. Other disk cache programs may have similar options to restrict their use of extended RAM at lower addresses.)

-fx000

Use -f to set the expanded memory page frame address to a hex value *x*. For example, to specify E000 as the page frame, use the command -fE000. You'll have to experiment to find a value that works for your system. Try also -fC000 or -fD000.

This option converts additional extended memory over the amount used by TD386 to EMS RAM. TD can then use this RAM to store a program's symbols. However, the converted memory is available *only* to TD—your program can't use this memory for its own EMS purposes. Use the option to debug large programs when you run out of room for the symbol table.

Hint: You do *not* have to use this option if you have an expanded memory card or emulator in your system. Also, the option will not work unless you also enable TDINST's `Options:Miscellaneous:Use expanded memory` setting.

-w

To avoid having to enter the -b, -e, and -f TD386 options described in this section for each new debugging session, specify -w to modify TD386.EXE's default values. For example, if you normally use -b, -e512, and -fE000 with TD386, change the defaults to these values by entering the command **td386 -b -e512 -fE000 -w**. Then, press ⟨**Enter**⟩ to accept the default path name where TD386.EXE is stored. Or, enter a different file name ending in .EXE to preserve the original file. Be careful when entering this command—the option doesn't warn you before overwriting any existing file of the same name. The new settings take effect the next time you run TD386.

Summary

This chapter lists tips for installing, configuring, and running TD. Every buggy program presents unique problems, and you may need to create many different configurations. Use the TDINST utility to select options that work best for most programs. Then, create TDCONFIG.TD files (either with TDINST or TD) to fine-tune the default settings.

TD can run on plain PCs and XTs or on AT-class systems with extended memory. TD286 can load most of the debugger into extended RAM, freeing system RAM for debugging large programs. TD386 can load a program and TD into virtual 8086 machines to free even more room for debugging. This also isolates the debugger from TD, thus preventing wayward instructions from overwriting TD's own code. All versions can use expanded RAM to store TD's overlays and a target program's symbol table.

A good way to use TD is to create a debugging workstation under control of Microsoft *Windows, DesqView,* or a similar multitasking DOS add-on. Or you can use the information in this chapter to run editors and other programs directly from TD. Anything you can do to limit the amount of time spent switching between editors, compilers, TD, and DOS can reduce the tedium of the design-compile-debug cycle.

This chapter also explains how to enable a mouse, how to load a language's on-line help for use inside TD, and how to use various command-line options to select debugging features.

Chapter 4

Windows, Menus, and Hot Keys

Turbo DEBUGGER is one of the most complex software packages that many programmers will ever own. Maybe that's why some are put off initially by TD's numerous windows and hundreds of commands. They mastered their compilers and editors in a few hours—why should it take so long to learn how to use TD?

The source of this common complaint, I believe, is that most programmers begin to learn their way around TD (and other debuggers) only after they've exhausted all other avenues for finding bugs in their code. Then, with deadlines looming, they turn to TD for help and are frustrated by their unfamiliarity with TD's windows, menus, and hot keys at a time when they're already burned up about not being able to find those blasted bugs.

If there's a recipe for failure, that one belongs in the haute cuisine of disasters. So, instead of waiting for trouble to boil before trying out TD's commands, you'll find debugging easier if you blend TD into your daily programming habits, and use it as a tool to examine code even before bugs occur. Then, when disaster strikes, you won't have to waste time learning how to set breakpoints, add variables to the `Watches` window, and enter expressions.

To help you master TD, this chapter is organized as a reference to TD's windows, menus, and hot-key commands. Portions of most TD displays are reproduced here, making this a good chapter to read when you're away from your keyboard. Don't try to memorize every detail that follows—skim the material your first time through so you can return for specific information later.

Sample Program

The TP sample spreadsheet program TCALC or the TC equivalent MCALC on your language master disks makes good multimodule demonstration programs for experimenting with TD's commands. (I used TCALC to prepare the figures in this chapter.) To compile TCALC with TP's command-line compiler, enter:

```
tpc /v /b tcalc
```

To compile TC's MCALC, enter:

```
tcc -v mcalc mcparser mcdisply mcinput mcommand mcutil
```

Then, enter **td tcalc** or **td mcalc** to load the program into TD. Press ⟨**F9**⟩ to run the program, ⟨**Ctrl**⟩-⟨**F2**⟩ to reset the demo to the beginning, and ⟨**Alt**⟩-**X** to quit TD. (We'll cover these commands in detail later, but that much will get you started.)

Unfortunately, there's no similar sample code for TASM users. Instead, you can use either one of the assembly language demos on TASM's master disk or a listing from an assembly language book. (CHARS.ASM or DT.ASM from my book, *Mastering Turbo Assembler,* is a good choice.)

The Scoop on Scope

All identifiers have a scope, a limit on their visibility to other parts of a program. Some identifiers are *global*—their scope extends throughout the entire program. Others are *local*—they are visible only while their declaring routines are active.

TD respects identifier scope. It always lets you specify global identifier names—for example, to inspect the value of a variable. But TD can't find local variables unless their declaring modules or routines are active. If you try to enter an identifier outside of its scope, you'll probably see a value listed as four questions marks **????**, or you'll receive an error message that the symbol can't be found. It is possible to override the current scope by prefacing a symbol with its module, procedure, or function name, separating identifiers with a **#** or a period. (See chapter 9 for details.)

Sometimes, TD's handling of locally scoped identifiers leads to problems. Although you can enter such identifiers at any time, TD recognizes them only when the declaring code runs. But TD can't know whether an identifier outside of its scope is spelled correctly, and any typing mistakes will go unnoticed. Don't be concerned about this, just be aware of how TD works. If TD refuses to recognize an identifier, make sure you've spelled it correctly.

Choose, or Select, Your Weapon

In general, to *select* something means to highlight it with a keyboard or mouse command. To *choose* something means to select the item and then enter a command that activates it. For example, you can select a command from a menu by moving the highlight bar to that command's name. But you choose the command by double-clicking its name or by pressing ⟨**Enter**⟩ after you select it.

The difference between selecting and choosing an item isn't always clear, but the distinction may be important at times.

Turbo Debugger's Display

TD usually begins with a display similar to the one in Figure 4.1. For reference, various window parts, which will be described later, are identified in the diagram. Global menu commands are along the top. (The triple-line symbol ≡ at the far left represents TD's System Menu. Other menus have names like File and Data.)

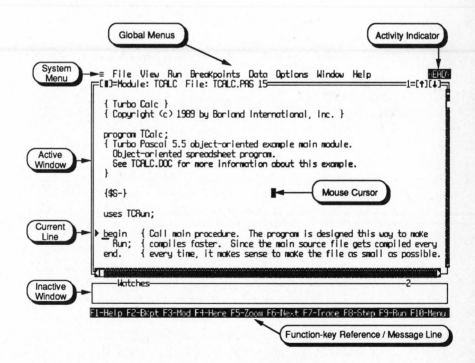

Figure 4.1. Typical starting display.

To the right of the global menu names is the *Activity Indicator,* which tells you what TD is doing. For example, in Figure 4.1, TD is `READY` to accept commands. Table 4.1 lists the meanings of other activity indicators.

Table 4.1. Activity indicators (upper left display corner).

Indicator	Activity or Meaning
ERROR	Error message showing; 〈Esc〉 to clear
HELP	On-line help is active; 〈Esc〉 to return
MENU	Menu line is active; 〈Alt〉-〈F10〉 returns
MOVE	Hold mouse button and drag to move window
MOVE/RESIZE	Use cursor movement keys to move or resize window
PLAYBACK	Playing back recorded keystrokes
PROMPT	Answer dialog box prompt; 〈Esc〉 clears
READY	Cursor in window; TD is ready for commands
READY...	TD is sorting the symbol table; wait
RECORDING	Macro recording in progress; 〈Alt〉-〈Minus〉 stops
RUNNING	TD is running, tracing, or stepping code
STATUS	Status dialog box is active; 〈Esc〉 clears
WAIT	Code is running or TD is busy; wait

The bottom display line shows TD's hot keys and also displays messages from time to time. Hold down 〈**Alt**〉 or 〈**Ctrl**〉 to see additional keys. Between the top and bottom two lines is TD's display field, which is normally filled with one or more windows displayed next to each other either in *tiled* fashion or overlapping. As Figure 4.1 shows, TD starts with two windows completely occupying this area—`Module` and `Watches`. There's nothing sacred about this initial organization, and you can change it to any other configuration by using an `Options` command to save a TDCONFIG.TD configuration file, as explained later.

If instead of `Module` and `Watches` TD displays the `CPU` or other window setup initially, the cause might be one of the following:

- You didn't compile and link your code with the correct options to add debugging information to the .EXE or .COM or other code file. See chapter 2 for help.

- TD can't find the source code files for the program. Use TDINST as explained in chapter 3 to specify a path to those files, or use an `Options` command as explained later in this chapter.

- You forgot to delete an old TDCONFIG.TD configuration file in which you saved a nonstandard window arrangement. Erase this file in the current directory or in TD's home directory.

- You used the -l command to start TD, causing the debugger not to execute the program's startup code. Use Run-menu commands to continue, or use the View:Module command to open the Module window to see your source code.

Windows

All TD windows are one of these four varieties:

- Menus
- Views
- Dialog boxes
- Inspectors

All four window kinds are related, but individual windows vary widely in the number and kinds of elements they contain. For example, some windows can move; others can't. One window might have a mouse scroll bar; another won't.

The following information explains in general how to use TD's four kinds of windows. After that are details about global menus, commands, and hot keys. Chapter 5 covers individual View-menu windows with their associated dialog boxes and commands. Inspectors are discussed as needed to explain how to investigate language data structures.

Menus

TD displays three kinds of menus, from which you can execute various commands:

- Global pull-down menus
- Local pop-up menus
- Submenus

There are nine *global pull-down menus* listed along the top of TD's display (see Figure 4.1). To open a global menu so you can see its commands, press ⟨**F10**⟩ and use ⟨**Cursor Left**⟩ and ⟨**Cursor Right**⟩ to highlight the menu you want. Then, press ⟨**Enter**⟩ or ⟨**Cursor Down**⟩ to open that menu. Or, instead of pressing ⟨**F10**⟩, you can press ⟨**Alt**⟩ plus the first letter of the menu name. You can also click the left mouse button after moving the mouse cursor to the menu name. To open the `System` menu, press ⟨**Alt**⟩-⟨**Space**⟩ or click the ≡ symbol.

Hint: Because Microsoft *Windows* reserves ⟨Alt⟩-⟨Space⟩ for its own use, under that program, press ⟨**Alt**⟩-**F**⟨**Cursor Left**⟩ to open the `System` menu.

If you have trouble opening a menu, the reason is probably that another window is expecting a response from you. Supply that response, or press ⟨**Esc**⟩ (possibly more than once), and then try to open the menu again.

When a global menu opens, it displays a list of commands (see Figure 4.2). Inside the menu, a highlight bar shows which command you'll execute if you press ⟨**Enter**⟩. Press ⟨**Cursor Up**⟩ and ⟨**Cursor Down**⟩ to move the highlighter up and down and ⟨**Home**⟩ and ⟨**End**⟩ to highlight the first and last commands. You can also use WordStar control keys A, S, D, F, E, and X to move around in menus. Or, press the highlighted letter key to execute a menu command directly. For example, to execute the `File` menu's `Resident` command, open that menu and press **R**.

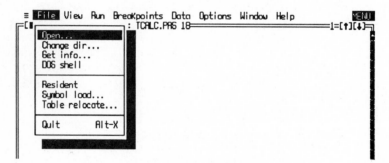

Figure 4.2.   Sample global pull-down menu.

Hint: The bottom display line describes the highlighted command in all menus, and a good way to learn more about TD is to open various menus and read those notes. For more extensive help, highlight a command and press ⟨**F1**⟩, then follow directions for using TD's on-line help window. (See "Help Menu" later in this chapter.)

To execute a command in an open global menu, you can also click the mouse cursor anywhere on the command name. Or, if you used the mouse to click open a menu, continue to hold the mouse button down while you drag the highlight bar up and down. Then, release the button when you get to the command you want. Press ⟨**Cursor Left**⟩ and ⟨**Cursor Right**⟩ to close the current menu and open one of its neighbors. Press ⟨**Esc**⟩ to close the menu and return to whatever you were doing. Or, you can click the mouse cursor anywhere outside of the menu border to close an open menu.

Inside the menu, as Figure 4.2 shows, some commands may be separated by horizontal lines. Commands within a segmented area are related in some way, but the lines have no special meaning. Also inside the menu are any hot-key assignments, shown to the right of a menu command. For example, in Figure 4.2, `<Alt>-X` is listed as the hot key for the `Quit` command. As you execute various menu commands, pay attention to these hot keys, which you can press to execute commands without opening their menus. Eventually, you'll memorize the hot keys for commands that you use most frequently. It's much easier to press **⟨Alt⟩-X** to quit TD than to type **⟨F10⟩fq** or other keys that do the same thing.

Notice also that some commands—for example, `Open` and `Change dir` in Figure 4.2—are followed by an ellipsis (...). This symbol tells you that executing the command opens a dialog box for selecting various TD features.

> This is a good place to point out a key TD feature. It's possible to execute many of TD's commands in uncountably different ways. Because different people have different skills and equipment—some are good typists, some have a mouse, others prefer using the keyboard—individuals will develop their own ways to run TD. Experiment with as many different possibilities as you can to find the commands that work best for you. I tend to use the mouse and keyboard about equally. So, the instructions here may reflect my personal bias. You may find other command sequences that work better for you.

Local pop-up menus belong to individual windows and list the commands that you can give to perform various actions on the information displayed inside that window. Each window has one or more local menus that pop up close to the text or mouse cursors, not in fixed locations. To open a local menu, first activate the window you want to use (make sure the window's border is a double line), then press **⟨Alt⟩-⟨F10⟩**. (**⟨Ctrl⟩-⟨F10⟩** also works.) For example, to open the `Watches` local menu (see Figure 4.3), press **⟨F6⟩** to activate that window and press **⟨Alt⟩-⟨F10⟩**.

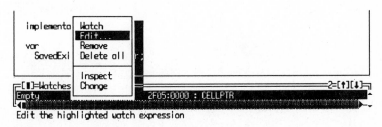

Figure 4.3.   Sample local pop-up window.

If you have a mouse, you can click the right button to open a local menu for the active window. To activate a different window, click the mouse cursor inside that window or anywhere on its border. To activate an inactive window and open its local menu, move the mouse cursor inside the window and click the right button twice. You can then choose commands by clicking their names, or hold down the button, drag the highlight bar, and release the button to execute the command.

When a local pop-up menu is open, execute commands using the same keystrokes and mouse movements described earlier for global menus. As with those menus, the bottom line describes each highlighted local command, and you can press ⟨**F1**⟩ for more extensive on-line help. Unlike global menus, local pop-ups can also move. Just click and drag the window border with a mouse, or press ⟨**Ctrl**⟩-⟨**F5**⟩ and use ⟨**Enter**⟩ and cursor movement keys to move windows and uncover whatever was hidden below. (See "Views" for more details about moving windows with keyboard commands.)

Also unlike global menus, all local menu commands have associated hot keys. To execute a local command directly, just press ⟨**Ctrl**⟩ and the highlighted letter of that command. For example, to execute the `Delete all` command in Figure 4.3, press ⟨**Ctrl**⟩-**D**. When the local menu is closed, you must press ⟨**Ctrl**⟩ plus a command's hot key. When the menu is open, press *only* the hot-key letter. (You can use TDINST to disable local command hot keys, as explained in chapter 3.)

Both global and local menus may have additional `submenus` (see Figure 4.4). A solid triangle (▶) to the right of a menu command—as in the `Another` and `Macros` commands in the figure—tells you that executing the command opens a submenu, which lists additional commands. Press ⟨**Esc**⟩ to close the submenu and return to the underlying menu. Or, press ⟨**Alt**⟩ and the letter of another global menu to close both menus and open another. To do the same with a mouse, either click on another menu name or click anywhere outside the menu border.

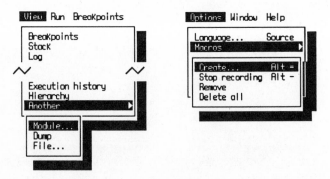

Figure 4.4.   Two sample submenus.

Another way to close a submenu is to click and hold the mouse button down while pointing to a visible command in the underlying menu. For example, with the `Options` menu's `Macros` submenu open (see Figure 4.4), you can click and hold on `Language` or `Macros` in the underlying menu to close the submenu. Then drag the mouse to another command or move it outside the menu and release to close both menus.

Views

Views are TD's main windows—places where most debugging activities occur. There are 14 of these views, each opened by executing a command from the global `View` menu. The following information generally applies to all 14 views. For details about individual view windows, see chapter 5.

What's in a Window?

Figure 4.5 illustrates the parts of a typical `View` window—in this case, a `Module` window that displays the source code for the OBJECTS.PAS file, positioned to line 205. Most `View` windows appear similarly, but they are different sizes and shapes and have different contents.

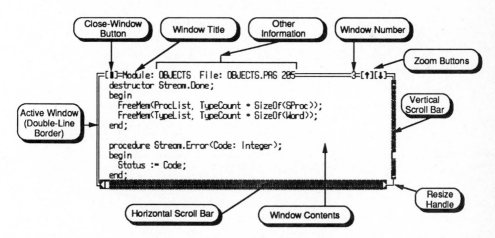

Figure 4.5. Parts of a typical View window.

Only one window at a time is the *active window*—identified by a double-line border. All input and commands from you affect the active window. *Inactive windows* have single-line borders. Output from TD may appear in active and inactive windows, but commands affect only the active one. For example, see the `Watches` window near the bottom of the display in Figure 4.1. Even though this window is inactive, TD still updates its contents when variables change values.

There are five ways to activate a specific window:

- Choose the window from the `Window` global menu. Open that menu in the usual way and select a window name as you do other commands. Or, with the `Window` menu open, press the digit key of that window's number.

- Open the window from the `View` menu. A new window always opens as the active window. If that window is already open, it will become active.

- Press ⟨**F6**⟩ to cycle through all open windows, activating each window in turn.

- Press ⟨**Alt**⟩**-n** where *n* is an open window's number.

- Click the mouse cursor anywhere inside a window or on its border. Of course, this works only if you can see at least part of a covered window. To activate a window that's completely hidden behind another, you must use one of the other four methods or move the other windows aside.

Mouse Window Commands

Many of the elements identified in Figure 4.5 are appropriate only if you have a mouse. You can still perform all TD commands directly from the keyboard— see "Keyboard Commands" later in this chapter. But a mouse makes life with TD windows so much easier, you may want to consider adding one to your system.

Most mouse movements are intuitive, and I assume you know how to move the mouse, click the buttons, and click and drag (hold the mouse button down while you move the mouse). The following tips are for using a mouse with TD windows (refer to Figure 4.5 as you read these):

- Click on the *close-window button* (upper left corner) to close the window. You don't have to press the button in the exact middle—anywhere on the two square brackets or the rectangle inside will do.

- To move a window, click anywhere on a single- or double-line border, hold the button down, drag the window outline to another location, then release the button.

- To resize a window, click and drag on the lower right single-line corner (the *resize handle*). When the window outline is the way you want it, let go of the button. If the window does not have a vertical scroll bar, you can click and drag anywhere along the right border to resize that window.

- Click or release the mouse button outside of an area to cancel a command chosen by accident. For example, suppose you click on the zoom down button when you meant to hit zoom up. If you're quick enough to realize your error before releasing the button, move the mouse aside and then release to cancel the command. (This trick also works with menus. When clicking and dragging in a menu, move the mouse cursor outside of the menu window and release the button to *not* choose any commands.)

- Double-click anywhere on the top window border to zoom a window to full screen. Double-click again to zoom back to the previous window size.

- Zoom buttons may appear in one of three styles (see Figure 4.6). Click on the zoom-up arrow to enlarge that window to cover the entire screen. Because that makes the window grow to its maximum size, it will then have only a zoom-down arrow. Click on that button to restore the window to its previous size. When both zoom-up and zoom-down arrows are visible, click on the zoom-down arrow to shrink the window to a small *icon,* which TD automatically positions in the lower right display corner. Icons have only zoom-up buttons. Click an icon's zoom-up arrow to restore the window to its previous size.

Figure 4.6.   Three zoom-button styles.

Using Scroll Bars

Many windows have vertical and horizontal scroll bars, which you can use to pan a window's contents up, down, left, and right. Some windows have only one bar and not the other. Others do not have scroll bars. The presence of a scroll bar is significant—it tells you that there is more to see beyond that window's borders. If a window doesn't have any scroll bars, then its contents are displayed in full.

Figure 4.7 shows a typical scroll bar, in this case a horizontal bar. (Vertical bars operate similarly, but they pan a window's contents up and down instead of left and right.) Click the left mouse button on one of the small triangles at either end of the scroll bar to scroll the contents one line (or other unit) at a time. Click repeatedly to scroll multiple lines or hold the mouse button down for a moment to scroll continuously until you release the button or until you move the mouse cursor aside.

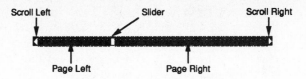

Figure 4.7. Typical scroll bar.

All scroll bars have a *slider,* a rectangular block that travels between the two triangles at the ends. The slider's position represents the relative position of the window's contents. For example, if the slider is about one-quarter of the way from the left, you can assume that there's about three-quarters more information hidden to the right. If the slider is in the middle, you're seeing the content's midpoint (more or less). When the slider is at either end of a scroll bar, you can assume you've reached the end of the window's contents in that direction.

To move to a specific location, click and drag the scroll bar slider and release the button when the slider is near the location you want. Because the slider only approximates the window's position, you'll probably miss the exact spot you want, so use this method to get close to where you want to go, and then use other scroll-bar commands to fine-tune your destination. To page left, right, up, and down, click inside the shaded parts on either side of the slider.

Hint: A handy trick is to position the mouse cursor to one side of a slider and click the left mouse button several times while being careful not to move the mouse. In most windows, this will jump back and forth between two pages of information—similar to pressing ⟨**Page Up**⟩ and ⟨**Page Down**⟩ repeatedly.

To page rapidly in any direction, click and hold the mouse button down inside the shaded region to either side of the scroll-bar slider. The window contents will continue to scroll in the same direction even *after* the slider passes the mouse cursor, making this a great way to scan quickly through a long source-code listing.

Window Panes

Many windows are divided into two or more *panes.* For example, as Figure 4.8 shows, the `CPU` window has five panes separated by vertical and horizontal lines.

Like windows, only one pane inside a window is active. To activate another pane, click the mouse button inside that pane's borders. Sometimes, an active

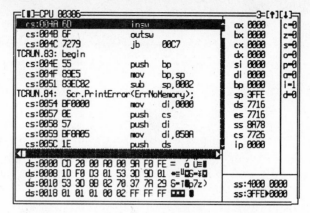

Figure 4.8. A CPU window is divided into five panes.

pane will have scroll bars—inactive panes never do. The active pane also will have a flashing text cursor or a highlight bar (or both).

Some window panes are strictly informational, for example, the right pane of the Breakpoints view. Such panes display various facts, but you can't activate them with the mouse.

Keyboard Window Commands

If you don't have a mouse, or if you don't like to use one, you can also drive TD with keyboard commands. These notes explain a few "key" concepts for manipulating windows. For more details on keyboard commands, see "Hot Keys" later in this chapter.

- Press ⟨F6⟩ to cycle between all open windows, activating each in turn. There are other ways to activate windows, but this key is usually the fastest.

- Press ⟨Alt⟩-⟨F3⟩ to close an active window. If you do this by accident for any window opened from the View menu only, press ⟨Alt⟩-⟨F6⟩ *immediately* after to reopen the closed window. (You can only recover one closed window this way.) Note: Previous TD versions assigned ⟨F3⟩ as the window-close key. This was changed to a double-key assignment to make it harder to close windows accidentally.

- Press ⟨F5⟩ to zoom a window to maximum size. Press ⟨F5⟩ again to zoom back to original size. To zoom a window to an icon, use the Window menu's Iconize/restore command. After that, you can activate the window and press ⟨F5⟩ once or twice to zoom to maximum and original sizes. Executing Iconize/restore on an active icon also zooms the window to its original size, but pressing ⟨F5⟩ is usually easier.

Moving Windows

Press ⟨**Ctrl**⟩-⟨**F5**⟩ to switch TD into "window-adjust" mode for the active window. (Note: In previous TD versions, ⟨Scroll Lock⟩ activated this mode.) After the window border changes to an unbroken single line, the bottom display line shows a list of some window movement and sizing keys. Here's a complete list:

- Press the cursor movement keys to move the window outline to a new position, then press ⟨**Enter**⟩ to fix the window at that spot. If you change your mind about moving the window, press ⟨**Esc**⟩. You can't move a window beyond TD's display limits—all windows must be fully visible.

- Use named function keys to move windows in giant steps—⟨**Home**⟩ to move fully left, ⟨**End**⟩ to move right, ⟨**Page Up**⟩ to move up, and ⟨**Page Down**⟩ to move down. These keys make it easy to move windows quickly out of the way or to send multiple windows to opposite corners.

- Press and hold ⟨**Shift**⟩ while using the cursor movement keys to resize a window. In general, you can change a window to any size, although some windows restrict their minimum and maximum dimensions.

- Press and hold ⟨**Shift**⟩ and use named function keys to resize windows to their minimum and maximum limits—⟨**Home**⟩ for the narrowest size, ⟨**End**⟩ for the widest, ⟨**Page Up**⟩ for the shortest, and ⟨**Page Down**⟩ for the tallest. (On my keyboard, these commands work only for these named keys on the numeric keypad with the ⟨Num Lock⟩-key light off, not the similar keys on an extended keyboard.)

Context Sensitivity

An important feature that applies to all TD windows is the concept of *context sensitivity.* At most times, TD is able to recognize various highlighted items, for example, text at the flashing cursor or at the position of the mouse cursor. This lets you point to something and give a command to operate on that item. For example, you can move the cursor (with or without a mouse) to a variable in a source-code listing displayed in the `Module` window and press ⟨**Ctrl**⟩-**I** to inspect that variable's contents. This is much faster than typing the variable's name.

Dialog Boxes

Dialog boxes, newly introduced in TD 2.0, make selecting program options much easier than in previous debugger versions. Dialog boxes collect various items in one handy window—for example, all the switches and settings associated with the display (see Figure 4.9). This lets you view all settings at a glance while changing only the options you need.

Figure 4-9.   A typical dialog box.

Using dialog boxes effectively takes practice. As with other windows, a mouse makes dialog-box handling much easier, and you may want to consider adding one to your system. You can select all options with the keyboard, but not as easily.

This section describes the parts, pieces, and commands associated with all dialog boxes. Individual dialogs are discussed along with the commands that activate them.

What's in a Dialog Box?

As Figure 4.9 shows, a dialog box's window looks like other windows. But a closer look reveals a few key differences:

- A dialog box lacks a resize handle in the lower right corner. You can't change the size of a dialog box. But you can move dialog boxes to new positions using the same commands that work for other windows.

- A dialog box lacks zoom buttons.

- A dialog box has at least one clickable button, usually labeled Ok, Yes, Cancel, or Help.

- Unlike other windows, dialog boxes do not have local pop-up menus. Pressing ⟨Alt⟩-⟨F10⟩ has no effect when a dialog box is active.

It's important to be able to distinguish dialog boxes from other windows because, when a dialog box is active, you can't issue other TD commands until you close the dialog box. This restriction is necessary because changing the settings in a dialog box affects TD's operation—so, you've got to complete your changes before continuing to use other debugger commands. Related to this is the fact that only one dialog box can be on the screen at a time.

No two dialog boxes are exactly alike, although they all use one or more parts listed in Figure 4.10. Depending on the kind of display you have, these parts may appear differently than shown here. For example, on monochrome displays, a default button is marked with a *chevron* character (»). On color screens, that same button is displayed in a different or brighter color than other buttons.

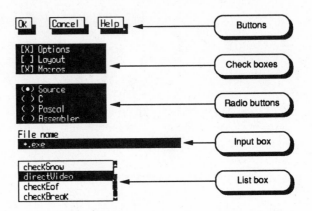

Figure 4.10.   Dialog-box parts.

Each dialog-box part has a specific purpose and controls options in a unique way. The following notes describe the parts listed in Figure 4.10. After that are instructions for using the keyboard and mouse to select a dialog's options.

- *Buttons* perform immediate actions. For example, the `Ok` button accepts the current settings and closes the dialog box. The `Cancel` button also closes the dialog box, but it restores the original settings. The `Help` button activates TD's on-line help to describe the dialog box's options. All dialog boxes have at least one button, usually named `Ok`.

- *Check boxes* select one or more options in a group. For example, in Figure 4.10, two check boxes select `Options` and `Macros` but not `Layout`.

- *Radio buttons* select one of several related options. They're called radio buttons because they resemble a car radio's push buttons. On the radio, you can tune into only one station at a time. In a dialog box, you can select only one radio button from a group. For example, in Figure 4.10, the `Source` option is selected. Selecting another button—`C`, `Pascal`, or `Assembler`— would deselect `Source` (similar to the way a radio button pops out when you press another).

- *Input boxes* are places where you can type information such as an expression, a file name, or an argument to be supplied to your program. TD saves a *history list* of your entries in most input boxes and lets you select previous entries from these lists the next time you activate this same dialog. More about this later.

- *List boxes* display lists of items for selection—for example, a list of file or module names. List boxes operate similarly to menus—use keyboard cursor movement keys and ⟨**Enter**⟩ to select highlighted items or double-click the left mouse button after moving the mouse cursor to the item you want. (Note: A quick double-click is necessary to select list-box items. A single click merely highlights that item. This differs from the way menu commands are selected by single clicks.) Alphabetized list boxes—for example, file and directory lists—let you select entries by typing partial names, what the *Turbo Debugger User's Guide* calls *incremental matching*. If MYCODE.EXE is listed among other files, none of which begins with MYC, you can type those three characters to highlight the name. In long lists, this may be faster than using cursor movement keys to move the highlight bar to that name.

Closing Dialog Boxes

You can press ⟨**Alt**⟩-⟨**F3**⟩ to close regular windows, but not dialog boxes. To close dialogs, you must press ⟨**Esc**⟩ or select another button or operation that closes the window. This may seem confusing at first, and until I discovered a small visual clue, I constantly pressed the wrong keys to close the wrong kinds of windows.

The trick is to look for a resize handle in the lower left corner of the window border. (See Figure 4.5.) If that corner is a double line, then the window is a dialog box, and you can close it by pressing ⟨**Esc**⟩. But if the corner is a single-line resize handle as it is in the Figure 4.5, you must press ⟨**Alt**⟩-⟨**F3**⟩ to close the window—⟨**Esc**⟩ won't work because this is not a dialog box.

There's one exception to this rule—you can press ⟨**Esc**⟩ or ⟨**Alt**⟩-⟨**F3**⟩ to close inspector windows even though they have resize handles.

Selecting Options with a Mouse

To activate a button, click and release the mouse button on the display button's highlighted text. The action doesn't take effect until after you release the button *without moving the mouse cursor*. This lets you cancel a button's action by moving the mouse cursor aside and releasing the button.

To select a check-box item, click anywhere in that item's text. You don't have to aim with 100% accuracy—for example, in Figure 4.10, you can click on any letter of Layout, inside the square brackets, or even on the brackets to check that item. Try this—it's a great time saver. Check boxes operate as toggles. Click once to select them; click again to turn them off.

To select a radio button, click inside the parentheses or on the button's label. This deselects the current radio button and selects the new one. Unlike check boxes, radio buttons are not toggles—at least one button in a group must be selected at all times.

Use the mouse to position the text cursor inside an input box and then enter your text. This is one time when you must take your hands off the mouse—unfortunately awkward, but unless you've got three hands, there's no alternative. Because ⟨Enter⟩ selects the Ok button, don't press that key to end typing unless you also want to accept all changes and close the dialog box. (See "Entering Text" below for more information about typing into input boxes.)

Selecting Options with the Keyboard

You can select all dialog items with keyboard commands. Although I prefer to use a mouse, at times I find it's easier to use the keyboard—especially when entering expressions and changing values, which require too much switching back and forth between the two input devices. Even if you have a mouse, it's a good idea to learn how to work with dialog boxes from the keyboard. These notes will help.

To select options in a dialog box, press that option's highlighted letter or number. Or, press ⟨**Tab**⟩ to move from one section to another—you can identify the current item by looking for the flashing cursor and by observing the labels. On color screens, the current item is displayed in a bright color; on monochrome screens, it's bracketed. To see this, open a dialog box and press ⟨**Tab**⟩ a few times. Press ⟨**Shift**⟩-⟨**Tab**⟩ to move in the opposite direction.

Press ⟨**Enter**⟩ to choose the dialog box's highlighted button, usually Ok or Yes. Press ⟨**Esc**⟩ to choose the Cancel button if there is one. Press ⟨**F1**⟩ to choose Help. You can also tab to the button you want and press ⟨**Enter**⟩, which leads to an ambiguity. For example, if the Cancel button is active, pressing ⟨**Enter**⟩ cancels the dialog box. But if *no* button is active, pressing ⟨**Enter**⟩ selects Ok; therefore, it's possible to press ⟨**Enter**⟩ to accept and to throw away your option settings! This can be terribly confusing. Just be sure that, if you're going to press ⟨**Enter**⟩ to select the Ok button, no other button is highlighted.

Tab to the check box you want to change and press ⟨**Space**⟩ to toggle the check mark on and off.

Radio buttons operate differently. First, tab to a group of radio buttons. Then use the cursor movement keys to select one button from the group. Unlike check boxes, you can press ⟨**Tab**⟩ to move from item to item. This is because check boxes function as individual items, but radio buttons function as a group—confusing until you get used to the difference.

Tab to an input box and type your entries. (See "Entering Text" after this section for more help with typing.)

Tab to a list box and use ⟨**Cursor**⟩ keys to select one of the listed items. Then press ⟨**Enter**⟩ to select that item (and usually close the dialog box).

Entering Text

At many different times, TD lets you enter text, usually into a dialog's input box. If you have a mouse, you can use it to position the flashing text cursor inside an input box. Just point to any character and click the left button. With or without a mouse, you can use the usual text-editing keys to move the text cursor as listed in Table 4.2.

Table 4.2.   Text editing keys.

Key	Purpose
⟨Cursor Up⟩	Select previous history entry
⟨Cursor Down⟩	Select next entry or highlight this one
⟨Cursor Left⟩	Move cursor left one character
⟨Cursor Right⟩	Move cursor right one character
⟨Delete⟩	Delete character at cursor
⟨Home⟩	Move to beginning of line
⟨End⟩	Move to end of line
⟨Page Up⟩	Move to first history entry
⟨Page Down⟩	Move to last history entry

TD lacks the insert/overstrike ability found in most editors and word processors. To replace characters, delete the old text and enter the new—you can't type over text to replace it.

When selecting text from a history list (see next section) or when TD inserts text in an input box automatically (which it frequently will do, for example, to enter a highlighted expression from your source text into an input box for editing), new typing replaces the old highlighted text. To keep that text, press ⟨**Cursor Left**⟩ or ⟨**Cursor Right**⟩ before pressing any other keys. This removes the highlighting so you can change the text without replacing it. To rehighlight the line, press ⟨**Cursor Down**⟩. (If there are multiple entries, this may select the next one. In that event, press ⟨**Cursor Up**⟩ to back up one line.) The text is again highlighted, and the next alphanumeric keypress will replace it.

History Lists

TD keeps track of the ten most recent entries into most dialog input boxes. (Use TDINST to change this number.) Histories in different input boxes are independent—each box keeps its own historical record. Figure 4.11 shows a sample history list as displayed by `Watches:Edit`.

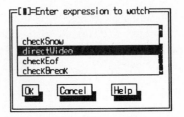

Figure 4.11.   Sample history list.

When you reuse an input box, you can select a stored history entry instead of retyping it. To do that, move the highlight bar with the cursor movement keys and press ⟨**Enter**⟩. Or, double-click the left mouse button while pointing to the entry you want. You might have to tab to the input box first. In small dialog boxes like the one in Figure 4.11, the input box is selected by default. In complex dialog boxes, another item might be selected at first.

To save room in dialog boxes with many other items, some history lists stay hidden until activated. If a small down arrow (see Figure 4.12) appears to the right of a single-line input box, there's a hidden history list waiting behind the scenes. To activate the list, press ⟨**Cursor Down**⟩. If you tab to another dialog item, TD hides the history list again, but it shows the selected entry in the input box.

Figure 4.12.   Input box with history list.

Some input boxes use history lists to let you type partial entries and then press ⟨**Ctrl**⟩-**N**. TD will search for a history entry that matches. If it finds one, it will complete the typing for you. For example, if `COUNTXYZ` is among a list of variable names, you can type **cou**⟨**Ctrl**⟩-**N** instead of entering the full identifier. At times, for example in a file-name dialog, pressing ⟨**Ctrl**⟩-**N** will open a list-box dialog with a set of symbols. Choose one of the displayed symbols to complete your entry.

Message Dialogs

A message window is a dialog box with no options, only a button or two and a message. Figure 4.13 shows a typical example—the "Terminated" message you see after running a program to completion.

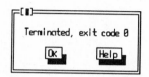

Figure 4.13.   Message dialog box.

Because message windows are dialog boxes, you must close them before you can use other TD commands or make other windows active. To close a message dialog, click the `window-close` or `Ok` buttons, or press **⟨Enter⟩**. Even though there's no `Cancel` button, you can also press **⟨Esc⟩** or **⟨Space⟩** to close.

> Hint: Before closing a message dialog box, click on `Help` or press **⟨F1⟩** for on-line help about why this message appeared.

Prompt Dialog Boxes

Some dialog boxes prompt for input but contain no other options except for the usual `Ok`, `Cancel`, and `Help` buttons. You'll often see these dialog boxes in response to various commands—for example, a command to change the value of a variable. Prompt dialogs also have history lists from which you can select previous entries. Figure 4.14 shows a sample prompt dialog box opened by the `File:Change dir` command.

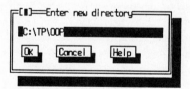

Figure 4.14.   Prompt dialog box.

When a prompt dialog box appears, the bottom display line shows the message "Enter item prompted for in dialog title." Read the window's title to know what TD expects you to enter. If you're still not sure what to enter, press **⟨F1⟩** for help.

Another kind of prompt dialog requires a yes or no answer. For example, if you choose the `Run:Arguments` command, after entering new command-line arguments, TD displays a prompt dialog that asks, "Reload program so arguments take effect?" This and similar dialogs have two buttons—`Yes` and `No`. Use a mouse to click the button you want, or press ⟨**Enter**⟩ or ⟨**Space**⟩ to choose `Yes`; press ⟨**Esc**⟩ to choose `No`. You can also press the **Y** or **N** keys to answer.

Inspectors

TD's fourth window variety is called an *inspector*. Inspectors are like magnifying glasses that let you view the inner workings of variables, memory locations, and subroutines. Inspectors also let you view lists of items linked by pointers, and they let you change the values of variables in memory. Figure 4.15 shows a sample inspector window open to a variable named `countByte` of type `BYTE`. The variable's current value is 76 in decimal, or $4C in hex.

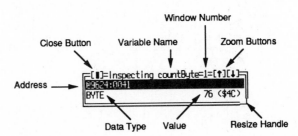

Figure 4.15.   A simple inspector.

Inspectors are like `View` windows—they have close and zoom buttons, they have a window number, and a resize handle. You can move, activate, and adjust the size of inspectors with mouse and keyboard commands as described earlier.

Inspectors differ from other windows by their ability to mold themselves to the data types of inspected items. If you view an array, the inspector shows the array's contents along with its index values. If you view a structure or record, the inspector shows the record's fields. And, if you view an object, the inspector shows data fields and methods in object classes and instances.

As Figure 4.15 shows, the first line in an inspector lists the item's segment and offset addresses (9624:0041). When this address line is highlighted, if you press ⟨**Enter**⟩, a second inspector opens to that address—a trick that's mostly useful for inspecting data addressed by pointers.

Figure 4.16 shows two inspectors opened to a Pascal record variable. In these and similar complex inspectors, you can move the highlight bar to any of the listed items to view its data type on the bottom line. If you then press ⟨**Enter**⟩, another inspector opens to show you more details about the highlighted item—in this example, the value of a field in the record (see the inspector to the right in the figure). You can continue to highlight and inspect individual items in complex data structures this way. There's no limit to the number of inspectors you can open. (But you may run out of memory at some point if you try to open too many inspectors at once.)

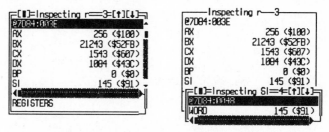

Figure 4.16. Two complex inspectors.

When inspecting variables with many parts, the top part of an inspector may scroll as you move the highlight bar up and down. If scroll bars appear, you can also use the mouse to scroll an inspector's contents. Inspector windows operate much like list boxes in dialogs, and you can use similar commands to control them.

To close an inspector, press ⟨**Esc**⟩ or ⟨**Alt**⟩-⟨**F3**⟩. If you've opened multiple inspectors to view the details of a complex data structure, press ⟨**Esc**⟩ to close only the topmost inspector window. Or press ⟨**Alt**⟩-⟨**F3**⟩ to close all open inspectors.

Chapters 20–22 list sample inspectors for all data structures in C, Pascal, and assembly language. Refer to those chapters for more information about using inspectors to view variables of different kinds.

Local Inspector Menu

Inspectors have their own local menus, activated in the usual way by pointing to the inspector window and pressing the right mouse button or by pressing ⟨**Alt**⟩-⟨**F10**⟩ when the inspector window is active. Figure 4.17 shows a sample local menu for an inspector open to a `Boolean` Pascal variable `DirectVideo`.

An inspector's local menu is divided into two sections. The commands in the top section perform minor surgery on the inspected item. The bottom commands affect the entire inspector window. All commands do not apply to all data types—for example, it's senseless to change the `Range` of a `Boolean` variable; you can change only the `Range` of an array. But don't be concerned about this—you'll learn how to apply these commands as you open inspectors to inspect variables of different kinds.

Remember that you can press ⟨**Ctrl**⟩ and a local command's highlighted letter to execute that command. For example, with an inspector active, press ⟨**Ctrl**⟩-**N** to select the `New expression` command. Also, because

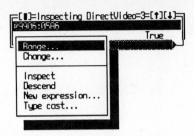

Figure 4.17.   An inspector's local menu.

inspector menus behave like other local menus, they can move—a useful trick to remember when the menu covers the inspected data. Just pick up the menu's window with a mouse or use keyboard commands to shove it aside. (Some people call TD's moveable menus "tear-off menus.")

The following notes describe how to use each command in an inspector's local menu. You'll find more details about these commands in other places in this book.

Range

This command changes the starting index and range of the indexed items in an array. Use it to limit or expand the amount of information displayed. Enter values separated by a comma. For example, type **5, 8** to list eight items beginning with the fifth, which might have an index value of 4 if the first array index is 0.

Change

This command changes the value of the highlighted item. If the address line is highlighted, the new value is stored in the entire variable. If another part of a variable is highlighted, only that part changes. This lets you highlight a field in a record or a character in a string and press ⟨**Ctrl**⟩**-C** to change its value. The changed value is stored directly in memory, so be sure that's what you want to do before using this command. If you receive the error message "Symbol not found," the value you entered is in the wrong form for this item. See chapter 9 for help on entering expressions for your language.

> Hint: This command is activated simply by typing any alphanumeric key. You never have to press ⟨**Ctrl**⟩**-C** to choose it—just start typing after highlighting an item to change. Try this. It saves a lot of time.

Inspect

Press ⟨**Ctrl**⟩-**I** to open another inspector window for the highlighted item or address. You can also press ⟨**Enter**⟩ to choose this command automatically. Multiple inspectors take memory, and you may not be able to use this command if you're short on RAM.

Descend

This command is similar to Inspect. Use it to view more details about a highlighted item. Unlike Inspect, however, the new inspector *replaces* the current inspector's contents, and there is no way to get the old contents back (except, of course, by reopening the original inspector.) Use Descend if you run out of memory when viewing multiple inspectors with the Inspect command.

New expression

Use this command to inspect another named variable when it's more convenient to enter the new item's name than it is to close the current inspector and open another one. The newly inspected item completely replaces the current inspector's contents.

Type cast

Enter a C or Pascal *type cast* expression to modify the data type of the inspected item, for example, to view a typed structure addressed by a generic pointer. If that pointer is p, and the type is t, then enter a C type cast such as (t *)p or (struct t *)p to view the data addressed by p as type t. Or, in Pascal, enter the expression t(p^) where t is a valid data type. See chapter 9 for more information about entering type casts.

> Hint: You can use this command during assembly language debugging if you first change Options:Language to C or Pascal.

Inspecting Objects

Because objects are special data types that encapsulate code and data, they have special inspector windows. As Figure 4.18 shows, there are two kinds of inspectors: one for instances (left) and another for object types or classes (right).

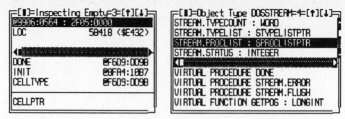

Figure 4.18.   Inspecting object instances and types.

Object inspectors are divided into two panes. At top are the object's instance variables; at bottom, method names and addresses. Highlight an instance variable and press ⟨**Enter**⟩ (or ⟨**Ctrl**⟩**-I**) to inspect that variable in more detail. For example, in Figure 4.18, you could highlight `LOC` and press ⟨**Enter**⟩ to view that field in this object.

To view the source code for object methods, press ⟨**Tab**⟩ to shift to the method area in the inspector window. Highlight a method name (for example, `INIT` in Figure 4.18) and press ⟨**Enter**⟩ twice—once to open a new inspector to that method and again to jump to the method's source code in the `Module` window.

Object Inspector Menus

Local menus in object inspector windows add a few new commands to those listed in Figure 4.17 and described earlier. When inspecting object instances (see Figure 4.18, left), there are two local menus, as shown in Figure 4.19. In that figure, the menu on the left appears when the top portion (showing instance variables) of the inspector is active. The menu on the right appears when the bottom portion is active (showing the object's methods).

Figure 4.19.   Object-instance inspector menus.

The two local menus are nearly identical—but only the one for the instance variables in the top of the object inspector contains the `Change` command. (You can't change object methods. You can change only instance field values.) The following notes describe how to use the local commands added to object inspectors.

Methods

This command toggles the bottom pane on and off. If on, that pane shows the object's methods. If off, the inspector shows only the object's instance variables. Hint: When inspecting complex objects, turning `Methods` off (press ⟨**Ctrl**⟩-**M**) lets you fit more information on-screen.

Show inherited

This command specifies whether to show inherited instance variables and methods if `Methods` equals `Yes`. This command is an excellent tool for comparing the instance variables and methods declared in this object with those declared in the object's ancestors.

Hierarchy

Press ⟨**Ctrl**⟩-**H** to open the `View:Hierarchy` window and highlight the inspected object's type (or class), showing where that object fits within the program's object tree. Because this opens a full `View` window, and not a dialog box, you have to press ⟨**Alt**⟩-⟨**F3**⟩, not ⟨**Esc**⟩, to close the window. See chapter 5 for more information about using the `Hierarchy` view.

Inspecting Object Types

In TP5.5 and TC++, object types or *classes* are conceptual—they don't exist anywhere in memory when a program runs. Object *instances,* which do exist in memory, are variables of their classes. Because of this difference, the inspector windows for object classes and variables differ, as do their local menus. Obviously, you can only `Change` an object instance's fields because only an object instance is stored in memory.

Normally, you can open inspector windows only to variables that exist in memory (and to procedures and functions, which, after all, are a form of data). But TD makes an exception for object types, which you'll often want to inspect. To do that, open the `View:Hierarchy` window either from the `View` menu or by executing the `Hierarchy` command while inspecting an object instance. Highlight an object type name in either window pane and press ⟨**Enter**⟩ or ⟨**Ctrl**⟩-**I** to open an inspector window for that type. As you'll see when you try this, an object-type inspector is similar to an object-instance inspector, but it shows the full instance variables and method names along with ancestor object names (if this type inherited parts from other objects).

As with other inspectors, you can highlight an object type's various items and press ⟨**Enter**⟩ or ⟨**Ctrl**⟩**-I** to open another inspector for that item. But, because the object type doesn't exist as a variable in memory, this works only for fields that are other objects (or pointers to objects). It's not possible to open inspectors for fields of other data types such as integers, strings, and real numbers.

When inspecting object types, the local menus for the top and bottom inspector panes contain only the three commands shown in Figure 4.20.

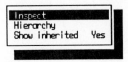

Figure 4.20.   Object-type inspector menu.

Inspect

This command opens an inspector window for another object type. It does not work for fields of other data types—only object types and pointers to object types. The resulting inspector functions is a new object-type inspector.

Hierarchy

This command shows the location of the inspected type in the `Hierarchy` window's tree. It is useful for switching back to that window rapidly without having to close the object-type inspector.

Show inherited

This command toggles inherited properties on and off. Use this command to compare the items defined in this object with those the object inherits from ancestor types.

Global Menus

This chapter began with a description of how to use TD's global menus, which are displayed on the top line of the screen (see Figure 4.1). The following information describes each of TD's global menus in the order they appear on that line and describes any related dialog boxes. Command hot keys are listed in parentheses.

Because some of this information applies to later chapters, the information here is brief and refers you to other places in this book. Also, some terms and concepts haven't been introduced—but that can't be helped. Use this section to become familiar with TD's global menus, commands, and dialog boxes. Then return to it later when you need help with specific commands.

> As in chapter 2, to avoid duplicating the information in the *Turbo Debugger User's Guide*, I've concentrated here on tips that explain why you might want to use one or another command. Remember also that you can highlight any command in TD and press ⟨**F1**⟩ for help.

System Menu (≡)

The System menu contains commands that have system-wide effects on TD's operation—plus one purely informational command. (See Figure 4.21.) Press ⟨**Alt**⟩-⟨**Space**⟩ to open this menu. (Microsoft *Windows* users must press ⟨**Alt**⟩-**F**⟨**Cursor Left**⟩ instead.)

Figure 4.21. System menu.

Repaint desktop

This command redisplays the global menu line, function key line, and all open TD windows. Use it to recover from a misbehaving program that overwrites some or all of TD's display.

> Hint: Memorize ⟨**Alt**⟩-⟨**Space**⟩**R** as the command to use if a program obliterates TD's display so much you can't even see the menu names. This might happen if you started TD with the -ds option or if you set Display:User screen updating to Swap with TDINST (see chapter 3).

Restore standard

This command restores all windows to their configuration when you first loaded your program into TD.

> Hint: If the `Watches` window stops expanding automatically for new variables, use this command to reactivate the expansion, which becomes disabled if you alter the size of the `Module` or `Watches` windows. The command is also useful to restore an expanded `Watches` window to its original small size. To do that, make `Watches` active, press ⟨**Ctrl**⟩-**D** to delete all variables in the window, and press ⟨**Alt**⟩-⟨**Space**⟩**S** to restore the original window sizes.

About

This command displays miscellaneous information about TD.

File Menu

Use `File` menu commands (see Figure 4.22) to open code files for debugging, to change directories, to view general information about a program you're debugging, to issue DOS commands, and to quit TD. You can also use commands in this menu to debug resident code, as chapter 19 explains.

Figure 4.22.   File menu.

Open

This command opens a dialog box (see Figure 4.23) and lets you select another code file for debugging. Enter a `File name`, select a name from `Files`, and view files in other `Directories`. The second to bottom line shows the current path and wild-card settings. The bottom line shows the selected file and its date, time, and size.

In addition to a file name, you can enter arguments and initiate I/O redirection in the dialog's `File name` prompt box. For example, enter a file name such as **myprog.exe arg1 arg2**. However, any arguments that have wild cards (for example, when debugging a directory-lister) are expanded by the dialog;

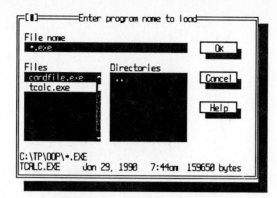

Figure 4.23. File:Open dialog box.

therefore, you must use the Run menu's Arguments command to enter arguments with wild cards.

Hint: At any time during debugging, press ⟨**Alt**⟩-**FO**⟨**Enter**⟩ or select a file name to reload a program. This has the same effect as quitting TD and restarting from DOS, but it is faster.

Change dir

This command opens a prompt box (see Figure 4.14). Enter the path name of any directory. You may specify either a drive, for example, C: or D:, along with the path or just the path. A good time to use this command is just before choosing File:Open when you want to load a program in a different directory and make that directory the new current one.

Get info

This command displays information about the code file loaded at startup or after using File:Open. (See Figure 4.24.) It shows the program name and its current runtime status. Various messages appear here, most of which have obvious meanings such as No program loaded, Control break, Breakpoint at..., Loaded..., Stopped at..., NMI Interrupt, Exception..., Divide by zero, Terminated, and Resident.

In the middle are system memory statistics (left) and EMS use (if TD has found some expanded memory to use). The User interrupts line shows any interrupts the target program is handling. Other items listed near the bottom

Figure 4.24.   File:Get info dialog box.

include the current DOS version, whether breakpoints are being set in hardware (80386 or 80486 systems only with an installed TDH386.SYS driver), and the date and time (to remind you, I suppose, how much time you've lost while hunting bugs).

The values for **Available** RAM are frequently 0 because of the way DOS allocates all memory to a loaded program. This doesn't mean you've run out of room. It just means DOS has given your code all available system RAM. If your program releases some RAM to DOS (or, for example, if in a TP program you use an **$M** directive to limit RAM use), then the **Available** figure might not be 0. The **Available** EMS value (if shown) lists how much EMS RAM is available to your program.

DOS shell

This command exits temporarily to DOS, swapping some RAM to disk to release the amount of memory specified by TDINST. Use it to issue DOS commands such as COPY and COMP. Enter **exit** at the DOS prompt to return to TD.

If the DOS screen doesn't work correctly when you choose this command, for example, if the display doesn't scroll as it normally does, the fault could be an installed ANSI.SYS or similar device driver. Try removing the driver. Or start TD with the -ds command-line option to prevent the debugger from using multiple video pages (see chapter 3).

Never load TSRs into memory after exiting to DOS. Run only small stand-alone utilities and DOS commands.

Resident

Makes TD "go resident" to allow debugging resident code. See chapter 19 for more information about this command.

Symbol load

This command loads a symbol table stored in a .TDS file. See chapters 2, 6, and 19 for information about preparing this file. Before using this command, you may have to start TD with an -sm# option to reserve space for symbols. (See chapter 3.)

Table relocate

This command relocates a symbol table's origin to the address of code already in memory. Usually that code is a TSR loaded before starting TD. Or it might be a device driver. (Chapter 19 explains more about using this command.)

Quit (⟨Alt⟩-X)

Press ⟨**Alt**⟩**-X** to quit TD and return to DOS. You can execute this command at just about any time, but not when a dialog box is active. If ⟨**Alt**⟩**-X** doesn't seem to work, press ⟨**Esc**⟩ and then try ⟨**Alt**⟩**-X** again. If that still doesn't work, press ⟨**Ctrl**⟩**-**⟨**Break**⟩⟨**Esc**⟩⟨**Alt**⟩**-X**. If you get no response, you may have crashed the debugger. Press ⟨**Ctrl**⟩**-**⟨**Alt**⟩**-**⟨**Del**⟩ to reboot. If you're still hung, click your heels three times and toggle the on/off switch.

View Menu

Chapter 5 describes the commands in this menu.

Run Menu

Commands in the Run menu (see Figure 4.25) execute the currently loaded program. Various choices let you run code up to breakpoints (see chapter 8), execute code fragments, single-step individual instructions, animate in slow motion, and even trace backwards to undo previously executed instructions. Other Run-menu commands let you enter program arguments and reset a program to its beginning.

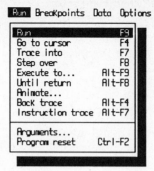

Figure 4.25.   Run menu.

Run (⟨F9⟩)

This command runs program from the line marked by ► in the Module window (see Figure 4.1). Code runs at full speed—except, perhaps, when an active breakpoint is set to monitor memory locations.

> Use this command to run a program up to a breakpoint, which you can set with the commands in the Breakpoints menu, described later in this chapter.

Go to cursor (⟨F4⟩)

Use the arrow keys to move the cursor, or click anywhere on a source-code line with the mouse, and press ⟨**F4**⟩ to run the program up to that line. The program must reach the marked location—if a statement skips the code at the cursor, pressing ⟨**F4**⟩ will have the same effect as ⟨**F9**⟩.

Trace into (⟨F7⟩)

Press ⟨**F7**⟩ to execute the single statement marked by ► in the Module window. If that statement calls a function, procedure, or assembly language subroutine, TD jumps to that routine and pauses, loading a different source-code file from disk if necessary. If process-ID switching is off (see chapter 3), then you can also trace into DOS int 21 function calls. Lines that contain multiple statements execute as a single command.

You can also use this command to trace into object methods. TD recognizes polymorphic method calls—those that are redirected through an array of method addresses called the VMT (Virtual Method Table).

> If pressing ⟨**F7**⟩ causes the **CPU** window to appear, TD can't find the source-code file for the module that contains the traced routine. In that event, either continue debugging on the machine-code level or, to return to your source, press ⟨**F3**⟩ and choose the previous module name. Set a breakpoint (press ⟨**F2**⟩) at the statement after the one you just traced and press ⟨**F9**⟩⟨**F2**⟩. This will execute the code for which the source is unavailable, halt after the routine returns, and remove the temporary breakpoint.

Step over (⟨**F8**⟩)

Press ⟨**F8**⟩ to execute the single statement marked by ► in the **Module** window. Unlike the similar **Trace into** command, **Step over** executes function, procedure, and assembly language subroutine calls as indivisible instructions. After the called routine finishes, the program halts at the next statement. Lines that contain multiple statements execute as a single command.

Use **Step over** to narrow a search for a bug in the early stages of debugging. First, run a suspect section of code by pressing ⟨**F8**⟩ to step over all subroutine calls. Then, when you find the subroutine where the bug appears, set a breakpoint at the statement that activates the routine, reset the program, and press ⟨**F9**⟩ to execute to that location. After that, press ⟨**F7**⟩ to trace into the routine and ⟨**F8**⟩ to step over more code until you find the low-level statement that's causing the problem.

> Despite this command's name, TD does not skip over the current instruction when you press ⟨**F8**⟩. It still executes the stepped-over routine. To skip a statement completely, move the cursor to the next statement below and type ⟨**Alt**⟩-**VC**⟨**Ctrl**⟩-**N**⟨**Alt**⟩-⟨**F3**⟩. This opens the **CPU** window, resets registers CS and IP to the new origin at the cursor, and closes **CPU**. If **CPU** is already active, just move the cursor to the next machine-code instruction to execute and press ⟨**Ctrl**⟩-**N**.

Execute to (⟨**Alt**⟩-⟨**F9**⟩)

Use this command to run a program up to a specific constant address. The program will halt when registers CS:IP equal the specified address. So, for the command to work, the program must reach the address that you enter. If you enter an offset value, TD automatically prefaces it with the code-segment value in CS. For example, TD interprets the Pascal hex value $017F as CS:$017F. Or, specify segment values explicitly as in $4000:$0800.

See chapter 9 for more information on entering address constants in C, Pascal, and assembly language.

You can also type a module name and line number such as **umod#100** to halt before executing the statement at that line. But it's usually easier to use Go to cursor (move the cursor and press ⟨**F4**⟩) for this purpose instead.

If you receive a runtime error when executing a program directly from DOS, note the address and load the program into TD. Then, press ⟨**Alt**⟩-⟨**F9**⟩ and enter an expression such as **(cs+0000):ffff** where 0000 is the runtime error's segment value and *ffff* is the offset. Because loading the program into TD positions the code to a different location than when that same program runs from DOS (unless you're running TD386), you must add the current code-segment register CS to the runtime error's segment value. If that doesn't work, you might have to press ⟨**F8**⟩ immediately after starting TD before using the Execute to command. This will execute any startup code and initialize CS to your program's code segment.

Until return (⟨Alt⟩-⟨F8⟩)

There are two main uses for this command. One, after pressing ⟨**F7**⟩ when you meant to press ⟨**F8**⟩ to step over a procedure or function call, press ⟨**Alt**⟩-⟨**F8**⟩ to run the program at full speed until the code returns to the statement following the one that called the routine. In that way, ⟨**Alt**⟩-⟨**F8**⟩ is a sort of "undo" command for Trace into. Two, use the command to finish executing a procedure or function after you've examined its initial statements.

> Press ⟨**Alt**⟩-**VS** to open the Stack window. The routine immediately below the highlighted line tells you the general location to which ⟨**Alt**⟩-⟨**F8**⟩ will return. If the Stack window shows no active subroutine calls, pressing ⟨**Alt**⟩-⟨**F8**⟩ does nothing.

Animate

Execute this command by pressing ⟨**Alt**⟩-**RN** or by choosing the Animate command from the Run menu. (Previous TD versions assigned hot key ⟨**Alt**⟩-⟨**F4**⟩ to this command. Version 2.0 now uses those keys for the Back trace command.) Enter the amount of delay in tenths of seconds to pause between each source-code line (or machine code if you're debugging in the CPU window). For example, enter 20 to pause for about 2 seconds between lines; enter 2.5 to pause for about a quarter second.

Use Animate to monitor a series of statements instead of pressing ⟨**F7**⟩ repeatedly. Then sit back and wait for a bug to appear. Press ⟨**Esc**⟩ to stop animating and then use other commands to fine-tune your search for a problem.

Back trace (⟨Alt⟩-⟨F4⟩)

New to version 2.0, `Back trace` is TD's "execution undo" command. Just press ⟨Alt⟩-⟨F4⟩ to run your program in reverse, undoing the effects of statements previously executed by pressing ⟨F7⟩ or ⟨Alt⟩-⟨F7⟩ or by using `Run:Animate`. You can also reverse most statements executed by pressing ⟨F8⟩, but you can't unravel a `LOOP`, a machine-code string instruction, or other statements treated as atomic by `Step over`. To get the most out of `Back trace,` use ⟨F7⟩ to execute several statements and press ⟨Alt⟩-⟨F4⟩ to undo that execution.

TD can reverse execute up to 400 statements, or 3000 if you have enough EMS RAM. Press ⟨Alt⟩-**VE** to open the `Execution history` window to examine the list of recorded statements. (See chapter 5 for more information about this window.)

Don't expect too much from `Back trace`. Obviously, it can't recall text sent to a printer or data written to disk. It also can't back up through a software interrupt `int` instruction unless you traced into that code by pressing ⟨Alt⟩-⟨F7⟩ (see `Instruction trace` in the next section). Despite these limitations, `Back trace` does let you back up to rerun a troublesome section, perhaps with new arguments.

> Pressing ⟨**F9**⟩ and executing software interrupts erases the `Execution history`; therefore, this puts ⟨Alt⟩-⟨F4⟩ out of action until you run a few more statements by pressing ⟨**F7**⟩ or ⟨Alt⟩-⟨F7⟩.

Instruction trace (⟨Alt⟩-⟨F7⟩)

When debugging C or Pascal source code in the `Module` window, press ⟨Alt⟩-⟨F7⟩ to open the `CPU` window and execute one machine-code instruction—usually one of several such instructions that the compiler generated for this high-level statement. This has the identical effect as pressing ⟨Alt⟩-**VC**⟨F7⟩. You can also use this command to trace a software interrupt `int` instruction.

Use the command in the final debugging stages after you've narrowed a problem to one or more statements and when you need to examine each machine-code instruction to understand why a high-level statement failed. For assembly language debugging, the command works, but it isn't that useful.

> Hint: After tracing into a procedure or function call by pressing ⟨Alt⟩-⟨F7⟩, to return to the source-code view and halt at the next statement, press ⟨**F6**⟩ repeatedly to make the `Module` window active. Then press ⟨**F8**⟩.

Arguments

Use this command to enter program arguments or to enable I/O redirection as you might do if executing the code from the DOS command line. Because this changes the startup conditions, TD asks if you want to "Reload program so arguments take effect?" Press ⟨**Enter**⟩ or click the Yes button. Press ⟨**Esc**⟩ or click **No** to cancel reloading and to throw away the new arguments—you must let TD reload the program for the new arguments to be accepted.

Reloading the program does not affect any variables added to **Watches** or any breakpoints set in code. This makes the **Arguments** command particularly handy for testing a variety of input data—for example, all the character switches that the program recognizes.

Remember that you can supply program arguments when starting TD. For example, you can enter **td mycode file** to debug a program file named MYCODE.EXE and supply the argument FILE. Use the **Arguments** command if you forget to supply a needed argument or to change the arguments that you entered before.

Program reset (⟨Ctrl⟩-⟨F2⟩)

Press ⟨**Ctrl**⟩-⟨**F2**⟩ to reset the program to its original startup condition. All breakpoints and watched variables remain active, so you can use this command to restart and investigate the effects of new input data or other operations.

> Hint: Activate the **Module** window and press ⟨**Ctrl**⟩-**O** immediately after pressing ⟨**Ctrl**⟩-⟨**F2**⟩ to bring the first source-code statement into view.

Breakpoints Menu

The **Breakpoints** menu (see Figure 4.26) lets you set breakpoints at specific locations or based on other conditions. When you execute a program by pressing ⟨**F9**⟩, TD halts the code before executing the statement at a breakpoint or after executing code that satisfies other conditions such as a variable reaching a specific value.

Don't confuse this menu with the **View** menu's **Breakpoints** command. Use the **Breakpoints** menu to set new breakpoints. Use the **View** menu's **Breakpoints** command to view and modify breakpoints already set. Normally, a breakpoint halts the program when it reaches a test location. But it's also possible to perform other breakpoint actions, call subroutines, and log expressions. (See chapter 8 for information about how to use breakpoints as part of a good debugging strategy.)

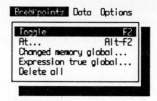

Figure 4.26. Breakpoints menu.

Toggle (⟨F2⟩)

The simplest way to set a breakpoint is to move the cursor to a source-code line and press ⟨**F2**⟩. Or, move the mouse cursor to either of the two blank columns to the left of any source-code statement and click the left mouse button when the mouse cursor changes from a square block to the symbol *. On monochrome monitors, the breakpoint shows in reverse video or is highlighted in some other way. On color monitors, breakpoint statements display in stop-sign red.

To remove a breakpoint, position the cursor and press ⟨**F2**⟩ again. You can toggle a breakpoint on and off as often as necessary. And, there's no limit to the number of breakpoints you can set simultaneously. (Actually, there may be an upper limit—TD has to record breakpoint information *somewhere* in a PC's limited memory. But the maximum number is probably so high that it's meaningless to consider.)

You may set a breakpoint only on statements for which the compiler generates machine code. This includes certain keywords and symbols such as **BEGIN** and **END** in Pascal or the braces { and } in C, which TD takes to represent any startup code appended by the compiler to the beginning of a subroutine; therefore, setting a breakpoint at the first statement in a procedure may have a different effect than setting one at the **BEGIN** or opening brace.

> Hint: The **Toggle** command accepts a certain amount of "slop"—the cursor can be anywhere on a line, it doesn't have to be positioned at the first character. Also, if the cursor is on a line that doesn't generate any machine code—for example, a comment or a function header—pressing ⟨**F2**⟩ sets a breakpoint at the first code-generating statement below. You don't have to move the cursor to that line.

At (⟨Alt⟩-⟨F2⟩)

Use this command to enter a constant address where you want the program to halt. You can also enter a module name and line number in the form **MODULE#250**.

Usually, pressing ⟨**F2**⟩ is easier than using this command to set breakpoints. But it might be useful for running code up to a runtime error location or to an address listing in a .MAP file. In that case, you may have to add your program's CS register value to the reported segment address—similar to the way you can specify a stopping address with the `Execute to` command in the `Run` menu.

Changed memory global

One of the most common and difficult bugs to fix is a bad pointer or other instruction that alters a memory location unexpectedly. Use the `Changed memory global` command to narrow your search for the source of this slippery bug.

When you choose the command, a dialog box prompts you for a memory address and count. Enter a constant expression followed by a comma and the number of elements you want to monitor. Normally, you'll specify the address as the name of a variable. For example, to halt the program if the `Temperature` rises (or falls), just enter that variable's name. To monitor more than a single variable—for example, an array of ten integers—follow the name of the variable by the count like this: **MyArray,10**.

The 10 here does not represent the number of bytes that are monitored. Instead, this is the count of elements of the variable's size. If TD recognizes `MyArray` to have 5-byte elements, the expression would set a breakpoint for 50 bytes.

You can also enter an explicit address such as DS:$0800,128 to monitor a block of 128 bytes. In C, use an expression such as DS:0x0800,128. See chapters 5 and 8 for more information on watching memory values.

The more bytes you monitor, the slower your code will run. If you have an 80386-based system, install the TDH386.SYS device driver to enable hardware debugging features, allowing code to run at full speed. You can execute either TD or TD386 for this purpose—it's the device driver that enables the special registers, not the virtual-mode capabilities in TD386.

Expression true global

This command sets a breakpoint to halt the program when a variable equals a specific value. For example, to trigger a breakpoint when an integer variable named `count` equals 99, choose this command and enter the expression **count = 10** in Pascal, **count = = 10** in C, or **count eq 10** in assembly language.

You can also monitor processor registers for specific values with this breakpoint option. In Pascal, enter **ax⟨⟩0**; in C, enter **ax! = 0**; and in assembly language, enter **ax ne 0** to halt the code if register AX is not zero. (See chapter 9 for help with entering other expressions in these three languages.)

> As with `Changed memory global`, this command may cause performance to drag unless you have an 80386-based system and have installed the TDH386.SYS device driver.

Delete all

Execute Delete all to remove all breakpoints from your program. To remove individual breakpoints, move the cursor to that location and press ⟨**F2**⟩. Or open View:Breakpoints, highlight any listed breakpoint, and press ⟨**Ctrl**⟩-**R**.

Data Menu

The four commands in the Data menu (see Figure 4.27) give you ways to inspect variables, evaluate expressions, add expressions to the Watches window, and examine function return values.

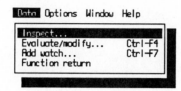

Figure 4.27. Data menu.

Inspect

Choose Inspect and enter the name of a variable that you want to examine in detail. If the variable is within the current scope, TD opens an inspector window and displays the variable's contents. If not, TD displays "Symbol not found." This means you can always inspect a global variable, but you can inspect local variables in C and Pascal only when their declaring procedures and functions are active.

Because the size, contents, and abilities of inspector windows depend on the examined data structure, it takes time to learn how to put these windows to the best use. For general information about inspector window features, see "Inspectors" earlier in this chapter. For detailed instructions for inspecting specific data structures in C, Pascal, and assembly language, see chapters 20–22.

> Usually, the easiest way to open an inspector window is to position the cursor on a variable name and press ⟨**Ctrl**⟩-**I**. Most often, you'll choose the Inspect command in the Data menu only when you can't easily find the variable name in your source code.

Evaluate/modify (⟨Ctrl⟩-⟨F4⟩)

Use this command to evaluate an expression, to examine a variable's value, or to change it. You can also use the command to call procedures and functions in your C and Pascal programs independently of the program's normal operation—a great way to run quick tests on a misbehaving subroutine.

When you press ⟨**Ctrl**⟩-⟨**F4**⟩ or choose `Evaluate/modify` from the `Data` menu, TD displays the dialog box in Figure 4.28. Three prompt boxes—`Expression`, `Result`, and `New value`—occupy most of this dialog box. The `Expression` area lets you enter new expressions to evaluate. The `Result` box shows the result of an expression after you choose the `Eval` button. And the `New value` space lets you enter a new value for a variable you entered into `Expression`. These three boxes can scroll horizontally if necessary to display long lines, indicated by left and right triangles at either end of the field. The top and bottom areas can scroll vertically, and they each have separate history lists of previous entries. Press ⟨**Esc**⟩ or click the close button to close the dialog box.

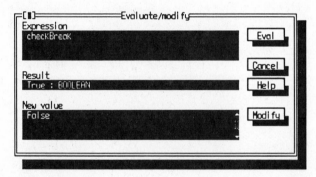

Figure 4.28.   Evaluate/modify dialog box.

To enter a new expression, tab to the `Expression` field and type the expression as it would appear in C, Pascal, or assembly language. You can also highlight an expression in the `Module` window and press ⟨**Ctrl**⟩-⟨**F4**⟩ to open `Evaluate/ modify` and copy the marked text to the `Expression` prompt box. Or just move the cursor to a variable name and open the dialog box. Choose `Eval` to evaluate the expression and display the result in the `Result` area. If the cursor is inside the `Expression` field, you can also press ⟨**Enter**⟩ to choose the `Eval` button.

If you evaluate a variable, you can change its value by moving to the `New value` field and entering another constant expression. For example, after typing **MyCount** into the `Expression` area and pressing ⟨**Enter**⟩ to examine that variable's value, tab to `New value` and enter **MyCount+1**. Then, choose `Modify` to evaluate that expression and assign its result to the variable in the `Expression` area. If the cursor is inside the `New value` field, pressing ⟨**Enter**⟩ chooses the `Modify` button.

Expressions can also call procedures and functions in C and Pascal programs. When it evaluates such expressions, TD pushes any required parameters and calls the routine—just as a statement in your program might do. Part 2 (especially chapter 9) explains how this works.

When an object method is active, enter `self` (or `this` for TC + +) into the `Expression` area. This is a good way to verify the class of an object, but `Inspector` windows are usually better for examining objects in detail.

Add watch (⟨Ctrl⟩-⟨F7⟩)

Press ⟨**Ctrl**⟩-⟨**F7**⟩ and enter a variable name or expression to add to the `Watches` window. If that window is closed, TD opens it. The expression or variable must evaluate to a constant—you can't enter expressions that cause side effects such as assigning a value to a variable or incrementing a variable with C's `++` and `--` operators. But you can watch expressions such as `MyCounter*2`. TD will then display the result of that expression, and it will update that value if `MyCounter` ever changes.

Rather than use this command, however, you may find it easier to move the cursor to a variable name and press ⟨**Ctrl**⟩-**W** to add that variable to `Watches`. (See chapter 5 for more information about this view window.) Use the `Add watch` command only if it's inconvenient to find a variable in the source code.

Function return

After halting a program inside a function, choose this command to examine the result that will be passed back to the function's caller. The command opens an `Inspector` window to a pseudo variable that represents the function's value, formatted according to the declared data type.

> Hint: Most function results are passed in registers, which you can also examine with the `View:Registers` command. Use that command along with `Function return` to verify that function results are stored in the expected registers.

Options Menu

The commands in the `Options` menu (see Figure 4.29) let you select various runtime parameters, create macros, change display formats, set directory paths, and perform other jobs that affect how TD operates. You can also save options in configuration files that you can reload during future debugging sessions to restore a custom configuration.

Language

Choose `Source` or one of the three languages—`C`, `Pascal`, or `Assembler` (assembly language)—from the dialog box shown in Figure 4.30. When this

Figure 4.29. Options menu.

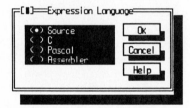

Figure 4.30. Expression Language dialog box.

option is set to `Source`, TD detects the language type automatically so you can enter expressions in that language's format. Use the other settings to force TD to accept expressions in a different format.

Hint: If you're more comfortable with C, but you have to debug a Pascal program, change **Language** to **C**. You can still debug the Pascal code as usual, but you can now enter hex values as **0x0800** and use other C constructions. Pascal programmers faced with debugging foreign C code can switch **Language** to **Pascal** to let TD recognize hex values such as $0800 and to format other expressions in a more familiar style.

Macros

The `Macros` command displays a submenu that you can use to create and delete macros (see the right half of Figure 4.4). TD macros can record and assign lengthy command sequences to ⟨Ctrl⟩ and other keys, which you can then press to run those commands.

Creating macros is easy. Just press **⟨Alt⟩-=** to begin recording and press the key to assign to this macro. Then, execute the commands to record. When you're done, press **⟨Alt⟩-⟨Minus⟩** to stop.

Using macros effectively is another matter. Because source-code changes, it's difficult to create general-purpose macros that work correctly under a range of conditions. Still, macros are useful. See chapter 16's sample macros for C, Pascal, and assembly language debugging.

You can record only TD commands in macros, not input typed into program variables. If you need that ability, use TDINST to switch on "Keystroke recording," or start TD with the -k option to record all keypresses and most mouse movements (see chapter 3).

Display options

Figure 4.31 shows the dialog box associated with this command. It's settings are similar to those for TDINST's `Display` command as described in chapter 3.

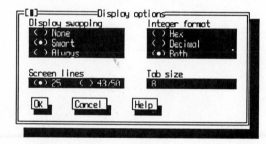

Figure 4.31. Display options dialog box.

Use the dialog box to change `Display swapping` to `None` (no output display), `Smart` (show output only when it changes or might change), or `Always` (show output between every statement).

Choose an `Integer format` to show values in `Hex` or `Decimal`. Use `Both` to display in both styles—usually the best choice unless you prefer one or the other and want to save a little horizontal display space.

Set `Screen lines` to `25` for most monochrome and CGA displays or to `43/50` for EGA and VGA displays that can display extra lines. The change takes effect as soon as you close the dialog box.

Set `Tab size` to the same setting that you use in your editor, from 1 to 32. The source code must have embedded tab characters for this setting to have an effect.

Path for source

Enter a path name with an optional drive letter where you store your program's source-code files. Enter multiple directory names separated by semicolons.

For large multimodule programs, I like to store various sections in their own directories. When debugging test programs inside those directories, I enter the pseudo directory name ".." in `Path for source`. Or, I use names such as "..\subx." This tells TD to look for additional source-code files in this directory's parent and in other subdirectories stemming from the same ancestor. I also avoid specifying drive letters such as C: and D:. That way, my configurations will work if I move my files to a different drive.

Save options

Choose this command and fill in the dialog box shown in Figure 4.32. Check off the items you want to save—`Options` to save all settings from other `Options`-menu commands, `Layout` to save the currently open `View`-menu window positions and sizes, and `Macros` to save any macros you created. Enter the file name, usually TDCONFIG.TD, in the `Save to` input field, then choose `Ok` to save the configuration to disk.

Figure 4.32. Save Configuration dialog box.

Be careful when typing the `Save to` file name—TD doesn't warn you before replacing an existing file. Some programmers name their configurations the same as their program, for example, SORT.TD for a program named SORT.C. This may be asking for trouble. If you accidentally supply the wrong file-name extension (.C instead of .TD), you could wipe out a source-code file.

If you change the output file name by accident, to return to the default TDCONFIG.TD, move to the `Save to` prompt box and press ⟨**Cursor Up**⟩ or ⟨**Cursor Down**⟩.

Restore options

Use this command to load a configuration file saved by the `Save options` command or created with TDINST as explained in chapter 3. The command opens a file dialog similar to the `File:Open` command's (see Figure 4.23) but displays files ending in .TD instead of .EXE. (You can change this by entering a new wild-card expression such as ***.tdx** or ***.td?**.)

Window Menu

Just about everything TD has to say is displayed in a window. Use the commands in the `Window` menu (see Figure 4.33) to move, resize, shrink, expand, close, and activate various TD windows. Some of these operations were covered earlier—see "Views" near the beginning of this chapter.

Figure 4.33.   Window menu.

Zoom (⟨F5⟩)

Press ⟨**F5**⟩ to expand the current window to full screen or to shrink it to its former size. I find the command especially handy for examining complex data structures in inspector windows—it's faster to zoom such windows to full screen temporarily than to use mouse and keyboard commands to make minor adjustments to the window size.

> Hint: Because large windows take more memory, this command may not work when debugging big programs. You can usually avoid this problem and conserve resources by zooming only one window at a time.

Next (⟨F6⟩)

Press ⟨**F6**⟩ to activate the next window in numerical sequence. I use this key to bring multiple inspector windows back into view after switching to `Module` to view some source code. Even though this means pressing ⟨**F6**⟩ several times, this is often easier than choosing the windows by other means as explained later in this section.

Next pane (⟨Tab⟩)

Press ⟨**Tab**⟩ to move from one pane to the next in windows that have more than one pane or in dialog boxes with multiple fields and buttons. This command does nothing for windows that have only single panes.

> Press ⟨**Shift**⟩-⟨**Cursor Left**⟩ or ⟨**Shift**⟩-⟨**Cursor Right**⟩ to move the cursor to the previous and next words in the `Module` window. Pressing ⟨**Tab**⟩ in TD does not move the text cursor to the next column as it does in most text editors, but these alternate keys make it possible to move around just as rapidly.

Size/move (⟨Ctrl⟩-⟨F5⟩)

Formerly attached to ⟨Scroll Lock⟩, the `Size/move` command lets you move and resize any window that has a resize handle in the lower right corner (see Figure 4.1). You can move but not resize dialog boxes. If you have a mouse, you'll probably never use this command. (In that case, remember ⟨Ctrl⟩-⟨F5⟩ as a possible macro key.)

Iconize/restore

Choose this command to reduce the current window to an icon, displayed as a tiny window near the bottom right of TD's display. Choose the command to expand an icon to its former size.

If you prefer to keep many `View`-menu windows open instead of choosing them individually as needed, convert them all to icons and use `Options:Save options` to store the `Layout` in a configuration file. When you restart TD, you can then use a mouse or keyboard command to expand the windows you want to use.

> After converting a window to an icon, it may disappear behind `Module` or `Watches.` If that happens, press ⟨**F6**⟩ to bring the icons forward so you can see them. Or, if this is a frequent problem, shrink `Module` and `Watches` one or two columns horizontally from the right to expose a sliver of the icon borders, which you can click with the mouse pointer to activate the windows.

Close (⟨Alt⟩-⟨F3⟩)

Press ⟨**Alt**⟩-⟨**F3**⟩ to close the current **View**-menu window. This does not work for dialog boxes. If the window is an inspector, pressing ⟨**Alt**⟩-⟨**F3**⟩ closes *all* open inspectors. To close only the active inspector window, press ⟨**Esc**⟩. (In previous TD versions, ⟨F3⟩ was the **Close** command's hot key.) See the next command for a way to undo the most recent close.

Undo close (⟨Alt⟩-⟨F6⟩)

If you accidentally close a **View**-menu or inspector (but not a dialog box), press ⟨**Alt**⟩-⟨**F6**⟩ to reopen the window to its former size, position, and content. You can restore only the most recently closed window—pressing ⟨**Alt**⟩-⟨**F6**⟩ again does not reopen other windows closed earlier.

> Hint: After opening multiple inspector windows, to close all but the one with the lowest window number, press ⟨**F6**⟩ or click on any *other* inspector to make it active, then press ⟨**Alt**⟩-⟨**F3**⟩⟨**Alt**⟩-⟨**F6**⟩. This can be handy when following a linked list to start over from the root node and follow a different path.

Dump pane to log

Choose this command to copy the information in the currently active pane of the active window to the **Log** window, opened by **View:Log**. See chapter 5 for more information about keeping logs and saving a log file to disk.

    I often use this command to prepare before-and-after tests. For example, after opening the **Registers** window, I'll dump one or both panes to the **Log** window. This gives me a snapshot of register and flag values as they existed at this place in my program. After running other statements, I can then compare the **Log** entry with the current values in **Registers**. (If you do this frequently, assign the command to a macro key. See chapter 16.)

User screen (⟨Alt⟩-⟨F5⟩)

Press ⟨**Alt**⟩-⟨**F5**⟩ to switch from TD's display to the program's output screen. To return to TD, press any key. The display output is frozen—all you can do is look.

    If this command doesn't work, check that **Options:Display options** is set to **Smart** or **Always**. If it's set to **None**, there is no display output to view. Also, TD disables **User screen** during remote and dual-monitor debugging (see chapter 17).

1 Module TCALC, 2 Watches

At the bottom of the Windows menu (see Figure 4.33) is a numbered list of all open View-menu and inspector windows. The list changes as you open and close windows, but it usually has the two entries listed here, Module (plus the module's name) and Watches.

To activate a listed window, you can open the Windows menu and press its number. This is the same number you can press along with ⟨**Alt**⟩ when the menu is *not* open. Usually, though, pressing ⟨**F6**⟩ or using a mouse to activate new windows is easier. The list is mostly helpful just for seeing what windows are open.

> The Windows menu can list up to nine window titles. When ten or more windows are open, the last menu command changes to Window pick. Choosing this command opens a dialog list box (see Figure 4.10) from which you can select the window you want to activate.

Help Menu

The last global menu lists three commands for TD's on-line help system. (See Figure 4.34.) The commands are easy to use. Just choose one of the Help menu's selections or press ⟨**F1**⟩. Then, follow the on-screen instructions to page among topics until you find the help you need.

Figure 4.34.   Help menu.

TD's help system is *context-sensitive*. This means you can activate a window or highlight a command and press ⟨**F1**⟩ at any time to view more information about that selection. For information about how to use on-line help, press ⟨**F1**⟩ twice.

Use the four cursor movement keys to select highlighted words in help-text screens, then press ⟨**Enter**⟩ to view more information about these topics. After threading your way among the facts you need, press ⟨**Esc**⟩ to close the help windows and return to what you were doing. To back out of a threaded journey through various help screens, press ⟨**Page Up**⟩ one or more times. See Table 4.3 for a complete list of keys you can use while viewing help screens.

Hint: Press ⟨**Alt**⟩-⟨**F1**⟩ to reopen the previous help screen after you close the on-line help system by pressing ⟨**Esc**⟩. This is a handy key to remember for flipping between another TD window and the help text that describes how that window works.

Table 4.3. On-line help keys.

Key	Action
⟨Alt⟩-⟨F1⟩	View previous screen (same as ⟨Page Up⟩)
⟨Ctrl⟩-⟨Page Up⟩	Return to first page opened this session
⟨Cursor Down⟩	Select highlighted topic below
⟨Cursor Left⟩	Select highlighted topic to left
⟨Cursor Right⟩	Select highlighted topic to right
⟨Cursor Up⟩	Select highlighted topic above
⟨Enter⟩	View help screen for highlighted topic
⟨Esc⟩	Close help screen and return to TD
⟨F1⟩	Open index to all help topics
⟨Page Down⟩	View next help screen*
⟨Page Up⟩	View previous screen (same as ⟨Alt⟩-⟨F1⟩)

*This works only when "PgUp/PgDn" appears in lower right corner.

Index (⟨Shift⟩-⟨F1⟩)

Press ⟨**Shift**⟩-⟨**F1**⟩ at any time to open TD's `Help Index` window. Then, use cursor and page movement keys or a mouse to choose topics from the displayed list.

Previous topic (⟨Alt⟩-⟨F1⟩)

When the on-line help system is open, pressing ⟨**Alt**⟩-⟨**F1**⟩ is the same as pressing ⟨**Page Up**⟩. The command takes you back through the help screens you visited previously.

This command is more useful after closing help by pressing ⟨**Esc**⟩. At any time after that, you can press ⟨**Alt**⟩-⟨**F1**⟩ to reopen the previous help screen.

Help on Help

Choose this command for an overview of TD's on-line help system. The information is the same as displayed when you choose the `Help on Help` entry in the help system index.

Hot Keys

As you learn to navigate TD's menus and windows, you'll find many commands that have *hot-key* assignments. Memorize as many of those keys as you can. You'll cut out a lot of rigmarole—opening menus, moving highlight bars, and choosing commands from pop-up lists.

This section will help you to learn TD's hot keys. Listed here are ⟨Ctrl⟩, ⟨Alt⟩, and all function key combinations (see Tables 4.4, 4.5, and 4.6). Unused combinations (marked *none* in the "Action" column) are available for assigning to macros (except for ⟨F11⟩ and ⟨F12⟩ on extended keyboards). Other suitable macro keys are ⟨Shift⟩-⟨F2⟩ through ⟨Shift⟩-⟨F10⟩.

For compatibility with Borland's integrated Turbo Pascal and Turbo C compilers and editors, ⟨Shift⟩-⟨F6⟩ performs the same action as ⟨F6⟩, ⟨Ctrl⟩-⟨F8⟩ sets breakpoints as does ⟨F2⟩, and ⟨Ctrl⟩-⟨F10⟩ and ⟨Alt⟩-⟨F10⟩ both open local menus. Unless you need both sets of keys, the duplicated entries make good choices for assigning to macros.

Table 4.4.   Function hot keys.

Key	Action
⟨F1⟩	On-line help text
⟨F2⟩	Toggle breakpoint at cursor on or off
⟨F3⟩	Open the `Pick a module` dialog box
⟨F4⟩	Execute program up to cursor
⟨F5⟩	Zoom (enlarge or shrink) window
⟨F6⟩	Uncover and make next window active
⟨F7⟩	Single-step, tracing *into* subroutine calls
⟨F8⟩	Single-step, stepping *over* subroutine calls
⟨F9⟩	Run program to a breakpoint or to completion
⟨F10⟩	Toggle between global menu and a window
⟨F11⟩	*None* (not available for macro assignment)
⟨F12⟩	*None* (not available for macro assignment)

This section does not list local-menu ⟨Ctrl⟩-letter keys. As explained earlier, every `View` window has its own local menu of commands, each of which has a highlighted character that you can press along with ⟨Ctrl⟩ to choose that command without first opening the menu. The best way to learn these hot keys is to open the menus or press the ⟨Ctrl⟩-key combinations to choose commands. Eventually, you'll memorize the keys for the commands you use most frequently.

If you have a mouse, you can click the left button to choose any function key displayed on TD's bottom line. You can also hold down ⟨**Alt**⟩ or ⟨**Ctrl**⟩ until that line changes (this takes a moment). Then, while still pressing that key, click the listed function. If you're good with a mouse, but not the world's best typist, you may find this method easier than pressing double-function keys.

Table 4.5. ⟨Alt⟩-Function hot keys.

Keys	Action
⟨Alt⟩-⟨F1⟩	Display or reopen previous help screen
⟨Alt⟩-⟨F2⟩	Set breakpoint options
⟨Alt⟩-⟨F3⟩	Close the active window (⟨Alt⟩-⟨F6⟩ recovers)
⟨Alt⟩-⟨F4⟩	Back trace through previous instruction traces
⟨Alt⟩-⟨F5⟩	View user screen (any keypress returns to TD)
⟨Alt⟩-⟨F6⟩	Reopen most recently closed **View** window
⟨Alt⟩-⟨F7⟩	Trace into machine code of current statement
⟨Alt⟩-⟨F8⟩	Run until return from subroutine
⟨Alt⟩-⟨F9⟩	Execute up to specified address or line
⟨Alt⟩-⟨F10⟩	Open local menu for current window

Table 4-6. ⟨Ctrl⟩-function hot keys.

Keys	Action
⟨Ctrl⟩-⟨F1⟩	*None*
⟨Ctrl⟩-⟨F2⟩	Reset program to startup conditions
⟨Ctrl⟩-⟨F3⟩	*None*
⟨Ctrl⟩-⟨F4⟩	Evaluate and modify expressions
⟨Ctrl⟩-⟨F5⟩	Activate window move and resize commands
⟨Ctrl⟩-⟨F6⟩	*None*
⟨Ctrl⟩-⟨F7⟩	Add a variable to Watches window
⟨Ctrl⟩-⟨F8⟩	Toggle breakpoint (same as ⟨F2⟩)
⟨Ctrl⟩-⟨F9⟩	Run program (same as ⟨F9⟩)
⟨Ctrl⟩-⟨F10⟩	Open local menu (same as ⟨Alt⟩-⟨F10⟩)

Summary

TD is a complex software package, and learning how to use its many windows, menus, and hot keys can be frustrating—especially when you have to find a bug now, not tomorrow. However, by weaving TD into your daily programming habits and by using the debugger as a tool to examine code even before bugs occur, you'll be ready to use the commands when bugs do surface.

This chapter is organized as a reference to most of TD's windows, menus, and hot keys. It also contains general information about using windows, dialog boxes, inspectors, the keyboard, and a mouse. Skim the chapter for an overview of TD's operations, then come back later for help with specific commands as you need it.

TD uses three kinds of menus: global menus, local menus, and submenus. Global menus are always available except when a dialog box is open. Local menus are associated with other windows. Submenus contain additional commands. Descriptions of global menus are listed in this chapter in the order the menus appear on the top line of TD's display.

The next chapter covers TD's most heavily used windows and commands from the View menu.

Views and Local Commands

Most of TD's power is concentrated in the `View` menu's 14 main commands (see Figure 5.1). Each of these commands opens a *view window,* described in this chapter in alphabetic order along with the window's associated local commands.

Most `View`-menu commands directly open their view windows—for example, `Watches` and `Registers`. Others (`Module` and `File`) first open a dialog box that prompts for various options to apply to those views. One command (`Another`) opens a submenu that lets you create additional copies of three other common views.

If you are reading this chapter out of order, you might want to glance at the beginning of chapter 4 for general help on using windows, choosing menu commands, and operating dialog boxes. Here are a few highlights from chapter 4 that will also help:

- Press 〈**Alt**〉-**V** to open the `View` menu. Then, press the highlighted letter of the command you want. For all `View` commands, this is the first letter of the command name. Press **C** to open the `CPU` view, **H** for the object `Hierarchy`, and so on. You can also use a mouse to choose commands.

- An ellipsis (...) in a menu command indicates that the command opens a dialog box. A small triangle (►) tells you the command opens a submenu.

- Press 〈**Esc**〉 to close a dialog box. Press 〈**Alt**〉-〈**F3**〉 to close a `View` window. You know it's a dialog box if the lower right corner is a solid double line. Only active `View` windows (and inspectors) have single-line resize handles at the lower right.

- TD normally opens the `Module` and `Watches` views when you start debugging. You'll rarely need to open these windows from the `View` menu.

- Press 〈**Alt**〉-〈**F10**〉 or 〈**Ctrl**〉-〈**F10**〉 to open a view's private menu of local commands. Or, instead of opening the menu, press 〈**Ctrl**〉 and a local

Figure 5.1.   View menu.

command's highlighted letter. A few commands also recognize ⟨**Delete**⟩ and ⟨**Insert**⟩ as alternate hot keys. Get in the habit of using these keys—they can save a lot of time. To help you learn them, this chapter lists hot keys in parentheses after the local command names.

- Press ⟨**F6**⟩ or use a mouse to activate an inactive window. Only one view at a time can be active, and all local commands apply only to that view.

How to Use This Chapter

Because this chapter is a reference to all View-menu commands, it mentions topics discussed elsewhere. So, if you come across something you don't understand, just skip it and go on. Don't try to memorize every detail here—skim the material the first time through and plan to come back later when you need help with specific commands.

Dozens of figures in this chapter illustrate many of TD's displays, making this a good chapter to read when you're away from your computer. Depending on the type of video adapter you have, the screens printed here might be different from those you see on your monitor. But all elements will be in the same places, and this shouldn't cause any problems.

Default Commands

Most views have default commands in their local menus that TD executes when the view's window is active and you simply start typing or when you press ⟨**Enter**⟩ or ⟨**Space**⟩. These commands are marked here by the word *(Default)*.

Default commands make TD seem almost intelligent, and they can save many wasteful keystrokes. For example, `Goto` is the `Module` window's default command; therefore, instead of pressing ⟨**Ctrl**⟩-**G** or opening the local menu and pressing **G**, you can simply type the name of a procedure or function to view. Once you learn these and other shortcuts, you'll never have to select these commands from their menus again.

Another View

Strictly speaking, `Another` isn't a view—it's a command that lets you open additional copies of three other views: `Module`, `Dump`, and `File`, explained elsewhere in this chapter. Choose `Another` and then choose an additional view from the submenu (see the bottom of Figure 5.1).

`Another` is needed because of the way `View` commands work. If, for example, you choose `Dump` a second time, it activates the *current* `Dump` window, bringing that window to the front if it's now hidden. It doesn't create another `Dump`. For this reason, only `Another` can open a second copy of these three windows. (It would serve no purpose to have second copies of the other views.)

You can use `Another` to open as many `Module`, `Dump`, or `File` windows as you need, limited only by the amount of memory available for TD to store internal data related to open windows.

Breakpoints View

The `Breakpoints` view displays facts about active and inactive *breakpoints*— stopping places or conditions where you want to halt a program for examination, log an expression, or call a subroutine. As Figure 5.2 shows, the `Breakpoints` window has two panes, but unlike other multipane windows, only the left pane has a local menu.

The right pane displays details about the highlighted breakpoint to the left. Move the highlight bar to select any breakpoint and read the information to the right. In Figure 5.2, the breakpoint named `Global_1` is set to go off when the expression `Reg.ax <> 0` is true. The breakpoint is enabled.

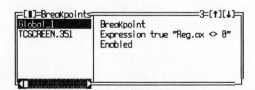

Figure 5.2. Breakpoints view.

If you've installed TDH386.SYS and if a breakpoint can use hardware debugging features on 80386 or 80486 processors, an asterisk in the left pane indicates that this breakpoint will not affect performance when you run the code by pressing ⟨**F9**⟩.

Don't confuse the `Breakpoints` view with the global `Breakpoints` menu. Use the view to examine breakpoints you set previously and to modify how those breakpoints work. Use the menu to set new breakpoints, as described in chapter 8. (It is possible, though not as easy, to set breakpoints with the view's local `Add` command, as explained later in this chapter.)

Local Breakpoints View Commands

There are six local commands that you can use when the `Breakpoints` view is active. (See Figure 5.3.) The following notes describe how to use each of these commands.

Figure 5.3.   Breakpoints local menu.

Set options (⟨Ctrl⟩-S)

This option opens the `Breakpoint options` dialog box illustrated in Figure 5.4. Use this command to examine or change the following options associated with this breakpoint.

- `Address`: Breakpoints in code are in the form #NAME#LINE or NAME.LINE where NAME is the module name and LINE is a line number. (The exact format depends on the current language.)

- `Action`: Set to `Break` to halt the program when the `Condition` to the right is true. Change to `Execute` and enter a function or procedure into the `Action expression` to run a subroutine when this breakpoint hits. Set to `Log` to log the result of an `Action expression`—usually a variable to examine at each breakpoint.

- `Action expression`: Enter an expression in your language's format (see chapter 9) to call a subroutine when `Action` is set to `Execute,` or to make an entry in the `Log` view. You can also enter an expression with an intentional side effect (a change to a global value) such as i++ in C.

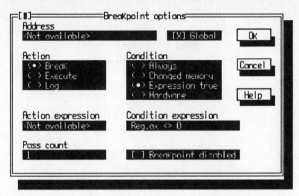

Figure 5.4. Breakpoint options dialog box.

Hint: To avoid trouble, it's usually best if a **Log** expression does not cause any side effects such as assigning a function result to a variable or using the C **++** and **--** increment and decrement operators. You may do this in unusual circumstances, but be aware that if you do, the breakpoint may affect the target program, complicating the search for a bug.

- **Pass count**: Change to ignore a breakpoint **Condition** until that condition occurs a certain number of times. For example, to break out of a loop after nine iterations, set a breakpoint on a statement inside the loop and change **Pass count** to 9. You can't set **Pass count** to 0 or to a negative value. Instead, use the **Breakpoint disabled** check box to disable a breakpoint.

- **Global**: After setting a breakpoint in code (usually by pressing ⟨**F2**⟩), you can enter a **Condition expression** for TD to evaluate when the breakpoint occurs. If you then turn on the **Global** switch, TD will monitor that condition between every source line (if **Module** is the active window) or between every machine-code instruction (if **CPU** is active). Because this will reduce TD's performance unless you have an 80386 or 80486 and are running TD386, there's few good reasons to change the **Global** setting—but you can examine it to find out how TD will monitor a breakpoint condition while a program runs.

Note: TD's use of the word "Global" confuses many people. A common code breakpoint is *not* global because TD creates it by inserting an interrupt instruction into the code; therefore, the debugger doesn't have to monitor the breakpoint's address. Instead, the breakpoint occurs when the program *itself* executes the interrupt instruction, which TD replaces with the original code when it handles the breakpoint. A global breakpoint requires TD to examine a memory location each time the debugger gains control from the target program. That's why global breakpoints cause performance to suffer the blues.

- `Condition`: Set to `Always` for breakpoints in code. Set to `Changed memory` to break when any of a range of memory bytes specified in `Condition expression` are changed. Set to `Expression true` to break when an expression becomes true— usually when a variable reaches a specific value as in Figure 5.4 where the break will occur when `Reg.ax` is not zero. Set to `Hardware` to enable the `Hardware options` local command if you're system has an 80386, 80486, or debugging board (see chapter 18).

- `Condition expression`: Enter an expression here when `Condition` is set to `Changed memory` or to `Expression true.` In the first case, the expression should be an address or label followed by a optional count of the number of items to examine. For example, the expression `MyCount,2` monitors 4 bytes if `MyCount` is a 2-byte integer. To monitor an entire variable such as an array, just enter its name. To monitor an unlabeled address, enter it in hex in your language's format. You can also specify segment registers and offsets such as CS:$0800 (Pascal), CS:0x800 (C), or CS:0800h (assembly language). When `Condition` is set to `Expression true`, TD evaluates the `Condition expression` before every source-code line (or machine-code instruction if the `CPU` view is active). The breakpoint `Action` is then taken if the expression is true.

Hint: Set `Changed memory` and enter a `Condition expression` to find a bug that's unexpectedly changing a memory location. Set `Expression true` and enter an expression to halt the code when a variable reaches or exceeds a *specific* value, for example, when an array index that's supposed to be limited to 99 is greater or equal to 100.

- `Breakpoint disabled`: Check this box to disable a breakpoint temporarily. Check it again to turn the breakpoint back on.

Hardware options (⟨Ctrl⟩-H)

Before you can use this command, you must install a hardware debugging board or have an 80386 or 80486 processor in your system as explained in chapter 18.

Add (⟨Ctrl⟩-A) (Default)

This option opens the `Breakpoint options` dialog (see Figure 5.4) so you can fill in a new breakpoint's details. In some cases, this might be easier than using the global `Breakpoints` menu commands to set breakpoints, especially if the `Breakpoints` view is already active. But usually, you won't add new breakpoints this way. Instead, use the methods described in chapters 4 and 8. For example, it's a lot easier to move the cursor to a source-code line and press ⟨**F2**⟩ to set a code breakpoint than it is to use the **Add** command and fill in the source-code line number manually.

> Hint: After loading a program into TD, open the **Breakpoints** view and enter the name of any procedure, function, or label. Because **Add** is the default action, just start typing. You don't have to choose the command from the menu. This will open the **Breakpoint options** dialog box and set a breakpoint at that address. Then, press ⟨**F9**⟩ to run the code to the breakpoint—a quick way to execute up to a routine when you know its name.

Remove (⟨Ctrl⟩-R, ⟨Delete⟩)

This command removes the breakpoint highlighted in the **Breakpoints** window. Be sure that's what you want to do—you'll have to reenter the breakpoint if you remove it accidentally.

> Hint: This is one of the few TD commands with two hot keys. You can press ⟨**Crtl**⟩-**R** or ⟨**Delete**⟩ to remove individual breakpoints.

Delete all (⟨Ctrl⟩-D)

This option removes all breakpoints of all kinds. Use this command to delete breakpoints only if the **Breakpoints** view is already active—the **Delete all** command in the **Breakpoints** global menu takes fewer keystrokes (⟨**Alt**⟩-**BD** instead of ⟨**Alt**⟩-**VB**⟨**Ctrl**⟩-**D**).

Inspect (⟨Ctrl⟩-I)

Highlight a nonglobal code breakpoint and press ⟨**Ctrl**⟩-**I** to view that source-code line in the **Module** window. If that window is not open, this command opens it.

Because **Module** usually occupies most of the display, when you press ⟨**Ctrl**⟩-**I**, the **Breakpoints** window appears to close, but it's just hidden behind **Module**. Press ⟨**F6**⟩ a few times to bring **Breakpoints** back into view.

> Note: This command doesn't work for global breakpoints that monitor memory locations and expressions. To examine those breakpoints, use **Set options** (press ⟨**Ctrl**⟩-**S**).

CPU View

The CPU view is one of TD's most complex. (See Figure 5.5.) Each of its five panes displays a different kind of information, and each has its own local menu of commands. Starting with the large pane in the upper left corner and proceeding clockwise, first is the Code pane, which shows a disassembly of your program's compiled or assembled machine code. Next is the Registers pane—a view of the 16- or 32-bit processor registers. After that comes a thin pane at the far right of the processor Flags. Below Registers and Flags is the Stack pane, showing the values currently pushed onto the system stack. To the left of that is the Dump pane, which you can use to view and change bytes, words, and other values anywhere in memory.

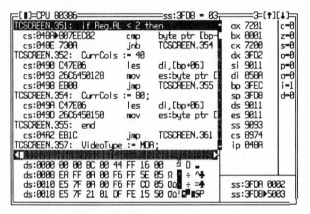

Figure 5.5.   CPU view.

Only two of the CPU's five panes are unique—the Code and Stack panes. The others are identical to the separate views Dump and Registers (which also contains the Flags pane). Turn to the descriptions of those two views in this chapter for more information about these sections of the CPU window. This section explains how to use the Code and Stack panes.

CPU Window Uses

Use the CPU view to examine and patch a program on its lowest level—the machine-code instructions that drive the 80x86 processor in your computer. Use it also to view and modify processor registers and flags, to examine the system stack, and to view a dump of bytes, words, and other values anywhere in memory.

When debugging assembly language code, some people prefer to use the CPU window instead of the source-code Module view. Because assembly language source-code statements directly translate into individual machine-code instructions and because much of assembly language programming involves setting registers and flags and manipulating the stack and bytes in memory, the `CPU` window is often convenient for debugging assembled machine code.

But when debugging high-level C and Pascal programs, the `CPU` window is mostly useful only when it becomes necessary to peer below the source-code level and look at the code the compiler has generated for your commands. For that reason, when debugging C and Pascal, you'll want to use the `Module` window at most times, switching to `CPU` only when:

- You want to trace machine not source code. When `CPU` is active, ⟨**F7**⟩, ⟨**F8**⟩, and other `Run`-menu commands execute processor instructions. When `Module` is active, those same commands trace source-code lines, which might be composed of many compiled machine-code instructions.

- You need to examine the registers or flags, for example, after returning from an assembly language subroutine or a call to a DOS function.

- You want to examine or modify a procedure or function's return address on the stack, or you want to alter a parameter passed to a routine on the stack.

- You want to execute individual machine-code instructions and watch their effects on bytes in memory.

- You want to patch the compiled code. The `CPU` window lets you assemble new instructions directly into memory, which might be useful for testing temporary fixes that you'll later add to your program's source.

Opening the CPU Window

Usually, use the mouse or press ⟨**Alt**⟩-**VC** to open the `CPU` window, similar to the way you choose other `View`-menu commands. Sometimes, however, the `CPU` window will open automatically when:

- You debug a program that lacks debugging information in its .EXE or .COM file. Unless this is what you want to do, quit TD and recompile according to the instructions in chapter 2. If the `CPU` window still appears, check that `Options:Path for source` lists the directory path name where you store your source-code files. If that's still no help, you may have used TDINST to set `Display:Beginning display` to `Assembler`. Change this back to `Source`, or use the -l- command line to run TD.

- You call a routine in a module for which source code is not available, for example, a library routine. If you do this by accident, close the `CPU` window (press ⟨**Alt**⟩-⟨**F3**⟩) and then press ⟨**Cursor Down**⟩⟨**F4**⟩ to run the program up to the next source-code statement.

- You break out of a program by pressing ⟨**Ctrl**⟩-⟨**Break**⟩. This will often interrupt a library routine without source-code and debugging information. Unless you want to continue debugging from that point, close the CPU window and press ⟨**Ctrl**⟩-⟨**F2**⟩ to reset.

The CPU view also exhibits a fair amount of intelligence. When you open CPU, it tries to show you something logical—the disassembled machine code for a selected statement in the Module window or a Dump of the bytes for an inspected data structure. But, if the window activates the wrong pane, just tab to the one you want.

CPU Code Pane

The Code pane is the large one in the CPU view's upper left corner. (See Figure 5.5.) In it is a disassembled representation of your program's compiled or assembled code. Usually, as the figure shows, the original source-code statements are displayed along with the machine-code instructions generated for those statements. (See the Mixed local command to change this pane's display format.) A small triangle (▶) marks the location of the instruction that will execute for the next Run-menu command.

When the highlighted instruction in this pane refers to a memory location—for example, as in the instruction mov [bp-01],al—the upper window border (near the center) shows something like SS:3FF7 = 5F. To the left of = is the effective address to which the instruction refers; to the right is the current byte or word value at that address. Use this information to confirm that values loaded into registers or written to memory are correct and that the addresses point where you think they should.

Examining code in the CPU view is a great way to learn how your compiler operates. Scanning the machine code for selected source-code statements can show you how the compiler executes a pointer reference, calls a function or procedure, or evaluates an expression. If you're curious about what code is *really* doing, this is the place to find out.

Assembly language programmers may notice a few discrepancies between source statements and disassembled machine code. This is because 80x86 assembly language often uses several mnemonics (symbolic names) for the same code. For example, je and jz refer to the same jump instruction. But TD always disassembles jz as the equivalent je.

> Hint: Along with the disassembly, the Code pane normally shows the machine-code bytes for those instructions. But, if you shrink the CPU window horizontally to less than about 60 characters wide, the bytes disappear! When you don't need to see the machine code, you can shrink CPU this way to pack almost as much information on-screen in a much smaller space.

Local CPU Code Pane Commands

Like most window panes, the `Code` pane has its own local menu of commands (see Figure 5.6). The next sections describe how to use each command.

Figure 5.6. Local menu in the CPU window's code pane.

Goto (⟨Ctrl⟩-G)

To examine other parts of a program, you can press the cursor and page movement keys, or you can use the `Goto` command to jump farther away. Enter an address such as **054Eh** (**$054E** for Pascal, **0x054E** for C), or if you know the line number, enter **#module#000** where *module* is the name of a source-code module and *000* is the line number, for example, #strio#124. (When debugging Pascal code, enter line numbers in the form MODULE.LINE.)

> Hint: Press ⟨**Ctrl**⟩-⟨**Cursor Left**⟩ and ⟨**Ctrl**⟩-⟨**Cursor Right**⟩ to shift the instruction displayed at the highlight bar in the `Code` pane. This is similar to using `Goto` to reposition the window and is helpful on the rare occasions where the disassembly becomes out of synch with the source code.

Origin (⟨Ctrl⟩-O)

This option returns to the current origin—the location of the instruction that will execute next when you use a `Run` command or press a hot key such as ⟨**F7**⟩, ⟨**F8**⟩, or ⟨**F9**⟩. Use this command after viewing other locations to get back to the program's current origin.

It's a good idea to use this command *before* entering expressions to make sure TD scopes any local symbols to the origin, not to another location in the code you happen to be viewing.

> Hint: After scrolling around in the **Module** window to view various source-code lines and opening the **CPU** window to view a disassembly of those statements, press **⟨Ctrl⟩-O⟨Ctrl⟩-V** to reset both windows, with **CPU** active.

Follow (⟨Ctrl⟩-F)

When a jump, call, or software interrupt instruction is highlighted in the **CPU**'s **Code** pane, press **⟨Ctrl⟩-F** to view that instruction's target location—the code that will be executed by the next **Run** command. You might think of **Follow** as a kind of "look before you leap" feature. It lets you look ahead into a subroutine before actually jumping into it.

After pressing **⟨Ctrl⟩-F** to view a target subroutine, press **⟨F7⟩** to execute the jump, call, or interrupt instruction that leads to this address. You can then continue debugging the subroutine. But *never* press **⟨Ctrl⟩-N** after **⟨Ctrl⟩-F** to make the target the new origin—unless, of course, you *don't* want the caller's return address to be pushed onto the stack.

Caller (⟨Ctrl⟩-C)

Press **⟨Ctrl⟩-C** to view the code that called the currently displayed subroutine. In order for this to work, that location's return address must be on the stack and a **call** must have been the most recently executed instruction. After pressing **⟨Ctrl⟩-C**, you can press **⟨Ctrl⟩-P** or **⟨Ctrl⟩-O** to return to the previous view.

Previous (⟨Ctrl⟩-P)

Press **⟨Ctrl⟩-P** to return to the location previously displayed in the **Code** pane before you used another command to move away from that spot.

> Hint: This command gives you a neat way to toggle between two disassemblies. For example, press **⟨Ctrl⟩-F** to follow (but not execute) a **call** instruction and then press **⟨Ctrl⟩-P** repeatedly to toggle between the two views.

Search (⟨Ctrl⟩-S)

Enter an assembly language instruction or a series of byte values to find. TD will start searching from the current address down. If it finds your search argument, it will reposition the **CPU Code** pane to that new location.

When entering byte lists, be sure to use the correct format for the current language. For example, to search for the two hex bytes 8E and 7F, enter

$8e $7f in Pascal, **0x08E 0x07F** in C, or **08Eh 07Fh** in assembly language. Also, beware of byte swapping in word and other multibyte values. To find the word value 8E7F, you must enter **$7F8E**, **0x7F8E**, or **07F8Eh** to account for the way these values are stored in memory.

You can also search for assembly language instructions, but in that case, you must enter an instruction that assembles to the bytes you want to find. TD doesn't search for the **text** of the instruction—it assembles the text and then searches for the resulting bytes. For example, if you enter the search argument **or al,al**, TD assembles that instruction and looks for the bytes 0Ah and C0h.

This means you can't search for conditional jumps because the offset locations are not the same for the starting and target addresses. If you search for **je tcscreen.450**, TD assembles the instruction and calculates the offset from the *current* location to line 450. Because that offset value is probably different where the instruction exists in the code, this kind of search usually fails.

Hint: Performing multiple searches for the same instruction is difficult because there is no "search again" command in this window pane. Fortunately, it's easy to create your own. For example, to find all occurrences of **int 21h**, after finding the first, press **⟨Cursor Down⟩⟨Ctrl⟩-S⟨Cursor Down⟩⟨Enter⟩**. Record those keys as a macro if you do this often.

View source (⟨Ctrl⟩-V)

Press **⟨Ctrl⟩-V** to view the source-code statement in the **Module** window associated with the highlighted machine-code instruction in the **CPU** window's **Code** pane.

Hint: Get into the habit of using this command if you frequently switch between the **CPU** and **Module** views—it's faster than closing the **CPU** window and then having to reopen it later. Press **⟨F6⟩** a few times or press **⟨Alt⟩** and the **CPU** window's number (usually 3) to return.

Mixed (⟨Ctrl⟩-M)

This command has three settings: **No**, **Yes**, and **Both**. Press **⟨Ctrl⟩-M** to cycle through each of these to change the format of the disassembled instructions in the **Code** pane. The results are purely visual and the settings have no other effects.

Hint: I use **Both** for C and Pascal, **Yes** for assembly language, and **No** when examining code for which I don't have the source text.

New cs:ip (⟨Ctrl⟩-N)

After highlighting an assembly language instruction, press **⟨Ctrl⟩-N** to copy the address of that instruction to registers CS (code segment) and IP (instruction pointer). This changes TD's origin—the location of the next instruction to execute.

Never reset the origin to an instruction inside a subroutine—that would skip the `call` instruction that pushes the caller's return address onto the stack. Do this only if you'll never execute that routine's return. For safety, place a breakpoint at the next `ret` or `retf` so that, if you press **⟨F9⟩** by accident, you'll avoid an almost certain crash.

Assemble (⟨Ctrl⟩-A) (Default)

Press **⟨Ctrl⟩-A** or just start typing to assemble a new instruction at the current location. When you press **⟨Enter⟩**, TD moves the highlight bar to the next line down; therefore, to enter multiple instructions, just type them one after the other, pressing **⟨Enter⟩** at the end of each line.

Use this command to enter short patches to code or to test small assembly language sequences. You can't save your changes to disk. Don't use this command to enter long subroutines—if you press **⟨Ctrl⟩-⟨F2⟩** to reset the code, TD will throw out all your patches. Also, you can't use the full-address forms of string instructions. Instead, you must use shorthand mnemonics like `lodsb` and `cmpsw`.

Hint: Add a small buffer to your program to provide space for entering assembly language patches. Use the `Data:Inspect` command to open an inspector window to the buffer, press **⟨Alt⟩-VC** to open the `CPU` view and press **⟨Tab⟩** to move to the `Code` pane. Press **⟨Ctrl⟩-G** and enter the first address shown in the `Dump` pane. You can then assemble instructions into the buffer without concern about overwriting other code in RAM. To execute the patch, use a `call far seg:ofs` instruction where *seg:ofs* is the segment and offset address of the patch, which should end with a far return instruction (`retf`).

If you make a mistake typing an instruction, you'll receive messages such as "Invalid instruction mnemonic" or "Symbol not found." To avoid having to retype the entire line, after erasing the error message, either press **⟨Space⟩** or press **⟨Ctrl⟩-A** and then press **⟨Cursor Down⟩** to highlight the previous text, which you can then edit in the usual way.

I/O (⟨Ctrl⟩-I)

After pressing ⟨**Ctrl**⟩-**I** or choosing I/O from the local menu, press **I**, **O**, **R**, or **W** to choose one of the submenu's commands: In byte, Out byte, Read word, or Write word. (See Figure 5.7.) Don't also press ⟨**Ctrl**⟩—let up on that key first. The "In" commands prompt you for the port number, which you can enter in decimal or hex. The "Out" commands prompt for a port number and a value to write to that port. Separate the two values with a comma. You can specify port numbers from 0 to 65,535.

> Hint: Be extremely careful with this command. It's like a rifle with a hair trigger— once you fire it, there's no way to recall the bullet. Even reading from some ports can affect circuits and devices attached to your system. For safety, reboot after using I/O.

Figure 5.7. I/O submenu for the CPU window's code pane.

CPU Registers Pane

The Registers pane in the CPU window shows the 80x86 processor's 16- or 32-bit registers. (See Figure 5.5.) The commands for this pane are identical to those for the Registers view, described later in this chapter.

CPU Flags Pane

The Flags pane in the CPU window shows the 80x86 processor's single-bit flag values. (See Figure 5.5.) There is only one local command in this pane, Toggle. To use it, highlight the flag you want to change and press ⟨**Ctrl**⟩-**T**.

> Hint: You can also press ⟨**Space**⟩ or ⟨**Enter**⟩ to toggle a flag value between 1 (on) and 0 (off).

CPU Stack Pane

The `Stack` pane in the `CPU` window's lower right corner shows 16-bit word values on the system stack. (See Figure 5.5.) A small triangle (►) marks the stack pointer's current location, the value most recently pushed onto the stack. This is the word that will be loaded into a register by the next `pop` instruction or into `ip` by the next `ret` (or the first of a pair of words to be loaded into `cs:ip` by the next `retf`).

> Hint: TD displays stack words in byte-swapped order. To view stack bytes as they are actually stored in RAM, tab to the `Dump` pane, press ⟨**Ctrl**⟩**-G**, and enter **ss:sp** for a byte-dump of the same values listed in the `Stack`.

Local CPU Stack Pane Commands

The `Stack` pane's local menu (see Figure 5.8) has five commands, described in the next sections.

Figure 5.8.   Local menu in the CPU window's stack pane.

Goto (⟨Ctrl⟩-G)

Use this command to position the stack to a new location. It's especially useful for examining pointer references to variables stored on the stack. For example, to see the stack location affected by the instruction `mov byte ptr [bp-13]`, press ⟨**Ctrl**⟩**-G** and enter **bp-$13** (**bp-0x13** for C or **bp-13h** for assembly language). Remember, the 13 is in hex, even though the `Code` pane doesn't list the value that way!

To scroll the `Stack` pane without moving the highlight bar, press ⟨**Ctrl**⟩-⟨**Cursor Left**⟩ and ⟨**Ctrl**⟩-⟨**Cursor Right**⟩.

When viewing stack locations, be aware that the stack pointer is always even (or, at least it should be). To return to a true representation of the stack after viewing odd-value addresses, press ⟨**Ctrl**⟩**-O**. To move quickly through the stack, enter an expression such as **sp+128** or **sp+1024**. You don't have to specify the stack segment register SS in the expression.

Hint: You don't have to view only the system stack in the Stack pane—you can also use it to view other locations as a list of words. For example, press ⟨**Ctrl**⟩**-G** and enter **ds:$0080** to view an array of integers or words in the data segment. I find that the Stack's vertical format makes viewing such arrays easier than the Dump pane, which displays values in a wide block. Unfortunately, the list is "upside down." So, to move *down* in memory (to higher addresses), you must press ⟨**Cursor Up**⟩. Of course, in RAM, *up* to one person might be *down* to another.

Origin (⟨Ctrl⟩-O)

Press ⟨**Ctrl**⟩**-O** to reset the Stack pane to the current SS:SP stack location. Use the command after scrolling, paging, or using other commands to view other stack positions.

Follow (⟨Ctrl⟩-F)

When a pointer on the stack represents an offset to another stack frame (a series of values pushed onto the stack usually by a high-level language subroutine), you can highlight the value and press ⟨**Ctrl**⟩**-F** to view that stack location. In the case where multiple pointers point to many such frames, you can trace through the stack quickly by highlighting the values and pressing ⟨**Ctrl**⟩**-F**. This command has the same effect as entering the pointer as an offset value with the Goto command.

Hint: Press ⟨**Ctrl**⟩**-P** to return to the previous view. Or, press ⟨**Ctrl**⟩**-O** to return to the stack origin after following a series of pointers.

Previous (⟨Ctrl⟩-P)

Press ⟨**Ctrl**⟩**-P** to restore the Stack pane to where it was before you used other commands to view different locations. The command works as a toggle— press ⟨**Ctrl**⟩**-P** two or more times to switch rapidly between two stack locations.

Change (⟨Ctrl⟩-C) (Default)

Press ⟨**Ctrl**⟩**-C** or just start typing to enter a new word value for the highlighted stack location. You can use this command to change arguments passed on the stack or to alter a return address. Remember to enter the value using the correct format for your language.

CPU Dump Pane

The Dump pane in the CPU window shows byte, word, and other values any-where in memory. (See Figure 5.5.) The commands for this pane are identical to those for the Dump view, described next.

Dump View

Figure 5.9 shows a typical Dump view window. Although at first glance, the contents of this window appear scatterbrained, the information divides log-ically into three columns: an address field (for example, ds:0000), eight hexa-decimal byte values stored beginning at that address, and eight ASCII characters representing those same bytes. These characters frequently look like gibberish unless the bytes are part of a string. You can ignore them most other times.

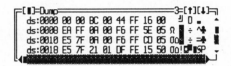

Figure 5.9.   Typical Dump view.

The address field may appear as in Figure 5.9 or as segment and offset values such as 735F:35D8. Watch for this—it tells you whether TD recognizes the displayed data as belonging to the program's global data segment addressed by **ds**. If an explicit segment address value appears, you are not looking at the data segment.

Because TD makes copies of certain memory locations, video display buffers, interrupt vectors, and the like, when using the Dump view to examine locations outside of a program, you may not be seeing the actual values stored in RAM when you look there. In other words, you can't see the values that TD uses from those locations. Instead, the Dump window always shows you the values that will be available to your code when it runs.

Scrolling the Dump Window

Use the cursor and page movement keys to scroll the text cursor inside the Dump window. Press ⟨**Home**⟩ and ⟨**End**⟩ to move the cursor to the beginning and end of a line. Press ⟨**Ctrl**⟩-⟨**Home**⟩ and ⟨**Ctrl**⟩-⟨**End**⟩ to move to the top and bottom of the window. Press ⟨**Ctrl**⟩-⟨**Page Up**⟩ to reset the current offset address to 0000, moving to the top of the current segment. To scroll the

window contents 1 byte at a time but keep the cursor stationary, press
⟨**Ctrl**⟩-⟨**Cursor Left**⟩ or ⟨**Ctrl**⟩-⟨**Cursor Right**⟩.

Local Dump View Commands

The `Dump` view has one menu of local commands (see Figure 5.10), three of
which have submenus with other commands.

Figure 5.10. Dump-view local menu.

Goto (⟨Ctrl⟩-G)

Use this command to position the `Dump` view to any address. If you enter only an
offset such as **$085E** (Pascal), **0x085E** (C), or **085Eh** (assembly language), TD
moves to that offset within the current segment. You can also specify explicit
segment and offset pairs such as **$72D0:$085E**, **0x72D0:0x085E**, or
72D0h:085Eh. Or, you can specify a segment register like this: **ds:$085E**.

In place of an explicit address, you can also enter the name of a variable. For
example, to dump the bytes of an array, enter its name with the `Goto` command.
In fact, you can enter other kinds of expressions, too. TD will evaluate the
expression and dump the bytes at the address that equals the result of the expression. You can even enter program line numbers such as **TCSCREEN.435** or
#DT#42 to dump the machine-code bytes associated for the statement at that line.

Search (⟨Ctrl⟩-S)

Press ⟨**Ctrl**⟩-**S** and enter bytes or ASCII text in quotes that you want to search
for in RAM. Separate multiple bytes with spaces. Surround ASCII text with
single quotes in Pascal, double quotes in C, or either in assembly language.

> Hint: Searches extend only to the end of the current segment. To continue a search
> in the next segment, add 1000 hex to the segment address with the `Goto`
> command. For example, if the current segment is 3500h, `Goto` 4500h:0 and repeat
> the search by pressing ⟨**Ctrl**⟩-**N**.

Next (⟨Ctrl⟩-N)

Press ⟨**Ctrl**⟩-**N** to repeat the most recent `Search`, starting from the current location and proceeding into the current segment (toward higher addresses).

> Hint: Press ⟨**Ctrl**⟩-⟨**Page Up**⟩ before ⟨**Ctrl**⟩-**N** to repeat a search for the entire segment beginning at address seg:0000.

Change (⟨Ctrl⟩-C) (Default)

Press ⟨**Ctrl**⟩-**C** or just start typing to insert one or more byte values starting with the byte above the flashing text cursor. Separate multiple bytes with spaces. Remember to enter each byte in a format that's suitable for your language—for example, **$FF** (Pascal), **0xFF** (C), and **0FFh** (assembly language).

You can also enter string data by typing a single (Pascal and assembly) or double (C and assembly) quote to choose the `Change` command. Then, enter your ASCII text, type a closing quote mark, and press ⟨**Enter**⟩ to insert the string into memory.

Use the `Display as` command to change the display format in the `Dump` window. You can then enter word, floating point, and other kinds of values instead of single bytes. If you don't change the display format before entering 16- and 32-bit values, you might accidentally change the wrong bytes if you fail to consider the 80x86's byte-swapped storage order for multibyte values. For these reasons, it's probably best to enter values in the currently displayed format.

> Hint: To use a mouse to choose this command, position the mouse cursor on the byte you want to change, press the right mouse button, and choose `Change`. But, be careful. If the mouse cursor moves before the local menu appears, you won't know that until you finish the command. Because this makes it too easy to deposit bytes at the wrong locations, I prefer to click the mouse left button to position the cursor. Then, I enter the new data.

Follow (⟨Ctrl⟩-F)

This command pops up a submenu with five additional commands. (See Figure 5.11.) Each command interprets the bytes at the text cursor as an address for displaying code in the `CPU` window or bytes at a different location in `Dump`. Code commands are at the top of the submenu; data commands are at the bottom. By using these commands, you can follow a list of items joined by pointer fields, trace pointers in the stack, and view buffers addressed by word segment values.

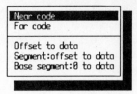

Figure 5.11. Submenu for the Dump view's Follow command.

The fastest way to choose these commands is to press ⟨**Ctrl**⟩-**FX** where *X* is the submenu command's first letter: N, F, O, S, or B. If you use these commands often, you might want to record those keystrokes as macros. The following notes explain how to use each of these subcommands:

- **Near code**: Opens or activates the `CPU` window to the current CS segment at the offset address equal to the word at the cursor. Most of the time, you'll use this command to trace a 16-bit near return value in the stack, although you can also use it to trace near calls, jumps, and 16-bit pointers to subroutines.

- **Far code**: Opens or activates the `CPU` window to the segment and offset address equal to the 32-bit value at the cursor. Use this command to inspect the code for a far return on the stack or to view the instructions addressed by any other 32-bit pointer.

> Hint: The 32-bit pointers are stored as two words with the offset value preceding the segment. The bytes in each of these word values are stored in swapped order. For these reasons, you might want to change the display format to words before using this command. That will make the values easier to read.

- **Offset to data**: Repositions the `Dump` view's contents to the current segment and offset value at the cursor. Because most C and Pascal pointers are stored as 32-bit values, you won't use this command often. But it shines when debugging assembly language programs, which frequently use arrays of offsets to address strings and other variables in the data segment. The `Offset` command lets you position the cursor on an array entry and press ⟨**Ctrl**⟩-**FO** to view the data at that address.

- **Segment:offset to data**: Repositions the `Dump` view's contents to the 32-bit segment and offset value at the cursor. The most common use for this command is to follow a linked list. Just position the cursor on the pointer value and press ⟨**Ctrl**⟩-**FS** to view the bytes at that location. You can then move the cursor to another pointer and repeat the command to view other linked items.

> Hint: Another good use for this command is to inspect arguments passed as 32-bit pointers on the stack to a procedure or function in C and Pascal programs. To do this, use the `Goto` command to view the stack (enter **ss:sp** for the address). Then, move the cursor to the pointer value and press ⟨**Ctrl**⟩-**FS**. The `Dump` window will then display the data addressed by the pointer.

- **Base segment:0 to data**: Repositions the `Dump` view's contents to the segment value at the cursor with an assumed offset of 0000. A good use for this command is to display the contents of buffers stored in their own segments—a typical setup for C and Pascal, but not uncommon in assembly language. Usually, a list of these buffers is stored as an array of word pointers in the global data segment. To view a buffer, move the text cursor to one of the word pointers and press ⟨**Ctrl**⟩-**FB**.

Previous (⟨Ctrl⟩-P)

After using another local command (but not cursor and page movement keys) to scroll the `Dump` view's contents, press ⟨**Ctrl**⟩-**P** to return to the previous display. The view keeps track of the last five `Goto` and `Follow` commands.

You can use the command as a toggle to switch between two views. For example, after pressing ⟨**Ctrl**⟩-**FS** to follow a 32-bit pointer that addresses another variable, press ⟨**Ctrl**⟩-**P** to view the previous item.

Display as (⟨Ctrl⟩-D)

Choosing this command brings up a submenu of commands that you can use to change the display format of the information in the `Dump` window. (See Figure 5.12.)

Figure 5.12.   Submenu for the Dump view's Display as command.

You might want to experiment with the available settings: `Byte`, `Word`, `Long`, `Comp`, `Float`, `Real`, `Double`, and `Extended`. Most have obvious meanings. `Long` is a 32-bit integer. `Comp` stands for *Composite Number*, an 8-byte integer value equivalent to TP's `Comp` data type.

Hint: Display values as words when examining pointers. That way, you won't have to swap bytes mentally to realize that 08 0F 00 01 actually refers to the address 0100:0F08. This is much easier to see if you display those bytes as the two words 0F08 0100, even though you still have to reverse the segment and offset values.

Block (⟨Ctrl⟩-B)

Choosing the `Block` command pops up a submenu of five other commands that `Clear`, `Move`, `Set`, `Read`, and `Write` multiple values in memory. (See Figure 5.13.) Use these commands to fill buffers, zero a data segment, or insert values into unused stack space.

Figure 5.13. Submenu for the Dump view's Block command.

Be careful when using these commands—they write and move values in memory and can easily destroy code and data, including bytes that belong to TD. Here's what each command does:

- `Clear`: Enter an address, a comma, and the number of bytes starting at that address that you want to clear to 0. For example, enter **ds:0,8** to clear the 8 bytes at ds:0000 through ds:0007.

Hint: To clear an entire variable in Pascal or C, enter its name, a command, and **sizeof(name)**. For example, to zero a buffer named `InBuf`, enter **InBuf,sizeof(InBuf)**.

- `Move`: Enter source and destination addresses plus the number of bytes to copy from the source to the destination. Except for overlapping moves where the source and destination areas share some of the same locations, this command does not change any bytes in the source.

- `Set`: Use `Set` to assign any byte value to a range of addresses. Enter an address, the number of bytes to set, and the value to insert in memory. For example, **ds:$0080, 10, $FF** sets 10 bytes starting at ds:0080 to hexadecimal FF.

Hint: You can fill backwards by subtracting from the current address. For example, to fill 100 bytes of unused stack space, enter the `Set` expression **ss:(sp - 100) ,100 ,255**. Take care not to fill too far backward, or you might erase other data, especially when using memory models that store global data and the system stack in the same segment. After running your program, use the `Dump` view to scan the stack—you'll see at a glance how much stack space your code used during the run.

- `Read`: Use this command to load data from a disk file into a block of memory. After choosing `Read,` enter or select a file name from the directory dialog box, then enter the address of the buffer and the maximum number of bytes (usually **sizeof(buffer)**) to load.

- `Write`: Use this command to write data to an existing or new file. After choosing `Write`, enter or select a file name from the directory dialog box and then type the address of the buffer and the number of bytes (usually **sizeof(buffer)**) to write to disk.

You can use the `Block:Write` command along with TD's built-in assembler to create small .COM program files. To do this, follow these steps:

1. Start TD with no file name. This opens the `CPU` window to the address CS:0100, the origin of all .COM programs.

2. Enter your program instructions. You don't need to select any commands to do this, just type the instructions and press ⟨**Enter**⟩ at the end of each line. You must compute address offsets manually. To make this easier, if the current address for the next instruction is 0108 and you need to jump forward from there to an unknown location, insert the temporary command **je 0108** and then fill in the correct offset later.

3. Note the address just after the last instruction in your program. You need this address to tell TD how many bytes to write to disk.

4. Press ⟨**Alt**⟩-**VD** to open the `Dump` window. Then, press ⟨**Ctrl**⟩-**G** and enter **cs:0100h** to view the bytes of the instructions you entered into the `CPU` view. The `Dump` window will display the address as `ds:0100` because CS = DS for .COM programs.

5. Press ⟨**Ctrl**⟩-**BW** to select the `Block:Write` command. Enter a file name, for example, **test.com**.

6. TD then prompts for an address and count. Enter the expression **cs:0100h, nh** where *n* is the address you noted earlier *minus* 100h. For example, if the address after the last instruction was 015F, enter **005Fh**.

Execution History View

If you like to ride backwards in subways and trains, you'll love the `Execution history` view, which shows you where your program came from to get to where it got. (Got that?) Even better, it lets you throw TD into reverse gear to undo execution one step at a time. This is useful for running multiple tests on code fragments and for resetting conditions before a bug appeared so you can test theories about the problem. You can also use this window to replay saved keystrokes leading up to a recorded event.

As Figure 5.14 shows, the `Execution history` view is divided into two panes. On top is a machine-code disassembly that shows the instruction you can undo. On bottom is a list of events, one for each time TD regained control after executing one or more instructions in your code. If you have EMS RAM, TD can save up to 3,000 instructions. If not, the limit is about 400 instructions.

Reverse Executing Code

Before you can run code in reverse, you have to execute one or more statements by pressing ⟨**F7**⟩, ⟨**F8**⟩, or ⟨**Alt**⟩-⟨**F7**⟩ or by using the `Run:Animate` command. Because of differences among these code-tracing commands, the effects on reverse tracing will vary. Use the `Run:Trace into` command (⟨**F7**⟩) for best results.

Reverse Execution Limitations

There are several limitations on the kinds of instructions you can reverse execute. As you might expect, you can't undo some operations—reading or writing bytes to I/O ports, for example. You also can't undo the effects of an interrupt service routine.

Local Execution History Commands

Figure 5.15 shows the local command menus for the top (the left screen in the figure) and bottom (the right screen in the figure) `Execution history` panes. Each of these commands is described next.

Figure 5.14.　Execution history view.

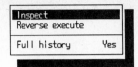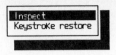

Figure 5.15.   Execution history view local menu.

Inspect (⟨Ctrl⟩-I)

Press ⟨**Ctrl**⟩-**I** to inspect the source-code line in the `Module` view associated with the highlighted machine-code instruction (top pane) or control event (bottom pane). If there isn't a source-code statement associated for the high-lighted item, TD may open the `CPU` window instead.

Reverse execute (⟨Ctrl⟩-R)

Highlight a machine-code instruction in the `Execution history`'s top pane and press ⟨**Ctrl**⟩-**R** to execute back to and including that command. For example, to undo the effects of the previous three instructions, press ⟨**Cursor Up**⟩ three times to and then press ⟨**Ctrl**⟩-**R**.

Full history (⟨Ctrl⟩-F)

Toggle this setting off if you don't want to collect every machine-code instruction in the `Execution history` view's top pane. When set to `Yes`, pressing ⟨**Alt**⟩-⟨**F4**⟩ reverses lines in the `Module` window and instructions in `CPU`. When set to `No`, pressing ⟨**Alt**⟩-⟨**F4**⟩ works in Pascal and C only for the `CPU` view, which has to be the active window during tracing.

> Hint: Switching `Full history` off adds a bit of speed to TD's tracing abilities, and it may conserve a little memory. Usually, however, you should leave it on to enable full back tracing.

Keystroke restore (⟨Ctrl⟩-K)

Highlight an event listed in the bottom pane of the `Execution history` view and press ⟨**Ctrl**⟩-**K** to repeat all keystrokes and significant mouse operations that led to that moment of debugging history. The command works only if you started TD with the -k command-line option or if you turned on keystroke recording permanently with TDINST (see chapter 3).

File View

Use the File view to examine the contents of a disk file. Choosing this command opens a dialog box to prompt for a file name, the same dialog that other file-related commands use. Figure 5.16 shows a sample view of a text file BUFSTM.ASM (top left) and that same text as assembled by Turbo Assembler to BUFSTM.OBJ (bottom right). Text files look very much like source code in a Module window, while other files look like a byte Dump. Feel free to examine any file on disk—TD will not overwrite the file or change it in any way.

When viewing binary data (as shown at the bottom right of Figure 5.16), address values in the first column are relative to the start of the file data. These addresses do not reveal where TD stores the file data in memory.

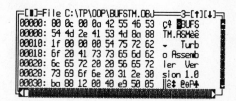

Figure 5.16. File views.

When viewing text data, the line number is shown after the file name in the window's top border. (It's 1 in the figure.) Use this number as a guide to find source-code lines referred to by TD in other windows such as Variables and CPU.

The text and binary File views are also useful for examining data files— those a program reads or those it creates. For example, if your code writes a text file, rather than quitting to DOS and using the TYPE command or another program to examine the file's contents, use TD's File view. You can then restart the code (press ⟨Ctrl⟩-⟨F2⟩), change input parameters or other conditions, and run another test. This should be much faster than switching between TD and DOS.

> Hint: Use the File view to examine C header files included in a module's source code. Or, create your own reference files and open them with this command to create custom on-line help screens.

File View Local Menu

Whether TD displays binary data or ASCII text in the File view, there are six local commands you can use when this window is active. (See Figure 5.17.)

Figure 5.17. File view local menu.

Goto (⟨Ctrl⟩-G)

Use Goto to enter a new line number for ASCII text files or offset address for binary data. If the number you enter is within range, TD will reposition the File view to the new location.

Search (⟨Ctrl⟩-S) (Default)

Press **⟨Ctrl⟩-S** or just start typing to enter a string you want to find in an ASCII text file or to locate a series of bytes in binary data. Unlike other TD commands that perform searches, the File:Search command does not require strings to be delimited with quote marks. But you do have to enter a byte series in the correct format for the current language, for example, **$F0** (Pascal), **0xF0** (C), or **0F0h** (assembly language).

> Hint: This command is useful for poking around in compiled programs for which the source code is not available. For example, to verify various messages while writing this book, I loaded TD.EXE into a File view window and searched for "Error" and similar strings that led me to other information.

Next (⟨Ctrl⟩-N)

After performing a Search command, press **⟨Ctrl⟩-N** to find the next occurrence of the search argument in the file. Press **⟨Ctrl⟩-⟨Page Up⟩** to move to the top of the file before pressing **⟨Ctrl⟩-N** if you want to repeat a search from the beginning.

Display as (⟨Ctrl⟩-D)

Press **⟨Ctrl⟩-D** or choose this command to toggle the `File` window between ASCII text and hexadecimal byte views. Usually, TD will display data in the correct format, but if it can't tell what a file MYSTUFF.XQP contains, it will display the contents in binary. In that case, press **⟨Ctrl⟩-D** to switch to the other format.

File (⟨Ctrl⟩-F)

The `File` local command is identical to the `File` command in the `View` menu. It opens a dialog box to prompt for a file name. If the file you specify exists, TD replaces the current `File` view with the contents of the new file.

> Hint: When examining files updated by a program, use this local command to reload the `File` view with a data file's current contents. TD does not update this window automatically—the `File` view represents a snapshot of a file's bytes at the time you loaded it from disk.

Edit (⟨Ctrl⟩-E)

If you specified an editor, a batch file, or another program with TDINST (see chapter 3), press **⟨Ctrl⟩-E** to run the program. TD passes to that program the name of the current file as an argument. This may be useful during debugging to make quick changes to one or more modules and to prepare input data for tests.

Hierarchy View

The `Hierarchy` view displays the relationships among an object-oriented program's object data types—or *classes* as they're known in C++. As Figure 5.18 shows, the window is divided into two panes—a list of object types on the left and a family-tree diagram of those same objects on the right.

Both panes understand the same keys for moving the highlight bar up and down. The cursor and page movement keys move the bar in the usual directions, **⟨Ctrl⟩-⟨Home⟩** moves to the top of the pane, **⟨Ctrl⟩-⟨End⟩** moves to the bottom, **⟨Ctrl⟩-⟨Page Up⟩** moves to the first object name, and **⟨Ctrl⟩-⟨Page Down⟩** moves to last.

Remember when using this window that you are viewing object *types,* not object *instances* (variables). The types do not exist in memory. Think of the information in this window as templates of a program's objects. Use it to browse objects and to examine their relations with one another.

> Hint: To document an object-oriented program, dump the `Hierarchy` window to a log file, which you can then print or store along with other program document files. First, open the `Log` view, press ⟨**Ctrl**⟩-**O**, and supply a name for the log file. Press ⟨**Alt**⟩-⟨**F3**⟩ to close `Log`. Then, press ⟨**Alt**⟩-**VH**⟨**Tab**⟩⟨**Alt**⟩-**WD** to copy the `Hierarchy`'s right pane to the log.

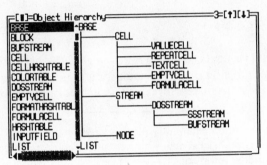

Figure 5.18. Hierarchy view.

C++ vs. Turbo Pascal

The `Hierarchy` view is similar for C++ and Turbo Pascal object-oriented programs. But when displaying C++ object classes, if those classes inherit from multiple ancestors, the view changes to display a `Parent Tree` pane below the usual two panes as shown in Figure 5.18. This new pane displays the parents for a highlighted class. Use this pane as you do the others. For example, you can highlight and select class names to view them in more detail, just as you can in the object list and tree panes.

> See chapters 20 and 21 for more information about viewing objects and classes in Pascal and C++ programs.

Hierarchy View Local Menu

Each of the `Hierarchy` view's two panes has a small local menu (see Figure 5.19). The left pane has two commands, the right has one. When debugging C++ programs that use multiple inheritance, a third local menu is available for the bottom `Parent Tree` pane. The following sections describe how to use these commands.

Figure 5.19. Hierarchy view local menus.

Inspect (⟨Ctrl⟩-I)

Press ⟨**Ctrl**⟩-**I** or just press ⟨**Enter**⟩ to open an inspector window for a highlighted object type in either of the two **Hierarchy** window panes. The command does the same job for all panes.

The object type's inspector window resembles an inspector for an object instance, but it displays only type information for data fields in the object, and it doesn't list the object's address. Remember, you are viewing only a template of an object, not an instance of that object in memory. Only variables have addresses, not data types.

Tree (⟨Ctrl⟩-T)

After highlighting an object type name in the left pane of the **Hierarchy** window, press ⟨**Ctrl**⟩-**T** to move to the right pane and highlight that same object type. This shows where that object type fits in the program's family tree of all other objects.

> Hint: The **Hierarchy** view's left pane recognizes incremental matching—just type the first few letters of any object type name to move quickly to that object. When you know an object's name, this may be faster than using the mouse or cursor movement keys.

Parents (⟨Ctrl⟩-P)

Tab to the bottom pane in a C++ program that uses multiple inheritance and press ⟨**Ctrl**⟩-**P** to toggle the setting from **Yes** to **No**. When set to **Yes**, multiple ancestors are displayed for a descendant class. If you don't need to see that information, change the setting to **No**.

This command is available only in C++ code. It is not available (nor is it needed) in Pascal programs.

Log View

Open the **Log** view to see entries made to the log buffer or file (see Figure 5.20). You can also use this command to start a new log and to write the current log information to disk.

Figure 5.20 shows a log of three items: the value of **Reg.ax**, the module and line number of a breakpoint (**TCSCREEN.351**), and a few register values. The value and breakpoint information are from breakpoints that I set and modified with the **Breakpoints** view's **Set options** local command, changing **Action** to

Log and entering the variable name Reg.ax as the Action expression. The register values came from the Registers view, copied to the Log by the Window:Dump pane to log command (press ⟨**Alt**⟩-**WD**).

> Unless you save log information to disk with the Open log file command, the log window can store at most about 50 lines. When it becomes full, new entries cause older ones to scroll into oblivion. You can change the maximum number of Log lines with TDINST (see chapter 3). But to conserve memory, it's usually better to save long logs to disk.

Figure 5.20.   Log view.

Log View Local Menu

With the Log view active, there are five commands you can use to open and close a log disk file, to add a comment, and to erase the current log information (see Figure 5.21). You can also turn off logging temporarily.

Figure 5.21.   Log view local menu.

Open log file (⟨Ctrl⟩-O)

Press ⟨**Ctrl**⟩-**O** to open a log file on disk and press ⟨**Enter**⟩ to accept the default file name or enter a new name. The default is the name of the current module with the extension .LOG. With a log file open, all entries in the Log window plus all newly logged information are written to disk. (The Log window still shows the most recent lines added to the log.)

You can log to only one file at a time. If you choose this command twice without first closing the log file, TD displays the message `Already logging to a file`.

> Hint: The window title normally says "Log." But when logging to a disk file, the title changes to something like "Log to TCALC.LOG." Watch this title. It tells you whether log information is being saved to disk.

Close log file (⟨Ctrl⟩-C)

If you don't want to continue recording logged information to disk, or if you want to start a new log file, press **⟨Ctrl⟩-C** to close the current log file. You don't have to execute this command before leaving TD. An open log file is closed automatically when you quit to DOS. You may also want to press **⟨Ctrl⟩-E** to erase any leftover lines in the `Log` window.

> Hint: Use the `File` view to open a saved log file and examine its contents. Because the `Log` window lacks a `Search` command, the `File` view is useful for searching through long logs for information.

Logging (⟨Ctrl⟩-L)

The `Logging` command acts as a toggle that switches logging on and off. When off, no new entries are saved in the `Log` window or file, and the message `(Paused)` is displayed in the window title. When on, logging resumes.

Use this command to speed up sections of code with many breakpoints that log `Action expressions`. When you need to get through such code quickly, temporarily switching off logging is faster than disabling breakpoints with `Breakpoints:Set options`.

Add comment (⟨Ctrl⟩-A) (Default)

Press **⟨Ctrl⟩-A** or just type to add a comment to the `Log` window or file. Whatever you type is added to the end of the current log.

Erase log (⟨Ctrl⟩-E)

Press **⟨Ctrl⟩-E** to erase the log information inside the `Log` window. This command does not affect any log information already written to disk.

Module View (⟨F3⟩)

If there's a main view in TD, this is it. The `Module` window (see Figure 5.22) shows your source code and breakpoints, and it lets you inspect and watch variables by selecting them from the text. When you start TD, this window opens by default and occupies most of the display—unless, that is, you configured TD to open with a different window combination. Also, if TD can't find the program's source-code file, it displays the `CPU` window instead of `Module`.

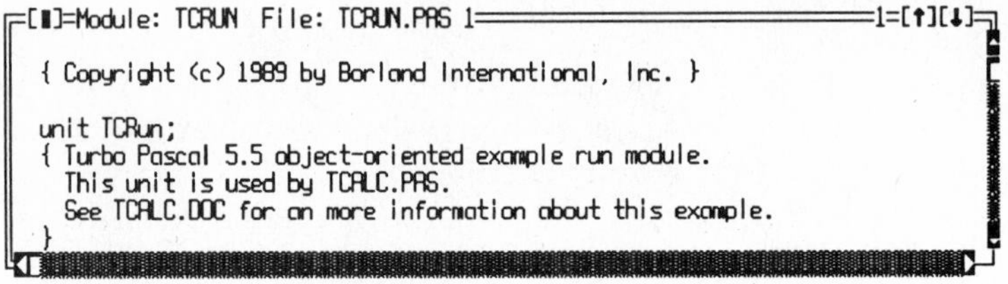

[■]=Module: TCRUN File: TCRUN.PAS 1
1=[↑][↓]
{ Copyright (c) 1989 by Borland International, Inc. }
unit TCRun;
{ Turbo Pascal 5.5 object-oriented example run module.
This unit is used by TCALC.PAS.
See TCALC.DOC for an more information about this example.
}

Figure 5.22. Module view.

Of all 14 TD views, only `Module` has an associated hot key. Press **⟨F3⟩** to open a *pick list* of module names (see Figure 5.23). You can then select a name in the usual ways, or type the first few letters of a listed entry and press **⟨Enter⟩** (or click `Ok`) to open that module.

> Hint: Opening a new module replaces the one now on view in the `Module` window. To view more than one module at the same time, use the `Another:Module` command.

[■]=Pick a module
OBJECTS
TCALC
TCCELL
TCCELLSP
TCHASH
TCINPUT
TCLSTR
TCMENU
TCPARSER
TCRUN
TCSCREEN
TCSHEET
TCUTIL
Ok
Cancel
Help

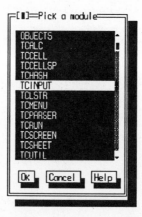

Figure 5.23. The Module view's pick list.

Module View Window Title

The `Module` view's title in the top window border shows the module name (TCRUN in Figure 5.22), and the file associated with this module—usually the same name plus an extension such as .PAS or .C. After this is the line number at the text cursor (*not* the mouse cursor).

At times, you might see the word (`Modified`) between the file name and line number. If so, this means the source-code file's date and time are later than the compiled code. When this happens, be prepared for strange occurrences—what you see on-screen may not be what you have in memory! Usually, this is caused by forgetting to recompile the code after making changes to source-code files or making the wrong directory current and loading an old compiled program into TD.

Module View Local Menu

Figure 5.24 shows the 11 local commands you can issue when the `Module` window is active. The following notes describe each of these commands.

Inspect (⟨Ctrl⟩-I)

Move the text cursor to an identifier. Usually this will be a variable name, but it can also be a function identifier or constant. Press **⟨Ctrl⟩-I** to open an inspector window for that identifier.

As mentioned in chapter 3, inspector windows mold themselves to the type of data they contain. See that chapter and also chapters 9 and 20–22 for more information about inspecting data types in C, Pascal, and assembly language.

> Hint: To dump the contents of a large buffer, move the cursor to the buffer's name and press **⟨Ctrl⟩-I⟨Alt⟩-VD**. This opens a Dump window to the same address as the inspector, giving you two views of the same information.

Figure 5.24. Module view local menu.

Watch (⟨Ctrl⟩-W)

The best way to use this command to add identifiers to the Watches view is to move the text cursor to a variable's name and press **⟨Ctrl⟩-W**. If the text cursor is not pointing to a symbol that TD recognizes, a prompt box will open in which you can type the identifier.

You don't have to highlight the entire variable name to add it to Watches. Also, the text cursor does not have to be under a name's first letter. If you have a mouse, click the left button anywhere on an identifier and press **⟨Ctrl⟩-W** to add it to Watches.

> Hint: If you have a mouse, you can click and drag the mouse pointer to highlight text in the Module window. If you don't have a mouse, press **⟨Insert⟩** and the cursor movement keys.

Module (⟨Ctrl⟩-M)

This command opens a pick list of module names (see Figure 5.23). It has the same effect as pressing **⟨F3⟩**—one key instead of two. So, the Module local command is one of a very few TD commands that you'll probably never use. Pick another module to replace the one now in the Module window or press **⟨Esc⟩** to cancel the command.

File (⟨Ctrl⟩-F)

When viewing modules with multiple source files—usually one or more include files inserted into a main program file with a compiler command—press **⟨Ctrl⟩-F** and select one of the listed files. This does not change the *module* currently on view. It selects which of two or more *files* that make up that module to display in the Module window.

To view a different module, use the Module command (or press **⟨F3⟩**). Also, this is not the correct command to view header files in C programs. To do that, use View:File.

> Hint: Use this command to find out if a module includes any other sources during compilation. If only one file name is listed after you press **⟨Ctrl⟩-F**, the current module includes no other files.

Previous (⟨Ctrl⟩-P)

Press ⟨**Ctrl**⟩-**P** to return to a previous location after scrolling away, using the `Goto` command, initiating a `Search`, or issuing any other command that changes the current position.

The command functions as a toggle—it doesn't let you page back through multiple locations. It can return to a previous module, though, so this is a quick way to reload a module after pressing ⟨**F3**⟩ to view a different source-code file.

To return to the current *statement,* not necessarily the previous view, press ⟨**Ctrl**⟩-**O**, not ⟨**Ctrl**⟩-**P**.

Line (⟨Ctrl⟩-L)

After pressing ⟨**Ctrl**⟩-**L**, enter a line number for the current module. If that number is in range of the lines in the module, TD will reposition the `Module` window to that new line.

This command is often helpful for inspecting code when you receive warnings from the compiler or from a C LINT program—a utility that combs "fuzzy" C code and reports questionable statements by line number. You can enter those numbers with the `Line` command and then type ⟨**Alt**⟩-**VC** to view the machine code for that statement.

The command is also useful for setting multiple breakpoints in code when you have a printed listing. Press ⟨**Ctrl**⟩-**L**, enter a line number, and press ⟨**F2**⟩ to set a breakpoint on that line. With a little practice, you can set a half dozen breakpoints in a module in a few seconds this way. It's much faster in some cases than scrolling through the text hunting for the lines you want.

Search (⟨Ctrl⟩-S)

Use this command to search for text in the current `Module`—similar to the way a text editor's search command works. If TD finds the argument you enter, it positions the `Module` window to that line. If not, it displays "Search expression not found."

You can use wild cards in search arguments. For example, the expression TC* finds all words beginning with TC. TC??? finds all occurrences of TCxxx where xxx are any characters. These wild cards are similar to those you can use with the DOS DIR command.

Hint: Searching begins from the current location. To hunt for text in the entire module, press ⟨**Ctrl**⟩-⟨**Page Up**⟩ before starting a new search.

Next (⟨Ctrl⟩-N)

After using the `Search` command, press ⟨**Ctrl**⟩-**N** to find the next occurrence of the search argument. If there are no more occurrences, TD displays "Search expression not found."

To repeat other previous searches, press ⟨**Ctrl**⟩-**S** and use the cursor keys to select a saved search argument from the history list.

Origin (⟨Ctrl⟩-O)

Press ⟨**Ctrl**⟩-**O** to display the statement that will execute for the next `Run` command. This is especially useful after paging away from a breakpoint or after viewing other modules. Also, after pressing ⟨**Ctrl**⟩-⟨**F2**⟩ to reset a program, press ⟨**Ctrl**⟩-**O** to display the program's first statement.

As with the `CPU` view's `Origin` command, it's a good idea to press ⟨**Ctrl**⟩-**O** *before* entering expressions to make sure TD scopes any local symbols to the origin, not to another location in the source code you happen to be viewing.

> Hint: The current statement is marked with a right-pointing triangle (►). If that symbol appears in the `Module` window, press ⟨**Ctrl**⟩-**O** to move the text cursor to the marked line. This may be easier than using cursor movement keys or the mouse to do the same.

Goto (⟨Ctrl⟩-G) (Default)

To find the source-code line associated with machine code at a specific address, enter that address and press ⟨**Enter**⟩. Because this is the default command, you don't have to press ⟨**Ctrl**⟩-**G** first—just start typing. The address can be anything that evaluates to a constant, but usually, you'll enter a procedure or function name, an assembly language label, or a line number such as **#mymodule#24** (or **mymodule.24** in Pascal). You can also enter an expression that refers to a pointer. As long as the expression evaluates to an address, `Goto` can use it.

Address values must be in a form that's suitable for the current language. TD prefaces offset values—for example, $0100 (Pascal), 0x0100 (C), or 0100h (assembly language)—with the current code segment CS. Or, you can enter an explicit address such as **CS:$085E** to find a source-code line after a runtime error that reports the source of the fault by address.

When searching for runtime errors this way, be aware that TD loads your program into a different area from where that same code runs when executed directly from DOS. For that reason, you may have to add the current value of CS to the segment value reported in the error. For example, for a runtime error at

02F0:0800, enter the address expression **(CS + $02F0):$0800** (using the appropriate formats for hex values in your language) to find the buggy source-code statement.

> Hint: Enter the name of any procedure or function (or fully qualified object method) to jump to that routine's source code. You don't have to choose any commands. Just make the **Module** view active and start typing. This is one of the fastest ways to hop around in a large program, provided, that is, you know the names of the subroutines you want to see.

Edit (⟨Ctrl⟩-E)

If you specified an editor name with TDINST (see chapter 3), you can press **⟨Ctrl⟩-E** to edit the current module. When you use this command, TD exits to DOS and appends the module's file name to the editor and path you entered with TDINST. If all goes well, this should load the module into your editor. When you are done making changes, quit your editor to return to TD. As I mentioned before, you can also use this command to run other programs and batch files. You don't have to use it to run only text editors.

Numeric Processor View

As you might expect, the **Numeric processor** view (see Figure 5.25) shows you the inner workings of a numeric data processor (NDP) such as an 8087, 80287, or 80387 (and, I assume, the on-board NDP on newer 80486 processors). But even if your system lacks a hardware NDP, also known as a math coprocessor, you can still use this view to inspect and manipulate an NDP emulator linked into your code.

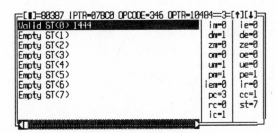

Figure 5.25. Numeric processor view.

The **Numeric processor** view is divided into three panes. The large pane on the left shows the NDP or emulator's internal registers stack—a small amount of memory inside the chip that stores intermediate values. The middle pane lists the NDP control flags. The right pane lists status flags. Refer to an Intel or other NDP reference for the meanings of these fields. (See Bibliography.)

NDP Stack Values

The register stack values in the left pane of the `Numeric processor` window are divided into three columns. The first column shows the register's status— `Valid`, `Zero`, `Special`, or `Empty`. The next column lists the register's index number, 0 to 7. The final column (which is blank if the status is `Empty`) shows the value stored in this register.

The Numeric Processor View's Window Title

The `Numeric processor` view's window title (see Figure 5.25) shows whether an `Emulator` or real NDP is being used (an 80387 in the figure). After this are three labels: `IPTR` (instruction pointer), `OPCODE` (operation code), and `OPTR` (operation pointer). `IPTR` addresses the current NDP instruction (the one just executed). `OPCODE` is the hex value of that instruction, and `OPTR` is the transfer address from that instruction. Not all instructions have such addresses.

The two `IPTR` and optional `OPTR` addresses are 20-bit absolute values. To convert these values to segment and offset logical pairs, lop off the last digit for the offset and append 0 to what's left for the segment. For example, if `IPTR` equals 010EF, it refers to the normalized logical address 10E0:F. (A normalized pointer's offset is within the range 0 to 15 decimal.)

> Hint: Open the **CPU** view, press ⟨**Ctrl**⟩-**G** to choose the `Goto` command, and enter a converted logical address to find the NDP instruction in memory. Remember to enter address values in a form that's appropriate for your language.

Numeric Processor View Local Menu

The `Numeric processor` view's left pane (see Figure 5.25) has three local commands. The middle and right panes have one each (see Figure 5.26). This section explains the view's local commands.

Figure 5.26.   Numeric processor view local menus.

Zero (⟨Ctrl⟩-Z)

Highlight a stack slot in the left pane and press **⟨Ctrl⟩-Z** to clear that value to 0.

> Hint: Pressing **0⟨Enter⟩** does the same job and might be easier if you're not a touch typist.

Empty (⟨Ctrl⟩-E)

Highlight a stack slot in the left pane and press **⟨Ctrl⟩-E** to empty that register. An empty register contains no value. This is not the same as setting the register to 0.

Change (⟨Ctrl⟩-C) (Default)

Highlight any stack slot in the left pane and enter a new value to insert in that register. This is the default command, so you can just start typing. You don't have to press **⟨Ctrl⟩-C** first.

You can enter integer values such as 1234 and 56, hex values in a form that's appropriate for your language ($FF, 0xFF, 0FFh, and so on), or floating point values in decimal (3.14159) or scientific notation (3.755e-2).

You can also enter an expression (see chapter 9). For example, to enter the value of a variable `NumLoops` into an NDP register, highlight the register's slot, enter the variable's name, and press **⟨Enter⟩**.

Toggle (⟨Ctrl⟩-T) (Default)

Highlight a flag in the middle or right `Numeric processor` panes and choose `Toggle` to flip that flag from 0 to 1, or from 1 to 0.

> Hint: Because this command is the default for these two `Numeric processor` panes, you can press **⟨Enter⟩** or **⟨Space⟩** to toggle a flag on and off. This is easier than pressing **⟨Ctrl⟩-T** or choosing this command from the local menu.

Registers View

Use the `Registers` view to examine and change register and flag values in your system's 80x86 processor. If your system has an 80386 or 80486, you can also choose whether to view registers as 16- or 32-bit values. Figure 5.27 shows both of these views.

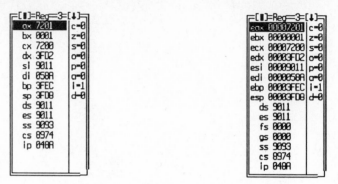

Figure 5.27.   16- and 32-bit Register views.

The `Registers` view is identical to the `CPU` window's `Registers` and `Flags` panes. The views are available separately to make it easy to inspect register and flag values without obscuring two-thirds of your display behind other `CPU` panes that you don't need to see. The local commands in the view and `CPU` panes are also identical.

Register View Local Menus

The two panes in the `Registers` view show register values (left) and flags (right). The following information describes the six local commands in these panes (see Figure 5.28).

Increment (⟨Ctrl⟩-I)

Highlight any register in the `Registers` view's left pane and press **⟨Ctrl⟩-I** to increment that register value by 1.

> Hint: Hold down **⟨Ctrl⟩-I** and let your keyboard's auto-repeat capability increase register values rapidly. This is sometimes easier than typing new values with the `Change` command. (Press **⟨Ctrl⟩-D** to decrement the register if you go too far.)

Figure 5.28.   Register view local menus.

Decrement (⟨Ctrl⟩-D)

Highlight any register in the `Registers` view's left pane and press ⟨**Ctrl**⟩-**D** to decrement the register's value by 1.

Zero (⟨Ctrl⟩-Z)

Press ⟨**Ctrl**⟩-**Z** to set a register to 0. I find it's easier to just type **0**⟨**Enter**⟩, but try it both ways.

Change (⟨Ctrl⟩-C) (Default)

To change the value of any register, highlight it, enter the new value, and press ⟨**Enter**⟩. There's never any good reason to choose this command from the local menu or to press ⟨**Ctrl**⟩-**C**. Just move the highlight bar and start typing.

Remember to enter new values in a form that's suitable for your language—for example, **$FACE** (Pascal), **0xFACE** (C), or **0FACEh** (assembly language).

> Hint: To set more than one register to the same value, enter the first normally, highlight the next, and press ⟨**Space**⟩⟨**Cursor Down**⟩⟨**Enter**⟩. This selects the previous entry from the `Change` command's history list for each register in turn.

Registers 32-bit (⟨Ctrl⟩-R)

Toggle this setting from `No` (16-bit registers) to `Yes` (32-bit registers) on systems that have 80386 or 80486 processors. Changing this setting has no effect on register values, and you can switch between the two views as often as you like.

Notice that in Figure 5.27 the 32-bit view also shows the additional two segment registers FS and GS, available only on 32-bit processors.

Toggle (⟨Ctrl⟩-T) (Default)

The `Flags` pane in the `Registers` view has only one command, `Toggle`, which you can choose by pressing ⟨**Ctrl**⟩-**T**.

> Hint: Because `Toggle` is the default command in the `Flags` pane, you can just highlight any flag and press ⟨**Enter**⟩ or ⟨**Space**⟩ to change it from 0 to 1 or from 1 to 0.

Stack View

The `Stack` view shows the chain of function, procedure, and object method calls that led to the current location. If no subroutine calls were made to arrive at this place in the program, the `Stack` view will be empty. You might want to open this view before tracing code with `Run`-menu commands. That way, you can see the hierarchy of nested subroutine calls as it develops.

When procedures and functions return to their callers, the list of entries in the `Stack` view shrinks. When the program makes new calls, it grows. For example, Figure 5.29 shows that module TCSCREEN has called a procedure (actually an object method call) named `INIT`. When `INIT` returns, that line will be removed from the window.

Figure 5.29.   Stack view.

The `Stack` view is also useful for spotting calls to procedures and functions that shouldn't be happening—or that are being made out of order. A quick glance at the `Stack` view shows you the full sequence of calls that led into the current subroutine.

The Stack view works only on a source-code level. You can't use this window to view calls and returns executed in the `CPU` window.

Stack View Local Menu

The `Stack` view has a simple local menu with two commands, described next (see Figure 5.30).

Inspect (⟨Ctrl⟩-I) (Default)

Highlight any line in the `Stack` view and press **⟨Ctrl⟩-I** to view that place in the program. This is a great way to follow the chain of function and procedure calls that led to a bug. Use the `Stack` view to trace back through those calls until you find what went wrong. Choosing this command activates or opens the `Module` window.

> Hint: Because `Inspect` is the default command, you can just press ⟨**Enter**⟩ to inspect a highlighted `Stack` entry. This is faster than choosing the command from its menu or pressing ⟨**Ctrl**⟩**-I**. Press ⟨**F6**⟩ a few times to return to the `Stack` view.

Figure 5.30.   Stack view local menu.

Locals (⟨Ctrl⟩-L)

The `Locals` command opens a `Variables` view window (described in the next section). Highlight a function, procedure, method name, or a recursive instance of a subroutine in the `Stack` window and press ⟨**Ctrl**⟩**-L** to see all local symbols available to the code at this point in time.

When `Variables` opens, it shows global symbols in the top pane, locals in the bottom. The highlight bar will rest on one of the local variables in the procedure highlighted in the `Stack` window. Press ⟨**Enter**⟩ to inspect those symbols in more detail.

Variables View

As a name, the `Variables` view is an understatement. This window shows not only variables, but all global and local program symbols available to TD (see Figure 5.31). In fact, this view *is* the symbol table, minus source-code line numbers.

The `Variables` view is divided into two panes. On top are global symbols: variables, constants, methods, procedures, and functions. On the bottom are the local symbols currently within the scope of an active procedure, function, or object method. The *Turbo Debugger User's Guide* calls the top section the *global pane* and the bottom the *static pane*.

```
╔[■]═Variables══════════════3═[↑][↓]╗
║TCRUN.PROGRAMOBJECT.INIT      @7D45:0040 ▲
║TCRUN.PROGRAMOBJECT.DONE      @7D45:015B ▒
║TCRUN.PROGRAMOBJECT.GETCOMMANDS @7D45:1F22 ▒
║TCRUN.PROGRAMOBJECT.SETDISPLAYAREA@7D45:207A▒
║TCRUN.PROGRAMOBJECT.DISPLAYALL @7D45:2193 ▼
║◄▓▓▓▓▓▓▓▓▓▓▓▓▓▓▓▓▓▓▓▓▓▓▓▓▓▓▓▓▓▓▓▓▓►
║CLEARSCREEN                   @8974:0000
║MOVETEXT                      @8974:0052
║SCROLLTEXT                    @8974:014D
║EGAINSTALLED                  @8974:0236
╚════════════════════════════════════╝
```

Figure 5.31.   Variables view.

Use the global pane to examine global variables and other global symbols at a glance. Because the symbols are grouped by module, this pane is a great way to inspect a series of variables. It's much faster than adding those same variables one by one to `Watches` or opening inspector windows for them. Use the static pane to view local variables declared inside procedures and functions.

Note: Before the `Variables` view will show a procedure or function's local symbols correctly, you must be sure to execute that routine's startup code. If the current line marker (▶) points to a Pascal procedure or function's `begin` or if it points to a C function's opening brace, then press 〈**F7**〉 or 〈**F8**〉 to see the local symbols in the bottom pane.

For C and assembly language programs, symbols in `Variables` are sorted alphabetically; therefore, you can use TD's incremental matching capabilities. As you type, the window automatically scrolls to symbols that begin with the letters you enter. To find C identifiers, you might have to type one or two leading underscores. Press 〈**Home**〉 to move the cursor to the beginning of a line (or 〈**Ctrl**〉-〈**Page Up**〉 to move to the top of the list) before starting a new incremental search.

Unfortunately, Pascal symbols are not sorted alphabetically, which disables incremental matching for programs in this language. Instead, symbols declared in the same units are listed together.

Variables View Local Menu

There are only two local commands in the `Variables` view, both of which are the same for the top and bottom panes (see Figure 5.32). The next sections explain how to use the commands.

Figure 5.32. Variables view local menu.

Inspect (〈Ctrl〉-I) (Default)

Press 〈**Enter**〉 to inspect a highlighted symbol in the top or bottom panes of the `Variables` view. You can also choose the command from its menu or press 〈**Ctrl**〉-I, but pressing 〈**Enter**〉 is easier. If that symbol refers to code, the command activates or opens the `Module` window and displays the source code associated with that symbol (usually a procedure or function name). (If the `CPU` window opens instead, then TD couldn't find the source-code file.) If the highlighted symbol refers to a variable, the `Inspect` command opens an inspector to show the variable's value.

Change (⟨Ctrl⟩-C)

Press **⟨Ctrl⟩-C** and enter a new value for a highlighted variable in the top or bottom panes of the `Variables` view. The command works only for variables— if you try to change a procedure or constant, TD will tell you the symbol "Cannot be changed."

Watches View

The `Watches` view lets you watch over one or more variables at any moment during a program's execution (see Figure 5.33). Even better, when tracing code with a `Run` menu command (usually by pressing ⟨**F7**⟩ or ⟨**F8**⟩), changes to variables made by statements are displayed instantly in `Watches`. For example, you can examine a loop index as it cycles from a minimum to a maximum value, watch a string take shape as a series of operations add characters to it, or watch the results of a complex expression. The `Watches` view lets you see all the individual values that make up these and other data structures.

Figure 5.33. Watches view.

When you first start TD, the `Watches` window occupies a narrow strip of real estate near the bottom of the screen, just under `Module`. As you add new symbols to the window, it automatically expands up to a limit specified with TDINST (see chapter 3). This lets you add several symbols to `Watches` without having to resize the window to see its contents.

> Hint: If you resize the `Module` or `Watches` window, `Watches` loses its magical ability to grow and shrink automatically. To restore this feature after adjusting either of these windows, choose the `System` (≡) menu's `Restore standard` command. This won't work, however, if you save a nonstandard window `Layout` with `Options:Save options`. When that happens, instead of quitting TD and deleting TDCONFIG.TD, save a new configuration *without* the `Layout` and then press ⟨**Alt**⟩-⟨**Space**⟩**S**.

Viewing Variables

Most symbols added to `Watches` are variables. As Figure 5.33 shows, the window displays the variable's name and value followed by a colon and data type. Unless you change `Options:Display options:Integer format`, integer values appear in decimal and in hex (in parentheses). Other variables display in appropriate forms.

Because `Watches` displays variables on single lines, complex items such as records and objects may be less than clear. In such cases, fields are strung together inside braces or parentheses, and separated by commas like this:

```
Reg (16,242,4400,1550,28216,...,6):Registers
```

Because fields are not labeled, this view is good only for a quick summary of the structure's values. For a better picture, highlight the line in `Watches` and press ⟨**Ctrl**⟩-**I** (see the `Inspect` local command later in this chapter).

Adding Symbols to Watches

There are many ways to add new symbol names to `Watches`, but the easiest is to move the text cursor to any character of a symbol (usually a variable name) in the `Module` window and press ⟨**Ctrl**⟩-**W**. You can also use the `Data:Add watch` command (press ⟨**Ctrl**⟩-⟨**F7**⟩) and type in a variable's name. Or, you can use the `Watch` local command in the `Watches` window.

When you add local symbols to `Watches,` if those symbols are not within the current statement's scope, TD displays its "unknown value" symbol—????. Later, when those variables come within the active scope, `Watches` will display their values. Unfortunately, this also means that TD doesn't catch typing mistakes. If you mistype an identifier—for example, `Clout` instead of `Count`—TD assumes the symbol hasn't come into scope, even though that will never happen.

You can also add expressions to `Watches`—you don't have to limit entries to plain symbols. For example, you can watch an expression such as `Count - 1`. TD evaluates the expression each time it displays the symbol's value; therefore, the displayed value in this example will always be one less than `Count`. This can be useful for monitoring loop indexes in code such as:

```
for Count := Min to Max do
  a[ Count - 1 ] := b[ Count - 1 ];
```

> Hint: When debugging object-oriented Pascal and C++ code, enter **self** (Pascal) or **this** (C++) into `Watches`. As you trace into various method calls, the window will show the instances of objects as they activate each method.

Watches View Local Menu

There are six local commands available in the `Watches` view, each described next (see Figure 5.34).

Figure 5.34. Watches view local menu.

Watch (⟨Ctrl⟩-W, ⟨Insert⟩) (Default)

Choose this command to enter the name of a variable to add to those in `Watches`. As mentioned before, there are easier ways to watch new symbols, but the command comes in handy when `Watches` is already active and you want to add another variable to the window.

> Hint: Because this is the default command, you can just start typing; you don't have to press ⟨**Ctrl**⟩-**W** or ⟨**Insert**⟩ first. Also, when entering many similarly named variables such as **var1**, **var2**, and **var3**, to save typing time, enter the first one and press ⟨**Enter**⟩. Then, press ⟨**Space**⟩⟨**Cursor Down**⟩ to select the previous entry from the command's history list. You can then edit the text to add the next variable.

Edit (⟨Ctrl⟩-E)

Highlight any line in `Watches` and press ⟨**Ctrl**⟩-**E** to insert the symbol into a small dialog box, where you can edit its name. When you're done, press ⟨**Enter**⟩ to replace the highlighted line with the edited symbol.

The command is useful for editing a complex variable so you can view one field from a record or an instance variable in an object. For example, using the earlier example for `Reg`, you could highlight that line, press ⟨**Ctrl**⟩-**W**, and change the symbol to `Reg.AH` to show only that field value.

> Hint: You can also press ⟨**Enter**⟩ instead of ⟨**Ctrl**⟩-**E** to call up this command. When `Watches` is active, think of ⟨**Enter**⟩ as the "Edit" key.

Remove (⟨Ctrl⟩-R, ⟨Delete⟩)

Highlight any line in `Watches` and press ⟨**Ctrl**⟩-**R** or ⟨**Delete**⟩. TD removes that line without disturbing any others.

Delete all (⟨Ctrl⟩-D)

Press ⟨**Ctrl**⟩-**D** to delete all lines in `Watches`.

Inspect (⟨Ctrl⟩-I)

Highlight a line in `Watches` and press ⟨**Ctrl**⟩-**I** to open an inspector window for that variable or other symbol. See chapters 3, 20–22, and others for more information about using inspectors.

The `Inspect` command is useful only for inspecting symbols that evaluate to memory addresses. You can still inspect an expression such as `Count - 1`, but, in that and similar cases, the inspector window opens to a constant value.

Hint: When watching `self` or `this` in `Watches` for object-oriented debugging, highlight that line and press ⟨**Ctrl**⟩-**I**⟨**Ctrl**⟩-**H** to see where the object instance fits in the hierarchy of other objects. I memorized this command by associating I and H with *Instance Hierarchy,* although that's not what the I stands for.

Change (⟨Ctrl⟩-C)

Press ⟨**Ctrl**⟩-**C** and enter a new value for the highlighted symbol in `Watches`. You can change the values of variables, but not expressions or functions.

Summary

The 14 commands in the `View` menu are some of TD's most powerful features. While debugging, you'll probably use these commands more frequently than others. `View`-menu commands open views (windows) that show a program's source code, variables, machine code, processor registers, and other information. TD normally opens two of these views, `Module` and `Watches`, at the start of each new debugging session.

Each view has a private menu of local commands, which perform various operations inside the current window. You can select these commands as you do others, but it's easier to press ⟨**Ctrl**⟩ plus the command's hot key. That way, you don't have to open the menus. Most views also assign one local command as an automatic default, selected when you just start typing. Learning these short-cuts can save a lot of time.

This chapter contains many tips for using all 14 `View`-menu commands. Hot keys and defaults are also listed for all local commands. Together, chapters 4 and 5 form a complete reference to TD's menus, windows, views, and hot keys.

Chapter 6

Using TD's Utility Programs

PACKED WITH TD are several utility programs. Use them to convert *CodeView* debugging information to TD's format, to display details about object-code and other files, to unpack archive files downloaded from bulletin boards, and to perform other jobs that make debugging a little less painful. (*Any* program that can help find bugs is welcome!)

This chapter is a reference to TD's utilities and command-line options. Each utility is listed in alphabetic order. As in previous chapters, instead of duplicating what you can find in the *Turbo Debugger User's Guide*, I've tried to concentrate on sharing tips that will help you get the most from these programs.

Displaying On-line Help

To display instructions for TDCONVRT, TDMAP, TDPACK, TDRF, TDSTRIP, TDUMP, and UNZIP, enter the program name with no arguments or option letters and press 〈**Enter**〉. For TDINST, TDNMI, and TDREMOTE, enter the program name plus **-?**. For example, to display TDREMOTE's instructions, enter:

```
tdremote -?
```

Or, to print a copy of the help text, enter:

```
tdremote -? >prn
```

Some programs also recognize -h as the "help" command-line option. Because the -? and -h commands are the same for all programs that use them, to save space here, these switches are not listed among other options.

Error Messages

The meanings of most error messages should be obvious, so I haven't duplicated them here. For more help with these messages, list or print the MANUAL.DOC file on one of the TD master disks.

About the Syntax Descriptions

This chapter lists the complete syntax for each TD utility. Square brackets represent optional items. The word *options* stands for one or more option letters, always preceded by a dash (-) or a slash (/). A vertical line means "or." For example, [.EXE|.COM] indicates that you can type either .EXE or .COM. Symbols such as ⟨*file*⟩, ⟨*infile*⟩, and ⟨*outfile*⟩ represent file names. The symbol ⟨*ext*⟩ represents any file-name extension. ⟨*#*⟩ stands for an integer value. An ellipsis (...) implies that you can repeat the previous item any number of times.

In general, TD's utilities operate similarly. But there are nagging inconsistencies. For example, TDCONVRT runs silently with the -s switch, while TDMAP requires -q to do the same. Also, help messages are inconsistent, listing combinations of upper- and lowercase letters preceded by slashes in some cases and dashes in others. To keep this chapter from looking too much like a flea market of command-line options, I've remodeled a few facts here and there. For that reason, you may notice several differences between this chapter and the instructions displayed by the utilities.

Most TD utilities are written as *filters* that write to the DOS standard output file. To pause long listings, you can pipe that output with a vertical bar character (|) to the DOS MORE filter, which must be in the current PATH. For example, enter **tdmem -v | more** to pipe TDMEM's *verbose* (-v) output to MORE. You can then press ⟨**Space**⟩ or ⟨**Enter**⟩ to view the information a page at a time.

TDCONVRT.EXE

Use this program to convert Microsoft *CodeView* debugging information in compiled and assembled code files to TD's format. As you'd expect, most Microsoft languages can add *CodeView* data to compiled code—similar to the way Borland languages add TD information. But several other compilers and assemblers can also create *CodeView* symbols. For those products, you can probably use TDCONVRT to prepare code for debugging with TD.

See chapter 2 for more information about using TDCONVRT with various compilers and assemblers.

TDCONVRT Syntax and Options

The complete syntax for TDCONVRT is:

```
tdconvrt [options] [<infile> [<outfile>]]
```

The default ⟨*infile*⟩ extension is .EXE. The default ⟨*outfile*⟩ extension is .TDS.

-c

This option creates a separate .TDS file containing the symbol table from ⟨*infile*⟩. If you don't specify an ⟨*outfile*⟩ name, it will have the same name as the input file, but with the extension changed to .TDS. For example, after compiling SAMPLE.C to SAMPLE.EXE, if you enter:

```
tdconvrt -c sample
```

TDCONVRT reads the *CodeView* information from SAMPLE.EXE and writes that same data to SAMPLE.TDS. It does not modify the original SAMPLE.EXE.

When you debug a *CodeView* .EXE and a .TDS file with the same file names in the same directory, TD first tries to read the debugging information from the .EXE file. If that data is not in TD format, it then looks for the .TDS file.

Hint: Use the -c option if you want to run *CodeView* and TD on the same program without having to recompile.

-sw

This option tells TDCONVRT to "shut up"—that is, to run silently. Use this command if you run TDCONVRT from a batch file or with MAKE, and you don't want to clutter the display with messages you don't care to read.

> MAKE is a utility program supplied with TASM, TP, TC, and many other compilers and assemblers. It reads a text file, called a *MAKE file*, which lists the dependencies between compiled and source code. MAKE uses this information to issue the minimum number of commands required to recompile and link a multimodule application.

TDDEV.EXE

Run TDDEV with no parameters for a list of character and block device drivers currently installed, probably by `DEVICE=` commands in CONFIG.SYS. The program is smart enough to detect any drivers installed after booting, in which case it displays "Detected device drivers patched in after CONFIG.SYS."

> See chapter 19 for help with device-driver debugging.

TDDEV Syntax and Options

The complete syntax for TDDEV is:

```
tddev [options]
```

-r

Specify the -r option for a "raw" report, listing additional facts about installed drivers, including strategy and interrupt entry point addresses.

TDINST.EXE

Run TDINST to modify various settings in TD.EXE, to create a custom TDCONFIG.TD configuration file, or to modify the parameters in an existing configuration.

TDINST Syntax and Options

The complete syntax for TDINST is:

```
tdinst [option] [<outfile>]
```

If you don't want to modify the original TD.EXE file, copy it to another file and specify that file's name as the optional TDINST ⟨outfile⟩. When you choose the `Save` command, TDINST will modify the file copy, not the original TD.EXE.

-c⟨file⟩

Use the -c option and a file name to edit a TDCONFIG.TD or other configuration file created earlier with TDINST or by using TD's `Options:Save options` command. Don't put any spaces between the option letter and the file name. For example, this loads BCFG.TD into TDINST for editing:

```
tdinst -cbcfg.td
```

When you `Save` the configuration, choose the `Save configuration file` subcommand to modify BCFG.TD or another file. Or, choose `Modify td.exe` to transfer the configuration to TD.EXE (or a copy of that file).

TDMAP.EXE

If your language can't generate TD or *CodeView* debugging information, but if it can create a .MAP file, you can use TDMAP to prepare the code for debugging with TD.

TDMAP reads a .MAP text file—a road map of a compiled or assembled program's symbols and line numbers. It translates the information in the .MAP file to TD's format and writes that information to the .EXE file to prepare it for debugging.

If TDMAP can't read your language's .MAP file, use the Turbo Linker (TLINK) /m option to create a sample .MAP file of a test program assembled with TASM. This will give you a template .MAP file to compare with the one from your language. In some cases, you might need to make minor fixups to convert foreign map files for TDMAP.

> See chapter 2 for examples of TDMAP in action.

TDMAP Syntax and Options

The complete syntax for TDMAP is:

```
tdmap [options] [<mapfile>[.MAP] [<outfile>] [options]]
```

Usually, you won't need to specify an ⟨*outfile*⟩, TDMAP assumes that file has the same name as ⟨*mapfile*⟩, but ends with the extension .EXE.

> If the .MAP file's date and time stamp is older than the .EXE file's, TDMAP displays a warning. To avoid this, use the TOUCH utility supplied with TASM to update the file's date and time.

-b

Unless you specify the -b option, TDMAP lists all variable types as word, or array of word. The option forces symbols to be of type byte or array of byte. Use the option if your language aligns variables to byte addresses.

This option reveals one of TD's weaknesses when debugging programs from languages that can't generate TD or *CodeView* debugging information directly. When debugging from a .MAP file, all symbols are represented as bytes or words. Even so, you can use type casts to convert selected variables to more readable forms. See chapter 9 for help.

-c

Use -c to tell TDMAP that map-file symbols are case-sensitive. With this option in effect, `MyVAR`, `myVar`, and `MYVAR` represent three *different* symbols. TDMAP's default is to ignore case differences.

> Hint: If you have trouble getting TD to recognize variable names and other symbols, try using combinations of TDMAP's -c option along with TD's -sc command.

-e⟨ext⟩

Some languages that recognize default file-name extensions create .MAP files with file names that lack extensions. For example, the .MAP file might refer to MYFILE, which the language assumes to mean MYFILE.C. So that TD knows this same detail, use options such as -eC and -ePAS. Don't type any spaces or a period between the -e and the extension's first character. The extensions can be in upper- or lowercase.

-q

Tell TDMAP to "be quiet"—that is, not to display a progress report while converting .MAP files. Because a large program can take several seconds to convert, using this option can speed the process. You might also use it to reduce display clutter when running TDMAP from a MAKE file.

TDMEM.EXE

Run TDMEM to display a system memory map, including a report of total and free expanded and extended memory. The program is especially useful for locating TSRs and other resident code for debugging (see chapter 19). In addition to other facts about various items in memory, TDMEM also displays each program's PSP (*Program Segment Prefix*) address, plus a list of "hooked vectors," in other words, interrupts that the TSR has redirected through its own routines. These facts can be vital for finding bugs that are caused by two or more conflicting TSRs.

TDMEM Syntax and Options

The complete syntax for TDMEM is:

```
tdmem [options]
```

-v

Use the *verbose* switch -v for a long-winded report, including the number of file handles allocated to a process.

TDNMI.COM

This utility installs a small resident program in memory that periodically (about two times a second) clears the nonmaskable interrupt on systems that mask out NMI for their own reasons. (Actually, it's impossible to mask the NMI. But it is possible to disable the ports that lead to the CPU's NMI pin, thus effectively masking the "nonmaskable" interrupt. TDNMI clears these ports.)

TDNMI also continually resets the breakout latch in a *Periscope* debugging board. This lets you press that board's breakout switch to activate TD.

> Note: Most people should *not* run this program. Install TDNMI once every time you boot only if you have a *Periscope* debugging board or if your system disables NMI. If you need to use the program, insert the line **c:\td\tdnmi** in AUTOEXEC.BAT. Replace C:\TD with the directory where TDNMI.EXE is stored.

TDNMI Syntax and Options

The complete syntax for TDNMI is:

```
tdnmi [<option>]
```

-p[⟨#⟩]

Specify -p to reset the *Periscope* board's breakout latch at the default address 0300h. Or, if you reconfigured your board, specify a different address immediately after -p, for example, -p310.

TDPACK.EXE

If you are having trouble debugging large programs, try running the code or symbol file through TDPACK. This will compress the debugging information in the file by combining duplicate strings and other items. With luck, this will free enough space so you can load the program into TD.

> If you still can't load the program, turn to chapter 3 for other ways to limit TD's memory use.

TDPACK Syntax

The complete syntax for TDPACK is:

```
tdpack [<file>[.EXE|.TDS|.COM]]
```

If you don't specify a file-name extension, TDPACK attempts to open
⟨*file*⟩.EXE. If that doesn't work, it tries to open ⟨*file*⟩.TDS. If you specify
.COM, TDPACK tries to open ⟨*file*⟩.TDS because it assumes you've created
.COM and .TDS files with TDSTRIP's -c and -s options. (Symbol tables are never
stored in .COM files; therefore, it would make no sense for TDPACK to operate
directly on .COM programs.) TDPACK has no command-line options.

See also TDSTRIP in this chapter and "Assembling .COM Programs" in
chapter 2.

TDREMOTE.EXE

Run TDREMOTE on a remote computer connected to a host system's RS-232
port by a serial cable. You can then use TD's -r option to debug programs in
remote mode, and you can use the TDRF utility to give simple commands to the
remote computer. (Chapter 17 describes how to use TDREMOTE.)

TDRF.EXE

After starting TDREMOTE on a remote computer connected to a host system's
RS-232 port by a serial cable, you can use TDRF to delete files, change directo-
ries, transfer files, and give other simple commands to the remote computer.
(Chapter 17 describes how to use TDRF.)

TDSTRIP.EXE

Use TDSTRIP to remove TD's symbol table from a compiled and linked .EXE
code file. You might do this to prepare "beta" test versions of your program
files that are identical to your own test copies minus the debugging information.

More often, however, you'll use TDSTRIP instead of the DOS EXE2BIN
utility to convert an .EXE file to a .COM-style code file with debugging information stored in a .TDS data file (see chapter 2). You can also use the program to
prepare .TDS files for debugging TSRs and device drivers (see chapter 19).

Note: Tests show that TDSTRIP does not always produce the same results as
recompiling a program without debugging information. A stripped code file is
probably safe for distribution, but if it were my code, I would still recompile it
before "pressing" the final master.

TDSTRIP Syntax and Options

The complete syntax for TDSTRIP is:

```
tdstrip [options] [<infile> [<outfile>]]
```

The ⟨*infile*⟩ may be an .EXE or .OBJ file that contains TD debugging information. The purpose and format of ⟨*outfile*⟩ depends on whether you specify the -s and -c options. See the descriptions of those options and "TDSTRIP Examples" later on for sample TDSTRIP commands.

-s

Specifying -s strips debugging information from ⟨*infile*⟩, which must have the extension .EXE. Exactly what happens to that information depends on whether you also specify -c and an optional output file name. (See "TDSTRIP Examples.")

-c

This option converts an .EXE file to a .COM file, similar to the way the DOS EXE2BIN utility works. Because .COM files can't store debugging information, you'll probably use -c and -s together to copy the symbol table to a .TDS file. You can then debug the .COM file with TD. The next section explains how this works.

> TDSTRIP can't convert every .EXE file to a .COM program. For a successful conversion, the program's origin must begin at offset 0100h, and it can't specify a stack segment or include any references that require "fix ups" at runtime.

TDSTRIP Examples

Even though TDSTRIP has only two options, it's difficult to use correctly. I've found that if I *don't* specify file-name extensions for ⟨*infile*⟩ and ⟨*outfile*⟩, but let TDSTRIP add them for me, I stay out of trouble. If you do specify extensions, be sure to use the correct ones, or you can easily create a .TDS data file named MYPROG.EXE, which, if you try to run it, will lead to a colossal crash.

The following sample command lines cover most TDSTRIP option and file-name combinations and should answer many questions about how to use the utility.

- To remove debugging information from SAMPLE.EXE, permanently losing that information, enter:

```
tdstrip sample
```

- To create NEWFILE.EXE without debugging information but without changing the original SAMPLE.EXE file (same as copying SAMPLE.EXE to NEWFILE.EXE and then typing **tdstrip newfile**), enter:

```
tdstrip sample newfile
```

- To strip debugging information from SAMPLE.EXE and transfer that same information to a new file named SAMPLE.TDS—useful for debugging TSRs—enter:

```
tdstrip -s sample
```

- To strip debugging information from SAMPLE.EXE and transfer that same information to a new file named NEWFILE.TDS, enter:

```
tdstrip -s sample newfile
```

- To strip debugging information from SAMPLE.EXE, create SAMPLE.COM, and delete SAMPLE.EXE—which also permanently throws away any debugging information—enter:

```
tdstrip -c sample
```

- To create NEWFILE.COM without changing the original SAMPLE.EXE— thus preserving debugging information in that file—enter:

```
tdstrip -c sample newfile
```

- To copy debugging information from SAMPLE.EXE to a new file named SAMPLE.TDS, creating SAMPLE.COM *and deleting* the original SAMPLE.EXE file—useful for preparing .COM programs for debugging— enter:

```
tdstrip -s -c sample
```

- To copy debugging information from SAMPLE.EXE to NEWFILE.TDS, creating SAMPLE.COM *and deleting* the original SAMPLE.EXE file, enter:

```
tdstrip -s -c sample newfile
```

TDUMP.EXE

TDUMP is a remarkable program that has all sorts of uses. With this single program, you can display an ASCII text file, examine bytes in data files, decipher an object-code file's internal format, print the debugging information added to an .EXE file, check a file's integrity, and perform other chores that can make debugging less painful.

TDUMP Syntax and Options

The complete syntax for TDUMP is:

```
tdump [options] [<infile> [<outfile>] [options]]
```

You must specify an ⟨*infile*⟩. Because TDUMP recognizes no default extensions, to dump SAMPLE.EXE you must type that file's full name. TDUMP writes its output to an optional ⟨*outfile*⟩ in ASCII text format. You can add one or more options either immediately after TDUMP or after the file names.

-a

This option tells TDUMP that ⟨*infile*⟩ contains ASCII text. The result is similar to a Dump window's byte list, but with each byte converted to a character. Any characters not in the ASCII range of 32–126 are displayed as periods.

-a7

This option displays characters in an ASCII text file with all high bits forced to 0. Use this option to dump *WordStar* and similar text files, which use the "extra" bit in characters as a formatting marker.

-b⟨#⟩

Start dumping at an offset equal to ⟨#⟩, expressed in the C language's hexadecimal format. For example, -b0x0100 starts dumping at hexadecimal offset 0100.

-e

Force executable code-file display, the default for files that end in .EXE. Use this option only when dumping executable code files that use a different file-name extension.

-el

Usually, when dumping an .EXE file with debugging information, TDUMP displays any line numbers and hex offsets in this format:

```
Line Numbers:
   7:01FAh       10:0203h        9:0217h       11:021Ah
```

Specify -el if you *don't* want to see this information.

-er

When dumping .EXE files, TDUMP normally displays relocatable address entries in the form:

```
Relocation Locations (1 Entry)
   0000:0001
```

Specify -er if you *don't* want to see this information.

-elr

This is shorthand for -el -er. Use it to not display line numbers and relocation details.

-b

Use this option to force TDUMP to display a file's contents as hexadecimal bytes and their ASCII equivalents—similar to the default format for a TD Dump window. This is the default setting for unrecognized file-name extensions. Use it only to display hex dumps for .EXE, .DLL, .OBJ, .LIB, and .TDS files, all of which TDUMP recognizes as containing formatted data. (.DLL stands for *Dynamic Link Library*, normally associated with OS/2. TD can't debug OS/2 code, but the presence of features like this suggests that such support might not be far away.)

-l

TDUMP displays the object-code modules in library files ending in .LIB. If your libraries end in a different extension, you must use this option to tell TDUMP that a file is a library. Otherwise, it will dump the file in hex.

-m

Use this option only with TC++ programs to *demangle* function and variable names in compiled code. If you don't use this option, these identifiers will appear in strange (mangled) forms, which, in a nutshell, allow C++ and C object-code files to be linked and processed by other utilities that normally recognize only C syntax. Use the -m option to dump compiled TC++ programs and view symbols the way you wrote them.

-o

TDUMP normally displays the formatted contents of object-code files ending in .OBJ. If your object-code files end in a different extension, you must use this option to tell TDUMP that the file contains object-code records. Otherwise, it will dump the file in hex.

-oc

This option verifies the checksum for object-file records. Or, at least that's what I *think* it should do. In the current TD 2.0 release, this option appears to have no effect.

-oiID

Object-code files (and library files that contain object-code modules) store records that list various facts. Each record is identified by an *Object File Record ID*.

To list only specific object-file records, specify the option -oiID. Replace *ID* with the record ID you want to see. This is very useful for extracting information from .OBJ and .LIB files. For example, for a list of an object file's segment definitions, enter the command:

```
tdump -oiSEGDEF sample.obj
```

Or, to display the public symbols in a library, enter:

```
tdump -oiPUBDEF sample.lib
```

You can also use more than one -oiID command to list multiple object-code records. Once you figure out the forms that are useful to you, enter them into a batch file so you don't have to look them up later. Consult a DOS technical reference for other record IDs (see Bibliography).

-oxID

Similar to -oi, this option lists all object-code records *except* the one identified. Use multiple -oxID commands to exclude more than one object-code record ID from the output.

Useful commands include **-oxCOMENT** (yes, there is only one *M*) and **-oxLINNUM**, which reduces TDUMP's usually lengthy output to a more manageable size.

-v

Specify -v (the *verbatim* switch) if you want to dump the "whole ball of wax" for an .OBJ file. The bytes from the file are dumped after each formatted object-code record. Using this option also suppresses comments normally added by TDUMP to document various object-code components. (This one is for programming "Hall of Famers" who can read object code as though it were Pascal or C. Don't bother with this option unless you *really* understand how .OBJ files are put together.)

UNZIP.EXE

To save disk space, many of TD's files are compressed into *archives,* identified by the file-name extension .ZIP. Use the UNZIP utility to extract one or more files from these packed archives on TD's master disks. Usually, the automated INSTALL program runs UNZIP for you. But, if you decide not to unpack archived files at that time, or if you're installing TD on floppy diskettes, you can run UNZIP manually on individual .ZIP files to extract the files you need.

You can also use UNZIP to extract files from archives downloaded from bulletin boards, *Compuserve, Bix,* and similar on-line services.

Warning: Some versions of this utility do not work properly with the popular PC-KWIK disk caches. If UNZIP hangs, reboot without the cache and try again. The problem is caused on 80386 or later machines by PC-KWIK's use of BIOS routines to access extended RAM. Unfortunately, not all BIOS implementations preserve the upper 16-bits of the 32-bit EAX register, which, apparently, UNZIP uses if available. Future versions of the cache and archiving software watch for and fix the conflict, so you may never run into this bug.

UNZIP Syntax and Options

The complete syntax for UNZIP is:

```
unzip [options] [<infile> [<outpath>] [<file>...]]
```

The ⟨*infile*⟩ must be a .ZIP file. You can't use this program to extract files from .ARC files, which use a different compression scheme. (Some other Borland language disks contain a program UNPACK.COM that can unpack these older-style archives.)

Specify an ⟨*outpath*⟩ such as C:\DEMOS to direct UNZIP's output to that directory. If you don't specify an ⟨*outpath*⟩, UNZIP deposits extracted files in the current directory.

To extract only specific files from an archive, list the file names after ⟨*infile*⟩ and an optional output path. Separate multiple file names with spaces. You can also use wild cards such as *.PAS to extract files with similar names.

> Hint: Copy a .ZIP file to a RAM drive and unpack the files there. This makes UNZIP *really* zip! You can then inspect each unpacked file and decide whether to copy it to a floppy or hard disk directory.

Some of the following options are not documented, but work in the version I used to write this chapter.

-c, -cm

When you just want to read the contents of an archive, use the -c (console) option to direct output to the display. Use -cm (console, more) to pause the display between pages. At the end of each page, press ⟨**Space**⟩ to continue, ⟨**Enter**⟩ for the next line, or ⟨**Esc**⟩ to advance to the next file. Press ⟨**Ctrl**⟩**-C** at any time to return to DOS.

> Hint: Press ⟨**Esc**⟩ to skip .EXE and other binary files, displayed as gibberish. I often run UNZIP with a command like **unzip -cm *.zip** to scan all archive files quickly in the current directory. Usually, this is faster than entering each file name individually.

-0

Use this option if you don't want UNZIP to warn you before overwriting an existing file.

-p

Similar to -c, this option directs output to the printer. Use it to print archived text files without having to extract those files from the archive.

-t

This option tests an archive's integrity. It displays a list of an archive's contents and verifies whether files can be safely extracted.

-v[b|c|d|e|n|p|s|r]

These options list an archive's contents. Use them to see a directory of a .ZIP archive without extracting the files it contains. Add an optional letter after -v to select brief output (b), and sort by CRC (c), by date (d), by extension (e), by file name (n), by percent of compression (p), by size (s), and in reverse order (r). For example, enter **unzip -vber tdexmple** for a brief list of an archive sorted in reverse order by extension.

> Note: UNZIP is a slightly modified version of PKUNZIP, published as pay-if-you-use-it shareware by PKWARE, Inc. (See Bibliography). This program and others are available on most bulletin boards and on-line services. Write to the company for more details and for information about utilities that let you create your own compressed archives.

Summary

TD's utility programs perform a variety of miscellaneous jobs. This chapter describes how to use TD's utilities, and it lists their command-line options. (See chapter 17 for help with TDREMOTE and TDRF.)

To display instructions for most utilities, enter the program's name and press ⟨**Enter**⟩. Or, specify the -? or -h command-line options.

Part Two

The Art of Debugging

Chapter 7

Developing a Debugging Strategy

I F YOU HAVE a modem, you probably know about *Compuserve*'s software *forums*—on-line bulletin boards where programmers can trade messages, tips, and techniques. Programming is a lonely craft, and the forums give programmers from all over the world a chance to meet and share ideas. Joining a forum is a great way to learn tricks of the trade and to get answers and suggestions about puzzling problems. It also makes interesting reading.

For example, I don't know how many times I've seen a message that goes something like this:

Everybody—I've discovered a bug in Turbo Pascal!!! In my 15,000-line point-of-sale package, I store linked data on the heap to categorize records according to subject, priority, etc. I use New() and Dispose() to manage the mess. Everything seems to be working just fine, but then something damages my list pointers. I'm sure it's not my code because I tested it. Is this a bug in the compiler? What should I do? —Confused.

Poor Confused. He or she has contracted a common ailment known as "the-compiler-is-bad syndrome." (Hardware engineers often catch a related "the-chip-is-bad virus.") True, compilers do have bugs. So do chips. But, most of the time, if something goes wrong, you'll find the culprit in your own work. There may be a bug in *Turbo Pascal,* but, more likely, the problem is hiding in Confused's "tested" code. Here's how I might respond:

Dear Confused—Can you isolate and upload a small section of your program that seems to be causing the problem? Maybe you've used a disposed pointer somewhere. —Tom

No one in his right mind would accept an invitation to go bug busting in a strange 15,000-line program. Before looking for goblins, the first step is to isolate the section of the code that's haunted. Often, after posting that advice, I'll receive a reply similar to this:

Tom—I started extracting code to upload and then, what do you know, I found the bug!!! You were right. I disposed a pointer and then used it two statements later (sigh). Everything's working now. Thanks so much for your help. — Confused No More.

I'll gladly accept credit for helping even though I didn't do anything. Confused found the bug simply by isolating suspect statements that had not been as thoroughly tested as Confused thought. If you remember nothing else from this book, remember to isolate your bugs. You'll be amazed at how much time that simple strategy alone can save during debugging.

After all, that's the goal of learning how to use TD—to let you quickly find bugs so you'll have time to pursue more valuable treasure. Nobody wants to waste efforts on fruitless crusades for bugs. But that's exactly what many programmers do. Instead of methodically searching for the cause of a bug, as soon as a problem appears, they load into TD all 38 modules of a 150K program that took six months to develop. Then, they single-step through each statement, hoping to discover just what has gone wrong.

Resist this natural urge to puzzle out the cause of a bug. Instead, learn how to use TD's tools and to apply the principles outlined in this chapter. Debug like you play chess. Plan ahead. Develop a strategy. And then go in for the kill.

The Elements of Debugging Style

Every programmer should read Brian W. Kernighan and P. J. Plauger's *The Elements of Programming Style* at least once a year. It's filled with gems like "Make it clear before you make it faster" and "Let the data structure the program."

But, while researching this book, I could find almost no similar advice for debugging. Could it be that, by not discussing the subject, programmers secretly hope the need for debugging will disappear? I can't answer that question. But, I can offer my own list of suggestions for developing a good debugging style—a condensed sampling of the front-line strategies that have saved my skin in countless bug battles over a dozen or so years:

- *Recognize that bugs are inevitable.* You may find a bug in the compiler, but you're more likely to find the error in your own code. Accept this. Everybody makes mistakes.

- *Let go of frustration.* That's easier to say than to accomplish, but when a bug plagues your code, instead of boiling over while hunting for the cause, take a short break, and then start fresh. Enjoy your work!

- *Use well-known programming algorithms.* There's no need to rediscover programming principles from scratch. Invest in books of algorithms, clip subroutines from magazine articles, purchase the top-rated toolkits for your language, and build your own procedure, function, and object-class libraries. You'll prevent many bugs by constructing code on existing frames instead of reinventing the wheels for each new project.

- *Isolate your bugs.* Don't just hunt through code looking for mistakes. Use TD to narrow bug searches first to a module, then to a subroutine, and finally to a statement or two. Divide and conquer.

- *Document your bugs.* When you discover a bug, carefully document the steps and input data that caused the error. You must be able to duplicate a program's bugs. That way, after fixing the problem, you can repeat those same steps to verify that your repairs are working. How else will you prove that the wicked bug is dead?

- *Develop repeatable tests.* Don't postpone testing and debugging until you've finished a large project. Test as you go. And, be sure to create your test code and data with the same care that you apply to your main work. Sloppy testing is a natural habitat for bugs.

Turbo Debugger's Tools

As you learned in part 1, TD has many commands, views, menus, windows, and other features. But among its many strengths, four main abilities offer the most power for developing useful debugging strategies:

- Breakpoints
- Code tracing
- Data inspection
- Expression evaluation

The following sections briefly introduce these four concepts, which you'll meet again in future chapters.

Breakpoints

All breakpoints have two parts: a *condition* and an *action*. Usually, the condition is simply the address of a machine-code instruction—often the first such code of a high-level C or Pascal statement. When the program reaches the *code breakpoint*'s address, TD executes the planned action, which normally halts the program so you can view variables and inspect other facts about misbehaving code. In addition to halting the program, breakpoint actions can also write information to the `Log` window or execute a subroutine.

TD sets code breakpoints by vectoring type 3 interrupts to its breakpoint handler. For each code breakpoint that you set, TD swaps the byte at the breakpoint location with an `int 3` software interrupt instruction (byte value CC hex). When the code executes the interrupt, TD's breakpoint handler gains control and swaps the original byte back to memory. After the handler executes the breakpoint action, to continue the program, TD restarts the code beginning at the breakpoint's address.

Actually, the process of handling code breakpoints is a little more complicated than that. After intercepting a type 3 interrupt, TD replaces the original byte that it saved when you set the breakpoint. To continue executing the program, the breakpoint handler decrements the IP value pushed onto the stack by `int 3` so that the next `iret` will execute the code at the breakpoint location. It then throws the processor into single-stepping mode (see the next section), executes the restored instruction at the breakpoint, regains control, again swaps CC hex with the byte at the breakpoint address (so that the handler will run if this location is reached later on), clears single-stepping mode, and continues execution. Luckily, TD handles these details automatically. You don't need to understand them to be able to use the debugger.

TD also lets you set two kinds of *data breakpoints*. The first of these, called a *changed-memory breakpoint,* periodically examines memory addresses for changes to values stored there. The second, called an *expression-true breakpoint,* monitors bytes in memory to become equal to specific values. When one of these data breakpoint conditions is satisfied, TD executes the planned action, just as it does for code breakpoints.

If your system has an 80386 or 80486 processor, and if you've installed TDH386.SYS or if you have a Trapper debugger board, TD can use the hardware's debugging registers and related features to set data breakpoints (see chapter 18). With the appropriate hardware, changes to monitored locations generate a *debug exception* (a type 1 interrupt) that activates TD's data breakpoint handler. Without this special help, TD can still set changed-memory and expression-true breakpoints, but it has to examine memory locations by brute force between source-code lines or machine-code instructions. This is why setting data breakpoints makes programs run slowly on systems with 8088, 8086, and 80286 processors.

Most often, you'll set code breakpoints to narrow the search for a bug. You'll create data breakpoints to find statements that are changing values unexpectedly or to discover how and why a variable reaches a specific value. For any of the three kinds of code and data breakpoint conditions, you can specify any one of the three possible actions to halt the program, make a log entry, or execute a subroutine—a total of nine breakpoint condition and action combinations.

See chapter 8 for more information about how to use each of the three kinds of breakpoint conditions and actions.

Code Tracing

All 80x86 processors can execute machine-code instructions one at a time—or, more correctly, they allow a program like TD to gain control *between* the execution of instructions. Called *single-stepping,* this feature is enabled when a program sets the *trap flag* (TF), which causes the processor to issue a type 1 interrupt after most instructions. (A few instructions, for example, assignments to segment registers, suppress the type 1 interrupt signal for the next instruction; therefore, these machine codes can't be traced.) When you use TD's Trace into, Step over, and Animate commands, the debugger intercepts the interrupt signal, letting you run programs one line or instruction at a time or in slow motion, which can help find bugs by slowing fast actions to inspectable levels.

Code tracing and breakpoints are natural partners. Many times, you'll set a breakpoint to halt a program at a test location, and then single-step through additional statements at that place. For this reason, chapter 8 discusses breakpoints and code tracing together.

Data Inspection

If you've never used a debugger before, you've probably inserted output commands in your program to display or print the values of variables at strategic locations. Or, perhaps you've written subroutines to save values in disk files for inspection after a test run.

Such methods should be entombed with hex pads, toggle switches, core dumps, and other relics from computing's pioneer days. With TD's abilities to inspect data structures of all kinds, you'll never have to use those old techniques again. Instead, you can inspect your program's variables in one of two main ways:

- Watching
- Inspecting

Both of these data inspection methods are similar. When you *watch* a variable by adding it to the Watches window, TD lists the variable's name, value, and data type on a single line. As you encounter breakpoints and use TD's code-tracing commands, you instantly see changes to all variables listed in Watches. If a variable changes unexpectedly or becomes equal to an unplanned value, you'll know immediately in which section of code that happened. You can also change the value of any variable to test the effects of new data on a program.

Inspecting takes the concept of watching variables one step further, showing you the intimate details of any variable from the simplest character to the most complex object-oriented structure you can devise. With TD's inspector windows, you can trace through a linked list, inspect an array, or examine the fields of a Pascal `record` or a C `struct`.

TD automatically updates inspector windows with new values as you execute code. You always see the *current* value of a variable in an inspector window. You can also use inspectors to enter new values into variables.

See chapter 4 for general information about using inspectors. Also see chapters 20–22 for details about inspecting specific data types in C, Pascal, and assembly language.

> Note: You can also watch and inspect C and Pascal procedures and functions. In that case, however, you see the subroutine's address and, if it's a typed function, the data type it returns. In other words, you can inspect code as data, but you can't change it.

Expression Evaluation

The fourth main debugging tool that you'll find especially helpful for developing useful debugging strategies is also one of TD's most versatile features. Along with breakpoints, code tracing, and data inspection, TD can evaluate just about any expression your compiler or assembler can parse (translate). You can use TD's expression evaluator to:

- Inspect and change variables, similar to the way you can perform those same tasks by watching and inspecting.

- Convert integers from hex to decimal and perform calculations. TD's expression evaluator makes a handy on-screen calculator.

- See the result of an expression before it executes. For example, if an expression is passed to a procedure or function, you can evaluate the expression's result without having to call the subroutine.

- Experiment with new expressions without having to recompile your program. You can copy an expression from your source code, make adjustments, and have TD evaluate the result. When the new expression passes muster, you can add the finished version to your source code.

- Call subroutines in your code independently of TD's other code-tracing capabilities. This lets you patch code on the fly and even create custom debugging commands.

You must take a great deal of care to use the last of these suggestions properly. In fact, many programmers will never need it. But imagine the control it offers. You can test the effects of a subroutine without having to run your program to the place where that subroutine is called—a fact that's useful when a bug crashes the code before reaching that spot. And, you can run "what if" tests to inspect what happens if you were to call a routine after a breakpoint halts the code.

Usually, you'll enter expressions or copy them from your source code into TD's `Evaluate/modify` dialog box (press ⟨**Ctrl**⟩-⟨**F4**⟩). But you can also evaluate expressions by adding them to the `Watches` window or to an `Inspector`. TD will then reevaluate the expression every time it gains control—in between every instruction if you want. Or, you can insert an expression as the action for a breakpoint, splicing code to call a subroutine when the breakpoint condition hits or just to save the result of the expression in the `Log` window. In fact, just about any time TD prompts for a constant value or an address, you can enter an expression.

When entering expressions, you must be careful to use data formats suitable to the current language. See chapter 9 for more information about how to enter expressions for C, Pascal, and assembly language.

Bug Species

Most bugs are unique. That's one reason they're so hard to find. Even so, all bugs belong to one of these three species:

- Syntax errors—program doesn't compile
- Runtime errors—program compiles but doesn't run
- Logical errors—program runs but doesn't work

Become familiar with these kinds of bugs and the differences between them. That way you'll avoid making the same mistakes over and over. Eventually, you'll be able to recognize classes of bugs by the symptoms they produce in a running program.

The following sections introduce these three bug species. Other chapters in part 2 recount instances of these bugs in programs and show how to use TD to find them.

Syntax Errors

A syntax error in the source code breaks the rules of the language. We should be able to trust the compiler to tell us of such mistakes. After all, it's the ultimate authority of language syntax, and no compiler worth its salt should generate code for a syntactically incorrect program.

Some programmers further divide syntax errors into two subspecies. First, there are syntax errors caused by using unsupported symbols—for example, typing **BEGN** instead of **BEGIN**, or using the keyword **ELSIF**, which you remembered from the Modula/2 book you read last year, but which doesn't exist in Pascal or C. Second, there are syntax errors caused by using supported symbols in the wrong ways—like expecting a Pascal procedure to return a value, which of course, it can't do.

But however you divide them, syntax bugs should be the easiest to find. And, in fact, you'll rarely have the opportunity to use TD to debug errors in syntax because the compiler will refuse to create the compiled code file until the source text is error-free.

Unfortunately, some kinds of syntax errors can still slip through the cracks, as you'll see in chapters 10 and 12 when you meet a few common bugs in C and Pascal. But most of the time, you'll catch syntax errors during compilation or assembly. TD can't help you find these kinds of bugs.

Runtime Errors

High-level languages like Pascal and C rely heavily on *runtime libraries* of stock routines that display text on screen, send characters to printers, read disk directories, handle file input and output, and perform other common jobs. When one of these routines receives illegal input or incorrect instructions, it generates a *runtime error.* This has one of two effects:

- The runtime error handler halts the program after displaying a message along with the address of the faulty statement.

- The runtime routine returns an error code to the program, which is expected to handle the error itself.

Other kinds of runtime errors occur when a program can't find its overlay file to load a portion of itself into RAM or when an expression performs an illegal operation—dividing by 0, for example. These and similar problems may activate runtime handlers in the operating system, causing the program to halt with a cryptic message.

Whatever the cause, a runtime error is embarrassing. It reveals the back-stage business that you so carefully attempted to hide. Any actor who has had the scenery fall over during Act 1 knows what it's like for a programmer to receive a report of a fatal runtime error. You know it's going to be a long night.

Finding and fixing runtime errors can be difficult. With TD, though, as long as you know the address where the fault occurred, you can set a breakpoint at that position and inspect the buggy statement. Usually, the runtime library's error handler reports this address.

Chapters 11–13 discuss ways to deal with runtime errors in C and Pascal. Assembly language programmers can use similar techniques.

Logical Errors

Most of the information in this book is directed at wiping out this third and most common kind of bug—an error in the program's logic. Such errors are frequently caused by poor design, sloppy programming, and carelessness. But, as I mentioned before, a few logical errors are *bound* to occur in anything but the simplest of programs. Programming a major application is just too difficult for anybody to expect to do it correctly on the first try.

TD can help you to locate logical errors by displaying the values of variables, running your code at slow speed, stopping on command at breakpoints, and letting you peer into memory as through a microscope in search of bugs hiding out in RAM. But even with all these features, TD still can't fix your bugs for you—an obvious but important fact to keep in mind. It's still up to you to decide *why* a statement is failing. The debugger can show you the conditions surrounding that failure. And this book's tips and hints can help you to acquire good debugging skills. But it's still your job to interpret the conditions and test results and to identify the source of your troubles.

Types of Runtime and Logical Bugs

Of all the runtime and logical errors you can make, most bugs seem to fall into six subcategories. When bugs occur, before loading the code into the debugger, I've found that it's often useful to classify runtime and logical errors as one of the following:

- Data-dependent bugs
- Intermittent bugs
- Moving-target bugs
- Fatal bugs
- Long-distance bugs
- Time-bomb bugs

While reading about these common kinds of bugs, keep in mind that there are no boldly drawn lines among the types, as there are among the three bug species described earlier. Identifying the kind of bug you have takes skill, guess work, and luck. But you can improve your odds at finding the cause of a problem by becoming familiar with the kinds of bugs that all programmers probably will face sooner or later.

Data-Dependent Bugs

A data-dependent bug is caused by a particular value or set of input data. With other data, the program runs with no errors.

The key to finding this kind of bug is to devise good input test data. Be sure to include values in the middle, at both ends, and outside of expected ranges.

TD's `Watches` and inspector windows are useful for finding the causes of data-dependent bugs. Or, if a specific value is giving you trouble, you might set an `Expression true global` breakpoint to find the statement that's assigning a specific value to a variable.

Intermittent Bugs

Intermittent bugs can drive anyone buggy. The symptom here is a program that fails, apparently for a different reason each time the code runs. Sometimes it works just fine. Then, just when you think all is well, the thing crashes again.

Cosmic rays? Probably not. Most of the time, this sort of problem is caused by an uninitialized variable. Because all variables have some value, if the code doesn't assign specific values to variables, they will have the values left in RAM by whatever was there before the program runs.

This bug also shows up at times after running a different program, not the one with the bug. Immediately after running that program, you execute the buggy code (which, up to now, you thought was working just fine). But this time, your program crashes, leading you to suspect the other program is causing the trouble.

Don't fall into this trap. The problem is more likely an uninitialized variable that's stored in a little-used area of RAM, maybe an area that's always equal to 0 except after running a huge word processor or spreadsheet. Your code crashes because, for instance, the formerly untouched variable now equals 243 instead of 0.

Another symptom of this problem occurs when a program crashes only just after compiling. Then, you run the same code and it works fine. Obviously, there's a bug in the compiler. Right?

Wrong. Nab this bug by devising repeatable tests that reproduce the error. Try to duplicate as many runtime conditions as you can and keep good notes about all the steps that lead to a bug's appearance.

Moving-Target Bugs

This bug is related to the intermittent kind, but instead of going away under different runtime conditions, it changes character. You might even be tricked into thinking you have two bugs when, in fact, there's only one.

Moving-target bugs exhibit two classic symptoms. In the first case, the bug shows up when you run the code from DOS. But, when you load the same code into TD, the bug changes to something else. In the second case, the bug changes when you add a new routine to the program—or, it progresses from an annoying problem to a full crash.

Uninitialized variables and pointers may be the cause of a moving-target bug. Any change to the program's load address—for example, loading the buggy code into TD—affects the bug by altering the values of uninitialized variables.

Running TD in remote mode or in virtual mode with an 80386 system is a good way to find a moving-target bug. Either of these methods helps to stabilize the runtime conditions under which you test your code.

Fatal Bugs

Unless you're debugging in remote mode, a fatal bug may crash your system and take the debugger with it. Even with TD286 or TD386, a nasty bug can still cause a failure. Only remote debugging can totally prevent the host system from crashing. Remember, TD and your code share the same memory, and in that case, there's nothing to prevent your code in all cases from destroying part of TD.

The worst case of this bug is one that damages your development system. For example, it's possible for a fatal bug to erase your hard drive, and there's nothing TD can do to recover your lost files. Using well-tested runtime libraries is the best preventive medicine against these kinds of bugs, which tend to show up more frequently for programmers who write low-level "systems" applications than those who write data base and other commercial software.

To find fatal bugs, the first step is to protect your development system. Because even an 80386 or 80486 system running in virtual mode isn't completely immune, the best solution is to use two computers and run TD in remote mode (see chapter 17). No bug can reach through an I/O port and destroy your hard drive or cause other damage. Of course, the remote system might suffer the same sorts of problems, but at least your main development computer is safe.

Long-Distance Bugs

Many people assume incorrectly that the source of a bug must be near to where the problem occurs. But that's not true for a long-distance bug, which sets conditions in motion that cause other statements to fail.

The classic case is a bad pointer that pokes random values into a subroutine that won't be called until much later. When that damaged code runs, the program crashes, leading you to hunt for a mistake in the routine. Of course, you won't find the problem there.

When this happens, trust your test procedures. If you've written careful tests, and you are sure that a subroutine is operating correctly, you will have to look elsewhere for the bug. If the code is crashing, you might set a `Changed memory global` breakpoint on the subroutine code itself. This will halt the program at the statement that's overwriting the code.

But if that doesn't work, you'll have to trace from the crash point back in time, investigating the sequence of events that led to the bug's appearance. Start by devising tests to run the code to just before the bug occurs. Then, use the `Stack` window and TD's `Run:Back trace` command to go back in time and investigate the events that caused the crash.

If you still can't locate the bug, set up check points at strategic spots where you can verify program parameters. Long-distance bugs are very hard to find because they may be caused by any statement and not show up until much later. The key is to attempt to discover the set of parameters that don't fit your expectations. If you can do that, you should be able to find the faulty statements.

Time-Bomb Bugs

The final logical and runtime bug type is actually a long-distance bug that reaches beyond your program's borders to affect another program. At first, the symptom of a time-bomb bug leads you to believe you've got an intermittent or moving-target problem. The bug doesn't always appear—it happens only occasionally.

But after investigating the problem, you still can find nothing wrong. And, besides, this program runs flawlessly on your partner's system. It only crashes for you (or for one customer and not another).

In such cases, you might have a time-bomb bug, its fuse lit by another program that you ran earlier. This treacherous surprise package explodes only after the buggy code finishes and you run the other program. For example, program A might change but fail to restore an interrupt vector in low memory. Other programs don't use that vector, so they run just fine. But program B does, and because of program A's mistake, the B crashes.

As with long-distance bugs, the first step is to trust your test procedures. After investigating program B, which doesn't have the bug, consider that the mistake may be in program A. To test that assumption, try to duplicate the bug, keeping good notes about all the programs you run until the bug appears. Reboot between programs and be suspicious about any program that ends prematurely, thus skipping code that restores low-memory vectors and other information left in RAM after the program returns to DOS. When you can duplicate the bug, use TD to examine program A's closing parameters and program B's input. Look for a common link between the two programs and narrow your search to statements that might affect that link.

Debugging Strategies

So far in this chapter, you've read about the elements that contribute to a good debugging style, you've met TD's main features for finding bugs, you've learned about the three species of bugs, and you've examined six common bugs that most programmers face sooner or later. It's time to assemble the pieces of that knowledge into a general debugging strategy that you can use for finding and fixing real bugs in real code.

Because each problem poses unique challenges, each requires a unique solution, and no single strategy will work in all cases. But no matter what problem you're facing, having a debugging strategy is always better than having none. And the strategies that work best for me usually include these four elements:

- Testing for bugs
- Stabilizing bugs
- Isolating bugs
- Repairing and retesting

Testing for Bugs

Of course, you know you've got to test your programs. But, how do you go about it? Do you write your code and then "play" with it? Do you use a program for a few hours? Or, do you give it to friends to try, and then assume all's well if no bugs appear?

There's nothing wrong with that kind of testing, and in fact, you should let others use your programs. They may find bugs or design flaws that you miss because you're too "close" to the project. Novices tend to find inconsistencies that experts naturally avoid.

But I'm talking about a different kind of testing—one that's designed to find the limits and flaws in code. The purpose of good testing is to force bugs to happen now so they won't happen later. And good test procedures play crucial roles in any debugging strategy.

Here are three hints that I try to remember when designing test procedures and data:

- Force bugs into the open
- Take good notes
- Test as you go

Force Bugs into the Open

Whether your tests are separate programs, a set of input data, or just a series of steps that you follow to exercise a section of code, design tests to force bugs to happen. Usually, you can do that by including data and procedures in the middle and at both ends—for example, using values like $0.001 and $999999.99 in a checkbook-balancing program, no matter how unlikely such values are in the real world. Test common cases, but don't neglect the uncommon ones.

Always save your tests and keep a log of their results. When you force a bug to appear, you can then repeat the test while executing the code in TD. Set breakpoints and examine variables at strategic locations. Then, force the bug into the open. Combined with good test data, TD will usually lead you straight to the source of the problem.

Take Good Notes

Use a data base system or your text editor to log your tests. Although this takes time, and you may be tempted to skip this step when deadlines are too close for comfort, good notes will almost always save more time in the long run than they take to create along the way.

Notes should include the date and time, the test procedure itself or its file name, the results of the test, and a description of any bug that you found. You should also add a note about what you plan to do about the bug, and then later, how you solved the problem. A glance at your past notes will help you to find bugs in other programs by refreshing your memory about problems you solved in the past.

Good notes also make it possible to duplicate test conditions under which bugs appear. See "Stabilizing Bugs" later.

Test as You Go

Don't wait until you're finished programming to begin testing and debugging. Test as you go. Use a top-down strategy in your tests, just as you do in your code. Test at high levels first to verify that procedures are working. Then, as you complete the lower subroutines, you can write tests for new sections without having to repeat your tests for the higher levels you've already tested.

Some people also suggest testing in both directions, first verifying that subroutines work correctly before adding them to a program and then testing the kit with the caboodle. Either way, the idea is to localize your tests to small sections as you complete them rather than use one grandaddy test bed for the entire project.

This can also simplify your debugging strategy by focusing your energy on small sections of the code at a time. When bugs appear, you can use TD's breakpoints and code-tracing commands to isolate buggy code and investigate the causes, without having to trace through a lot of programming that has nothing to do with the problem you're trying to find.

Stabilizing Bugs

When a test forces a bug into the open, the next step is to stabilize the problem. You can't fix a bug that hops around all over the place. First, you've got to nail it down so it stays put.

The best way to stabilize a bug is to devise a repeatable test that always forces the bug into the open. This may be difficult if the bug is the intermittent or moving-target variety, but resist the urge to skip this step for bugs that won't hold still. Most will if you can duplicate runtime conditions exactly. And, that's the key. Reboot, fill RAM with known values, and use TD to initialize variables. Do whatever you can to pin a bug in place. This might take time, but it will make debugging easier—and less frustrating.

Isolating Bugs

You've completed your tests and forced a bug into the open. You've carefully documented the test procedure and you've stabilized the problem. The bug stays put—it always shows up for the same input.

You're now ready to find out what's causing that bug. Load the program into TD and isolate the problem. To do that, you may have to set breakpoints at random locations, or you might be able to start examining one section of a large program, skipping other parts that you tested before. Narrow your search to a module, then to a procedure in that module. Then, start examining the statements in that procedure. TD's keystroke-recording ability is especially helpful for this. See chapter 16.

Postpone single-stepping the code with trace commands as long as possible. Tracing takes time, so try to get close to a problem before using the `Trace into` and `Step over` commands. Concentrate on finding *where* a bug occurs, not *why* it happens.

Often, you'll discover your mistake this way before you complete the hunt. Just narrowing a search seems to help people to reconsider their program's design, focusing their mental energy on the problem. Solutions to bugs just pop out.

Repairing and Retesting

You've found the bug! And now that you know what's wrong, you can fix the problem. If you're still unsure about why the problem occurred, verify that you're using your language's syntax correctly. Any uncertainty at this point should send you straight to your reference manuals. Before fixing a bug, be absolutely sure you've correctly identified the cause.

After fixing the problem, don't neglect to retest your program, using the same test data and following all the steps outlined in your notes. Be sure you can prove without a doubt that you've eliminated the bug. Don't just assume it's gone.

And don't forget to update your notes and to document the change in your source code. I frequently convert buggy statements into comments, so I can compare new programming with old. Or, even better, use a version control program to keep track of all source-code changes. Armed with your notes and test procedures, you can then step back in time to just before you fixed a bug in case it shows up again later, or if another bug surfaces that you suspect was caused by fixing the other one.

Keep your tests, notes, and old program versions. In time, you'll build a custom data base that will help you to devise new debugging strategies the next time disaster strikes.

Summary

Programmers learn the value of a good programming style, but even experts often fail to realize that a good debugging style is equally important. Recognize that bugs are inevitable, let go of frustration, use well-known algorithms, isolate bugs, take good notes, and use the same care in writing test procedures that you use in all your projects.

TD has many commands, of course, but among them, four often prove to be the most useful for debugging: breakpoints, code tracing, data inspection, and expression evaluation. The next several chapters discuss these areas in detail.

Three species of bugs affect code: syntax, runtime, and logical errors. The last two of these further divide into six kinds of common bugs: data-dependent bugs, intermittent bugs, moving-target bugs, fatal bugs, long-distance bugs, and time-bomb bugs. The purpose of a good debugging strategy is to identify a bug by species and kind. Only then can you begin to find and fix the problem.

Each problem is unique, so it's difficult to create general formulas to find and fix bugs. But a good debugging strategy should include four elements: testing, stabilizing, isolating, and repairing. Be your own "beta" tester. Stabilize a bug so it holds still while you search for its cause. Isolate buggy code; don't waste time puzzling out problems. And, after you locate a bug and fix it, repeat your tests to prove a problem is gone for good. Don't forget to document the fixes you make.

With these elements of a good debugging style in mind, you're ready to explore how to use TD's breakpoints and code-tracing capabilities. The next chapter explains how to put these two most powerful TD tools to work.

Chapter 8

Breakpoints and Code Tracing

IF THERE'S a common feature that all debuggers share, it's a breakpoint. A breakpoint is like a checkpoint in a rally. It forces the action to stop at planned intervals so you can keep tabs on the race—that is, the race to find bugs.

As described in chapter 7, breakpoints have two parts: a condition and an action. When the condition is satisfied—for example, when the program reaches a certain location or when an expression becomes true—TD carries out the programmed action. That action might halt the program, execute a subroutine, or log the value of a variable.

After TD halts a program at a breakpoint, you'll often use code-tracing commands to execute one or more additional statements. Breakpoints let you find out roughly where a problem is located. Tracing can take you straight to a bug's hideout. Because these two TD features often go hand in hand, this chapter describes them together. It also explains how to use breakpoints to log expressions and splice code to try out repairs from inside the debugger.

Breakpoints, Tracepoints, and Watchpoints

If you've used another debugger, you may be familiar with the words *breakpoint, tracepoint,* and *watchpoint.* TD doesn't use these terms, but it has all the same abilities. In TD:

- A classic breakpoint is the same as a code breakpoint set by TD's `Toggle` command (press ⟨**F2**⟩) to halt a program or perform another action just before the program executes an instruction at a planned address.

- A tracepoint is similar to a `Changed memory global` breakpoint, triggered when a monitored memory location changes value.
- A watchpoint is like an `Expression true global` breakpoint, triggered when a monitored memory location changes to a specific value.

Debugging with Code Breakpoints

After you've forced a bug into the open and stabilized it with a repeatable test, the next step is to isolate the bug. At this stage, you know that the program isn't working, but you don't know why it has failed. To answer that question, the first step is to isolate the buggy statements that have gummed up the works.

The following sections describe ways to use code breakpoints for that purpose. To set a code breakpoint, move the text cursor to any line in the `CPU` or `Module` windows and press ⟨**F2**⟩. Or, if you have a mouse, click in either of the two blank columns to the left of a source-code line. (See chapters 4 and 5 for other ways to set breakpoints.)

Isolating a Bug

Use a divide-and-conquer approach to isolate a bug to the smallest possible section of code. One obvious way to do this is to set a breakpoint somewhere in the middle of a program and then press ⟨**F9**⟩ to run to that place. If the bug still appears, set another breakpoint halfway back and repeat. If it doesn't show, set a breakpoint farther into the code and run.

While setting out your traps, keep in mind that the goal is to pinpoint the source-code statement that causes the bug to appear. These tips will help you to narrow the search:

- Press ⟨**Ctrl**⟩-⟨**F2**⟩ to reset the program before beginning the next test run. This does not erase existing breakpoints. They stay set until you remove them.
- Sometimes, it's useful to run the program with no breakpoints and press ⟨**Ctrl**⟩-⟨**Break**⟩ to halt when a bug appears. If this opens the `CPU` window, to get back to the source-code view, activate the `Module` window, move the cursor to a location somewhere after the place where you halted the code, and press ⟨**F4**⟩. If that doesn't work, try setting one or more breakpoints and press ⟨**F9**⟩. You may have to repeat these steps several times to narrow your search to a small section that you can then examine in detail.
- Use the -k command-line option (see chapter 3) to enable keystroke recording when you start TD. You can then use the `View:Execution history`

command's bottom pane to play back all events leading to the moment a bug arrives on stage. After opening that window, press ⟨**Tab**⟩ to move the highlight bar into the bottom pane, select the event to reenact, and press ⟨**Ctrl**⟩-**K**.

Breaking in Procedures and Functions

Pascal and C procedures and functions (I'll call them all subroutines here) usually begin with startup instructions that allocate space on the stack for local variables and prepare register BP for addressing those variables and any arguments passed to the routine. To examine the startup code:

- Position the cursor on the procedure or function declaration (not the first statement in its body) and press ⟨**F2**⟩. TD will show the breakpoint on the Pascal **BEGIN** keyword or on a C function's opening brace. This tells you the breakpoint is set to go off before the first statement executes.

- Press ⟨**F9**⟩ to run the code. When the breakpoint hits, press ⟨**Alt**⟩-**VC** to open the **CPU** window. You can then trace the machine-code startup instructions for this subroutine.

It's also useful to set breakpoints at the beginning of every subroutine in a module. The brute force method uses the **Module** window's **Search** command (press ⟨**Ctrl**⟩-**S**). Enter **procedure** or **function** as the search argument. As you locate each subroutine, press ⟨**F2**⟩⟨**Ctrl**⟩-**N** to set a breakpoint there and move to the next routine. When you run the code, it will halt at the beginning of each subroutine. (See "Data Breakpoint Tricks" later in this chapter for a different method to break in subroutines.)

> To view all local variables within the scope of each routine, open the **Variables** view (press ⟨**Alt**⟩-**VV**). Then, press ⟨**F9**⟩ to run. When the program breaks at the start of each procedure or function, the bottom window pane shows all arguments passed to routines plus other items reachable from this location. (If you halted the program before a subroutine's startup code, you must press ⟨**F8**⟩ or ⟨**F7**⟩ to execute those instructions before the window will show the correct information.)

Examining Program Exit Conditions

You can also set breakpoints at the ends of subroutines, which is especially useful for examining function return values. To do that, **Search** for **procedure** or **function** as in the previous section, but press ⟨**Cursor Up**⟩ a few times to move the cursor to the previous Pascal routine's **END** or a C function's closing brace before setting the breakpoint. When you press ⟨**F9**⟩ to run, the subroutines will halt before they return to their callers. You can then use the `Data:Function return` command to examine the return values for functions.

Finding a Runtime Error

When a runtime error handler halts a program due to an I/O error or another cause, it usually reports the address where the problem occurred. To find the statement at that address, press ⟨**Alt**⟩-⟨**F2**⟩ to set a breakpoint at the reported location, then press ⟨**F9**⟩ to run to that place.

If that doesn't seem to work, the error handler may be reporting a *relative* segment address. To find the true location when running the program in TD, press ⟨**Alt**⟩-⟨**F2**⟩ and add the CS register to the reported segment value. For example, if the reported address is `3400:0800`, enter **(cs+$3400):$0800** in Pascal or **(cs+0x3400):0x0800** in C.

> Hint: You can enter similar expressions with the `Goto` command in the `Module` view. This positions the cursor to the offending statement without requiring you to run the code up to that spot.

Breaking into OOP Methods

Set breakpoints in Pascal and C++ object methods the same way you set breakpoints in non-OOP code. When the breakpoint hits, you can then use the `Data:Evaluate/modify` command (press ⟨**Ctrl**⟩-⟨**F4**⟩) to call other methods for the object instance that led to the breakpoint location. For example, after opening the `Evaluate/modify` window, you might enter **self.listEmpty()** to see the effect of that method for this object instance. For methods that declare no parameters, the empty parentheses tell TD to call the method instead of merely reporting its address. In C++, use *this* instead of *self*.

You can also call non-OOP routines this way (see "Splicing Code" later in this chapter). But the technique is particularly useful for debugging object methods because of the way objects encapsulate their data and code. In well-written OOP code, calling a method out of turn should affect only the current object instance.

Another useful technique is to open an inspector window for the current object when a breakpoint halts the action inside a method. To do that, move the cursor to a blank character and press ⟨**Ctrl**⟩-**I** or use the `Data:Inspect` command. Then, enter **self** for Pascal or **this** for C++. Or, choose `View:Variables`. The bottom pane of this window shows the `self` or `this` parameter passed to all object methods, although it doesn't show as much detail as an inspector window.

Code Breakpoint Tricks

As chapter 7 explains, to set breakpoints in code, TD replaces a single byte at the breakpoint address with an int 3 instruction (CC hex). When the program reaches that location, the software interrupt activates TD, which copies the original byte back into RAM so that, when you execute the instruction, it runs as it normally would if the code had never stopped.

You can take advantage of this fact to place permanent breakpoints in code, which, in some cases, might be easier to set in the source-code text than to use TD commands. To do this in Pascal, insert the statement:

```
inline( $CC );
```

For Turbo C, use the statement:

```
asm int 3
```

In assembly language, use:

```
int 3
```

Or, use another method to insert the CC hex byte into the code. You can set as many of these breakpoints as you need. TD won't highlight the locations as it does for other breakpoints, and it won't let you modify their actions with the local commands in the Breakpoints view. But, when you press ⟨**F9**⟩ to run the program, it will halt at each of the permanent breakpoint locations.

Debugging with Data Breakpoints

There are two kinds of data breakpoints you can set. One kind monitors memory locations for changes to bytes stored there. Another monitors memory for specific values.

In general, the first kind—set by the Changed memory global command in the Breakpoints global menu (not the View window command with the same name)—is most helpful for finding a statement that changes data or code without permission. Often, this is the result of using an uninitialized pointer, but it might also be caused by an array index that's addressing elements beyond the space allocated to the array. After identifying the addresses where the unauthorized change is occurring, enter the address and number of bytes to monitor. For example, in Pascal, enter something like **cs:$0F00,$100**. In C, use **cs:0x0F00,0x100**, and in assembly language, **cs:0F00h,0100h**.

If a variable is changing unexpectedly, just enter the variable's name. Despite the `Change memory global` command's prompt message "Enter memory address, count," you don't have to enter the count. Suppose you have a 1,000-byte array of 4-byte long integers `ArrayOfPlenty`. To monitor the entire array, just enter its name. Or, to monitor only a portion, enter an expression like **ArrayOfPlenty[n],c**, where n is the index of the first entry in the array and c is the count of those items you want to monitor—64 to monitor the first 256 bytes, for example, (256/4).

When you know the address and the bad value that's showing up, for example, when an index `count` becomes equal to 100 when you know it should never be greater than 99, choose `Expression true global` in the `Breakpoints` global menu and enter an expression such as **count > 99**. TD will evaluate that expression repeatedly, and when the result is true, it will execute the programmed action. Usually, this will take you right to the spot that's incrementing `count` once too many times.

Entering Expressions

When you enter *segment:offset* address expressions in various TD commands, use a form that's appropriate for the current language (see chapter 9). If you enter only the offset, TD considers that value to be relative to the current value of CS.

But you don't have to enter explicit address values. You can also enter a module name and line number such as **#SCRMOD#100** or, in Pascal, **SCRMOD.100**. Or, if a pointer addresses the location you need, you can dereference its value to pass the address to TD. For example, when TD prompts for an address, in Pascal, you might enter **p^**; in C, ***p**.

Yet another way to enter an address is to refer to a label, for example, a procedure or function name. Just enter the procedure name, which TD evaluates as an address. You don't need to preface the name with ❾ as you do in Pascal, or with **&** as you must in C.

> When entering address and other constant expressions, be careful not to introduce side effects. For example, don't enter **x = 5** in C when you meant to specify **x = = 5**. The first expression sets x to 5; the second tests whether x *equals* 5. In Pascal, don't use **:=** in expressions. In assembly language, use **EQ** and similar keywords, not **=**.

Hardware and Software Differences

When setting `Changed memory global` and `Expression true global` breakpoints, be aware that TD scans memory locations and evaluates expressions between every statement or machine-code instruction. Because that takes time, these data breakpoints can make the program run slowly. The more addresses and expressions you enter, the slower the code goes. In fact, searching for an elusive bug that's changing bytes at random in a large buffer could take hours—far too long to be useful in many cases.

The following notes describe a few ways to add back some of the speed that data breakpoints steal.

Speeding Software Data Breakpoints

The best solution when data breakpoints slow execution is to install the TDH386.SYS device driver on an 80386- or 80486-based system (see chapter 3). You can then take advantage of this processor's special debugging registers, which can monitor up to four addresses for read and write instructions. All systems with 80386 or 80486 processors, including those with 80386SX processors, have this capability.

An even better choice is to install a hardware debugging board, which gives you a wider range of methods for examining memory locations (see chapter 18).

When TD can use either of those two hardware solutions, it displays an asterisk (*) next to the breakpoint in the Breakpoints view. You can also request hardware assistance for a breakpoint by clicking the Hardware condition in the Breakpoint options dialog box (press ⟨Ctrl⟩-S after opening the Breakpoints view and highlighting a current breakpoint).

> Hint: A faster way to open the Breakpoint options dialog is to move the cursor to any breakpoint highlighted in the Module window and press ⟨Alt⟩-⟨F2⟩. This takes you to the same dialog box as choosing View:Breakpoints, selecting a breakpoint in that view, and pressing ⟨Ctrl⟩-S.

But what if you don't have an 80386 an 80486 or a hardware debugging board? In that case, there's no way to prevent the code from executing more slowly. But there are a few things you can do to minimize sluggishness:

- Make sure the Module, not the CPU, window is active before running the code. That way, TD will evaluate breakpoint expressions between source-code lines. With CPU active, the debugger does that between every machine-code instruction, which takes more time.

- Limit evaluation to a specific address. To do this, first set a code breakpoint to any source-code line. Choose View:Breakpoints and press ⟨Ctrl⟩-S to Set options. Change Condition to Changed memory and enter an address or variable name in Condition expression. Or, change Condition to Expression true and enter the expression that you want TD to evaluate at this address. Either way, TD will now examine the condition you specified *only* when the program reaches this breakpoint location. Of course, you can use this trick only if you know where to set the code breakpoint. But, when you do, this is a great way to add speed to data breakpoints.

- Avoid referring to local variables in expressions. This causes TD to work harder to evaluate expressions because it can't compute addresses in advance as it can for global variables. Setting a `Changed memory global` breakpoint for a local variable declared in a procedure or function usually causes a worse slowdown than setting a similar breakpoint on a global symbol.

- Before setting data breakpoints, try to narrow your bug search as much as possible by using code breakpoints. This will improve speed by limiting the number of statements TD has to execute while monitoring memory locations and evaluating expressions.

- Limit the number of bytes monitored. When examining an array, instead of watching the entire variable, enter an expression such as **a[0],5** to examine the first five elements. Or, monitor a *related* variable instead of the data that changes. For example, in Pascal, to trap changes to strings, you might just as well examine the string length by entering **s[0]** for a `Changed memory global` breakpoint. This will be a lot faster than watching every byte in a 255-character string variable. (But it might also miss a bug that's causing the string to change without also changing its length.)

String Comparisons

Talking about strings, you can monitor them for changes but not for specific values. In other words, you can set a `Changed memory global` breakpoint with an expression equal to a string identifier, but you can't set an `Expression true global` breakpoint to monitor when, for example, a string equals 'XYZ'.

However, you can accomplish almost the same result entering a complex expression such as **(s[1] = 'X') and (s[2] = 'Y')** to set a breakpoint when the first two characters in **s** are 'X' and 'Y'. This may produce a few false breaks for string values that don't exactly match the one you're looking for, but the method works well enough in most cases. (In C, use expressions like **(s[0] = = 'X') && (s[1] = = 'Y')**.)

Breaking on Register Values

You can enter expressions to set breakpoints for when registers change or when they become equal to a certain value. For instance, you might enter **es** into a `Changed memory global` breakpoint to halt a program if that data segment register ever changes value. Because Pascal and C statements often use that register to load pointer values, this may help you to arrest a delinquent pointer bug.

At times, it may also be useful to watch for when two registers are equal to each other. To do this, choose `Expression true global` and enter an expression such as **ds = es** in Pascal, **ds = = es** in C, or **ds EQ es** in assembly language. In C, you can also refer to pseudo registers such as **_AX** and **_DX**, but the leading underscores are not required.

Similarly, to find instructions that change but fail to restore a register value, enter an `Expression true global` breakpoint expression such as **ds 〈〉 es**. Or, use an explicit value as in the expression **ds 〈〉 $76F0** to nab a statement that changes the data segment register. This can be useful for identifying the source of a long-distance bug by finding instructions that change the data segment register, causing statements that appear correct in the source code to write data to the wrong locations in memory.

Data Breakpoint Tricks

To narrow a search for a bug quickly, it's often useful to halt a program or perform another breakpoint action at the beginning and end of every procedure and function in C and Pascal.

Because most high-level subroutines begin by assigning the stack pointer to register BP, you can often do this by entering **bp** as the expression for the `Changed memory global` command in the `Breakpoints` menu. Then, press 〈**F9**〉 to run the program, which will halt at every change to BP. Because procedures and functions typically restore BP before they return to their callers, this method halts the program at the start and end of most subroutines. (If other code changes BP, the program may also make a few unplanned stops, but this shouldn't cause any problems.)

Logging Expressions

For all breakpoints, you can tell TD to log the result of an expression as the action to perform when the breakpoint hits. You can do this for code and data breakpoints, and there are different reasons you might want to use this technique for each of the two kinds of breakpoint conditions.

To prepare a breakpoint to log an expression, first set the breakpoint as you normally do—usually by pressing 〈**F2**〉, clicking the left mouse button, or by choosing `Breakpoints:At` and entering an address expression. Next, press 〈**Alt**〉**-VB**〈**Ctrl**〉**-S** to open the `Breakpoints` view and set the option for this breakpoint. (To do this for several breakpoints, highlight each one in the window before pressing 〈**Ctrl**〉**-S**.)

You should see the `Breakpoint options` dialog box. Set the `Action` radio buttons to `Log` (press ⟨**Tab**⟩ and use the cursor movement keys to select a labeled button). Press ⟨**Tab**⟩ again and enter an expression in `Action expression`.

TD will evaluate the expression and log its value. Possible action expressions you can enter include:

- The name of a variable. TD will write the variable's value to the log at each breakpoint.
- The result of a C or Pascal function, either in the program or in a runtime library linked to the code. For example, in Pascal, enter **IoResult()** (note the required empty parentheses) to log the result of that function at each breakpoint. Be careful to consider the side effects that this may cause, for example, changing a global variable.
- A literal value such as 0 or 1. This can be useful when you want to log many code breakpoints in a long program just to see whether certain sections are executed, but without halting the code. Enter all the breakpoints, then change each to log the digit as the expression. (It doesn't matter what digit you use, but you have to enter something—TD can't log an empty expression.) After running the program, open the `Log` window to see which of your breakpoints were executed.

There are other possibilities, and each problem will suggest its own solutions. The following sections include additional hints that may help you decide how to log different kinds of information.

Logging Multiple Variables

You can set as many breakpoints as you want, but only one per address. This means you can't log the results of more than one expression for a code breakpoint set to a certain statement. For example, there's no easy way to log the value of two variables i and j for a single breakpoint inside a loop.

One way around this dilemma is to write a string function that returns monitored variables in character form. Here's a sample in Pascal:

```
function ijStr( i, j : integer ) : string;
var si, sj : string[6];
begin
   str( i, si );
   str( j, sj );
   ijStr := si + ' ' + sj
end;
```

The `ijStr` function returns a string with the values of i and j converted to characters. Unfortunately, because Turbo Pascal strips unused code while compiling, you also have to enter a statement such as **writeln(ijStr(0, 0));** somewhere so the function is available when you load the program into TD.

After doing that, set a breakpoint and modify it to log the expression **ijStr(i, j)**. This calls ijStr at each breakpoint, converts the variables to a string, and records the result in the Log window.

Logging Complex Expressions

When a conditional expression controls a program loop, rather than halt the code inside the loop to examine conditions for each iteration, you can save time by logging an expression instead. That way, the code runs at full speed, and you can view the finished report in the Log window after the loop finishes. For example, suppose you've written the following `while` loop in C:

```
while (--argc > 0)
   printf("Argument #%d : %s\n", argc, argv[argc]);
```

Set a breakpoint on the `while` statement and change the breakpoint to log **argc** as the action expression. Be aware that the logged value is saved *before* the expression is evaluated; therefore, you have to subtract 1 mentally from the recorded values to account for the decrement operator (`--`). But don't try to fix the problem by logging the expression **--argc**. That would change `argc` every time TD evaluates the expression and throw the `while` loop out of whack. (This is an example of a side effect that you should avoid except in special cases. See "Splicing Code" later.)

Logging "Self" in OOP Code

To log a series of method calls for various object instances, set a code breakpoint on a method's declaration or first statement and press ⟨**F9**⟩ to halt the program at the first call to that method. (Use `View:Hierarchy` to find a program's methods.) Then, open the `Breakpoints` view and press ⟨**Ctrl**⟩-**S**. Set `Action` to `Log` and enter **self** or **this** in C++ as the `Action expression`. Press ⟨**F9**⟩ again to restart the program. All subsequent method calls will now be logged, giving you a complete record of all objects that call that method.

When entering **self** or **this** as an action expression, the program's current location must be inside a method before TD will accept the key word. In other words, as with other symbols, **self** or **this** must be within the current scope before you can use it in an expression.

> Hint: Because this tip may produce reams of data, you might want to open a log file (press ⟨**Ctrl**⟩-**O** in the Log view) before running the program.

Side Effects

Because expressions can call functions and assign values to variables, they might cause *side effects*. For example, if you log an expression **f(x)**, TD calls f() when it evaluates the expression, just as the program code might call that same subroutine. If the function changes a global variable, it could affect the program's operation. It might even introduce a bug where none existed before!

The same is true of expressions that assign values to variables. Usually, it's not wise to log expressions of the form **v = k** where *v* is a variable, *k* is a constant value or another expression, and = is the assignment operator or statement in your language.

To avoid side effects in action expressions, ask yourself if the expression evaluates to a constant and whether it calls any functions. If so, proceed cautiously, and carefully compare results with and without the breakpoint enabled to be sure that you haven't introduced a side effect accidentally.

Splicing Code

Now that I've posted fair warnings about the dangers of side effects in expressions, I'll turn completely around and show how doing exactly that can sometimes be useful for debugging. When used this way, a side effect is called a *code splice*.

To splice code, set a breakpoint in the usual way, then press ⟨**Alt**⟩-**VB** to open the `Breakpoints` view. Press ⟨**Ctrl**⟩-**S** to set the breakpoint's options and then change `Action` to `Execute`. Next, enter an `Action expression`, which should call one or more functions, assign a value to a variable, or both. When the breakpoint hits, TD will evaluate the expression and, in the process, execute the side effect. The program now runs as though a *new* statement (the splice) at that position performed this same action.

The following sections suggest a few ways to put this interesting technique to work. Unfortunately, the method is available only to Pascal and C programmers; you can't splice assembly language code, at least not as easily. (It might be possible to call assembly language routines by inserting `call` instructions in an unused area of memory and then executing those calls. But this is probably more trouble than it's worth.)

Splicing Pascal Code

After isolating a bug to a few statements, you can use a code splice to test possible solutions to the problem. Of course, you can exit TD, modify the source code, compile, and reload the program for testing. But many times you can insert temporary splices to test your assumptions without leaving the debugger.

For example, consider the buggy Pascal program in Listing 8.1, SPLICE1.PAS. After running the code, you discover there are two bugs: variable `count` is never initialized, and the wrong variable (`i` instead of `count`) is incremented inside the `while` loop.

Listing 8.1.   SPLICE1.PAS (with bugs).

```
program splice1;
var
   count, i : integer;
begin
   while count < 100 do
   begin
      writeln( 'Count = ', count );
      i := i + 1
   end;
end.
```

Of course, in this small example, you could just as easily modify and recompile the source to fix the errors. But a run-through of the steps required to splice a temporary fix demonstrates a technique that's often useful in more complex situations:

1. Set a code breakpoint on the first line of the `while` statement, press ⟨**F9**⟩ to run the program to that line, move the cursor to `count`, press ⟨**Ctrl**⟩-**I**, and enter an initial value, for example, 10. This takes care of the missing initialization statement that should precede the loop.

2. Toggle the breakpoint from step 1 off—you don't want to halt the code while the loop executes now that you've initialized `count`.

3. Set a new code breakpoint on the statement that increments `i`. There's no simple way to prevent that from happening, but you can patch the code to increment the correct variable.

4. Press ⟨**Alt**⟩-**VB**⟨**Ctrl**⟩-**S** to open the `Breakpoint options` dialog. Change `Action` to `Execute`, and enter **count := count + 1** for the `Action` expression.

5. Press ⟨**Enter**⟩ to close the dialog box and ⟨**Alt**⟩-⟨**F3**⟩ to close the `Breakpoints` window. Then, press ⟨**F9**⟩ to run the patched code, which now executes the `while` loop correctly.

Splicing C Code

Splicing C programs is similar to splicing Pascal. As an example, Listing 8.2, SPLICE1.C, has the same two bugs as Listing 8.1. It neglects to initialize `count`, and it increments the wrong variable inside the `while` loop.

Listing 8.2.   SPLICE1.C (with bugs).

```c
#include <stdio.h>
main()
{
   int count, i;

   while (count < 100)
   {
      printf( "Count = %i\n", count );
      i++;
   }
}
```

To patch SPLICE1.C with a temporary splice, follow the five steps in the previous section for Pascal. But in step 4, enter the expression **count + +** to increment `count`. When you press ⟨**F9**⟩ to run the modified code, you'll see that it now works correctly.

Splicing Procedure and Function Calls

Calling procedures and functions in Pascal or C action expressions is another way to put code slicing to use. The technique is especially good for initializing a series of variables that would take too much time to set manually in the `Watches` view or `Inspector` windows.

First, write the procedure, which includes statements to assign test values to variables. You can also add statements to prompt you for new values at runtime. Be sure to call the procedure at least once in the program (preferably near the beginning) to prevent the compiler from throwing away the "unused" subroutine.

Next, set a code breakpoint at the beginning of the section where you've isolated a bug. Modify the breakpoint to execute an expression and enter the initialization procedure's name (or C `void` function's name) followed by a set of empty parentheses, for example, **CustomInits()**. TD will then call the procedure every time it reaches the breakpoint, assigning new test values at this location.

Setting the Pass Count

Select any breakpoint in the `Breakpoints` view (press ⟨**Alt**⟩-**VB**), open the `Breakpoint options` dialog box (press ⟨**Ctrl**⟩-**S**), tab to the `Pass count` input box, and enter any value from 1 to 32767. Press ⟨**Enter**⟩ to close the dialog window.

From then on, every time the breakpoint condition is satisfied, if `Pass count` is greater than 1, TD subtracts 1 from the current count and lets the program continue. (In other words, it ignores the breakpoint.) When `Pass count` equals 1, TD executes the breakpoint action.

The following notes describe a few practical uses for `Pass counts` greater than 1.

Verifying a Loop Index

One way to verify that a loop index is within range is to set an `Expression true global` breakpoint for an expression like `index > maxIndex`. But there's another way to accomplish the same job with a `Pass count` that doesn't slow performance on non-80386 systems.

First, set a code breakpoint at the first statement inside the loop you want to check, for example, on the `writeln` statement in Listing 8.1 or the `printf` line in Listing 8.2. Then, change the `Pass count` for this breakpoint to the maximum number of times *plus 1* that the loop should execute. If the loop ever runs more than its official limit, the breakpoint will halt the program. If the breakpoint doesn't hit, then the loop is operating within its defined parameters, and the index value is probably okay.

Finding Unauthorized Variable Assignments

When hunting for a statement that's changing a variable unexpectedly, you can set a `Changed memory global` breakpoint for that variable as described earlier. But when many other statements also assign values to the same variable, the breakpoint may halt the program dozens or hundreds of times, reducing the effectiveness of this technique.

A possible solution is to set the breakpoint's `Pass count` to a high value and run the code. If the bug does not appear, double `Pass count` and repeat the test. If the problem shows, halve the count. By repeating this process, you can quickly find the statement that's not supposed to modify the variable, while skipping past most others that are.

Locating Unwanted Recursions

One of the nastiest surprises is a procedure or function that calls itself unexpectedly, often because a function name incorrectly appears on the right side of an assignment expression inside the function. Usually, this kind of bug is easy to find because the program halts with a stack overflow at the buggy statement.

But a subtle form of this problem can be more difficult to debug—an unwanted *mutual recursion*, where another procedure or function calls back the one that called it in the first place. To find out where the code is going wrong, after isolating which subroutine is running more often than it should, insert a breakpoint in the routine and set the **Pass count** to 2 or higher. The first call to the routine will be ignored. The next (if count is 2 initially) will halt the program. Use the **View:Stack** command (press ⟨**Alt**⟩-**VS**) to find the source of the unwanted recursion. The procedure or function name should appear inside the window.

Debugging with Code Tracing

TD's **Run** menu gives you several ways to execute code. They're all useful, but five of those commands let you run one statement, or even one machine-code instruction, at a time. This extreme level of control—called *code tracing* or *single-stepping*—is one of the most productive debugging tools in TD's toolkit.

You met these commands earlier in chapter 4, and you've used them in other places. But for those who need a quick refresher, the five code-tracing commands covered in this section (with hot keys in parentheses) are:

- **Animate**—Runs code in slow motion. Use it to slow a complex passage so you can see exactly where a bug hatches.
- **Back trace (<Alt>-<F4>)**—Traces individual instructions in reverse. Use it to undo the steps that led to a bug.
- **Instruction trace (<Alt>-<F7>)**—Opens the **CPU** window and executes a single machine-code instruction for the current source-code line in the **Module** view. Use this command to examine the code generated by the compiler for a high-level-language statement and to trace into **int** software interrupt instructions.
- **Step over (<F8>)**—Executes a subroutine call or software at full speed then halts when the routine returns. Use this command to step over procedure and function calls.
- **Trace into (<F7>)**—Traces into a subroutine call or software interrupt. Use this command to follow procedure and function calls to their destinations.

The following sections describe some of the ways you can use these commands to carry out your debugging strategy.

Tracing and Stepping

Be sure to understand the difference between tracing and stepping. When you press ⟨**F7**⟩ to trace into a procedure, function, or subroutine call, TD executes the **call** instruction and stops. You'll see the instructions for that subroutine, with source code if available or in disassembled machine code if not. You can then continue to trace instructions in the routine.

When you press ⟨**F8**⟩ to step over a procedure, function, or assembly language subroutine call, TD executes the `call` instruction at full speed. Then, when the called routine returns, TD again halts the code so you can continue tracing. The effect of this is identical to setting a breakpoint for the instruction following the one that calls the subroutine and pressing ⟨**F9**⟩.

If the current instruction is not a call to a subroutine, then pressing ⟨**F7**⟩ or ⟨**F8**⟩ has the same effect. To avoid confusing the two keys, I usually trace all code by pressing ⟨**F7**⟩ and use ⟨**F8**⟩ only when I don't want to trace into a subroutine. This also gives the best control for tracing code in reverse (see "Debugging with Back Tracing" later in this chapter).

You can also use ⟨**F7**⟩ and ⟨**F8**⟩ to narrow a search for a bug. During the early stages of a debugging session, press ⟨**F8**⟩ to step over all subroutine calls on the outer program level until you determine roughly where the bug occurs. Set a breakpoint at that location (or just before) and press ⟨**Ctrl**⟩-⟨**F2**⟩ to reset the program. This will not remove the breakpoint. Next, press ⟨**F9**⟩ to run the program at full speed up to the marked subroutine call and press ⟨**F7**⟩ to trace into that call. You can then repeat these steps until you find the source of a bug. This avoids tracing a lot of other statements needlessly, but it works best with code that's written in top-down fashion, where each program level contains numerous calls to the next level down.

Using Instruction Tracing

If you're programming in C or Pascal, I'd suggest using the `Instruction trace` command as a last resort. Try to debug your code on the source-code level in the `Module` window. It's much easier (usually) to find bugs by tracing statements in the same language that you used to write them. Trust the compiler. It probably does *not* have a bug, and you probably do *not* have to examine the machine code generated for high-level statements to determine what's gone wrong.

But don't hesitate to break that rule when you've exhausted other avenues and need to step into the wonderful world of assembly language to understand what the code is doing on the lowest level. To do this, position the cursor on any high-level statement and press ⟨**Alt**⟩-⟨**F7**⟩ to open the `CPU` window and execute one machine-code instruction. You can then continue tracing with ⟨**F7**⟩ and ⟨**F8**⟩, although now only individual processor instructions will be executed, not high-level source-code lines. To return to the source level, press ⟨**Ctrl**⟩-**V** (`View source`).

Don't use this command when you only want to view the compiled code for a high-level statement. To do that, you can open the `CPU` window (press ⟨**Alt**⟩-**VC**). Press ⟨**Alt**⟩-⟨**F7**⟩ for an `Instruction trace` to open `CPU` *and* execute one instruction, for example, a procedure or function call that you want to debug in disassembled form.

Another time to use `Instruction trace` is when you need to trace into a software interrupt `int` instruction. See "Tracing into DOS and BIOS Code" later in this chapter.

Animation

I prefer to use this command when debugging in remote mode (see chapter 17) or when using two monitors. But you can use it at any other time to run code in slow motion, like flipping the pages of a paper cartoon.

And that's a good analogy. If you're not debugging remotely and if the program displays a lot of text, TD will switch between its own and the output displays so much that you may have trouble seeing the results. To eliminate display jitters, use `Options:Display options` to set `Display swapping` to `None` before choosing `Run:Animate`. (Of course, you now can't switch to the output display by pressing ⟨**Alt**⟩-⟨**F5**⟩. The program still writes to the display; you just can't see it.)

When you choose `Run:Animate`, you're prompted for a delay value in 10th-second intervals. You can enter any value from 0 to 71—beyond that, code runs as though you entered 0. (I found this limit by trial and error. It's not an officially documented maximum.) The default value of 3 delays about a 1/3 second between instructions. I often enter 10, which gives me a better chance to follow the code flow. Anything above 20 (a 2-second delay) causes too much of a slowdown to be useful.

Hint: Before using this command, decide whether you want to animate on the source- or machine-code levels. Open the **Module** window to animate high-level source-code statements. Open **CPU** only if you want to animate individual machine-code instructions.

When it starts animating, TD executes multiple trace-into commands, just as though you pressed ⟨**F7**⟩. But instead of halting the code after each trace, TD pauses and then "presses" ⟨**F7**⟩ again. Press ⟨**Esc**⟩ to stop the action. (This may take a moment when using high delay values.)

I find animation to be useful for debugging two kinds of programs: graphics and those that build complex text displays. (It's probably also useful for putting embedded systems through the paces, but I'm not a hardware engineer, so I can't say for sure.) Animation is especially useful with TD running on one system while the buggy code runs remotely on another. With this setup, you can animate a section of code, sit back, and watch the result until a bug appears. Keep your finger poised on ⟨Esc⟩, ready to halt the program as soon as you find the bug. Then, use back tracing to step back to the statement that's causing all the trouble.

> Hint: During early stages of a debugging session, an animation value of 0 can be very useful for isolating where a bug appears. It's probably not a good idea to run the entire program this way, but you might animate a module or two and press ⟨**Esc**⟩ to stop when you've located where the bug occurs.

Debugging with Back Tracing

The first rule to remember before trying to use TD's `Back trace` command (press ⟨**Alt**⟩-⟨**F4**⟩), is: You can't trace back in time until you trace forward into the future. You can use any one of the five tracing commands listed earlier, but you'll get the best results from TD's `Trace into` command (press ⟨**F7**⟩). Using that command prepares nearly *every* instruction for back tracing.

The `Animate` command also records events for back tracing, letting you run code in slow motion and press ⟨**Esc**⟩ when a bug appears. When doing this, you'll often execute one or two statements too many. If that happens, just back trace until you find the buggy statement.

Another good use for back tracing is to run repeated tests on a section of code for different input data. You can repeat loops, function calls, and other statements over and over, each time changing associated variables listed in the `Watches` or `Inspector` windows.

Back Tracing Machine Code

To back trace through machine-code instructions, open the `CPU` window before pressing ⟨**Alt**⟩-⟨**F4**⟩. It doesn't matter whether you traced the code originally at the source- or machine-code levels—TD always lets you trace back through machine-code instructions disassembled in `CPU`. (This works because TD traces source-code lines by single-stepping the associated machine-code instructions at high speed; therefore, each of those recorded instructions is available for back tracing.)

In the late stages of a bug search, use this technique to examine the effects of undoing machine code. For example, after tracing through several statements and locating a bug, open the `CPU` window and press ⟨**Alt**⟩-⟨**F4**⟩ to undo the machine-code instructions for the buggy statement. Although this shouldn't be necessary in most cases, it can reveal why a high-level statement is misbehaving when you can't figure that out by examining the source-code text.

> Hint: To view a list of instructions available for back tracing, press ⟨**Alt**⟩-**VE** to open the `Execution history` window. You can then highlight any instruction and press ⟨**Ctrl**⟩-**R** to travel back to that moment in time.

Back-Tracing Limitations

Back tracing can't undo every instruction. In particular, you can't trace back through:

- Any of the following machine-code instructions: in, out, insb, insw, outsb, and outsw.

- A procedure or function that you stepped over by pressing ⟨**F8**⟩.

- Any software interrupts (int machine-code instructions) that you didn't trace by pressing ⟨**Alt**⟩-⟨**F7**⟩.

- I/O statements that write data to disk, send text to the printer, read or write data to I/O ports, and perform other obviously "undoable" actions.

Tracing into DOS and BIOS Code

Normally, TD prevents you from tracing into DOS and BIOS calls. It's rare that a bug hunt will lead into these dark woods, but if you must make the journey (or if you're just curious and you like to poke around in system code), here are a few hints that will help you to enjoy—and, with luck, to *survive*—the trip.

- Disable TD's process-ID switching with the -i- command-line option or by using TDINST (see chapter 3). This will allow you to trace into DOS routines. But it also forces your program and TD to use the same limited number of DOS file handles, so you might not be able to accomplish the trick if your program opens several files simultaneously.

- Press ⟨**Alt**⟩-⟨**F7**⟩ to trace into a software int instruction such as the ubiquitous int 21h DOS-function call. You can't trace into software interrupts by pressing ⟨**F7**⟩.

- Before tracing into a system routine, set a breakpoint after the int instruction that calls the DOS or BIOS routine. That way, you can probably press ⟨**F9**⟩ to get back to your program after you're done poking around. And do try to get back. Quitting TD after halting a system routine is not a good idea. It could cause DOS, your computer, or both to become unstable.

- Setting breakpoints inside DOS is *very* dangerous. Don't do it! (If you must try this, reboot as soon as possible.)

- For the best protection, trace DOS routines only when debugging in remote mode. This will protect your development system. Remember, there's no way to predict the effects of halting DOS or the BIOS during a critical operation. You can do a lot of damage if you're not careful.

Summary

All debuggers let you set breakpoints, usually to halt the code so you can examine variables and other conditions at strategic locations. This chapter explains how to use breakpoints in C, Pascal, and assembly language debugging.

Code tracing, or single-stepping, gives you complete control over a program's execution. You can trace into or step over subroutine calls. You can also animate code, running it in slow motion to reveal bugs doing their dirty work. After tracing code, you can back trace most instructions in reverse, undoing their effects.

Breakpoints and tracing are natural partners. Often, you'll set a breakpoint, run the code up to that location, and then trace additional statements one by one until you pinpoint where a bug is hiding.

Be sure to understand the difference between tracing and stepping. Press ⟨**F7**⟩ to trace into subroutine calls. Press ⟨**F8**⟩ to step over those calls. Using ⟨**F7**⟩ and choosing the `Run:Animate` command are best if you want to take advantage of TD's back-tracing abilities.

In addition to halting at a breakpoint, you can also have TD log an expression. This is a good method to use along with several breakpoints or inside loops. By logging the values of variables at many breakpoint locations, you can run the program at full speed and then choose `View:Log` to see a full activity report later.

Usually, it's best to avoid side effects, often caused by breakpoint expressions that call program functions. But when used with care, side effects let you splice new procedures into programs to test the effects of procedure and function calls at breakpoint locations.

Tracing into DOS routines is tricky business. Don't do it unless you have to—it can make DOS unstable, causing damage to hard drives, erasing files, and leading to other miseries. For safety, trace into DOS and BIOS system routines only when debugging in remote mode.

Chapter 9

Evaluating Expressions

EXPRESSIONS IN PROGRAMS can range from simple calculations like (i + 1) to complex formulas that simulate events in the real world. To help you debug expressions, TD has a full expression evaluator that can calculate the result of just about any C, Pascal, or assembly language expression.

TD's expression handler makes it possible to test the results of expressions (or parts of expressions) without having to execute program statements. You can also enter an expression at any time TD prompts for a number or an address. To TD, anything that returns a value is an expression. So, if the debugger asks you to supply a count—perhaps as the second parameter of a `Changed memory global` breakpoint—instead of typing a literal number, you can enter **(marbles - 1)**. TD will evaluate that expression and use the result, thus saving you the trouble of counting your `marbles` and subtracting 1.

You can also use TD's expression-handling capabilities as an on-line calculator. To do that, open the `Data` menu's `Evaluate/modify` dialog box (press ⟨Crtl⟩-⟨F4⟩) and enter any expression. I like to use this dialog box to convert between hexadecimal and decimal values. I can also enter characters in quotes to determine their ASCII values.

If you first highlight an expression in the `Module` window (use a mouse, or press ⟨**Insert**⟩ and the cursor movement keys) and press ⟨**Ctrl**⟩-⟨**F4**⟩, TD will copy the expression text to the `Evaluate/modify` window's `Expression` pane. You can then press ⟨**Enter**⟩ or click the `Eval` button to evaluate the expression and display its result. This gives you a quick way to test expressions in programs without having to execute code or retype long expressions.

But that's not all. In addition to being able to evaluate nearly any C, Pascal, or assembly language expression, TD can also call compiled C and Pascal functions and procedures. Similar to the code-splicing technique described in chapter 8, this lets you execute portions of your program independently of other statements. Just insert a function's name in an expression wherever a variable or constant of that same data type might appear. To call a procedure or a `void` C function, attach empty parentheses to its name as in, for example, **DoThisNow()**.

This chapter explains how to enter these and other kinds of expressions during debugging sessions. The first part of the chapter lists general information. The rest details expression formats for C, Pascal, and assembly language.

If you read the entire chapter, you may notice a few sentences repeated here and there in the C, Pascal, and assembly language parts. Please excuse the redundancies, which (I hope) make it easier to find information about a specific language's expression formats.

Language and Format

To TD, an *expression* is anything that returns a value. An expression can be the name of a variable like `pieCount` or a literal number like 156 or 3.14159. It can also be an address, usually written in hexadecimal in a format that's suitable for the language selected in the `Options` menu.

Expressions can also be complex, using parentheses and operators from the current language. You can even assign the result of an expression to a variable. Instead of quitting TD, assigning different values to variables, recompiling the program, and reloading the code into TD, you can use expressions to enter a series of values to change variables "on the fly."

Changing an Expression's Format

Usually, TD will display an expression result appropriately. It displays characters as text, real numbers in floating point or scientific notation, addresses separated into segment and offset parts, and integers in hex and decimal. (If you want to see only hex or decimal values, use `Options:Display options` to change the `Integer format` setting.)

Usually, TD's default formats give the best results, but not always. For example, you may want to examine the address of a variable in the `Watches` window instead of that variable's value. To do that, append a capital letter *P* to the variable name as in the expression **pieCount,P**. If the expression evaluates to a pointer or an array, you can also add a repeat count as in **p,d,10**, which displays 10 decimal bytes addressed by pointer `p`. Notice that `p` is not dereferenced as it would be if you wrote `p^`. See Table 9.1 for other options you can use to change an expression's display format.

> The *TD User's Guide* indicates that repeat counts should come *before* the formatting letter, but my tests show that this is not correct—the count should follow the letter. Also, some of the options, for example, f[#], do not always seem to produce the expected results. For these reasons, if a formatting option doesn't let you see a variable in the format you need, you might try using a type-cast expression to convert the variable's data type to another form.

Table 9.1. Expression formatting options.

Option	Description
c	Display strings in extended ASCII
d	Decimal integer
f[#]	Floating point (# = optional number of digits)
h	Hexadecimal (same as x)
m	Display memory as hex byte list
md	Display memory as decimal byte list
P	Pointer (segment:offset)
s	Quoted, null-terminated string
x	Hexadecimal (same as h)

> Hints: Use the h and d formats to show selected variables in hex and decimal instead of changing the `Integer format` setting with `Options:Display options`, which affects all variables. Add an optional digit after f, for example, type **f8** or **f10**, to see that many significant digits. Specify a small repeat count to limit the amount of information TD displays horizontally in the `Watches` window.

Line Numbers

Whenever TD requests an address, you can enter a line number in the form:

`[[#]module[#file]]#000[#ident]`

Replace *module* with a module name, *file* with a file name for multifile modules, *000* with the line number in decimal, and *ident* with an identifier in that module and file. The identifier can be any global symbol. You must type the # character, which you can replace with a period if that doesn't conflict with other uses for the current language. Usually, you don't have to precede the module name with #, and, in fact, that can cause problems in Pascal expressions where this character prefaces control codes in strings. Try it both ways to find the format that works for your program. Here are a few samples:

#150	Line 150 in the current module
prog.300	Line 300 in module PROG
#prog#x.inc#25	Line 25 in PROG's Include file X.INC
prog#25#i	Variable i at line 25 in PROG

The last line is handy when you need to select one of several variables declared on a single line.

When supplying a literal line number is inconvenient, you can also enter line-number expressions in this alternate format:

`[#module[#file]][#proc]#ident`

After the optional module and file names, replace *proc* with a procedure or function identifier, followed by a local symbol *ident*. For example:

counter	Local symbol counter
prog#volume	Function or procedure volume in PROG
#prog#x.inc#q	Variable q in PROG's X.INC include file
prog#volume#v2	Variable v2 in volume

C Expressions

When entering C expressions, be aware that identifiers are case-sensitive. If TD complains that it can't find a symbol, be sure you've typed the symbol correctly. You do not have to enter a leading underscore, even though the Variables window may list a variable that way—for instance, _myCounter. If TD can't find an identifier, it appends an underscore and looks in the symbol table again. But watch out for variables that begin with double underscores as in _ _huge_dble. In that case, you must enter at least *one* underscore for TD to find the symbol. (If this gives you trouble, and if your programs don't rely on case sensitivity, you might want to use TDINST to turn off case-sensitive symbols as explained in chapter 3.)

You can also type register names such as **AX** and **ES** in expressions. However, when those names conflict with other program symbols, you may have to preface them and other registers with an underscore as in **_CS** and **_BX**. When entered that way, the symbols refer to Turbo C's *pseudo register* names, which TD recognizes when the current language is C. Because C is case-sensitive, these register names *must* be in uppercase.

Operators

You can use all of C's usual numeric operators, array brackets [] (vectors), unary operators, and the assignment symbol =. You can also combine operators to create shorthand assignments such as += and *=. Because you're probably familiar with the purpose of these and other operators, I won't describe them here. See the *Turbo Debugger User's Guide* and your language reference manual for a complete list of operators and their precedences. In general, you can combine operators, variables, and constants using the same formats as in your program's source code.

When entering 32-bit addresses, use a colon (:) to separate the segment and offset parts. Although the *Turbo Debugger User's Guide* suggests using a double colon (::) for this purpose, a single one works equally well. As far as I've been able to tell, :: has no practical value. For example, to specify two 16-bit values as a 32-bit address, enter expressions like **ds:bx**, **__DS:0x80**, and **(__ CS + 0x0100):0x00F0**. The parentheses are required because the colon in TD has a higher precedence than +.

Numeric Expressions

TD assumes that constant values in numeric C expressions are in decimal. Precede digits with a capital **O** for octal, or with **0X** or **0x** for hexadecimal. Append a capital **L** for long 32-bit integers.

Enter floating point values in the usual way—3.14159. Use scientific notation for very large and small values—2e10 and 5.8e-12.

String Expressions

Surround single characters with single quotes and character strings with double quotes. Represent control codes with C escape sequences—for example, \t for tab, \n for new lines, \\ for \, \x00 for a hex value 00, and so on.

> Hint: Use the `Data:Evaluate/modify` command and enter characters such as '**A**' and '**$**' to display their ASCII values in decimal and in hex.

Type Casting

When you want TD to treat an identifier of one data type as though it were another, use a *type cast*. Usually, you'll do this to tell TD that a `void` pointer actually addresses `int`, `char`, or data of another type. Specify the data type in parentheses followed by the identifier to convert. For example, (int *)p casts p as a pointer to int, while *(int *)p casts and dereferences the pointer to return the addressed integer value.

You can also use a cast when debugging code to which you've added symbolic information from a .MAP file (see chapter 2). In that case, TD considers all variables to be bytes or words, and you can use casts to let TD know what those variables actually are. For example, (double)level tells TD to treat level as though it were of type double.

Side Effects

As described in chapter 8, side-effect expressions are useful for assigning values to variables and for splicing code with temporary breakpoint patches. A side-effect expression calls a C function, which may change a global variable. Or, it assigns the result of a function to a variable. When entering expressions that cause side effects, be sure to use = only when you want to assign the result of the expression on the right to the variable or address on the left. Use == to test for equality.

You can pass parameters to functions just as you do in source-code statements. Specify literal values, expressions, or symbolic arguments, but don't end the line with a semicolon. For example, this calls a function reset with three arguments, a literal value (255), a pointer variable named cp, and a constant MAX:

```
reset( 255, cp, MAX)
```

To call functions with no parameters, follow the identifier with empty parentheses, for example, **do_something( )**. If you don't attach the parentheses, TD replaces do_something with the *address* of that symbol—it doesn't call the function code.

Pascal Expressions

Except for set expressions and string concatenation using either the concat function or the string addition operator (+), TD can evaluate nearly any Pascal expression. Unlike C, Pascal symbols are not case-sensitive, so you can enter an identifier as maxvalue even though that symbol might be spelled MaxValue in the program source code.

You can also refer to register names like AX and DS in expressions as long as you haven't defined other symbols with those same names. If this is a problem, switch languages temporarily to C with Options:Language and attach an underscore as in _CS to refer to C's pseudo registers. After entering the expression—you'll have to use C data formats—remember to switch the current language back to Source or Pascal.

Operators

You can use all of Turbo Pascal's usual numeric operators, array brackets [ ], unary operators, and the assignment symbol :=. Because you're probably familiar with the purpose of these and other operators, I won't repeat them here. See the *Turbo Debugger User's Guide* and your language reference manual for a list of operators and their precedences. In general, you can combine operators, variables, and constants using the same formats as in your program's source code.

Enter 32-bit address values with a colon (:) separating the segment and offset parts. For example, to specify two 16-bit values as a 32-bit address, enter expressions like **ds:bx**, **ds:$0080**, and **(cs + $0100):$00F0**. The parentheses are required in this sample because the colon in TD has a higher precedence than other operators.

Numeric Expressions

TD assumes that constant values in numeric Pascal expressions are in decimal. Precede digits with a dollar sign ($) for hexadecimal values such as **$0F00** and **$FA9E**.

Enter floating point values in the usual way, for example, 3.14159. Use scientific notation for very large and small values such as 2e10 and 5.8e-12.

String Expressions

The only restriction on string expressions is concatenation—you can't create single strings out of multiple parts using `concat` or the string addition operator (+).

If you must use string concatenation in TD, write your own string function that returns two or more string arguments as a single string value. You can then call the function in an expression.

Surround characters and strings with single quotes, just as you do in Pascal source code. Precede control characters and extended ASCII values with # as in this sample string, which includes two "bell" controls:

```
'Ring'#7' the'#7' bell'
```

Calling String Functions

To determine a string's length, enter an expression such as **length(s)** in the `Evaluate/modify` dialog box. Because the `length` function returns an integer value, TD allows it. Unfortunately, the debugger doesn't recognize other string functions and procedures such as `Copy` and `Delete`. Therefore, you can't call these routines in expressions.

But, like many rules, this one's made to be broken—just write your own replacement string procedures and functions and call those in expressions instead of the originals. For example, in Listing 9.1, STRFUNC.PAS, `xCopy` and `xDelete` call their counterparts `Copy` and `Delete`. This adds `xCopy` and `xDelete` to the program's symbol table, giving TD the information it needs to call these routines.

Listing 9.1.   STRFUNC.PAS.

```
(*
**     Purpose: Test string functions
**     Author:  (c) 1990 by Tom Swan.
*)

program stringFunctions;
var
   s : string;

function xCopy( s : string; index, len : word ) : string;
begin
   xCopy := copy( s, index, len )
end; { xCopy }

procedure xDelete( var s : string; index, len : word );
begin
   delete( s, index, len )
end; { xDelete }

begin
   s := xCopy( s, 1, 0 );   { Prevents stripping xCopy }
   xDelete( s, 1, 0 );      { Prevents stripping xDelete }
   s := 'abcdefghijklmnop'
end.
```

Notice that the first two statements in STRFUNC's main block make purposeless calls to `xCopy` and `xDelete`. This prevents TP's linker from stripping the functions from the compiled result.

After loading the test program into TD, press ⟨**F8**⟩ to step past the assignment to string s. Press ⟨**Ctrl**⟩-⟨**F4**⟩ to open the `Evaluate/modify` dialog box. Then, enter a few test expressions such as **xCopy(s,1,4)** and **xDelete(s,2,3)**. Enter **s** and press ⟨**Enter**⟩ to inspect the string variable's current value.

Type Casting

When you want TD to treat an identifier of one data type as though it were another, use a *type cast*. Usually, you'll do this to tell TD that a generic Pascal `pointer` actually addresses an array, a record, or data of another type. Specify the data type followed by parentheses around the identifier to convert. For example, `string(p^)` casts the variable that `p` addresses as a string, while `integer(p^)` casts that same data as an integer value.

> Just as this book was about to be printed, Borland decided to delete TD's capability to use expressions such as `string(p^)` and `integer(p^)`, features that worked in previous TD releases and in all TD2 prereleases that I tested. These constructions are perfectly legal in TP, and, therefore, the debugger should recognize them. But, even though these formats no longer work, I left this information here in hopes that a later release will restore this omission. If you program in Pascal, and if you want these features back, as I do, tell Borland!

Casts are also useful to force TD to convert numeric expressions to one of Turbo Pascal's five integer types: `ShortInt`, `Byte`, `Integer`, `Word`, and `LongInt`. For example, TD assumes that 100 is a `ShortInt`—the smallest type that can hold that value. To represent 100 as a 32-bit long integer, enter **LongInt(100)** in an expression.

Side Effects

As chapter 8 explains, side-effect expressions are useful for assigning values to variables and for splicing code with temporary patches. A side-effect expression calls a Pascal procedure or function, which may change a global variable. Or, a statement might assign a function's value to a variable. Either way, the result is a side effect. To cause side effects intentionally in TD expressions, use Pascal's assignment operator `:=` to assign the result of an expression on the right to a variable or address on the left.

You can also pass parameters to procedures and functions just as you can in source-code statements. Specify literal values, expressions, or symbolic arguments, but don't end the line with a semicolon. For example, this calls a procedure `reset` with three arguments, a literal value (**255**), a pointer variable named `cp`, and a constant `MAX`:

```
reset( 255, cp, MAX)
```

To call procedures and functions with no parameters, follow the identifier with empty parentheses, for example, **do__something()**. If you don't attach the parentheses, TD returns the *address* of do_something—it doesn't call the procedure or function code.

Assembly Language Expressions

Expressions in assembly language differ from those in Pascal and C in a major way—they are evaluated at assembly time, not when the assembled program runs. Unlike C and Pascal compilers, which translate expressions into machine-code instructions that calculate expression results at runtime, the assembler reduces expressions to constant values during assembly. Consequently, all values in an expression must also be constants, not variables.

Even so, while it supports typical assembly language expressions, TD can also evaluate expressions that you can't insert into an assembly language program—unless, that is, you write your own expression parser. For example, if you declare a variable `Count` with the `dw` directive, you can enter the expression **(Count * Level) / 2** in the `Data` menu's `Evaluate/modify` window even though there's no easy way to enter similar expressions directly into the program's source code.

You can also enter register values in expressions. 8-bit registers display as type `byte`; 16-bit registers, as type `word`; and 32-bit registers, as type `dword`.

A useful trick is to set a breakpoint for specific register values. For instance, to halt before returning to DOS via `int 21h`, enter an `Expression true global` breakpoint for the expression `ah eq 04ch`. When you press ⟨**F9**⟩ to run the program (it will execute more slowly than normal), the code will stop when `ah` equals 04Ch, DOS's program-terminate function number. Of course, if the program ends via another method, it won't stop, which may also be useful to know.

> Hint: The symbol **$** stands for the current location. For a continual update on the address of the next instruction to execute, insert the expression **cs:$** into the `Watches` view.

Operators

You can use all of TASM's and MASM's usual numeric operators, unary operators, comparison operators (`EQ`, `NE`, `LT`, `LE`, `GT`, and `GE`), and the assignment symbol `=`. Because you're probably familiar with the purpose of these and other operators, I won't repeat them here. See the *Turbo Debugger User's Guide* and your language reference manual for a list of operators and their precedences.

Remember always to use `EQ`, not `EQU`, in comparisons for equality. `EQU` associates a value and a constant in the source code—it has no meaning in TD. To compare two symbols, enter an expression such as **(v1 EQ v2)**. To assign a new value to a variable, use the `=` operator like this: **v1 = 5**.

Enter 32-bit address values with a colon (**:**) separating the segment and offset parts. For example, to specify two 16-bit values as a 32-bit address, enter expressions such as **ds:bx**, **ds:0080h**, and **(cs + 0100h):00F0h**. Actually, the parentheses aren't needed in this last case as they are in C and Pascal expressions because the colon has a lower precedence than + when the current language is set to `Assembler`.

> Note: Apparently, TD follows TASM's Ideal mode to determine operator precedence, while the *Turbo Debugger User's Guide* incorrectly lists operators according to their precedence levels in MASM mode. To avoid confusion, it's probably best to use parentheses instead of relying on a certain precedence order when entering assembly language expressions into the debugger.

Numeric Expressions

TD assumes that constant values in numeric assembly language expressions are in hexadecimal. Be aware of this—the default radix (number base) in TASM and MASM is decimal unless you've used the `RADIX` command to change it. This means that expressions copied from the source code into a prompt box may not produce the same result as when the assembler evaluates that same expression.

One way to resolve potential conflicts (except when using the `RADIX` command) is to always specify a value's radix—both in the source code and in TD expressions. End hexadecimal values with **h**, decimal values with **d**, octal values with **o** or the more conspicuous **q**, and binary values with **b**. You may use upper- or lowercase letters. In all cases, you must begin a number with a digit. This is a hexadecimal value: 0F09Ch. This is an alphanumeric symbol: F09Ch.

Enter floating point values in the usual way, for example, 3.14159. Use scientific notation for very large and small values such as 2e10 and 5.8e-12.

String Expressions

You can display strings declared with `DB` and delimited with single or double quotes, but you can't assign new string values in expressions. Assembly language has no string assignment operator, and neither does TD when the current language equals `Assembler`.

One way around this problem is to open an `Inspector` window for the label that identifies the string. You can then enter quoted characters such as **'p'** and **'@'** to modify the string. Or, after opening the `Inspector`, press ⟨**Alt**⟩-**VD** to open a `Dump` window listing the bytes and characters in the string. Move the cursor to the character display at right and enter the new string delimited with double or single quotes.

> A bug in TD prevents entering single-character quoted strings into **Dump** windows when **Language** is set to **Assembler**. The **Dump** window accepts strings such as **'ab'** and **'abc'**, but it rejects single-character expressions like **'x'** and **'y'**. Perhaps this problem will be fixed in a future release.

Side Effects

There's no way to call assembly language subroutines in TD expressions. You can do that only in C and Pascal programs. You can assign expressions to variables, however, using the **=** operator as explained earlier. But using side effects to splice code and to call routines independently of other statements is a high-level operation that TD does not support when the current language is set to **Assembler**.

Object-Oriented Expressions

In expressions, you may refer to Pascal object types or C++ classes, object instances, methods, and fields. (For simplicity, I'll refer to them all as types.) Use periods to separate related identifiers. For example, `list.delete` might refer to a method `delete` in the object `list` type, while `myList.empty` might refer to an `empty` function or data field in an object instance named `myList`.

Always keep in mind the difference between object types and instances. You can't use the value of a field in an object type because that field doesn't exist anywhere in memory until the object is *instantiated*, that is, allotted space as a variable. You can't use an object type's fields in expressions. Only variables have values, not data types.

To refer to object types and instances outside of the current scope, you may have to qualify the object expression. To do that, you can append a module name to an object type or instance, and you can refer to local variables and nested procedures and functions (Pascal only). Use dot notation to separate individual parts, according to this scheme:

```
[module.]instance|type[.field|.method][.local symbol]
```

As usual, brackets represent optional items. Replace *module* with a module name to refer to objects in a module outside of the current one. The *instance* may be a variable or a pointer to an object. Or, you can specify an object *type*. After that, you can refer to a *field* or *method* in the object, plus any *local symbol* defined in that method. This might be a local variable, or in Pascal, a nested procedure or function.

Calling Object Methods

You can call object methods in C++ and Pascal programs just as you can other procedures and functions. But there's a catch. Because objects encapsulate their code and data, an object only exists after it's been instantiated. Although the object method's code is stored along with other subroutines of the program, you can execute those methods in expressions only by referring to an instance of the object type.

This restriction makes better sense when you consider that object methods typically read and write data field values in objects. Because those fields don't exist in memory until the object type is instantiated as a variable, executing an object method outside of any reference to an object instance could cause serious problems. You'd be reading and writing data in fields that don't yet exist anywhere in memory.

So, the first rule to remember is, if you want to call object methods in expressions, you must execute the program up to a place where one or more object instances are available. One way to do this is to set a breakpoint inside a method. When the program halts, open the `Data` menu's `Evaluate/modify` window and enter an expression such as **self.currentItem( )**. (C++ uses the keyword `this` instead of `self`.) Without the empty parentheses, TD would display the address of *self.currentItem*. With the parentheses, TD calls the `currentItem` method. If the current object instance is of type `list`, then typing **list.currentItem** is perfectly acceptable—it represents the address of that method in this object type. But entering **list.currentItem( )** causes TD to report an "Illegal procedure or function call" because it makes no sense to call a method in an object type.

You can also pass arguments to methods in parentheses. For example, you might execute methods by entering expressions such as **self.setX(10)** and **self.setAll(pastHead)**. Again, without parentheses, TD would evaluate *self.setX* and *self.setAll* as the addresses of those methods. With the parentheses, TD calls the methods and, in these examples, passes the listed arguments.

It's also possible to call methods for specific objects. To do that, run the code until the object comes into scope—perhaps as a result of the program reaching a local declaration inside a procedure or function, or after a statement allocates heap space to an object pointer. You can then call methods with expressions. If `menu` is an initialized object instance, you can call methods in the object by entering expressions such as **menu.displayMenu( )** and **menu.nextItem( )**.

Summary

TD can evaluate just about any C, Pascal, or assembly language expression. Whenever TD asks for a number or an address, you can enter an expression. You can test expression results in the `Evaluate/modify` dialog box, and you can use that window as an on-line calculator. In C and Pascal, you can even call procedures and functions in expressions to execute code independently of other statements.

Expression syntax depends on the `Language` setting in the `Options` menu. Normally, TD selects the appropriate language automatically. But you can always change the setting if, for example, you prefer to enter expressions in C's format while debugging assembly language code.

Source-code line numbers can substitute for addresses and, in some cases, are easier to enter. Separate module, file, line number, and identifier symbols with # or, if it doesn't present any conflicts, a period.

Each language—C, Pascal, and assembly language—has its own expression format. In general, TD can evaluate nearly any expression that you might use in a program. With few exceptions, all operators, numeric data types, and strings are available. You can also cast C and Pascal pointers to inform TD what data types those pointers address.

Side effects are an important debugging tool, but they require care to use properly. A side effect can occur when a function changes or is assigned to a global variable. Side effects in TD let you call functions in expressions to test code independently of other statements. You can also call Pascal procedures and C `void` functions.

In object-oriented Pascal and C++ programs, it's possible to call object methods, but only when an object instance of that object's type is within the current scope. Object types don't exist in memory, so it doesn't make sense to reference object fields until the objects are instantiated.

Chapter 10

Common C Bugs

BECAUSE OF C's wide lexical freedom, bugs in C programs frequently arise from statements that compile correctly but don't perform up to snuff. In other words, C lets programmers get away with source-code murder, and it often takes a sophisticated debugger with the nose of a bloodhound (TD) plus an experienced detective with the intuition of a Sherlock (that's you) to track down the villainous bugs responsible for a C program's demise.

So, when the tables turn on your C code, start your investigation with the tips in this chapter. Chances are you'll find the culprit among the common C bugs listed here. I collected many of these problems from various C programming books and other sources (including my own list of colossal blunders). Of course, it's not possible to list every error that you can make in C programs. But even if your bug isn't here, you can at least use this chapter to eliminate the more likely causes.

> Note: I used TC2 to compile the sample code in this chapter; therefore, some of the code and error messages may be unique to that compiler. But all of the bug descriptions are general and should apply to most modern C-language compilers.

Going to the Source

Every programmer knows that simple typing errors frequently cause bugs. But instead of looking for simple, unexciting typos in source code, programmers often waste time hunting for more exotic disasters such as uninitialized pointers, array-index range errors, and accidental function recursion. We'll examine those and other fancy bugs in a moment, but when trouble brews, it's wise to begin your search by first going directly to the simple source.

Transposed Comment Brackets

Because C's comment brackets use the two symbols * and /, if you accidentally transpose one of those characters, the other may become part of the comment, causing it to extend to the *next* closing bracket. For example, consider this typical fragment:

```
for (count = 0; count <= 9; count++) {   /* Fill array /*
   a[count] = count;    /* Assign count to array */
}
```

At first glance, this `for` loop appears to initialize an array of integers with the values 0 through 9. But the comment at the end of the first line incorrectly ends with `/*` when it should end with the closing comment bracket `*/`—a simple transposition that incorrectly extends the comment from `/* Fill...` to the end of the *next* line at `...array */`.

Because of the error, the compiler reads the assignment to `a[count]` as part of the comment; therefore, that statement is never compiled, and it doesn't execute. When you run the buggy program, the array appears to be filled with random values, and you may be tempted to look for a bad pointer that's trashing the array contents when the actual cause is far simpler.

If you are using TC, one way to locate a bad bracket is to enable nested comments with the -C option. If the code compiles correctly without that switch but generates spurious errors with the switch turned on, then a bad comment bracket is almost surely at fault. For example, compiling the previous `for` statement with -C produces an "Unexpected end of file" error and two "Compound statement missing" errors. Compiling without that switch produces no error messages. Notice that these errors do not refer directly to the actual problem, but to the faulty syntax that the compiler notices as a result of the bad comment. It's still up to you to realize why these errors occurred.

In some cases, that can be difficult, especially when the bad comment extends over several lines. In that case, load the program into TD and press ⟨**F7**⟩ or ⟨**F8**⟩ to single-step sections of code. Or, use the `Run:Animate` command to execute a module in slow motion while you watch for the cursor to jump over statements that were accidentally converted into comments.

Mismatched Braces and Parentheses

Similar to a bad comment bracket—and just as common, if not more so—is a mismatched set of braces or parentheses. In most cases, the compiler will flag such errors, but more often than not, the resulting error messages are anything but helpful. Here's a typical example:

```
for (i = 1; i <= 10; i++) {
   printf("\n"); }  /* ??? */
   for (j = i; j <= 10; j++) {
      printf("%d ", j );
   }
}
```

The closing brace at the end of the first `printf()` statement should not be there. When compiled, this innocent-looking character produces a flood of error messages, all of which begin with the line that follows the code fragment. Be aware of this—the compiler may not notice such problems until long after passing the mistake.

Simple typos like this one are easy to spot. But in a complex section of code with many nested statements, you can have a devil of a time identifying which brace or parenthesis is out of order. Of course, if the code won't compile, TD can't help you locate the problem. So, the best course of action is to run the source code through a brace and parentheses counter, which you can find on most on-line bulletin boards, from *Compuserve*, or in a commercial C toolkit. You might also use a *LINT* program, which reads through a C source-code listing and performs a more thorough syntax analysis than provided by most compilers.

Else with Wrong If

I classify this error with other source-code typos even though most C references list it as a logical mistake. But the problem usually is not one of poor logic. More often, the cause of a misplaced `else` statement is just sloppy typing, as this fragment demonstrates:

```
if (count <= 10)
   if (j == count)
      printf("j = count");
else
   printf("count > 10\n");
```

The `if` statement is supposed to test whether `count` is less or equal to 10. If so, a second `if` compares `j` and `count`. If those two variables are equal, `printf()` displays a message that j = count. But if `count` is greater than 10, a second `if` statement displays count > 10.

Or does it? Running the code when `count` equals 11 does not display any message because the `else` statement logically attaches to the second, not the first, `if`. Even though the programmer aligned the `else` with the first `if`— perhaps in a hurry to get that statement entered before closing time—the compiler sees the program differently. The correct code is:

```
if (count <= 10) {
   if (j == count)
      printf("j = count");
}
else
   printf("count > 10\n");
```

By surrounding the inner if statement with braces, the else now applies to the first if as it should.

This mistake is especially hard to find in deeply nested if statements. When you suspect the code is bugged by this sort of problem, use TD to step through the logic, add the control variables (count and j in this example) to the Watches window or open an inspector for them, and set a breakpoint (press ⟨**F2**⟩) on the first if. Then, run the code to that place (press ⟨**F9**⟩). Use the Change command to assign test values to the variables—press ⟨**Ctrl**⟩-**C** with the variable highlighted in Watches or just type the new value with the inspector window active. After that, single-step the code by pressing ⟨**F8**⟩ and observe the results.

All Things Being Equal

How many times have you typed = when you should have typed ==? If not many, go to the head of the class. But if you make this common C mistake often, don't worry. At least you're in good (and numerous) company.

Of course, you probably know that the single equal sign = is C's assignment operator. In an expression, the value on the right of = is assigned to the variable on the left. For example, this assigns 123 to an integer variable k:

```
k = 123;
```

That's harmless enough, but it's not so innocent when a similar construction appears in a if statement, as in this faulty example:

```
k = 100;
if (k = 1) printf("k = 1\n"); /* ??? */
```

The control expression (k = 1) assigns 1 to k, probably not what the programmer intended. Because this means that k will always equal 1 at this place in the program, when the statement runs, no matter what value k has initially, printf() always reports k = 1. To correct the mistake, use the equality operator in the control expression:

```
if (k == 1) printf("k = 1\n");
```

Most compilers warn about this error. (TC reports a "Possibly incorrect assignment" for the previous example.) But many programmers turn off this and other warnings to prevent too much "chatter" from the compiler. The easy solution, of course, is to leave the warning enabled. But there's a good reason you might want to disable it. Because all expressions have values, a typical C trick is to write statements like this:

```
if ((k=getk())!=0)
   do_something(k);
```

The expression `((k = getk())!=0)` performs work (it assigns the result of a fictitious function `getk()` to k), and it also has a value, the same value assigned to k. This is an example, then, where = in a control expression is correct because the if statement is *supposed* to check the value of the expression to determine whether to execute `do_something()`. If `getk()` returns 0, k is set to 0, and the if statement regards the result as false. If `getk()` returns 1, k is set to 1, or nonzero, C's value for true.

While the C language allows (even encourages) this kind of tricky business, many compilers generate warnings for it. However, because the technique is common, the messages are usually meaningless, so many programmers turn them off. Unfortunately, if you do that—for example, by using a `-w-pia` compiler switch with TC—the previous incorrect if statement will go unnoticed, leading to a hard-to-find bug.

A good way to use TD to find this error is to set a `Breakpoints:Changed memory global` breakpoint for `k,1`. (The 1 means "1 word," the size of an int variable in TC.) Then press ⟨**F9**⟩ to execute the code, which will halt at all changes to k. (In a large program, you might want to start by running the program to a logical stopping place, for example, the beginning of a suspected function. Then, set the global breakpoint and press ⟨**F9**⟩ to continue.) You may have to press ⟨**F9**⟩ more than once to skip legitimate assignments to k, including any automatic initializations. But this experiment will find any bad if statements. Just keep pressing ⟨**F9**⟩ and examining each stopping point to be sure that the code is supposed to assign a new value to k.

Path-Name Problems

Exasperating conflicts can occur in path-name strings because DOS uses the backslash (\) as a directory-name separator. This causes trouble because C uses that same character as an escape mechanism to insert control characters in ASCII strings. For a variable declared as `char *filename`, a common mistake is to assign a path name such as:

```
filename = "c:\tc\alpha\newstuff"; /* ??? */
```

Who would think that such an innocent-looking statement could cause so much trouble? Yet that's exactly what it does. Because \t represents a tab character, \a the bell, and \n a new line (carriage return and line feed in DOS), printing this string with printf() displays:

```
c:      clpha ewstuff
```

Many C programmers, when they see scrambled output like that, immediately think "bad pointer." But don't be fooled. The errors are simple typos, which you can easily correct by doubling the backslashes:

```
filename = "c:\\tc\\alpha\\newstuff";
```

Misplaced Semicolons

It takes time and patience to learn where semicolons go in C programs. The compiler traps most mistakes that involve semicolons—C's statement terminator—and you can learn to prevent most problems by studying a good C tutorial and by reading samples of healthy C code. Sometimes, though, misplaced semicolons can lead to deceiving error messages. For example, a typical mistake is to define a function prototype like this:

```
void do_something(int kk);
```

Using a text editor's cut-and-paste commands, you then copy the prototype declaration to the function's implementation, accidentally forgetting to delete the semicolon. Because of this, the compiler reports a "Declaration syntax error" when it tries to compile:

```
void do_something(int kk);  /* ??? */
{
    printf("\n\nInside do_something. kk=%d\n", kk);
}
```

A similar mistake, which the compiler does not catch, causes a far more difficult bug to find. Beginners are especially prone to this one because they haven't yet learned that semicolons terminate statements, not control structures. For example, a common mistake is to write a for loop this way:

```
for (count = 1; count <= 10; count++);  /* ??? */
    printf("count=%d\n", count);
```

The semicolon at the end of the first line is perfectly legal but usually senseless. Because C permits null statements, the result is a do-nothing loop that initializes `count` to 1 and repeatedly increments `count` until it equals 11. The `printf()` statement is then executed a single time instead of ten times as intended.

Removing the misplaced semicolon fixes the error, which you can locate with TD by single-stepping the code and examining the control variable `count`.

Another similar bug that causes the program to halt in its tracks, forcing you to reboot, is sometimes the fault of a misplaced semicolon in a `while` loop such as:

```
count = 1;
while (count <= 10); { /* ??? */
    count++;
    printf("count=%d\n", count);
}
```

The statement `while (count <= 10);` is syntactically legal, but it's almost certainly unintended. Because of the semicolon, the `while` loop executes a null statement repeatedly while `count` is less than or equal to 10. Because `count` never changes, the system hangs.

TD makes it easy to find this kind of error. Just run the code until it hangs and press ⟨**Ctrl**⟩-⟨**Break**⟩. If you're lucky to hit the exact moment when the loop repeats, the debugger will show you the statement that's executing over and over. Usually, though, you'll break into a disassembled instruction displayed in the `CPU` window. If that happens, press ⟨**Cursor Up**⟩ until you see your C source code, then press ⟨**F6**⟩ to bring the `Module` window back into view. That should locate the buggy code. You might also be able to press ⟨**F8**⟩ repeatedly to return to the source-code view. But even these keys may not return you to `Module` if you're trapped inside a subroutine for which source is not available. In that case, you have little choice but to repeat the experiment until you break into a module that TD recognizes.

Accidental Function Redefinition

The C compiler should warn against accidentally reusing an identifier that's already associated with a library function. But if functions don't do what you think they should—especially if you've just begun to use a new library—check whether you have accidentally redefined a function name.

Some libraries add prefixes to their function names, a simple device that goes a long way toward avoiding conflicts. For example, in a graphics library, there might be functions such as `gr_line`, `gr_point`, and `gr_circle`. If every library followed a similar convention, you could easily avoid name conflicts by never using the same `gr_` prefix for your own identifiers.

To find errors caused by reusing function names, set a breakpoint (press ⟨**F2**⟩) on the function call that appears to be broken. Then press ⟨**F9**⟩ to run the program up to that place and single-step through the function by pressing

⟨**F7**⟩. If the **CPU** window appears, then you probably have not redefined the library function. But, if the **Module** window jumps to one of your own functions, compare its name with those in the libraries you are using. You might just find a duplicate.

Problems with Variables

It's hard to imagine a useful C program that doesn't declare any variables. Even the rare module that lacks its own variables may use private data that belongs to runtime library routines.

TD gives you several ways to examine a program's variables—for example, inspector windows, the **Watches** and **Variables** views, and expression evaluation in the **Evaluate/modify** dialog box. You can also set data breakpoints to monitor changes to values in memory. Use these and other features to search for bugs in variables. As the following sections explain, there are more than a few common pitfalls.

Uninitialized Variables

One of the most feared bugs is the dreaded uninitialized variable. (Don't scream.) In C, *global* variables—those declared outside of **main()**—are initialized to 0 at runtime. But *automatic* variables—those declared inside a function—are not initialized. This means that if you create an automatic variable like this:

```
int apples;
```

the compiler generates code to allocate stack space for **apples** at runtime. Because that space is not initialized, **apples** will have whatever value was left in that same location by a previous operation. To initialize **apples**, you can declare it to have a starting value:

```
int apples = 10;
```

Or, you can include an assignment statement in the code:

```
int apples;
...
apples = 10;
```

Either way, just giving variables initial values can often prevent bugs from cropping up later.

But, while carefully initializing variables can prevent bugs, recognizing that a problem is caused by an uninitialized variable is not so easy. The classic symptom is a bug that seems to have a life of its own. When you run the program, a variable takes on a strange value. Then, you insert new programming, or you enable debugging statements with a command-line directive. When you run the code, `apples` stabilizes to 0. What's going on?

In such cases, you may not be initializing `apples` properly. This causes the variable to assume values left on the stack, and because of the stack's volatile nature, `apples` may have different values at different times while the program runs. Also, the presence of new programming might alter the location of the code, data, and stack segments, thus affecting the variable's position and its value. Uninitialized variables are sensitive to the slightest breeze. Even minor alterations to the source code may flush a bug into the open air.

Another symptom of an uninitialized variable is code that runs differently on two systems. Often, this will lead you to suspect a hardware failure on one of the computers, or you might conclude there's a bug in the BIOS. But the real cause could be an uninitialized variable. If the two systems differ in any way—if they load different DOS versions, read a different set of TSRs into RAM, or install different device drivers—then they will "assign" different values to uninitialized variables.

Finding uninitialized variables takes patience—especially in code with hundreds or thousands of variables to check. TD can help, as the next section explains, but before loading the program into the debugger, it's wise to stabilize runtime conditions. For example, you could reboot before testing. Or, you could write a utility to fill RAM with known values. By stabilizing runtime conditions, you'll be able to duplicate the bug on demand and simplify your search for the cause.

C compilers should warn you if they detect variables used before appearing on the left side of an assignment. Even so, it's possible for uninitialized array elements, pointers, and other structures to slip through the C parser and cause a bug.

Finding Uninitialized Variables

When you suspect that an uninitialized variable is causing a bug, the first step is to identify which variable is at fault. Sometimes, the answer will be obvious—for example, if the program displays the wrong date, obviously you'll want to examine the program's date variables.

At other times, however, you won't know which variable to observe. You might suspect an array-index value or a record field in a linked list, but you won't know which of many possible variables is the source of the bug.

A good way to proceed is to isolate the bug to as small a section of code as possible. Then, open the `Variables` window (press ⟨**Alt**⟩-**VV**) and set a `Changed memory global` breakpoint for the pseudo register **__BP**. When you press ⟨**F9**⟩ to run, the code will halt at the beginning of all functions that refer to automatic variables and function parameters on the stack. (You may have to repeat this experiment for registers **__SI** and **__DI** to find functions that store local variables in these registers.) As you run the code, watch the bottom pane of the `Variables` window—it will show you the values of all automatic variables and function parameters.

You may also want to add specific variables to the `Watches` window and observe their values while you single-step the code by pressing ⟨**F7**⟩ or ⟨**F8**⟩. Or, open an inspector window for an even closer look at a variable's value.

Stabilizing a Changing Variable

One of the most distressing bugs is the kind that changes a variable at random while a program runs. This can be caused by an uninitialized variable allocated at different locations at different times. Because those locations have different values, the symptom of this problem resembles the effect of a bad pointer that's overwriting memory.

One way to find such problems is to locate all statements in a program that change a certain variable. You could add the variable to the `Watches` view for observation, but a faster method is to log accesses to one or more variables while the code runs. This creates a report of all statements that affect those variables. For example, follow these steps to create a log for a variable named k:

1. Use `Breakpoints:Changed memory global` to set a breakpoint to k. Just enter the variable's name—despite the prompt, you don't have to specify its size in bytes.

2. Select `View:Breakpoints` and press ⟨**Ctrl**⟩-**S** to `Set options`. Change `Action` to `Log` and set `Action expression` to the variable's name, k. This will log every change made to that variable. Repeat this for each variable you want to monitor.

3. Press ⟨**F9**⟩ to run the program to completion, then press ⟨**Alt**⟩-**VL** to view the `Log` window. You'll see a history of all source-code lines that changed k. To examine those lines, switch to the `Module` window, press ⟨**Ctrl**⟩-**L**, and enter a line number. Or, refer to a printed listing. (Note: The logged lines may refer to statements after the ones that changed the variable.)

You might also want to write the log to disk. After step 2, press ⟨**Alt**⟩-**VL** and ⟨**Ctrl**⟩-**O** to open a log file. Specify the default file name or enter a different one. (You must open the log file *before* making too many log entries, or old ones might scroll out of the in-memory log's limited space.) When you quit TD, the log is automatically saved to disk. Here's a sample of a log file I created by following those steps:

```
Turbo Debugger Log
Stopped at _main
At #VAR#36 k = int 1 (0x1)
At #VAR#52 k = int 2 (0x2)
At #VAR#36 k = int 3 (0x3)
At #VAR#52 k = int 4 (0x4)
Terminated, exit code 0
```

Starting with the third line (ignore the first two), each log entry indicates where k was changed. `#VAR#36` refers to module `VAR.C` at line 36, where the `int` variable k was changed to 1. Other log entries, such as the "Terminated" message here, indicate breakpoint locations and other events.

Mishandling Global Variables

Good code uses global variables only when absolutely necessary. For example, using a global variable as the control in a `for` loop is almost always a bad idea. If that loop calls a function that also changes the global variable, problems are certain to arise. If k is global, then even this innocent-looking code is prone to catching a bug:

```
for (k = 1; k <= 10; k++) {
   do_something();  /* ??? */
}
```

If `do_something()` modifies k, this loop will fail. But if `do_something()` does not change k, the loop will execute correctly. In fact, the only way to certify that this loop will run without error is to limit the scope of k, preventing access to that variable from inside `do_something()`.

Whenever a bug search leads to a global variable, you should consider whether that variable needs to be global. If it does not need to be global, convert it to an automatic variable inside the functions that need it. Or, define the variable as `static` to limit its scope to a module or function. Use globals only where a variable must retain its value between function calls.

If you suspect that two or more functions use the same global variables in conflicting ways, log changes to that variable as explained in the previous section. This will give you a history of activity for the variable and may help you to find the conflict.

Confusing Automatic and Static Variables

Variables declared outside of `main()` are global. They are initialized to 0 and retain their values between function calls. Variables declared inside functions, including `main()`, are allocated temporary space on the stack or are stored inside a processor register. Because automatic variables do not retain their values between function calls, they must be reinitialized every time the function runs.

But don't confuse static and automatic variables, both of which may be declared inside a function. For example, this function declares an automatic variable r of type `float`:

```
void auto_var()
{
    float r;
    r = 3.14159;
}
```

Because r is automatic, it must be initialized at each call to `auto_var()`. Contrast this to a similar function that declares r as `static float`:

```
void static_var() {
    static float r;
    r = 9.51413;
}
```

A static variable is allocated *global* space; therefore, its value is initialized to 0, and it does not change between function calls. In fact, a static variable declared this way is identical to a global variable except for one difference: only the function in which the variable is declared may use the variable.

A common error is to assume that, if two functions declare static variables of the same name, they refer to the same variable in memory. They do not—a fact that you can prove by opening an inspector window for each variable. If you try this, you'll see that the addresses of identically named static variables in separate functions are different.

Also, when using TD to examine static variables, be aware of a subtle difference between the `Watches` and inspector windows. When you open an inspector to a specific variable, it will always refer to that same variable even if the code enters another function that declares another static variable of the same name. But, when you add a static variable to `Watches`, that variable will refer to the value that falls within the current scope. In other words, if you want to examine the values of static variables available to a function, add them to `Watches`. But if you want to examine a static variable at a specific address, use an inspector.

> Hint: To inspect variables listed in **Watches**, press ⟨**F6**⟩ to activate that view, highlight the variable, and press ⟨**Ctrl**⟩-**I**.

Confusing Static and Extern

Another common confusion involves the keywords `static` and `extern`. As the previous section explains, if two functions declare identically named static variables, those variables are stored at different memory addresses. There are, in fact, two separate variables, even though they have the same name. But in a multi-module program, you'll often want to allocate space for a variable in one module and then refer to that variable from inside others. This is what `extern` is for.

If you are having trouble getting your functions to reference a global variable in another module, you may be using `extern` incorrectly. Or, you may be confusing it with `static`. To solve the problem, it helps to remember that only one module may allocate space for a variable. For example, suppose that you declare `int xcount` outside of `main()`. Then, in a separate module, you write a function `extern_var()` that needs to reference that same global variable. To accomplish that, write the function this way:

```
void extern_var()
{
    extern int xcount;
    /* ... function statements */
}
```

Because of `extern`, the compiler knows that `xcount` will be allocated in another module, and it assumes that the address of the variable will be supplied when all modules are linked to the final code file. It would be a mistake to use `static` for this purpose, which would create two distinct variables in memory, both named `xcount`.

Use inspector windows to examine `extern` and `static` variable addresses and to make sure that the variables that you think refer to the same memory locations actually do.

Arrays

Problems with arrays are most often caused by improper indexing; therefore, the place to begin searching for array bugs is with the array's index variable. The following sections describe how to handle this and other common array problems that plague C programmers. But if you still can't find the bug, turn to the section on pointers for more information about debugging arrays.

Something for Nothing

You always get something for nothing in C arrays. That is, there is always a value stored at index location [0]. If you declare an array of 10 integer values, the array indexes range from 0 to 9, *not* from 1 to 10. A common mistake is to misunderstand this and write code such as:

```
int a[10];
int i;
for (i = 1; i <= 10; i++)  /* ??? */
   a[i] = 0;
```

In this sample, if i is not a register variable, it is physically located after the end of the array a. (At least it was in one test with TC.) Because the for loop mistakenly cycles index i from 1 to 10 when it should have used values from 0 to 9, the final assignment when i equals 10 overwrites the index variable, resetting it to 0! This causes the entire loop to restart, thus hanging the computer until you reboot or, if you're executing the program in TD, until you press ⟨**Ctrl**⟩-⟨**Break**⟩.

This example demonstrates how sensitive C arrays are to index range problems. Even a simple mistake can hang the system. Avoid similar trouble by remembering that [0] is always the first index position in a C array and that the last legal position is always equal to the number of elements declared minus 1. (Pascal programmers who switch to C are particularly prone to making this mistake because arrays in Pascal may be indexed starting with 1 or any other integer value.)

Index-Range Errors

The example in the previous section is only one of a class of bugs known as index-range errors. In C programming, it's your responsibility never to use index values outside of an array's declared size. Doing so may overwrite other variables or code in memory, causing serious bugs and crashes. In fact, if you experience a major crash, it's often wise to start looking for the problem by examining arrays and array indexes. Experience suggests that the tiniest mistakes in array indexing can produce the most spectacular crashes. In other words, with array-index errors, you often get the most bang for your bug.

One way to trap range errors is to use the `Breakpoint:Expression true global` command to set a breakpoint for out-of-range index values. For example, if i is an integer index for a 100-element array, enter the expression:

```
(i < 0) || (i > 99)
```

That will trigger a breakpoint at any time i's value is outside of its legal range. And this usually will take you directly to the statement that's writing beyond the declared array range.

When this approach is not convenient, you might set a `Changed memory global` breakpoint to monitor a few bytes before or after the array in memory. This can locate a statement that accidentally writes to a location outside of the array's allocated space. To set the breakpoints, use inspector windows to determine the starting and ending addresses of the array and then enter adjusted addresses and byte counts into the `Changed memory global` prompt box to monitor values just beyond the array boundaries. Or, instead of calculating the addresses manually, you can specify "illegal" array indexes. For instance, to monitor the bytes before and after an array `int a[10]`, set two breakpoints, one for `a[-1]` and another for `a[10]`. You can also use larger and smaller array indexes and specify an element count to monitor more space around the array.

Problems with Pointers

Pointers in C have taken the blame for more bugs than any other feature in the language. But I often wonder whether that criticism is deserved or imagined. While it's true that pointers allow you to address and, therefore, change any byte in memory, it doesn't necessarily follow that simply using pointers opens the door for all sorts of bugs to crawl in. Pointers can cause bugs, but so can other misused language features.

But it's certainly true that, when a pointer is at fault, finding and fixing the problem can be extremely difficult. A bad pointer might even overwrite the debugger, causing it to crash, unless, that is, you're debugging in remote mode, or you're running TD386 on an 80386- or 80486-based system. (See chapters 3, 17, and 18.)

So, don't avoid pointers because "they cause bugs." Pointers don't cause bugs; programmers do. You can learn to use pointers safely, and you can use TD to find errors caused by wayward pointers, as the following sections explain.

Uninitialized Pointers

The most common pointer bug stems from code that uses an uninitialized pointer variable. When looking for this problem, keep these four pointer facts in mind:

- A pointer is a *variable*. It is stored somewhere in memory.
- A pointer has a *value* stored in the pointer variable.

- The pointer's value is an *address,* which points to another location in memory.

- The location to which the pointer points has a *data type,* just like any other variable.

> Hint: One way to guard against pointer bugs is to use **const** to tell the compiler to reject assignments to pointer variables. To do that for a pointer **p** to a variable **v**, use a declaration such as ***const p = &v;**.

Finding Uninitialized Pointers

Uninitialized pointers can exhibit a variety of symptoms, and it's impossible to list every possible characteristic. But some of the more common signs are:

- A variable changes value even though no statement directly writes to that variable.

- A function that runs correctly most of the time suddenly crashes.

- A function fails to return to its caller. Instead, another section of the program magically runs.

- The program runs just fine. But after the program finishes, DOS crashes.

All of those effects might be caused by a pointer that writes data to memory locations that don't "belong" to the pointer. Because a pointer can address any spot in RAM, it can change bytes in DOS, alter a low-memory interrupt vector, wreck a return address on the stack, destroy code, or poke new values into other variables.

Finding the cause of such errors can be difficult. You can't set a breakpoint for a specific pointer value because you don't know what that value is. And you can't watch every memory byte for changes. That would produce too many halts for other statements that have legitimate reasons for changing values.

TC, other compilers, and LINT syntax checkers issue warnings if they encounter statements that use pointers before they are initialized. These checks can help, but they're not foolproof. Even if your code compiles with no warnings, it could still contain an uninitialized pointer error. For example, if the pointers are embedded in a `struct` like this:

```
struct node {
   /* ... other data */
   struct node *left;
   struct node *right;
};
```

and if you declare a variable np of type **struct node**, the compiler does not warn about the assignment tnp.left = tnp.right, even if those two pointers have not been initialized.

Hint: If your pointers are automatic variables declared inside a function (including **main**), then you can use the same technique described earlier to find other uninitialized variables. Set a **Changed memory global** breakpoint for **_BP**, select **View:Variables**, and press ⟨**F9**⟩ to run. Watch for senseless pointer values at the start of each function.

Finding NULL Pointers

Global and static pointers are initialized to **NULL** when the program runs. But using these pointers can lead to disaster, overwriting the low-memory interrupt vector table beginning at address 0000:0000, the value associated with **NULL**.

To find **NULL** pointers, you can't set an **Expression true global** breakpoint for **myptr = = NULL**. That doesn't work because **NULL** is #defined as a macro in STDIO.H, and TD doesn't allow you to refer to macros this way. Instead, enter the expression **myptr = = 0:0**. When you press ⟨**F9**⟩ to run the code, TD will halt the program at every spot where myptr equals **NULL**. Change **= =** to **!=** to find statements that assign values to **NULL** pointers.

Not Allocating Space to Pointers

Closely related to uninitialized pointers is the common mistake of forgetting to allocate memory space by calling malloc() or another memory-allocation library routine before using the pointers. This error frequently occurs with character strings, which are usually addressed by pointers declared like this:

```
char *string;
```

Elsewhere, assign and display a string with:

```
string = "Rudolph the Red-Nosed Reindeer";
printf("%s", string);
```

What's not evident is the hidden business in such code that leads to many string-pointer bugs. Assigning "Rudolph..." to the **string** pointer appears to break the earlier rule that pointers should be initialized before being used. Why don't you have to call malloc() to create space to store the string?

The reason is that assignments of string constants to pointers in C assign the *address* of those constants to the string pointer variables. The actual characters are stored in a fixed location in memory, and the assignment does not copy characters from there to somewhere else.

You can prove this to yourself by opening an inspector window to `string`. Notice that, when you execute the assignment, the variable's address changes in the inspector window to the location where the character string is stored.

Flunking Pointer Arithmetic

C's pointer arithmetic capabilities let you add and subtract values from pointers, which is often handy as an alternative to common array indexing. For example, if you define the following variables:

```
float a[10];
int i;
float *fp;
```

you can then display the array contents with this typical `for` loop:

```
for (i = 0; i <= 9; i++)
   printf("a[%d]=%f\n", i, a[i]);
```

But, you can also use a pointer `fp` to do the same job:

```
for (fp = a; fp <= &a[9]; fp++)
   printf("%f\n", *fp);
```

The key here is the increment operation `fp++`, which advances the pointer to the next array element, not to the next byte in memory. Pointer arithmetic in C always accounts for the pointer's data type. If the pointer addresses a 4-byte variable (as it does here), then incrementing the pointer in a C expression actually adds 4 to the pointer's address value when the code runs. This is easy to forget because the `++` operator increments integer variables by 1. Applying that operator (and its counterpart `--`) to a pointer increments and decrements the pointer by the size of the addressed item. Forgetting this detail is sure to lead to bugs.

Pointers and Automatic Variables

Remember that automatic variables are temporary—they exist in memory only while their declaring function is active. When the function returns to its caller, any memory used by automatic variables is reclaimed for use during other function calls and to store return addresses.

One mistake that programmers often make is to assign the address of an automatic variable to a pointer. There is nothing wrong with doing so, as long as you are careful not to use that pointer after the function ends. Because automatic variables no longer exist after that time, using pointers to the variables' former addresses can easily overwrite other data and return addresses on the stack.

This error sometimes sneaks up on programmers when they pass arguments by address to function parameters. For example, suppose you write the following function:

```
void make_float()
{
   float fp;

   fp = 3.14159;
   make_trouble(&fp);
}
```

Function `make_float()` declares a single floating point automatic variable `fp`. It then assigns a value to `fp` and calls `make_trouble`, which takes a pointer to type `float`:

```
void make_trouble(float *fp) {
   global = fp; /* ??? */
   /* ... other code */
}
```

If variable `global` is another `float *fp` pointer in which the function saves the address of its parameter for another statement's later use, this code is walking on dangerously thin ice. The bug occurs when the caller to `make_float` exits, causing the space originally allocated on the stack for `fp` to be reclaimed and leaving `global` addressing a now unprotected location in the stack. Writing a value to `*global` could change a variable belonging to another function. Worse, if `global` happens to point to a return address, changing its value could alter the course of history—that is, the history of your function calls and returns.

Finding this kind of mistake is difficult, even with TD. The debugger can help you to narrow the problem to a section of code. It can slow the code with tracing and animation commands so you can observe the effects of actions that otherwise pass too quickly. But the best medicine in this case is prevention. Either avoid passing the addresses of automatic variables to pointer parameters or never design your functions to save those pointers in global variables. When you must write such code, be sure to document functions to which automatic variables should not be passed by address.

Not Disposing Allocated Space

After allocating space to a pointer by calling `malloc()` or one of its relatives, when you're done using that space, you should call `free()` (or the appropriate derivative) to dispose the unused space. If you receive out-of-memory errors after a program has been running for a time, failing to dispose unused memory might be the cause. Check that all calls to `malloc()` are matched by calls to `free()`.

Using Disposed Memory

Related to the previous out-of-memory bug is the common mistake of using a pointer after its allocated space has been disposed. Because `free()` and its derivatives return a memory block to the pool of unallocated bytes in the heap, using a disposed pointer can produce the same kinds of problems as using other uninitialized pointers.

One way to prevent such errors is to set disposed pointers to `NULL` immediately after calling `free()`. You can then use TD to find illegal uses of disposed pointers by following the earlier suggestions for finding `NULL` pointers.

Functions

Some of the more common bugs that are associated with functions are: forgetting to return a value for all possible exit paths, confusing value and variable (passed by address) parameters, being victimized by a hidden side effect, and accidentally falling into an unwanted recursion. This section examines these typical function traps in detail.

Forgetting a Return Value

Except for `void` functions, you must remember to execute a `return` statement for all possible exit paths. Although it's rare to forget a `return` altogether, it's fairly common to fail to cover all the bases. For example, suppose you have these definitions:

```
enum boolean { NO, YES };
enum boolean answer(char *prompt);
```

You then write the `answer` function, which is supposed to return `NO` or `YES` depending on whether you press **N** or **Y** in response to a prompt:

```
enum boolean answer(char *prompt)
{
    int c;

    printf("%s (y/n)? ", prompt);
    c = toupper( getchar() );
    if (c == 'Y')
        return YES;
    else if (c == 'N')    /* ??? */
        return NO;
}
```

The problem here is that the programmer neglected to consider what would happen if somebody types a character other than N or Y. In that case, the function simply ends without executing a `return`. To fix the mistake, you could repeat the call to `getchar()` until it returns N or Y, or you could change the `if` statement to:

```
if (c == 'Y')
    return YES;
else
    return NO;
```

The function still ends for any keypress other than N or Y, but now it defines a return value for every possible condition.

Of course, this example is a simple one, and in this case, covering all the bases isn't that difficult. This kind of bug is more common in large functions with many nested `if` statements, which you can test with TD to determine whether the function returns values for all possible exit paths.

To do that, position the cursor on the function's closing brace and press ⟨**F2**⟩. This sets a breakpoint to just before the function ends. Then, press ⟨**F9**⟩ to run the code. When the program halts, use `Data:Function return` to examine the function's value. Repeat this experiment for different sets of input data.

Note: Before rerunning a test with new input data, close the `Function return` window. If you don't, the window may not show the correct value at the next breakpoint. Or, choose `Data:Function return` a second time even if the window is already open (you don't have to close the window first). This forces TD to update the information in the window to show the current return value for the active function.

Confusing Calls by Value and Reference

Technically, all C function arguments are passed by value. C has no equivalent to Pascal's `var` parameter declarations. In C, all function parameters receive copies of passed arguments—a scheme that seems simple enough but can lead to trouble when those values are pointers.

Confusing the two kinds of arguments—those that are passed by value and those that are passed by reference—can lead to all sorts of nasty surprises. Even though ANSI C function prototypes can help prevent mistakes before they do any damage, it's still possible to fool the compiler with code such as:

```
void parameters(long *p1, long *p2)
{
   /* ... statements */
}
```

Function `parameters` declares two pointer parameters to `long` integers, `p1` and `p2`. To pass the address of two `long` arguments `x` and `y` to the function, use a statement similar to this:

```
parameters(&x, &y);
```

That correctly passes the addresses of `x` and `y` to `parameters`. But errors sometimes occur when programmers confuse the address operator (`&`) with a pointer cast. For instance, this is *not* correct:

```
parameters((long *)x, (long *)y);   /* ??? */
```

The first example correctly uses `&` to pass the address of the two variables to the function. The second example incorrectly casts the *value* of the variables into pointers—a mistake that can have serious consequences if the function writes values to those phony addresses. In fact, this error can produce all the horrors of an uninitialized pointer, and because the compiler freely allows recasting variables this way, it does not warn that anything is amiss.

Here's a good way to find this kind of mistake. After loading the program into TD, set a breakpoint on the function you want to monitor. Add the function's parameters to the `Watches` window, which displays the values as `????` because the variables are not yet in scope. This is normal—the actual data will show up later on when the function runs.

Next, press 〈**F9**〉 to run the code and, when it halts, use the `View:Stack` command to list the currently active function calls. Highlight the call immediately below the monitored function, and press 〈**Ctrl**〉**-I** to inspect that source-code line. Then, open an inspector window for each of the arguments in the statement that called the function.

Now, compare the addresses of those variables with the addresses of the function parameters in `Watches`. In all cases, the addresses should match. If they don't, you may have passed an argument by value when you should have passed it by reference.

Function Side Effects

Functions that alter global variables are generally considered to be bad form, although in practice, the technique can be useful. But it can also cause serious bugs, as this code fragment demonstrates:

```
int err;

int error_code()
{
    int temp;

    temp = err;
    err = 0;
    return(temp);
}
```

Function `error_code()` returns the value of a global integer variable `err`, to which another function (not shown) assigns an error code that indicates the success or failure of a preceding I/O operation. As a means of enabling future I/O, `error_code()` resets `err` to 0.

The scheme works well enough, but problems begin if another function calls `error_code()` incorrectly. For example, suppose `err` equals 10 from a previous I/O operation. This is the *wrong* way to check for that error:

```
if (error_code() != 0)
    printf("ERROR: code #%d\n", error_code()); /* ??? */
```

The `if` statement calls `error_code()` to check whether `err` is 0. (Presumably, the global variable `err` is not made available for direct use to other functions.) If the error code is not zero, `printf()` displays a message. But it also calls `error_code()` again to display the error code number. Because the previous call resets `err` to 0, the program always displays:

```
ERROR: code 0
```

This is a good example (and a bad case) of a *function side effect*—a function that affects future runtime behavior by changing global values.

Finding a function side effect requires careful monitoring of the afflicted global variables. This is difficult because you may not know what those variables are, and their symbols may be hidden in a compiled library for which you don't have the source code. If you do have the source or know the addresses of the variables, you can set a `Changed memory global` breakpoint to halt when statements change their values. Or, use `Expression true global` in cases when you know exactly what to look for—in the previous sample, a statement that sets `err` to 0.

In a complex expression where you suspect a function side effect, a good test is to assign all function values to automatic variables and then use the variables in expressions instead of calling the functions directly. Use TD to try out several sets of input data for both forms of the function. If the results differ, the cause might be a function side effect.

Unwanted Recursion

Recursion is a useful feature in C that lets functions call themselves. As a general programming concept, recursion also simplifies "housekeeping" details for some kinds of algorithms—for example, a tree search that works by calling itself at each node in a linked list until finding a target item.

Unwanted recursions are not at all useful. When a function calls itself by accident, the results can range from odd behavior to a fatal stack overflow. Sometimes, programmers accidentally cause an unwanted recursion by writing expressions that use the function's name on the right side of an assignment:

```
result = 2 * f();
```

Normally, this would cause no trouble. But if that statement appears *inside* function `f()`, the compiler generates code to call `f()`, which evaluates the expression, which again calls `f()`, and so on. Usually, the symptom of this problem is a stack-overflow error when the numerous return values, parameters, and automatic variables fill the stack to capacity. Use TD to isolate the place where the error occurs, then trace the code. You'll easily spot where the function calls itself.

A more subtle kind of unwanted recursion—and one that's much more difficult to find—occurs when a function `a()` calls `b()`, which calls `a()` back again. This is called a *mutual recursion*. When it occurs unintentionally, the program may halt with a stack overflow as it can for a plain recursion. But the more common symptoms are incorrect values from expressions or strangely repeating operations that should run only once.

After using TD to narrow the problem to a small section of code, run the affected area to a breakpoint or use the `Run:Animate` command to execute the program in slow motion while you watch the source code in the `Module` window. You might also want to open the `View:Stack` window, which lists function calls. Any accidental recursions should then be obvious.

Numerical Errors

It's difficult to categorize numerical errors—there are countless numbers of bugs that can arise from poorly written expressions. However, a few show up with regular frequency. If you are having trouble with expression results, check these first.

> Hint: Use the `Data` menu's `Evaluate/modify` dialog box to test expressions. To copy an expression from the source text to the dialog box's `Expression` pane, press ⟨**Insert**⟩ and move the cursor (or use a mouse) to highlight the expression in the `Module` view. Then, press ⟨**Ctrl**⟩-⟨**F4**⟩, and press ⟨**Enter**⟩ or click the `Eval` button to evaluate the result.

Bad Operator Precedence

Mistakes with operator precedence can cause so many problems, I prefer to use parentheses lavishly in expressions to force the evaluation order I want. For example, I rarely write expressions like this:

```
x = n + 4 / x;
```

Instead, I'd write the logically equivalent expression:

```
x = (n + 4) / x;
```

For most values of n and x, the two expressions are *not* equivalent. Instead, because division has a higher precedence than addition, most compilers evaluate the former expression as:

```
x = n + (4 / x);
```

But even if that's what I meant to write, I'd include the parentheses to make my intentions clear. It's too easy to introduce bugs by assuming the wrong evaluation order in a complex expression.

Putting the Hex On

You must be careful to express constants in the appropriate radix. The compiler can catch an assignment such as `count = fa29` because it assumes that `fa29` is an identifier. But it can't catch `count = 7659` if you meant that value to be hexadecimal. To assign the correct value, you must write `count = 0x7659`.

Unless you change the default `Integer format` with `Options:Display options`, TD displays values in decimal and hexadecimal. Because this can help you to spot a radix error, it's probably best not to change the default setting. Instead, use the formatting options (see chapter 9) to display selected variables in the format you want.

File Handling

There are countless bad turns you can make in programs that read and write data to disk files. But, before embarking on an extended debugging session to find your mistakes, eliminate the possibilities listed in this section.

Forgetting to Close Open Files

As a rule, you should close all open files before a program ends. This ensures that the DOS directory entry for the file is properly updated and that any data held in memory is flushed to disk. It also releases DOS file handles for future use.

But if you are using a modern C compiler and DOS 2.0 or later, this error isn't that likely to occur because most programs end via DOS function 0x4C, which automatically closes any open file handles before passing control back to COMMAND.COM. Other functions, such as 0x31 (terminate-and-stay-resident), do not close open files. And, for that reason, it's wise to close your files explicitly—especially when building library functions that you might use later in a resident program.

The symptom of a failure to close file handles is a reduction in the number of available DOS handles for new files; therefore, the error frequently shows up later when you run the next program and execute a statement that attempts to open a new file. If that fails due to a lack of file handles, the problem may be in an earlier function, or it might even be in another program that you ran before this one.

Not Checking for I/O Errors

I'm always amazed at the amount of code that fails to take I/O errors into account. Disks do become full, write-protect tabs are sometimes covered when they should be uncovered, and disk sectors can become unreadable. Careful programmers test for I/O errors after every significant I/O operation.

In C programs that use file streams, `ferror()` tests for I/O errors. After detecting errors that way, a common mistake is to forget to call `clearerr` to allow future I/O to continue. Another mistake is forgetting that `rewind` clears any unserviced I/O errors.

Neglecting to Use Pointers in scanf( )

Except for the initial formatting string, all arguments in `scanf()` calls must be pointers to variables. A common error is to write code like this:

```
int count;

printf("? ");
scanf("%d", count); /* ??? */
```

While this appears to prompt for an integer value `count`, because that variable is passed incorrectly by value to `scanf()`, the result is a serious bug. At best, `count` will not have the value entered by the operator. At worst, the system will crash when `scanf()` writes data over other variables, code, or the stack. The correct way to write the previous sample is:

```
printf("? ");
scanf("%d", &count);
```

In this case, `&count` passes the *address* of `count` to `scanf()`, which fills in the variable with a value from the standard input, usually the keyboard.

Remember too that string arrays are pointers; therefore, you can pass them directly to `scanf()`. For a string declared as `char s[80];`, use this expression to input text:

```
scanf("%s", s);
```

The string variable `s` is an array, which is equivalent to a pointer; therefore, specifying `&s` in this case would be incorrect as that would pass the address of the pointer, not the array. As this demonstrates, it's not enough just to hunt for `scanf()` function calls with arguments not prefaced with `&`. You must also examine the data types of the arguments to find mistakes. (Inspector windows are good for this.)

Bad Breaks

A `break` statement causes a loop or a `switch` statement to terminate immediately. This section discusses a few of the more common bugs associated with `break`.

Nested Breaks

When `break` executes, the currently active `for`, `while`, or `do` loop ends. A common bug is caused by executing a `break` at the wrong level in a deeply nested set of loops. Although contrived, the following code demonstrates the problem:

```
for (i = 1; i < 10; i++) {
   printf("\n%d: ", i);
   for (j = 1; j < 10; j++) {
      printf("%d ", j);
   if (i >= 5) break;   /* ??? */
   }
}
```

This fragment should write five sets of ten values, but it halts early by a `break` when `i >= 5`. From the indentation, it appears as though the programmer intended the `break` to exit the outermost loop, but because it executes while the inner `for` is active, the program displays:

```
1: 1 2 3 4 5 6 7 8 9
2: 1 2 3 4 5 6 7 8 9
3: 1 2 3 4 5 6 7 8 9
4: 1 2 3 4 5 6 7 8 9
5: 1
6: 1
7: 1
8: 1
9: 1
```

Loading the program into TD and tracing the code proves that the outer loop continues to run even after executing `break`. Only the inner loop is prevented from finishing.

Having found the problem, the fix is to move the `break` to the correct level:

```
for (i = 1; i < 10; i++) {
   printf("\n%d: ", i);
```

```
    for (j = 1; j < 10; j++)
        printf("%d ", j);
    if (i >= 5) break;
}
```

Now, when the program runs, it displays the correct results:

```
1: 1 2 3 4 5 6 7 8 9
2: 1 2 3 4 5 6 7 8 9
3: 1 2 3 4 5 6 7 8 9
4: 1 2 3 4 5 6 7 8 9
5: 1 2 3 4 5 6 7 8 9
```

Broken Continuations

Related to a bad `break` is a bug caused by confusing `break` and `continue`. A `continue` statement causes the currently active loop to start with the next iteration; `break` exits the loop immediately. Single stepping a few test loops in TD is a good way to learn the difference between `break` and `continue` and to determine whether you've used the wrong one.

Forgetting Break in a Switch Statement

In a `switch` statement, executing `break` jumps to the statement that follows the `switch`. There are two places where this use of `break` typically leads to bugs.

The first occurs when a `break` is purposely left out of `switch` in order to allow multiple selectors to activate a code section. For example, suppose you want to execute a series of statements from a different "entry point" depending on the value of an integer i. If i equals 3, you want to execute statements 3, 4, and 5; if it's 4, you want to execute statements 4 and 5; if it's 5, you want to execute only statement 5. A `switch` statement is the ideal choice for solving this kind of problem:

```
i = 3;
switch (i) {
    case 1 : printf("case 1\n"); break;
    case 2 : printf("case 2\n"); break;
    case 3 : printf("case 3\n");
    case 4 : printf("case 4\n");
    case 5 : printf("case 5\n"); break;
    default : break;
}
/* ... execution continues here after break */
```

Cases 3 and 4 "fall through" to the next statements, allowing multiple selectors to activate a statement series at different starting points. The other cases end with `break`, which passes control to the statement that follows the `switch`.

There is nothing wrong with using `break` this way, but the program is prone to developing a bug if the design changes later and you forget to take into account all the consequences of the programmed fall-throughs. Of course, in a simple example such as this, any errors are easy to see. But typical `switch` statements can occupy pages of printout listings, and they can be nested inside each other, making bugs hard to find.

Remember also to include a `break` as the `default` value, as in the previous sample, even when not strictly needed. The extra `break` occupies very little room and costs nothing in runtime performance. But it can trap errors caused by bad input values to the `switch` statement.

> Hint: Set a breakpoint on the default `break`, and the program will halt if the `switch` statement ever receives an out-of-range selector.

Summary

C is a well-respected language with many useful features. But it also allows programmers to get away with source-code murder. Bugs in C range from simple typos to uninitialized variables, mishandled arrays, bad pointers, problems with function parameters, and other problems.

Getting to know the common C bugs in this chapter is a good way to prevent them from occurring in your own code. And, when bugs do happen, you can use this knowledge to help find the source of the problems with TD.

Chapter 11

Hands-On Debugging for C

To GAIN EXPERIENCE in the art of debugging, there's nothing like a little on-the-job training. In this chapter, you'll enter a buggy *Turbo C* program—a UNIX-like replacement for the DOS DIR command—which is long enough to be interesting, but not so long as to discourage you from typing it into your editor. Then, you'll follow the steps outlined in chapter 7 to develop a debugging strategy for five mischievous bugs. After fixing each problem, you'll retest the code to be sure the bugs stay dead.

You can also use this chapter as a self test of the information you've learned so far. After reading about each bug, watch for this note:

Self test: Stop reading now.

When you see that message, stop reading and try to find and fix the problem. Continue reading after you've discovered the solution or if you're stuck and need more help. Don't be concerned if you can't find all the bugs on your own. It's more important to try and fail than never to try at all.

Note: Some of the text in this chapter also appears in the hands-on debugging sessions for Pascal and assembly language in chapters 13 and 15. Despite these similarities, the programs and bugs in each of these chapters are *different*—you can read one chapter and take the self test, or read them all.

Debugging Strategy Review

Before turning to the buggy program, it will be helpful to review the steps of a good debugging strategy from chapter 7. Remember to apply these steps if you're taking the self test.

The key to all debugging strategies is to avoid hunting through code looking for errors. Try not to figure out the cause of a bug. Develop good tests and use TD to divide and conquer. Force bugs into the open where you can trap them. Don't be clever, be methodical.

Briefly, here are the four steps that you should follow to find and fix each bug in this chapter's sample program. You might also want to reread "Debugging Strategies" near the end of chapter 7:

- *Test:* Design good tests to force bugs to appear. Don't just "play" with the program. Use the same care to write test procedures and to create test data that you use for the main code. Test extreme ranges and take good notes. (If this were a real program in development, you would also want to test as you go rather than wait until the program is done to begin testing.)

- *Stabilize:* Write down the steps required to reproduce the problem. If you can't cause a bug to repeat, you won't be able to prove later that you've fixed the mistake. Always nail your bugs to the ground before attempting to fix them.

- *Isolate:* Use TD to isolate the section of code that's causing the problem. Divide and conquer. Concentrate on finding *where,* not *why,* a bug appears. Work quickly until you've narrowed the search to a reasonably small section that you can examine in finer detail.

- *Repair:* You've found the bug. Quit TD and fix the mistake. But, before continuing to program (or to move on to the next bug in this chapter's simulation), be sure to document what you did to repair the mistake. And, most important, repeat your earlier tests to verify that the bug is gone for good.

The Program

Enter Listing 11.1 and save it in a file named LS.C. Remember not to enter the line numbers added for reference along the left border. Then, compile to LS.EXE with the integrated *Turbo C* editor and compiler as explained in chapter 2, or use this command to compile with the command-line compiler:

```
tcc -v ls
```

You may use either *Turbo C* 2.0 or *Turbo C++* 1.0 to compile the sample program.

Note: After finding each bug and making the suggested changes to LS.C, enter that same command to recompile the modified listing.

Listing 11.1. LS.C (with bugs).

```
 1:  /*
 2:  **     Purpose: List files (WITH BUGS!)
 3:  **     Author:  (c) 1990 by Tom Swan.
 4:  */
 5:
 6:  /* ---- Include header files */
 7:  #include <stdio.h>
 8:  #include <mem.h>
 9:  #include <dos.h>
10:  #include <dir.h>
11:
12:  /* ---- Define constants */
13:  #define  NUM_COLUMNS    5
14:  #define  COLUMN_WIDTH   15
15:  #define  FNAMESTR_LEN   12
16:
17:  /* ---- File date bit fields */
18:  typedef struct DATEFIELD {
19:     unsigned day : 5;
20:     unsigned month : 4;
21:     unsigned year : 7;
22:  } dateField;
23:
24:  /* ---- File time bit fields */
25:
26:  typedef struct TIMEFIELD {
27:     unsigned int hour : 5;
28:     unsigned int minute : 6;
29:     unsigned int second : 5;
30:  } timeField;
31:
32:  /* ---- Linked list entries */
33:  typedef struct ITEM *itemPtr;
34:  typedef struct ITEM {
35:     itemPtr next;
36:     char attr;
37:     timeField time;
38:     dateField date;
```

```
39:    long size;
40:    char name[13];
41: } item;
42:
43: /* ---- Function prototypes */
44: void getOptions(int argc, char *argv[]);
45: void instruct(void);
46: int  isFile(char *path);
47: void fixPath(char *path);
48: itemPtr newItem();
49: void readDirectory(void);
50: int  itemCmp(const void*, const void*);
51: void sortDirectory(void);
52: void writeBlanks(int numBlanks);
53: void writeDate(dateField date);
54: void writeTime(timeField time);
55: void writeAttributes(char attr);
56: void writeItem(itemPtr p);
57: void displayByRows(void);
58: void displayByCols(void);
59:
60: /* ---- Options and their default values */
61: enum boolean { FALSE, TRUE };
62: enum boolean OPT_ALLFILES = FALSE;
63: enum boolean OPT_HELP = FALSE;
64: enum boolean OPT_LONG = TRUE;
65: enum boolean OPT_ROWORDER = FALSE;
66: enum boolean OPT_SORT = FALSE;
67: enum boolean OPT_UPPERCASE = FALSE;
68:
69: /* ---- Global variables */
70: itemPtr *indexArray;        /* Pointer array for sorting */
71: char path[79] = "*.*";      /* Path name and default value */
72: itemPtr root;               /* Directory list pointer */
73: int dirCount;               /* Number of list entries */
74:
75: /* ---- The main program function */
76: main(int argc, char *argv[])
77: {
78:    getOptions(argc, argv);
79:    if (OPT_HELP)
80:       instruct();
81:    readDirectory();
82:    if (dirCount == 0)
83:       printf("\n%s\n", "No files");
```

```
84:      else {
85:         sortDirectory();
86:         if (OPT_ROWORDER || OPT_LONG)
87:            displayByRows();
88:         else
89:            displayByCols();
90:      }
91:      return 0;
92:  }
93:
94:  /* ---- Interpret command-line options */
95:  void getOptions(int argc, char *argv[])
96:  {
97:      unsigned char ch;
98:      char *p;
99:
100:     while (--argc > 0) {
101:        p = *++argv;
102:        if (*p != '-' && *p != '/')
103:           strcpy(path, p);            /* Set path or wild card */
104:        else {
105:           if (strlen(p) == 1)
106:              ch = '?';                 /* If no option letter */
107:           else
108:              ch = *(p + 1);            /* else ch == option letter */
109:           switch (toupper(ch)) {
110:              case 'A' :
111:                 OPT_ALLFILES = TRUE;
112:                 break;
113:              case 'H' :
114:                 OPT_HELP = TRUE;
115:                 break;
116:              case 'N' :
117:                 OPT_SORT = FALSE;
118:                 break;
119:              case 'R' :
120:                 OPT_ROWORDER = TRUE;
121:                 break;
122:              case 'W' :
123:                 OPT_LONG = FALSE;
124:                 break;
125:              case 'U' :
126:                 OPT_UPPERCASE = TRUE;
127:                 break;
128:              default:
```

```
129:                    OPT_HELP = TRUE;
130:                    break;
131:              }
132:          }
133:      }
134: }
135:
136: /* ---- Display instructions and halt */
137: void instruct(void)
138: {
139:    printf("\nUsage: LS [option...] [argument] [option...]\n");
140:    printf("\nLS displays a list of files in the current\n");
141:    printf("directory, or in the directory specified by\n");
142:    printf("an optional path and wild-card argument.\n");
143:    printf("Options are:\n\n");
144:    printf("-a   All files\n");
145:    printf("-h   Display this help message\n");
146:    printf("-n   Do not sort file names\n");
147:    printf("-r   Row order (implies -w)\n");
148:    printf("-u   Uppercase display\n");
149:    printf("-w   Wide listing\n");
150:    printf("-?   Same as -h\n\n");
151:    printf("Example: ls -a -w \\mywork\\*.c\n");
152:    exit(0);
153: }
154:
155: /* Return TRUE if path is a file or contains wild cards */
156: int isFile(char *path)
157: {
158:    FILE *f;
159:
160:    if (strchr(path, '*') != NULL || strchr(path, '?') != NULL)
161:       return(TRUE);
162:    else {
163:       if ((f = fopen(path, "r")) == NULL)
164:          return(FALSE);
165:       else {
166:          fclose(f);
167:          return(TRUE);
168:       }
169:    }
170: }
171:
172: /* ---- Prepare path for directory search */
173: void fixPath(char *path)
```

```
174:  {
175:      unsigned char lastch;       /* Last char in path */
176:
177:      if (!isFile(path)) {
178:          lastch = path[strlen(path)-1];
179:          if (lastch != ':')                /* e.g. "a:" */
180:              if (lastch != '\\')           /* e.g. "\path\" */
181:                  strcat(path, "\\");       /* Append '\' */
182:          strcat(path, "*.*");              /* Append wild card */
183:      }
184:  }
185:
186:  /* ---- Return pointer to new list item */
187:  itemPtr newItem()
188:  {
189:      return ((itemPtr) malloc(sizeof(item)));
190:  }
191:
192:  /* ---- Read directory into linked list */
193:  void readDirectory(void)
194:  {
195:      struct ffblk fb;       /* File search block */
196:      int searchAttr;        /* Search attribute */
197:      int done;              /* True when search is done */
198:      itemPtr p;             /* Pointer to list items */
199:
200:      root = NULL;              /* Start new list */
201:      if (OPT_ALLFILES)        /* Determine search attribute */
202:          searchAttr = 0x3F;        /* All files and directories */
203:      else
204:          searchAttr = 0x10;        /* Normal files and directories */
205:      fixPath(path);
206:      done = findfirst(path, &fb, searchAttr);
207:      while (!done) {
208:          if (root == NULL) {
209:              root = newItem();           /* Insert first list item */
210:              p = root;                   /* Address item with p */
211:          } else {
212:              p->next = newItem();        /* Insert other list items */
213:              p = p->next;                /* Move p to new item */
214:          }
215:          p->next = NULL;              /* Mark end of list */
216:          memcpy(&p->attr, &fb,
217:              sizeof(item) - sizeof(itemPtr)); /* Copy item to list */
218:          if (!OPT_UPPERCASE)
```

```
219:              strlwr(p->name);         /* Convert name to lowercase */
220:          dirCount++;                  /* Count entries in list */
221:          done = findnext(&fb);
222:        }
223:  }
224:
225:  /* ---- Compare two directory names for qsort() */
226:  int itemCmp(const void *item1, const void *item2)
227:  {
228:      return(strcmp(
229:          (*(itemPtr *)item1)->name,
230:          (*(itemPtr *)item2)->name ));
231:  }
232:
233:  /* ---- Prepare directory index and sort entries */
234:  void sortDirectory(void)
235:  {
236:      itemPtr p;             /* Pointer to list items */
237:      unsigned int i;        /* Array index */
238:
239:  /* Prepare array of pointers to listed items */
240:      if (dirCount > 0) {
241:          indexArray =
242:              (itemPtr *) malloc(dirCount * sizeof(itemPtr));
243:          p = root;
244:          i = 0;
245:          while (p != NULL) {
246:              indexArray[i++] = p;     /* Add pointer to index */
247:              p = p->next;             /* Move p to next item */
248:          }
249:
250:  /* Sort the pointers array by file name */
251:          if (OPT_SORT && dirCount > 1)
252:              qsort(&indexArray, dirCount, sizeof(itemPtr), itemCmp);
253:      }
254:  }
255:
256:  /* ---- Send numBlanks blanks to std out */
257:  void writeBlanks(int numBlanks)
258:  {
259:      while (--numBlanks >= 0)
260:          putchar(' ');
261:  }
262:
263:  /* ---- Write a file's date */
```

```
264:   void writeDate(dateField date)
265:   {
266:      printf("%4d-%02d-%02d",
267:          date.month, date.day, date.year + 80);
268:   }
269:
270:   /* ---- Write a file's time */
271:   void writeTime(timeField time)
272:   {
273:      unsigned hour;
274:      char *ampm;
275:
276:      hour = time.hour;
277:      if (hour >= 12) {
278:         if (hour != 12)
279:            hour = hour - 12;
280:         ampm = " pm";
281:      } else
282:         ampm = " am";
283:      printf("%4d:%02d%s", hour, time.minute, ampm);
284:   }
285:
286:   /* ---- Write a file's attributes */
287:   void writeAttributes(char attr)
288:   {
289:      char *s = "  ------";
290:
291:      if (attr & FA_RDONLY) s[2] = 'r';
292:      if (attr & FA_HIDDEN) s[3] = 'h';
293:      if (attr & FA_SYSTEM) s[4] = 's';
294:      if (attr & FA_LABEL)  s[5] = 'v';
295:      if (attr & FA_DIREC)  s[6] = 'd';
296:      if (attr & FA_ARCH)   s[7] = 'a';
297:      printf("%s", s);
298:   }
299:
300:   /* ---- Write one directory item */
301:   void writeItem(itemPtr p)
302:   {
303:      unsigned int width;
304:
305:      if (!OPT_LONG)
306:         width = COLUMN_WIDTH;
307:      else
308:         width = FNAMESTR_LEN + 1;
```

```
309:     printf("%s", p->name);
310:     writeBlanks(width - strlen(p->name));
311:     if (OPT_LONG) {
312:        if (p->attr & FA_DIREC)
313:           printf("<DIR>   ");   /* <DIR> + 3 blanks */
314:        else
315:           printf("%8ld", p->size);
316:        writeDate(p->date);
317:        writeTime(p->time);
318:        writeAttributes(p->attr);
319:     }
320:  }
321:
322:  /* ---- Display directory in row order */
323:  void displayByRows(void)
324:  {
325:     unsigned int i;
326:
327:     if (dirCount > 0) {
328:        printf("\n");
329:        for (i = 1; i <= dirCount; i++) {
330:           writeItem(indexArray[i - 1]);
331:           if (i % NUM_COLUMNS == 0 || OPT_LONG)
332:              printf("\n");
333:        }
334:        if (!OPT_LONG && dirCount % NUM_COLUMNS != 0)
335:           printf("\n");
336:     }
337:  }
338:
339:  /* ---- Display directory in column order */
340:  void displayByCols(void)
341:  {
342:     unsigned int rows, i, j;
343:
344:     if (dirCount > 0) {
345:        printf("\n");
346:        rows = (dirCount / NUM_COLUMNS);
347:        if (dirCount % NUM_COLUMNS != 0)
348:           rows++;
349:        for (i = 1; i <= rows; i++) {
350:           j = i;
351:           while (j <= dirCount) {
352:              writeItem(indexArray[j - 1]);
353:              j += rows;
```

```
354:              }
355:              if (j > dirCount)
356:                  printf("\n");
357:          }
358:      }
359:  }
```

Hands-On Debugging Sessions

Each of the following sections begins with a description of a bug in LS.C. The descriptions simulate the early stages of debugging when you know that something isn't operating as expected, but you don't know exactly what has gone wrong. Perhaps a customer telephoned to complain about a strange occurrence, or you've added new programming, and the code, which seemed to work correctly until now, suddenly failed. All you know at this stage is that the program isn't working. You don't know why.

If you're taking the self test, after reading the description of the bug, put the book aside and try to find and fix the mistake on your own. Then, whether or not you're taking the self test, follow the step-by-step numbered sections to run through the TD commands that I used to locate the bug. Do this even if you've successfully located the bug on your own. That way, you can compare your debugging strategy with mine.

Be careful to keep LS.C up to date. Some of the later bugs depend on earlier ones, and you must complete sections 1 through 5 in that order, or the step-by-step instructions will be meaningless. A useful plan is to copy LS.C to LSTEST.C for taking the self tests. Make your own changes only to LSTEST.C. Then, after finishing each self test, compile and load the current LS.C file into TD, and follow the step-by-step debugging demonstrations after the "stop reading" note. Make the changes suggested in the text directly to LS.C. You can then copy the partially debugged LS.C again to LSTEST.C to take the next bug's self test.

You might also want to copy the original, unmodified LS.C to another file, perhaps named LSBUG.C, so you or someone else can repeat the hands-on demonstrations in the future without having to retype the listing. This will also let you start over in case you mix up the files. If that happens, just copy the master LSBUG.C to LS.C and make the suggested changes to LS.C up to the point where you stopped.

Note: Line numbers in the text refer to Listing 11.1 as printed in this chapter. After you make the first set of changes to LS.C, your editor's line numbers may not match those in the listing. For that reason, when I suggest adding new statements, for example between lines 45 and 46, use the printed listing as a guide to locate the place in your up-to-date LS.C file where you should make those changes.

Using LS.C

If the program didn't have any bugs, it would list the files in the current or another directory. Similar to the UNIX LS command, the program understands the options listed in Table 11.1. Of course, you'll have to find and fix the bugs in the program before these options will work.

Table 11.1.   LS.C options.

Option	Description
-a	All files, including those normally hidden
-h	Display helpful instructions
-n	Do not sort file names
-r	Display wide listing in row order
-u	Uppercase display (normally lowercase)
-w	Wide listing in column order
-?	Same as -h

How LS.C Works

Finding bugs is always easier when you're familiar with the code. If LS.C was your program, you'd have a good idea where to look for certain kinds of bugs. But, because you've never seen this program before, debugging its statements will be more difficult than normal. These notes will help fill that gap.

Many of LS's functions have obvious purposes—setting various options, displaying instructions, preparing wild cards and path names for directory searching, and converting directory information to the proper formats for display. Because the program sorts the directory by file name (unless you've turned off sorting with the -n option) it has to read all file names into memory, sort them, and then display the information.

To do that, LS stores directory entries on a linked list (see Figure 11.1). Each listed entry contains the name of a file plus other information such as its date, time, and size (see `struct item` at lines 34–41). A single pointer named `root` (line 72) addresses the first entry of the list. Another variable `dirCount` (line 73) counts the number of entries in this list. If `root == NULL` or `dirCount == 0`, the list is empty.

For easy sorting, LS also prepares an array of pointers `indexArray` (line 70) that addresses the items in the linked list. As Figure 11.1 shows, each array element points to one linked list entry, giving LS two ways to access the directory information stored in memory. It can follow the `next` fields in the list, hopping from one directory entry to the next, or it can run through all entries in the indexed array. Sorting is kept fast by rearranging the pointers in `indexArray` rather than shuffling the larger directory items or fussing with the list's `next` links. This also makes it easy for the program to display sorted and unsorted file lists. (For example, you could revise the program to display both kinds of lists without having to reread the directory from disk. Don't try this before fixing the bugs, though!)

Another global variable `path` at line 71 addresses the requested path and wild card such as C:\MYWORK\ *.C that you can enter as an argument when running LS. If you enter no such argument, `path` defaults to the string "*.*".

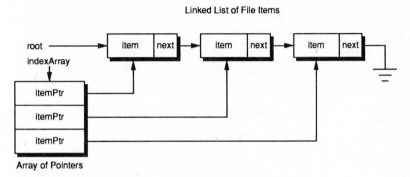

Figure 11.1. LS stores file entries in a linked list.

Bug Number 1

You've just completed the first version of LS.C, and you're ready for a test run. You should have debugged the code as you programmed each new function, but you were in a hurry to finish before the weekend. Now, you've got trouble.

When you compile and run the program by typing **ls** and pressing ⟨**Enter**⟩ at the DOS prompt, you discover a serious problem—the display looks somewhat like a directory, but its contents are unreadable. Something is trashing the directory names. Could this be caused by a bad pointer?

Self test: Stop reading now.

Bug number 1—Test

You've already performed the only primary test possible for now—running the program. Because it fails so miserably, there's not much else you can do to test the code at this stage.

Bug number 1—Stabilize

Even though testing seems pointless (you know the program is broken), a *repeatable* test is a major element in all good debugging strategies. Without a repeatable test, you'll have no way to verify that you've fixed a bug after you discover what's wrong. Here's the stabilizing test that I devised:

1. Create a temporary directory named TEMP with the DOS command **md temp**. Use the command **copy ls.c temp** to copy a test file to the directory so LS has at least one file name to list.

2. Enter the command **ls temp** to list the contents of the TEMP directory.

3. Enter the command **dir temp** to use the DOS DIR command to list the same directory. Compare the results from step 2. They should list similar information.

This simple but effective test stabilizes the bug in three ways. It prepares useful test data (the TEMP directory). It describes how to run LS to reproduce the problem. And, it provides a way to verify whether the program works (using DIR). The next step is to find the cause of the bug.

Bug number 1—Isolate

Obviously, the program's output is faulty. This might be caused by a bug in the output routines, or it could be caused by faulty input. Or, both input and output routines could be broken. When faced with similar situations, remember to divide and conquer. Don't peer into every corner looking for bugs. Isolate their nesting grounds so you can smoke them out.

Since input precedes output, let's first be sure that the program is reading the directory correctly. There's no sense wasting time investigating the output routines until we determine whether the input is getting in. Follow these steps:

1. Load LS.EXE into TD by typing the command **td ls temp**. (Supplying the temp argument now is easier than using the Run:Arguments command in TD later, which would have the same effect.)

2. Because root addresses the linked list of file-name entries (see Figure 11.1), it seems like a good idea to monitor that pointer's value. Our first goal is to examine how the file list forms. To add root to the Watches view, move the cursor up a few lines to any character in the identifier root (line 72) and press ⟨Ctrl⟩-W. The window shows the pointer's data type and its current value, ds:0000.

3. Press ⟨F8⟩ to step over each statement in main() until root's value changes. (I had to press ⟨F8⟩ four times.) This proves that readDirectory() is changing root—the expected behavior.

4. The directory should now be in memory, stored in the list that `root` addresses. To find out if that's so, press ⟨**F6**⟩ to make `Watches` the active window and then press ⟨**Ctrl**⟩-**I** to inspect the `item` addressed by `root`. Notice that, although the inspector window lists the correct field names for a directory item, the contents are gibberish. Obviously, `readDirectory()` is not preparing the linked list as it should.

5. We need to dig deeper to investigate how `readDirectory()` forms the list. To do that, press ⟨**Esc**⟩ to close the inspector window and ⟨**F6**⟩ to make `Module` the active window again. Move the cursor up one line to `readDirectory()` and press ⟨**F2**⟩ to set a breakpoint on that line. Press ⟨**Ctrl**⟩-⟨**F2**⟩ to reset the program and press ⟨**F9**⟩ to run. When the breakpoint stops the program, press ⟨**F7**⟩ to trace into `readDirectory()`. (This is a typical sequence. First, step over various statements looking for changes to variables or other events. Then, set a breakpoint just above that location, rerun the program, and trace into a suspicious function call.)

6. The cursor should now be on the entry to `readDirectory()`. Next, let's find out exactly where `root` changes. Press ⟨**Alt**⟩-**BC** to set a `Changed memory global` breakpoint and enter **root** into the prompt box. Press ⟨**Enter**⟩ or click the `Ok` button to close the box. You don't have to specify `root`'s size—TD uses the variable's size as the default `count` value.

7. Press ⟨**F9**⟩ to continue running the program. In a moment, the breakpoint halts the program at `#LS#210`. (The line number may be different on your screen.) Press ⟨**Enter**⟩ to clear the breakpoint message window and notice that a statement has just assigned to `root` the address of a new item, allocated by function `newItem()`. To examine that item, press ⟨**F6**⟩ to make `Watches` current and then press ⟨**Ctrl**⟩-**I**. So far so good—the program hasn't assigned any information to the new item, so the gibberish inside the structure is expected.

8. The program is paused inside the `while` loop that reads directory information from disk. Press ⟨**Cursor Down**⟩ twice to highlight the `attr` field in the inspector, then type **0** and press ⟨**Enter**⟩. This initializes the field value so we can detect any changes made to it. Often, when variables appear to be assigned scrambled information, it's a good idea to initialize suspect variables this way. Otherwise, it's easy to miss where the faulty assignment occurs. To continue looking for that assignment, press ⟨**F7**⟩ four times to trace each statement while you watch the `attr` field in the inspector window for changes. (Notice that you can trace the code even though the inspector is the top window—you don't have to make `Module` the active window to do this.)

9. The inspector's contents change after the call to `memcpy` at line 216. But the information inside the newly allocated item is still gibberish; therefore, we know the bug occurs somewhere in the previous four lines, probably at `memcpy`.

10. Some programmers at this point would trace the machine code to `memcpy`, hoping to find a mistake in the runtime library. Don't do this—at least not until you've verified that you have used that routine correctly.

11. So, let's look at the source of the data for `memcpy`. Because we've already executed that line, press **⟨Alt⟩-⟨F4⟩** to go back one step, undoing the effects of the function call. Notice that this also resets the data inside the inspector. Press **⟨F6⟩** to make `Module` the active window. Move the cursor to the line that calls `memcpy` (it should already be on that line), press **⟨Alt⟩-BD** to delete old breakpoints, and press **⟨F2⟩** to set a breakpoint at the new location. This will let us examine each loop as it reads one directory entry from disk.

12. So we can view those entries, move the cursor to the `f` in `&fb`, the argument passed as the source of the memory move. (At this point, local variable `fb` holds raw directory information read from disk.) Press **⟨Ctrl⟩-I** to open an inspector window for this information.

13. Notice that the file name is the single-character string `.\0`, which represents the current directory. (If you don't see this string, make sure that `Options:Language` is set to `Source`.) Press **⟨F9⟩** to run another loop and the string changes to `..\0` representing the directory on the previous level. Press **⟨F9⟩** again. This time, the name field equals `LS.C\0`. From these tests, it seems as though the program is reading directory information into `fb` correctly.

14. Where was that inspector to `root`? Press **⟨Alt⟩-3** to bring its window forward and compare the two structures. (You may have to rearrange the windows so you can see both at the same time. If you accidentally closed the inspectors, open two of them for `root` and `fb` using the `Data:Inspect` command.) Obviously, the two records are different, even though the `memcpy` function should have assigned the contents of `fb` to the item addressed by `root`. No doubt about it, this is the bug.

Notice that the first field in `fb` is `ff_reserved`. The real information begins at the next field—`ff_attrib`. And this is the problem. As now written, the call to `memcpy` transfers information from the *start* of `fb` instead of from the beginning of the `ff_attrib` field. The program reads the directory information correctly but assigns the wrong bytes to the items on the linked list.

Bug number 1—Repair

As it often happens, the repair is easy once you've located the source of the trouble. Quit TD (press **⟨Alt⟩-X**) and load LS.C into your editor. Then, change line 216 to:

```
memcpy(&p->attr, &fb.ff_attrib,
```

Recompile (**tcc -v ls**) and run the repeatable test (**ls temp**). You should now see normal file names and other directory information. Run the DOS DIR command on the same directory (**dir temp**) to prove that the bug is fixed. Apparently, it is. But, the program still isn't working correctly. LS and DIR now show the same basic information, but the file times are different.

Bug Number 2

After fixing the first bug in LS, you retested the program and discovered another problem—DOS DIR and LS report different times for the same files. This is common. You fix one bug, and another surfaces. Good! This shows that your testing strategies are flushing out bugs before your customers will see them.

Of course, the bad news is: you have another bug to fix.

Self test: Stop reading now.

Bug number 2—Test

To provide a few more test files, enter the DOS command **copy ls.* temp**. Or, copy a few files from another directory. For a completely thorough test, you could prepare dummy files with various dates and times including midnight and noon. But you don't have to do that for this demonstration.

Bug number 2—Stabilize

The steps for stabilizing this bug are the same as before—enter the commands **ls temp** and **dir temp**. You may also want to print copies of these test results for reference while debugging. To do that, assuming you have a printer, of course, enter the commands **ls temp >prn** and **dir temp >prn**. If you don't have a printer, refer to Figure 11.2. (Of course, the file dates and times will be different on your display.)

```
                                           C:\>dir temp

                                           Volume in drive C is HARD DISK C
       C:\>ls temp                         Directory of  C:\TEMP

       .          <DIR>   4-25-90  16:47 pm  ----d-    .           <DIR>         4-25-90  11:47a
       ..         <DIR>   4-25-90  16:47 pm  ----d-    ..          <DIR>         4-25-90  11:47a
       ls.c        9422   3-27-90   4:49 am  ----da    LS    C      9422         3-27-90  10:49a
       ls.obj      3624   4-25-90   7:49 am  ----da    LS    OBJ    3624         4-25-90  11:49a
       ls.exe     11060   4-25-90   8:49 am  ----da    LS    EXE   11060         4-25-90  11:49a
                                                        5 File(s)  19742720 bytes free
```

Figure 11.2. Sample directories of TEMP.

Notice that the file sizes and dates appear to be correct. This suggests that most of the program is working. Only the file times are wrong. The job, then, is to isolate the section of buggy code that's responsible for displaying file times.

Bug number 2—Isolate

Type **td ls temp** to load LS into TD. Again, supplying the **temp** argument now is easier than using a command to do that later. Because we know that something is wrong with the file times, we may as well start investigating the code that's responsible for displaying those times. Follow these steps:

1. Press ⟨**Ctrl**⟩**-G** to choose the Module window's Goto command. Enter **writeTime** and press ⟨**Enter**⟩ to jump to that routine's source. (This is a handy way to hop to specific functions. When you know the function names, using Goto is much faster than paging through a long file looking for subroutines.)

2. Press ⟨**F2**⟩ to set a breakpoint on the function declaration (line 271 in the listing). We want to examine time arguments passed to the function, so move the cursor to the t in time at the end of this line and press ⟨**Ctrl**⟩**-I** to open an inspector window for this parameter.

3. Oops! TD displays the error message "Cannot access an inactive scope." This makes sense. No statement has called writeTime; therefore, its parameters don't yet exist. Press ⟨**Esc**⟩ to clear the error message and press ⟨**F9**⟩ to run the program up to the breakpoint you set earlier. (The cursor should still be on time.) Press ⟨**Ctrl**⟩**-I** again. This time, the inspector opens because the parameter is "visible" within the current scope.

4. If you printed a directory listing, compare it with the information in the window. (If you don't have a printer, refer to Figure 11.3. Of course, the information shown here will differ from the text on your display.) The inspector shows the time for the first file. Compare that time with DIR's output (Figure 11.2 if you don't have a printer). It looks as though the values for struct's hour and second fields at far right in the window are reversed. (The hour is in 24-hour time.)

5. Note the struct values and press ⟨**F9**⟩. This runs the program to the next writeTime call. Press ⟨**Alt**⟩-⟨**F5**⟩ to view the program's display. Compare the file time with the values you noted, not the values now on-screen. Note

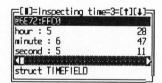

Figure 11.3.   Sample time inspector.

those values for later. Again, `hour` and `second` are reversed. Press ⟨**Enter**⟩ to return to TD's screen.

6. Repeat step 5 once or twice more. In each case, the fields are reversed—the `second` field equals the correct hour as displayed by DIR. Good testing strategies along with TD's ability to examine function arguments took us straight to the buggy code.

Bug number 2—Repair

We've proven that the `dateField` structure's `hour` and `second` fields are reversed. To repair the damage, change that structure's definition at lines 26–30 to:

```
typedef struct TIMEFIELD {
    unsigned int second : 5;
    unsigned int minute : 6;
    unsigned int hour : 5;
} timeField;
```

Recompile and repeat the test to be sure that DIR and LS display the same file times. You might also want to compare the new structure with your DOS reference's description of the time field in a directory entry (not shown here).

Bug Number 3

To the right of every file's date and time, LS is supposed to display the file's attributes. But, as it now operates, LS marks all file entries as directories (with a lowercase d). Worse, trying LS on other directories shows that some entries have the archive bit set; others don't, making it difficult to pin this bug down.

Table 11.2 lists the attribute settings that LS should display for files, directories, and volume labels. But something is causing the program to show the wrong facts.

Table 11.2. LS file attributes.

Attribute	Meaning
a	Archive bit (file is not backed up)
d	File is a directory
h	File is hidden
r	File is marked read-only
s	System file
v	Volume label

> **Self test:** Stop reading now.

Bug number 3—Test

LS seems to have a moving-target bug, one that changes depending on the input fed to the program. In fact, when tested on some directories, the attribute information appears to be correct.

At such times, when your tests indicate that a bug comes and goes as it pleases, list your observations, paying no attention to order. Then, use that knowledge to stabilize the bug. For example, you might observe that:

- When at least one archive marker (a) appears, all subsequent files have the same marker.

- Directories that contain only directories list correctly. Normal files in subdirectories are marked incorrectly as directories.

- In some directories, other false attributes appear. For example, some files are marked as hidden even though they're not.

> Note: It may be difficult for you to simulate all of these effects. Your files are different from mine, and the results of running LS will therefore differ, too. Don't worry about these differences—they won't affect the following hands-on demonstration. If you have a hard drive, try entering **ls -a** \. That should demonstrate that LS is not healthy.

Bug number 3—Stabilize

After recording your observations, look for facts that will help stabilize the bug. In this case, the fact that all files in subdirectories are marked incorrectly as directories gives a simple repeatable test. The other observations may be caused by other bugs, or they might all be related. But to reduce the test to manageable levels, it helps to pick *one* repeatable event and ignore the others.

This is a good rule of thumb to follow. When a bug exhibits many faces, choose one for debugging. By narrowing your sights to one characteristic, you'll simplify the debugging strategy. Then, after fixing that bug, if the others disappear, you can safely assume they were related. If not, you have your next debugging session cut out for you.

If your version of DOS has the ATTRIB command, follow these steps to reproduce the directory and archive flag bugs (or, maybe it's the same bug). If your DOS version doesn't have this command, use a commercial DOS utility to change the archive bit as described here or skip the next four steps and continue reading at "Bug number 3—Isolate." (This will not affect the hands-on demonstration.)

1. Using the TEMP subdirectory from previous tests, enter **attrib -a temp \ *.*** or use a DOS utility to turn off the archive flags for all files in TEMP.

2. Enter **ls temp**. Notice that all files are listed as directories, but none of the archive flags is set.

3. Set the archive bit of the first file in TEMP. For example, if that file is LS.C, type **attrib +a temp \ ls.c**. (You can also use a DOS utility to perform this step.)

4. Enter **ls temp** again. All files are still listed incorrectly as directories. But now, all files also have their archive flags set, even though we set that flag for only one file.

This test describes every step required to reproduce the bug. It takes advantage of the earlier observations that all files are marked as directories and that after one file's archive flag is set, other files show the same flag. The steps are repeatable, nailing down this elusive bug so we can find and fix it.

Bug number 3—Isolate

In a normal setting, you would now load the program into TD and repeat the previous test procedures to reproduce the bug. However, because some DOS versions don't have an ATTRIB command, the following notes skip this part of the debugging strategy. But no matter. TD can still help find the bug.

1. Load LS into TD with the command **td ls temp**.

2. Earlier, you used the Goto command to locate a function's source. Here's another way that's handy when you can't remember the function's exact name. In this case, let's suppose that you know the name begins with "write." Press **⟨Alt⟩-VV** to view the program's variables (actually, the window shows all global and local symbols, not only variables). Because C adds an underscore to symbols, enter **_w**. If you make a mistake, press **⟨Home⟩** and start over. As soon as you type the two characters, the window shifts to the first matching entry. You should see the symbol `_write`. Press **⟨Cursor Down⟩** to highlight the next line (`_writeattributes`) and then press **⟨Enter⟩**. This takes you directly to that function's source.

3. The cursor should be on `writeattributes`' declaration. The function uses one `char` parameter `attr`, which contains a file's attribute bits. A local string

pointer s addresses a string of two blanks plus six dashes—the default settings for a file with no flags. Six `if` statements test bits in `attr` and assign appropriate letters to the string before a call to `printf` displays the result.

4. Apparently, the `if` statements are not setting the correct flags; therefore, let's test the before and after conditions for each call to this function. Because this report will be lengthy, to save time, we'll dump the information to the `Log` view.

5. First, set a breakpoint on the function declaration at line 287 in the original listing. (The cursor should be on that line. If so, just press ⟨**F2**⟩.) Then, without moving the cursor, press ⟨**Alt**⟩-⟨**F2**⟩ to open the `Breakpoint options` dialog box for this breakpoint. Use a mouse or press ⟨**Tab**⟩ and ⟨**Cursor Down**⟩ twice each to change `Action` to `Log`. Then, press ⟨**Tab**⟩ again and enter **attr** as the `Action expression`. Press ⟨**Enter**⟩ to accept your changes. Instead of halting the program, when the program reaches the breakpoint's location, it will now log the value of `attr` for each file that LS lists.

6. Next, set two more breakpoints by moving the cursor and pressing ⟨**F2**⟩— one at the first `if` statement (line 291) and another at `printf` (line 297). As you set each breakpoint, repeat step 5 to change the `Action` to `Log`, but this time enter **s** as the `Action expression` for both breakpoints. (You can set both breakpoints and then modify the options, or do them one at a time.) This will log the string value before and after the `if` statements assign characters to the string.

7. Press ⟨**F9**⟩ to run. Notice that the program operates more slowly as the breakpoint actions write information to the `Log`. When you see the "Terminated" message, press ⟨**Enter**⟩ to clear that window. Then, press ⟨**Alt**⟩-**VL** to open the `Log` window and press ⟨**F5**⟩ to expand the view to full screen.

Note: If TD displays "Not enough memory for selected operation," press ⟨**Esc**⟩ to close the error-message window and then press ⟨**F6**⟩ two or more times to make `Variables` active. Press ⟨**Alt**⟩-⟨**F3**⟩ to close that view, press ⟨**F6**⟩ again until `Log` is active, and then press ⟨**F5**⟩ to zoom the window to full screen.

---

8. You are now seeing the before, during, and (almost) after pictures of each call to `writeAttributes` (see Figure 11.4). The `attr` values appear to be correct—`0x10` is a directory, `0x20` indicates the archive flag is set, and `0x00` is correct for normal files. (A good DOS reference explains these values.) But the before and after strings are odd. At the second call to `writeAttributes` (about eight lines down), the initial string has the same value as it did just before the previous call ended. We've found the bug. The

function is supposed to initialize the string at the beginning of each call. Instead, it uses the left-over string values from previous executions.

```
Turbo Debugger Log
At _writeAttributes attr = char '\x10' 16 (0x10)
At #LS#291 s = char * ds:03AF "  ------"
At #LS#297 s = char * ds:03AF "  ----d-"
At _writeAttributes attr = char '\x10' 16 (0x10)
At #LS#291 s = char * ds:03AF "  ----d-"
At #LS#297 s = char * ds:03AF "  ----d-"
At _writeAttributes attr = char ' ' 32 (0x20)
At #LS#291 s = char * ds:03AF "  ----d-"
At #LS#297 s = char * ds:03AF "  ----da"
At _writeAttributes attr = char '\0' 0 (0x00)
At #LS#291 s = char * ds:03AF "  ----da"
At #LS#297 s = char * ds:03AF "  ----da"
Terminated, exit code 0
```

Figure 11.4. Partial log of calls to writeAttributes.

Bug number 3—Repair

Notice from Figure 11.4 that the `char` variable in `writeAttributes` (line 289 in the original listing) addresses location `ds:03AF` (which might be different on your system). But the variable is supposed to be local to the function—and that's the key to understanding the source of this error.

The declaration `char *s` and the string assignment do not copy the characters from that string to the variable—they merely assign the *address* of the string constant to `s`. Because there is only one copy of the string in memory, any changes are permanent.

Knowing this, the fix is obvious. The function must copy the string constant into another variable, and then insert any flag characters into the fresh copy. To make this change, quit TD, load LS.C into your editor, delete line 289 and, in its place, insert these lines:

```
static char *source = "  ------";
char s[9];

strcpy(s, source);
```

The first line defines a `static char` pointer named `source`, which addresses a constant string of two spaces and six dashes. The second line creates a local `char` pointer s with enough space to hold the eight-character string plus a null terminator. The third line copies the constant string (and its terminator) to the local variable addressed by s.

Now that the string is a proper local variable on the stack, into which the string constant is copied on each call to `writeAttributes`, the problem with file name attributes is gone. After making these changes, run the earlier tests to verify that the attributes display correctly.

Bug Number 4

While finding and fixing the previous three bugs, you may have noticed another one—file names are not sorted alphabetically. And the -n option, which is supposed to turn off sorting, seems to have no effect. (To see the problem, try the commands **ls** and **ls -n**.)

In your own code, when you discover other problems while searching for a bug, note them for later. Resist the temptation to fix every bug in sight. That will only complicate the current debugging strategy. And, if you fix two or more problems at once, you could introduce new errors that your test procedures won't catch.

Self test: Stop reading now.

Bug number 4—Test

Good test data and good debugging strategies go hand in hand. Test data can come from various sources, but often, it's necessary to create some with another program.

For example, Listing 11.2 creates dummy files in the TEMP subdirectory for testing LS's sorting abilities. Save the listing as MAKETEMP.C and compile with the command **tcc maketemp**. Don't run the program yet.

Listing 11.2.   MAKETEMP.C.

```
 1:  /*
 2:  **     Purpose: Make test files in TEMP subdirectory.
 3:  **     Author:  (c) 1990 by Tom Swan.
 4:  */
 5:
 6:  /* ---- Include header file */
 7:  #include <stdio.h>
 8:
 9:  /* ---- Function prototype */
10:  void makefile(char *fname);
11:
```

```
12:  main()
13:  {
14:      makefile("temp\\test.007");
15:      makefile("temp\\zzzzzzzz.zzz");
16:      makefile("temp\\gggggggg.ggg");
17:      makefile("temp\\test.020");
18:      makefile("temp\\s.z");
19:      makefile("temp\\mmmmmmmm.mmm");
20:      makefile("temp\\ssssssss.sss");
21:      makefile("temp\\a.a");
22:      makefile("temp\\test.001");
23:      makefile("temp\\aaaaaaaa.aaa");
24:      makefile("temp\\b");
25:  }
26:
27:  /* ---- Create a file named fname */
28:  void makefile(char *fname)
29:  {
30:      FILE *f;
31:
32:      if ((f = fopen(fname, "w")) == NULL)
33:          printf("%s%s\n", "Error opening ", fname );
34:      else
35:          fclose(f);
36:  }
```

Bug number 4—Stabilize

Follow these steps to create test data for the sorting bug:

1. Enter **del temp**, answer **Y** to the "Are you sure?" prompt from DOS, and then run MAKETEMP (Listing 11.2) to create test files in the empty TEMP subdirectory. If you receive any errors, check that TEMP is in the current directory. If not, enter **md temp** and then run MAKETEMP again.

2. Type **ls temp** to list the files in TEMP. They should be sorted alphabetically, but, obviously, they are not.

3. Type **dir temp** and compare the DOS directory. LS and DIR list files in the same order.

Bug number 4—Isolate

Let's review what we know about LS so far. We know the files are loaded into memory correctly. We know the program can display file names. We also know that the DOS DIR command lists files in the same order as LS, implying that no sorting is taking place. (That's confirmed also by the fact that the -n option doesn't seem to work.)

These observations give valuable clues for debugging. If we assume that no sorting is taking place, then the cause is either a problem with the program's options switches or in the way it calls the library `qsort()` function. The first problem is easy to check, and in fact, doesn't require loading the program into TD. As you can see from the original listing, line 66 sets `OPT_SORT` to the value `FALSE`. But, this should be `TRUE` in order to have the program sort file names by default.

To repair this obvious mistake, load LS.C into your editor, and change line 66 to:

```
enum boolean OPT_SORT = TRUE;
```

Recompile (**tcc -v ls**) and test. Despite fixing the obvious mistake, when you enter **ls temp**, files still aren't sorted correctly. (You may even see some gibberish again on screen.) We may as well assume that `qsort()` works—the library routine may have a bug, but the problem is more likely to be found in way LS calls that routine.

So, let's check the data structures first, then examine how `qsort()` acts on them:

1. Load LS into TD with the command **td -k ls temp**. This passes the TEMP subdirectory name to LS and enables keystroke recording, which we'll use in a moment.

2. We want to test the before and after effects of calling `sortDirectory` at line 85 in the original listing. Move the cursor down to that line (use the cursor movement keys), and press ⟨**F2**⟩ to set a breakpoint there. Then, press ⟨**F9**⟩ to run the program up to that line, halting the program before calling `sortDirectory`.

3. As you recall, LS uses two data structures: a linked list of file entries and an array of pointers that address each entry (see Figure 11.1). To sort the file names, instead of moving the items in the linked list, the sorting routine is supposed to rearrange the pointers in the array.

4. To investigate why this isn't working correctly, first, let's examine the linked list, addressed by `root`. Press ⟨**Alt**⟩-**DI**, type **root**, and press ⟨**Enter**⟩ to open an inspector window to the first item in the list. The top line of the inspector shows the address of the `root` pointer, followed by the address to which the pointer points. It also shows the fields in this item. To examine the next list node, move the highlight bar down one line to the `next` pointer field and press ⟨**Enter**⟩. This opens another inspector window for the item addressed by that field. Repeat this step—highlight `next`

in the new window and press ⟨**Enter**⟩. Notice that the name field shows the file name for this entry. Continue opening inspectors until the next field equals ds:0000, the value that represents NULL and marks the end of the list.

Note: If you see the message "Not enough memory for selected operation," press ⟨**Esc**⟩ two times and then, instead of pressing ⟨**Enter**⟩ to open a new inspector, highlight the next field and press ⟨**Ctrl**⟩-**D** to choose the inspector window's local Descend command. This *replaces* the contents of current inspector with the next item from the list and, therefore, does not require TD to allocate additional memory for another window. Continue highlighting next fields and pressing ⟨**Ctrl**⟩-**D** until next equals ds:0000.

---

5. Apparently, the linked list is sound—all the file names are there. Close all inspectors by pressing ⟨**Alt**⟩-⟨**F3**⟩.

6. Press ⟨**F8**⟩ to step over the call to sortDirectory. Then, examine the indexArray array of pointers, which that function is supposed to initialize and sort. To do this, press ⟨**Alt**⟩-**DI**, type **indexArray** into the prompt box, and press ⟨**Enter**⟩.

7. The array appears to hold only one item at [0], but this is understandable—lines 241–242 allocate only as much memory to the array as needed to hold one pointer for each linked list item, a fact that TD can't know because this calculation is made at runtime. To see the entire array, you have to tell TD the array's current size. Press ⟨**Ctrl**⟩-**R** to select the Range command, press ⟨**Backspace**⟩ once or twice to erase the default range of 5 or 10, enter **dirCount**, and press ⟨**Enter**⟩. (The complete entry should read 0, dirCount.) As lines 241–242 show, LS allocates dirCount * sizeof(itemPtr) bytes to the array. Because TD already knows the array elements are item pointers, you need to tell the debugger how many items (not bytes) to display. Specifying dirCount instead of a literal value is the simplest way to do this.

8. Use a mouse (or ⟨**Ctrl**⟩-⟨**F5**⟩, ⟨**Shift**⟩-⟨**Cursor**⟩, and ⟨**Enter**⟩ keys) to resize the inspector (see chapter 4) to show all 13 elements from [0] to [12]. To examine the data at the addresses in those array positions, move the highlight bar down to any bracketed index and press ⟨**Enter**⟩. After viewing that item, press ⟨**Esc**⟩ to close the inspector window, move the highlight bar to another index, and press ⟨**Enter**⟩. Repeat several times. Notice that the file names are identical to those you examined in the linked list earlier.

9. These examinations tell us that the linked list and the array of pointers contain the expected information. Obviously, then, indexArray's pointers aren't being sorted by sortDirectory. Because we've gone past that

function call, press ⟨**Alt**⟩-⟨**F4**⟩ to back up one statement, and then press ⟨**F7**⟩ to trace into `sortDirectory`. (Leave the `indexArray` inspector open.)

10. You should now see `sortDirectory`'s source code in the `Module` window. (Move the `indexArray` window aside if necessary.) Press ⟨**F6**⟩ twice to make the `Module` window current, move the cursor down to the call to `qsort` (line 252 in the original listing), and press ⟨**F2**⟩ to set a breakpoint there. Then, press ⟨**F9**⟩ to run the program up to that location. We want to investigate what `qsort` does to `indexArray`; therefore, press ⟨**F6**⟩ again to bring the inspector window back into view. Note the addresses in the array and press ⟨**F8**⟩ to step over `qsort`, which should rearrange the addresses in the array. But the addresses didn't change. Why?

11. To find out, we need to dig further into the call to `qsort`, but because this is a library routine, probably coded using instructions that delete TD's event history, we can't back up by pressing ⟨**Alt**⟩-⟨**F4**⟩ as we did earlier. Instead of repeating the previous nine steps manually, press ⟨**Alt**⟩-**VE** to open the `Execution history` view. Press ⟨**Tab**⟩ to move the highlight bar into the bottom pane of this window, which, because we started TD with the -k option, displays recorded events. Press ⟨**Cursor Up**⟩ once to highlight the breakpoint at the call to `qsort`, then press ⟨**Ctrl**⟩-**K**. Thanks to TD's keystroke recording, this repeats all the keystrokes you entered up to that point in time. After a few moments, the action stops with the cursor poised at the `qsort` function call.

12. Press ⟨**Alt**⟩-**VC** to open the `CPU` window, then press ⟨**F7**⟩ seven times to trace each instruction up to (but not including) `call_qsort`. These instructions push arguments onto the stack for the function call. Before tracing that call, let's examine the arguments on the stack, displayed in the lower right pane. Because C pushes function arguments in reverse order, the stack pointer should address the first item in `indexArray`. On my display, the stack shows the address 0778 hex. (This and other addresses may be different on your screen.) To verify this address, press ⟨**F6**⟩ to bring back the `indexArray` window and note the address below the window's top border. (If the window is gone, press ⟨**Alt**⟩-**DI** and enter **indexArray**.) On my display, this line shows `ə63C8:0778 : ds:0A80`. The first address (63C8:0778) shows where the `indexArray` pointer is stored. The second (ds:0A80) shows where that pointer points. But the stack contains the *pointer's* address; therefore, `qsort` is sorting the wrong data! The call to `qsort` should push the pointer's *value,* not its *address*. By isolating the problem and comparing addresses, we found the bug.

13. To verify this without leaving TD, we can patch the argument on the stack. Note the correct address at right on the first line of the inspector (`ds:0A80` for me), press ⟨**F6**⟩ three times to make `CPU` the active window and then press ⟨**Tab**⟩ three times to highlight the stack pane in the lower right corner. Enter the value of the pointer—0x0a80 for me, but probably different for you. Just type this value and press ⟨**Enter**⟩ to change the

word on the stack. Don't forget to preface the hex value with **0x**. Verify that the stack entry changes to the value you enter.

14. Press ⟨**F9**⟩ to run the program to completion. Press ⟨**Enter**⟩ to clear the "Terminated" message. Then, press ⟨**Alt**⟩-⟨**F5**⟩ to view the output. The directory is now sorted correctly. Press ⟨**Enter**⟩ to return to TD.

Bug number 4—Repair

In this case, we know the cause of the bug, and we've already verified the fix by patching a qsort argument on the stack. The bug is caused by passing the value, not the address, of indexArray to qsort. To correct the problem, quit TD, load LS.C into your editor, and change line 252 to:

```
qsort(indexArray, dirCount, sizeof(itemPtr), itemCmp);
```

In other words, remove the **&** from the **&indexArray** argument. All else stays the same. Recompile and test. TEMP and other directories are now sorted correctly.

Bug Number 5

The program seems to be working much better now. Directories are sorted, dates and times appear to be correct, and file sizes compare with the information reported by DOS DIR. It's time to print the labels and ship the product. Right?

Almost. A beta tester just phoned at 4:55 pm on Friday afternoon (and, naturally, you're leaving for the mountains tomorrow) to report that the -r option isn't working. According to the program's documentation, this option is supposed to display a wide directory in row order. Unlike the -w option, which lists files sorted in columns like a newspaper's, the -r option should display files similar to DIR's /w option.

Strangely enough, however, when *combined* with -w, the -r option works as it should! In other words, as the beta tester reported, the command **ls -r temp** fails to produce the expected wide directory, but the two commands **ls -w temp** and **ls -r -w temp** work correctly. You try those three commands and discover the report is correct. Unless you can find and fix the bug quickly, it's goodbye mountains.

Self test: Stop reading now.

Bug number 5—Test

This bug brings up the difficult question, "How much testing is enough?" You can't feed LS and most other programs every possible input value they might have to handle. There's probably not enough time in the universe (not to mention this evening) for that.

Even limiting the tests to all valid program options is impractical—there are 127 unique combinations of LS's seven option letters. (In other words, we can assume that -n -u give the same results as -u -n.) But if option order does matter, it would take 13,699 tests to cover all possible combinations of just seven options! (That is, $7 + (7 \times 6) + (7 \times 6 \times 5) + ... + (7 \times 6 \times 5 \times ... \times 1)$.)

Devising good tests that cover midrange and extreme cases is the only reasonable answer to this common dilemma. It's just not possible to test every possible input combination. In this simulation, at least we're lucky to know which options work and which don't. But, in "real life," it's often necessary to choose reasonable subsets of all input values to find similar bugs. This points out how important it is to create test data with great care. The success of your programs may depend on it.

Bug number 5—Stabilize

Armed with the TEMP subdirectory from the previous test plus the beta tester's report, we can design a stabilized test procedure:

1. Enter **ls temp**. The directory displays normally.

2. Enter **ls -w temp**. The directory displays correctly in column order.

3. Enter **ls -r temp**. The directory should display in row order. Instead, it shows the same results as in step 1.

4. Enter **ls -r -w temp**. The directory displays correctly in row order. This is the result that should be given for step 3.

Bug number 5—Isolate

The stabilized test suggests an action plan: find and compare the statements that generate the good and bad results. Because some option-letter combinations work correctly, while others don't, comparing the good actions to the bad may tell us what's wrong:

1. Load LS into TD with the command **td ls**. You don't need to supply the TEMP directory name this time.

2. Move the cursor to OPT_ALLFILES (line 62 in the original listing). Press ⟨**Ctrl**⟩-**W** to add this option to the Watches window. Then, move the cursor down to the next option (OPT_HELP) and press ⟨**Ctrl**⟩-**W** to add it to Watches. Repeat these steps four more times to add all seven OPT variables to the window.

3. Press ⟨**Ctrl**⟩-**O** to return to the origin in the Module view. Then, move the cursor to if (OPT_HELP) (line 79) just below the call to getOptions and press ⟨**F2**⟩ to set a breakpoint there. This will stop the program so we can inspect the option settings in Watches. Press ⟨**F6**⟩ to make Watches the active window to make it easy to copy the values to the Log view for later inspection.

4. Type ⟨**Alt**⟩-**RA** and enter the command-line argument **temp**. Press ⟨**Enter**⟩, then press ⟨**Enter**⟩ again to answer Yes to the "Reload program..." prompt, and press ⟨**F9**⟩ to run the program up to the breakpoint. Press ⟨**Alt**⟩-**WD** to dump the current window (Watches) to the Log view.

5. Repeat all keypresses in step 4 three more times with one difference: Each time, substitute for **temp** the test arguments **-w temp**, **-r temp**, and **-r -w temp** from the stabilized test procedure. This copies the entire series of test results to Log, making it easy to compare them.

6. To do that, press ⟨**Alt**⟩-**VL** to open the Log window and press ⟨**F5**⟩ to zoom the window to full screen. You should see four sets of option variables—one set for each of the previous test runs.

7. We know that the last set of values (for options -r -w) represents the values that should be used for the third test (-r). The first two sets show values for tests that work correctly. So, compare the last two sets. The last set should equal the third, but, obviously, it doesn't. OPT_LONG is TRUE in the third set but FALSE in the fourth. This is the reason the directory displays in long form with the -r switch—OPT_LONG should be FALSE to make the directory display in wide style.

8. The next step, then, is to trace into getOptions to see how the program sets options for the -r option. Press ⟨**Alt**⟩-⟨**F3**⟩ to close the Log window, ⟨**F6**⟩ to make Module the active window, and ⟨**F2**⟩ to clear the breakpoint at the if statement. Press ⟨**Alt**⟩-**RA** and enter **-r temp** as the command-line argument, then press ⟨**Enter**⟩ twice to accept the new arguments and reload the program.

9. Press ⟨**F7**⟩ twice to trace into the call to getOptions. Move the cursor to the switch statement (line 109) and press ⟨**F2**⟩ to set a breakpoint there. Press ⟨**F9**⟩ to run up to the breakpoint and move the cursor to ch, the variable that should hold option letters entered as the program's arguments. Press ⟨**Ctrl**⟩-**I** to open an inspector window. This shows the option character to be 'r', which is correct.

10. Press ⟨**Esc**⟩ to close the inspector and press ⟨**F7**⟩ three times to follow the switch statement's logic. It correctly selects case 'R', sets OPT_ROWORDER to TRUE, and hops back to the top of the while.

11. Press ⟨**F7**⟩ four more times to examine the next argument. This time, the program calls strcpy to copy the argument text to the global path. Press ⟨**F7**⟩ once more, and the code jumps to the end of getOptions. Look at the option settings in Watches. OPT_LONG is still TRUE, but it should be false. We've confirmed the bug. OPT_LONG should be set to FALSE to display a wide directory for the -r option.

Bug number 5—Repair

Quit TD and load LS.C into your editor. The obvious repair is to add this statement between lines 120 and 121 (just below OPT_ROWORDER = TRUE):

```
OPT_LONG = FALSE;
```

Although that works, notice that the next case executes this same statement; therefore, another repair is possible, one that employs an infamous C programming trick. Just remove the break statement at line 121, letting the case for 'R' *fall through* to the case for 'W'. You don't need to enter the assignment to OPT_LONG after all. (If you did that, delete the line.)

Often, a problem in a switch statement is caused by a missing break. But, this time, just the opposite caused the bug—an extra break that wasn't needed. Careful comparisons of variables and a repeatable test procedure revealed the cause of the bug.

Be sure to try the **ls -r** and **ls -w** commands to determine whether the bug is fixed. (And, enjoy your trip to the mountains.)

Summary

This chapter lists a buggy program (LS.C), describes five bugs, and shows how to use TD to find the source of each problem. You can use the chapter as a hands-on demonstration of debugging techniques or as a self test of what you've learned so far. (See chapters 13 and 15 for similar hands-on sessions using Pascal and assembly language.)

Chapter 12

Common Pascal Bugs

OF ALL high-level languages, Pascal does more than most to guard against common programming errors. Pascal's strong type-checking and other checks and balances help ensure that assignments and variables passed to procedures and functions are the correct data types. And, in *Turbo Pascal*, automatic range- and stack-checking options can trap problems during compilation and at runtime, preventing many common bugs from taking hold in finished code.

This chapter explores Pascal's well-known (and a few not so well-known) bugs and shows how to use TD to find them. The material is organized by complexity, starting with simple errors in Pascal etiquette and progressing to more scandalous blunders that have been known to crash even the most carefully arranged events in Pascal programs.

Typos and Other Ink Spots

More than a few bugs are caused by simple typing mistakes. Misplaced comment brackets, poor indentation, and accidental redefininition of standard procedures and functions are almost always caused by typos. Like an ink spot on a music score, even one misplaced symbol can throw a Pascal program's orchestration out of tune.

The Case of the Missing Comment Bracket

Unfortunately, TD can't help you to find the first and, perhaps, most common Pascal source code typo. Even so, this bug pops up all the time, and it deserves a dishonorable mention here.

Whenever I receive a strange syntax error message during compilation, I usually find a misplaced comment bracket somewhere. A common symptom of this problem is the *disappearing procedure*, illustrated in Listing 12.1, BADBRACE.PAS.

Listing 12.1.   BADBRACE.PAS (with bugs).

```
 1:  program badBrace;
 2:  var i : integer;
 3:
 4:  procedure something( var i : integer );
 5:  begin
 6:    if i < 100 then inc( i )
 7:      else i := 0;
 8:  end; { something )
 9:
10:  procedure somethingElse;
11:  begin
12:    writeln( 'Value of i = ', i );
13:  end; { somethingElse }
14:
15:  begin
16:    i := 100;
17:    something( i );
18:    somethingElse;    { Unknown identifier error! }
19:  end.
```

Compiling BADBRACE with TP produces `Error 3: "Unknown identifier"` at the last statement before `end`. The error message is no help, however, because the actual mistake occurs much earlier in line 8 at the end of procedure `something`, where a right parenthesis appears instead of the correct right brace. Because Pascal comments may extend over multiple lines, the faulty comment continues to the next right brace—in this case, to the end of the next procedure, `somethingElse`; therefore, the compiler "sees" all of `somethingElse`'s statements as a long comment. Because those statements aren't compiled as instructions, an error occurs when another statement tries to call the procedure. To fix the problem, change line 8 to:

```
8:  end; { something }
```

To determine whether a missing comment bracket is ruining the day, use your editor's search command to locate right and left braces. You can then match them visually. Or, run the GREP utility (located on your TP diskettes) to display all lines with left braces—you might quickly spot a mistake that you may easily miss by hunting through 10,000 lines of source text. (This works only if the program uses single-line comments.) Here's what GREP displayed when I fed it BADBRACE.PAS, using the -n option to display numbered lines containing the character {:

```
C:>grep -n { badbrace.pas
File BADBRACE.PAS:
8        end; { something )
13       end; { somethingElse }
18          somethingElse;   { Unknown identifier error! }
```

ELSE with Wrong IF-THEN

Nested `for` loops are easy prey for a misplaced `else` clause—an error that can be difficult to find. Listing 12.2, BADELSE.PAS, shows a classic case.

Listing 12.2.   BADELSE.PAS (with bugs).

```
1:   program badElse;
2:   uses crt;
3:   var
4:      ch : char;
5:      fileSaved : Boolean;
6:
7:   function answerYes( message : string ) : Boolean;
8:   begin
9:      write( message );
10:     ch := readKey;
11:     writeln( ch );
12:     answerYes := ( ch = 'Y' ) or ( ch = 'y' )
13:   end;
14:
15:   begin
16:     fileSaved := FALSE;
17:     if not fileSaved
18:     then
19:        if answerYes( 'Save file? ' )
20:           then writeln( 'Saving file' )
21:     else
22:        writeln( 'Ending program: file is saved' )
23:   end.
```

BADELSE emulates the way some programs prompt you to save changes to a disk file before quitting. If `fileSaved` is false, the program displays "Save file?" If `fileSaved` is true, the program skips the prompt and tells you the file is saved—or, at least, that's what should happen. (The sample doesn't actually write any file data, so don't be concerned about erasing something by accident.) When you answer **N** to the "Save file?" prompt, instead of quitting as it should, the program displays "Ending program: file saved."

Obviously, BADELSE has a bug—apparently caused by line 22 executing for the wrong condition, that is, when `fileSaved` is false. That line should execute only when `fileSaved` is true. Now that the bug is out in the open and stabilized by a repeatable test, the next step is to load the program into TD and look for the cause.

First, set a breakpoint on the statement (line 22) that's executing out of place. Then, open the `View` menu's `Breakpoints` window and press ⟨**Ctrl**⟩-**S** to set the breakpoint's options. Change `Condition` to `Expression true` and enter **not fileSaved** under `Condition expression`. Press ⟨**Enter**⟩ to close the window and then press ⟨**F9**⟩ to run the program. Answer **N** to the prompt, and after the breakpoint stops the program, examine the conditions that led to that statement running at the wrong time.

The fix in this case is to add `begin` and `end` keywords to force the `else` clause to go with the appropriate `then`. This takes extra space and typing time, but there's no runtime penalty for bracketing single statements, and it's a good way to avoid this common problem. Here's how to fix BADELSE's lines 16–22:

```
if not fileSaved then
begin
    if answerYes( 'Save file? ' ) then
    begin
        writeln( 'Saving file' )
    end
end else
    writeln( 'Ending program: file is saved' )
```

In larger programs where multiple statements run at the wrong times, use TD to identify the misplaced `else`. In general, follow these steps:

1. Set a breakpoint on the statement that appears to be executing at the wrong time.

2. Modify the breakpoint with the `View:Breakpoints` and `Set options` commands to be triggered on `Expression true`, with a `Condition expression` equal to the conditions that should *not* be true for this statement.

3. Run the code until it fails. Examine all nested `if` statement control variables. This should tell you which nested statement is attached to the wrong `else`.

Disappearing Standards

Here's the situation. You've been using Turbo Pascal for years. Then, all of a sudden, a familiar library routine fails. For example, Listing 12.3, STANDARD.PAS, prompts for a name and address. Line 36 then calls the standard string procedure `insert` to change "Tom Jones" to "Mr/Mrs Tom Jones." But, when you run the program, instead of that result, every name comes out as "1:Mr/Mrs." What's going on?

Listing 12.3. STANDARD.PAS (with bugs).

```
 1:  {$V-}
 2:  program standard;
 3:
 4:  type
 5:     rec = record
 6:        name : string[40];
 7:        address : string[40];
 8:     end;
 9:
10:  var
11:     r : rec;
12:
13:  procedure insert( s : string; var d : string; n : integer );
14:  var
15:     temp : string[8];
16:  begin
17:     str( n, temp );
18:     d := temp + ':' + s;
19:  end;
20:
21:  procedure insertName( r : rec );
22:  begin
23:     { insert new record in data base }
24:     writeln( r.name );
25:     writeln( r.address );
26:     writeln( 'Inserted' );
27:     writeln;
28:  end;
29:
30:  procedure getrec( var r : rec );
31:  begin
32:     write( 'Name? ' );
33:     readln( r.name );
34:     write( 'Address? ' );
```

```
35:     readln( r.address );
36:     insert( 'Mr/Mrs ', r.name, 1 );
37:  end; { getrec }
38:
39:  begin
40:     getrec( r );
41:     insertName( r );
42:  end.
```

Investigating the bug, you first check the syntax for the `insert` statement at line 36, and it appears to be correct, inserting "Mr/Mrs" into `r.name` at index position 1. But, something is causing `r.name` to change unexpectedly—and, that's the key to finding the error. Load the program into TD and follow these steps to find the statement that changes `r.name`:

1. Choose the `Breakpoints:Changed memory global` command and enter **r.name** as the breakpoint expression. Despite the prompt in the window title, you don't have to enter a *count*—TD monitors the entire variable by default.

2. Press ⟨**F9**⟩ to run, and enter **Tom Jones**. The program breaks at line 34. No problem there. The `readln` statement at line 33 is supposed to change `r.name`.

3. Press ⟨**F9**⟩ again to continue. Enter Mr. Jones's address when prompted. Surprisingly, this triggers another breakpoint at line 19.

Look closely at the `Module` window. You've found the bug. Lines 13–19 redefined the `insert` procedure, which you added to insert line numbers into another section of the program (not shown in this simplified example). Just by accident, the redefined routine has the same name and identical parameters as the library standard, which you intended to call from line 36.

The fix is easy—rename the new `insert` routine and try not to use standard procedure and function names for your own code in the future. Unfortunately, as the number of standard routines in TP's library grows, it's becoming harder to avoid making this mistake. Try to be as familiar as you can with TP's library. The more you know about existing identifiers, the less frequently you'll experience a problem with disappearing standards.

Variable Dilemmas

All variables exist somewhere in memory, and as a result, until you assign a value to a variable, it will have whatever value happens to be at that address when the variable comes into scope. The so-called *uninitialized variable* is actually initialized for you by whatever was left at that memory location by another process. An uninitialized variable has an *unpredictable* value, not a nonexistent one. Until you assign it a value, there's no way to predict what a variable's initial value will be.

Uninitialized variables often cause bugs that seem to be alive. They hide from your attempts to catch them—a mark of the intermittent or moving-target varieties introduced in chapter 7. First, you run a program and it fails. Then, you add a statement like this to display a test value:

```
writeln( 'Testing. count = ', count );
```

And the bug disappears! But when you remove the test line, the bug does not come back as you expect. So, you conclude, maybe the problem was just a "glitch." Chalk one up for cosmic rays. Then, later on—maybe even days later—you make another change and there's that bug again.

Frustrating, isn't it?

Luckily, this common mystery is not difficult to solve. Whenever you notice that conditions change after you add a seemingly innocent statement, the cause is almost always an uninitialized variable. (But see the section on pointer bugs later in this chapter.) The new statement causes addresses of other statements to change and, therefore, may affect the starting value of the uninitialized variable at its new memory location. Even a small change to the program can cause the compiler or editor to run differently, thus filling different sections of memory with new values that are left in RAM when the program runs.

A little medicine can prevent future headaches. Always initialize your variables, even when this means executing a few more statements than necessary.

But when that's impractical, resist the urge to load the program into TD and start poking around. You'll rarely find the bug that way. Instead, make every possible attempt to stabilize the error. Reboot. Write a program to fill memory with zeros before executing the buggy program. Duplicate as many runtime conditions as you can to force the bug into the open. Only after you can repeat the problem should you load the program into TD. Then, use code breakpoints to isolate the section of code that's causing the trouble and look for uninitialized variables.

It may also be useful to log assignments to one or more variables while the code executes. Doing this may show you which variables are not assigned initial values when they should be. For example, here's a printout of the activity log for changes made to r.name in STANDARD.PAS (Listing 12.3):

```
Turbo Debugger Log
At STANDARD.34 r.name = 'Tom Jones' : STRING[40]
At STANDARD.36 r.name = 'Tom Jones' : STRING[40]
At STANDARD.19 r.name = '1:Mr/Mrs ' : STRING[40]
Terminated, exit code 0
```

After loading STANDARD.EXE into TD, follow these steps to create this log:

1. Use the `Breakpoints:Changed memory global` command to set a breakpoint to `r.name`.
2. `View` the `Breakpoints` window and press ⟨**Ctrl**⟩-**S** to `Set options`. Change `Action` to `Log` and set `Action expression` to **r.name**.
3. Press ⟨**F9**⟩ to run the program. Enter sample data. When the program ends, press ⟨**Alt**⟩-**VL** to view the `Log` window.

You might also want to write the log to disk. After step 2, open the log file by pressing ⟨**Alt**⟩-**VL**⟨**Ctrl**⟩-**O**. Choose the default file name or enter a different one.

Global Variable Wars

Use global variables only where strictly required. Never declare simple globals for multiple subroutines to use. The most common conflict occurs in innocent-looking code like this:

```
for i := 1 to 100 do
    something;
```

If `i` is a global variable and if procedure `something` also uses `i`, the `for` loop may go haywire. Using global variables this way is almost always a bad idea. A better plan is to declare loop controls as local variables in procedures and functions.

A good way to resolve a global variable conflict is to set a breakpoint to occur every time a suspect variable changes value. That way, you can examine all statements that affect the variable—you'll probably find that two or more procedures refer to the same global variable by mistake.

To do this, load the program into TD and add the variable to the `Watches` window so you can monitor its value. Then, choose `Breakpoints:Changed memory global`, which prompts you to enter an address. Just enter the variable's name—despite what the prompt says, you don't need to know the address. (TD evaluates a variable name as an expression, reducing it to that variable's address in memory.) Now, press ⟨**F9**⟩ to run the program. Every time the variable changes, the `Module` window will display the statement that made the change.

Home on the Range Error

Accessing array indexes outside of an array's declared boundaries can lead to all sorts of disasters by overwriting other variables or code in memory. If variables seem to change on their own when other unrelated statements execute, a likely cause is an array-index fault, also known as a *range error*.

The best medicine against range errors is to use Turbo Pascal's {$R+} switch to generate automatic checks for assignments to subrange variables and to array indexes. Illegal values will then halt the program with a runtime error.

If you suspect an array-indexing range error has occurred, and you don't want to switch on automatic runtime checks, use the Breakpoint menu's Expression true global command and enter an expression such as:

```
(index < 0) or (index > 99)
```

Run the code by pressing ⟨**F9**⟩. The program will halt if index is not within the range 0 to 99.

How to Find a Runtime Error

Follow these steps to locate the source of a runtime error:

1. Note the address in an error message such as Runtime error 105 at 0084:0026.

2. Load the program into TD or reset (press ⟨**Ctrl**⟩-⟨**F2**⟩⟨**Ctrl**⟩-**O** to view the main program module). The reported runtime error address is relative to this module, so it's important to have it in view in the Module window.

3. Press ⟨**Ctrl**⟩-**G** and enter the reported address in hexadecimal, adding the code-segment register CS. Don't forget the dollar sign—Pascal's hexadecimal indicator. In this case, you would enter **(cs + $84:$26)**.

4. In the Module window, you should now see the statement after the one that caused the error. If the bug's cause is still not obvious, set a code breakpoint (⟨**F2**⟩) at this location or a little earlier, reset (⟨**Ctrl**⟩-⟨**F2**⟩), and run (⟨**F9**⟩). You can then use other TD commands to examine variables and statements that led to the problem.

Looping Once Too Many Times

Related to array-indexing problems is a loop that loops once too often. Most programmers learn the hard way not to write code like this:

```
const
   count = 100;
var
   a : array[ 0 .. count - 1 ] of integer;
   i : integer;
```

```
begin
   for i := 0 to count do
      a[i] := i;
end.
```

That program has a serious bug. Although the programmer carefully declared a constant `count` representing the number of items to store in an array, the array is indexed starting at 0, not 1; therefore, the highest possible index value is 99, not 100. The range 1..100 and the range 0..99 both cover 100 values. The range 0..100 covers 101 values—the number of times the faulty `for` loop executes, which is clearly a mistake. The correct loop is:

```
for i := 0 to count - 1 do
   a[i] := i;
```

However, because you may forget to subtract 1 from `count` in all such cases, it's usually wise to add two more constants:

```
const
   count = 100;
   lowindex = 0;
   highindex = count - 1;
var
   a : array[ lowindex .. highindex ] of integer;
```

By specifying the index limits in the `const` section, you reduce the likelihood of introducing errors later. You can now rewrite the `for` loop:

```
for i := lowindex to highindex do
   a[i] := i;
```

Finding loops that execute too many times is similar to finding out-of-range index values. Monitor the control variables with breakpoint expressions and in the `Watches` window. Or, enter a `Changed memory global` breakpoint for an expression such as **a[maxIndex + 1]**, which halts the program if a statement assigns a value just after the end of the array—probably the most common form of this mistake.

Procedural Predicaments

The concept of a subroutine is probably one of the oldest *paradigms* (conceptual models) in computer programming. Pascal uses two kinds of subroutines: procedures and functions. Procedures run where their names appear in statements. Functions run where their names appear in expressions. For simplicity, I'll refer to both kinds as *procedures* in this section.

Mixing Variable and Value Parameters

Pascal programmers often confuse value and variable parameters declared in procedures. The two key points to remember are:

- A *value parameter* is a copy of a variable's value passed to a procedure; therefore, changing the parameter inside the procedure does not affect the original variable.

- A *variable parameter* is passed as the address of a variable; therefore, changing the parameter inside the procedure also changes the original because it refers by address to the original variable.

The classic symptom of a value- or variable-parameter mixup resembles the uninitialized variable ailment described earlier. Despite the fact that you carefully initialized your global variables, the code fails with index-range errors, pointer problems, and other ills. Just about any kind of bug can be caused by an uninitialized variable, so this is a difficult problem to pinpoint.

One solution is to monitor suspect variables at the beginning and end of every procedure. To do this, set a `Changed memory global` breakpoint on register BP. Because BP is set equal to SP at the start of every procedure and then restored before the procedure finishes, this trick is a handy way to halt the program at the beginning and end of every procedure. Press ⟨**F9**⟩ to run and choose `View:Variables` to examine arguments passed to value and variable parameters.

You may also want to log values passed to procedures instead of halting the code. To do this, choose the `View:Breakpoints` command, highlight the breakpoint you set earlier, and press ⟨**Ctrl**⟩-**S** to set `Action` to `Log` and `Action expression` to the name of a parameter to monitor. Run the program and then press ⟨**Alt**⟩-**VL** to view the logged information. This will show all values passed to this procedure's parameter.

String Length Problems

Procedures that process string parameters are most useful when they can work on strings of any length. For example, the classic procedure to convert (or "bump") a string to uppercase is:

```
procedure bumpstrup( var s : string );
var i : integer;
```

```
begin
   for i := 1 to length( s ) do
      s[i] := upcase( s[i] )
end; { bumpstrup }
```

By declaring parameter s of type string, which is equivalent to the maximum-length string of 255 characters, the procedure can accept strings of any length. Even so, the following does not compile:

```
var s20 : string[20];
begin
   s20 := 'abcdefg';
   bumpstrup( s20 );
end;
```

Turbo Pascal rejects the 20-character string argument passed to bumpstrup because the procedure's parameter is declared as a variable string of 255 characters. If the procedure changes any byte in the string beyond s[20], it could overwrite memory addresses that don't belong to the original string. Of course, the for loop in bumpstrup prevents this, but the compiler isn't smart enough to make that observation; therefore, the fix is to turn off string-length checking when calling the procedure:

```
{$V-} bumpstrup( s20 ); {$V+}
```

That compiles and runs, but it also introduces the danger that bumpstrup may now write beyond the declared length of s20. If, for example, the for loop in bumpstrupx were changed to:

```
for i := 1 to 255 do
   s[i] := upcase( s[i] );
```

the code would merrily overwrite the data at s[21] to s[255] despite the fact that the official end of the string is at s[20].

To find out if a string-length error is causing a bug, try changing all short string-variable declarations such as string[20] to plain string types. Then rerun the code. If the bug disappears, examine all procedures with var string parameters, using TD to monitor index values and string lengths in the Watches window.

Another good way to find these kinds of errors is to set an Expression true global breakpoint on the string length. Enter an expression such as **length(s) > 20** to halt the program if the string length ever grows beyond its declared limit. Or, instead of a literal maximum length value, use the expression **length(s) >= sizeof(s)**, which has the same effect.

Functional Foul Ups

A misused function is at the bottom of many subtle bugs. Because functions are used like constants in expressions, they can obscure their effects on a program. A bug that appears to be caused by the expression may actually be the result of a function that changes a global variable or that calls a critical system routine at the wrong times. Such bugs have definite symptoms described here that, when you come to recognize them, will help you to find and fix the problems.

Side Effects

The classic side effect is a function that changes a global variable on which the function depends. The standard `IoResult` function is an prime example. For example, this does not work:

```
{$I-}
begin
   assign( f, 'FILENAME' );
   reset( f );
   if IoResult <> 0 then
   begin
      writeln( 'Error #', IoResult ); { ??? }
      halt( IoResult )
   end;
end.
```

Errors detected by the `reset` statement cause `IoResult` to return a nonzero value. The `if` statement tests for that condition and halts the program if any errors occur. No problem there. But running the code always displays "Error #0" no matter what caused `reset` to fail. Why?

This problem is due to misunderstanding `IoResult`'s *intentional* side effect. When an I/O error occurs, `reset` and other I/O routines store an error code in an integer system variable named `InOutRes`. `IoResult` returns this value, but it also resets the value to 0—an action that's required to allow future I/O operations, which examine `InOutRes` to see if any pending errors are unresolved. If the function didn't do this, you'd have to reset the internal value with a program statement after every I/O error. `IoResult` saves you that trouble by doing this automatically, but in the process, it introduces the side effect that every subsequent call to the function with no intervening I/O operation always returns 0.

Finding the source of similar side effects is difficult. For instance, in the previous sample, you may incorrectly assume that the `writeln` statement is at fault and waste time debugging the code at this place in the program. To avoid making that mistake, when examining expressions that call functions, inspect or watch all global variables used by the functions. Add those variables to a Watches window or set Changed memory global breakpoints on selected variables to monitor when they change.

After stabilizing a side-effect bug, use a temporary variable to store the function result. This usually repairs the problem. For example, you can correct the previous code with:

```
{$I-}
var
    resultCode : integer;
begin
    assign( f, 'FILENAME' );
    reset( f );
    resultCode := IoResult;
    if resultCode <> 0 then
    begin
        writeln( 'Error #', resultCode );
        halt( resultCode )
    end;
end.
```

This Way Out

Designing Pascal functions is like designing prisons. You must be sure to guard all the exits. Every function should return a planned value for every possible escape route, or the result will be a serious breach of security, as demonstrated by this criminally dysfunctional function:

```
function f( n : integer ) : integer;
begin
    if n >= 0
        then f := { some calculated value }
end;
```

The mistake here is that n might be negative—a condition the function ignores. Some programmers "fix" this problem with a sternly worded comment in the source code:

```
{ Function f. Note: parameter n MUST BE POSITIVE! }
```

But that, of course, isn't much help in preventing bugs. If the function is buried in a 100,000-statement library, you and other programmers may never read that comment. A better approach is to change the parameter type to restrict input to legal values. For example, if you change n to type **word**, the compiler will reject negative arguments passed to the parameter. This neatly prevents bugs and has no effect on runtime performance.

When that's not possible, try these steps to find bad function results:

1. Add a temporary statement at the start of the function, setting the result to a default value. In this example, you could insert **f := -1;**.

2. Recompile and load the program into TD.

3. Set a code breakpoint (press **⟨F2⟩**) on the function's end; keyword. This will halt the program just before the function returns to its caller.

4. Press **⟨Alt⟩-VB** to view the Breakpoints window and select Set options (press **⟨Ctrl⟩-S**) to change Condition to Expression true. Then, set Condition expression to **f = -1**. This alters the breakpoint to halt the program only when the function identifier equals the default value. Press **⟨Enter⟩** to close the Breakpoints window.

5. Optionally add various parameters and local variables to the Watches window. In this example, you'd probably want to watch parameter n.

When you press **⟨F9⟩** to run the program, it will halt every time the function is ready to exit without having assigned a return value different from the assigned default. You can then use the View:Stack command to find the expression that called the function with the bad input arguments.

Unwanted Recursion

A stack overflow error might be caused by too little stack space, but when increasing the stack size with an {$M} directive doesn't make the bug go away, you should immediately suspect an unwanted recursion. This can happen in a function that mistakenly uses the function identifier on the right side of an equation. For example, suppose you need a custom random-number generator (even though Turbo Pascal already has one). You might begin with the standard approach illustrated in Listing 12.4.

Listing 12.4. RANDOM.PAS.

```
1:  {$N+,E+}              { Coprocessor or emulation }
2:  program stacked;
3:  uses crt;
4:
5:  const
6:     MAXLONG = $7FFFFFFF;
```

```
 7:  var
 8:      seed : longInt;
 9:
10:  function random( var seed : longInt ) : double;
11:  const
12:      M = 25173;
13:      C = 13849;
14:  begin
15:      random := seed / MAXLONG;
16:      seed := ( M * seed + C ) mod MAXLONG;
17:  end; { random }
18:
19:  begin
20:      write( 'Seed? ' );
21:      readln( seed );
22:      while not keypressed do
23:          write( random( seed ):20:8 )
24:  end.
```

Although RANDOM seems to work correctly, you decide to experiment. What if, you ask, you were to randomize the **seed** inside the function? (This may not produce useful random sequences, but it illustrates a common problem.) Perhaps you could change line 15 to:

```
random := random( seed ) / MAXLONG;
```

But, when you run the program, you immediately receive error 202, "Stack overflow." In fact, the program no longer displays any random values. If you receive this message while running TD (reported as "exit code 202"), the cursor should be positioned near the location of the problem. If you ran the code from DOS, to find the source of the error, load the program into TD, press ⟨**F8**⟩ to step past any startup code and type ⟨**Ctrl**⟩-**G**. Enter the reported error address relative to CS:0000. For example, if the error was reported at 0032:0143, enter **(cs + $32),$0143** to locate the statement that caused the stack to overflow. Remember to specify hexadecimal values with preceding dollar signs even though the error doesn't display hex values that way.

When you receive a stack overflow—especially after making a change to a function statement—you should immediately suspect that an unwanted recursion is at fault. Check whether you accidentally used the function name in the right hand part of an assignment, as I did in this example, causing **random** to be called each time **random** begins running. The same problem can also occur in procedures that inadvertently call themselves in statements.

Mutual Madness

The unwanted recursion described in the previous section is not hard to find. The symptom of a stack overflow is immediate, and it points directly to the offending statement.

More difficult is an *unwanted mutual recursion*—an effect that occurs when one function calls another that eventually calls the original function back. This traps the mutual functions in a so-called infinite loop, which ends with abrupt finality when the stack runs out of space.

If you've tried the suggestions in the previous section, but still can't locate the problem, you may have been victimized by an unexpected mutual recursion. To find out if this is the case, load the program into TD, and follow these steps:

1. Set a `Changed memory global` breakpoint for **sp**, the stack pointer register. This will trigger the breakpoint whenever SP changes.

2. Modify the breakpoint by using the `Set options` command in the `Breakpoints` window (press ⟨**Alt**⟩-**VB**⟨**Ctrl**⟩-**S**). Change `Action` to `Log` and set `Action expression` to **sp**, which will record the value of SP every time the breakpoint's condition is satisfied.

After these steps, run the program (press ⟨**F9**⟩) until the stack overflows. Then, press ⟨**Alt**⟩-**VL** to view the log. You may see something like this:

```
Turbo Debugger Log
At MUTUAL.18 sp = 1020 ($3FC) : WORD
  .
  .
  .
At MUTUAL.8 sp = 534 ($216) : WORD
At MUTUAL.FIRST sp = 530 ($212) : WORD
At MUTUAL.14 sp = 528 ($210) : WORD
At MUTUAL.SECOND sp = 524 ($20C) : WORD
At MUTUAL.8 sp = 522 ($20A) : WORD
At MUTUAL.FIRST sp = 518 ($206) : WORD
At MUTUAL.14 sp = 516 ($204) : WORD
At MUTUAL.SECOND sp = 512 ($200) : WORD
Terminated, exit code 202
```

Program MUTUTAL (not shown) calls procedures FIRST and SECOND over and over until it blows up the stack, ending the program with exit code 202. Examining those two routines is sure to turn up an accidental mutual recursion.

Note: Even though this trick generates an overwhelming stream of data, you don't have to write the Log to disk. You want to see only the tail end of the log anyway, so it doesn't matter if you lose the earlier entries.

When using this technique, be aware that it can take a long time. Setting breakpoints on register values requires TD to examine processor registers after each statement, causing the program to run at a snail's pace, even on fast 80386- or 80486-based machines. To save time, try to isolate the problem to one module, run the code up to that place, and then start logging breakpoints on SP.

You might also be able to save time by forcing stack overflow errors to occur sooner. To do that, add the compiler directive {$M 1024,0,0} (changing 0,0 to the minimum and maximum amount of heap space you need). This sets up a small 1,024-byte stack. If the program fails before the bug surfaces, you may have to increase this value.

Another possibility is to set an Expression true global breakpoint for sp < $300 instead of the method described in step 2. That won't improve performance by much, but it may reduce the size of the log file by logging entries only after SP becomes dangerously low.

Interactive Side Effects

Functions that perform I/O of any kind are prone to another common error, which I call an *interactive side effect*. This problem occurs when a multipart expression accidentally calls the same function more than once. A typical case is a statement that calls the Crt unit's readKey function:

```
if ( readKey = 'Y' ) or ( readKey = 'y' )
   then writeln( 'Answer is Yes' )
   else writeln( 'Answer is No' );
```

That will never work! The multiple calls to readKey require double key-presses where only one is needed. Keep an eye out for similar expressions. They may look healthy, but they're about to come down with a bug.

In a very complex expression, it may not be obvious that multiple calls to functions are being made. To find out, run the code up to the expression. Then, press ⟨F7⟩ to single-step through the expression parts. You'll quickly spot any functions that are executing more than once.

Pointer Pointers

Turbo Pascal pointers are composed of two 16-bit halves: a segment value and an offset. Pointers may point to any location in a PC's 1-megabyte address space—a versatility that's both useful and dangerous when misdirected. Uninitialized pointers can address bytes in a program's code segment and data segment, in the stack, or even inside DOS. If you assign a value to one of those locations, you could damage your code, other data, or DOS itself.

Uninitialized Pointers

An uninitialized variable is bad enough, but an uninitialized pointer is like an arrow fired blindly into the air. There's no telling where it will come down or what it will hit.

Because pointers can address any location in RAM and, therefore, might change bytes belonging to data and code, the symptoms of an uninitialized pointer are varied and difficult to catalog. Here are a few of the classic signs that misused pointers are known to cause:

- The program crashes, forcing you to reboot. Sometimes, you can recover only by turning power off and on.
- DOS develops strange quirks after running the program.
- The program runs correctly once. Subsequent runs fail.
- Variables change unexpectedly.
- Procedures and functions return to the wrong addresses.
- Procedures and functions run magically even though no statement or expression calls them.
- The program crashes when executed from DOS, then runs without fault in TD.

Crashes and DOS problems are most likely caused by assigning values to pointers that address bytes in a code segment. Changing those bytes by accident can produce delayed effects that can throw a bug search off track. A bad pointer that wrecks a subroutine not called until much later is extremely difficult to find.

Another symptom is a program that runs correctly one time but then fails to run the next. This is often caused by an uninitialized pointer that has a predictable value after compiling—which leaves memory initialized to one set of values—but then takes on a different value after the program loads other data into RAM. On subsequent runs, the pointer has a different value than on the first.

A variable might change unexpectedly because of a pointer that addresses the variable's memory space. This problem is not as difficult to locate. Set a `Changed memory global` breakpoint on the variable to halt the program when the variable changes.

If a procedure or function suddenly executes even though no statement called it, or if a routine returns to an unexpected location, an uninitialized pointer might be the cause. The most likely bug is a pointer that addresses the stack segment—easily located by setting a breakpoint on the pointer's segment value (see the next section). Less frequently, a pointer might change a machine-code `ret` instruction to something else, causing a fall-through from one routine to the next in RAM.

Programs that crash when executed from DOS but then run flawlessly in TD may be caused by an uninitialized pointer that overwrites the interrupt vector table in low memory, beginning at address 0000:0000. Because a `nil` pointer in Pascal has this same value, and because Pascal does not prevent assignments via pointers equal to `nil`, such assignments can easily modify the vector table—a bug that may not surface until after the program ends. (This is a good but nasty example of the time-bomb bug introduced in chapter 7.) Because TD saves and restores a portion of the interrupt vector table, running the code under the debugger's control can cause this bug to disappear. But running the same code from DOS does not restore the damaged vectors, thus causing a future crash.

Finding Nil Pointers

Finding `nil` pointers is not always easy. If you know the variable name, set an `Expression true global` breakpoint and enter the expression **p = nil**. This will halt the code at any time the pointer equals `nil`.

Usually, however, you won't even know which pointer is causing the trouble. You can't set breakpoints on all the pointers in your program!

One little-known way to trap assignments to `nil` pointers is to set an `Expression true global` breakpoint expression to **(es = 0) and (di = 0)**. That works because TP generates code to load pointer addresses into ES:DI for assignments. Monitoring the register values will halt the code after the machine-code instruction (usually `les`) that loads the `nil` pointer address into the two registers.

Finding Uninitialized Pointers

When your code develops a bug and if the program uses pointers, there are several steps you can take to determine if an uninitialized pointer is the cause. First, because pointers usually address variables allocated in the heap by `new`, you can set a breakpoint to halt the program or to log an expression for every statement where a certain pointer addresses a value outside of the heap.

To do this for a pointer p, set an `Expression true global` breakpoint to the expression **seg(p^) ⟨ seg(heapOrg^)**, which halts the program for every statement where p addresses RAM below the heap. This includes all of DOS, the program's data, and code. The carets in the expression dereference the pointers, causing `seg` to return the segment address of the memory location to which `p` points. Without the caret, `seg(p)` returns the segment address of the pointer variable. The `heapOrg` typed constant pointer from the `System` unit locates the start of heap memory.

If you suspect a bad pointer is changing a return address or other value on the stack, you can watch for this condition by setting a similar breakpoint to **seg(p^) = ss**, which executes the breakpoint action if the segment address of the value addressed by `p` ever equals the value of the stack segment register.

Disposed Pointers

The flip side of the uninitialized pointer coin is a bug caused by a statement that uses a disposed pointer. Pascal's `dispose` procedure returns to the heap the memory that `new` allocates to a pointer. Unfortunately, `dispose` does not change the pointer value; therefore, after executing `dispose(p)`, the pointer `p` still addresses the same memory as it did before. However, that memory is now on the heap's free list of disposed spaces, which might be reallocated to other pointers by subsequent calls to `new`.

Bugs caused by using a disposed pointer will show up only if later statements allocate that same memory to fresh pointers. Assignments will then write values to memory locations addressed by more than one pointer at the same time—an insidious condition that can cause all sorts of trouble.

Because disposed pointers have perfectly legitimate address values even though the memory at those locations is not available for the program's use, finding this condition is a challenge. One approach is to take advantage of a Pascal feature that in other circumstances is best avoided—the ability to redefine library routines. For example, add the replacement `dispose` procedure to your program and recompile:

```
procedure dispose( var p );
var
    pp : pointer absolute p;
begin
    system.dispose( pp );
    pp := nil;
end;
```

Next, load the code into TD. Add selected pointer variables to `Watches` or set `Expression true global` breakpoints for expressions such as p = nil. (Or, use the ES:DI trick mentioned earlier.)

Every call to `dispose` is now routed through the custom replacement, which uses an untyped parameter to accept pointers of all types. The parameter is redefined as a `pointer absolute` for passing to `system.dispose`, which handles the memory deallocation as usual. The final statement resets the pointer to nil, allowing breakpoints to detect subsequent assignments to disposed pointers.

Note: This technique will not work with object-oriented programs that use Turbo Pascal's extended dispose procedure. Use the method only for non-OOP pointer debugging.

Unnormalized Pointers

A pointer is *normalized* when its offset value is in the range 0000 to 000F hexadecimal (0 to 15 in decimal). Unnormalized pointers have offset values greater than 000F hex. Because 80x86 processors address memory in 16-byte chunks, or paragraphs, it's possible for unnormalized pointers with different values to address the same bytes in memory. But normalized pointers are unique—there's only one normalized pointer address value per byte in RAM.

For that reason, programs can compare, add, subtract, and perform other operations on normalized pointers—operations that fail if the pointers are not normalized. For example, a simple calculation can subtract two normalized pointers to determine the number of bytes between two addresses. But if the pointers are unnormalized, that same formula will usually give the wrong answer.

Many of TP's system routines do not normalize pointers before using them. This saves time but can also cause bugs. The most notorious of these routines is FreeMem, which returns a certain number of bytes to the heap. Usually, you'll use the procedure this way:

```
FreeMem( p, 100 );
```

That returns 100 bytes to the heap at the address where p points. But, the procedure works correctly only if p is normalized. Suppose you have these type declarations:

```
aPtr = ^anArray;
anArray = array[1..100] of integer;
```

If you then declare variables p and p2 of type aPtr, you might execute code to allocate a 100-integer array and then dispose its higher half, perhaps to conserve memory when you don't need the full array:

```
new( p );
p2 := @p^[50];
FreeMem( p2, 100 ); { ??? }
```

The code appears to be unblemished, but there's a worm in the apple. First, `new` allocates a full-sized array and assigns its address to `p`. An assignment statement uses the `@` operator to set `p2` to the address of the array's midpoint. And `FreeMem` disposes 100 bytes (50 integers) at that address.

But that's not what happens. Because `@` returns an unnormalized pointer, `FreeMem` miscalculates the number of bytes to return to the heap, and the program will probably crash.

Sometimes this error can go unnoticed for many statements. Other times it will appear immediately. When it occurs, you may be able to find the cause by setting an `Expression true global` breakpoint for the expression **ofs(p^)>15**. Don't forget the caret (**^**), which passes to `ofs` the address to which `p` points. Without the caret, the expression would pass the address where the pointer variable is stored.

After entering the expression, run the program by pressing ⟨**F9**⟩. It will halt whenever `p`'s offset value is unnormalized. (You may have to press ⟨**F8**⟩ at the beginning of the program to initialize DS so TD can correctly locate `p` and other variables. This might produce false breakpoints at startup, which you can safely ignore.)

Finding the mistake is the difficult part. Fixing it is easy—normalize the pointer before passing it to `FreeMem` or to other system routines. To do that, include this function in your code:

```
function normalize( p : pointer ) : pointer;
begin
   normalize := ptr( seg(p^) + ( ofs(p^) div 16 ), ofs(p^) mod 16 )
end; { normalize }
```

To correct the buggy call to `FreeMem` listed earlier, change that statement to:

```
FreeMem( normalize(p2), 100 );
```

Misunderstanding MemAvail and MaxAvail

Be sure that you understand the difference between `memAvail` and `maxAvail`, both of which tell you how much space is available on the heap but differ in how they calculate that space:

- `memAvail` returns the total amount of free space available.
- `maxAvail` returns the size of the largest available heap space.

Normally, you should use `maxAvail` to determine whether enough space is available for a new pointer-addressable variable. For example, if `pr` addressed a record type `rec`, it's not a good idea to write:

```
if memAvail >= sizeof( rec )
   then new( pr );
```

Instead, call `maxAvail` to determine if there's a space large enough to hold a variable of `rec`'s size:

```
if maxAvail >= sizeof( rec )
   then new( pr );
```

The difference is important because previous calls to `dispose` may have left gaps in the heap. In that case, the total amount of available memory may be greater than the largest available space. If that largest space is smaller than the size of `rec`, calling `new` will cause a runtime out-of-memory error (code 203).

If you receive that error while running the code from DOS, use TD's `Goto` command in the `Module` window to locate the statement where the error occurs (see "How to Find a Runtime Error" earlier in this chapter). If that location calls `new` or `getMem`, check earlier statements to see whether you called `memAvail` when you should have called `maxAvail`.

But if you discover that you did check `maxAvail` correctly, then you are most likely experiencing the effects of a badly fragmented heap. Some say this is a bug in Pascal, but it's more of a design flaw than an outright error. Fragmentation is caused by disposing many small-size pointer-addressable variables. This fragments heap memory while also causing the free list to steal space for its own use. You might want to consider storing small variables in larger buffers allocated by `new`. That will reduce the size of the free list and create larger holes in memory of the same size, which will help to prevent fragmentation.

Out-of-Memory Bugs

Of course, running out of memory is a problem. But I have in mind a different out-of-memory quirk that I call the "water, water everywhere" bug. This problem is not caused directly by a memory shortage. It occurs when a program disposes too many variables in order to make room in a full heap. This leads to "memory, memory everywhere, but not a drop to dispose."

Or, rather, there's not enough memory to insert new entries into the free list that keeps track of disposed bytes in the heap. This can happen when the heap is full or nearly so and you call `dispose` to make room for new variables. Because the heap is full, TP is unable to expand the free list to record the newly disposed memory addresses, thus preventing the disposal for the same reasons that prompted the program to make room!

When using TD to trace the cause of an apparent memory shortage, if you end at a `dispose` statement that appears to release plenty of space, your code may have been pumped dry by a "water, water everywhere" bug. Plug the hole in the dike by setting `System.Freemin` to a higher value divisible evenly by 8. Calls to `new` and `getmem` will then fail if the space between `HeapPtr` and `FreePtr` is less than `FreeMin`, thus reserving more room for free-list entries.

Numerical Puzzles

There are countless numbers of numerical bugs, but a few show up with predictable frequency. For instance, you may discover that an assignment from an expression to a variable does not give the expected value. After using TD to isolate the appropriate statements, you still don't know why the result is wrong. Now what do you do?

One answer is to write a few other expressions to test your assumptions. Of course, you can write small programs for this purpose, but don't forget about the `Data` menu's `Evaluate/modify` command, which lets you enter test expressions. This is a great place to run quick tests and to feed new input values into formulas.

You can also load expressions directly from the source code into the `Evaluate/modify` window. To do that, highlight the expression in the `Module` view by clicking and dragging the mouse. Or, position the cursor on the expression's first character and press ⟨**Insert**⟩⟨**End**⟩ to highlight the line. Use the cursor movement keys to adjust the amount of highlighted text so you don't copy a semicolon if there is one at the end of the line. Press ⟨**Ctrl**⟩-⟨**F4**⟩ to open the `Evaluate/modify` dialog box and copy the highlighted text to the `Expression` pane. Then, press ⟨**Enter**⟩ to calculate the result. Beware of expressions that use functions—TD will call the function code, which might cause a side effect if it contains statements that change global variables.

> Hint: When evaluating test expressions, if you receive the message "Initialization not complete," press ⟨**Esc**⟩ to close the dialog box, press ⟨**F8**⟩ to execute the program's startup code, and then try `Evaluate/modify` again.

Misplaced Operator Precedence

Expecting specific operator precedences in expressions can lead to obscure code. For that reason, I rarely rely on a language's defined precedence order for numerical and other operators. Instead, I prefer to use parentheses in expressions to make my intentions perfectly clear—even when parentheses aren't required. For example, for most values of n and x, this expression

```
x := ( n + 4 ) / x;
```

is not equivalent to

```
x := n + 4 / x;
```

Because division has a higher precedence than addition, TP and most other compilers evaluate the expression as:

```
x := n + ( 4 / x );
```

But even if that's what I meant to write, I would add the parentheses. They help prevent bugs that might occur if I make changes to the expression later.

TD helps find badly written expressions by monitoring variables and letting you enter test expressions. But, unless you already suspect that you've written the expression incorrectly, there's not much else TD can do. However, if you know the range that an expression *result* should have, you may be able to locate the problem with an `Expression true global` breakpoint. For example, in the previous sample expressions, if x should always range from 0 to 99, enter a breakpoint expression such as **(x ⟨ 0) or (x ⟩ 99)**, which will halt the code any time x steps out of bounds.

Negative Words

Expecting unsigned word values to become negative is a common numerical problem with a classic symptom—a hung computer. For example, consider this loop:

```
while w >= i do
begin
   { something }
   dec( w );
end;
```

If i is an integer and w is a word, then if i is negative, w will always be greater or equal to i. As a result, the loop will execute "forever"—that is, until you pull the plug.

To find what's causing the computer to hang, reboot and load the program into TD. Run the code until it hangs, then press ⟨**Ctrl**⟩-⟨**Break**⟩ to break out of the loop. Usually, this will cause the CPU window to open because you'll most likely interrupt execution between two machine-code instructions, not necessarily between two high-level statements. If this happens, switch to the Module view, move the cursor to a statement close to where the break occurred, and press ⟨**F4**⟩ to continue running the program up to that line. You may also be able to press ⟨**F8**⟩ repeatedly until source-code statements reappear in the CPU view. But, unfortunately, that may require single-stepping too much code to be practical.

Another possibility is to choose `Run:Animate` and enter **0** to select the shortest possible delay value. Press ⟨**F9**⟩ to continue running and be ready to press ⟨**Esc**⟩ (or another key) as soon as you see source-code lines appear in the window. This may take a few long moments. (It also may not work at all if you're unlucky enough to have halted inside a machine-code routine that's looping, waiting for a keypress or other input.)

I've also had some success with this problem by setting an `Expression true global` breakpoint for **cs = $1234** where $1234 equals a code-segment value in the compiled program. Use the `CPU` window to determine this value before running the code. Then, if pressing ⟨**Ctrl**⟩-⟨**Break**⟩ brings up the `CPU` view, enter the breakpoint expression and press ⟨**F9**⟩ to continue running. In a multisegment program, use an expression such as **(cs) = $1234)** where $1234 is the lowest code segment used by the program's code. After the breakpoint hits, you may still have to press ⟨**F8**⟩ a few times to get back to the source if the code-segment value you specify includes routines in the runtime library.

Whichever method you choose, after getting back to the source, check whether the code is executing inside a loop. If so, examine the control variables (**w** and **i** in this example) and be especially wary of any mixed integer and word combinations.

Putting the Hex On

Programs are sometimes vexed by numbers that should be expressed in hex but are actually interpreted as decimal values. The compiler can report incorrect values only for constants that use hex letters A to F. Assignments such as `i := FA29` don't compile because Turbo Pascal "sees" FA29 as an identifier that begins with F. It doesn't realize that FA29 should be a hexadecimal value written as $FA29.

Other mistakes such as `i := 100` compile without error, even though you intended to write `i := $100`, which has a different result. In decimal, 100 is 100. But $100 is 256.

As with other numerical errors, you can use TD's `Watches` and `Evaluate/ modify` windows to check for decimal values that should be in hex. Because these and other windows display integers in both decimal and hex unless you change the `Integer format` setting with `Options:Display options`, such mistakes are often easy to spot by simple observation.

Integer Wrap Around

Pushing your system to the max is fine, but pushing integer variables past their maximum limits can have serious consequences. For example, adding 1 to 32767, the maximum positive integer value, produces different results depending on the expression. If **i** is an integer, then this does not compile:

```
i := 32767 + 1;
```

But the compiler accepts the next statements, which appear to produce the same result:

```
i := 32767;
i := i + 1;
```

Adding 1 to i (or using the equivalent statement inc(i)) equals $-32{,}768$ because of the wrap-around effect produced by carries within a fixed number of bits. The first statement doesn't compile because the compiler evaluates the constant expression 32767 + 1 as a longInt—not an integer. Because longInt values are 32 bits long, the addition is perfectly legal. But, the assignment to the 16-bit i is not.

Finding this type of mistake isn't too difficult. You might set a breakpoint to halt the program if i = maxInt. Then, after the break, press ⟨F7⟩ to single-step the code up to the place where i is incremented past its maximum value. Or, you could watch for a change in sign, monitoring the expression i < 0 in an Expression true global breakpoint.

Mishandling Files

File handling is one of those subjects that every programming language seems to do differently. On the surface, the commands are usually similar—there are open, close, read, and write operations, plus other ways to manipulate files, usually by calling DOS functions. But, underneath these apparent standards are subtle deviations that can lead to bugs.

Many times, file-handling bugs are caused by changes to the language. For example, in early versions of Turbo Pascal, closing a closed file had no bad effects. Now, it can lead to serious problems, as explained a bit later. If your code ran correctly before but now fails when recompiled with a new compiler version, run don't walk to your references and carefully review the current set of file-handling specifications.

Forgetting to Close a File

Always close your files when you're done with them. Some languages, but not TP, specify that files are closed automatically at the ends of procedures that declare local file variables. Others, including TP, close all open files when the program ends.

When programs halt unexpectedly due to a runtime error #4 (too many open files), the fault is probably one of these:

- One or more procedures fails to close a file variable declared locally in the procedure.

- The number of files exceeds DOS's maximum of 15 per process. This maximum remains fixed even if n is set to a larger value in a CONFIG.SYS FILES=n command, which specifies the maximum number of files for all concurrent processes. Each process is still limited to 15 files.

- The CONFIG.SYS FILES command is missing or is set to a low value.

- The program is executed as a DOS filter or in a pipe, which steals one file handle away from the program.

To examine file details, add a uses dos; declaration to your program and watch or inspect **fileRec(f)**, where *f* is the name of any file variable. Or, use **textRec(tf)**, where *tf* is a variable of type text. These type cast expressions expose the details inside file variables that are normally hidden from view.

You can also set Expression true global breakpoints for a file f using expressions such as **fileRec(f).mode = fmClosed** to locate closed files or **fileRec(f).mode < > fmClosed** to locate those that are open.

Delayed File Errors

File I/O errors sometimes occur at the strangest times. Usually, the problem is caused by misunderstanding how the {$I} option affects file errors. For example, consider the buggy Listing 12.5, BADCLOSE.PAS, which detects whether a file exists.

Listing 12.5.   BADCLOSE.PAS (with bugs).

```
 1:  program badClose;
 2:
 3:  type
 4:     s65 = string[65];    { file names }
 5:
 6:  {$I-}
 7:  function fileExists( fileName : s65 ) : Boolean;
 8:  var
 9:     f : file;
10:  begin
11:     assign( f, fileName );
12:     reset( f );
13:     fileExists := IoResult = 0;
14:     close( f );    { ??? }
15:  end; { fileExists }
16:  {$I+}
17:
```

```
18:  var
19:     filename : s65;
20:
21:  begin
22:     write( 'Enter file name to check ' );
23:     readln( filename );
24:     if fileExists( fileName )
25:        then writeln( filename, ' exists' )
26:        else writeln( filename, ' does not exist' );
27:     writeln( 'End of program' );
28:  end.
```

When you run BADCLOSE, enter an existing file name (BADCLOSE.PAS is a good choice). The program correctly reports that the file exists. Then, run the program again and enter a nonexistent file name such as **XXX**. This time, you receive "Runtime error 103 at 0000:013A" (or something similar).

To find the source of this data-dependent bug, load the program into TD or press ⟨**Ctrl**⟩-⟨**F2**⟩ to reset if you already did that. Then, press ⟨**Ctrl**⟩-**G** and enter **cs:$013A** (replace $013A with the reported address) to jump to the statement that caused the runtime error.

Strangely enough, that statement is `writeln` at line 26. (The cursor will be on line 27 because the reported runtime error address is just after the offending statement.) Something is causing a standard and presumably well-debugged library routine to halt the code!

Some programmers at this point would waste time tracing through the machine code for `writeln`. (They must be spelunkers at heart.) Resist taking such journeys to the center of your own code—at least until you've exhausted simpler possibilities near the surface. A better plan is to isolate all statements for which the `System` unit's `InOutRes` typed constant is not 0. This is the value that `IoResult` returns; therefore, setting a breakpoint for this condition effectively inserts a check on `IoResult` at every statement in the entire program.

To perform this test, reset the program (press ⟨**Ctrl**⟩-⟨**F2**⟩), choose the `Breakpoints:Expression true global` command, and enter the expresion **InOutRes⟨⟩0**. Then, press ⟨**F9**⟩ to run the program. Enter a nonsense response for the file-name prompt to duplicate the runtime error. The code will break inside `fileExists` at line 13. This is *not* the bug—the very next line checks `IoResult`, causing `fileExists` to return true or false depending on whether the `reset` at line 12 succeeded. That's exactly what should happen.

So, press ⟨**F9**⟩ again to continue. When you do that, you may be surprised to hit a second breakpoint at line 15. Something is causing the function to end with `InOutRes` not equal to 0, a condition that causes the *next* I/O operation to fail due to Turbo Pascal's requirement that pending I/O errors prevent future I/O until `IoResult` clears the internal error code.

The pea that's causing all the discomfort must be the statement between the assignment to the `fileExists` function identifier and `end`—the `close` statement at line 14. Because the previous `reset` failed, file `f` is not open; therefore, the `close` generates an I/O error. However, because I/O error checking was switched off at line 6, the problem goes unnoticed until later at `writeln`.

There are a number of ways to fix this mistake, but the most reliable is to check `IoResult` after `close`, adding this statement between lines 14 and 15:

```
if IoResult <> 0
   then { ignore the error };
```

Overlay Obstacles

When it loads an overlay from disk, Turbo Pascal's overlay manager requires all active procedures and functions to be compiled with the {$F +} far-code switch. This switch causes the compiler to generate far `call` and `ret` instructions, which push and pop full 32-bit return addresses on the stack.

The overlay manager enforces this requirement in order to allow multiple overlays to call each other. At such times, the program may have to shuffle one or more overlays in and out of the overlay buffer. To prevent `ret` instructions from returning to code that's no longer in memory (and what a bug that would be), the overlay unit patches return addresses on the stack to return to a subroutine inside the overlay manager. Upon intercepting one of those patched returns, the manager reloads the appropriate overlay module from disk and completes the return. Making those patches requires the overlay code to examine procedure stack frames while searching for a return address. That code is designed to recognize only 32-bit far addresses; therefore, all procedures and functions must be activated with far calls.

Forgetting to compile your code with the {$F +} switch is the most probable cause of bugs in overlay handling. Remember that, even if procedure A calls procedure B, which calls procedure C, which calls another routine in an overlay, procedures A, B, and C must all be compiled with {$F +}. For this reason, Borland recommends placing that switch at the top of the program. But, strictly speaking, you need to use the switch only for code that might lead to an overlay being loaded into memory.

Over Initialization

You must call `OvrInit` before using overlays in a program, but only do that one time! A common mistake is to call `OvrInit` from inside the overlay module. If that procedure is then called several times, the program will eventually fail—a good example of an intermittent bug that shows up only after running the same code many times.

Sluggish Overlays

When you have many small units in a program, the tendancy is to convert them all to overlays in an attempt to make the program run in as small a space as possible. Don't do this. You may cause your code to develop a bad case of lethargy—a bug that falls in the intermittent category because it appears only after the program runs correctly for a while. A slowdown is usually due to one of these causes:

- The overlay buffer is too small. A larger buffer will reduce disk activity and, therefore, improve program speed.
- Multiple overlays are being loaded from inside a `for`, `while`, or `repeat` statement, which can drastically cut performance, especially when RAM space is cramped.
- The disk drive might be failing. This forces DOS to reread tracks many times until the operation succeeds.

Except for a hardware problem, TD can help you to fine-tune overlay performance by monitoring activity for two `Overlay` unit typed constants, `OvrTrapCount` and `OvrLoadCount`. When combined with Turbo Pascal 5.5's new probation-reprieve memory management scheme, the correct values for those two variables will help to keep frequently used overlays in memory longer. This can give an overlaid program a tremendous performance boost.

To monitor the two variables, load your program into TD and make the `Watches` window current. Then, type the names of the two variables. Or, set a separate `Changed memory global` breakpoint for each of the variable names. Then, open the `Breakpoints` window and press 〈**Ctrl**〉**-S** to `Set options`. Change `Action` to `Log` and `Action expression` to the variable name. (Both `Action expression` and `Condition expression` should refer to the same variable.) Close the window and run the program. Then, inspect the log (press 〈**Alt**〉**-VL**). (I find it best to log the variables and inspect the results after testing.)

The following guidelines will help you to adjust the two parameters for better overlay performance. (This text is extracted from my book, *Mastering Turbo Pascal 5.5*.)

- `OvrLoadCount` measures the number of times units are loaded from disk. Aim for the lowest possible value, indicating that units are staying in memory longer. You can usually reduce a high `OvrLoadCount` by increasing the overlay buffer size with `OvrSetBuf`.
- `OvrTrapCount` counts two items: the number of times units are loaded from disk and the number of times units are accessed while on probation. Each count represents one interception by the `Overlay` manager of a call to a unit that either is not in memory or is on probation. If `OvrTrapCount` increases at

nearly the same rate as `OvrLoadCount`, then the probation-reprieve scheme is not working well—try increasing the probation area size by calling `OvrSetRetry`. You might also need a larger overlay buffer. If `OvrTrapCount` increases at a greater rate than `OvrLoadCount`, then more units are being reprieved—a good sign that you're headed in the right direction. If `OvrTrapCount` increases while `OvrLoadCount` advances slowly or not at all, you've probably hit the ideal configuration. You might even try reducing the buffer and probation sizes to minimize memory use.

Summary

Knowing the most common bugs in your favorite language can help you to avoid repeating the same mistakes over and over. And, it can help you to recognize certain kinds of bugs by their symptoms. When bugs occur, as they almost always do, the more you know about their characteristics, the better prepared you'll be to use TD to find the causes so you can fix them.

This chapter lists many of Pascal's most common bugs, and it shows how to use TD to flush them out. Bugs in Pascal code can range from simple typos, to uninitialized pointers, to problems with overlays—difficulties that most Pascal programmers run into sooner or later.

Chapter 13

Hands-On Debugging
for Pascal

To BECOME a master gardener, you've got to get your hands dirty. And so it is with debugging. To master the art of debugging *Turbo Pascal* programs, there's no substitute for a little hands-on experience searching for harmful bugs in muddy code.

Similar in design to chapter 11's hands-on debugging sessions for *Turbo C*, this chapter demonstrates how to use TD to find real bugs in real TP code. First, you'll enter a buggy program, which is long enough to be interesting, but not so long as to discourage you from typing it into your editor. Then, you'll follow the steps outlined in chapter 7 to develop a debugging strategy for six devilish bugs. After fixing each problem, you'll retest the code to be sure the bugs stay dead.

You can also use this chapter as a self test of the information you've learned so far. After reading about each bug, watch for a note like this:

> **Self test:** Stop reading now.

When you see that message, stop reading and try to find and fix the problem. Continue reading after you've discovered the solution or if you're stuck and need more help. Don't be concerned if you can't find all the bugs on your own. It's more important to try and fail than never to try at all.

> Note: Even if you already read chapter 11, you can take the self tests and follow the demonstrations in this chapter. The program and bugs are completely different (as they are in chapter 15's hands-on sessions for assembly language). However, if you didn't read chapter 11, you might want to scan that chapter's review of debugging strategies from chapter 7 before continuing.

The Program

Type in Listing 13.1 and save as CAL.PAS. Don't enter the line numbers along the left border added for reference. Then, compile to CAL.EXE with the integrated TP editor and compiler as explained in chapter 2, or use this command to compile with the command-line compiler:

```
tpc -v cal
```

Note: After finding each bug and making the suggested changes to CAL.PAS, enter that same command to recompile the modified listing.

Listing 13.1.   CAL.PAS (with bugs).

```
 1:  (*
 2:  **    File:    cal.pas (WITH BUGS!)
 3:  **    Purpose: Display 6-month calendars
 4:  **    Author:  (c) 1990 by Tom Swan.
 5:  *)
 6:
 7:  program cal;
 8:
 9:
10:  uses   crt, dos;
11:
12:
13:  const
14:
15:
16:  { ---- Miscellaneous constants }
17:
18:    NULL          = #0;       { Null character }
19:    BLANK         = #32;      { Blank character }
20:    LOWEST_YEAR   = 1980;     { Lowest legal year }
21:    HIGHEST_YEAR  = 2099;     { Highest legal year }
22:
23:
24:  { ---- Key constants returned by getKey function }
25:
26:    KEY_ENTER  = #13;      KEY_ESC   = #27;
27:    KEY_HOME   = #140;     KEY_LEFT  = #144;
28:    KEY_RIGHT  = #146;     KEY_PGUP  = #142;
29:    KEY_PGDN   = #150;     KEY_INS   = #151;
30:
```

```
31:
32:  { ---- Set of months with 30 days (the 'hath 30' months) }
33:
34:      HATH_THIRTY : set of 1 .. 12 = [ 4, 6, 9, 11 ];
35:
36:
37:  { ---- Names of months as character strings }
38:
39:      MONTH_NAMES : array[ 1 .. 12 ] of string[ 9 ] =
40:        ( 'January', 'February', 'March', 'April',
41:          'May', 'June', 'July', 'August', 'September',
42:          'October', 'November', 'December' );
43:
44:
45:  { ---- Number of days to the first of each month. }
46:
47:      DAY_OF_YEAR : array[ 1 .. 12 ] of word =
48:        ( 0, 31, 59, 90, 120, 151, 181, 212, 243, 273, 304, 334 );
49:
50:
51:  { ---- Names of week days as character strings. }
52:
53:      DAY_NAMES : array[ 0 .. 6 ] of string[ 9 ] =
54:        ( 'Sunday', 'Monday', 'Tuesday', 'Wednesday',
55:          'Thursday', 'Friday', 'Saturday' );
56:
57:
58:  var
59:
60:      today        : dateTime;     { Today's date }
61:      targetdate   : dateTime;     { First month to display }
62:      userQuits    : Boolean;      { TRUE to quit program }
63:
64:
65:  { ---- Return key press }
66:
67:  function getKey : char;
68:  const
69:      KEY_OFFSET = 69;  { 128 + readKey value for F1 (59) }
70:  begin
71:      getKey := readKey;
72:      if keypressed and ( getKey = NULL )
73:        then getKey := chr( ord( readKey ) + KEY_OFFSET );
74:  end; { getKey }
75:
```

```
76:
77: { ---- Return TRUE if low <= n <= hi }
78:
79: function inRange( n, low, hi : integer ) : Boolean;
80: begin
81:    inRange := ( low <= n ) and ( n <= hi )
82: end; { inRange }
83:
84:
85: { ---- Return TRUE if year is a leap year }
86:
87: function leapYear( year : word ) : Boolean;
88: begin
89:    if year mod $100 = 0
90:       then leapYear := ( year mod 400 ) = 0
91:       else leapYear := ( year mod 4 ) = 0
92: end; { leapYear }
93:
94:
95: { ---- Return last day of month for year and month in date d }
96:
97: function lastDay( d : dateTime ) : word;
98: begin
99:    with d do
100:    begin
101:       if month in HATH_THIRTY
102:          then lastDay := 30 else
103:       if month <> 2 then lastDay := 31 else
104:          if leapYear( year )
105:             then lastDay := 29
106:             else lastDay := 28
107:    end { with }
108: end; { lastDay }
109:
110:
111: { ---- Return true if date d is a legal (existing) date }
112:
113: function legalDate( d : dateTime ) : Boolean;
114: begin
115:    legalDate := FALSE;  { Default value for early exits }
116:    with d do
117:    begin
118:       if not inRange( month, 1, 12 )
119:          then exit;
120:       if not inRange( year, LOWEST_YEAR, HIGHEST_YEAR )
```

```
121:        then exit;
122:      legalDate := inRange( day, 1, lastDay( d ) )
123:    end { with }
124: end; { legalDate }
125:
126:
127: { ---- Return 0=sun, 1=mon, ..., 7=sat for date d. Assumes
128: that date is legal. }
129:
130: function dayOfWeek( d : dateTime ) : word;
131: var
132:    oldYear, oldMonth, oldDay, dow : word;
133: begin
134:    getDate( oldYear, oldMonth, oldDay, dow );
135:    with d do
136:    begin
137:      setDate( year, month, day );
138:      getDate( year, month, day, dow )
139:    end; { with }
140:    setDate( oldYear, oldMonth, oldDay );
141:    dayOfWeek := dow
142: end; { dayOfWeek }
143:
144:
145: { ---- Get today's date }
146:
147: procedure getToday( var today : dateTime );
148: var yy, mm, dd, dow : word;
149: begin
150:    getDate( yy, mm, dd, dow );
151:    with today do
152:    begin
153:      year := yy;
154:      month := mm;
155:      day := dd
156:    end { with }
157: end; { getToday }
158:
159:
160: { ---- Add one month to date d. Note: The day is not
161: changed, which could result in an illegal date if day > 28 }
162:
163: procedure nextMonth( var d : dateTime );
164: begin
165:    with d do
```

```
166:     if month < 12
167:     then
168:        inc( month )
169:     else
170:        begin
171:           month := 1;
172:           inc( year )
173:        end { else }
174: end; { nextMonth }
175:
176:
177: { ---- Subtract one month from date d. Note: The day is not
178: changed, which could result in an illegal date if day > 28 }
179:
180: procedure prevMonth( var d : dateTime );
181: begin
182:     with d do
183:     if month > 1
184:     then
185:        dec( month )
186:     else
187:        begin
188:           month := 12;
189:           dec( year )
190:        end
191: end; { prevMonth }
192:
193:
194: { ---- Show one calendar at x, y = top left corner }
195:
196: procedure showCal( x, y : word; d : dateTime );
197: var
198:     showDay, weekday : integer;
199:     currentmonth : Boolean;
200:
201:     procedure showMonthHeader( x, y : word; d : dateTime );
202:     var
203:        doy : integer;    { Day of year }
204:     begin
205:        lowvideo;
206:        gotoxy( x, y );
207:        with d do
208:        begin
209:           doy := DAY_OF_YEAR[ month ];
210:           if leapYear( year ) and ( month >= 3 )
```

```
211:              then inc( doy );
212:            write( year, BLANK:13, doy:3 );
213:            gotoxy( (x + 10) -
214:                ( length( month_names[ month ] ) div 2 ), y );
215:            highvideo;
216:            write( month_names[ month ] )
217:        end; { with }
218:        gotoxy( x, y + 1 );
219:        write( '--------------------' );    { 20 dashes }
220:        gotoxy( x, y + 2 );
221:        write( ' S  M  T  W  T  F  S' );
222:    end; { showMonthHeader }
223:
224: begin
225:    with d do
226:    begin
227:        day := 1;
228:        currentmonth := ( year = today.year   ) and
229:                        ( month = today.month );
230:        showMonthHeader( x, y, d );
231:        y := y + 3;
232:        weekday := dayOfWeek( d );
233:        gotoxy( x + ( weekday * 3 ), y );
234:        for showDay := 1 to lastDay( d ) do
235:        begin
236:            if currentmonth and ( showDay = today.day )
237:               then highvideo
238:               else lowvideo;
239:            write( showDay:2, BLANK );
240:            inc( weekday );
241:            if weekday >= 7 then
242:            begin
243:                weekday := 0;
244:                inc( y );
245:                gotoxy( x, y )
246:            end { if }
247:        end { for }
248:    end { with }
249: end; { showCal }
250:
251:
252: { ---- Show calendars starting from date d (with day = 1) }
253:
254: procedure showCals( d : dateTime );
255: const
```

```
256:     XCAL = 5;         { Top left x coordinate of first calendar }
257:     YCAL = 3;         { "    "   y    "       "    "    "    }
258: var
259:    i : integer;
260: begin
261:    if not legalDate( d ) then d := today;
262:    d.day := 1;
263:    for i := 0 to 5 do
264:    begin
265:       showCal( XCAL + (i mod 3) * 25, YCAL + (i div 3) * 10, d );
266:       nextMonth( d )
267:    end { for }
268: end; { showCals }
269:
270:
271: { ---- Prompt for year to display }
272:
273: procedure getNewDate( var d : dateTime );
274: begin
275:    gotoxy( 1, 23 );
276:    clreol;
277:    write( 'Year ? ' );
278:    readln( d.year );
279:    d.day := 1;
280:    d.month := 1
281: end; { getNewDate }
282:
283:
284: { ---- Initialize global variables }
285:
286: procedure initialize;
287: begin
288:    if lastmode <> mono
289:       then textcolor( brown );
290:    userQuits := FALSE;
291:    getToday( today );
292:    targetdate := today;
293: end; { initialize }
294:
295:
296: { ----- Display instructions }
297:
298: procedure instructions;
299: begin
300:    gotoxy( 1, 23 );
```

```
301:      textcolor( white );
302:      lowVideo;
303:      write( '>Esc|Enter-Quit, Home-Today,' );
304:      write( ' Left|Right-month, PgUp|PgDn|Ins-year ' );
305:  end; { instructions }
306:
307:
308:  begin
309:      initialize;
310:      repeat
311:        clrscr;
312:        showCals( targetdate );
313:        instructions;
314:        with targetDate do
315:        case getKey of
316:          KEY_ESC, KEY_ENTER : userQuits := TRUE;
317:          KEY_HOME : targetDate := today;
318:          KEY_INS  : getNewDate( targetDate );
319:          KEY_PGUP : dec( year );
320:          KEY_PGDN : inc( year );
321:          KEY_LEFT : prevMonth( targetDate );
322:          KEY_RIGHT : nextMonth( targetDate );
323:        end; { case }
324:      until userQuits;
325:      gotoxy( 1, 24 )
326:  end.
```

Hands-On Debugging Sessions

Each of the following sections begins with a description of a bug in CAL.PAS. The descriptions simulate the early stages of debugging when you know that something isn't operating as expected, but you don't know exactly what has gone wrong. Perhaps a customer telephoned to complain about a strange occurrence, or you've added new programming, and the code, which seemed to work correctly until now, suddenly failed. All you know at this stage is that the program isn't working. You don't know why.

If you're taking the self test, after reading the description of the bug, put the book aside and try to find and fix the mistake on your own. Then, whether or not you're taking the self test, follow the step-by-step numbered sections to run through the TD commands that I used to locate the bug. Do this even if you've successfully located the bug on your own. That way, you can compare your debugging strategy with mine.

Be careful to keep CAL.PAS up to date. Some of the later bugs depend on earlier ones, and you must complete sections 1 through 6 in that order, or the step-by-step instructions will be meaningless. A useful plan is to copy CAL.PAS to CALTEST.PAS for taking the self tests. Make your own changes only to CALTEST.PAS. Then, after finishing each self test, compile and load the current CAL.PAS file into TD and follow the step-by-step debugging demonstrations after the "Stop reading" note. Make the changes suggested in the text directly to CAL.PAS. You can then copy the partially debugged CAL.PAS again to CALTEST.PAS to take the next bug's self test.

You might also want to copy the original, unmodified CAL.PAS to another file, perhaps named CALBUG.PAS, so you or someone else can repeat the hands-on demonstrations in the future without having to retype the listing. This will also let you start over in case you mix up the files. If that happens, just copy the master CALBUG.PAS to CAL.PAS and make the suggested changes to CAL.PAS up to the point where you stopped.

> Note: Line numbers in the text refer to Listing 13.1 as printed in this chapter. After you make the first set of changes to CAL.PAS, your editor's line numbers may not match those in the listing. For that reason, when I suggest adding new statements, for example between lines 45 and 46, use the printed listing as a guide to locate the place in your up-to-date CAL.PAS file where you should make those changes.

Using CAL.PAS

If CAL.PAS did not have bugs, it would display 6-month calendars (see Figure 13.1) and let you press several keys to view and enter other months and years.

```
1990    March      59    1990    April      90    1990    May       120
--------------------    --------------------    --------------------
 S  M  T  W  T  F  S     S  M  T  W  T  F  S     S  M  T  W  T  F  S
             1  2  3     1  2  3  4  5  6  7           1  2  3  4  5
 4  5  6  7  8  9 10     8  9 10 11 12 13 14     6  7  8  9 10 11 12
11 12 13 14 15 16 17    15 16 17 18 19 20 21    13 14 15 16 17 18 19
18 19 20 21 22 23 24    22 23 24 25 26 27 28    20 21 22 23 24 25 26
25 26 27 28 29 30 31    29 30                   27 28 29 30 31

1990    June      151    1990    July      181    1990    August    212
--------------------    --------------------    --------------------
 S  M  T  W  T  F  S     S  M  T  W  T  F  S     S  M  T  W  T  F  S
                1  2     1  2  3  4  5  6  7              1  2  3  4
 3  4  5  6  7  8  9     8  9 10 11 12 13 14     5  6  7  8  9 10 11
10 11 12 13 14 15 16    15 16 17 18 19 20 21    12 13 14 15 16 17 18
17 18 19 20 21 22 23    22 23 24 25 26 27 28    19 20 21 22 23 24 25
24 25 26 27 28 29 30    29 30 31                26 27 28 29 30 31

>Esc|Enter-Quit, Home-Today, Left|Right-month, PgUp|PgDn|Ins-year
```

Figure 13.1. Sample CAL.PAS display.

Table 13.1 lists the keys and associated commands you can use to control CAL.PAS. Unfortunately, however, the program doesn't work, so many of these commands will fail until you find and fix the bugs in the code.

Bug Number 1

Here's the scene. You've just added new programming to CAL.PAS. You've compiled the program, and you're ready for a test run. The program starts as it should, and the display appears as expected. But when you try the commands in Table 13.1, you discover that the only keys the program recognizes are ⟨Esc⟩ and ⟨Enter⟩. Other commands don't work. (Actually, because the current month is showing, ⟨Home⟩ may or may not be working. There's no way to tell.)

Table 13.1. CAL.PAS keys and commands.

Key	Command
⟨Cursor Left⟩	Go back one month
⟨Cursor Right⟩	Go forward one month
⟨Enter⟩	Quit program and return to DOS
⟨Esc⟩	Same as ⟨Enter⟩
⟨Home⟩	Display current month and year
⟨Insert⟩	Enter a new year
⟨Page Down⟩	Go forward one year
⟨Page Up⟩	Go back one year

Obviously, the program isn't calling the procedures for those commands as it should. Or, could something else be wrong?

Self test: Stop reading now.

Bug number 1—Test

The test to reproduce this bug covers a lot of ground. That can't be helped, however. Until we can execute the program's commands, we can't test whether those commands work. So, the full test merely describes the problem:

1. Run the program.

2. Press ⟨**Insert**⟩, ⟨**Home**⟩, ⟨**Page Up**⟩, ⟨**Page Down**⟩, ⟨**Cursor Left**⟩, and ⟨**Cursor Right**⟩. None of these keys appears to work. (⟨**Home**⟩ might be working, but it's impossible to tell.)

3. Press ⟨**Esc**⟩ or ⟨**Enter**⟩ and the program ends. This is correct.

The full test describes the bug in detail—in fact, the initial test is the bug description. But it's still too broad to be useful for debugging. We need to stabilize the problem before hunting for the cause.

> Note: Ignore any other bugs you may notice. Concentrate on one problem at a time—in this case, the inoperative command keys.

Bug number 1—Stabilize

You've identified the bug, and you might be tempted to skip this step and start debugging. But the test in the previous section covers too much territory. Also, we haven't done anything to duplicate runtime conditions that might be causing the error.

A good way to satisfy these goals and stabilize a bug is to select a subset of the full test. In other words, instead of just pressing all keys to see if they work, a more exacting strategy will let us work quickly to find the bug's source.

So, let's pick one of the broken commands, assuming that the same bug is responsible for causing that and the other function key to fail. That assumption may be wrong—each key could be failing for a different reason. (After all, at least two keys work!) Still, it seems more likely that we'll find one bug, not four or five. Here's the plan:

1. Run the program.

2. Press ⟨**Esc**⟩. The program should end.

3. Run the program again.

4. Press ⟨**Page Up**⟩. The calendar should display the previous year. Instead, the year does not change.

Notice that the refined test includes instructions about how to run the program, how to perform a command that works, and how to duplicate a known problem. The steps also list what should happen along with what doesn't. Together, the stabilized test duplicates the runtime conditions needed to reproduce the bug while providing a useful comparison to make during debugging.

Bug number 1—Isolate

It's time to load the program into the debugger and narrow the problem to as small a section of code as possible. Remember to compile the source with the proper switch to insert debugging information, then type **td cal** to start TD. You should see the program's source code in the `Module` window.

Next, follow these steps to isolate the bug. Remember, the goal is to work quickly, using the tests developed in the previous two sections.

1. Move the cursor to anywhere on the line inside the `case` statement that begins with the constant `KEY_PGUP` (line 319 in the listing), and set a code breakpoint there (press ⟨**F2**⟩). We want to find out why the `KEY_PGUP` key fails, so that `case` selector is the logical place to start.

2. Because this line decrements the `year` field in `targetDate` (the displayed calendar's date), it's probably a good idea to monitor this value in the `Watches` window. To do that, press ⟨**F6**⟩ to make `Watches` current and enter **targetDate.year**. You don't have to choose any commands, just start typing and press ⟨**Enter**⟩. Then press ⟨**F6**⟩ to switch back to the `Module` window.

3. Press ⟨**F9**⟩ to run the program. When the calendar display appears, press ⟨**Page Up**⟩ to duplicate the bug.

4. The code stops on the breakpoint. Notice that the year displayed in `Watches` is correct. Next, we want to verify whether the statement advances the year. So, press ⟨**F8**⟩ to step over the code. (You could also press ⟨**F7**⟩, but if the statement called a procedure or function, you'd want to step over that call the first time through. Remember, the goal is to divide and conquer. Don't start tracing into subroutines until you're reasonably certain that you're in hot pursuit of a bug.)

5. Oh, no. The year didn't change. And, the cursor moved to the next `case` selector. This is clearly wrong. After executing a selected case, the program should move to the end of the `case` statement; therefore, the only possible conclusion is that the `KEY_PGUP` statement did not execute.

6. To test that assumption, set another breakpoint on the `KEY_ESC` selector (move the cursor up to line 316, just below `case`, and press ⟨**F2**⟩). Press ⟨**F9**⟩ to run, then press ⟨**Esc**⟩. When the breakpoint stops the code, press ⟨**F8**⟩ as you did before. This time, the cursor jumps to the `until` clause in the `repeat` statement, the correct behavior after the selected `case` statement executes.

7. The `case` statement seems to work, so perhaps the problem isn't with the program commands after all. Instead, it looks as though the proper `case` selectors aren't generated for the expected keystrokes. Those selectors come from `getKey`, called by `case`. So, let's turn our attention there.

8. To test the assumption that `getKey` is at fault, press ⟨**Ctrl**⟩-⟨**F4**⟩ to open the `Evaluate/modify` dialog box. Type **KEY__ PGUP** and press ⟨**Enter**⟩ to see the value of this selector. (Perhaps the key constant values are wrong.) But, no, the value is ASCII #142, the correct value for ⟨Page Up⟩.

9. So, let's test the `getKey` function. While still viewing the `Evaluate/modify` window, type **getKey( )** and press ⟨**Enter**⟩. The program display appears when the expression executes the function. (The entire program isn't running, at this point, only `getKey`.) Press ⟨**Page Up**⟩, the faulty key. In a moment, the `Result` pane in the `Evaluate/modify` window shows that `getKey()` returned #0—not the expected value of #142 that we determined in the previous step.

10. Try executing `getKey` again. You don't have to type it—just press ⟨**Enter**⟩ with the cursor on `getKey()`. When the calendar appears, press ⟨**Esc**⟩, one of the two keys that we know works. As expected, the window shows the correct value for this key, ASCII #27.

11. Apparently, `getKey` works for some keys but not for others. Press ⟨**Esc**⟩ to close the `Evaluate/modify` window. Clear old breakpoints (⟨**Alt**⟩-**BD**) and reset the code (⟨**Ctrl**⟩-⟨**F2**⟩). Move the cursor to line 315 (press ⟨**Ctrl**⟩-**L**, type **315**, and press ⟨**Enter**⟩) and set a new breakpoint (press ⟨**F2**⟩) on that line. It's time to trace `getKey` to see what's wrong with the function.

12. Press ⟨**F9**⟩ to run. At the breakpoint, press ⟨**F7**⟩ to trace into `getKey`. Press ⟨**F7**⟩ once more to execute the function's invisible startup instructions, then press ⟨**F7**⟩ again to trace the first statement, which calls the system routine `readKey` to get the next keypress.

13. You should again see the program's display. Press ⟨**Page Up**⟩, the key that's causing all the trouble.

14. So far, so good, the program returns from `readKey` and prepares to execute the next line. So, let's continue tracing—there are only a few statements here, and we may as well examine each one in detail. Press ⟨**F7**⟩ once more.

15. Whoops! The cursor jumped to `begin`. Now, what could that mean? There's only one answer—the function just called itself. Examine the `if` statement that you traced. The expression (`getKey = NULL`) is the culprit. It calls the function rather than doing what it should—testing for the null character (#0) that precedes all function keys returned by `readKey`. We've found the bug—an unexpected recursion inside the function.

Bug number 1—Repair

To fix the problem, quit TD (⟨**Alt**⟩-**X**) and load CAL.PAS into your editor. Add a `char` variable for the `if` statement to examine. This modifies the function to return the next keypress only if the first equals #0, indicating that a named function key was pressed. To make these changes, replace lines 67–74 in the original CAL.PAS listing with the following text:

```
function getKey : char;
const
   KEY_OFFSET = 69;  { 128 + readKey value for F1 (59) }
var
   ch : char;
begin
   ch := readKey;
   if keypressed and ( ch = NULL )
      then getKey := chr( ord( readKey ) + KEY_OFFSET )
      else getKey := ch
end; { getKey }
```

After repairing the buggy function, recompile CAL.PAS (**tpc -v cal**) and repeat the stabilized test. Run CAL and press ⟨**Page Up**⟩. This time, the year advances as planned. Also try the other function keys. They seem to work, too. Apparently, our assumption that there was one bug, not four or five, was correct.

Bug Number 2

If you have a color monitor, you undoubtedly noticed from the previous demonstration that every time you press a key, the display changes from color to black and white. I purposely avoided mentioning this problem until now for a good reason.

Very often while testing for one bug, you'll notice another. When that happens, make a note about it, then continue working on the first bug. Don't hop around fixing everything in sight. If you do, you may introduce other errors, and you'll destroy the effectiveness of your test procedures.

If you don't have a color monitor, you won't even know that this new bug exists. Readers with monochrome screens may think that gives color-display owners an unfair advantage, but if you were writing a commercial program, you'd want to test it on as many different system configurations as possible. But even if you can't locate a color monitor, you can still follow the step-by-step demonstration for finding the bug.

Self test: Stop reading now.

Bug number 2—Test

This time, the test is simple. Any key, it seems, causes the problem. No matter what you type, the screen switches from living color to dull black and white after the first keypress.

When faced with similar problems, I usually press as many keys as possible, both alone and in combination with ⟨Ctrl⟩, ⟨Alt⟩, and ⟨Shift⟩. This takes only a few seconds, and it often forces other bugs into the open—for example, a command that executes for the wrong key.

Some programmers perform their keyboard tests in the most violent fashion, literally smashing their fist onto the keys (but not too hard) to test the program's input procedures. I prefer less brutal tests, but the point is, no matter what input test you devise, you can't check every possible combination of all keys! It's probably good enough to test only the alphanumeric keys plus a few extremes—function keys, keypad digits with ⟨Num Lock⟩ on and off, cursor movement keys, and so on. Good tests don't have to include every possibility. A sensible cross section will do.

Bug number 2—Stabilize

As with the first bug, after testing reveals a problem, stabilize the error with repeatable steps. Here are the ones I selected:

1. Run the program.
2. Press ⟨Esc⟩. The program ends normally.
3. Run the program again.
4. Press **A**. The display changes to black and white.

Why did I choose to press the A key in step 4? Why not use a program function key such as ⟨Home⟩ or ⟨Page Down⟩?

The reason is that I noticed from the earlier tests that both the A key and ⟨Page Down⟩ produced the same result. Because the program recognizes ⟨Page Down⟩ as a command, but does not recognize the A key, it seems reasonable to conclude that the operation selected by ⟨Page Down⟩ is not causing the problem. For this reason, choosing the A key gives us a head start by narrowing the bug search even before loading the code into TD.

Bug number 2—Isolate

Armed with a repeatable test, load CAL into TD, this time specifying the -k command-line option to enable keystroke recording. (Enter the command **td -k cal**.) Then, follow these steps to isolate the cause of the disappearing color display:

1. Because the bug occurs after pressing a key, the logical place to divide the code is the same as it was for the previous mistake—on the `case` statement at line 315. (Remember, line numbers here refer to the listing printed in this chapter. Because you modified CAL.PAS, line numbers in your editor and in TD may not match.) Move the cursor to that line, set the breakpoint there (press ⟨**F2**⟩), and then press ⟨**F9**⟩ to run.

2. The program will halt almost immediately. When it does, press ⟨**Alt**⟩-⟨**F5**⟩ to examine the output screen. It's in color, which is no surprise—you haven't completed the steps to reproduce the bug. So, press ⟨**Enter**⟩ to return to TD's display, then press ⟨**F9**⟩ to continue running. This calls `getKey` for the next keypress. Press the A key to duplicate the bug, and the program halts at the same breakpoint location. Press ⟨**Alt**⟩-⟨**F5**⟩ to check the display again. Now it's in black and white! Press ⟨**Enter**⟩ to return to TD.

3. At this point, we know only that the bug occurs somewhere between `repeat` at line 310 and `until` at 324. The next step, then, is to narrow the search further to discover whether the problem appears before or after the current breakpoint on `case`. That's easy enough. Just set another breakpoint at `until` (line 324). Move the cursor to that line and press ⟨**F2**⟩.

4. Clear the output display by opening the `Evaluate/modify` window (press ⟨**Ctrl**⟩-⟨**F4**⟩). Enter **clrscr( )** and press ⟨**Enter**⟩ to call that system routine. (When trying this at other times, if you receive the message "Initialization not complete," close the window, press ⟨**F8**⟩, and repeat the command. This executes runtime startup code, so TD can locate and call system routines.) Press ⟨**Esc**⟩ to close the `Evaluate/modify` window and ⟨**Alt**⟩-⟨**F5**⟩ to check that the display is clear. Press ⟨**Enter**⟩ to return to TD.

5. Next, press ⟨**Ctrl**⟩-⟨**F2**⟩ and ⟨**F9**⟩ to reset the program and run. Again, the program stops at `case`, and the output screen is in color as it was before. (Check it by pressing ⟨**Alt**⟩-⟨**F5**⟩ and then ⟨**Enter**⟩ to return to TD.) Press ⟨**F9**⟩ to run and then press the A key. The code stops at `until`. Check the output (press ⟨**Alt**⟩-⟨**F5**⟩ and ⟨**Enter**⟩). It's still in color, so we can assume that the error occurs above `case`. This also eliminates `getKey` as a candidate. (The problem could have been caused by the earlier bug fix, but that does not appear to be the case.)

6. Of the three statements between `repeat` and `case`, we can safely eliminate `clrscr`. The problem might be in a system routine like this one, but that's not very likely. More likely, the bug is in `showCals` (line 312) or `instructions` (line 313). We can ignore everything between `case` and `end` because the A key is not one of the listed `case` selectors.

7. By setting breakpoints and repeating the stabilized test, we've narrowed the search in short order to two statements. So far, the hunt has remained entirely on the program's outer level, letting us quickly eliminate entire

sections of code. But now, it's time to dig deeper to find out which statement is at fault. To duplicate the buggy conditions, press ⟨**Alt**⟩-**FO**, enter **cal**, and press ⟨**Enter**⟩. This reloads the program and clears all breakpoints—easier than using other commands to do the same job. Move the cursor to the line that calls showCals (312 in the listing) and press ⟨**F2**⟩ to set a breakpoint there. This routine is the likely candidate since it displays the calendars.

8. But, let's be sure. Press ⟨**F9**⟩ to run. The code halts at showCals. Press ⟨**F8**⟩ to step over the procedure and check the output (press ⟨**Alt**⟩-⟨**F5**⟩). It's in color. Press ⟨**Enter**⟩ to return to TD and press ⟨**F9**⟩ to continue. Press the A key to duplicate the bug. Then press ⟨**F8**⟩ once more and check the output (⟨**Alt**⟩-⟨**F5**⟩). The screen is in black and white. Obviously, the second call to showCals is causing the problem. Press ⟨**Enter**⟩ to return to TD.

9. Reset the program (press ⟨**Ctrl**⟩-⟨**F2**⟩) and repeat step 8 up to the *second* time the instructions tell you to press ⟨**F8**⟩. But this time, instead of that key, press ⟨**F7**⟩ to trace into the showCals procedure. (If you get mixed up at this point, just repeat step 9.) You should see showCals' source code in the Module window.

10. A quick glance at showCals shows that this procedure merely calls showCal in a for loop to display each month's calendar. Let's trace into the first of those calls. To do that, move the cursor down a few lines to showCal and press ⟨**F4**⟩ to execute up to that line. Then press ⟨**F7**⟩ to trace into the procedure.

11. You now see showCal's source code. Check the output again to be sure there's nothing there (press ⟨**Alt**⟩-⟨**F5**⟩ and then press ⟨**Enter**⟩ to return to TD). Next, let's find the first statement that writes something to the screen. Press ⟨**F8**⟩ to step over individual lines and check the output by pressing ⟨**Alt**⟩-⟨**F5**⟩ and ⟨**Enter**⟩ after each line executes. Aha! The call to showMonthHeader shows the top part of the first calendar in black and white. (If you don't have a color monitor, stop pressing ⟨**F8**⟩ after executing showMonthHeader.)

12. Unfortunately, we've stepped too far to trace back through showMonthHeader. But, because we enabled keystroke recording, it's possible to repeat all the steps that led up to that point. To jump back one step in time, first press ⟨**Alt**⟩-**VE** to open the Execution history window. Press ⟨**Tab**⟩⟨**Cursor Up**⟩ to highlight the call to showMonthHeader in the bottom pane. Then, press ⟨**Ctrl**⟩-**K** to repeat the keystrokes that led to this stopping place. This may take a few seconds. When TD stops, the cursor will be positioned on the call to showMonthHeader.

13. Press ⟨**F7**⟩ to trace into that procedure. Then, as you did earlier, press ⟨**F8**⟩ to step over each source line and check the output for changes by pressing ⟨**Alt**⟩-⟨**F5**⟩⟨**Enter**⟩. The first such change comes at line 212

(write(year, ...)), which displays the year and number of days in the year to the first of the current month. After executing that statement, check the output by pressing **⟨Alt⟩-⟨F5⟩⟨Enter⟩**. It's in black and white.

14. But, wait a minute. We haven't executed any statements that change display colors. And, it's impossible for the display to switch to black and white on its own. We've traced the code to the lowest level—a write statement in the runtime library, which we may as well assume works correctly. The only conclusion is disheartening. We've been on a wild goose chase!

15. It happens. But, because you've adopted a methodical approach to debugging, you can easily return to a previous assumption and continue debugging. Our efforts aren't yet wasted. Earlier, the search narrowed to one of two procedures, showCals and instructions. The problem isn't in showCals. It must be in...

16. Instructions? Let's find out. Press **⟨Alt⟩-VE** to open the Execution history window again, press **⟨Tab⟩** to move to the bottom pane, then press **⟨Ctrl⟩-⟨Page Up⟩** to jump to the first recorded line. Press **⟨Cursor Down⟩** five times to highlight the first call to instructions and press **⟨Ctrl⟩-K** to replay all keystrokes up to that call. When the action stops, press **⟨F7⟩** to trace into instructions. Look at the code (lines 298–305). The textColor statement at line 301 sets the output to white. Now, everything makes sense. The instructions procedure runs after the first call to showCals; therefore, the output changes to black and white only after showCals has one shot at displaying the calendar in color.

17. By the way, this is a good example of a long-distance bug—a problem that appears in one place but is caused by a statement in some other location. We found the bug this time, not by tracing to it but by eliminating the only other possible path.

Bug number 2—Repair

This bug is caused by an inconsistent design—a typical problem when a global setting (the text color in this case) requires temporary changes (to show calendars in one color but instructions in another). There are usually two approaches you can take to prevent this kind of problem:

- Save and restore the current setting in each routine that changes it.
- Or, make each routine responsible for selecting the setting it needs.

Either solution will work—but I prefer the second. That way, every routine is responsible for setting its own display colors. To fix the program, quit TD, edit CAL.PAS, and move lines 288 and 289 (if lastmode...then) from their present positions inside initialize to between lines 224 and 225 in showCal (just after begin and before with d do). Now both showCal and instructions follow the same scheme—changing the text color as needed. Don't forget to recompile and retest!

Bug Number 3

Things are looking up. You've tried all of the program's commands, and the code seems to be working well. Time to cut the master and start shipping disks to customers. Right?

Not exactly. Remember that the primary goal of good testing is to force bugs into the open air. How do you know the program is working? Perhaps there are hidden bugs waiting for certain input or other conditions. All may seem well. But it's time to put that assumption to the test—the torture test, that is.

For some reason, bugs often hide at the limits in code. Formulas that normally work give incorrect results when fed extreme values. Arrays blow up when indexes reach either end. Programs crash when memory fills. So far, you haven't tested CAL.PAS at its limits. For example, it's probably a good idea to display a few calendars for the two constant values at lines 20 and 21, which define the earliest year as 1980 and the highest as 2099—limits imposed by DOS date routines.

On one such trial, you press ⟨**Page Up**⟩ to travel back in time to 1980. Then you press ⟨**Page Up**⟩ again just to verify that the program stops at that year. But instead of stopping there, the calendar resets to the current year. Worse, ⟨**Page Up**⟩ suddenly stops working. In fact, other function keys fail at this point too. (But sometimes, they start working again!) Could this be a result of the earlier change to getKey?

Self test: Stop reading now.

Bug number 3—Test

This looks serious. The program fails at its outer limits, and as soon as one problem appears, others follow—the keyboard stops working. Things aren't looking up after all. In fact, they seem to be getting worse.

The test has already forced the bug into the open, so we can skip directly to the next stage in the debugging strategy.

Bug number 3—Stabilize

Let's review the facts. Pressing ⟨**Page Up**⟩ a number of times to display early years causes the program to fail after reaching the lower limit of 1980. Pressing that same key only once or twice doesn't seem to cause any trouble. So, to stabilize the problem, the first step is to determine the minimum number of trials required to reproduce the bug.

That's a good rule of thumb. When a sequence of repeated events leads to a bug, try to find the smallest number of events that causes the problem. Hunt for the cause by repeating the test in TD. After fixing the problem, retest the program to be sure the bug is gone. This is the strategy we'll follow. If CAL is running, quit to DOS, then:

1. Run CAL and press ⟨**Page Up**⟩ until the year equals 1980.

2. Press ⟨**Page Up**⟩ again. The calendar changes to the current year.

3. Press ⟨**Page Up**⟩ again. The key no longer works.

4. Press ⟨**Esc**⟩ to end. This key works.

Bug number 3—Isolate

Load CAL into TD with the command **td cal**. Follow these steps to isolate the cause of this bug:

1. Because we know the number of steps that reproduce the problem, the first step is to run the code to just before the problem appears. To do this, first set a breakpoint at the `case` selector for `KEY_PGUP` at line 319 in the original listing—move the cursor to that line and press ⟨**F2**⟩. Then, with the cursor still on the same line, press ⟨**Alt**⟩-⟨**F2**⟩ to set this breakpoint's options.

2. Press ⟨**Tab**⟩ or use the mouse to highlight the `Pass count` input box in the `Breakpoint options` dialog box. Then, type 11—the minimum number of keypresses required to reproduce the error. (Note: It's 1990 as I write this. Increase the pass count by one for each later year.) Press ⟨**Enter**⟩ to accept the change.

3. Press ⟨**F9**⟩ to run. Press ⟨**Page Up**⟩ 11 times or the number you entered for the pass count. The code will halt at the suspect location. Setting the pass count allowed us to get to this place in the code quickly.

4. Let's examine the target date's year. Move the cursor to any character of `targetDate` on the line above and press ⟨**Ctrl**⟩-**W** to add the variable to the `Watches` window. As you can see, the first field in the date record equals 1980.

5. Trace the current line by pressing ⟨**F8**⟩. The year changes to 1979. But that seems wrong. Why then does the calendar display the current year? To find out, run the code by pressing ⟨**F9**⟩ again. Press ⟨**Page Up**⟩ to complete the stabilized test and press ⟨**Alt**⟩-⟨**F5**⟩ to examine the program's display. The year on screen is still the current one, but when you press ⟨**Enter**⟩ to

return to TD and then press ⟨**F8**⟩ to step over dec(year) again, targetDate's first field changes to 1978.

6. Apparently, showCals is not displaying the same date as the one passed to it at line 312. Let's trace into that routine and see whether targetDate is reaching its intended target. Set a breakpoint on the call to showCals (move the cursor to line 312 showCals(targetDate) and press ⟨**F2**⟩) and then press ⟨**F9**⟩⟨**F7**⟩ to run the code and trace into the procedure.

7. Press ⟨**F8**⟩ to step over the procedure's startup code. (Always remember to perform this step after tracing into a procedure or function in which you want to examine passed arguments.) Move the cursor to either of the two references to parameter d on this line and press ⟨**Ctrl**⟩-**W** to add d to Watches. It's now easy to compare this date with targetDate.

8. The dates are the same. But look at the first statement. If the procedure determines that d is not a legal date, it sets it equal to today. We know that d is not legal—1978 is earlier than the programmed lower limit; therefore, press ⟨**F8**⟩ to see if the statement assigns today to d. And, yes, it does. This is why, when passed an illegal date, the displayed calendar shows today's year.

9. And now we see the problem. Obviously, targetDate is not changed after the assignment of today to d. The showCals procedure should pass that value back to the caller to keep the dates in synch.

Bug number 3—Repair

To fix the bug, quit TD, edit CAL.PAS, and add var to the showCals declaration at line 254, changing that line to:

```
procedure showCals( var d : dateTime );
```

Recompile and run the program, then press ⟨**Page Up**⟩ to repeat the earlier test. But, what's this? Something else appears to be wrong. Now, years don't change by ones—the wrong months pop up on screen. Try ⟨**Cursor Left**⟩ and ⟨**Cursor Right**⟩ to move from month to month. Those keys don't work either. Instead of fixing the problem, we've made it worse!

At such moments, don't be alarmed. I cooked up this surprise to demonstrate the value of good test procedures. What if you had added the var declaration, assumed the problem was fixed, and then added a few other new features? You might then have assumed that the new code had produced the bug, when it was the simple three-letter change you made earlier. Many programmers fall into this trap. Don't be one of them.

Also, when a bug fix seems to worsen a problem—as it often does—it's usually a good idea to remove it and return to the previous version. Debugging rarely follows the cleanly outlined steps you might find in a textbook (but, obviously, not this one). In practice, debugging is a messy business. Be prepared to undo your changes when you discover they don't work.

But was the earlier bug search wasted? No. We determined that the program reduces the `year` field in `targetDate` as expected. But the code allows `year` to go beyond the programmed limit of 1980. This is a major design flaw—the program should prevent `targetDate` from becoming illegal in the first place.

Apparently, there are two appropriate repairs to this lack of error handling that our debugging strategy exposed. One is to insert checks in the code before every change to `targetDate` to ensure that it never becomes illegal. For example, you could change line 319 to:

```
KEY_PGUP : if year >= LOWEST_YEAR then dec( year );
```

That's the approach many programmers take, and it's not wrong. But it may introduce other bugs by spreading the program's error checks over a wide area. For that reason, I prefer to repair this kind of problem by simply resetting `targetDate` to its formerly legal value if it ever becomes illegal. To make my fix, load CAL.PAS into your text editor and add this variable declaration between lines 61 and 62:

```
savedDate : dateTime;    { Current legal date }
```

Then, add this assignment between the original lines 313 and 314 (between `instructions` and `with targetDate do`), preserving `targetDate` for resetting later:

```
savedDate := targetDate;
```

Also add this two-line statement between lines 323 and 324 (between `end` and `until`) to test `targetDate` and reassign it the saved date value if the adjusted date is illegal:

```
if not legalDate( targetDate )
   then targetDate := savedDate
```

Be sure to remove the `var` that you added earlier to `showCals` at line 254. Then, recompile and retest. Now when you press ⟨**Page Up**⟩, the calendars stop at 1980 as they should.

Bug Number 4

You just finished adding error handling to prevent a serious bug when the year became less than the lowest legal year, 1980. This should also take care of any possible problems at the other end when the year is greater than the upper limit, 2099. Right?

Absolutely not. One of your beta testers just reported that when December 2099 is displayed in the upper left corner, the following months begin on the wrong days. You try the experiment and discover the report is correct. How can that be?

Self test: Stop reading now.

Bug number 4—Test

Be sure always to test your programs at their extreme ranges. Never assume that fixing a problem for one extreme will repair other problems. Test low, middle, and high values to force bugs to appear.

To verify the beta tester's report, run CAL, press 〈**Insert**〉, enter **2099**, and press 〈**Cursor Right**〉 to bring December 2099 to the upper left corner. Notice that January 2100 is displayed next to December, even though we added code earlier to limit dates to legal ranges. (2099 should be the last year displayed.) Worse, the calendar shows all months starting with January 1, 2100 beginning on the same day.

Bug number 4—Stabilize

The repeatable test to stabilize the bug is:

1. Run the program.
2. Press 〈**Insert**〉, enter **2098**, and press 〈**Enter**〉. We don't want to enter 2099 here because the beta tester reported using the cursor keys to bring the problem dates into view. This may or may not be significant, so we'll do the same. Entering **2098** keeps the problem month off screen, no matter what the current month is.
3. Press 〈**Cursor Right**〉 until December 2099 is in the upper left corner. January 2100 (which shouldn't be displayed) shows the wrong days. So do February through May 2100, which also should be rejected as illegal dates.

Bug number 4—Isolate

This time, a check of a good DOS manual reveals the cause of the problem—DOS can't handle dates beyond December 31, 2099. The program should prevent displaying illegal dates after then. At first, we might suspect a problem with the `legalDate` function at line 113. But rather than waste time pondering the function's algorithm, let's use TD's ability to set breakpoints for specific values and find out where in the code illegal dates are getting through. Follow these steps:

1. Load CAL.EXE into TD with the command **td cal**. Because `showCals` takes care of displaying calendars, let's find out whether an illegal `targetDate` is ever passed to that procedure. To do this, move the cursor to the call to `showCals` (line 312 in the printed listing) and press ⟨**F2**⟩ to set a code breakpoint there.

2. Without moving the cursor, press ⟨**Alt**⟩-⟨**F2**⟩ to set this breakpoint's options. Tab to `Condition` and press ⟨**Cursor Down**⟩ twice to toggle `Expression true`, then press ⟨**Tab**⟩ again and, as the `Condition expression`, enter **targetDate.year⟩2099**. Press ⟨**Enter**⟩ to accept the changes you made to the breakpoint.

3. Press ⟨**F9**⟩ to run the program. Even though you set a breakpoint to monitor a memory location for a specific value, the program runs at full speed (or nearly so). This is because you limited the expression evaluation to a single line in the source. If you don't have an 80386-based system or a hardware debugging board, this is a good way to use `Expression true` breakpoints without affecting program performance.

4. Repeat the stabilized test to force the bug to appear (bring December, 2099 to the upper left corner). Nothing happens, proving that an illegal `targetDate` year is not passed to `showCals`. Good. This eliminates that section of code and lets us trace further into `showCals` to locate the problem.

5. Press ⟨**Esc**⟩ twice to end CAL and remove TD's termination message. The cursor should still be on the line that calls `showCals`. Press ⟨**F2**⟩ to remove the breakpoint, then press ⟨**Ctrl**⟩-⟨**F2**⟩ to reset. Move the cursor to any letter in `showCals` and press ⟨**Ctrl**⟩-**G**⟨**Enter**⟩ to `Goto` that routine's source code. (Remember this handy shortcut for hopping to the source of a procedure or function. It's usually easier than paging through text looking for a specific routine.)

6. Let's repeat the earlier test to find an illegal date in the `for` loop that displays the six calendars. Move the cursor down five lines to the place inside the loop that calls `showCal`, press ⟨**F2**⟩ to set a breakpoint, and press ⟨**Alt**⟩-⟨**F2**⟩ to set options. Press ⟨**Tab**⟩ to move to `Condition` and ⟨**Cursor Down**⟩ twice to set `Expression true`. Press ⟨**Tab**⟩ again and enter **d.year⟩2099** as the `Condition expression`. Press ⟨**Enter**⟩ to close the options dialog window. (This is nearly the same test we performed for `targetDate` earlier, but it narrows the search further to each calendar as it displays.)

7. Press ⟨**F9**⟩ to run. You may notice that the code runs slower than before. This is because setting breakpoints for local variables requires more

processing than for globals. (On fast systems, you may not be able to tell the difference.) Repeat the stabilized test procedure to bring December 2099 into view. You won't be able to complete these steps—as soon as January 2100 scrolls into view at the lower right corner, the breakpoint halts the program, and TD displays `Breakpoint at CAL.271 "d.year>2099" true`. (The line number may be different.)

8. Press ⟨**Esc**⟩ to clear the breakpoint message. There's no need to go further. The code should not pass illegal dates to `showCal`, but it does. Despite the test for illegal dates that we inserted before, the call to `nextMonth` just after the current breakpoint increments the date past its upper limit. The program's error-handling needs more work.

Bug number 4—Repair

Searching for this bug with TD taught us two facts about the program. One, an illegal initial date is not passed to `showCals` in the program's outer loop (at line 312). But, two, an illegal date is passed to `showCal` from inside `showCals` at line 265.

This implies that two changes are required. First, line 261 (`if not legal-Date...`) is useless. We've proven that illegal dates aren't passed to this procedure, so we may as well remove the statement—it has no effect on the program. Load CAL.PAS into your editor and delete that line.

A better place to check for illegal dates—in fact, the only correct place in this example—is before calling `showCal`. To do that, insert this line between lines 264 and 265 (between the `for` loop's `begin` and the call to `showCal`):

```
if not legalDate( d ) then exit;
```

Compile and run the stabilized test. This time, when December 2099 comes into view, `showCals` exits before displaying the illegal dates, leaving those calendars blank.

Bug Number 5

Just when you think you've found all the bugs, a beta tester phones to report a runtime error for "certain date values" entered after pressing ⟨**Insert**⟩. When you ask which date fails, the tester says, "Jan 1996."

"But," you say, "You're not supposed to enter month names, only years with this command." The tester thanks you for the advice and hangs up, leaving you with a nagging suspicion that you've forgotten something important. So, you try the reported bug, and sure enough, the program halts with a runtime error 106.

> **Self test:** Stop reading now.

Bug number 5—Test

The first question that comes to mind is, "Is this problem specific to the input value 'Jan 1996', or do other input values cause the same problem?" To find out, press ⟨**Insert**⟩ and enter a few other month names and years. Finding that they all halt the program, try other text—your name, random characters, and other bad input. In all cases, the result is the same.

Bug number 5—Stabilize

Since all character input seems to cause the same problem, it's only necessary to pick one sequence that you know fails. For this, we may as well use the beta tester's example:

1. Run CAL.
2. Press ⟨**Insert**⟩ to select the change year command.
3. Enter **Jan 1996**.
4. The program halts with `Runtime error 106 at 0000:0661` (the address may be different).

Bug number 5—Isolate

Isolating a runtime error is easy. The runtime error handler has given you the address, which you can pass to TD to find the statement that's causing the trouble. Follow these steps:

1. Load CAL.EXE into TD with the command **td cal**. Press ⟨**Ctrl**⟩-**G** to select the `Module` view's `Goto` command. Enter the error address **$0661** (use the value from your screen) and press ⟨**Enter**⟩ to jump to that location. The dollar sign tells TD that this is a hexadecimal value.
2. The cursor is now at the line just after the one that caused the problem—the call to `readln` at line 278 in the original listing. Just to make sure we've found the source of the trouble, set a breakpoint at `readln` (move the cursor up one line and press ⟨**F2**⟩), then press ⟨**F9**⟩ to run.
3. Press ⟨**Insert**⟩. The breakpoint stops the program before the `readln` call. Press ⟨**F9**⟩ to continue and enter **Jan 1996**. When you press ⟨**Enter**⟩, the

program halts and TD displays `Terminated, exit code 106`. This proves that the call to `readln` is causing the bug.

Bug number 5—Repair

Some programmers, upon discovering that a bug occurs during a call to a system routine like `readln`, immediately criticize the language for the failure. Or, they waste time tracing the routine's machine code looking for a bug.

But, the chance of finding a bug in well-tested system code is small. More likely, the problem is in the way the program uses that code. You may disagree with the design of a system procedure or function, but if it follows its published specifications, it doesn't have a bug. It just doesn't work as you may wish it did.

For that reason, this is the time to turn to your language manuals. When you do, you find that `readln` is *supposed* to fail for character input to numeric variables. The bug isn't in `readln`, but rather in the program's use of that routine. To read a numeric variable without halting for a bad input value, you must read a string and convert it to an integer value. This gives the program complete control over input so it can deal appropriately with bad data.

A quick fix isn't possible this time. Instead, the `getNewDate` procedure needs redesigning. Quit TD, edit CAL.PAS, and insert this new procedure in place of lines 273–281 in the original listing:

```
procedure getNewDate( var d : dateTime );
var
   s : string[4];
   x : integer;
begin
   gotoxy( 1, 23 );
   clreol;
   write( 'Year ? ' );
   readln( s );
   if length( s ) > 0 then with d do
   begin
      val( s, d.year, x );
      day := 1;
      month := 1
   end
end; { getNewDate }
```

The revised `getNewDate` reads new years into a four-character string `s`, and if that string's length is not 0, calls `val` to convert the string to an integer, saving the result in `d.year`. The program ignores the error code `x` that `val` returns—from other bugs and tests, we know that the program's error handling will prevent displaying illegal dates. So, even if `getNewDate` returns an out-of-range year, the program will not fail. (Of course, you may want to test this claim!)

Bug Number 6

Another beta tester reports that February 2048 should have 29 days, but the calendar displays it as having 28. The year 2048 should be a leap year. But, obviously, the program's leap-year function needs repair.

Self test: Stop reading now.

Bug number 6—Test

This problem brings up a difficult question: How much testing is enough? There's no easy answer. In this program, it's reasonable to test all February calendars between 1980 and 2099 to check whether each displays the correct number of days. But is it reasonable to test every month of every year? Probably not.

The solution is to develop confidence in your test procedures and data. Don't test only the finished code. Test low-level functions such as `leapYear`, which in this case appears to be broken. Allowing this untested function into the program led to a nasty bug that could have been prevented by good testing. But now that we've found another bug, let's use TD to isolate it.

Bug number 6—Stabilize

The stabilized test is simple:

1. Run CAL.
2. Press ⟨**Insert**⟩ and enter **2048**.
3. Press the cursor movement keys if necessary to bring February into view. The month should have 29 days, but it shows 28.

Bug number 6—Isolate

The bug search is already narrowed to a single function. Let's use TD's ability to call functions out of context to find out why the code fails. Follow these steps:

1. Load CAL.EXE into TD with the command **td cal**. Press ⟨**F8**⟩ to execute the program's startup code and then press ⟨**Ctrl**⟩-⟨**F4**⟩ to open the `Evaluate/modify` window.

2. Call the `leapYear` function with various test values. For example, enter **leapYear(2048)**. When you press ⟨**Enter**⟩, the `Result` pane reports `False` for this expression—which is not correct. 2048 is a leap year. Try other years: **2047**, **1980**, **1996**, and **2000**. These values appear to give the correct results.

3. The next step is to examine `leapYear` in finer detail to discover why it doesn't work as expected. Press ⟨**Esc**⟩ to close the `Evaluate/modify` window, then press ⟨**Ctrl**⟩-**G** to select the `Goto` command. Enter **leapYear** and press ⟨**Enter**⟩ to display that function's source code.

4. Move the cursor to the line that begins `if year...` and press ⟨**F2**⟩ to set a breakpoint there. Press ⟨**Alt**⟩-⟨**F2**⟩ to set this breakpoint's options. Tab to `Condition`, press ⟨**Cursor Down**⟩ twice to select `Expression true`, press ⟨**Tab**⟩ again, and enter **year=2048** as the `Condition expression`. Press ⟨**Enter**⟩ to accept the change. Notice that TD allows you to set a breakpoint for a variable (the `year` parameter) that does not yet exist. As long as the cursor is inside a procedure or function, TD can recognize the scope of that routine; therefore, it allows the breakpoint for the variable that will come into scope only when this routine is active.

5. Press ⟨**F9**⟩ to run. When the program display appears, use the cursor movement keys to bring February of the *current* year into view. Then, press ⟨**Insert**⟩ and enter **2048**. The program should halt with the message `Breakpoint at CAL.93 "year=2048"` true. (The line number may be different.)

6. Press ⟨**Enter**⟩ to clear the message. Examine the code carefully. The first statement tests whether the remainder of dividing the year by $100 is 0. But this is the wrong radix! The value should be 100 decimal to account for leap year centuries that are evenly divisible by 400 (2000, for example). The bug is a single character, **$**.

7. Because $100 is 256 in decimal, and because 2048 happens to be the only year in the range 1980 to 2099 that's evenly divisible by 256, this accounts for why other leap years are displayed correctly except for this one. The program "thinks" 2048 is the turn of a century. And, because 2000 is divisible by 4, even though the function is wrong, it gives the right result for that year.

8. You could fix the problem easily enough, but let's complete the demonstration using the `CPU` window to add a temporary patch to the code. Press ⟨**Alt**⟩-**VC** to open that window and then press ⟨**Cursor Down**⟩ a few times to highlight the machine-code instruction `mov cx,0100`. Type **mov cx,64** and press ⟨**Enter**⟩ to modify this instruction to load the correct

divisor into CX. Press ⟨**Alt**⟩-⟨**F3**⟩ to close the CPU window and press ⟨**F2**⟩ to erase the breakpoint.

9. Press ⟨**F9**⟩ to run. February 2048 now has 29 days as it should.

Bug number 6—Repair

The final repair is the simplest of them all. Quit TD, edit CAL.PAS, and remove the dollar sign from $100 at line 89.

Summary

This chapter lists a buggy Pascal program, describes six bugs, and shows how to use TD to find the source of each problem. You can use the chapter as a hands-on demonstration of debugging techniques or as a self test of what you've learned so far.

After completing this chapter, you may want to go back and retest the finished program to make sure all of the (known) bugs are gone. Also, after adding new features to CAL, you can run the same tests to force new bugs into the open.

Chapter 14

Common
Assembly Language Bugs

B ECAUSE YOU CAN MAKE the same kinds of mistakes in assembly language as you can in C and Pascal, this chapter does not repeat the obvious—for example, looping one too many times and overwriting code and data by using an out-of-range array index. Instead, the following sections concentrate on errors that are common and *unique* to assembly language programming.

Note: The source code in this chapter requires *Turbo Assembler* 2.0 (TASM), which is supplied with *Turbo Debugger and Tools* 2.0. In general, though, most of the information that follows applies to other assemblers such as the *Microsoft Macro Assembler* (MASM) and *OptASM*.

Typos and Ink Spots

In all programming languages, bugs frequently occur due to simple typing mistakes. However, because assembly language comments begin with a semicolon and extend to the end of the line, it's unlikely that a misplaced comment bracket will cause the same level of damage as in C and Pascal. Still, assembly language programmers are prone to making other kinds of typos that are just as difficult to find.

Instruction Operand Order

One of the most common typographical blots in assembly language is a simple but disastrous reversal of operands in certain instructions, typically `mov`:

```
mov    cx, ax    ; copy ax into cx
```

In that and other two-operand instructions, the transfer of data is from right to left. In this example, the value of AX is copied into CX. People who are unfamiliar with Intel 80x86 instructions often think this is backwards—that the instruction reads as though it transferred CX to AX. But that's not the way the instruction works—`mov cx,ax` transfers AX to CX.

To avoid making this mistake, memorize this general scheme, which applies to most two-operand instructions:

instruction *destination, source*

Knowing about this mistake is one thing—finding it is another. Often, the telling symptom is a register that changes unexpectedly. To find the mistake, you can use the Breakpoint menu's `Changed memory global` command to set a breakpoint for every time the register changes, but beware that executing a long program with such a command may generate too many spurious breakpoints to be useful. If the bad value is consistent—for example, CX is zeroed unexpectedly—use the `Expression true global` command with an expression such as **cx eq 0** to set your traps.

A trick that sometimes works is to examine registers (press ⟨**Alt**⟩-**VR**) after the bad register value shows up. Look for other registers with the same value and set an `Expression true global` breakpoint for **cx eq ax** or **es eq ds**. This may help you to locate the instruction that's assigning AX to CX when it should have assigned CX to AX.

Popping the Wrong Registers

For every `push`, there should be a corresponding `pop` (unless you adjust the stack pointer by other means). If you push these three registers:

```
push   ax
push   bx
push   cx
```

Then, sometime later, you should pop those registers in the reverse order:

```
pop    cx
pop    bx
pop    ax
```

Occasionally, errors in pushing and popping creep in after modifying a subroutine and inserting a new `push` instruction, perhaps after adding a loop that changes a previously unused register. Then, you either forget to add a corresponding pop or you insert the instruction in the wrong place. Either way, your program's goose is cooked.

The first mistake—forgetting the pop—almost always sends the code into limbo. When I modify a subroutine and it blows up, I often find a missing pop to be the cause. But if I can't locate the mistake in the source text, I set a breakpoint on the first and last instruction in the subroutine and inspect the stack pointer SP in the CPU or Registers window to confirm that my pushes and pops match.

The second mistake—inserting a pop in the wrong location—is more difficult to locate. The symptom in this case is a register suddenly changing value—similar to what happens when you reverse the *destination* and *source* operands. A trick that I use is to open the Registers window at the start of a routine (or before a series of push instructions), and then execute the Window menu's Dump pane to log command. I then trace through several instructions or execute the code to a breakpoint, and compare the Log and Registers windows side by side. (A mouse helps arrange the windows on screen.) A quick glance shows any discrepancies among the pushed and popped registers.

If these kinds of errors plague your code, you might want to use a macro or TASM 2.0's new single-line, multiple-instruction push and pop instructions, which let you write code like this:

```
push    ax bx cx
  .
  .
  .
pop     cx bx ax
```

Confusing Offsets and Variables

MASM (and TASM when not in IDEAL mode) allows an ambiguous form of variable addressing that leads to many assembly language bugs. If the data segment defines a word variable named Counter, then this statement loads the variable's value into BX:

```
mov     bx, [Counter]
```

The brackets tell the assembler to generate the correct instruction to load the value at the address where Counter is stored. But MASM syntax also allows you to write the same instruction without the brackets:

```
mov     bx, Counter
```

That's harmless enough—unless you meant to load the offset address of `Counter` into BX. Just removing the brackets is not enough. To correct the problem, you must also add the `offset` keyword:

```
mov     bx, offset Counter
```

If you forget the `offset`, TASM warns you of the danger only when assembling in `IDEAL` mode, so this can be easy to miss in MASM-style code. Because the missing `offset` probably loads the wrong address into the register, subsequent instructions that use the register as a pointer can overwrite other data at the wrong location. This may wreck the code or even the stack, depending on the value of `Counter` and how segments are ordered. If your code unravels like haywire, a mixed up offset and variable reference might be the cause.

Prevention is the best medicine in this case. To avoid confusing offsets and variables, force yourself to surround all variable references with brackets. That way, you'll be less likely to forget to include the `offset` qualifier when you need to use the address of a variable instead of its value. You can also use TASM's `IDEAL` mode, which requires brackets around all variable references.

Finding the source of a variable reference that should have used `offset` is a tough job that requires setting a breakpoint for all instructions that read that variable's address. You still have to figure out which of those instructions is wrong, but at least this method gives you a head start. Unfortunately, monitoring memory reads requires hardware-debugging assistance (see chapter 18). TD can monitor changes to specific memory locations, but it can't find all accesses to a certain address without help from the hardware.

If you do have a hardware debugging board or an 80386 or 80486 processor, follow these steps to set a breakpoint to find all reads to a specified address:

1. Open the `Breakpoints` window from the `View` menu (press ⟨**Alt**⟩-**VB**).

2. Press ⟨**Ctrl**⟩-**A** to add a new breakpoint. Select the `Global` and `Hardware` options, then press ⟨**Enter**⟩ or click `Ok` to close the window.

3. Press ⟨**Ctrl**⟩-**H** to modify hardware options, set `Address match` to `Equal`, and enter **Counter** as the `Address value`. Leave the other default values as they are. Press ⟨**Enter**⟩ or click `Ok` to close the window.

4. Execute the code by pressing ⟨**F9**⟩. The breakpoint will halt the program at every reference to `Counter`.

By following those four steps, you can quickly locate all instructions of the form `mov bx, [Counter]` and `mov bx, Counter`. Look for an instruction that should have been written `mov bx, offset Counter`.

Common Program Errors

Crack assembly language programmers can write the most amazingly clever code. But assembly language can also lead programmers into bug-infested woods where even top professionals spend much of their time fighting goblins. You'll prevent many disasters if you avoid the following demons.

No Return to DOS

Assembly language programs never die; they just fade back to DOS. Forgetting to provide an exit path for every possible condition that might end a program will surely lead to a colossal crash.

The usual way to end most assembly language programs is to call DOS function 4Ch with code similar to this:

```
Exit:
        mov     ah, 04Ch        ; DOS function: Exit program
        mov     al, [exitCode]  ; Return exit code value
        int     21h             ; Call DOS.  Terminate program
```

Byte variable exitCode holds a value to return to DOS as an error indicator, which tells the calling process whether an error occurred. When running programs from DOS, you can inspect the error value in a batch file by examining ERRORLEVEL. (Most DOS references explain how to do this.)

There are other ways to end programs, but none as sound, so there's no need to list them here. If your programs use other means, you'd be smart to bring them up to date.

If that doesn't ease your woes, you've got to find where the program is flying off into outer space. Do that by dividing the code into arbitrary sections until you narrow the search to a small section that you can then trace one instruction at a time. One way to do this is to open the CPU window and patch in jmp near Exit—or from other segments, jmp far Exit—instructions.

To make the patch, move the highlight bar to an appropriate location and start typing. You might also have to enter one or more nop instructions after the patch to keep the disassembled code in synch with your program.

> Hint: Press ⟨**Ctrl**⟩-**M** to toggle the Mixed setting to No in order to see a disassembly of the patched instructions; other settings show the original source code even after you enter patches, which can be confusing.

After running the program to completion, press ⟨**Ctrl**⟩-⟨**F2**⟩ to reset. That also removes the previous patch. You can then patch in another jump nearer to the crash site. By repeating this process, it shouldn't take long to narrow the problem to a small section, which you can then trace or `Animate` while watching various program variables.

Stack Missing or Too Small

Be sure to declare a stack of an appropriate size unless you're writing a .COM program, which combines the code, data, and stack into a single 64K or smaller segment. During development, or if the code hangs, declare a large stack with the directive:

```
STACK    16384    ; 8192 is also a good choice
```

Declaring more stack space than needed is a useful debugging tool. Try this as one of your initial tests when a program catches a bug. If the problem disappears, it may be caused by too little stack space.

Also, by adding this simple test to your list of standard debugging steps, you'll find those times when you simply forget to declare a stack. Although the linker warns about this condition, the warning message may scroll off screen before you read it, especially when you're assembling large programs with TASM's MAKE utility.

Misunderstanding Uninitialized Data

Assembly language variables are usually stored in data segments, of which there are two basic kinds: initialized and uninitialized. Most often, segment registers DS and ES locate data-segment starting addresses, leading to bugs if you forget to initialize and preserve these register values.

It's wise to take the word "uninitialized" seriously. Uninitialized variables have no predetermined values, and programs that fail to recognize that are on a sure path to trouble.

In assembly language, a question mark defines an uninitialized value. For example, to define space for a single uninitialized byte, you can write:

```
aByte    DB    ?
```

The problem is, many programmers assume that `aByte` and other "uninitialized" variables are set to 0 when the program runs. They make that assumption because, when `aByte` is sandwiched between two other initialized variables, the assembler reserves space for the variable by inserting one or more 0 bytes:

```
aWord   DW  1h
aByte   DB  ?
aString DB  '(c) 1920. No Rights Reserved'
```

Declared that way, the uninitialized `aByte` is set to 0 because, in order to include the values for `aWord` and `aString` in the .OBJ file, the assembler has to reserve space for `aByte`. By design, the assembler assigns 0 bytes to that space; therefore, even though `aByte` is declared as an uninitialized variable, it is "initialized" to 0 at runtime.

Danger looms if, later on, you remove `aString` or shift it to another spot. If that places `aByte` among the last uninitialized variables defined, space for `aByte` is no longer reserved in the object-code file's data segment:

```
aString DB  '(c) 1920. No Rights Reserved'
aWord   DW  1h
aByte   DB  ?
```

The modified program no longer reserves space for `aByte`, and as a result, `aByte`'s starting value equals the left over value stored at that location. It's no longer safe to assume that the uninitialized value will be set to 0 by default.

TD adds to the confusion because, when you assemble the code with full debugging information, uninitialized variables are preset to all 0 bytes—even when they are declared last. Only when you execute the program directly from DOS are uninitialized values assigned uninitialized memory space.

If the program exhibits buggy behavior when executed directly from DOS, but if that bug disappears when executed under the debugger, you should immediately suspect that an uninitialized variable is at fault.

A good way to combat such bugs is to use the `UDATASEG` directive to collect all uninitialized variables in the same location. This will help you to verify that your program properly assigns values to all variables in uninitialized data segments.

Misunderstanding ASSUME

A common snafu is misunderstanding the role of `ASSUME` in segment addressing. `ASSUME` is a directive to the assembler—it doesn't generate any machine code, and, therefore, the directive has no effect at runtime. `ASSUME` tells the assembler that a segment register has been or will be initialized to the address of a declared segment. This lets the assembler choose the correct machine-code formats for instructions that refer to variables in that segment.

Some programmers place a single `ASSUME` inside the code segment before the first instruction. For example, this is a typical directive:

```
ASSUME  cs:cseg, ds:data, es:extra, ss:stackSeg
```

That's fine, and it defines the segment locations early for easy reference. But it's still the program's responsibility to load the segment registers with the correct values. All that `ASSUME` does is to tell the assembler what registers the program will use to address variables in segments. (Registers CS and SS are initialized at runtime by DOS. You don't have to initialize them with program instructions.)

If the program changes DS or ES, it must also tell the assembler about the change. Use `ASSUME` to do this as in this fragment:

```
mov     ax, extra2        ; Initialize es to address
mov     es, ax            ;  of extra data segment
ASSUME  es:extra2         ; Tell assembler where es points
```

You must load the register *and* tell the assembler about the change with `ASSUME`.

Unexpected Register Changes

When a register changes value unexpectedly, it's usually due to one of two causes: an interrupt service routine (ISR) that fails to preserve modified register values or an instruction such as `mul ax, [value]`, which changes both AX and DX, even though only AX is shown in the source code. Other culprits include string instructions such as `stosb` and `lodsw`, which modify the string index registers SI and DI.

You can often distinguish between the two different cases by running the code several times. If the bug appears at random times, it's most likely due to a faulty ISR. But if the bug appears consistently at the same location, check your assembly language reference for all register effects for instructions in that code section. Pay special attention to `imul`, `mul`, and string instructions. They seem to give assembly language programmers the most trouble with unexpected changes to register values.

It is possible to set a `Changed memory global` breakpoint for a suspected register, but due to the heavy reuse of most registers in assembly language code, this often produces an overwhelming series of breaks that are more confusing than helpful. Do what you can to isolate the bug to as small a section of code as possible before setting breakpoints for specific registers. Then, press ⟨**Alt**⟩-**BE** and enter an expression such as **ax eq 042h** to halt the code when that value appears in AX. (See chapters 8 and 9 for help with breakpoints and assembly language expressions.)

Undocumented Registers

Don't be too trusting of documented register use. Test your code to be sure that subroutines preserve the expected register values.

This can even be a problem with well-known DOS routines. For example, this typical fragment writes ASCII characters ending with $ to the standard output:

```
mov dx, offset message
mov ah, 09h
int 21h
```

A well-known and trusted DOS reference does not mention that calling DOS function 09h also changes AL, but it does.

Flag Foul-Ups

Symptoms of mishandled flags can range from the simple to the complex. One signpost is a subroutine or other code section that runs under the wrong conditions. For example, if a certain routine should execute only when Level is less than 10 but runs unexpectedly when that variable is greater than 10, you may have failed to preserve flags that are set during a previous comparison. (Also see "Jumping Into the Fire" later on.)

A good way to watch for flag changes is to open the CPU window and press ⟨Tab⟩ to activate the flag pane—the skinny one at the upper right. Then, use the Window menu's Dump pane to log command to make a copy of the current flag values. You can then open the View menu's Log window to inspect flag settings and compare them after you step through various code sections. Once you master this trick, you'll find it's a lot easier than jotting down flag values on paper.

Segment Snags

Suddenly, your variables disappear, or they change values. Your code seems to be suffering from a loss of memory, and you are at a loss to explain why. Or, values that you store at one location magically shift to another.

What's the matter? Probably, you've got a segment-related bug, often caused by mishandling a segment register. This can cause the program to read and write data at a different segment base than intended, causing all variables to change suddenly. When that happens, look for the following common causes.

Using the Wrong Segment Register Value

You probably realize that you must initialize your segment registers, usually by executing these simplified memory-model instructions at the beginning of your program:

```
        IDEAL
        DOSSEG
        MODEL   small
        STACK   256
        CODESEG
Start:
        mov     ax, @data       ; Initialize DS to address
        mov     ds, ax          ;  of data segment
        mov     es, ax          ; Make es = ds
```

This is not a complete program, but it shows a typical startup sequence. Errors will occur, of course, if you forget to initialize DS (and ES if needed), but more often, segment-addressing bugs arise from other code that changes DS or ES and does not restore their values.

If you suspect that DS is being changed at the wrong time, load your code into the debugger and press ⟨**F8**⟩ to step over the instructions that initialize the segment registers. Open the `CPU` or `Registers` window and then set an `Expression true global` breakpoint to the expression **(cs eq 2AFDh) and (ds ne 2B01h)**.

In place of 2AFDh, use the current value of CS shown in the `CPU` or `Registers` window. In place of 2B01h, use the current value of DS. You must monitor *both* CS and DS to avoid breaking when code outside of the program changes DS.

Next, close the `CPU` or `Registers` window or press ⟨**F6**⟩ to switch back to the source-code view. Then, run the program by pressing ⟨**F9**⟩. The code will halt at any instruction in your program that changes DS to a value other than `@data`.

Using the Wrong Default Segment Register

Certain instructions are intimately tied to specific segment registers. For example, `lods` always loads a byte or word at DS:SI, unless an explicit override specifies ES instead of DS. Similarly, `stos` normally stores a byte or word at ES:DI.

But it's the instructions, and not the index registers SI and DI, that are linked to segment registers DS and ES by default. A common misunderstanding is to assume that DI always represents an offset from the segment addressed by ES because `stos` normally uses ES:DI. It doesn't. Consider a simple `mov`:

```
mov    ax, [word ptr di]
```

When used like that in a register-indirect reference, DI's default segment is DS, not ES. To refer to data in a segment addressed by ES, you must use an explicit override:

```
mov    ax, [word ptr es:di]
```

Common symptoms of a misused default segment register include the inability to find initialized data, strings that display garbage on screen, and other illnesses that suggest the program is having trouble locating its data.

Many times, the cure is simple. Just set DS and ES to the same segment. If your troubles go away, then you've probably written code that expects the wrong default register for some instructions. Of course, you can't apply this technique if you need to use ES to address a second data segment or if the program modifies ES frequently.

A good way to check that instructions are referring to the expected segment register is to single-step portions of the program while viewing the CPU window. At every memory read and write, the border just above the code pane shows the segment, offset, and value at the computed address before the highlighted instruction executes. Use this feature to verify that your segment expectations are what you think they should be.

Ignoring Data Segment Starting Offsets

You can use TD to monitor your program's data segments. First load your program and press ⟨F7⟩ or ⟨F8⟩ to step through the instructions that initialize DS and ES. Open a Dump window, press ⟨Ctrl⟩-G, and enter **ds:0** or **es:0** to display bytes at these addresses.

When you do that, you may be surprised to discover that the first variables declared in your program aren't necessarily located at DS:0000 or ES:0000. If the segment is aligned by BYTE or WORD, the first byte of the segment's first variable might be at offset 08h or 0Eh or at another value. Only when data segments are aligned to PAGE or PARA are the starting offsets guaranteed to begin at 0. This is a normal consequence of 80x86 memory segments, which always begin on fixed 16-byte address boundaries, called *paragraphs*. To align segments to addresses between paragraphs requires the segments to be positioned at an offset from the closest fixed boundary below (at a lower address).

Figure 14.1 illustrates how misunderstanding this arrangement can lead to serious bugs. Register CS addresses the base of the program's code segment. Register DS addresses the data segment. But because the data segment is WORD aligned (or, it might be BYTE aligned), the byte at DS:0000 actually addresses the tail end of the overlapping code segment. Changing the bytes starting at DS:0000 will modify some of the program's instructions!

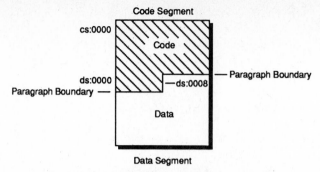

Figure 14.1.   Overlapping code and data segments.

To determine whether this is causing the bug, set a `Changed memory global` breakpoint for **ds:0, offset firstVar - 1**, where `firstVar` is the first variable declared in the data segment. The offset address of that variable minus one equals the number of overlapping bytes in both segments. Setting a breakpoint to watch for changes will trap any instruction that overwrites the tail end of the program's code.

Unexpected Segment Wrap Around

A similar problem to the one described in the previous section occurs when an instruction or a loop writes data to multiple segment locations, incrementing an offset value, usually in a register. For example, suppose you define a 24-byte array and fill that array with 0 bytes this way:

```
        xor     ax, ax
        mov     bx, offset array
        mov     cx, 12
aa10:
        mov     [word bx], ax
        add     bx, 2
        loop    aa10
```

There are better ways to write this kind of loop, but the sample clearly demonstrates a common mistake. If `array` is located near the end of a 64K data segment and if the wrong loop count is assigned to CX, then adding 2 to BX might cause the index value to wrap around from 0FFFFh to 0. Because DS:0 overlaps a portion of the preceding code segment in memory, the effect is to wipe out one or more instructions.

Load the code into TD and set a `Changed memory global` breakpoint for **ds:0,n** where n is the number of bytes to monitor. This will trap the instruction that's writing data to addresses that don't belong to the data segment.

Procedural Predicaments

A procedure (a subroutine) isn't as neatly packaged in assembly language as procedures and functions are in C and Pascal. In assembly language, a procedure is any series of instructions that ends with ret or retf. Procedures help modularize a program, but because the assembler enforces few rules for creating procedures, they also invite several common mistakes.

Unexpected Fall-Through

The most prevalent procedure error is an unexpected fall-through, caused by forgetting to end a procedure with ret or retf. Programmers who are more comfortable with C and Pascal often make this error because high-level languages do not require termination instructions at the end of a procedure or function. (In a way, this problem resembles a bug caused by a missing return statement in a C function that returns a value.)

If your program seems to develop a mind of its own, you may be experiencing this sort of trouble. For example, consider these two subroutines:

```
; ----   Return ax = ax + bx + cx
PROC    AddReg
        add     ax, bx          ; ax <- ax + bx + cx
        adc     ax, cx          ; Forgot ret instruction!
ENDP    AddReg
; ----   Display message
PROC    Welcome
        mov     dx, offset Message
        mov     ah, 9
        int     21h
        ret                     ; AddReg returns here!
ENDP    Welcome
```

Because AddReg doesn't return to its caller, the program continues with procedure Welcome after the second adc instruction. Welcome displays a message defined in the data segment:

```
DATASEG
Message     db  13, 10, "Care for a game of chess?", '$'
```

But, because of the bug, every time you call AddReg to add AX + BX + CX, the computer asks "Care for a game of chess?"

The mistake in this example is obvious, but in a large program with many modules or multiple code segments where adjacent subroutines in the assembled code might not be next to each other in the source, if you can't find the missing return by eye, set a breakpoint in the unexpected routine (Welcome in this example). Then, open the CPU window and press ⟨**F9**⟩ to run the program until it stops. You'll probably find that you should have inserted a ret or retf just above that point. If a return is there, then you may have called the wrong subroutine. In that case, press ⟨**F8**⟩ to step over the current routine's code until it returns. That will take you back to just after the bad call.

Uninitialized Register Parameters

An obvious, but still frequent, error is forgetting to pass the correct input values in the registers required by a procedure. To check input values, you can add registers to Watches or press ⟨**Alt**⟩**-VR** to view them in the Registers window. Or, you can view the CPU window, which has its own Registers pane. That way, you can inspect any input flag values, too.

Multiple Entry Points and Exit Paths

A good rule of thumb is to provide single entry and exit points in all procedures. Of course, rules are made to be broken, and this rule is broken more often than most by clever assembly language programmers bent upon squeezing their code into the smallest possible space.

Technically, there's nothing wrong with a procedure that has multiple entries and exits—as long as you stay on guard for bugs. The number one guideline is to provide an exit for every possible input condition, which is not always easy to do in complex code.

To check out a procedure with multiple entries and exits, use the CPU window to assign test values to registers and then execute a call to the subroutine by pressing ⟨**F8**⟩. Unfortunately, you can't use the Data menu's Evaluate/modify command to call assembly language subroutines out of context as you can in C and Pascal. But there is a way to simulate that ability. Follow these steps:

1. Run the code up to a call instruction that calls the test procedure. Open the CPU window and press ⟨**Ctrl**⟩**-G**. Enter the current instruction pointer IP displayed in the registers pane near the top left corner of the window. For example, if the current location is CS:001B, enter **cs:001bh**. (Don't forget the trailing h to indicate that this is a hexadecimal value.) The highlight bar should not move.

2. Press ⟨**Tab**⟩ and enter values passed to the subroutine in registers. Press ⟨**Tab**⟩ again and set any required flags. Then press ⟨**Shift**⟩-⟨**Tab**⟩ once or twice to get back to the disassembly pane.

3. Press ⟨**F8**⟩ to step over the `call` instruction, simulating TD's ability to call subroutines out of context in C and Pascal. (If you press ⟨**F7**⟩, you would trace into the subroutine. To execute the routine at full speed, ⟨**F8**⟩ is the correct key.) When the subroutine finishes, examine any returned registers or other events you need to monitor.

4. To prepare for another test, press ⟨**Ctrl**⟩**-G,** hit ⟨**Cursor Down**⟩, and then press ⟨**Enter**⟩⟨**Ctrl**⟩**-N**. This repositions the highlight bar to the `call` instruction and sets CS:IP to that location. You can then set new values in registers and flags and repeat from step 2.

These steps reset the origin to the `call` instruction so you can call the same subroutine many times without having to reset the entire program. You might also be able to press ⟨**Alt**⟩**-**⟨**F4**⟩ (the `Back trace` command's hot key) or use keystroke recording to perform similar tricks, undoing the effects of `call`s and other instructions. (See chapter 16.)

By the way, step 4 makes an excellent macro. Before executing step 4 the first time, press ⟨**Alt**⟩**-=** to turn on the macro recorder and choose a key for the macro (⟨**Alt**⟩**-R** for "Reset" is a good choice). After pressing ⟨**Ctrl**⟩**-N**, press ⟨**Alt**⟩**--** (⟨**Alt**⟩ and the hyphen (-) key) to stop recording. From then on, instead of doing step 4, press ⟨**Alt**⟩**-R** to reset the program to just before the `call`. When you're done testing, you might want to use the `Save options` command in the `Options` menu to save this macro for next time.

Returning Near and Far

Every call to a near procedure (in the same code segment) must be matched by a near return. Every call to a far procedure (in a different code segment) must be matched by a far return. Near calls and returns push and pop 16-bit address offsets on the stack; far calls and returns push and pop 32-bit segment and offset addresses.

If you always use `PROC` directives, and optionally specify `near` or `far`, TASM can generate the correct `call` and `ret` instructions automatically. But it's also possible to create a subroutine without `PROC`:

```
subx:   push    ax
        ; instructions for subroutine
        pop     ax
        retf
```

If you call this routine from within current code segment, the assembler will not generate a far `call` instruction. TASM doesn't know that the subroutine returns via `retf`, so it incorrectly uses a near `call`. It's up to you to use the correct `call` instruction:

```
call    far subx
```

Two common symptoms often appear for this bug. The first is a system crash, caused by "returning" to a far address from a near call. Sometimes, a crash will not occur if other calls left the correct segment address on the stack, in which case the telling mark is a stack pointer that advances 2 bytes too many for each subroutine call as extra words are popped from the stack.

The second common symptom is a stack that slowly loses space, often caused by a near return to a far call that happens to be in the same segment. For example, you might have a series of far library procedures that are called both from other segments and by local routines in the same segment. In that case, the routines must end with `retf` instructions and must be called by `call far routine` instructions no matter where the call originates.

Because the offset portion of the return address is pushed onto the stack last by a `call far` instruction, a near `ret` in the same segment works but also leaves the segment address unpopped. A handy way to find all `ret` and `retf` instructions is to search for those symbols in the `CPU` window (press ⟨**Ctrl**⟩**-S**). Because these two returns evaluate to single-byte machine codes 0C3h (`ret`) and 0CBh (`retf`), you can search for them by name. This will also locate any `ret` instructions in far `PROC`s for which the assembler generates `retf` machine codes.

Not Preserving Registers Around Calls

One of the leading causes of "the chip is bad fever" is a mysteriously changing register. I caught a dose of that bug one time while using a computer (not a PC) that used an interrupt to update a processor register repeatedly as a random-number seed. One time, I forgot that fact and noticed that the register was changing at random. Assuming that the chip had developed a bad case of the jitters, I decided to replace it with a new processor. Luckily, I remembered the interrupt just before popping out the "faulty" chip.

A more common cause of a register that changes mysteriously is a subroutine that modifies the register but fails to preserve its value. You may be able to trap this error by setting a `Changed memory global` breakpoint on the register, but first try to isolate the mistake to as small a section as possible. Because of the limited number of registers in 80x86 processors, setting breakpoints for changed registers often produces too many halts to be useful.

Jumping Into the Fire

TD makes life with conditional jumps so much easier, I usually test my code in the debugger during development instead of waiting for bugs to appear. This helps me to avoid two of the most common errors with conditional jumps, described next.

Wrong Jump Sense

It's easy to mix up conditional jumps like `ja` (jump if above, unsigned) and `jg` (jump if greater, signed). For example, when comparing negative values, using the wrong jump causes the program to fail as this sample demonstrates:

```
xor     ax, ax      ; set ax = 0
cmp     ax, -1      ; is ax > -1?
ja      Exit        ; jump if ax > -1 (??)
```

The `ja` is not correct. It should be `jg`. The program fails because 0 is greater than −1, but 0 is not above −1, which in unsigned decimal equals 65535 (0FFFFh).

Long-distance conditional jumps are even more error-prone than single jumps like that one. Typically, when jumping farther than about 127 bytes forward or backward, it's necessary to combine two jump instructions this way:

```
cmp     ax, -1      ; is ax <= -1?
jg      @@10        ; jump if ax > -1
jmp     Error       ; jump if ax <= -1
@@10:
```

Reversing the sense of the conditional jump—using `jg` instead of `jle`—and then following the conditional with an unconditional `jmp` has the same effect as `jle Error`, but allows the target label to be farther away.

One way to prevent errors when designing such code is to use TASM's **JUMPS** directive, which inserts long-distance jumps as needed automatically when the target label is too far away for a single conditional jump to reach.

Another way is to use TD to examine flags in test cases. Remember that conditional jumps are based on certain flag settings. For instance, `jg` is carried out only if the sign flag `sf` equals the overflow flag `of` and if the zero flag `zf` is 0. Compare these values with an assembly language reference's flag settings for conditional jumps.

Misplaced Local Labels

Watch out for local labels such as `@@10:` and `@@Continue:` in the wrong position. Because local labels can be duplicated throughout a program, be sure to aim your jumps at the targets you want to hit.

The assembler can catch one of the most common local-label mistakes. Suppose you write a subroutine to call another routine ten times:

```
PROC    DoSub
        mov     cx, 10
@@Temp:
        call    Subroutine
        dec     cx
        jnz     @@Temp
        ret
ENDP    DoSub
```

If another place in the program executes `call DoSub`, the routine calls `Subroutine` (not shown) ten times. You then realize that if you load CX with another value, you can call the temporary local label to execute `Subroutine` any number of times:

```
mov     cx, 2       ; load count into cx
call    @@Temp      ; call DoSub's temp label (??)
```

The trouble is, this doesn't assemble because `@@Temp:` is trapped inside `DoSub`; therefore, the label is not visible (to TASM, that is) outside of the procedure. Local labels exist only up or down to the nearest nonlocal label, and the assembler gives an "Undefined symbol" error when you try to assemble the source.

But the assembler does not catch another common local-label problem. The trouble begins when you write a loop similar to the previous sample to call a `Subroutine` (or perform another action) a certain number of times:

```
        xor     ax, ax
@@Repeat:
        call    Subroutine
Entry2:
        dec     ax
        jnz     @@Repeat
  .
  .
  .
@@Repeat:
```

Here, the problem occurs because local label `@@Repeat` appears at the correct place in the loop but is repeated later. The program assembles with no errors, but the `jnz` refers to the *second* `@@Repeat:` when it should jump to the first. The code is syntactically correct because local labels may be repeated between other nonlocal labels such as `Entry2:`. But it doesn't run as expected.

Tracing or stepping over (press ⟨**F7**⟩ or ⟨**F8**⟩) through this kind of sequence quickly points out such errors. When doing that in the **CPU** window, up and down arrows appear next to highlighted jump instructions if the jump will be taken. If the arrows don't appear, then the instruction after the jump will execute next. This lets you preview the effect of a jump without actually jumping.

String Sins

String instructions `lods`, `movs`, `stos`, `cmps`, and `scas` plus their alternate no-operand forms are useful for filling, moving, comparing, and performing other operations on byte strings. When combined with repeat prefixes `rep`, `repe`, `repz`, `repne`, and `repnz`, a single instruction can affect thousands of bytes.

Such power adds speed to machine code. But, when applied carelessly, these instructions can also wipe out an entire segment in a flash. So, if your program has a bug and you are using string instructions, the error might be among the following common mistakes.

Expecting CX = 0 to Reach an Entire Segment

Because a repeat prefix such as `repnz` examines CX before executing the next string instruction, if CX equals 0 initially, the instruction is skipped. That means you can't fill an entire 64K segment addressed by ES with code such as:

```
xor     al, al      ; set al = 0 (fill value)
mov     cx, 65535   ; assign count to cx
mov     di, 0       ; assign offset address to di
cld                 ; clear direction flag
repnz   stosb       ; fill segment less 1 byte
```

That fills the addresses from ES:0000 up to and including ES:FFFEH with 0 bytes. To fill the last byte, you must follow this sequence with another unrepeated `stosb`.

A useful method for examining code like this is to open a **Dump** window to the area being filled or moved by other string instructions. Use the **Goto** command (press ⟨**Ctrl**⟩-**G**) to position the window to the area to watch. Then, trace or step through the instructions. The **Dump** window will show the results.

It's also helpful to fill areas with known values when performing string-instruction tests. For example, before filling a buffer, I often set all bytes to 0ffh so I can easily see if any bytes are skipped by the code. Rather than write a loop to do this, use the **Dump** window's **Block:Set** command to fill memory with byte values. Be careful with the command—it writes values directly to any locations you specify. To fill the entire segment at ES:0 with 0ffh bytes, enter the Set expression **es:0,65535d,0ffh**.

Trusting String Operands

String instructions may include operands that specify source and destination labels. Even so, you still have to load the necessary registers and set the direction flag for the instructions to work. The operands are permitted only so the assembler can check whether the labels are addressable by the currently ASSUMEd segment registers. A typical mistake is to write:

```
ASSUME  es:_DATA
        mov     cx, 10      ; load count into cx
        xor     al, al      ; load fill value into al
repnz   stos    [byte es:destination]   ; fill array (??)
```

This is very dangerous! The code tells the assembler that ES: addresses the global data segment and that the program will store 10 zero bytes in an array named destination. The assembler reports no errors, but the code has a whopping bug because it fails to initialize the destination index register DI and to clear the direction flag so that stos will increment the index for each repnz repetition. Here's the correct way to write the loop:

```
ASSUME  es:_DATA
        mov     cx, 10
        xor     al, al
        mov     di, offset destination
        cld
repnz   stos    [byte es:destination]
```

Even though stos specifies the destination label, a mov or other instruction still has to initialize DI to the same offset address. Also, a cld instruction clears the DF flag to make certain that DI will be incremented.

The symptom of a string-instruction operand problem can be a subtle quirk or a horrendous crash. If you are using operands this way, set breakpoints on your string instructions and run your code until it halts. Then, open the Registers or CPU windows to check that all registers are properly initialized.

> Hint: Press ⟨**F7**⟩ to execute repeated string instructions one iteration at a time. Press ⟨**F8**⟩ to execute all repetitions. Just before pressing those keys, you might want to change SI, DI, and CX to experiment with different index and count values rather than reassemble the code.

Bad Direction Flag Setting

Always precede every repeated string instruction with `cld` (to increment index registers SI and DI) or `std` (to decrement the registers). Don't just execute a single `cld` at the start of your program and assume that the DF flag won't ever change. Other subroutines may not preserve DF's value.

Confusing Default Segment Registers

Another common string error can occur when you expect the wrong default segment register to be used. For example, `stosb` and other forms of `stos` store bytes at ES:DI; therefore, you must initialize ES to the segment that contains the variable at the offset in DI. If only DS is initialized to the program's data segment, the string instruction could easily overwrite data or code anywhere in memory.

One way to avoid trouble is to set DS and ES to the same data segment address early on. That way, you can use string instructions freely to fill, move, and compare bytes in global variables. This is a good idea when assembling stand-alone programs that specify `MODEL small` at the start, in which case there is only one global data segment unless you specify another with `FARDATA`.

You can get back into trouble, though, if you later switch to another memory model or if you decide to use multiple data segments. Code that used to work correctly may then require extensive changes to initialize segment registers before each string operation.

Interrupt Intricacies

An interrupt service routine is similar to a common subroutine except that, instead of being called from a program statement, it runs due to an external event that triggers the processor to suspend its current activity and jump to a *vector address* stored in low memory. Software interrupts such as the famous DOS function call `int 21h` and the ROM BIOS video interrupt `int 10h` are even more like subroutines because program statements call them explicitly. But hardware interrupts, which can run at any time, give people the most trouble.

The key to ISR success is to understand that a hardware interrupt might occur at any time (except when expressly prohibited by clearing the interrupt-enable flag with `cli`, but more on that later). Because the ISR might run between any instruction in a program—even between instructions in DOS or in the ROM BIOS—you must reset every modified register and flag to the same values as when the ISR began.

Usually, bugs in ISRs show up as intermittent faults. Under one set of conditions, a certain problem appears. Under another, it goes away or changes character. It's impossible to describe one set of circumstances that signifies an ISR bug. But, if your program uses interrupts, problems might be from one of the following common causes.

Destroying Register Values

Because TD saves and restores the first 48 interrupt vectors, if you set any of those vectors to your own ISR, an external event will activate that ISR only if you run the code by pressing ⟨**F9**⟩. The debugger also restores these same vectors before returning to DOS—so if your program changes one or more vectors, you don't have to restore their values.

While usually helpful, these features can make it difficult to detect the most common kind of ISR bug—failing to preserve every modified register. Flag values are saved and restored automatically by the processor during interrupt handling. You don't have to preserve flags yourself. But if the ISR doesn't preserve a register, all kinds of bad things are likely to happen.

To examine the before and after register values in an ISR, set a breakpoint on the ISR's first instruction and run your program by pressing ⟨**F9**⟩. After the breakpoint halts the program, open the `Registers` window and execute the `Window` menu's `Dump pane to Log` command. Open, resize, and align the `Log` window so you can easily compare register values. Then, run the ISR up to `iret` and verify that all registers are preserved.

Disabling Interrupts

If you want other interrupts to be able to interrupt an ISR, you must execute `sti` as one of the ISR's initial instructions. When you are having trouble getting an interrupt to run as expected—for example, if a serial I/O routine loses characters even at slow baud rates or if a clock ISR loses time—the fault may be in another ISR that fails to enable interrupts by executing `sti`. If that ISR takes a long time to finish, no other maskable interrupts will be processed until the next `iret`. For that reason, it pays to check that all active ISRs properly execute `sti` before wasting time hunting bugs in healthy code.

Forgetting to Restore Interrupt Vectors

Always restore all changed interrupt vectors except in cases when a program installs resident code that remains in memory while other programs run. In other cases, you should reset all interrupt vectors before returning to DOS. (See chapter 19 for more information about debugging TSRs and other resident programs.)

If DOS or other programs develop bugs after your program runs, a changed interrupt vector may be at fault. Also, when debugging ISRs, if you aren't 100% sure that interrupt vectors are reset properly, reboot before running your code in TD. Otherwise, the first 48 vectors will be restored to their buggy values when the debugger returns to DOS. In fact, under these circumstances, code that runs just fine in the debugger may develop a bug only when you run other code!

Problems like these are sometimes easier to fix by writing short test programs to put ISRs through the paces (either in the debugger or from DOS). A neat debugging trick is to deactivate the external interrupt by executing `cli` in the test code and then call your hardware interrupt with a software `int` instruction. This lets you debug the ISR code as though it were a plain subroutine (it still has to end with `iret`, though).

Numerical Puzzles

Expression handling in assembly language is far more tedious than in C and Pascal. If you must use assembly language to crunch numbers, watch out for the following common "gotchas."

Not Extending the Sign Bit

When mixing signed bytes and words, be sure to extend the sign bit properly. Don't get caught in this trap:

```
mov     al, -1      ; set al = -1
mov     bx, 5       ; set bx = 5
add     ax, bx      ; ax <- ax + bx (??)
```

Here, the intention is to add a byte in AL to a word in BX. The trouble is, the first `mov` assigns a value only to AL, leaving the high byte of AX (AH) uninitialized. If AX is 07F04h before this fragment, the addition ($-1 + 5$) will equal 32,511.

To fix the mistake, insert `cbw` after the first `mov` to convert the signed byte in AL to a signed word in AX.

Radix Mistakes

Adopt a standard radix and stick to it. I use decimal in all cases except where hex seems more appropriate—filling memory with all 0ffh bytes, constructing logical AND and OR masks and setting specific bits in bytes and words. I learned to count my toes before I learned to count computer bits, so decimal is more natural to me. Besides, this is the default setting for TASM and MASM.

Many assembly language programmers prefer hexadecimal, however, and they change the default radix to hex by adding a `RADIX 16` directive to their programs. There's nothing wrong with that, but remember that you still have to add a trailing h to all hex values that end in a b, which the assembler and TD recognize as the binary radix modifier.

Watch out for this problem. Even after changing the radix to hex, the value 101B equals 5 in binary; it does not equal the expected 4,123 in decimal! To write that value correctly in hex, you still have to use 101Bh with a trailing h even though you changed the default radix.

> Hint: Mistakes in radix often show up in the `Watches` and inspector windows. The `Data` menu's `Evaluate/modify` command is also helpful as a decimal-to-hex converter—use it often to check that values are what you think they should be.

Debugging Mixed-Language Code

C and Pascal programs that call assembly language subroutines, whether included in line with the source code or from external modules, can experience the same kinds of bugs as unmixed code. As far as debugging is concerned, there isn't anything special about mixing languages.

Of course, you must be careful to follow the recommended designs for writing assembly language subroutines. Common errors include failing to preserve the stack frame pointer BP, adjusting the stack pointer by the wrong number of bytes in a `ret` instruction, and failing to preserve registers. (Watch out for SI and DI in mixed-language C programs. Those may be used as C's register variables.)

When debugging *Turbo C* programs, TD automatically switches to show C and assembly language source code in the `Module` view. For this to work, you must be sure to assemble, compile, and link with the options that add debugging information to all modules (see chapter 2).

When debugging *Turbo Pascal* programs, however, TD does *not* show an assembly language view—even if you assembled the object-code modules correctly. Unfortunately, the built-in TP linker strips debugging information from .OBJ modules when it combines them with the compiled Pascal code. We can only hope that a future TP release will fix this problem.

> Hint: When TD switches from C to assembly language, if `Options:Language` is set to `Source`, as it usually is, you must enter expressions in assembly language format. When TD switches back to C, you must use C's format again. If you find this to be confusing, choose another setting for `Options:Language`.

Summary

It's possible to write some classy code in assembly language, but it's also possible to introduce subtle bugs that are extremely difficult to find. Assembly language is a cryptic language that demands utmost attention to detail. The slightest mistake can lead to disaster.

This chapter lists many kinds of common assembly language bugs that are both common and unique. Of course, you can also make most of the same errors in assembly language as in C and Pascal, so if you're reading this chapter out of order, you might also want to read chapters 10 and 12 for descriptions of other common bugs.

Chapter 15

Hands-On Debugging for Assembly Language

Bugs in assembly language code often do more damage than similar problems in other languages. Because an assembly language program is in complete charge of the computer, the slightest disturbance can send the code spiraling out of control—all the more reason to apply the debugging strategies and principles outlined in this book and demonstrated in this chapter.

Similar in design to the hands-on debugging sessions in chapters 11 and 13 for *Turbo C* and *Turbo Pascal*, the following sections demonstrate how to use TD to find bugs in *Turbo Assembler* code. First, you'll enter a buggy program, which is long enough to be interesting, but not so long as to discourage you from typing it into your editor. Then, you'll follow the steps outlined in chapter 7 to develop a debugging strategy for three fiendish bugs. After fixing each problem, you'll retest the code to be sure the bugs stay dead.

You can also use this chapter as a self test of the information you've learned so far. After reading about each bug, watch for a note like this:

Self test: Stop reading now.

When you see that message, stop reading and try to find and fix the problem. Continue reading after you've discovered the solution or if you're stuck and need more help. Don't be concerned if you can't find all the bugs on your own. It's more important to try and fail than never to try at all.

Note: Even if you already read chapter 11 or 13, you can still take the self tests and follow the demonstrations here. Parts of these chapters are the same, but the programs and bugs are unique. If you didn't read chapter 11, you might want to scan that chapter's review of debugging strategies from chapter 7 before continuing.

The Program

As you learned in chapter 7, a good plan for stabilizing bugs caused by unini-tialized variables and pointers is to set all available memory to 0 before running the buggy code. That way, uninitialized variables will have known values, which you can search for with the debugger.

The next three listings make up a program, ZEROMEM, that you can use for this purpose. Before running tests on buggy code, use ZEROMEM to clear old values out of memory. Or, you can incorporate the program into your own projects. This may be all you need to stabilize a bug that refuses to hold still.

Although filling bytes with values should be a simple job, because the 80x86 divides memory into 64K segments, filling address ranges over multiple segments is difficult to accomplish with good speed. For that reason, I decided to base ZEROMEM on a general-purpose module FILLMEM.ASM (Listing 15.1) that can fill any range of addresses with values, from a single byte up to all available RAM. Unfortunately, however, the module has a few rough spots that need polishing.

To expose those defects, I also wrote a test program, FILLTEST.ASM (Listing 15.2). Before running the final ZEROMEM.ASM program (Listing 15.3), the subroutines in FILLMEM will have to pass FILLTEST's tests.

Enter all three listings now, but don't assemble and run ZEROMEM.ASM yet—I'll let you know when to do that. Use these commands to assemble and link the other two modules, FILLMEM and FILLTEST:

```
tasm /zi fillmem
tasm /zi filltest
tlink /v filltest fillmem
```

You may want to insert those lines into a batch file named MT.BAT (for Make Test). You can then enter MT to assemble and link instead of typing each line.

Note: After finding each bug and making the suggested changes, enter these same three commands to reassemble and relink. Or, run the **MT** batch file if you created it.

Listing 15.1. FILLMEM.ASM.

```
1:  %TITLE "Fill-memory module. TASM 2.0 Ideal mode"
2:
3:  ;**      File:    fillmem.asm (WITH BUGS!)
4:  ;**      Author:  (c) 1990 by Tom Swan.
5:
6:           IDEAL
```

```
 7:          MODEL    small
 8:          CODESEG
 9:          PUBLIC   CalcDistance, FillMemory, Normalize
10:
11:  ;-----------------------------------------------------------
12:  ; CalcDistance            Calculate distance between two pointers
13:  ;-----------------------------------------------------------
14:  ; Input:
15:  ;        es:di = normalized pointer number 1
16:  ;        ds:si = normalized pointer number 2
17:  ; Output:
18:  ;        dx:ax = 32-bit unsigned result. If es:di = ds:si, the
19:  ;        result = 1. If es:di < ds:si, the result is undefined.
20:  ; Registers:
21:  ;        ax, dx
22:  ;-----------------------------------------------------------
23:  PROC    CalcDistance
24:          push     bx cx di si    ; Save modified registers
25:          mov      ax, si         ; Copy si to ax for subtraction
26:          sub      ax, di         ; ax <- si - di (signed)
27:          cwd                     ; Convert to 32-bit ax:dx
28:          mov      si, ds         ; Copy ds to si, es to di--can't
29:          mov      di, es         ;  subtract segment registers.
30:          sub      si, di         ; si <- ds - es (# paragraphs)
31:          xor      di, di         ; Zero high order 32-bit result
32:          mov      cx, 4          ; Assign loop count
33:  @@10:
34:          shl      si, 1          ; Multiply segment value by 16
35:          rcl      di, 1          ;  over 32-bit result si:di
36:          loop     @@10           ; Loop on cx
37:          add      ax, si         ; Add offset value to
38:          adc      dx, di         ;  32-bit result in dx:ax
39:          pop      si di cx bx    ; Restore saved registers
40:          ret                     ; Return to caller
41:  ENDP    CalcDistance
42:
43:  ;-----------------------------------------------------------
44:  ; FillBytes               Fill number of bytes at any address
45:  ;-----------------------------------------------------------
46:  ; Input:
47:  ;        cx = number of bytes to fill (must be <= 0fff0h)
48:  ;        dl = byte value to use for fill
49:  ;        es:di = normalized starting address for fill
50:  ; Output:
51:  ;        none
```

```
52: ; Registers:
53: ;       ax, cx, di, es
54: ;-----------------------------------------------------------
55: PROC    FillBytes
56:         jcxz    aa10            ; Exit if count = 0
57:         cld                     ; Clear direction flag
58:         repnz   stosb           ; Fill cx bytes at es:di
59: aa10:
60:
61: ; ----  Fall through to Normalize pointer in es:di
62:
63: ENDP    FillBytes
64:
65: ;-----------------------------------------------------------
66: ; Normalize               Normalize pointer in es:di
67: ;-----------------------------------------------------------
68: ; Input:
69: ;       es:di = any 32-bit address value
70: ; Output:
71: ;       es:di normalized so that offset in di is in
72: ;       the range 0000 to 000Fh. Formula is
73: ;       segment = (segment + (offset / 16))
74: ;       offset  = (offset % 16)   (% = "modulo")
75: ; Registers:
76: ;       ax, es, di
77: ;-----------------------------------------------------------
78: PROC    Normalize
79:         push    bx cx           ; Save registers
80:         mov     ax, di          ; Copy di (offset) to ax
81:         mov     cl, 4           ; Calculate offset / 16
82:         shr     ax, cl          ;  by shifting right x 4
83:         mov     bx, es          ; Copy es to bx
84:         add     ax, bx          ; ax = ax + bx
85:         mov     es, ax          ; Copy result back to es
86:         and     di, 0fh         ; Calculate offset % 16
87:         pop     cx bx           ; Restore registers
88:         ret                     ; Return to caller
89: ENDP    Normalize
90:
91: ;-----------------------------------------------------------
92: ; FillMemory             Fill memory with any byte value
93: ;-----------------------------------------------------------
94: ; Input:
95: ;       dl = byte value to use for fill
96: ;       es:di = starting address for fill
```

```
 97: ;           ds:si = ending address for fill
 98: ; Output:
 99: ;           Area from es:di up to and including ds:si filled
100: ;           with dl bytes. If ds:si = es:di, 1 byte is filled.
101: ;           If ds:si < es:di, no filling occurs.
102: ;           After, es:di = address of byte after ds:si
103: ; Registers:
104: ;           ax
105: ;-------------------------------------------------------------
106: PROC    FillMemory
107:         push    bx cx dx di si es  ; Save most registers
108:
109: ; ----   Normalize the two addresses in es:di and ds:si, so that
110: ;        their offset values are in the range 0000 to 000Fh.
111:
112:         push    es ds               ; Save es, push ds
113:         pop     es                  ; Set es <- ds
114:         xchg    di, si              ; Swap di and si
115:         call    Normalize           ; Normalize ds:si in es:di
116:         push    es                  ; Push result in es
117:         pop     ds                  ; Set ds <- es
118:         xchg    di, si              ; Swap di and si back
119:         pop     es                  ; Restore es
120:         call    Normalize           ; Normalize es:di
121:
122: ; ----   Fill as many almost full segments as possible. The
123: ;        division keeps the program running fast, while
124: ;        simplifying the logic that would be required to fill
125: ;        full 65,536-byte segments  when the starting offset
126: ;        might not be zero.
127:
128:         push    dx                  ; Save fill value on stack
129:         call    CalcDistance        ; dx:ax <- count of bytes to
fill
130:         mov     bx, 0fff0h          ; bx <- fill-loop maximum count
131:         div     bx                  ; ax <- dx:ax div 0fff0h
132:         mov     bx, dx              ; Assign remainder to bx
133:         pop     dx                  ; Restore fill value to dl
134:         mov     cx, ax              ; Assign fill-loop count to cx
135:         jcxz    aa20                ; Skip loop if count = 0
136: aa10:
137:         push    cx                  ; Save count for next loop
138:         mov     cx, 0fff0h          ; Set count to maximum
139:         call    FillBytes           ; Fill cx bytes at es:di
140:         pop     cx                  ; Restore loop count
```

```
141:            loop     aa10              ; Repeat until cx = 0
142:    aa20:
143:            mov      cx, bx            ; Assign remainder in bx to cx
144:            call     FillBytes         ; Fill remaining bytes
145:            pop      es si di dx cx bx    ; Restore registers
146:            ret                        ; Return to caller
147:    ENDP    FillMemory
148:
149:            END                  ; End of fillmem.asm text
```

Listing 15.2.   FILLTEST.ASM.

```
 1:    %TITLE "Test fillmem module"
 2:
 3:    ;**     File:    filltest.asm
 4:    ;**     Author:  (c) 1990 by Tom Swan.
 5:
 6:    ; Note: Run in TD. If exit code = 0, no errors detected, else
 7:    ;       exit code equals the failed test number.
 8:
 9:            JUMPS
10:            IDEAL
11:            MODEL    small
12:
13:    STKSIZE EQU      4096              ; Stack size in bytes
14:
15:            STACK    STKSIZE
16:
17:    cr      EQU      13
18:    lf      EQU      10
19:
20:    SEGMENT DSeg Para Public 'DATA'
21:
22:    exitCode        db       0
23:
24:    ; ----   TEST1: 1-byte fill
25:
26:    t1s     db       'TEST1',cr,lf,'$'
27:    t1x     db       0ffh
28:    t1      db       0ffh              ; Area to fill
29:    t1y     db       0ffh
30:
31:    test1   dw       offset t1s        ; Address of test name
32:            dw       offset t1x + 1    ; Address to start fill
33:            dw       offset t1y - 1    ; Address to end fill
```

```
34:          dw       offset t1y - offset t1
35:
36:  ; ----   TEST2: 2-byte fill
37:
38:  t2s     db       'TEST2',cr,lf,'$'
39:  t2x     db       0ffh
40:  t2      dw       0ffffh           ; Area to fill
41:  t2y     db       0ffh
42:
43:  test2   dw       offset t2s
44:          dw       offset t2x + 1
45:          dw       offset t2y - 1
46:          dw       offset t2y - offset t2
47:
48:  ; ----   TEST3: 4096-byte fill
49:
50:  t3s     db       'TEST3',cr,lf,'$'
51:  t3x     db       0ffh
52:  t3      db       4096 dup (0ffh) ; Area to fill
53:  t3y     db       0ffh
54:
55:  test3   dw       offset t3s
56:          dw       offset t3x + 1
57:          dw       offset t3y - 1
58:          dw       offset t3y - offset t3
59:
60:  ENDS    DSeg
61:
62:          CODESEG
63:
64:  ; ----   From FILLMEM.OBJ:
65:
66:          EXTRN    FillMemory:proc
67:
68:          ASSUME   ds:DSeg
69:
70:  Start:
71:          mov      ax, DSeg               ; Initialize DS and ES to
72:          mov      ds, ax                 ;  address of data seg
73:          mov      es, ax
74:
75:  ; ----   Run tests, which jump to Exit with exitCode = test #
76:  ;        if any errors are detected.
77:
78:          mov      bx, offset test1       ; Address test1's data
```

```
79:        call    PerformTest         ; Perform test
80:        mov     bx, offset test2    ; Repeat for other tests
81:        call    PerformTest
82:        mov     bx, offset test3
83:        call    PerformTest
84:
85:        mov     [exitCode], 0       ; No errors
86:  Exit:
87:        mov     ah, 04Ch            ; DOS terminate function
88:        mov     al, [exitCode]      ; Load ERRORLEVEL code
89:        int     21h                 ; End
90:
91:  ; ---- Perform the fill test
92:
93:  PROC   PerformTest
94:        inc     [exitCode]          ; Identify test number
95:        mov     dx, [bx]            ; Display test message
96:        mov     ah, 9               ;  via DOS function 9
97:        int     21h                 ; Call DOS function
98:        mov     di, [bx + 2]        ; es:di = start address
99:        mov     si, [bx + 4]        ; ds:si = end address
100:        xor     dl, dl              ; dl = fill value (0)
101:        call    FillMemory          ; Fill es:di to ds:si
102:        cmp     [byte es:di - 1], 0ffh  ; Test byte before fill
103:        jne     Exit                ; Jump if changed
104:        cmp     [byte ds:si + 1], 0ffh  ; Test byte after fill
105:        jne     Exit                ; Jump if changed
106:        cmp     [byte es:di], 0     ; Test first/single byte
107:        jne     Exit                ; Jump if <> 0
108:        mov     cx, [bx + 6]        ; cx = fill area size
109:        xor     al, al              ; al = fill value (0)
110:        repe    scasb               ; scan rest of fill area
111:        jcxz    @@10                ; Exit if cx = 0
112:        jmp     Exit                ; Else jump to error
113:  @@10:
114:        ret                         ; Return to caller
115:  ENDP   PerformTest
116:
117:        END     Start           ; End of program / entry point
```

Listing 15.3. ZEROMEM.ASM.

```
1: %TITLE "Zero available memory. TASM 2.0 Ideal mode."
2:
3: ;**    File:   zeromem.asm (WITH BUGS!)
```

```
 4:  ;**     Author:  (c) 1990 by Tom Swan.
 5:
 6:          IDEAL
 7:          MODEL   small
 8:
 9:  STKSIZE EQU     256                 ; Stack size in bytes
10:
11:          STACK   STKSIZE
12:
13:          DATASEG
14:
15:  lowAddr         dd      far ptr 0       ; First address filled
16:  highAddr        dd      far ptr 0       ; Last address filled
17:
18:          UDATASEG
19:
20:  msgHello        db      'ZEROMEM: Filling memory...', '$'
21:
22:          CODESEG
23:
24:  ; ----  From FILLMEM.OBJ:
25:
26:          EXTRN   FillMemory:proc
27:
28:  Start:
29:          mov     ax, @data           ; Initialize DS to
30:          mov     ds, ax              ;  address of data seg
31:          mov     dx, offset msgHello ; Display welcome message
32:          mov     ah, 9               ; DOS function: print
33:          int     21h                 ; Call DOS
34:          call    GetAddresses        ; Find fill begin, end
35:          les     di, [lowAddr]       ; Initialize es:di
36:          lds     si, [highAddr]      ; Initialize ds:si
37:          xor     dl, dl              ; Assign fill byte (0) to dl
38:          call    FillMemory          ; Fill memory with dl
39:          mov     ax, 04C00h          ; DOS function: Exit
40:          int     21h                 ; Call DOS
41:
42:  ;----------------------------------------------------------
43:  ; GetAddresses         Calculate high and low fill addresses
44:  ;----------------------------------------------------------
45:  ; Input:
46:  ;       es = PSP segment address (offset assumed to be 0000)
47:  ; Output:
48:  ;       lowAddr = address one byte beyond stack
```

```
49: ;       highAddr = highest address allocated to program
50: ;       Note: assumes that highest possible stack address
51: ;             is < 0fffeh.
52: ; Registers:
53: ;       ax
54: ;--------------------------------------------------------------
55: PROC    GetAddresses
56:         mov     [word lowAddr+2], ss       ; Set lowAddr to byte
57:         mov     [word lowAddr], STKSIZE    ; after end of stack
58:         mov     ax, [es:2]                 ; Get address from PSP
59:         dec     ax                         ; Correct value in ax
60:         mov     [word highAddr+2], ax      ; Copy to variable
61:         mov     [word highAddr], 0fh       ; Assign offset
62:         ret                                ; Return to caller
63: ENDP    GetAddresses
64:
65:         END     Start                      ; End of program / entry point
```

Hands-On Debugging Sessions

Each of the following sections begins with a description of a bug in FILLTEST.ASM. The descriptions simulate the early stages of debugging when you know that something isn't operating as expected, but you don't know exactly what has gone wrong. In this case, problems have been revealed by running FILLTEST, which puts FILLMEM's subroutines through their paces. Only after passing all tests will you trust the low-level routines enough to assemble and run ZEROMEM.

> Note: FILLTEST.ASM declares a data segment DSeg using TASM's SEGMENT directive instead of the usual simplified memory model DATASEG (see line 20 in Listing 15.2). This causes variables to be aligned to a segment paragraph boundary, duplicating the offset positions of those variables under different runtime conditions. If FILLTEST didn't do this, some of the bugs in this chapter might show up differently on different machines. Aligning the test data keeps the tests "honest"— a good tip to remember when debugging your own code.

If you're taking the self test, after reading the description of a bug, put the book aside and try to find and fix the mistake. Then, whether or not you're taking the self test, follow the step-by-step numbered sections to run through the TD commands that I used to locate the error. Do this even if you've successfully located the bug on your own. That way, you can compare your debugging strategy with mine.

Be careful to keep FILLMEM.ASM up to date. Some of the later bugs depend on earlier ones, and you must complete sections 1 through 3 in that order, or the step-by-step instructions will be meaningless. A useful plan is to copy FILLMEM.ASM to MYFILL.ASM for taking the self tests. Make your own changes only to MYFILL.ASM. Then, after finishing each self test, compile and load the current FILLMEM.ASM file into TD and then follow the step-by-step debugging demonstrations after the "Stop reading" note. Make the changes suggested in the text directly to FILLMEM.ASM. You can then copy the partially debugged FILLMEM.ASM again to MYFILL.ASM before taking the next bug's self test.

You might also want to copy the original, unmodified FILLMEM.ASM to another file, perhaps named FILLBUG.ASM, so you or someone else can repeat the hands-on demonstrations without having to retype the listing. This will also let you start over in case you mix up the files. If that happens, just copy the master FILLBUG.ASM to FILLMEM.ASM and make the suggested changes to FILLMEM.ASM up to the point where you stopped.

Note: Line numbers in the text refer to the listings as printed in this chapter. After you make the first set of changes to FILLMEM.ASM, your editor's line numbers may not match those in the listing. For that reason, when I suggest adding new statements, for example between lines 45 and 46, use Listing 15.1 as a guide to locate the place in your up-to-date FILLMEM.ASM file where you should make those changes.

Using FILLMEM and FILLTEST

Before turning to the first bug, you'll need to understand how the FILLTEST program and the FILLMEM module work. Here's a brief summary of FILLMEM's subroutines:

- `CalcDistance` calculates the number of bytes between two addresses, which must be normalized (their offsets must be in the range 0 to 15). Pass the starting address in ES:DI and the ending address in DS:SI. If these addresses are the same, `CalcDistance` should return 1, not 0. After calling the subroutine, DX:AX equals the 32-bit unsigned integer result with the low-order value in AX. Registers AX and DX are subject to change. Other registers are preserved.

- `FillBytes` fills any range of addresses within one segment. Set CX to the number of bytes to fill, DL to the value to store in those bytes, and ES:DI to the starting address. The value in CX must be less than or equal to 0FFF0h, which simplifies filling segments that are not aligned on paragraph boundaries, but which also limits the maximum range to 65,520 bytes. `FillBytes` modifies AX, CX, DI, and ES. Other registers are preserved.

- `Normalize` converts any address in ES:DI to a unique value, called a *normalized address*, useful for some kinds of operations—for example, calculating the distance between two bytes in RAM. After calling `Normalize`, the address in ES:DI points to the same physical location in memory, but its offset is guaranteed to be within the range of 0 to 15. The subroutine may change AX, ES, and DI. It preserves other registers.

- `FillMemory` performs memory fills between two addresses, no matter how distant. The subroutine can fill a single byte or multiple segments. Set DL to the value to use for filling, ES:DI to the starting address, and DS:SI to the ending address. `FillMemory` changes only AX. Other registers are preserved.

The FILLTEST program (see Listing 15.2) puts those four subroutines through their paces. Three sets of variables labeled TEST1, TEST2, and TEST3 store the name of the test as an ASCII$ string (see line 26 in Listing 15.2), followed by three variables: a check byte (labeled 'x'), an area to fill, and another check byte (labeled 'y'). The addresses of these items are then stored in four word variables labeled by the test name (for example, see `test1` at lines 31–34).

FILLTEST displays the test name, fills the test area, scans that area to determine if the fill worked, and verifies that the check bytes surrounding that area were not disturbed. The main program performs these actions by using BX as a pointer to the test-data addresses and calling the subroutine `PerformTest` (see lines 78–83).

That subroutine (lines 93–115) calls DOS to display the test name, prepares ES:DI and DS:SI to address the area to fill, and then calls `FillMemory` in the FILLMEM module. After that, `PerformTest` verifies that the fill worked. If so, the subroutine returns normally. If not, it jumps directly to label `Exit` at line 86. This leaves the `exitCode` byte variable set to the test number, which is either passed back to DOS as an error code or displayed in TD's "Terminated, exit code" message box. If TD reports an exit code of 0, then all tests passed; otherwise, the value represents the number of the failed test.

Bug Number 1

On your first FILLTEST trial run, you realize something is amiss. First, the program displays only the TEST1 message, suggesting a failure in that routine. Second, when you load FILLTEST into TD and run, the debugger reports an exit code of 1.

> **Self test:** Stop reading now.

Bug number 1—Test and Stabilize

Unlike the C and Pascal hands-on demonstrations in chapters 11 and 13, we've already stabilized the bug in this chapter by running FILLTEST. Even so, it's important to list the steps required to reproduce the bug:

1. Load FILLTEST into TD with the command **td filltest**.
2. Press ⟨**F9**⟩ to run the test.
3. The program halts with "exit code 1," suggesting a failure in TEST1.

To avoid repeating those obvious steps, this will be the last "Test and Stabilize" section. Use these same steps to test and stabilize each of the three bugs in this chapter.

Bug number 1—Isolate

The next step is to isolate the problem to find out where the code is misbehaving. Follow these steps.

1. The program is already loaded into TD. (If not, perform the three steps under "Bug number 1—Test and Stabilize" now.) If the "Terminated" message window is still visible, press ⟨**Esc**⟩. Then, press ⟨**Ctrl**⟩-⟨**F2**⟩ to reset.

2. Because the first test fails, it makes sense to monitor test number 1's variables. Press ⟨**F6**⟩ to make `Watches` the current window, type **t1x**, and press ⟨**Enter**⟩. Notice that you don't have to choose a command—just start typing. Also enter **t1** and **t1y**. As you can see, each of these values equals 255 (FFh). Press ⟨**F6**⟩ to return to the `Module` view.

3. Now, let's find out where `PerformTest` fails. First move the cursor down about nine lines to `mov bx, offset test2` and press ⟨**F2**⟩ to set a breakpoint there (after the first call to `PerformTest`). Experience teaches that before tracing into low-level assembly language routines, it's a good idea to set a breakpoint so that you can return to a known location later. Next, press ⟨**F7**⟩ five times to trace into `PerformTest`. Then, move the cursor down about seven lines to `call FillMemory` and press ⟨**F4**⟩ to run up to that

location. Press ⟨**F8**⟩ to step over the `call`. This should clear test variable **t1** to 0, but it doesn't, meaning that we are faced with the job of finding the cause of an event that doesn't occur.

4. This suggests a failure in the fill algorithm, so let's review what we know about FILLMEM's subroutines. As explained earlier, `FillBytes` (lines 43–63 in Listing 15.1) is responsible for filling address ranges within a single segment; therefore, we may as well begin searching FILLMEM at this lowest level by checking how `FillBytes` operates.

5. To do that, you could press ⟨**F3**⟩ to choose TD's `View:Module` command, select module "fillmem," and then search for the `FillBytes` subroutine. But there's an easier way: just enter the routine's name **fillbytes**. This automatically selects the `Module` view's `Goto` command. After you press ⟨**Enter**⟩, it switches modules and hops directly to the subroutine's first instruction, `jcxz aa10`. (Go ahead and enter **fillbytes** now and press ⟨**Enter**⟩. Notice that the module name changes in the window's top border.)

6. Press ⟨**F2**⟩ to set a breakpoint on the `jcxz` instruction. Then, press ⟨**Ctrl**⟩-⟨**F2**⟩ to reset the program and ⟨**F9**⟩ to run the test up to the breakpoint. Notice how in all of these steps, we are digging deeper into the code, running up to a strategic location, observing the results, resetting, and then following the logic farther down. With luck, this will take us to the bug's hideout.

7. The program is now paused inside the call to `FillBytes`. To examine the arguments passed to the subroutine, press ⟨**Alt**⟩-VR to view the `Registers` window. Immediately, we spot a problem—CX should specify the number of bytes to fill, 1 for this single-byte test. But the `Registers` view shows CX equal to 0000.

8. A quick patch proves whether setting CX to 1 fixes the problem. Move the highlight bar down to `CX 0000`, type **1**, and press ⟨**Enter**⟩. CX's value should change to 0001.

9. Close `Registers` (press ⟨**Alt**⟩-⟨**F3**⟩), then press ⟨**F9**⟩ to run. The program halts at the breakpoint we set earlier, and the test byte at **t1** now equals 0 as it should. Also, `PerformTest` didn't halt this time with exit code 1.

Bug number 1—Repair

By definition, when ES:DI and DS:SI address the same location, FILLMEM's `FillMemory` subroutine is supposed to fill exactly 1 byte by setting CX to 1 and calling `FillBytes`. Because that isn't happening, the cause must be in `CalcDistance`, which should return 1 for the "distance" between two equal addresses.

In other words, to find the number of bytes between two addresses X1 and X2, `CalcDistance` should calculate (X2 − X1) + 1. Instead, a `sub` instruction (line 26) subtracts the two offsets but fails to add 1 to the 16-bit result before converting it to 32 bits with `cwd`.

To fix the problem, quit TD, load FILLMEM.ASM into your editor, and add the following line between original lines 26 and 27 in procedure `CalcDistance` after the instruction `sub ax,di`:

```
inc   ax        ; Equal addresses are 1 byte distant
```

Assemble and link (or run the MT batch file). Then, enter **filltest** at the DOS prompt to retest. TEST1 now passes as expected, but, obviously, our work is unfinished. The program never makes it past TEST2.

Bug Number 2

This is typical. You fix one bug and another one pops out of nowhere. But this is good news—your tests are forcing bugs into the open. Better to do that now than to let a customer find a problem for you.

Getting back to work, you load the modified FILLTEST into TD and discover that the program now ends with exit code 10. (Type **td filltest** to start TD, then press ⟨**F9**⟩.) That's strange. There are only three tests, not ten. Has FILLTEST caught a bug?

Self test: Stop reading now.

Bug number 2—Isolate

This bug has all the symptoms of an uninitialized variable or pointer. Apparently, the `exitCode` variable is being trashed. Let's find out where that's happening.

1. Load FILLTEST into TD with the command **td filltest**. If TD is already running, press ⟨**Esc**⟩ to clear the message window if it's visible, then press ⟨**Ctrl**⟩-⟨**F2**⟩ to reset. Add variables `exitCode`, `t2x`, `t2`, and `t2y` to `Watches`. To do that, either move the cursor to each of those variables (lines 22 and 39–41 in Listing 15.2) and press ⟨**Ctrl**⟩-**W**, or press ⟨**F6**⟩ to make `Watches` the current window and enter each name as you did in the previous demonstration. Be sure to switch back to `Module` (press ⟨**F6**⟩ again) before continuing.

2. Next, set a breakpoint to find where `exitCode` is set to 10—the value that TD reports when the program ends. Press ⟨**Alt**⟩-**BE** and enter **exitCode eq 10d**. This sets an `Expression true global` breakpoint that will halt the code at the instruction that sets `exitCode` to 10. Notice how the trailing d specifies 10 as a decimal value. This is necessary because TD's default value is hexadecimal when debugging assembly language.

3. Press ⟨**F9**⟩ to run. In a moment, the program stops with the same "Terminated" message as before. But that's strange. It should have halted as soon as `exitCode` became equal to 10—long before the program ended. Press ⟨**Esc**⟩ to clear the message box, then look at the variables in `Watches`. The `exitCode` is 2, not 10. Also, test location `t2` is set to 0 as expected, and the check bytes at `t2x` and `t2y` are undisturbed. There doesn't seem to be anything wrong with the test variables.

4. What can these observations mean? There's only one answer: the variables aren't being trashed after all. Instead, the program has lost track of its data—a sure sign that a subroutine has changed a data segment register and failed to change it back.

5. Let's test that assumption. Press ⟨**Alt**⟩-**BD** to delete all breakpoints and then press ⟨Ctrl⟩-⟨F2⟩ to reset the program to its beginning. Press ⟨Ctrl⟩-**O** to position the cursor to the origin in case the line at that location is not on screen. (Notice that the variables remain visible in `Watches` after resetting.)

6. Move the cursor down several lines to the *second* `call` to `PerformTest`—the one that's broken. Press ⟨**F4**⟩ to run up to that location. Then, press ⟨**Alt**⟩-**BC**, type **ds**, and press ⟨**Enter**⟩ to set a `Changed memory global` breakpoint for that register. This will halt the code after any instruction changes DS.

7. Press ⟨**F9**⟩ to run. In a moment, a message appears giving the breakpoint number (there is only one), the module name, and a line number (`#fillmem#119` on my screen, but possibly a different number on yours). Press ⟨**Esc**⟩ to clear the message window.

8. The instruction that changed DS is above the cursor: `pop ds`. Notice also that the variables in `Watches` now have the values ????, indicating that even TD can't find them. Move the cursor up a few lines to find out which subroutine we're in. It's `FillMemory`, and the `push` instruction at line 107 obviously fails to save DS. Also, obviously, we've found the bug.

Bug number 2—Repair

It's not hard to fix bugs when you know what causes them. In this case, the repair adds DS to the `push` and `pop` instructions in `FillMemory`. Quit TD, load FILLMEM.ASM into your editor, and change original line 107 to:

```
push  bx cx dx di si ds es
```

Also change original line 145 to:

```
pop   es ds si di dx cx bx
```

After assembling and linking, load FILLTEST into TD and press ⟨**F9**⟩ to run. This time, the "Terminated" message box displays "exit code 0," indicating that the three tests passed. Press ⟨**Esc**⟩ to clear the message box, then press ⟨**Alt**⟩-⟨**F5**⟩ to check the program's output. You should see all three test names. Press any key to return to TD.

Bug Number 3

With FILLMEM completely debugged (we hope), it's time to assemble and run ZEROMEM.ASM (Listing 15.3). To do that, quit TD if it's running and enter these commands:

```
tasm /zi zeromem
tlink /v zeromem fillmem
```

Then, enter **zeromem** to run the program. A message tells you that ZEROMEM is filling memory, and after a brief moment, the DOS prompt returns. Apparently, the code is working correctly. Just to be sure, load ZEROMEM into TD and examine a few locations with the Dump view. To your surprise, you discover that available memory is set to anything but the expected zeros. Considering the careful tests we've conducted, how can this be?

Self test: Stop reading now.

Bug number 3—Isolate

To isolate this bug, we need a way to examine the memory that ZEROMEM is supposed to set to 0. A macro will help perform that job quickly:

1. If you didn't load ZEROMEM into TD, do that now with the command **td zeromem**. Move the cursor down several lines to the second int 21h instruction (below mov ax, 04C00h), and press ⟨**F2**⟩ to set a breakpoint for returning to this spot later.

2. Move the cursor up a couple of lines to call FillMemory and then press ⟨**F4**⟩ to run up to that location. The program is now paused just before any filling occurs.

3. To examine the memory areas that should be filled, press ⟨**Alt**⟩-**VD** to open the `Dump` view and press ⟨**F5**⟩ to zoom the window to full screen.

4. Press ⟨**Alt**⟩-**=** to start recording a macro. Press ⟨**Ctrl**⟩-**A** for the macro key assignment. (If a message asks for permission to overwrite an existing macro, answer "Yes" by pressing **Y**.) The activity indicator at the upper right should now display `RECORDING`. Press ⟨**Ctrl**⟩-**G** to choose the `Goto` command, enter **es:0**, press ⟨**Enter**⟩, press ⟨**Ctrl**⟩-⟨**F4**⟩, type **es = es + 1000h**, and press ⟨**Enter**⟩⟨**Esc**⟩. Stop recording the macro by pressing ⟨**Alt**⟩--. The upper right corner should display `READY`. (If you make a mistake while entering the macro, press ⟨**Alt**⟩-- to stop recording and then repeat this step over from the beginning.)

5. You have just entered a macro to display the beginning of the segment addressed by ES and then added 1000h to that register to prepare for displaying the *next* segment. Press ⟨**F8**⟩ to execute the `call` to `FillMemory`, where the program is now paused. Notice that you can do this even though the `Dump` window recovers the display. Scan the bytes in the `Dump` view by pressing ⟨**Page Down**⟩ a dozen or more times. As you can see, some bytes are set to 0, but most aren't.

6. To scan the next segment, press ⟨**Ctrl**⟩-**A**. This runs the macro you entered, positions the `Dump` view to the current ES:0 address, and adds 1000h to ES for the next time. Notice how the segment address at far left advances by 1000h. Use ⟨**Page Down**⟩ to scan this new segment. Repeat several times (press ⟨**Ctrl**⟩-**A** and ⟨**Page Down**⟩) until you reach the end of available memory—on most systems, when the segment address is greater or equal to A000. To find the exact maximum address, press ⟨**Alt**⟩-**VR** to open `Registers`. ZEROMEM assigns the ending address to DS:SI. Close `Registers` by pressing ⟨**Alt**⟩-⟨**F3**⟩.

Note: If you quit TD, you'll lose the macro you entered in the previous steps. To save it, press ⟨**Alt**⟩-**OS** and **M** to select the `Macros` check box. Press ⟨**Enter**⟩ to write TDCONFIG.TD to disk. The next time you start TD, you can open the `Dump` view and press ⟨**Ctrl**⟩-**A** to run the macro.

Now that we have a way to examine the memory that ZEROMEM is supposed to fill, the next step is to find out why the program fails to live up to its promise. The obvious approach is to set a `Changed memory global` breakpoint for the starting address and halt the code at the instruction that's changing this byte to the wrong value. That would take us directly to the buggy code.

However, because FILLMEM uses a repeated string instruction to perform the fill (see line 58 in Listing 15.1), this kind of breakpoint works only on 80386- and 80486-based systems that install the TDH386.SYS device driver to enable hardware debugging registers. A more general, but slower, method that works for all systems follows.

7. Press ⟨**F6**⟩ a couple of times to return to the `Module` view. Press ⟨**Ctrl**⟩-⟨**F2**⟩ to reset the code, move the cursor up to the `call FillMemory` instruction, and press ⟨**F4**⟩ to run up to that spot.

8. Press ⟨**F6**⟩ to reactivate the `Dump` window, press ⟨**Ctrl**⟩-**G** to select the `Goto` command, enter **es:di**, and press ⟨**Enter**⟩. If the `Dump` view is zoomed to full screen, shrink it by pressing ⟨**F5**⟩ so you can see the `Module` window behind.

9. Next, choose the `Run:Animate` command (press ⟨**Alt**⟩-**RN**). Then, keeping your eye on `Dump`, press ⟨**Enter**⟩ to animate with the default value 3 (3/10-second delays). As soon as the byte values in the center of `Dump` begin to change, press ⟨**Esc**⟩ to stop animating. This will take about 10 or 15 seconds.

10. The current instruction in the `Module` window is `repnz stosb`, which performs the filling for FILLMEM. Open the `Registers` view (⟨**Alt**⟩-**VR**) to inspect the fill value being used in AL. As you can see, this value is not 0, and now the problem is clear. The `FillBytes` subroutine should have copied the fill value passed in DL to AL before executing `repnz stosb`.

11. Let's try a patch to prove that assumption. Press ⟨**Alt**⟩-⟨**F3**⟩ to close `Registers`. Press ⟨**F6**⟩ twice to activate `Module`, move the cursor up one line to the `cld` instruction, and press ⟨**F2**⟩ to set a breakpoint there. Press ⟨**Alt**⟩-⟨**F2**⟩ to modify that breakpoint's options. Press ⟨**Tab**⟩ twice and use ⟨**Cursor Down**⟩ to change `Action` to `Execute`. Press ⟨**Tab**⟩ once more and enter **al = dl** for the `Action expression`. Press ⟨**Enter**⟩ to accept this change and close the `Breakpoint options` dialog box.

12. You have just inserted an expression that patches `FillBytes` to perform a missing instruction. To test the patch, reset the program (press ⟨**Ctrl**⟩-⟨**F2**⟩), press ⟨**F6**⟩ to bring the `Dump` window back into view, and press ⟨**F9**⟩ to run. When the program reaches the breakpoint you set earlier, zoom the `Dump` view to full screen (⟨**F5**⟩). The values are all 0s. Use the ⟨**Page Down**⟩ key to examine more of this segment. Then, press ⟨**Ctrl**⟩-**A** to examine other segments as you did before. (The first time you do this, you may see a few bytes in the stack segment, identified by SS in the left column. Filling starts after the stack, so this is normal.)

Note: If you examine all available RAM, sooner or later, you'll run into a series of nonzero values, probably FF FF FF... Note the address of the first value. (For me, it was 9DD9:2270). Normalizing this address equals the end of RAM, or in my case, A000:0000. If you want, you can confirm this by passing the unnormalized address to the `Normalize` procedure in FILLMEM (lines 65–89).

Bug number 3—Repair

As with most bugs, once you locate the cause, the repair is easy. Quit TD, load FILLMEM.ASM into your editor, and insert the following line between original lines 56 and 57 in Listing 15.1 (between jcxz @@10 and cld):

```
mov  al, dl          ; Assign fill value to AL
```

Be sure to assemble and link *both* FILLMEM and ZEROMEM. The complete commands are:

```
tasm /zi fillmem
tasm /zi zeromem
tlink /v zeromem fillmem
```

Then, load ZEROMEM into TD and repeat steps 1 to 6 at the beginning of this section to fill and examine memory. If you saved the macro earlier, in place of step 4, press ⟨**Ctrl**⟩**-G** to choose the Dump view's Goto command and enter **es:0** to position the window to the starting address for the fill. Then, continue with steps 5 and 6.

Note: This final bug (if there is such a thing) demonstrates the danger of using incomplete tests. FILLTEST failed to test FILLMEM's ability to fill multiple segments, a problem that surfaced only after running ZEROMEM. A better test would not have stopped after filling only a few test variables.

Summary

This chapter lists a buggy assembly language program, describes three bugs, and shows how to use TD to find the source of each problem. You can use the chapter as a hands-on demonstration of debugging techniques or as a self test of what you've learned so far.

After you iron out its bugs, the ZEROMEM program also makes a useful utility for setting all available RAM to 0 bytes, which can help stabilize uninitialized variables and bad-pointer bugs in other programs. Run ZEROMEM before loading programs into TD for debugging.

Part Three

Advanced Debugging Topics

Chapter 16

Macros and Keystroke Recording

Td CAN RECORD and play back keystrokes in one of two ways. It can associate a series of commands with a *macro key* that you can press to execute those commands. Or, it can record all keystrokes from the beginning of a TD session so you can replay those keys to relive a moment of debugging history.

Because macros and keystroke recording are related but used differently, this chapter covers them both. The first section explains how to enter and use macros as part of a debugging strategy. It also includes several sample macros that you can enter and save in a TD configuration file. The second section describes how to use keystroke recording.

Macros

A macro can save time by reducing a series of TD commands to a keypress or two. When creating your own macros, the main points to remember are:

- A macro can repeat only TD commands. If one of those commands executes a target program's instruction that prompts for input, any keys that you press in response are not saved in the macro.

- While recording a macro, the keys you press perform their usual actions. Before creating a new macro, you must load a program, open windows, and perform any other setup chores required by the macro's commands. Recording a macro doesn't just "go through the motions." Each command executes as you enter it.

- Unfortunately, there is no way to edit a macro after you've created one. If you make a mistake while entering a macro's keystrokes, you must start over. (If that mistake is minor, however, you may be able to leave the error in the macro without any harm.)

How to Enter Macros

Press ⟨**Alt**⟩-= (hold down ⟨**Alt**⟩ and press the unshifted = key). When you release those keys, TD's activity indicator in the upper right corner changes to PROMPT, and a window appears with the message, "Press key to assign macro to."

Press any unused key for the macro. Good choices are ⟨**Shift**⟩ plus a function key ⟨**F1**⟩ to ⟨**F10**⟩, unused control keys, or unusual symbol keys such as ~, }, and **!**.

If you choose a macro key that's already used for another macro, TD asks "Overwrite existing macro on selected key?" Answer **Y** to replace the macro assignment with the new keystrokes. Or, answer **N** to cancel macro recording. If you answer **N**, you can start over by pressing ⟨**Alt**⟩-= and selecting a different key assignment.

When macro recording begins, the activity indicator changes to RECORDING. Enter the TD commands that you want to associate with this macro key. The commands operate as they normally do, so you must be sure to open windows and perform other preliminary setups before starting to record.

When you're done, press ⟨**Alt**⟩-- (hold down ⟨**Alt**⟩ and press the unshifted dash or hyphen key, not the minus key on a numeric keypad). The activity indicator at the upper right corner should return to READY, indicating that TD is no longer recording keystrokes for this macro. You can now press the assigned macro key to rerun the commands you just entered.

Keys for Macros

Be careful not to assign a macro to a TD hot key. If you do, the macro key will replace the original key's operation. For example, if you assign a macro to ⟨**Ctrl**⟩-**I**, you'll no longer be able to position the cursor to a variable's name in the Module window and press those keys to open an inspector window, showing the variable's value. However, you can still use the associated Inspect command by choosing it from a menu.

Table 16.1 lists 28 unused keys that don't conflict with TD's current hot-key assignments. Generally, the shifted function keys make the best choices and are recommended by Borland for assigning to macros. But the other keys should be available on most keyboards. You might want to copy this table and enter your own macro assignments in the blank spaces for reference. With one exception, the ⟨Ctrl⟩-letter key combinations near the end of the table are unused by local menus in view windows. A few windows, for example, the flags pane in Registers, assign ⟨Ctrl⟩-T to a Toggle command. Because you can choose that command simply by pressing ⟨**Enter**⟩ or ⟨**Space**⟩, ⟨Ctrl⟩-T makes a good macro key. The same is true for other ⟨Ctrl⟩-letter key combinations that you never or seldom use.

Table 16.1. Suggested macro keys.

Keys	Description*
⟨Shift⟩-⟨F1⟩	
⟨Shift⟩-⟨F2⟩	
⟨Shift⟩-⟨F3⟩	
⟨Shift⟩-⟨F4⟩	
⟨Shift⟩-⟨F5⟩	
⟨Shift⟩-⟨F6⟩	
⟨Shift⟩-⟨F7⟩	
⟨Shift⟩-⟨F8⟩	
⟨Shift⟩-⟨F9⟩	
⟨Shift⟩-⟨F10⟩	
⟨Ctrl⟩-⟨F1⟩	
⟨Ctrl⟩-⟨F3⟩	
⟨Ctrl⟩-⟨F6⟩	
⟨Ctrl⟩-⟨F8⟩	
⟨Ctrl⟩-⟨F9⟩	
⟨Ctrl⟩-⟨F10⟩	
⟨Ctrl⟩--	
⟨Ctrl⟩-⟨Enter⟩	
⟨Ctrl⟩-J	
⟨Ctrl⟩-Q	
⟨Ctrl⟩-T	
⟨Ctrl⟩-U	
⟨Ctrl⟩-X	
⟨Ctrl⟩-Y	
⟨Ctrl⟩-@	
⟨Ctrl⟩-^	
⟨Ctrl⟩-]	
⟨Ctrl⟩-|	

*Fill in this table to document your macro key assignments.

Note: Keys ⟨Ctrl⟩-⟨F8⟩, ⟨Ctrl⟩-⟨F9⟩, and ⟨Ctrl⟩-⟨F10⟩ perform the same jobs respectively as ⟨F2⟩ (**Breakpoints:At**), ⟨F9⟩ (**Run:Run**), and ⟨Alt⟩-⟨F10⟩ (**Local**). The three ⟨Ctrl⟩ function key combinations are duplicated for compatibility with other Borland products, but if that's not important to you, they make good choices for macros. Also, when using ⟨Ctrl⟩-@ and ⟨Ctrl⟩-^, you don't have to press ⟨Shift⟩.

Saving and Restoring Macros

To save the current set of macro assignments, choose `Options:Save options` (press ⟨**Alt**⟩-**OS**). Press **M** or use a mouse to select the `Macros` option in the `Save Configuration` dialog box, and then press ⟨**Enter**⟩ or click the `Ok` button to create the TDCONFIG.TD file in the current directory.

The other options in the dialog box select whether to save `Options` (for example, the number of display lines, the language, and the path for source files), plus `Layout` (the current crop of open view windows, their positions, and sizes). You can check these options on or off to save other items along with macros in TDCONFIG.TD.

You can also change the TDCONFIG.TD file name by tabbing to the `Save To` area in the `Save Configuration` dialog box and typing a different name. Or, use the DOS RENAME command to change the file name after quitting TD.

After saving macros (and other items) in a configuration file, you can reload that file to restore its settings and macros. There are three ways to do this:

- Start TD normally with TDCONFIG.TD in the current directory. TD will load that file automatically if it exists. If TDCONFIG.TD is not in the current directory, then TD looks for the configuration file in the TDINST `Turbo directory` and then in debugger's home path, usually C:\TD.

- Use the -c command-line option to load a different configuration file when you start TD. For example, to load MACROS.TD and debug a program called MYCODE.EXE, use the command **td -cmacros.td mycode**. Notice that there is no space between -c and the configuration file name.

- After starting TD, choose `Options:Restore options` (press ⟨**Alt**⟩-**OR**) and select or enter a configuration file name.

Macros and Debugging

Macros are good for repeating any sequence of commands that you execute regularly. While debugging, if you notice that you are entering the same commands over and over, you might want to convert them into a macro.

The following sections describe some of the uses I've found for macros while debugging various programs. Most of these macros are temporary—I enter them while debugging and don't save them to disk. Or, I sometimes save these macros in a TDCONFIG.TD file and then, after debugging the code, erase the file.

Opening views

I get a little tired of pressing ⟨**Alt**⟩-**V** plus a view's hot key to open a window, especially after doing that a few hundred times. If I know I'm going to open the

`Dump` view frequently, I'll assign the keys ⟨**Alt**⟩-**VD** to a macro. To those keys I might also add ⟨**F5**⟩ to zoom the window to full screen. And, if I want to inspect data at a certain location, I'll insert a `Goto` command.

For example, the sequence to open a `Dump` window, zoom it to full screen, and use `Goto` to view bytes addressed by DS:SI is:

`<Alt>-=`	Start macro recorder
`<Shift>-<F1>`	Assign macro key
`<Alt>-VD`	Choose `View:Dump`
`<F5>`	Zoom to full screen
`<Ctrl>-G`	Choose `Goto` command
`DS:SI<Enter>`	Enter address
`<Alt>--`	Stop recording the macro

> Note: Other macros in this chapter are listed similarly, with keystrokes to the left and brief descriptions to the right. Enter only the keys at left and press ⟨**Enter**⟩ only where that key appears. In place of the second line ("Assign macro key"), you may use any of the key combinations from Table 16.1.

Reprogramming TD's hot keys

Although TD lacks the native ability to change its hot-key command assignments, if you don't like TD's choice of keys, you can always reprogram them with macros. For instance, because I never press ⟨**F10**⟩ to open global menus, I reassign that key as a macro that opens the `Breakpoint options` dialog box. Then, after setting a code breakpoint at a source-code line, I press ⟨**F10**⟩ to open the dialog box, which lets me select different conditions and actions for this breakpoint. Enter these keystrokes to create the macro:

`<Alt>-=`	Start macro recorder
`<F10>`	Assign macro key
`<Alt>-VB`	Choose `View:Breakpoints`
`<Ctrl>-S`	Choose `Set options`
`<Alt>--`	Stop recording the macro

> Hint: Notice that I did not use the existing hot key ⟨Alt⟩-⟨F2⟩ as the macro sequence to open the dialog box. Now that I've reassigned ⟨F10⟩ to do this, I can use ⟨**Alt**⟩-⟨**F2**⟩ for another macro. Or, I could leave the original definition alone if I wanted both keys to perform the same action.

I also frequently use macros to add hot keys to commands that have none—for example, `Window:Dump pane to Log`. To avoid choosing that command over and over from the `Window` menu, I create a macro for the sequence ⟨**Alt**⟩-**WD**. Then, when I want to dump a window pane's data to the `Log`, I just press the macro key.

Repeating test sequences

Macros are also useful for creating repeatable tests—one of the key elements of a successful debugging strategy. To do this, load your program into TD and start recording a macro. You can assign the macro to any key, but I usually choose ⟨**Shift**⟩-⟨**F9**⟩ because of the way TD uses ⟨F9⟩ and variations for other "run" commands.

Next, use TD commands to run the code to a stopping place immediately before a bug appears. Stop recording the macro. Save the macro to disk so you can restart the same sequence after quitting and restarting the debugger (or in case of a serious crash that forces you to reboot).

After tracing the buggy code, to perform another test, press ⟨**Alt**⟩-**FO** and enter or select the program's name. This reloads the buggy program and resets other TD conditions to their original startup values. After that, press the macro key to rerun the program up to where you stopped before.

Even better, because macros ignore keystrokes entered as input for the target program, this method lets you rerun test patterns with new data. When the code reaches an input statement, the macro will pause. Enter the new information and press ⟨**Enter**⟩ (or continue the buggy program by other means). The macro will then pick up from where it stopped.

Entering watch and inspector expressions

It can be tedious to enter numerous variable names or to select them from the source code in the `Module` window. To make this easier to do, I start recording a macro. Then I add my variables to `Watches`, or I open inspector windows to view their values. When I'm done, I stop recording the macro and save it in TDCONFIG.TD. The next time I load that same program, I can then press the macro key to load the same set of data into `Watches`.

There are several ways to implement this tip. You can record the keystrokes needed to search for variables in modules, position the cursor, and press ⟨**Ctrl**⟩-**W** or ⟨**Ctrl**⟩-**I** to watch and inspect values. You could also use the `Data:Inspect` and `Data:Add watch` commands and enter each variable name. But I find the technique works best by using this sequence of commands:

`<Alt>-=`	Start macro recorder
`<Ctrl>-<F1>`	Assign macro key

`<Alt>-VW`	Activate `Watches` view
`v1<Enter>`	Enter first variable name
`v2<Enter>`	Enter second variable name
`...`	Enter more variable names
`vn<Enter>`	Enter last variable name
`<Alt>-VM<Enter>`	Activate `Module` view
`<Alt>--`	Stop recording the macro

After switching to the `Watches` view, enter a variable name—which automatically selects the window's default local `Watch` command—and then switch back to `Module`. Notice that the macro commands select `Watches` and `Module` from the `View` menu rather than have you press ⟨**F6**⟩ or ⟨**Alt**⟩ and the window's number. Because of this and because variables are listed by name, the macro will work under a variety of conditions, for example, even if the `Watches` view is closed.

Setting multiple breakpoints

When you have several breakpoints to set, rather than do that for each new debugging session, you can record the necessary keystrokes in a macro. After that, load the target program and press the macro key to set out your traps for the next test run.

When setting breakpoints with macros, be aware that the `Breakpoints:At` command (⟨F2⟩) operates as a toggle. Pressing ⟨**F2**⟩ sets or removes a breakpoint at the cursor position in the `Module` window. For this reason, if you rerun a macro that sets breakpoints, it will *remove* the breakpoints set previously.

Sometimes this can be useful. For example, you might record the steps required to set the last 6 out of 12 breakpoints as a macro. You can then press the macro key to toggle those 6 breakpoints on and off without disturbing the others.

When you don't want a macro to toggle breakpoints, use the `File:Open` command to reload the target program. Unlike `Run:Program reset` (⟨Ctrl⟩-⟨F2⟩), reopening the program with the `File` menu command erases all current breakpoints, which you can then set again by running the macro.

Problems with Macros

Macros replay their keystrokes blindly. Unless all conditions are the same when you replay a macro as they were when you recorded the original keys, the results may not be what you expect.

This is frequently a problem when you press a macro key while a dialog box is active. Because dialog boxes inhibit global menu commands, any macro keystrokes that choose commands will produce strange results or be ignored. One way to avoid this trouble is to begin all macros by pressing ⟨**Esc**⟩ one time after starting to record. Because that key closes an active dialog window, but is usually ignored at other times, the effect is to allow the macro to work even when a dialog box is on screen.

When creating macros, it also helps to keep in mind these other limitations and quirks:

- You can record up to 256 keystrokes for a single macro, provided, of course, that TD has enough memory to store those keys.

- Mouse clicks and movements are not stored in macros. While recording a macro, TD ignores any commands entered with a mouse.

- Macros can't call other macros. The effects of pressing another macro's key while recording a new macro are unpredictable.

- There is no way to edit existing macros, and there is no way to display a macro's keystrokes. Keep good notes about the macros you enter. That way, you'll be able to retype them later if necessary.

- If you accidentally press the wrong macro key while recording a macro, stop recording, and choose the `Options:Macros:Remove` command (⟨**Alt**⟩-**OMR**). Press the macro key that you typed by accident to restore that key to its original use. Use `Options:Macros:Delete all` (⟨**Alt**⟩-**OMD**) to erase all macro definitions and restore all keys. (Be careful with this command. Unless you saved your macros to disk, after deleting them, there is no way to get them back.)

Sample Macros

The next sections describe a few sample macros that you can enter and store in a TD configuration file. For best results, erase or rename any existing TDCON-FIG.TD files to avoid conflicts. (Be sure to check for a configuration file in TD's home directory.) I've suggested macro key assignments for all macros in this section, but you can change these to any of the keys listed in Table 16.1.

In addition to the listed keystrokes, you may also have to answer the prompt "Overwrite existing macro on selected key." If you see that message, press **Y** or click the `Yes` button and then continue typing.

> Note: Start TD and load a sample program before entering these macros. Unless the instructions say otherwise, you can use any listing in this book. Or, if you're familiar enough with TD's commands, use one of your own programs. After entering one or more macros, remember to choose `Options:Save options` to save the keystrokes in a configuration file. TD does not warn you if you quit the debugger without saving your macros.

Display hidden windows—⟨Shift⟩-⟨F1⟩

If you have a mouse, you've probably discovered that clicking inside the `Module` window causes any inspectors and other view windows to run and hide. Enter the following macro to bring all hidden windows back into view:

`<Alt>-=`	Start macro recorder
`<Shift>-<F1>`	Assign macro key
`<Alt>-1`	Bring first window forward
`<Alt>-2`	Bring next window forward
`<Alt>-3`	And so on, ...
`<Alt>-4`	
`<Alt>-5`	
`<Alt>-6`	
`<Alt>-7`	
`<Alt>-8`	
`<Alt>-9`	... up to the last window
`<Alt>--`	Stop recording the macro

You can enter this macro even if there are less than nine windows open. TD ignores ⟨Alt⟩-digit key combinations for nonexisting window numbers.

The next time inspector and view windows disappear behind `Module`, either after clicking the mouse or using other commands, press ⟨**Shift**⟩-⟨**F1**⟩ to bring them all forward again. If you want to try this now, open several inspectors to a few test variables, press ⟨**Alt**⟩-**1** or click the mouse pointer inside `Module` to make it the active window (which hides the inspectors), and press ⟨**Shift**⟩-⟨**F1**⟩.

Skip over statements—⟨Shift⟩-⟨F2⟩

The TD commands `Run:Trace into` (⟨F7⟩) and `Run:Step over` (⟨F8⟩) execute the current instruction and stop. If that instruction calls a procedure, function, or subroutine, pressing ⟨**F7**⟩ traces *into* that routine. Pressing ⟨**F8**⟩ executes the call at full speed, stopping after that call returns.

What's missing is the capability to skip an instruction and not execute its machine code. Of course, this can have negative effects on the program, but it can also make a useful debugging tool that will let you investigate what happens if you remove one or more instructions.

Before entering this macro, load a sample program into TD, press ⟨**F8**⟩, and position the cursor to the first of at least two source-code statements in the `Module` view. This is important—the macro works correctly only where there are at least two adjacent lines that generate machine code. After positioning the cursor, press ⟨**F4**⟩ to run the program to this location. (If the cursor is already at the current location, skip that step.)

The current-statement marker (▶) and cursor should now be on the same line, and there should be at least one program statement below that line. Press ⟨**Cursor Down**⟩ to move to the statement below, and then enter the macro:

`<Alt>-=`	Start macro recorder
`<Shift>-<F2>`	Assign macro key
`<Alt>-VC`	Open the CPU view
`<Ctrl>-N`	Reset CS:IP to the new origin
`<Alt>-<F3>`	Close the CPU view
`<Alt>--`	Stop recording the macro

To use this macro, move the cursor to any source-code line below the current one and press ⟨**Shift**⟩-⟨**F2**⟩. The current instruction and those up to the cursor will be skipped. This is similar to the way ⟨F8⟩ works except that *no code is executed*. The new current instruction will be the one to which you moved the cursor before running the macro. Choosing any Run-menu command will continue the program starting with that line.

> Note: Before running this macro, be sure that the cursor is on a source-code line that generates at least one machine-code instruction and that the Module window is active. Also, never use this macro to skip a return from a procedure or function—this will almost certainly cause problems if you continue running the program.

Reset and return to origin—⟨Shift⟩-⟨F3⟩

When you press ⟨**Ctrl**⟩-⟨**F2**⟩ to choose the Run:Program reset command, TD reloads the program but leaves the cursor at the place where the program stopped during the previous session. Sometimes this can be useful. For example, after resetting, you can move the cursor up a line or two and press ⟨**F4**⟩ to rerun the code up to that earlier statement.

Even so, after resetting, I often press ⟨**Ctrl**⟩-**O** to return the cursor to the origin. For that reason, I combined the two commands into a "super reset" macro:

`<Alt>-=`	Start macro recorder
`<Shift>-<F3>`	Assign macro key
`<Ctrl>-<F2>`	Reset the current program

| `<Ctrl>-O` | Move cursor to origin |
| `<Alt>--` | Stop recording the macro |

After entering this macro, during a debugging session, you can press ⟨**Ctrl**⟩-⟨**F2**⟩ as usual to reset and leave the cursor where it is, or press ⟨**Shift**⟩-⟨**F3**⟩ to reset and move the cursor back to the program's first statement.

Hint: After ⟨Ctrl⟩-O, you can also insert other commands to close `View`-menu windows, execute the `System` menu's `Repaint desktop` or `Restore standard` commands, or perform any other tasks that you want to attach to TD's standard `Program reset` command.

Open views as icons—⟨Shift⟩-⟨F4⟩

Because I usually open the same few windows for every debugging session, I discovered that I could save time by using a macro to open those views at the touch of a key. Also, shrinking the windows to icons reduces display clutter while arranging the views along the right border where I can select them easily with a mouse. (If you don't have a mouse, you can do the same by pressing ⟨**F6**⟩ or ⟨**Alt**⟩ plus the window's number and then pressing ⟨**F5**⟩.)

Enter the following macro to create three icons for the `Breakpoints`, `Log`, and `CPU` views. You can replace my ⟨**Alt**⟩-**Vx** commands with those that open the views you need, or you can add additional views. Just be sure to follow each `View`-menu command with ⟨**Alt**⟩-**WI** to shrink the window to an icon.

`<Alt>-=`	Start macro recorder
`<Shift>-<F4>`	Assign macro key
`<Alt>-VB`	Open the `Breakpoints` view
`<Alt>-WI`	Reduce window to an icon
`<Alt>-VL`	Open the `Log` view
`<Alt>-WI`	Reduce window to an icon
`<Alt>-VC`	Open the `CPU` view
`<Alt>-WI`	Reduce window to an icon
`<Alt>--`	Stop recording the macro

The next time you start TD, press ⟨**Shift**⟩-⟨**F4**⟩ to open these same windows and shrink each one to an icon. Initially, the icons will be hidden behind the `Module` and `Watches` views. Press ⟨**F6**⟩ to bring them forward.

> Hint: If you also entered the "Display Hidden Windows" macro (⟨**Shift**⟩-⟨**F1**⟩), you can press those keys after pressing ⟨**Shift**⟩-⟨**F4**⟩ to bring all icons into view.

Erase user screen—⟨Shift⟩-⟨F5⟩

Between debugging sessions, TD does not clear the program's display. Unless the target program does this, whatever was on screen will be there the next time you choose the `Window:User screen` command (⟨**Alt**⟩-⟨**F5**⟩).

Use the following macro to add an "Erase User Screen" command to TD. The macro works by calling *Turbo Pascal*'s or *Turbo C*'s `clrscr` procedure. (TP programs must add a `uses crt` declaration. TC programs must include the CONIO.H header and must call `clrscr()` at least once in the program.) If you are using a different language, you may be able to call a similar library subroutine (or write one) that erases the display.

Before creating the macro, load a test program into TD and press ⟨**F8**⟩ to execute any runtime initialization routines. Then, enter these keystrokes:

`<Alt>-=`	Start macro recorder
`<Shift>-<F5>`	Assign macro key
`<Ctrl>-<F4>`	Open the `Evaluate/modify` dialog box
`clrscr()`	Enter the procedure or function name
`<Enter>`	Evaluate (call) the routine
`<Esc>`	Close the dialog window
`<Alt>--`	Stop recording the macro

> Note: Before using this macro, you must execute the target program's runtime initializations. Do this by pressing ⟨**F8**⟩ after loading the code into TD or after resetting. Running the macro before initializing the program does no harm, but it won't clear the display.

Start a new log file—⟨Shift⟩-⟨F6⟩

I like to keep a log file open at all times while debugging so I can dump information to the `Log` view and not have to worry about old text scrolling out of reach. The following macro lets me open a new log file at the start of a debugging session.

Before entering the keystrokes, make sure there are no .LOG files in the current directory. Then, type these commands:

`<Alt>-=`	Start macro recorder
`<Shift>-<F6>`	Assign macro key
`<Alt>-VL`	Open **Log** view
`<Ctrl>-C`	Close log file if one is open
`<Ctrl>-E`	Erase log window (optional)
`<Ctrl>-O`	Open a new log file
`<Enter>`	Accept the default file name
`<Alt>-<F3>`	Close the **Log** view
`<Alt>--`	Stop recording the macro

You can now close the log file by pressing ⟨**Alt**⟩**-VL** and ⟨**Ctrl**⟩**-C**. In the future, to start a new log, press ⟨**Shift**⟩**-**⟨**F6**⟩. If a NAME.LOG file already exists in the current directory where NAME is the file name of the program's main module, TD will display "Overwrite NAME.LOG?" Answer **Y** to start a new log of the same name. Or, if you press **N**, you can enter a new log file name. When you see this prompt message, because the macro has finished replaying its keystrokes, you'll have to close the **Log** window manually by pressing ⟨**Alt**⟩**-**⟨**F3**⟩.

> Note: The log file remains open and information is written to the **Log** whether or not that view is open.

Snapshot—⟨Shift⟩-⟨F7⟩

At various times while debugging a program, I run the following macro to take a "snapshot" of the **Module**, **Watches**, and **CPU** views. The macro stores the text from each of those views in a log file named SNAPSHOT.LOG, erasing any old file of that name. I can then print that file, view it with the **View:File** command, or rename it to save a copy for future reference.

Load a sample program and make the **Module** window current before entering these keystrokes to create the "snapshot" macro:

`<Alt>-=`	Start macro recorder
`<Shift>-<F7>`	Assign macro key
`<Alt>-VL`	Open **Log** view
`<Ctrl>-C`	Close log file if one is open
`<Ctrl>-E`	Erase log contents
`<Ctrl>-O`	Open a new log file
`<Enter>`	Accept the default file name

`<Enter>`	Allow overwriting old snapshot
`<Alt>-<F3>`	Close the `Log` view
`<Alt>-1`	Activate the `Module` view
`<Alt>-WD`	Dump pane to log
`<Alt>-2`	Activate `Watches` view
`<F5>`	Zoom to full screen
`<Alt>-WD`	Dump pane to log
`<F5>`	Zoom back to normal size
`<Alt>-VC`	Open `CPU` view
`<F5>`	Zoom to full screen
`<Alt>-WD`	Dump disassembly pane to log
`<Tab>`	Move to next pane
`<Alt>-WD`	Dump registers to log
`<Tab>`	Move to next pane
`<Alt>-WD`	Dump flags to log
`<Tab>`	Move to next pane
`<Alt>-WD`	Dump stack to log
`<Tab>`	Move to next pane
`<Alt>-WD`	Dump memory dump to log
`<Tab>`	Move to first pane
`<F5>`	Zoom back to normal size
`<Alt>-<F3>`	Close `CPU` view
`<Alt>-VL`	Open `Log` view again
`<Ctrl>-C`	Close log file
`<Ctrl>-E`	Erase log contents
`<Alt>-<F3>`	Close `Log` view
`<Alt>--`	Stop recording the macro

OOP instance inspector—⟨Shift⟩-⟨F8⟩

In object-oriented Pascal or C++ programs, after halting inside a call to a method, I often want to inspect the object instance that made the call. The next macro makes this easy by opening an inspector window for the `self` (Pascal) or `this` (C++) hidden argument passed to all methods.

Before entering the macro, you must load a program that declares at least one object with at least one method. Set a breakpoint inside that method and press ⟨F9⟩ to execute up to that place. Then, type these keystrokes:

Key	Action
`<Alt>-=`	Start macro recorder
`<Shift>-<F8>`	Assign macro key
`<Alt>-VS`	Open the `Stack` view
`<Ctrl>-L`	View local variables
`<Ctrl>-<Page Down>`	Move to last item in window
`<Enter>`	Open `self` or `this` inspector
`<Alt>-VS`	Activate `Stack` view
`<Alt>-<F3>`	Close `Stack` view
`<Alt>--`	Stop recording the macro

Alternatively, you could replace the keys from ⟨Alt⟩-VS to ⟨Alt⟩-⟨F3⟩ with **⟨Alt⟩-DI** and use the commands **self⟨Enter⟩** for Pascal or **this⟨Enter⟩** for C++. But I like the longer version for two reasons. One, it works with both Pascal and C++ object methods, and two, it opens the `Variables` view to show other method parameters and variables within the current scope.

> Note: Run this macro only after pausing the program inside a method and after executing that macro's startup code. After running the macro, press **⟨Alt⟩-⟨F3⟩** twice to close the inspector and `Variables` windows.

Forward and reverse gears—⟨Keypad +⟩ and ⟨Keypad –⟩

Most keyboards have a separate numeric keypad with + and – keys. Because you can always enter those characters with the + and - keys on the main keyboard, if you don't mind giving up the keypad equivalents, they make handy forward and reverse "gear shift" macros.

Enter the following keystrokes to assign the `Trace into` (⟨**F7**⟩) and `Back trace` (⟨**Alt**⟩-⟨**F4**⟩) commands to keypad + and –. Be sure to press those keys on the keypad, not on the main keyboard:

Key	Action
`<Alt>-=`	Start macro recorder
`<Keypad +>`	Assign macro key
`<F7>`	Execute trace into command
`<Alt>--`	Stop recording the macro
`<Alt>-=`	Start macro recorder
`<Keypad ->`	Assign macro key
`<Alt>-<F4>`	Execute back-trace command
`<Alt>--`	Stop recording the macro

You can now press ⟨**Keypad +**⟩ and ⟨**Keypad −**⟩ to trace forward and backward in code. And, you can still use the original keys ⟨**F7**⟩ and ⟨**Alt**⟩-⟨**F4**⟩. Remember that back tracing has some limitations, for example, you can't reverse gears through a software interrupt instruction or through any library routine that executes an interrupt. But most of the time, you can press those keys to trace program statements forward and back. I find the macros much easier to use than ⟨F7⟩ and ⟨Alt⟩-⟨F4⟩.

Note: The only drawback is that, after creating the macros, to enter expressions, you must remember to press the + and - keys on the main keyboard. The macros disable the keypad + and − keys for all other uses.

Repeat test—⟨Shift⟩-⟨F9⟩

As I mentioned earlier, I usually reserve this macro key to create repeatable tests while debugging. For that reason, I don't assign it to a permanent macro.

CPU search next command—⟨Shift⟩-⟨F10⟩

If you do a lot of assembly language programming, you may have noticed that the `CPU` view has a `Search` command (⟨**Ctrl**⟩-**S**) but lacks a `Search next` operation like the one in the `Module` view. To search for several machine-code instructions takes too many keystrokes for my tastes, so I created my own `Search next` command with a macro.

Before typing these keystrokes, load any program (it doesn't have to be written in assembly language) and press ⟨**Alt**⟩-**VC** to open the `CPU` view. Press ⟨**Ctrl**⟩-**S** to start a search, enter **push bp**, and press ⟨**Enter**⟩. If you receive a message such as "Syntax error" or "Search expression not found," press ⟨**Esc**⟩. Then, enter these keystrokes to create the macro:

`<Alt>-=`	Start macro recorder
`<Shift>-<F10>`	Assign macro key
`<Cursor Down>`	Move cursor to next instruction
`<Ctrl>-S`	Start a search
`<Cursor Down>`	Select previous search argument
`<Enter>`	Search for next occurrence
`<Alt>--`	Stop recording the macro

After entering the macro, the next time you open the `CPU` window and search for an assembly language instruction, press ⟨**Shift**⟩-⟨**F10**⟩ to locate the next occurrence of the same search argument.

This macro is also useful for locating the starts of Pascal and C subroutines, as long as those routines allocate stack space for local variables. First, start a new search for **push bp**. If you find that instruction, press ⟨**Ctrl**⟩-**V** to see the associated high-level source code in the Module view. Press ⟨**F6**⟩ a few times to return to CPU, then press ⟨**Shift**⟩-⟨**F10**⟩ to search for the next occurrence of that same instruction. You can then press ⟨**Ctrl**⟩-**V** again to see the next routine's source.

> Note: This is the end of the sample macros section. If you are entering each macro as you read about it, be sure to choose Options:Save options, press **M** to select **Macros**, and press ⟨**Enter**⟩ to save the macros in TDCONFIG.TD. You might want to make a copy of that file to preserve the macros for future debugging sessions.

Keystroke Recording

Both macros and keystroke recording save keypresses for playing back later. But although these TD features seem to be twins, they have very different personalities.

While macros can associate one or more events with many different macro keys, there is only one keystroke recording session in progress while TD is running. Keystroke recording operates as a kind of endless tape inside TD that records every event as it occurs. Unlike macros, keystroke recording saves all keypresses from the first command you give after loading a program into TD until you quit, including any keys you press in response to a program's prompts.

Borland calls keystroke recording their "instant replay" feature, and that's not a bad description. Keystroke recording lets you reenact events up to where the ball slips out of your program's hands, and the computer cries "foul."

Enabling Keystroke Recording

As chapter 3 explains, there are two ways to enable keystroke recording. If you always plan to use the feature, you can switch it on with TDINST for every debugging session. Or, you can give the -k command-line option when you start TD. For example, to debug a program named OODRAW.EXE and enable keystroke recording, start TD with the command:

```
td -k [other options] oodraw
```

Either way, the result is a file called OODRAW.TDK in the current directory. (The file is always named the same as the buggy program's main module but with the extension .TDK.) After quitting TD, you can erase this file without harmful effects.

Execution History View Review

As chapter 5 explains, the bottom pane of the `Execution history` view displays the events saved by TD's keystroke recording facility. Press ⟨**Alt**⟩-**VE** to open this window and then press ⟨**Tab**⟩ to move the highlight bar into the bottom pane.

After performing those steps, you can move the highlight bar to any line and then choose one of two local commands. Press ⟨**Ctrl**⟩-**I** to `Inspect` the source-code line for this recorded event. Or, press ⟨**Ctrl**⟩-**K** to reload the program and replay all keystrokes up to that moment. When you do that, the replayed keys plus those you press after the replay stops are again saved in the `Execution history`'s bottom pane. A good way to think of this is to imagine a tape inside TD that you can rewind and replay by pressing ⟨**Ctrl**⟩-**K**. After stopping the tape, you can then press the record button (using any `Run`-menu command) to start recording new material from that location.

> Note: The top pane of the `Execution history` view shows events that the `Run:Back trace` command can execute in reverse. Even though this pane is in the same window, it has no direct relationship to keystroke recording. The two panes may at times show similar events, however.

Keystroke Recording and Debugging

Because keystroke recording saves and replays all keystrokes, it's ideal for running repeat tests on buggy code. The following sections list a few tips for using this feature as part of an overall debugging strategy.

Keystroke recording and breakpoints

Start TD and enable keystroke recording. Set two or more breakpoints to narrow a search for a bug and run the code up to the breakpoints. Based on your observations, open the `Execution history` window, select a breakpoint location, and press ⟨**Ctrl**⟩-**K** to repeat the steps that led to that place. Then, trace deeper into the code (usually by pressing ⟨**F7**⟩), set more breakpoints, and repeat.

This technique is especially helpful when you have to press keys and supply other data to let the buggy code proceed to the next breakpoint location. With keystroke recording, you have to type such input only once. TD will replay those keys and commands perfectly every time from then on.

Keystroke recording and animation

Another way to use keystroke recording to narrow a bug search is to run the code with the Run:Animate command. Because this command operates by issuing Trace commands as though you pressed ⟨**F7**⟩ repeatedly, each animated statement is saved in the Execution history's recorded keystrokes.

While animating a section of code, be ready to press ⟨**Esc**⟩ or another key to stop executing. Then, open the Execution history window, select a prior trace point, and press ⟨**Ctrl**⟩-**K** to rerun the program up to that location.

Or, if that takes too much time, press ⟨**Ctrl**⟩-**I** to inspect the source code at any recorded trace, press ⟨**F2**⟩ to set a breakpoint at that location, and then press the keys ⟨**Ctrl**⟩-⟨**F2**⟩ to reset and ⟨**F9**⟩ to run up to this breakpoint location. You can then continue tracking a bug from this spot.

Keystroke recording and code tracing

Many programs are composed of a series of calls to procedures, functions, and subroutines. When trying to find which of those calls has a bug, a good plan of action is to enable keystroke recording and follow these steps:

1. Press ⟨**F8**⟩ to step over procedure and function calls until the bug appears.
2. Open the Execution history view and move the highlight bar up one or more lines to the faulty call.
3. Press ⟨**Ctrl**⟩-**K** to replay all steps up to but not including this call.
4. Press ⟨**F7**⟩ to trace into the call. Then, repeat from step 1 until you locate the bug.

When debugging programs written in strict top-down fashion, these steps can take you straight to a bug with amazing speed. Instead of tracing every statement in sight, use keystroke recording along with the Step over and Trace into commands in the Run menu to divide and conquer a bug's territory.

> Hint: I sometimes open the Execution history window before pressing ⟨**F8**⟩ and ⟨**F7**⟩ to trace code. Each trace point then appears inside the window's bottom pane, giving me a quick way to review the steps that led to the program's current statement.

Keystroke recording and inspectors

Open inspector windows by positioning the cursor in the Module view and pressing ⟨**Ctrl**⟩-**I** or by using the Data:Inspect command. With keystroke recording enabled, you can then replay these steps to reopen your inspectors for a new test run.

When you choose the `Keystroke restore` command in the `Execution history` view's bottom pane, TD closes all open inspectors. Therefore, when you replay keystrokes, TD will open fresh inspector windows for these same variables.

Creating Repeatable Test Procedures

Recorded keystrokes saved in a .TDK file are available the next time you start TD with keystroke recording enabled for this same module. This means you can run through a debugging session, quit TD, and recompile your source code. Then, when you restart the debugger, open the `Execution history` view and replay the previous keystrokes to repeat your test procedure.

When doing this, you'll notice the line "End of recording" in the bottom window pane. Highlight this line and press **⟨Ctrl⟩-K** to get back to your previous stopping place. Or, highlight a different line to return to an earlier moment.

Obviously, this feature has limits. If you make drastic changes to the code, TD might not be able to replay the commands required to get back to a specific location. Also, you may prefer to clear recorded keystrokes before starting a new debugging session. In that case, be sure to erase the .TDK file before running TD.

Problems with Keystroke Recording

Using keystroke recording is mostly intuitive. Even so, there are a few hidden gotchas that you should keep in mind when using this feature:

- Program arguments entered with `Run:Argument` are not reset when replaying keystrokes. This means that any arguments entered after the event to which you return will be used on this new test run. If those new arguments change the course of history, they could affect TD's ability to get back to a previous stopping place.

- Mouse clicks and movements are not saved along with keystrokes. Use a mouse only for commands that you want keystroke recording to ignore.

- The number of keystrokes that can be recorded is limited only by the amount of disk space available. Be sure to have plenty of free space on disk before starting TD with keystroke recording enabled.

- Data written to disk may affect replayed keystrokes if the program rereads that data. For example, you may not be able to repeat a test run for a program that modifies input data in a file because, on the next run, the program will try to process the modified data.

Using Macros and Keystroke Recording

Because macros and keystroke recording save keystrokes, they can conflict. Usually, you'll have no trouble using both features while debugging. But if you do run into difficulties, the following notes may help:

- If you create a macro while recording keystrokes and then replay those keys, TD will attempt to recreate the macro. In this event, you may see a message box that asks "Overwrite existing macro on selected key?" If so, answer **N**. This seems to allow the playback to continue.

- If you replay recorded keystrokes, one of which runs a macro, that macro will again run. However, if that macro traces statements beyond the one to which you intended to return, the program will not halt at the expected location. Instead, execution will continue past that location until the macro stops replaying.

For these reasons, I find it's best to create macros without keystroke recording enabled. Also, when recording keystrokes, I avoid using macros that trace code—except for simple ones like the ⟨Keypad +⟩ and ⟨Keypad −⟩ macros described earlier.

Summary

Macros let you associate TD keystrokes with macro keys, usually ⟨Shift⟩ and a function key ⟨F1⟩ through ⟨F10⟩. With macros, you can quickly replay complex command sequences, invent custom commands, reopen a series of inspector windows, and perform other repeatable activities. This chapter explains how to enter macros and lists several sample macros that you can enter and save in a TDCONFIG.TD configuration file.

Keystroke recording also saves keystrokes, but unlike macros, this TD feature can save keypresses given in response to program prompts. Also unlike macros, there is only one keystroke recorder, enabled by switching this option on with TDINST or by using the -k command-line option.

With keystroke recording enabled, you can open the Execution history window, press ⟨**Tab**⟩ to activate the bottom pane, and highlight any recorded moment. You can then press ⟨**Ctrl**⟩**-I** to inspect that event's source code or ⟨**Ctrl**⟩**-K** to replay all keystrokes that led to this place. This makes keystroke recording ideal for designing repeatable tests and for replaying events that led to a bug.

Chapter 17

Remote and Dual-Monitor Debugging

IF YOU ARE fortunate to have two PCs (they can be XTs, ATs, or other models), you can run TD in remote mode. This lets you execute buggy code on a remote system while the debugger runs locally on your main development computer.

Or, if you have two display adapters with video buffers located at different addresses, you can configure TD to display its output on one monitor while you view the program's graphics and text displays on the other.

These setups, explained in this chapter, offer several advantages over TD's normal single-computer operation. The main benefits for a remote hookup are:

- Both displays are visible at the same time—you no longer have to press ⟨**Alt**⟩-⟨**F5**⟩ to view your code's output. (In fact, those keys are disabled in remote mode.) TD's windows appear on the main system while the remote computer shows the target program's display. This makes remote debugging especially useful for testing graphics programs or those programs that create complex text screens.

- The target program's input comes from the remote system's keyboard. While debugging, you issue TD commands as usual on the local computer, but you type input to the program on the remote keyboard. Because the two keyboards (and other peripherals such as printers and a mouse) are isolated, hardware conflicts between TD and the target program are eliminated. This is especially helpful when debugging input routines, TSRs, and device drivers. (See chapter 19.)

- Programs that are too large to fit in RAM along with TD on one system can usually be debugged in remote mode. All but a small amount of memory (about 20K) is available on the remote. TD shares the local system's RAM with itself and the program's symbol table. Also, TD can use local EMS RAM for symbols, making a remote link ideal for debugging very large programs. Symbols occupy no space on the remote computer's disk or memory.

- Remote debugging prevents haywire bugs from crashing the debugger, which can easily happen on a single system, especially when not running TD386. Even if the remote system crashes, it's unlikely to affect TD's local operation. (I suppose that a buggy program could issue a TD command via the remote link and cause the local system to hang. But the possibilities of this happening are "remote.")

- The remote link prevents serious damage to the local development system's disk and other devices. There is virtually no way for a buggy program running on a remote computer to affect the development system's disk—for example, by writing absolute sectors or by performing another hardware-specific operation. Of course, buggy code can still erase files and perform other mischief on the remote machine. But at least the main computer is well protected from harm by the remote link.

There are a few disadvantages with remote and dual-monitor debugging. For one, there's the cost of the second system or display hardware. For another, remote debugging can't take advantage of TD386's ability to set hardware breakpoints on 80386 and 80486 processors.

A third disadvantage is the time it takes to transfer the target program's compiled or assembled code to the remote computer. When running in remote mode, TD takes a little longer to get going than it does when executed locally. Also, you have to transfer to the remote system any data and text files required by the target code, which adds more time to the debugging process. These disadvantages are usually minor, however, and the steps are easily automated with a batch file.

Dual-monitor debugging doesn't offer as many advantages as a remote link between two computers, but if you have the appropriate hardware, TD can display its own screens on one monitor while the program's output appears on the other. Also, with this setup, you can take advantage of hardware debugging registers on an 80386 or 80486 processor and still see both screens, which isn't possible in remote mode.

This chapter explains how to hook up two systems or two monitors for remote and dual-monitor debugging. For a remote link, you'll need two computers with one serial I/O port each, a cable, and appropriate connectors. For dual-monitor debugging, you'll need color and monochrome adapters (or the equivalent internal circuits) and two displays. If you have only a single system with one display, you can't use these TD features. But you might still want to scan this chapter to determine if adding a second computer or investing in another monitor will be worthwhile.

The Right Connections

As with many endeavors, it pays to have the right connections. That's especially true when hooking two computers' RS-232 serial I/O ports: COM1 or COM2. (If your system has additional COM3 and COM4 ports, TD can't use them. You must use COM1 or COM2.)

For a successful remote link, the first step is to prepare or purchase a serial cable with the necessary pin connections. Successful communications requires the *transmit data* (pin 2) and *receive data* (pin 3) lines to talk to each other; therefore, a straight-through or "ribbon" cable between two identically configured I/O ports probably won't work. (Note: Some systems have 9-pin to 25-pin adapters that cross pins 2 and 3. In that case, because the two lines are already crossed, a straight-through cable may work.)

There might be a PC clone somewhere that breaks that rule, but to connect most systems, you'll need what's usually called a *null-modem* cable, which simply means that pins 2 and 3 are crossed between the two connectors. This configuration lets the speaker (transmitter) talk to the listener (receiver).

> Warning: Before attaching any cables, make absolutely sure that you know which are the RS-232 serial ports on the back of your computer. Unfortunately, other devices sometimes use connectors that look like serial ports, and attaching a remote link to the wrong device could damage one or both computers. For that reason, it's a good idea to test your serial ports with an inexpensive modem or with a "loop-back" plug and associated diagnostic software that you may have received on a system disk. Connect the two computers only after you've positively identified the RS-232 serial ports on each.

Figure 17.1 shows the connections to make between two 25-pin (also called DB-25) connectors. It doesn't matter which end you plug into which computer, but be sure to check whether you need male pins or female sockets. This is the correct cable to use when connecting most XTs and PCs. (When connecting this cable to a single 9- to 25-pin adapter, make sure that only the adapter or the cable, but not both, crosses pins 2 and 3.)

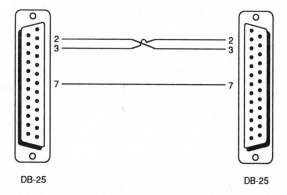

DB-25   DB-25

Figure 17.1. 25-pin to 25-pin serial connections.

Figure 17.2 shows the connections to make between 25-pin and 9-pin connectors found on most AT-class and 80386 (or 80486) systems. Use this cable to connect most AT systems to a spare PC or XT.

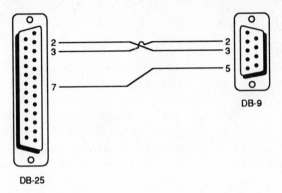

DB-25

Figure 17.2.   25-pin to 9-pin serial connections.

Figure 17.3 shows the connections to make between two 9-pin connectors. In most cases, this is the correct cable to use for hooking up two AT-class systems.

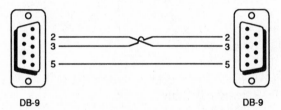

DB-9   DB-9

Figure 17.3.   9-pin to 9-pin serial connections.

When making your own cables, you can leave unlisted pins unconnected. With prefabricated cables, try the connection first before cutting unused wires. In most cases, other pins can be connected without affecting the remote link as long as at least the pins listed here are attached.

> Hint: Use a short cable—if possible, less than 50 feet long. With good quality, shielded cable, you might be able to extend this recommended maximum. But for best results, the shorter the cable the better.

Testing the Remote Link

After buying or preparing your serial cable, attach the two systems and run the test described in this and the next two sections. The local system needs a fully installed copy of TD plus miscellaneous files in a directory that's listed in a DOS PATH command. The remote system needs only the TDREMOTE.EXE utility, which can be in the current directory, on a floppy disk, or in a PATH subdirectory. You do not have to install TD on both computers.

After you've copied TDREMOTE.EXE to your remote computer, type **tdremote** and press ⟨**Enter**⟩ on the remote keyboard. You should see:

```
TD Remote Program Loader Version 2.0 ...(c) 1988, 1990 Borland Intl
Waiting for handshake (press Ctrl-Break to quit)
```

Next, switch to the local system, type **tdrf dir** and press ⟨**Enter**⟩. (TDRF is TD's Remote File Utility—more on this program later.) If all is working correctly, you should see a directory of the remote computer on the local system's display. You'll probably also see and hear disk activity on both systems.

> Note: If the preceding test works, skip the instructions in the next two sections, which you need to complete only if the default configuration fails. Continue reading at "Configuring TD for Remote Debugging."

Configuring TDREMOTE

If the test in the previous section failed, you'll need to configure TDREMOTE (TD's Remote Program Loader) on the remote system. You may also need to configure TDRF on the local system as explained in the next section. Or, the problem could be a bad cable or a faulty serial port. Whatever the cause, the following tests will help you to determine and cure the problem.

On the remote system, if TDREMOTE is currently "Waiting for handshake," press ⟨**Ctrl**⟩-⟨**Break**⟩ to return to the DOS prompt. Verify which remote serial port is connected on the remote computer—either COM1 or COM2. If it's COM1, restart TDREMOTE with this command:

```
tdremote -rp1
```

Or, if the cable is attached to COM2, use this command:

```
tdremote -rp2
```

Next, back again at the local system's keyboard, enter **tdrf dir** and press ⟨**Enter**⟩. If you see "Waiting for handshake" and don't receive a directory listing from the remote, press ⟨**Ctrl**⟩-⟨**Break**⟩ on the local system and go on to the next section now to configure TDRF. Leave TDREMOTE running on the remote computer.

If you do see a directory, you'll want to save this configuration for next time. To do that, first press ⟨**Ctrl**⟩-⟨**Break**⟩ on the remote keyboard to return to DOS. Then, restart TDREMOTE with the same -rp command-line option plus -w. This writes the tested configuration directly to TDREMOTE.EXE. For example, if you determined that COM2 works on the remote system, enter:

```
tdremote -rp2 -w
```

TDREMOTE will then prompt for the name of the program code file to modify. Press ⟨**Enter**⟩ to accept the default file name or enter a different name if you want to store the modifications to a copy of TDREMOTE.EXE, leaving the original program file untouched.

Configuring TDRF

After checking the remote system's serial port and restarting TDREMOTE with an appropriate option, do the same on the local system with TDRF. For example, if you determine that the local system is connected to COM1, enter this TDRF command:

```
tdrf -rp1 dir
```

Notice that, in addition to the command-line option, you must also issue a TDRF command such as DIR. If the cable is attached to COM2, enter:

```
tdrf -rp2 dir
```

If neither of these commands works, you either have a bad cable, or your serial ports can't handle a high-speed 115 Kbaud rate. Repeat the TDREMOTE and TDRF commands from this and the previous sections, but this time, add one of the two "speed" options **-rs2** or **-rs1** to retest your connections at 38.4 Kbaud and 9,600 baud. If you still are having trouble, and if the cable is not faulty, one or both serial ports may need repairs.

> Note: Two of TD's published remote baud rates (9,600, 40K, and 115K) are approximate. The true values are 9,600 (-rs1), 38,400 (-rs2), and 115,200 (-rs3) baud. You don't need to be aware of these precise rates for most remote debugging sessions, but they may be important for system designers to know, especially when debugging embedded systems software and for running custom PC hardware in remote mode.

After you can successfully display a remote directory, use the -w command as explained in the previous section to write TDREMOTE's options permanently to disk for the next time. For example, on the remote system, enter:

```
tdremote -rp1 -rs2 -w
```

Substitute the -rp⟨#⟩ and -rs⟨#⟩ options from your tests. Then, on the local system, execute a similar command, again writing the options to disk. You might enter something like this:

```
tdrf -rp2 -rs2 -w
```

You'll be prompted for the name of the program code file to modify. Press ⟨**Enter**⟩ to accept the default file name or enter a different name if you want to store the modifications to a copy of TDRF.EXE, leaving the original program file untouched.

As a final test, start TDREMOTE on the remote computer (don't enter any command-line options this time) and then enter **tdrf dir** on the local system. If you receive a directory from the remote computer, you're ready to begin remote debugging.

TDRF and TDREMOTE Command-Line Options

Table 17.1 lists all TDREMOTE and TDRF command-line options. For additional help, type **tdremote -h**. For help with TDRF, type **tdrf** and press ⟨**Enter**⟩. Whatever settings you choose, remember that TDREMOTE and TDRF must operate at the same speed.

Configuring TD for Remote Debugging

Before debugging in remote mode the first time, run the TD installation program TDINST and choose the Options and Miscellaneous commands. Set Remote link port to the I/O port to which the cable is attached on the local system—COM1 or COM2. Leave Link speed set to 115 Kbaud unless you changed it earlier to run TDRF. TD must be set to operate at the same speed as TDRF and TDREMOTE. Do not enable Remote debugging unless you plan to run TD exclusively in remote mode.

> Hint: If you will always debug a certain program remotely, you might want to enable the **Remote debugging** option and save this configuration in a TDCON-FIG.TD file in the current directory. But, usually, you should leave this box unchecked. That way, you can continue to use TD in single and in remote modes. If you select this setting, start TD with the option -r- when you don't want to run the debugger in remote mode.

Table 17.1.   TDREMOTE and TDRF command-line options.

Option	Description
-rp⟨#⟩	Set COM port (1 = COM1, 2 = COM2)
-rs⟨#⟩	Set baud rate (1 = 9,600, 2 = 38.4K, 3 = 115.2K)
-w	Write options to .EXE file
-h	Display help
-?	Same as -h

Debugging a Program in Remote Mode

To debug a program in remote mode, make sure your systems are connected properly and then start TDREMOTE on the remote computer. You should see the same copyright and "Waiting for handshake..." messages as listed earlier.

Return to the local keyboard, compile your program, and start TD with the -r option—unless you enabled **Remote debugging** with TDINST, in which case -r has no effect. For example, after compiling a program named MYTEST.PAS (not listed here—the steps are similar for other programs), enter this command at the local keyboard:

```
td -r mytest
```

If you're sharp, you'll see the message "Waiting for handshake from TDREMOTE (ctrl-break to quit)" on the local computer. But, if that message isn't soon replaced by TD's display, the remote link is not working and you may need to configure TDRF and TDREMOTE as explained earlier.

The first thing TD does when started in remote mode is check if the target file is already on the remote computer. If not, or if the date of an existing file is earlier than the date of that same file on the local system, the debugger asks, "Program out of date on remote, send over link?" Usually, you should type **Y**, click **Yes**, or press ⟨**Enter**⟩ to answer. When you do that, the debugger copies the target file—MYTEST.EXE in this case—to the current directory on the remote computer's disk.

If you answer no to the prompt, TD will display "Error loading program" because it won't find the program's code file on the remote's disk. This might also happen if you mistype the program's name. Press ⟨**Esc**⟩ to clear the error message and then use `File:Open` (⟨**Alt**⟩-**FO**) to load the correct .EXE file. You are still communicating with the remote system, and it's not necessary to quit and restart TD in order to begin debugging. (You can also load several files in succession to debug more than one program in remote mode. Each file will be transferred to the remote for debugging.)

While TD is transferring an .EXE or other code file to the remote, you'll see these messages on the remote's display:

```
Link established
Reading file "MYTEST.EXE" from Turbo Debugger
2176 bytes downloaded
Download complete
Loading program "MYTEST.EXE" from disk
Program load successful
```

Only the target-code file is transferred to the remote system—the source-code text files remain on the local computer's disk where TD can find them. The symbol table is stripped from the code file before the transfer to save time; therefore, the file on the remote does not contain any debugging symbols. If the target file already exists and is not out of date, you'll see only the last two messages. During these file-transfer stages, you may receive an error message if, for example, there isn't enough room on the local system to hold the target-code file. The *Turbo Debugger User's Guide* explains these error messages.

Provided all goes well, you should be looking at the `Module` window and seeing the source code to MYTEST.PAS or another program. The remote display remains stuck where it is for the moment because the program hasn't begun executing yet. You can now press ⟨**F7**⟩ and ⟨**F8**⟩ on the local keyboard to single-step through the code. You can also use other TD commands, just as you do when debugging on a single system. In fact, all TD commands except `Window:User screen` (⟨**Alt**⟩-⟨**F5**⟩) operate identically in remote mode as they do in single-computer debugging sessions. The only significant difference is that TD's and the program's displays appear on their own monitors. Also, you must remember to use the remote keyboard to answer prompts and enter information required by the buggy program.

Other than these few differences, running TD in remote mode is no different from running a local setup. You can issue all TD commands, use a mouse to open and move windows, add variables to `Watches` windows, inspect memory areas, and perform other debugging operations.

> Note: As mentioned earlier, you can't set hardware breakpoints while debugging in remote mode, even if the remote system has an 80386 or 80486 processor and installs TDH386.SYS at boot time. For this reason, even with fast computers, data breakpoints set with the **Changed memory global** and **Expression true global** commands in the **Breakpoints** menu cause the target code to execute slowly.

File I/O and Remote Debugging

Because TD transfers only the target-code file automatically, it's your responsibility to copy any data or other files that the target program requires. Remember, the code file runs on the remote system under the supervision of TDREMOTE while the debugger runs locally; therefore, you must create the necessary conditions on the remote system that would exist if the code was executing from DOS. TD automatically transfers only the program's .EXE file.

When debugging programs that read other data files, use the TDRF utility to copy those files to the remote system before starting TD. (See the next section in this chapter for details about TDRF commands.) For example, to copy a file named MYDATA.DAT to the remote system and begin remote debugging for MYTEST.EXE, enter the two commands:

```
tdrf t mydata.dat
td -r mytest
```

The **tdrf t** command copies MYDATA.DAT from the local system to the remote disk drive in the current directory. Then, **td -r mytest** tells TD to debug MYTEST.EXE over the remote link. If you have many files to transfer, or if you have to give several TDRF commands each time you start debugging, you can save time by storing the necessary commands in a batch file named D.BAT (or another name) in your program's working directory. You can then run the batch file to begin a new remote debugging session.

Debugging Keyboard Input Routines

Remote debugging makes testing keyboard input routines easier than on a single system where TD and the program have to share the same keys. Although TD does a great job of staying out of the program's way, there are times when two keyboards are practically required to solve a sticky input problem.

For example, it's difficult to create reliable tests for investigating input from the type-ahead buffer, where keypresses are stored before the program's input statements have a chance to read those key values. On a single system, if the target code isn't running, every keypress is directed to TD; therefore, the only way to stuff keys into the type-ahead buffer for the buggy program to read is to run the code—but, then, you can't see what the debugger is doing.

A remote link is the answer. After starting TD in remote mode, run the code up to a breakpoint or other stopping place. The activity indicator should display **READY**. Next, switch to the remote system and enter the keys you want to insert into the type-ahead buffer. Nothing will happen. Back on the local system again, use TD **Run**-menu commands to trace or run various input statements, which will read the keypresses you typed a moment ago into the remote's type-ahead buffer. This will give you a close-up picture of how the program handles input from the buffer.

TDRF Commands

Table 17.2 lists TDRF's commands, all of which are single letters, listed in the leftmost column. You can enter full name commands such as **dir** and **cd** if you prefer, but TDRF ignores all but the command's first letter. The table also lists the operation that TDRF performs, the minimum and maximum number of arguments allowed, the equivalent DOS commands, and an example of the command in action.

Table 17.2. TDRF commands.

Command Letter and Operation		Args	Equivalent DOS Command	Example
c	Change directory	0-1	CD or CHDIR	tdrf c c: \ tp
d	List directory	0-1*	DIR	tdrf d
e	Erase file	1*	ERASE or DEL	tdrf e *.bak
f	Copy from remote	1-2*	COPY	tdrf f newdat.dat
k	Remove directory	1	RD or RMDIR	tdrf k \ temp
m	Make directory	1	MD or MKDIR	tdrf m \ newtemp
r	Rename file	2	RENAME	tdrf r x.txt x.bak
t	Copy to remote	1-2*	COPY	tdrf t readme.doc

* File specifications may include wild card characters * and ?.

For the commands in Table 17.2 to work, the remote system must be running TDREMOTE. After issuing a command, you'll see the results on the local display, not on the remote computer. On the remote screen, you'll see only "Link established" and "Link broken" messages, indicating that TDREMOTE is communicating successfully with TDRF.

Be careful when using the two copy commands *f* and *t* not to reverse the direction of the transfer. To copy a file *from* the remote to the local system, use the *f* command. To copy a file *to* the remote from the local computer, use the *t* command. These commands do not warn you before removing an existing file on the destination drive, and it's easy to erase data accidentally by copying in the wrong direction. So, be careful.

Some commands require no parameters. For example, a useful command is **tdrf c**, which prints the current directory of the remote computer, similar to the way CD with no parameters works from DOS. Enter **tdrf d** for a listing of the files in the remote's current directory.

You may use wild card characters * and ? in file specifications with all commands except *c k m* and *r*. For example, to list all .PAS file names in the current directory, enter **tdrf d *.pas**. To copy all files from the current path to the remote computer, enter **tdrf t *.***.

Dual-Monitor Debugging

Monochrome displays—including the original IBM Monochrome Display Adapter (MDA) and most Hercules brand monochrome cards and clones—receive their characters from a video buffer located at segment address 0B000h. Because the Color Graphics Adapter (CGA) and its descendants—Enhanced Graphics Adapter (EGA) and Video Graphics Array (VGA)—use a text buffer at a different segment address, 0B800h, it's possible for both kinds of video hardware to operate peacefully in the same computer.

Even though DOS can use only one display at a time, each video circuit remains "alive" while the computer is on. For this reason, simply storing ASCII character codes in the correct buffer causes text to appear on that display adapter's screen. TD uses this trick to display its output on the other display—the one that DOS isn't using—letting you debug code on one computer but see TD's and the program's output on separate monitors.

Two monitors are especially good for debugging graphics programs, where it's often necessary to trace or animate in slow motion a series of graphics statements while you watch the effect take shape on the program's screen. This is also a good way to debug subroutines that display text windows (like TD's) and other complex text screens. Even better, unlike remote-mode debugging, dual monitors on an 80386- or 80486-based system let you see both displays at once and still be able to set hardware breakpoints.

> Hint: When plugging two video cards into the same system, It's usually a good idea to insert **mode co80** and **mode mono** commands into AUTOEXEC.BAT. On some systems, TD may not be able to run in dual-monitor mode until you execute these or similar commands to initialize the video hardware. Make sure MODE.COM is in the current path before giving the commands.

Using Two Monitors

To test whether your two display adapters and monitors can run simultaneously, enter the commands **mode co80** and **mode mono**. These commands should switch DOS back and forth between the two screens. If this doesn't work, you may not be able to use TD's dual-monitor abilities.

After getting the two displays working, load a test program into TD with the command **td -do test**. The -do command-line option switches on TD's Other display setting to send TD's output to the alternate monitor. The program's output will appear on the display that DOS normally uses.

To enable dual-monitor debugging permanently, use the TDINST Display command to set User screen updating to Other display. Write the configuration to TD.EXE to use dual monitors for all debugging sessions or save the new setting in a TDCONFIG.TD configuration file in the current directory.

Switching Displays

Most systems require you to set a system switch to select one of your video adapters as the primary display. But, regardless of this switch's setting, you can always select the other display for debugging using the following commands to debug a program called NAME.EXE:

- Type **mode co80** and **td -do name** to run TD on the monochrome monitor and to see the program's output on the color display.
- Type **mode mono** and **td -do name** to run TD on the color display and to see the program's output on the monochrome screen.

In other words, when you use the -do switch, TD's output always goes to the alternate display, while the program's screen appears on the monitor that is active when you start the debugger.

Problems with Dual-Monitor Debugging

Aside from incompatible video hardware that prevents TD from using dual monitors, there are two problems that you might run into when debugging in this mode:

- If the target program writes directly to the alternate display, it might destroy TD's screen. Use the System menu's Repaint desktop command to recover. (If you can't see TD's menus, press ⟨**Alt**⟩-⟨**Space**⟩**R**.)
- When using an older CGA card to drive the alternate display (the one on which TD's output appears), you might have to disable Fast Screen Update

with the TDINST `Display` command to eliminate interference patterns 2(snow). However, if the snow doesn't bother you, *enable* this option for faster screen updates.

Summary

Running TD in remote or dual-monitor modes lets you view TD's and the program's outputs on separate displays. This makes these special configurations, described in this chapter, ideal for debugging code that creates complex graphics or text screens, especially when you need to trace statements and observe their visual effects.

Remote debugging isolates the local development system from the remote computer, thus eliminating hardware conflicts and helping to prevent buggy programs from damaging your main system. A remote link is also useful for debugging keyboard input routines, TSRs, and device drivers.

In addition to the TDREMOTE program, which must be running on the remote system for remote-mode debugging, you can use the TDRF utility to transfer files, list directories, and perform other tasks on the remote computer.

Successful dual-monitor debugging requires two video adapters (or equivalent internal circuits) that receive characters from different memory addresses. With this setup, TD's display appears on the alternate monitor, letting you view the program's output on the currently active display.

Chapter 18

Hardware-Assisted Debugging

BUSY PROGRAMMERS need fast tools for chasing bugs. At most times, TD and an AT-class system offer more than adequate speed, but when monitoring memory with `Changed memory global` breakpoints, even a fast 80386-based system can slow to a traffic-snarling creep. Getting out of this kind of jam and solving a few other tricky problems described in this chapter require the features that only hardware-assisted debugging can provide.

Despite common hearsay, "hardware-assisted debugging" doesn't have to mean investing in a circuit board that costs three times the price you paid for your computer. If your system has an 80386 processor, it already has many of the features found in more costly products. Or, if your system has an earlier processor such as an 8086 or 8088, there are ways for getting a little hardware help to fix broken programs without having to break your bank account.

While examining these subjects, I'll also take the opportunity to dip into a few related hardware topics, explaining how to use TD to debug embedded systems, how to install and use a breakout switch, how to set breakpoints in ROM (Read-Only Memory) code, and how to add a panic button to systems that lack a reset switch.

Internal and External Hardware Debugging

Hardware-assisted debugging comes in two varieties: internal and external. The internal variety refers to special debugging features built into 80x86 processors. The external kind usually takes the form of a circuit card that you can plug into a peripheral slot.

TD can take advantage of both internal and external hardware-debugging components. In fact, many people don't realize that TD uses hardware-debugging features that are available on all 80x86 processors. If these options didn't exist, neither would TD!

Single-Stepping and the Trap Flag

You're probably familiar with TD's most basic hardware-assisted debugging feature, called single-stepping, used by the `Trace into` (⟨**F7**⟩) command. Available on all 80x86 processors, single-stepping works by generating a type 1 interrupt between most instructions. TD enables single-stepping by setting the processor's *trap flag* and directing the subsequent type 1 interrupts to an internal subroutine. By this hardware trick, the debugger gains control of the target code *between* nearly every instruction.

On systems with processors earlier than the 80386, TD sets this same flag to implement `Changed memory` and `Expression true` breakpoints (see chapter 8). By intercepting control after most instructions, TD can monitor memory locations, and if a breakpoint condition is satisfied, it can halt the code or perform another action. This is why these data breakpoints make program code run slowly. It's as though you inserted a `call` instruction to a complex subroutine between every instruction in your program.

Breakpoint Interrupt

80x86 processors also reserve interrupt type 3 as the *breakpoint interrupt,* the second kind of hardware-debugging capability found in all PCs, regardless of make or model. TD uses this hardware feature to set breakpoints in the program's code. When you set a code breakpoint, TD swaps an `int 3`'s single-byte machine code (0CCh) with the byte at the breakpoint's location. When the program reaches this spot, the processor executes the interrupt, which transfers control to TD. Using some additional hocus pocus, TD eventually replaces the original instruction to allow the code to continue; therefore, when you examine the program's machine code, you'll never see the `int 3` instructions that TD inserts. (See chapter 7 under "Turbo Debugger's Tools" for a more detailed description of how TD handles code breakpoints.)

> Note: You can insert temporary `int 3` instructions in your code to create "forced" breakpoints, but don't use this interrupt for other purposes. If you do, you may not be able to debug the program with TD or other debuggers. Also, it's probably a good idea to remove `int 3` instructions before executing the program from DOS.

Internal Debugging Registers

The hardware-debugging story took a major turn with the introduction of the 80386 processor, to which Intel added several new features. Among these was a bank of *debugging registers,* specifically reserved for setting breakpoints that in the past required an expensive in-circuit emulator (ICE) or caused software debuggers like TD to execute code at a snail's pace when monitoring a program's data.

On systems with 80386, 80386SX, or 80486 processors, TD can use these on-board debugging registers to set sophisticated data breakpoints. Of the eight 32-bit registers available (labeled DR0 through DR7), four can store addresses of locations in memory to monitor a variety of conditions. The other registers are either reserved or used for various control operations, for example, to distinguish between data-read and data-write breakpoints. (If you want to know more about these hardware-debugging features, Intel's 80386 and 80486 reference manuals describe them in detail. See the Bibliography.)

If your computer has an 80386 or later processor, all versions of TD can use the debugging registers to set sophisticated data breakpoints. All you have to do to enable this capability is to insert the line **DEVICE = C: \ TD \ TDH386.SYS** into the CONFIG.SYS file. (Replace C: \ TD with the path where you installed TD.) The next time you boot, the device driver will be loaded into RAM, ready for TD's use.

Remember that all versions of TD can use the debugging registers on 80386- and 80486-based machines. You do not have to run TD386 to enable hardware-assisted debugging, a common misconception. However, if you also have additional extended RAM, as chapter 3 explains, you can run virtual-mode TD sessions by starting the debugger with the TD386 supervisor. This configuration lets you set breakpoints using more sophisticated address-matching conditions than are possible with plain TD and TD286. We'll look at those differences in more detail later. For most purposes, you can install the TDH386.SYS device driver to take advantage of hardware-debugging features with similar benefits on all 80386, 80386SX, and 80486 systems while running plain TD, TD286, or TD386.

Note: You may be able to install the TDH386.SYS device driver even if you are running a memory manager like *QEMM.SYS* or a multitasker such as *DesqView*, *Windows/386*, or *Windows 3.0* in *386 Enhanced* mode, all of which prevent TD286 and TD386 from running. With the device driver installed, you can still set hardware breakpoints while running plain TD—you just can't run TD286 and TD386. According to Borland, TD should be able to use debugging registers in a multitasking environment without conflicts unless multiple copies of the debugger attempt to set hardware breakpoints simultaneously. In that event, all bets are off.

Hardware-Debugging Boards

If your computer does not have an 80386 or later processor, or if you need more sophisticated debugging features, you may want to consider purchasing a hardware debugger circuit board. These products, of which there are several brands, typically come with banks of protected RAM for storing debugging software (not TD), a *breakout switch* for cutting down a hung program, plus other features that tap into the computer's address bus to give detailed pictures of low-level goings on.

At this time, only one such external hardware-debugging board—the *Trapper,* manufactured by Purart, Inc.—can communicate directly with TD. (See Bibliography.) If you have an original PC, XT, or AT, you can install a Trapper board in an empty slot (a "short slot" will work) to add hardware-debugging features to your system similar to those on an 80386. You can also use the board's breakout switch to bring up TD from a hung program. Although the Trapper board can set only a single hardware breakpoint, it offers additional features such as fast I/O and instruction-fetch traps that even TD386 can't perform with the same agility.

Other debugging boards with more extensive features (and higher price tags to match) are available from various manufacturers. Probably, the most popular of these are manufactured by The Periscope Company. Their Periscope debuggers are well known and well regarded among professional programmers. (For this chapter, I tested the *Periscope III* model on an original IBM XT.)

Unfortunately, as good as they are, Periscope debugging boards come with their own software; they do not make good use of TD. It's possible to install a Periscope debugger and run TD on the same system, but it's not possible (or at least it's not easy) to make TD communicate directly with the hardware debugger's features. A major drawback is TD's inability to use the model III's real-time trace buffer, which can record up to 8K of "bus events," providing snapshots of the internal happenings for individual machine cycles. Earlier versions of TD hinted at providing this feature, but, apparently, that hint remains in Borland's suggestion box. For that reason, companies like Periscope have chosen not to implement device drivers that would allow TD to communicate with these more sophisticated hardware debuggers, even though Borland has always made the device-driver interface available to developers.

Despite these limitations, though, it is possible to use a Periscope model I or III's breakout switch to interrupt execution and return to TD from a hung program. To enable the switch for Periscope's default port address of 0300h, type this command or add it to AUTOEXEC.BAT:

```
tdnmi -p
```

Or, if you changed the board's address, add it to -p, but do not type a colon as you must with the similar Periscope PS.COM software option. For example, to enable the breakout switch at address 0380h, use the command:

```
tdnmi -p380
```

Setting Up for Hardware-Assisted Debugging

Choosing the right combination of hardware and software is always difficult. If you're shopping for hardware, the following suggestions will help you to plan a strategy for adding hardware-assisted debugging features to your development system:

- An 80386-, 80386SX-, or 80486-based computer is probably the best all-around choice. All versions of TD can use the special debugging registers on these processors to set up to four hardware breakpoints for a variety of conditions.

- Any computer with an 80386 or better processor plus at least 700K of extended RAM can run TD and a target program in virtual mode under control of TD386. This arrangement adds additional levels of hardware-debugging features that are as good as or better than similar options found on external ICE hardware costing much more.

- If you have a PC, XT, or AT class computer, and you don't plan to upgrade to an 80386 or better system soon, a Trapper board offers a relatively inexpensive way to add hardware-assisted debugging features to your machine. Despite the Trapper's limit of a single hardware breakpoint, the board can monitor I/O instructions, and it can even let you set breakpoints in ROM code by monitoring instruction fetches. Also, the Trapper's break-out switch comes in handy for getting back to TD from a hung program.

- A Trapper board might also be useful when installed in an 80386 or better system. In general, while TD386 and the TDH386.SYS device driver offer superior hardware-debugging assistance, they do so with a small loss of speed for I/O and some kinds of data breakpoints. A Trapper board provides these same services while allowing the program to run at full speed.

- The principle drawback to using a Trapper board in an 80386 or better system is that you must run plain TD or TD286. With TD, the debugger and your code share the same 640K of system RAM. By running TD286 on an 80386 system, you can still make use of extended RAM and Trapper's features. (This is also a good setup for an 80286 AT with extended RAM.) But, because Trapper comes with its own TD device driver, it can't work along with TDH386.SYS and TD386. Even so, you can still install the Trapper card, load TDH386.SYS, and run TD386. In that case, the virtual-mode TD just ignores the Trapper hardware.

- Periscope and other external hardware debuggers offer even higher, but pricey, levels of sophistication. Unfortunately, these boards do not fully cooperate with TD. You may be able to use TD and an external debugger in the same computer, and you can use a Periscope model I or III's breakout switch to interrupt a hung program and return to TD. But, don't expect TD to use the board's other features, for example, to set hardware breakpoints, monitor instruction fetches, store symbols in on-board RAM, or access a real-time trace buffer.

The Hardware Breakpoint Options Dialog

With a Trapper board installed, or after booting to load the TDH386.SYS device driver on a system with an 80386 or better processor, TD enables the `Hardware breakpoint` command in the `Breakpoints` menu. Choosing this command opens the `Hardware breakpoint options` window (see Figure 18.1). This same dialog box is also available by choosing `View:Breakpoints`, highlighting an existing hardware breakpoint, and pressing **⟨Ctrl⟩-H** to use the local `Hardware options` command. (If another hardware debugger becomes available, it probably will include a device driver that will enable these same commands.)

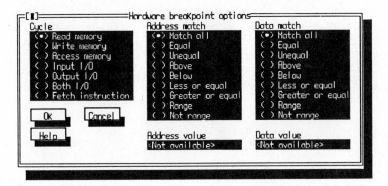

Figure 18.1.   The Hardware breakpoint options dialog box.

You can use the `Hardware breakpoint options` dialog box to set new hardware breakpoints or to modify existing ones. As Figure 18.1 shows, three sets of radio buttons let you select among seven `Cycle`, nine `Address match`, and nine `Data match` options—a total of 567 different combinations. However, the actual number of hardware breakpoint types you can set will be less than this maximum because the Trapper board and the TDH386.SYS device driver do not support all possible settings. Also, some combinations have no practical value (for example, matching all addresses and all data values for read/write `Access memory` cycles—sort of like begging for grid lock at high noon in Times Square). TD displays the error message "Can't set that sort of hardware breakpoint" for unsupported combinations.

After opening the dialog window, to set a hardware breakpoint, first select a `Cycle`, for instance, a `Write memory` operation to inspect a value stored in RAM. This type of breakpoint requires selecting an `Address match` option, usually `Equal`, which monitors the specified cycle type for a specific address. When you select any button except `Match all` from the `Address match` group, TD enables the `Address value` input box. Move the cursor to that area and enter an address or variable name, using the expression format for the current language. For example, you might enter **dataArray[10]** to set the breakpoint for an array element at index 10.

After selecting `Cycle` and `Address match` options, if you also want to restrict the breakpoint to a *specific* data value, you may select a `Data match` button. This group of buttons is *always* optional—you may select `Match all` to match any data value for a certain cycle type and address. Or, if you select a different `Data match` setting, TD enables the `Data value` input box. In that case, move the cursor to the box and enter a value, using the expression format that's suitable for the current language. For example, if you're debugging a *Turbo Pascal* program, to watch for the value FF hex, you would enter **$FF** into this box.

After setting these breakpoint options, click the `Ok` button with a mouse or just press 〈**Enter**〉. Click `Cancel` or press 〈**Esc**〉 if you change your mind. You can also select the `Help` button for on-line messages about the dialog's settings.

> Hint: Tab to one of the three radio button groups before pressing 〈**F1**〉 or clicking `Help` to get help with a specific set of options.

How to Set Hardware Breakpoints

After booting to install the TDH386.SYS device driver, or a similar driver supplied with a Trapper hardware-debugging board, you can load a program into TD, TD286, or TD386 and set hardware breakpoints. (You can't run TD386 when the Trapper device driver is installed, however.)

Use `File:Get info` to verify that TD recognizes the existence of hardware-assisted debugging (the `Breakpoints` setting should display `Hardware`). To set a new hardware breakpoint, you can use one of four methods:

- Use the `Breakpoints:Changed memory global` command to monitor any address or variable for changes. TD will use the device driver to set this breakpoint in hardware. If you've exceeded the maximum number of hardware breakpoints (1 for Trapper, 4 for TDH386.SYS), TD will set the breakpoint in software as it normally does, which may slow the program.

- Use the `Breakpoints:Hardware breakpoint` command to open the `Hardware breakpoint options` dialog box. Then, select the settings you want as described in the previous section. Unlike the `Changed memory global` command, with this method and those that follow, the breakpoint will be accepted only if you have not exceeded the hardware's capacity for new breakpoints.

- Open the `View:Breakpoints` window and press ⟨**Ctrl**⟩**-A** to add a new breakpoint. This opens the `Breakpoint options` dialog box (see Figure 5.4). Toggle `Global` on, and then set `Condition` to `Changed memory`, enter an address expression in `Condition expression`, and press ⟨**Enter**⟩. (This has the identical result as the less complicated `Breakpoints:Changed memory global` command.)

- Open `View:Breakpoints`, press ⟨**Ctrl**⟩**-A**, toggle `Global` on, and set `Condition` to `Hardware`. Press ⟨**Enter**⟩ and note that the window displays "Breakpoint, Not set, Enabled." To finish the breakpoint, highlight it and press ⟨**Ctrl**⟩**-H**, selecting the local `Hardware options` command. This opens the `Hardware breakpoint options` dialog box, identical to using the `Breakpoints:Hardware breakpoint` command.

After setting the hardware breakpoint, open the `View:Breakpoints` window (it may already be open depending on which of the previous methods you decide to use). The new breakpoint will be listed as `Global_1*` or similar, with the asterisk confirming that the device driver successfully fielded the breakpoint. If the asterisk does not appear, the breakpoint is not set in hardware.

When you highlight a hardware breakpoint in `Breakpoints'` left pane, the right pane displays lines similar to these:

```
Breakpoint
Hardware Write memory
Addr: Equal a[0]
Data: Match all
Enabled
```

The first line identifies the breakpoint action, which you can change by pressing ⟨**Ctrl**⟩**-S** and setting `Action` to `Break`, `Execute`, or `Log`. (You don't have to halt the program with hardware breakpoints. You can use them to splice code and log expressions, as chapter 8 explains.)

The middle three lines of the breakpoint's description list the cycle, address match, and data match that you selected from the `Hardware breakpoint options` dialog box. The last line shows `Enabled` or `Disabled`. To toggle this setting, highlight the breakpoint, press ⟨**Ctrl**⟩**-S**, and change the `Breakpoint disabled` check box. Other lines may also appear in the window listing other breakpoint options.

Hint: It's often easier to disable a breakpoint temporarily than it is to delete and reenter it later, for example, after resetting the code to repeat a debugging test. By the way, the keystrokes to disable or enable a highlighted breakpoint in the `Breakpoints` view make a good macro: ⟨**Ctrl**⟩**-S D** ⟨**Enter**⟩.

Modifying Existing Hardware Breakpoints

You can modify existing hardware breakpoints in two ways. First, open the View:Breakpoints window and highlight the breakpoint you want to change. Then, press ⟨**Ctrl**⟩-**S** to open the Breakpoint options dialog. At this point, you can change the Action, Action expression, Pass count, or Breakpoint disabled settings.

However, don't change the breakpoint's Condition (which should be listed as Hardware), toggle the Global check box, or enter an Address or Condition expression. If you choose any of these options, you'll be prevented from modifying the cycle, address match, and data match settings in the Hardware breakpoint options dialog box.

You can also highlight a hardware breakpoint in the Breakpoints view window and press ⟨**Ctrl**⟩-**H**. This opens the Hardware breakpoint options dialog box (Figure 18.1). You can then select new settings for the breakpoint as you do when creating a new breakpoint.

Accessing and Changing Memory

After setting a Changed memory global breakpoint, either by using that command in the Breakpoints global menu or by setting the Changed memory radio button in the Breakpoint options dialog box, even if TD sets the breakpoint in hardware, you cannot open the Hardware breakpoint options dialog box (Figure 18.1) to modify this breakpoint's settings.

This restriction makes sense when you consider that a Changed memory breakpoint does exactly what its name suggests: it monitors a memory location for a *change* to the value currently stored there. For example, suppose you set a Changed memory breakpoint (in hardware or in software) for an array account with the value at indexed position [0] equal to 50 and then execute these Pascal statements:

```
account[0] := 50;
account[0] := 100;
```

The Changed memory breakpoint will be triggered only for the second statement because the first writes the same value to account[0].

However, setting a hardware breakpoint with Cycle = Write memory, Address match = Equal, and Address value = account[0], will activate the breakpoint for both assignments—a subtle difference that may be important when searching for bugs that destroy memory areas. Only a hardware breakpoint can detect an instruction that writes a value to a memory location that already equals that same value.

Expression True vs Hardware Breakpoints

As chapter 8 explains, you can set Expression true global breakpoints to evaluate an expression as the breakpoint's condition. TD never sets these breakpoints in hardware, and for that reason, using this command in the global Breakpoints menu may cause the code to run slowly.

With hardware assistance, you can often get the same results of an expression breakpoint with no slowdown. First, use any of the methods listed earlier to open the Hardware breakpoint options dialog box (Figure 18.1). Then, select Cycle, Address match, and Data match radio buttons, and enter expressions and values into the Address value and Data value input boxes, using settings that duplicate the breakpoint expression.

For example, instead of setting an Expression true global breakpoint for **yCoord >= 480**, create a new hardware breakpoint. Set Cycle to Write memory, Address match to Equal, and Data match to Greater or equal. Enter **yCoord** into the Address value box and **480** into Data value. TD will then halt the code or perform another action after any statement writes a value of 480 or greater to yCoord, regardless of that variable's current value.

Using hardware-debugging features to simulate Expression true global breakpoints this way takes more time and care, but the results are worth the effort. With the breakpoints set in hardware, the code now runs at full speed.

> Hint: This tip works best on systems with 80386 or better processors, an installed TDH386.SYS device driver, and TD386. Other configurations restrict the kinds of hardware breakpoints you can set and, therefore, limit the kinds of expressions you can simulate with hardware options. See "Problems With Hardware-Assisted Debugging" later in this chapter.

Selecting Hardware Breakpoint Options

Tables 18.1, 18.2, and 18.3 describe each of the three banks of radio buttons in the Hardware breakpoint options dialog box (Figure 18.1). The tables also list the conditions under which a breakpoint action will be taken. Table 18.2's Address match options apply to the currently selected Cycle. Table 18.3's Data match options apply to the currently selected Cycle and Address match. For Address and Data match options not equal to Match all, you must enter Address and Data value expressions into those input boxes before TD will accept the breakpoint. Depending on your hardware and the version of TD you are running, some combinations of options listed in these tables may not be recognized.

Table 18.1. Hardware breakpoint cycle options.

Cycle	Breakpoint Action Occurs...
Read memory	After a read from memory
Write memory	After a write to memory
Access memory	After a read or write from or to memory
Input I/O	After an `in` instruction executes
Output I/O	After an `out` instruction executes
Both I/O	After an `in` or `out` instruction executes
Fetch instruction	When the processor fetches an instruction

Table 18.2. Hardware breakpoint address match options.

Address Match	Breakpoint Action Occurs...
Match all	After all matching cycles
Equal	For the specified address value only
Unequal	For any other address except this one
Above	For all addresses above this one
Below	For all addresses below this one
Less or equal	For this address and those below
Greater or equal	For this address and those above
Range	For an address and count such as `a[10],5`
Not range	For all addresses outside of a range

Table 18.3. Hardware breakpoint data match options.

Data Match	Breakpoint Action Occurs...
Match all	For all matching cycles and addresses
Equal	For the specified data value only
Unequal	For any value except this one
Above	For all values above (greater than) this one
Below	For all values below (less than) this one
Less or equal	For this value and those that are less
Greater or equal	For this value and those that are greater
Range	For any values within a range such as 10,20
Not range	For any values outside of a range

Table 18.4 lists the combinations of hardware options from Tables 18.1, 18.2, and 18.3 that are available for various hardware configurations.

The Trapper options are available only with TD and TD286, not TD386. The TD/TD286 and TD386 settings require a system with an 80386 or better processor and an installed TDH386.SYS device driver.

Table 18.4.   Hardware breakpoint option combinations.

Option	Trapper	TD/TD286	TD386
Cycle:			
Read memory	Yes	No	Yes
Write memory	Yes	Yes	Yes
Access memory	Yes	Yes	Yes
Input I/O	Yes	No	Yes
Output I/O	Yes	No	Yes
Both I/O	Yes	No	Yes
Fetch instruction	Yes	Yes	Yes
Address match:			
Match all*	No	No	No
Equal	Yes	Yes	Yes
Unequal	No	No	No
Above	Yes	No	Yes
Below	No	No	Yes
Less or equal	No	No	Yes
Greater or equal	Yes	No	Yes
Range	Yes	Yes	Yes
Not range	No	No	No
Data match:			
Match all	No	Yes	Yes
Equal	No	Yes	Yes
Unequal**	No	No	No
Above	No	Yes	Yes
Below	No	Yes	Yes
Less or equal	No	Yes	Yes
Greater or equal	No	Yes	Yes
Range	No	Yes	Yes
Not range**	No	No	No

   * For hardware that supports I/O breakpoints, this setting may equal `Match all`. However, this may cause recursive entries into the debugger due to TD386's own I/O instructions. In most cases, it's best to select `Equal` and specify an I/O address to monitor in the `Address value` input box.

  ** To simulate an `Unequal` data match, set two hardware breakpoints for the same cycle, address, and data value, with a data match of `Above` for the one and `Below` for the other. Use a similar trick to set a `Not range` data match, but set the "Above" breakpoint to the higher and the "Below" breakpoint to the lower range of values.

How Hardware-Assisted Debugging Works

There isn't room here to describe in detail how hardware breakpoints work on the processor level with an 80386 or with a hardware debugger. In general, though, an active hardware breakpoint causes one of two actions to occur when the breakpoint's condition is satisfied:

- In the case of a Trapper or other external hardware debugger, a satisfied breakpoint condition triggers a nonmaskable interrupt (NMI), which the debugger's device driver intercepts. The driver then passes control to TD, which executes the breakpoint action. The device driver ignores NMI signals that come from another device, allowing more than one use of this interrupt line.

- With TDH386.SYS installed on systems with 80386 or better processors, a satisfied breakpoint condition causes the processor to generate an interrupt type 1—the same interrupt generated for single-stepping when the trap flag is set. TD intercepts this interrupt, determines the cause, and executes the breakpoint action.

The results are similar in both cases. However, because the Trapper or similar board uses the NMI approach while TDH386.SYS uses a type 1 interrupt, the effects of hardware breakpoints under various configurations will differ in subtle ways.

For example, because Trapper uses NMI, the board can intercept a breakout switch signal and call TD, letting you press the button to interrupt a hung program. But when using TDH386.SYS on a system that also has a Trapper or Periscope debugger installed, in order to use the breakout switch, you must also load the TDNMI resident utility. That program intercepts the NMI signal from the debugging hardware and activates TD.

Another difference between the two hardware techniques involves code tracing. Using a Trapper board and device driver, it's possible to trace, step, and animate code and still be able to set hardware breakpoints reliably. No matter how you run the code, if the breakpoint condition is satisfied, it will interrupt the program or perform another action.

TDH386.SYS and all versions of TD do not work the same way. With these configurations, setting a hardware breakpoint and tracing, stepping, or animating code will cause the breakpoint condition to be missed! This happens because, when running in single-step mode, the processor generates a type 1 interrupt signal after every instruction, preempting the use of this interrupt for a hardware breakpoint.

Normally, these differences are minor and won't affect your debugging strategies. But, I have found the Trapper board to be useful for animating a section of code in slow motion and still be able to set hardware breakpoints. This is not possible to do with any version of TD, whether or not the TDH386.SYS device driver is installed.

Problems with Hardware-Assisted Debugging

It may be useful to keep the following problems and limitations in mind when using hardware breakpoints:

- 80386 or better systems with TDH386.SYS installed are limited to four hardware breakpoints using any version of TD. With a Trapper board, the limit is one hardware breakpoint.

- According to Borland, TDH386.SYS hardware breakpoints may be set for an address range from 1 to 16 bytes with TD and TD286. However, the actual limit may be less depending on how the data is aligned. TD386 and the Trapper board impose no practical limits on the range of hardware breakpoints.

- Some computers use NMI to communicate with peripheral cards (for example, to enable a video mode) and for other purposes. On these systems, you may have to install the TDNMI utility to resolve these conflicts.

- Instruction-fetch breakpoints may cause "false triggers" because of the way 80x86 processors load, or fetch, multiple instructions. This means that some instructions may activate the breakpoint even if those instructions are not executed. For example, an instruction following a conditional jump that is not taken may still cause the breakpoint action to occur if the processor fetches all of those instructions together.

- Because of the way the Trapper and other external hardware-debugging boards work, there may be a small delay between the time the breakpoint condition is satisfied and TD's appearance. This happens because a few cycles execute between the time the device driver asserts NMI and when TD receives that signal, a problem known as *NMI latency.* For that reason, when the breakpoint action halts the code, the actual cause of a problem might be a few instructions away in either direction (because the latency period may have allowed the code to repeat a loop before TD halts execution.)

- You may see a "Device driver stuck" error when setting hardware breakpoints to monitor local variables allocated by C and Pascal on the stack. This problem occurs when a breakpoint causes the device driver to be entered recursively due to its own use of a few bytes of stack space. When those bytes overlap the addresses of the local data, the device driver may discover that it has interrupted itself, in which case it reports the error. You can usually fix the problem by disabling the breakpoint temporarily and tracing a few instructions to execute the procedure or function's startup code, which allocates stack space for use by local variables. Also, be aware that setting hardware breakpoints for unallocated stack data belonging to inactive procedures and functions may cause similar problems.

Debugging with Hardware Breakpoints

One of the most common uses for a hardware breakpoint is to find an instruction that's overwriting some data that should not be changed at this place in the program. In other words, you know the data is wrong, and you know where that data is, but you don't know the location of the faulty code.

By setting a hardware breakpoint to halt the code when the data changes, and then running the program, TD will stop at the instruction that's causing the damage. Most of the time, you can use a `Changed memory global` breakpoint for this purpose. But, often, it's best to use the methods described earlier to set `Cycle`, `Address match`, and, possibly, `Data match` options to find all reads and writes to a certain location or range of addresses.

However, the flip side of the hardware-debugging coin has a darker face. When you know the place in the program, but you don't know where the bad data is coming from, hardware assistance may be of no help. For example, after narrowing a bug to a procedure or function that receives arguments from various places, you still may have no idea why the caller is passing the bad data to the subroutine. The problem could be in other code that created the conditions affecting the caller. In such cases, hardware breakpoints won't locate the trouble because you don't know the bad data's address, which you need in order to set the breakpoint. In this case, try using the `Stack` window to investigate the subroutine's callers. This may give you a clue about where to look for the source of the bad data.

The following sections list sample programs in C and Pascal and show how to use TD to trap memory reads and writes—typical situations that are well suited for hardware-assisted debugging. (You can also set hardware breakpoints for assembly language using similar methods.) The demonstrations will help you to understand the kinds of conditions that hardware breakpoints can detect. To follow the step-by-step instructions, your computer must have an 80386 or better processor, and you must install the TDH386.SYS device driver. You may run TD, TD286, or TD386 (the memory-read test requires TD386). Or, you can use a Trapper board and TD or TD286.

Hardware Breakpoints and C

Enter Listing 18.1 and compile with the *Turbo C* command **tcc -v harddemo**. Then, follow the step-by-step instructions after the listing to test hardware breakpoints with C.

Listing 18.1. HARDDEMO.C.

```
1:  #include <stdio.h>
2:
3:  int i;
```

```
 4:   int a[100];
 5:
 6:   main()
 7:   {
 8:       puts( "Press <Enter> to begin test..." );
 9:       i = getchar();   /* Wait for keypress */
10:
11:       puts( "Test #1: Read" );
12:       i = a[50];
13:
14:       puts( "Test #2: Write" );
15:       a[50] = 0;
16:
17:       puts( "Test #3: Read/Write" );
18:       a[50] = a[50];
19:
20:       return 0;
21:   }
```

After compiling the program, load it into TD with the command **td386 harddemo**. (If you run plain TD or TD286, you won't be able to complete the read-memory test unless you have a Trapper board installed in your computer.) Next, follow these steps:

1. Press ⟨**Alt**⟩-**BH** to open the Hardware breakpoint options dialog box. Press ⟨**Tab**⟩ to move to Address match (leaving Cycle set to Read memory) and then press ⟨**Cursor Down**⟩ to select Equal. Press ⟨**Tab**⟩ again and enter **a[50]** for the Address value. When you press ⟨**Enter**⟩, TD accepts this breakpoint, which will halt the code for any reads from the array at index position 50. (If you receive an error message, your system can't set this kind of breakpoint. Press ⟨**Esc**⟩ twice to erase the message and close the dialog window. Then, skip to step 7.)

2. Press ⟨**Alt**⟩-**VB** to view this breakpoint's parameters. You should see Global_1* in the window pane at left, and a description of the breakpoint at right. Remember, the asterisk (*) indicates that this is a hardware breakpoint.

3. Close the Breakpoints view window (⟨**Alt**⟩-⟨**F3**⟩) and press ⟨**F9**⟩ to run the program. Press ⟨**Enter**⟩ to begin the test. Almost immediately, the first breakpoint halts the code. Press ⟨**Esc**⟩ to clear the message window. If TD displays the CPU window, press ⟨**Ctrl**⟩-**V** to view the related source-code statement. (This may or may not happen depending on the kind of system you have, which version of TD you are running, whether you have a Trapper board, and so on.)

4. The memory-read test has correctly identified the first access to a[50]. Note that only a hardware breakpoint can detect this condition—software data breakpoints are not able to detect reads from memory.

5. Press ⟨F9⟩ to continue the program. A second breakpoint halts the code. Press ⟨Esc⟩ and, if CPU opens, ⟨Ctrl⟩-V. The cursor should be on or near the third assignment, which again reads from a[50]. The second test is skipped because it writes to the array; it doesn't read a value from it.

6. For the next test, reset the program by pressing ⟨Alt⟩-FO and entering **harddemo** (or selecting the program from the file list). You can use other methods to reset, but this approach is easier when you also want to clear all breakpoints.

7. Press ⟨Alt⟩-BH to reopen the hardware dialog box. This time, press ⟨**Cursor Down**⟩ to set Cycle to Write memory. Then, press ⟨Tab⟩, press ⟨**Cursor Down**⟩ to select Equal for Address match, press ⟨Tab⟩ once more, and enter **a[50]**. When you press ⟨**Enter**⟩, TD sets a breakpoint for memory writes to a[50].

8. Press ⟨F9⟩ to run and ⟨**Enter**⟩ to start the test. When the breakpoint hits, press ⟨Esc⟩ (plus ⟨Ctrl⟩-V to return to the source code if CPU opens). Notice the position of the cursor—just after (or, possibly, on) the assignment to a[50]. This time, the memory read from that location was skipped.

9. Press ⟨F9⟩ to continue. A second breakpoint halts the code. (Press ⟨Esc⟩ and, if necessary, ⟨Ctrl⟩-V.) The final test reads and writes to a[50], an action that the memory-write breakpoint easily traps.

10. Repeat from step 6, but this time, after opening the dialog box, press ⟨**Cursor Down**⟩ twice to set Cycle to Access memory. Select the other settings as you did before. When you press ⟨F9⟩ to run, you'll receive three breakpoints, one for each assignment. As this shows, a hardware breakpoint is the only way to detect both reads and writes from a memory location.

11. A final test shows the difference between changed-memory and other kinds of hardware breakpoints. Reload the program (press ⟨Alt⟩-FO and select or enter **harddemo**). Press ⟨F6⟩ to switch to the Watches window and enter **a[50]**. Press ⟨Ctrl⟩-C to change this array element's value to **1**. Press ⟨F6⟩ to switch back to the Module view.

12. Set a Changed memory global breakpoint (press ⟨Alt⟩-BC) and enter **a[50]** into the prompt box. Press ⟨Alt⟩-VB and notice how this breakpoint's information differs from the other hardware kind. Also, as the asterisk proves, TD automatically detected and used the hardware's debugging capabilities. Close the Breakpoints window (⟨Alt⟩-⟨F3⟩) and press ⟨F9⟩ to run. When you press ⟨**Enter**⟩ to begin the test, you receive a breakpoint after the assignment of 0 to a[50]. (Press ⟨Esc⟩ and, if necessary, ⟨Ctrl⟩-V to return to the source-code view.) Press ⟨F9⟩ again, and the

program ends, skipping the assignment to `a[50]` at line 20. Even though this statement also writes to the array, it doesn't *change* the value stored there. For that reason, the `Changed memory global` breakpoint does not halt the code.

13. Press ⟨**Esc**⟩ to clear the "Terminated" message. The value of `a[50]` should now be 0 in `Watches`. Press ⟨**F9**⟩ and **Y** to reset and run the code (leaving the previous breakpoint set). This time, when you press ⟨**Enter**⟩ to start the test, the program runs to completion. The breakpoint does not halt the code because the two assignments to `a[50]` did not change the value stored there. Press ⟨**Esc**⟩ to remove the "Terminated" message and ⟨**Alt**⟩-**X** to quit TD and return to DOS.

Hardware Breakpoints and Pascal

Enter Listing 18.2 and compile with the *Turbo Pascal* command **tpc -v harddemo**. Then, follow the step-by-step instructions in the previous section to test using hardware breakpoints with Pascal.

Listing 18.2.   HARDDEMO.PAS.

```
 1:  program hardDemo;
 2:
 3:  var
 4:
 5:      i : integer;
 6:      a : array[ 0 .. 99 ] of integer;
 7:
 8:  begin
 9:
10:      write( 'Press <Enter> to begin test...' );
11:      readln;  { Wait for keypress }
12:
13:      writeln( 'Test #1: Read' );
14:      i := a[50];
15:
16:      writeln( 'Test #2: Write' );
17:      a[50] := 0;
18:
19:      writeln( 'Test #3: Read/Write' );
20:      a[50] := a[50];
21:
22:  end.
```

Using I/O Breakpoints

The steps to set I/O breakpoints are the same as for other kinds of hardware-assisted traps. For example, to locate an input instruction for a certain port address, set `Cycle` to `Input I/O`, change `Address match` to `Equal`, and enter the port address into the `Address value` input box. If you want to watch for a specific data value from that port, also change `Data match` to `Equal` and enter the value into the `Data value` input box.

Set other I/O breakpoint combinations using similar commands. To find both input and output instructions, select `Both I/O` for the `Cycle`. In that case, you'll probably also want to select a range of port address values to monitor (for example, **0x03F8,8** in C's format to trap I/O for ports from 03F8 to 03FF hex).

> Note: Although TD accepts an `Address match` setting of `Match all` for I/O breakpoints, this may cause problems with TD386, and for that reason, isn't recommended. When monitoring I/O, it's usually best to specify one or more port addresses.

Using Instruction-Fetch Breakpoints

After installing the TDH386.SYS device driver or a Trapper board, you can set *instruction-fetch* breakpoints to halt code or perform other actions when the processor loads instructions at specified addresses for execution.

To use a Trapper board's instruction-fetch breakpoints, you'll need to purchase an optional "umbilical cable" that plugs into an 8087 or 80287 math coprocessor socket. (You may use the cable with or without a math chip also installed.) The cable allows the Trapper to monitor the computer's bus for instruction fetches. If you don't need to set these kinds of breakpoints, you don't need the cable.

Instruction-fetch breakpoints are typically used to set code breakpoints in ROM subroutines. Because TD swaps `int 3` (0CCh) machine codes with program bytes to implement code breakpoints, the `Breakpoints:Toggle` command (⟨**F2**⟩) won't work for instructions that are permanently chiseled into a ROM's stone-cold circuits.

For example, suppose you want to halt a program when it calls a certain ROM BIOS routine. (You can use Listing 18.1 or 18.2 to try this.) After loading the program into the virtual-mode debugger with TD386, press ⟨**Alt**⟩-**BH** to open the `Hardware breakpoint options` dialog box. Set `Cycle` to `Fetch instruction` and change `Address match` to `Greater or equal`. Then, enter the address **0xF000:0000** (or **$F000:0000** for Pascal). Press ⟨**Enter**⟩ or click `Ok` to set the breakpoint. When you run the code by pressing ⟨**F9**⟩, TD will halt execution of any ROM code at or above that address.

Note: When running TD or TD286, you must set `Address match` to `Equal` or `Range`, which is limited to 16 bytes. For this reason, with these versions of the debugger, you must know the exact ROM address within 16 bytes to set instruction-fetch breakpoints.

Another less common use for an instruction-fetch breakpoint is to trap data that another statement accidentally calls as "code." Finding this kind of bug is difficult because it usually crashes the system. As always, the first step is to narrow the problem to a small section of code. Then, set an instruction-fetch breakpoint to monitor selected areas of data. This requires an accurate address map of the program's segments, and you'll probably have to repeat the test several times before locating the data that's executing as "code."

When you successfully trap the bad call to the program's data, the `CPU` view will open. At that time, you can examine the stack pane in the lower right corner to determine where the call came from. Or, use the `Stack` view to inspect a C or Pascal program's currently active procedures and functions. This should tell you the location that called the data.

Debugging Embedded Systems

An *embedded system* is a broad term that usually refers to a highly specialized computer incorporated (embedded) in some sort of device—for example, a performance panel in an automobile, an audio mixing board, or a laser printer.

In most cases, the embedded system's software is stored in ROM on board the device. That software has to be debugged, perhaps by running simulations on a PC before committing the code to its final form. But the real test comes after burning the code into ROM, when, of course, the really tricky bugs often decide to announce their presence. Unfortunately, the stock TD can only debug code running on a PC. It can't help you to debug software after it's embedded inside custom hardware.

An interesting product, *Paradigm Locate,* from Paradigm Systems (see Bibliography) offers a unique solution to this problem. Without going into every detail here—some of which are highly advanced—*Locate* lets system designers embed the functional equivalent of the TDREMOTE utility inside the custom hardware. By then running TD in remote mode (see chapter 17), the debugger is fooled into thinking that it's communicating with a remote PC, when in fact, it's actually talking to an embedded system that has been modified to include the few resources of a PC that TD requires.

The main advantage with this setup is cost—it should be less expensive to simulate a remote PC for debugging embedded systems than it would be to purchase an in-circuit emulator or to create other hardware for debugging purposes. The only disadvantage, which is minor, is that the device must include a serial I/O port that's compatible with a PC's baud rates. For most designs, the tradeoff of being able to use TD to debug a custom device's software will more than offset the costs of including an extra I/O port.

> Note: I'm not a hardware engineer, so I'll leave the description of Paradigm's *Locate* package with that brief description. For more information, contact Paradigm Systems.

Installing a Panic Reset Button

Another product that deserves mention here is the *Irata Reset* switch sold by Irata Systems, Inc. (see Bibliography). Some newer computers come with reset switches on the front panel, but most older PCs and XTs lack a similar "panic button."

A reset switch has nothing to do with TD, of course, but if you are as frustrated as I was at having to flip the big red power switch after repeated program crashes, you may want to consider installing an *Irata* button. With the switch mounted (either on the back panel or through a hole that you can drill in the front of the case), you can press the button to reboot. It's a real time saver, and it helps reduce wear and tear on the power switch, which, if it breaks, may require replacing the system's more expensive power supply.

> Warning: If you're the slightest bit nervous about working around power supplies inside your computer, get help or don't install this switch. The product comes with only minimal instructions, so you'll need to know your way around your PC's circuits, or you could damage your computer.

Writing a Debugging Device Driver

It's unlikely that you'll need to write your own hardware device driver, but if you want to try your hand at this difficult task, you'll find the specifications in a file named MANUAL.DOC on a TD master diskette. The text in this file also makes interesting reading for those who want to know more about how the TDH386.SYS device driver implements hardware-assisted debugging for 80386 and later-model processors.

In the past, Borland has hinted that a future TD release would expand the debugger's use of a TDHDEBUG device driver—the name of the installed driver in RAM. At present, however, TD can access driver subroutines only to set breakpoints as described in this chapter. It still can't perform two of the promised expansions:

- Support for a real-time trace-back buffer.
- Access to a hardware debugger's RAM, probably for storing large symbol tables.

Perhaps a future version of TD will enable these options, which would make a marriage between Turbo Debugger and a Periscope or other hardware-debugging board, if not made in heaven, at least more likely to succeed.

Summary

Two kinds of hardware-assisted debugging let TD set sophisticated breakpoints for memory read, write, I/O, and instruction-fetch operations. Internal hardware on board 80386, 80386SX, and 80486 processors add in-circuit emulator capabilities to TD. External hardware debuggers such as the Trapper and Periscope peripheral boards are also useful for adding similar features to PCs, XTs, and ATs.

Every 80x86 processor has at least some form of hardware-assisted debugging, for example, a trap flag that throws the computer into single-step mode. But only an 80386 or later processor has special debugging registers that TD can access via the TDH386.SYS device driver to set complex data breakpoints with the Hardware breakpoint options dialog box.

With all of these setups, there are several ways to set hardware breakpoints. If possible, TD will automatically use the hardware to assist a Changed memory global breakpoint, which can locate changes to existing values in memory. Or, for more control, you can use the Hardware breakpoint command in the Breakpoints menu to select Cycle, Address match, and Data value options.

Other kinds of hardware-assisted debugging are available to trap I/O instructions and to monitor the processor's instruction fetches, useful for setting breakpoints in ROM code. Related hardware-assistance topics in this chapter include the ability to use TD for embedded systems debugging, and the installation of a panic reset button.

Chapter 19

Debugging
Resident Programs

Iɴ THE PAST, a hardware debugging board was a practical necessity for trapping bugs in resident code. Because a hardware debugger hides in the board's protected RAM, this setup lets you place breakpoints inside resident subroutines to halt execution, for example, when the device driver receives a call from DOS or when a Terminate-and-Stay-Resident program (TSR) pops up on screen.

Starting with version 2.0, TD can now run as a kind of super TSR, simulating the way a hardware debugger stays out of DOS's way. With TD hiding in the background, the debugger is ready to halt resident code at breakpoints and to monitor other conditions for device drivers and TSRs. You can also load and relocate a program's symbol table to debug TSRs and device drivers that were loaded into memory before starting TD.

This chapter explains how to use these new TD commands to debug TSRs and device drivers written in assembly language. (You can use the same techniques to debug resident C and Pascal programs, too.) The chapter lists a few typical bugs that infest resident code, and it also covers related topics of debugging interrupt service routines (not always possible with TD) and "exec-ed" child processes.

TSRs—A Quick Review

DOS has always had the capability to load TSRs, which, unlike common .EXE and .COM programs, sit in memory awaiting an activation signal such as a special keypress or another external event. When that happens, the TSR typically pops up in a text window and performs its duties. Then, usually after you give the TSR another command, the program restores the display and other conditions to their original states to allow the interrupted process to continue.

In this way, TSRs give DOS a limited measure of multitasking—or, at least, the capability to share resources with more than one program simultaneously loaded into memory.

There are two varieties of DOS TSRs: *active* and *passive*. An active TSR monitors an external device (usually the keyboard) and watches for a specific command to float by. Most often, that command is a combination of keypresses such as ⟨Alt⟩-⟨Shift⟩ or ⟨Ctrl⟩-⟨Shift⟩ that the TSR recognizes as an activation signal.

After receiving the activation signal, most active-type TSRs do not begin running immediately. Instead, they set a flag in memory that causes the TSR to activate itself later, often at the next *timer-tick* interrupt. Because the TSR may be activated at any time—and, therefore, it may have interrupted a DOS or BIOS subroutine—a well-written TSR should delay its activation to allow other processes to finish. This is especially true of interrupted DOS functions, many of which are not *reentrant* (able to be interrupted and restarted). Failing to allow for this condition is probably the number one cause of TSR bugs.

A passive-type TSR is not as finicky. Unlike the more complex active type, passive resident code does not monitor external events. Instead, a passive TSR sleeps until another program sends it a wake-up signal. Because the other program controls when that occurs, conflicts with uninterruptible DOS and BIOS routines are unlikely. The passive TSR operates much like a subroutine library except that it remains in RAM instead of being linked to every program that needs the TSR's routines.

Despite these operational differences, active and passive TSRs have nearly identical forms and are loaded into RAM using similar techniques. Both TSR varieties are composed of two sections: the *transient portion* and the *resident portion*. Successful TSR debugging requires a good understanding of how these two sections cooperate to load a TSR into memory:

- The TSR's transient portion contains instructions that install the TSR's resident portion in RAM. To do that, the transient code calls DOS function 31h, which raises the address where DOS normally loads new programs. Some TSRs issue the alternate `int 27h` instruction instead of calling function 31h. Either way, DOS protects the resident code from being overwritten by another program, allowing the TSR to remain in memory while awaiting its wake-up call. Active-type TSRs also usually change an interrupt vector or perform another action that will allow the resident portion to recognize the activation signal. Passive TSRs don't need to perform this step.

- The TSR's resident portion contains code, data, and sometimes a private stack that remains in memory after the transient portion ends. In most cases, an active-type TSR's resident code is written as an interrupt service routine (ISR) that intercepts keypresses or other external events that will activate the TSR. Passive TSRs can also be ISRs, but they are usually not tied to a hardware interrupt signal. Instead, a program calls a passive TSR with a software `int` instruction, similar to the way DOS functions are called with `int 21`.

Debugging TSRs

Because TSRs load themselves into memory, past TD versions could not examine a TSR's code and data symbolically. It was possible to debug the TSR's transient loader with TD, but not the resident portion—except, that is, in the CPU view's machine-code disassembly.

TD 2.0 changes that with features that emulate a hardware debugger's capability to run in the background. By using TD's new `Resident` command, you can load a TSR, return to normal DOS operation, give the TSR's activation signal, and then investigate variables, examine source code, set breakpoints, and evaluate other conditions in resident code and data.

Figure 19.1 illustrates how TD shares memory with a TSR. If you're using TD386, the debugger and TSR each runs in a separate virtual 8086 address space, duplicating the conditions that exist when loading the resident program directly from DOS. TD286 can also free system RAM by loading the debugger into extended RAM. You can use any of these TD versions to debug TSRs.

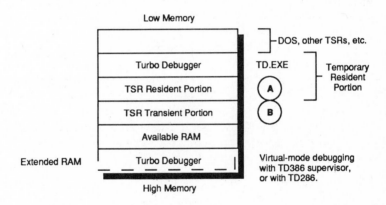

Figure 19.1. TD shares RAM with a TSR being debugged.

When you load the TSR's code into TD and press ⟨**F9**⟩ to run, the transient portion (labeled B in the figure) installs the TSR's resident part (A) in RAM just as it does when you run the program from the DOS command line. You can debug the transient code as you do any other program, set breakpoints on source-code statements, watch and inspect variables, and perform other debugging tasks. However, before you can debug the transient portion, you'll need to perform a few extra steps.

> Hint: When debugging TSRs, iron out any wrinkles in the transient loader before hammering the lumps in the resident portion. It's probably not wise to debug both parts simultaneously.

After the loader finishes, press ⟨**Esc**⟩ to clear the message "Resident, Exit code 0." If you receive any other message, the TSR has not been installed, and you'll have to investigate why that happened by debugging the transient loader. Only after receiving the "Resident" message can you proceed to debug the resident code and data.

Next, set breakpoints for resident statements to halt the TSR or perform other actions at strategic locations. Then use the `File:Resident` (⟨**Alt**⟩-**FR**) command to make TD resident in RAM. Looking again at Figure 19.1, you can see that this new *Temporary Resident Portion* consists of the debugger plus the TSR's own resident code and data.

At this point, you should see the DOS command line. Depending on how much memory your system has and whether you are using TD, TD286, or TD386, you can give DOS commands, run programs, and perform other tasks as you normally do. TD remains in memory along with the TSR, which you can activate by pressing the appropriate keys or by running another program to issue the interrupt signal that calls one of the TSR's subroutines. When the TSR hits a breakpoint, TD pops into view. After you're done examining variables, single-stepping statements, and using other TD commands, continue the program by pressing ⟨**F9**⟩.

When you're finished debugging, to unload the resident debugger, run the TSR up to a breakpoint—or, from the DOS command line, press ⟨**Ctrl**⟩-⟨**Break**⟩ twice. When you then press ⟨**Alt**⟩-**X** to quit, TD unloads itself and the TSR's resident portion, returning the system to the conditions that existed before the debugging session began.

But if the TSR changes any hardware settings, or if it alters interrupt vectors above 2F hex, TD may not be able to restore every last detail to original form. For this reason, in some circumstances, you may still have to reboot or perform other actions after quitting TD.

> Note: TD can remove itself and an installed TSR from RAM whether or not the TSR has an "unload" command.

A Sample TSR Program

A hands-on demonstration of a TSR debugging session will help you to understand how to use TD's `File:Resident` command to debug resident code. In this section, you'll assemble, load, and debug a sample TSR using the methods outlined previously. To save space, the TSR is a mere shell. Even so, it contains many of the parts and pieces found in complete applications. Note: You can use most of the same steps in this section when debugging TSRs written in Pascal and C.

To assemble the sample TSR, enter Listings 19.1, 19.2, and 19.3. Make sure that Turbo Assembler's directory is in the current path. Then, type these commands:

```
tasm /zi common
tasm /zi /m loadtsr
tlink /v loadtsr common
tasm /zi call64
tlink /v call64
```

> Note: Don't run any of the sample TSR programs just yet. They are designed to work together, and they may fail if executed out of order. Turn to "Debugging the Sample TSR" after the listings for instructions about loading the assembled programs into TD.

Listing 19.1. COMMON.ASM.

```
 1:  ;**
 2:  ;**      Purpose: Common routines for ASM programs.
 3:  ;**      Author:  (c) 1990 by Tom Swan.
 4:  ;**
 5:  ;**      To compile:
 6:  ;**       tasm /zi common
 7:  ;**
 8:
 9:  COMMON_code     SEGMENT para public 'CODE'
10:                  ASSUME  cs:COMMON_code, ds:nothing, es:nothing
11:                  PUBLIC  HexDigit, IntToHex
12:
13:  ;-------------------------------------------------------------
14:  ; HexDigit      Convert 4-bit value to ASCII hex digit
15:  ;-------------------------------------------------------------
16:  ; Input:
17:  ;       dl = value limited to range 0..15
18:  ; Output:
19:  ;       dl = ASCII hex digit equivalent
20:  ; Registers:
21:  ;       dl
22:  ;-------------------------------------------------------------
23:  HexDigit        PROC    near
24:
25:          cmp     dl, 10          ; Is dl < 10 (i.e. hex 'A')?
26:          jb      HD_10           ; If yes, jump
27:          add     dl, 'A'-10      ; Else convert to A...F
```

```
28:          ret                     ; Return to caller
29:  HD_10:
30:          or      dl, '0'         ; Convert digits 0 to 9
31:          ret                     ; Return to caller
32:
33:  HexDigit        ENDP
34:
35:  ;------------------------------------------------------------
36:  ; IntToHex       Convert unsigned integer to ASCII hex string
37:  ;------------------------------------------------------------
38:  ; Input:
39:  ;       ax = 16-bit value to convert
40:  ;       cx = minimum number of digits to output
41:  ;       es:di = address of string large enough to hold result
42:  ; Output:
43:  ;       es:di = address of byte after last inserted character
44:  ; Registers:
45:  ;       ax, bx, cx, dx, si, di
46:  ;------------------------------------------------------------
47:  IntToHex        PROC    near
48:
49:          mov     bx, 16          ; Radix = 16 (hex)
50:          xor     si, si          ; Set digit-count to zero
51:          jcxz    ITH_20          ; If cx=0, jump to set cx=1
52:  ITH_10:
53:          xor     dx, dx          ; Extend ax to 32-bit dxax
54:          div     bx              ; ax<-axdx div bx; dx<-remainder
55:          call    HexDigit        ; Convert dl to ASCII digit
56:          push    dx              ; Save digit on stack
57:          inc     si              ; Count digits on stack
58:          loop    ITH_10          ; Loop on minimum digit count
59:  ITH_20:
60:          inc     cx              ; Set cx = 1 in case not done
61:          or      ax, ax          ; Is ax = 0? (all digits done)
62:          jnz     ITH_10          ; If ax<>0, continue conversion
63:          mov     cx, si          ; Set cx to stack char count
64:          jcxz    ITH_40          ; Skip next loop if cx=0000
65:          cld                     ; Auto-increment di for stosb
66:  ITH_30:
67:          pop     ax              ; Pop next digit into al
68:          stosb                   ; Store digit in str; advance di
69:          loop    ITH_30          ; Loop for cx digits
70:  ITH_40:
71:          ret                     ; Return to caller
72:
```

```
73: IntToHex        ENDP              ; End of procedure
74:
75: COMMON_code     ENDS              ; End of COMMON code segment
76:                 END               ; End of COMMON module
```

Listing 19.2.   LOADTSR.ASM.

```
 1: ;**
 2: ;**     Purpose: Sample TSR for Mastering Turbo Debugger
 3: ;**     Author:  (c) 1990 by Tom Swan.
 4: ;**
 5: ;**     To compile:
 6: ;**       tasm /zi /m loadtsr
 7: ;**       tlink /v loadtsr common
 8: ;**
 9:
10: ;----- Equates
11:
12: TSRInt          equ     64h       ; TSR's interrupt number
13: STACK_SIZE      equ     100h      ; TSR's stack size
14: CR              equ     13        ; ASCII carriage return
15: LF              equ     10        ; ASCII line feed
16: STDOUT          equ     1         ; Standard output handle
17:
18: ;-------------------------------------------------------
19: ;                ---- Resident Portion ----
20: ;-------------------------------------------------------
21:
22: TSR_group       GROUP   TSR_code, TSR_data, TSR_stack
23:
24: ;----- The TSR's code segment
25:
26: TSR_code        SEGMENT byte public 'TSRCODE'
27:                 ASSUME  cs:TSR_group, ds:TSR_group
28:
29: ;----- The TSR's Interrupt Service Routine
30:
31: TSR_isr         PROC    far
32:
33: ;----- Switch to the TSR's private stack
34:
35:         sti                       ; Allow interrupt servicing
36:         push    ds                ; Save ds on current stack
37:         push    cs                ; Address TSR group with
38:         pop     ds                ;  ds (same as cs)
```

```
39:
40:          mov     Old_sp, sp        ; Save sp and ss in the
41:          mov     Old_ss, ss        ;  TSR's data segment
42:          mov     ss, TSR_ss        ; Load new stack segment and
43:          mov     sp, TSR_sp        ;  offset values into ss:sp
44:
45:          push    ax                ; Save other registers
46:          push    bx                ;  used by this TSR
47:          push    cx                ;  on the TSR's stack
48:          push    dx
49:
50:   ;----- Display message (note the TSR_group override!)
51:
52:          mov     bx, STDOUT        ; Load DOS handle into bx
53:          mov     cx, MESSAGE_LEN ; Load string length into cx
54:          mov     dx, offset TSR_group:Message ; Address message
55:          mov     ah, 40h           ; Call DOS function 40h
56:          int     21h               ;  to display string
57:
58:   ;----- Restore registers saved on TSR's private stack
59:
60:          pop     dx
61:          pop     cx
62:          pop     bx
63:          pop     ax
64:
65:   ;----- Reset to original stack and restore ds, dx
66:
67:          mov     ss, TSR_group:Old_ss ; Restore saved stack
68:          mov     sp, TSR_group:Old_sp ;  registers to ss:sp
69:          pop     ds                ; Restore ds from old stack
70:          iret                      ; Return from interrupt
71:
72:   TSR_isr         ENDP
73:   TSR_code        ENDS
74:
75:   ;----- The TSR's data segment
76:
77:   TSR_data        SEGMENT word public 'TSRDATA'
78:
79:   psp             dw      0         ; TSR's psp segment address
80:   DOSversion      dw      0         ; Major and minor version number
81:   Old_ss          dw      0         ; Storage for old stack seg (ss)
82:   Old_sp          dw      0         ; Storage for old stack ofs (sp)
83:   TSR_ss          dw      seg TSR_stack   ; TSR's stack seg (ss)
```

```
84: TSR_sp          dw      STACK_SIZE      ; Initial stack ofs (sp)
85: Message         db      CR, LF, 'TSR Activated: code-'
86: MsgCode         db      '0000:0000 data-'
87: MsgData         db      '0000:0000 stack-'
88: MsgStack        db      '0000:0000', CR, LF
89: MESSAGE_LEN     =       $ - Message
90:
91: TSR_data        ENDS
92:
93:
94: ;----- The TSR's stack segment
95:
96: TSR_stack       SEGMENT word stack 'STACK'
97: private_stack   db      STACK_SIZE dup(?)
98: TSR_stack       ENDS
99:
100: ;-------------------------------------------------------------
101: ;                    ---- Transient Portion ----
102: ;-------------------------------------------------------------
103:
104: ;----- The TSR loader's code segment
105:
106: LOADER_code     SEGMENT para public 'CODE'
107:                 ASSUME  cs:LOADER_code, ds:TSR_data, ss:TSR_stack
108:                 EXTRN   IntToHex:proc
109:
110: ;---- The TSR loader's main procedure
111:
112: Load_TSR        PROC    far
113:
114:         mov     ax, seg TSR_data ; Initialize ds to address
115:         mov     ds, ax          ;   the TSR's data segment
116:         call    CheckVersion    ; Abort if DOS version = 1.x
117:         jnc     LTSR_10         ; Jump if cf = 0 (no error)
118:         mov     al, 1           ; Select error message #1
119:         jmp     ErrorExit       ; End program if DOS 1.x
120: LTSR_10:
121:         mov     psp, es         ; Save psp segment for TSR
122:         push    es              ; Save PSP address on stack
123:         push    ds              ; Save TSR data segment
124:
125: ;----- Install interrupt service routine
126:
127:         mov     al, TSRInt      ; Get current vector for
128:         mov     ah, 35h         ;   the TSR's interrupt number
```

```
129:          int      21h                ;  using DOS function 35h.
130:          mov      bx, es             ; Copy segment address to bx
131:          or       bx, bx             ;  and test if bx = 0.
132:          jz       LTSR_20            ; Jump if vector is not used
133:          pop      ds                 ; Restore TSR data seg to ds
134:          pop      es                 ; Restore PSP address to es
135:          mov      al, 2              ; Set error code number
136:          jmp      ErrorExit          ; And exit with error message
137:   LTSR_20:
138:          mov      ax, seg TSR_code ; Set ds to TSR's code
139:          mov      ds, ax             ;  segment.
140:
141:          ASSUME   ds:TSR_code
142:
143:          mov      dx, offset TSR_isr ; Set dx to TSR's int service
144:          mov      al, TSRInt         ;  routine, and set the
145:          mov      ah, 25h            ;  interrupt vector for TSRint
146:          int      21h                ;  with DOS function 25h.
147:          pop      ds                 ; Restore TSR data segment
148:
149:          ASSUME   ds:TSR_data
150:
151:   ;----- Insert TSR addresses into the message string
152:
153:          push     ds                 ; Set es = ds for addressing
154:          pop      es                 ;  strings with es:di
155:          mov      ax, seg TSR_group  ; ax <- TSR group segment
156:          push     ax                 ; Save ax for later
157:          mov      bx, offset TSR_isr ; bx <- TSR code offset
158:          mov      di, offset MsgCode ; Address code addr in string
159:          call     InsertAddress      ; Insert ax:bx into string
160:
161:          pop      ax                 ; Restore ax from stack
162:          push     ax                 ;  and save ax again
163:          mov      bx, size TSR_code  ; bx <- TSR data offset
164:          mov      di, offset MsgData ; Address data addr in string
165:          call     InsertAddress      ; Insert ax:bx into string
166:
167:          pop      ax                 ; Restore ax from stack
168:          mov      bx, size TSR_code + size TSR_data ; bx=stack ofs
169:          mov      di, offset MsgStack ; Address stack addr in str
170:          call     InsertAddress      ; Insert ax:bx into string
171:
172:   ;----- Terminate and stay resident
```

```
173:
174:            mov     ax, seg LOADER_data ; Initialize ds to loader's
175:            mov     ds, ax              ;  data segment
176:
177:            ASSUME  ds:LOADER_data
178:
179:            mov     dx, offset doneMsg ; Display "TSR Loaded" message
180:            mov     ah, 09h            ;  by calling DOS print-
181:            int     21h                ;  string function.
182:            pop     ax                 ; Restore PSP seg addr to ax
183:            mov     dx, cs             ; dx <- Transient start addr
184:            sub     dx, ax             ; dx <- Resident size
185:            mov     ax, 3100h          ; DOS terminate function
186:            int     21h                ; Terminate, stay resident
187:                                       ; al = 0 (return code)
188: Load_TSR       ENDP
189:
190: ;-------------------------------------------------------------------
191: ; ErrorExit              Exit with error message and code in al
192: ;-------------------------------------------------------------------
193: ; Input:
194: ;       al = error code 1..n
195: ;       ds = address of TSR's data segment
196: ;       es = psp segment address (DOS 1.x only)
197: ; Output:
198: ;       none. program halted.
199: ; Registers:
200: ;       none preserved
201: ;-------------------------------------------------------------------
202: ErrorExit      PROC    near
203:
204:            ASSUME  ds:TSR_data
205:
206:            push    DOSversion          ; Save DOS version on stack
207:            push    ax                  ; Save error code on stack
208:            mov     ax, seg LOADER_data ; Initialize ds to loader's
209:            mov     ds, ax              ;  data segment
210:
211:            ASSUME  ds:LOADER_data
212:
213:            mov     dx, offset errorMsg ; Address "ERROR: " string
214:            mov     ah, 09h             ; DOS print-string function
215:            int     21h                 ; Display error lead-in
216:            pop     ax                  ; Restore error code to al
```

```
217:          push     ax              ; Save code again
218:          cmp      al, 1           ; Does error code = 1?
219:          jne      test2           ; If not, check next code
220:          mov      dx, offset errmsg1 ; Address error message 1
221:          jmp      Exit            ; Display message and exit
222: test2:
223:          cmp      al, 2           ; Error code 2
224:          jne      default
225:          mov      dx, offset errmsg2
226:          jmp      Exit
227: default:
228:          mov      dx, offset defaultmsg ; Default error code
229:
230: ;----- Display message and exit. Error code still in al.
231:
232: Exit:
233:          mov      ah, 09h         ; DOS print-string function
234:          int      21h             ; Display error message
235:          pop      ax              ; Restore error code to al
236:          pop      bx              ; Restore DOS version to bx
237:          cmp      bl, 2           ; Is it ver. 2.x or higher?
238:          jb       ExitDOS1x       ; Jump for versions 1.x
239:
240: ;----- End program for DOS 2.x and higher
241:
242:          mov      ah, 4ch         ; DOS terminate with code
243:          int      21h             ; End with error code in al
244:
245: ;----- End program for DOS 1.x
246:
247: ExitDOS1x:
248:          push     es              ; Push es onto stack
249:          xor      ax,ax           ; Set ax to 0000
250:          push     ax              ; Push 0000 (stack=es:0000)
251:          retf                     ; Far return exits program
252:
253: ErrorExit      ENDP
254:
255: ;-------------------------------------------------------------
256: ; CheckVersion          Test DOS version
257: ;-------------------------------------------------------------
258: ; Input:
259: ;        ds = address of TSR's data segment
260: ; Output:
```

```
261: ;        TSR_data:DOSversion = version number
262: ;        ax = version number
263: ;        cf = 0 = DOS version 2.x or higher
264: ;        cf = 1 = DOS version 1.x
265: ; Registers:
266: ;        ax
267: ;-------------------------------------------------------------
268: CheckVersion    PROC    near
269:
270:         ASSUME ds:TSR_data
271:
272:         mov     ah, 30h              ; DOS get-version function
273:         int     21h                  ; Get DOS version
274:         mov     word ptr DOSversion, ax ; Save in TSR data seg
275:         cmp     al, 02h              ; Test major revision number
276:         ret                          ;  cf = 0 if al >= 2
277:                                      ;  cf = 1 if al < 2
278: CheckVersion    ENDP
279:
280: ;-------------------------------------------------------------
281: ; InsertAddress           Insert seg:offset address into a string
282: ;-------------------------------------------------------------
283: ; Input:
284: ;        ax = segment address
285: ;        bx = offset address
286: ;        es:di = address of 9-character string (minimum size)
287: ; Output:
288: ;        ax:bx inserted in hex into string at di
289: ;        es:di = address of byte after last inserted character
290: ; Registers:
291: ;        ax, bx, cx, dx, si, di
292: ;-------------------------------------------------------------
293: InsertAddress   PROC    near
294:
295:         push    bx              ; Save offset value on stack
296:         call    IA_10           ; Insert segment into string
297:         inc     di              ; Skip colon (:)
298:         pop     ax              ; Restore offset to ax
299: IA_10:
300:         mov     cx, 4           ; Specify minimum of 4 digits
301:         call    IntToHex        ; Convert ax to hex at es:di
302:         ret                     ; Return to caller
303:
304: InsertAddress   ENDP
```

```
305:   LOADER_code    ENDS
306:
307:   ;----- TSR loader's data segment
308:
309:   LOADER_data  SEGMENT word public 'DATA'
310:
311:   doneMsg          db        CR,LF,'TSR Loaded',CR,LF,'$'
312:   errorMsg         db        CR,LF,'ERROR: ', '$'
313:   errmsg1          db        'Requires DOS 2.0 or later',CR,LF,'$'
314:   errmsg2          db        'Interrupt vector in use',CR,LF,'$'
315:   defaultmsg       db        'Unknown cause',CR,LF,'$'
316:
317:   LOADER_data    ENDS
318:                  END     Load_TSR
```

Listing 19.3.   CALL64.ASM.

```
 1:  ;**
 2:  ;**      Purpose: Demonstrate how to activate LOADTSR
 3:  ;**      Author: (c) 1990 by Tom Swan.
 4:  ;**
 5:  ;**      To compile:
 6:  ;**        tasm /zi call64
 7:  ;**        tlink /v call64
 8:  ;**
 9:          DOSSEG
10:          .MODEL    small
11:          .STACK    256
12:
13:  ;----- Equates
14:
15:  TSRInt          equ       64h       ; TSR's interrupt number
16:
17:          .CODE
18:  Start:
19:          mov       ax, @data       ; Initialize DS to address
20:          mov       ds, ax          ;  of data segment
21:          int       TSRInt          ; Activate resident code
22:  Exit:
23:          mov       ax, 04C00h      ; DOS function: Exit program
24:          int       21h             ; Terminate with al=exit code
25:
26:          END       Start           ; End of program / entry point
```

Debugging the Sample TSR

Before running the sample TSR, check that you have at least these five files in the current directory: COMMON.ASM, LOADTSR.ASM, LOADTSR.EXE, CALL64.ASM, and CALL64.EXE. Then, start TD with the command **td loadtsr**. In a moment, you should see the TSR's source code in the main Module window.

Notice that the cursor is positioned on the TSR's entry point, in this case, at the instruction under label Load_TSR. This duplicates the conditions that exist just before the TSR transient portion begins running when you execute the program from DOS. If you now press ⟨**F9**⟩ to run, the transient loader will install the TSR's resident code and data in memory.

Go ahead and do that—press ⟨**F9**⟩ to install the TSR. You should receive the message "Resident, exit code 0." (If you receive another message or exit code, skip ahead to "Resetting the Interrupt Vector," then try again.) Press ⟨**Enter**⟩ or ⟨**Esc**⟩ to clear the message window.

As explained earlier, the transient code's main job is to install the TSR's resident portion. LOADTSR accomplishes this at lines 143–146 in Listing 19.2 by calling DOS function 25h, which changes interrupt 64h's vector (represented by constant TSRInt) to address the TSR's interrupt service routine, TSR_isr (lines 31–72). The instructions at lines 183–186 assign the resident portion's size in paragraphs to DX before calling DOS function 31h to terminate and make that much of the program resident in RAM. The other instructions in the program insert the TSR's code, data, and stack addresses into a string (lines 85–88) displayed when the resident code runs.

Setting TSR Breakpoints

If you are following along with TD, the TSR is now installed in memory, and the debugger is idle. The next step is to set a few breakpoints inside the resident code so that, when you activate the TSR, TD can regain control to let you examine variables and to perform other debugging rites and rituals. Use ⟨**Page Up**⟩ and the cursor movement keys (or a mouse) to position the cursor at the entry to procedure TSR_isr, the sti instruction (line 35 in Listing 19.2.) Press ⟨**F2**⟩ to set a breakpoint at that line. Then, press ⟨**Alt**⟩-**FR** (File:Resident), which pushes TD into the background and returns the DOS prompt.

After using the Resident command, you should see the message "TSR Loaded." You can now give DOS commands (for example, type **dir** for a directory) and run other programs. But, despite appearances, TD and LOAD-TSR are still in memory, waiting for an activation signal.

In this case, you can give that signal by running the CALL64 program (Listing 19.3), which includes an int 64h instruction, the interrupt number that activates LOADTSR's resident code. As soon as you type **call64** and press ⟨**Enter**⟩, you again see TD's screen with the cursor positioned at the breakpoint you set earlier.

If you press ⟨**F9**⟩ now, the resident code finishes, and the DOS prompt reappears. Notice that when you do this, the TSR displays a message that lists the addresses of the resident code, data, and stack segments. These addresses may be helpful for debugging various TSR parts and pieces, and you might want to include similar code in your own programs.

To get back to TD, press ⟨**Ctrl**⟩-⟨**Break**⟩ twice. (If this opens the CPU window, close it by pressing ⟨**Alt**⟩-⟨**F3**⟩.) Then, to quit the debugger and return to DOS, press ⟨**Alt**⟩-**X**.

When you quit TD after having installed a TSR, the debugger unloads the TSR's resident portion, resets interrupt vectors from 00 to 2Fh, unloads itself from RAM, and exits. This restores most conditions to their original states that existed before you began this debugging session. You can then edit the TSR, recompile, and continue debugging.

Resetting the Interrupt Vector

Resident programs are likely to do just about anything, including actions that TD can't reset automatically. If you are following along on your computer, you just installed a TSR, ran the code to a breakpoint, and exited to DOS. If you now type **td loadtsr** to start another debugging session, and press ⟨**F9**⟩ to run, instead of "Resident, exit code 0," TD displays the message "Terminated, exit code 2." This indicates that something is preventing the TSR's transient code from installing the resident portion. Let's use the debugger to find out what's wrong.

First, press ⟨**Esc**⟩ to clear the termination message and then press ⟨**Ctrl**⟩-⟨**F2**⟩ to reset the program to its startup conditions. Because termination error codes are passed back to DOS in register AL, we need to set a breakpoint on that condition to track down the conditions under which this error occurs.

Press ⟨**Alt**⟩-**BE** and enter **al eq 2** to set a breakpoint to halt the program when register AL equals 2, the value of the reported error. Then, press ⟨**Alt**⟩-**VR** to use View:Registers (or open the CPU window) and change register AX to 0000 (just type **0** and press ⟨**Enter**⟩). This will prevent a false breakpoint from occurring in case AL already equals 2 from a previous operation.

You can now press ⟨**F9**⟩ to run the program, which should halt at about line 136. Press ⟨**Esc**⟩ and ⟨**F6**⟩ once or twice to bring the Module view forward. The instruction just before the breakpoint's location is mov al, 2; therefore, it's a program instruction that's causing the error, not another kind of bug. Examining a few lines above this location reveals that error code 2 is set when interrupt 64h's vector is in use. Because TD resets only vectors 0 through 2Fh, even after unloading the TSR and the debugger, interrupt 64h's vector remains in place. So, the transient loader refuses to run the second time.

Now that we know why that happens, the fix is easy—write a short utility (see Listing 19.4, RESET64.ASM) to reset the interrupt vector and run that program between debugging sessions. Assemble the program with the commands:

```
tasm /zi reset64
tlink /v reset64
```

Listing 19.4. RESET64.TSR.

```
 1:  ;**
 2:  ;**       Purpose: Reset interrupt vector 64h to 0000:0000
 3:  ;**       Author:  (c) 1990 by Tom Swan.
 4:  ;**
 5:  ;**       Note: Run this program before debugging LOADTSR.EXE.
 6:  ;**             Do NOT run while LOADTSR is resident.
 7:  ;**
 8:  ;**       To compile:
 9:  ;**         tasm /zi reset64
10:  ;**         tlink /v reset64
11:  ;**
12:           DOSSEG
13:           .MODEL    small
14:           .STACK    256
15:
16:  ;----- Equates
17:
18:  TSRInt          equ      64h        ; TSR's interrupt number
19:  CR              equ      13         ; ASCII carriage return
20:  LF              equ      10         ; ASCII line feed
21:  STDOUT          equ      1          ; Standard output handle
22:
23:           .DATA
24:  Message         db   CR,LF,'Interrupt vector 64h reset',CR,LF,'$'
25:
26:           .CODE
27:  Start:
28:           xor     dx, dx          ; dx <- 0000
29:           mov     ds, dx          ; ds <- 0000
30:           mov     al, TSRInt      ; Reset TSR's interrupt
31:           mov     ah, 25h         ;   vector by calling
32:           int     21h             ;   DOS function 25h.
33:
34:  ;----- Display confirmation message
35:
36:           mov     ax, @data       ; Address data segment
37:           mov     ds, ax          ;   with ds
38:           mov     dx, offset Message ; Address message string
39:           mov     ah, 09h         ; Call DOS function 9
40:           int     21h             ;   to display string
```

```
41:   Exit:
42:           mov     ax, 04C00h      ; DOS function: Exit program
43:           int     21h             ; Terminate with al=exit code
44:
45:           END     Start           ; End of program / entry point
```

After assembling and linking RESET64, from the DOS command line, type **reset64** and press ⟨**Enter**⟩ to run the program, which should display the message, "Interrupt vector 64h reset." You can then restart TD and run LOAD-TSR as explained before.

In other situations, you may have to perform similar reinitializations before you will be able to debug a TSR after the first trial run. Or, you might have to reboot. Of course, a well-written TSR should be able to remove all traces of itself from memory. But, because TD has taken over the tasks of unloading the TSR's resident portion, the TSR's own unloading routines may not have the opportunity to run; therefore, when debugging complex TSRs, you may still need to devise custom procedures similar to RESET64 for resetting conditions between debugging sessions.

Alternate TSR Debugging Methods

At times, running the TSR's transient loader inside TD may be inconvenient. For example, as demonstrated in the previous section, making TD and the TSR resident at the same time can prevent the TSR's unloader from resetting interrupt vectors and other critical items. (The sample program in this chapter doesn't have an unloader, but the effect of not being able to reset the vector illustrates the difficulty.) Also, because installing the TSR from inside TD positions the TSR above any other resident programs, the methods just described can't be used to investigate conflicts that occur only when the TSR is installed earlier than other resident programs.

Another TD command, `File:Table relocate`, can deal with those sorts of problems by moving the relative address of the program's debugging symbols to another location in memory. (The symbols don't actually move, of course. Relocating the program's symbols merely tells TD to associate those symbols with data at a new address.) This lets you debug a resident program installed before running TD.

Loading the TSR from DOS

To see how this technique works, reboot to make sure the sample TSR isn't already in memory. Then, follow these steps to load and debug LOADTSR (Listing 19.2) using `Table relocate`:

1. Run LOADTSR from the DOS command line to install the sample TSR in memory. You should see the message "TSR Loaded." If not, reboot or run RESET64 to clear the interrupt 64h vector, then try again.

2. Next, run CALL64 to display the TSR's code, data, and stack segment addresses. Write down the code segment address—you'll need it in a moment.

3. Enter the command **td loadtsr** to start TD and load the assembled TSR. *Do not run the program.*

4. Open the `View:CPU` window (⟨**Alt**⟩-**VC**) and type two instructions, pressing ⟨**Enter**⟩ after each: **int 64h** and **int 3**. You don't have to select a command first—when viewing the `CPU` window, you can just start typing to patch in new machine-code instructions. The first instruction activates the TSR and the second is a fail-safe interrupt that will call TD in case you forget to set a breakpoint inside the TSR's resident code. (Note: You can skip this step when debugging active TSR's that are awakened by key-presses. The patch is needed only for this chapter's sample.) Close the `CPU` window by pressing ⟨**Alt**⟩-⟨**F3**⟩.

5. Open the `View:Variables` view (⟨**Alt**⟩-**VV**). The window shows the variables of the program as loaded in TD—not those that belong to the TSR you installed earlier.

6. Choose `File:Table relocate` (⟨**Alt**⟩-**FT**) and enter the code-segment address you noted earlier. Remember to use assembly language notation for hex values. For example, if the TSR reported a code-segment address of 3E8B, enter **03e8bh** as the segment address value for `Table relocate`.

7. When you enter the segment address, the values in `Variables` change to the actual TSR's data. You are now viewing the code and data values of the resident code installed before starting the debugger.

8. Press ⟨**Tab**⟩ to move the cursor into the lower window pane and highlight the TSR's entry point at label `tsr_isr`. Press ⟨**Enter**⟩ to view the source-code line at this location.

9. Press ⟨**F2**⟩ to set a breakpoint on the TSR's first instruction.

10. Press ⟨**F9**⟩ to run the patched `int 64` instruction and activate the TSR, which will halt at the breakpoint. You are now seeing the conditions as they exist when the TSR is activated from DOS, and you can use other TD commands to inspect variables, patch subroutines, and evaluate expressions.

11. After debugging, press ⟨**Alt**⟩-**X** to quit TD and return to DOS. Because you loaded the TSR separately, its resident portion remains in memory. You can prove this by running CALL64 again.

12. Because the sample TSR does not have the ability to unload itself from memory, you may want to reboot now to remove the resident code from RAM.

When debugging your own programs, keep in mind that after you relocate the TSR's symbol table, any symbols that refer to code and data in the TSR's transient portion are invalid. This will not cause problems if you remember not to execute transient subroutines or change any data that doesn't belong to the TSR's resident segments. As Figure 19.2 shows, after relocation, transient symbols can even address portions of TD! Storing new values to those locations may cause serious problems.

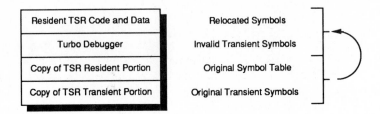

Figure 19.2.   Repositioning the symbol table for a TSR's resident code and data may invalidate symbols for the transient portion.

> Note: You can use the TDMEM utility program (see chapter 6) to locate TSR code-segment addresses for repositioning debugging symbols. However, the addresses reported by TDMEM may need adjusting for TD's use, and for that reason, it's best to include programming in the TSR to report the resident code's address as demonstrated here.

Loading a Separate Symbol Table

There's another, and perhaps better, way to debug a TSR that is already resident before starting TD. With this method, you transfer the program's debugging symbols to a separate file and then load that information into the debugger. This also takes less RAM and, therefore, may allow you to debug larger TSRs.

To experiment with this technique, reboot to unload the sample TSR. Then, follow these steps:

1. Run LOADTSR as you did earlier to install the sample TSR in memory. Also run CALL64 and note the reported address of the TSR's code segment. Next, use the command **tdstrip -s loadtsr.exe** to transfer debugging information from LOADTSR.EXE to a new file named LOADTSR.TDS.

2. Enter **dir loadtsr.tds** to determine the size of the symbol table file. Double the file size and round down to the nearest 1,000 bytes to find the approximate amount of memory required to hold the symbols. For example, if the

file size is 1,810 bytes, the symbols will take about 3K. (Note: Borland recommends using a value of about 1.5 times the size of the symbol table file.)

3. Start TD with the -sm option to reserve space for the program's symbols, using the value you determined in the previous step. For example, to reserve 3K for symbols, enter **td -sm3**. Do *not* specify a file name to load.

4. Press ⟨**Esc**⟩ or ⟨**Enter**⟩ to erase TD's startup message. Execute `File:Symbol load` (⟨**Alt**⟩-**FS**) and select or enter the name of the symbol table file, in this example, LOADTSR.TDS. If you receive the error message "Not enough memory to load symbol table," quit the debugger and increase the value for -sm.

5. Use `File:Table relocate` (⟨**Alt**⟩-**FT**) to enter the TSR's code-segment address reported earlier by CALL64, for example, **017a3h**. You should see the `CPU` window change to display the TSR's instructions. To open the `Module` window, you may have to press ⟨**F3**⟩, select `loadtsr`, and press ⟨**Enter**⟩ and ⟨**F5**⟩ to zoom the display to full screen. You can now set breakpoints, view variables, and use other commands to debug the TSR.

6. After setting at least one breakpoint (on `sti` at line 35 in Listing 19.2 if you're following along), you can now activate the TSR in one of two ways. You can patch in and run instructions as you did earlier to call a subroutine in the resident code, or you can use `File:Resident` (⟨**Alt**⟩-**FR**) to push TD into the background. With this second (and probably better) method, the DOS prompt reappears, and you can press the TSR's activation keys to wake up the code. (For this demonstration, simulate that action by running CALL64.) When the program reaches a breakpoint, TD comes out of hiding to perform the breakpoint action, usually halting the program so you can inspect various conditions.

Debugging TSRs in Remote Mode

Another good way to debug TSRs is to connect two systems with an RS-232 serial cable and execute TD in remote mode (see chapter 17). This setup allows the TSR to run on the remote system while you simultaneously view TD's display on the local screen. Remote debugging also isolates the resident code from the debugger, thus avoiding conflicts and crashes that can occur when both programs share the same memory.

There are two ways to debug a TSR in remote mode. The first uses TD's resident capabilities. The second repositions a TSR symbol table over a TSR that was installed on the remote system before you started the debugger. The following sections explain how to use both of these methods.

Resident Remote Debugging

Follow these steps to debug a TSR on a remote system while you view TD's output on a local display. For test purposes, you can use Listings 19.1 through 19.4, or you can substitute your own TSR code in place of LOADTSR:

1. Make sure the two computers are properly connected. To verify that, type **tdremote** on the remote system and **tdrf d** at the local keyboard. You should see a listing of the files in the remote system's current directory.

2. Transfer miscellaneous files needed by the TSR to the remote system. If you are running the sample TSR, enter **tdrf t reset64.exe** and **tdrf t call64.exe** to copy those two auxiliary programs to the remote.

3. With TDREMOTE still running on the remote computer, start TD on the local system using the command **td -r loadtsr**. If you see a message asking permission to "send over link?," answer "Yes" (press ⟨**Enter**⟩). In a moment, you should see the program's source code in the `Module` window on the local screen.

4. Press ⟨**F9**⟩ on the local keyboard to run the TSR's transient loader and install the resident portion in the remote computer's memory. If you are using the sample TSR, you should see the message "TSR loaded" on the remote display. On the local screen, you should see a window with the message "Resident, exit code 0." Press ⟨**Esc**⟩ on the local keyboard to erase this message.

5. The TSR is now loaded into the remote system's RAM, and the debugger is running locally. Using the local keyboard, set one or more breakpoints in the TSR's resident code. If you're following along with the sample TSR, set a breakpoint on the `sti` instruction after label `tsr_isr` at line 35.

6. Next, on the local system, choose `File:Resident` (press ⟨**Alt**⟩-**FR**). Because you are debugging in remote mode, this makes TDREMOTE go resident on the remote computer—it does not make TD resident locally as with single-system TSR debugging. You should see the DOS prompt reappear on the remote computer, and you can now switch to that keyboard and give DOS commands or run other programs. TDREMOTE remains in memory, ready to intercept breakpoints and to send the local system a signal that will awaken TD. Until then, TD is inactive and won't accept any commands locally. (You can press ⟨**Ctrl**⟩-⟨**Break**⟩ on the local keyboard to regain control if the remote system hangs.)

7. On the remote keyboard, run the CALL64 program to activate the sample TSR. (Or, press your own TSR's hot keys.) When the program reaches a breakpoint, TDREMOTE wakes up TD on the local system, and you can switch back to that keyboard to examine variables, make patches, and use other TD commands.

8. Press ⟨F9⟩ locally to continue running. You can then switch over to the remote keyboard again and press the TSR's hot key (or run CALL64). When finished debugging, run the TSR up to a breakpoint or press ⟨Ctrl⟩-⟨Break⟩ on the local keyboard to regain control. Then, press ⟨Alt⟩-X locally to quit TD and return to DOS. This restores both the remote and local systems to their states before starting TD. The remote system should display the message "Link broken," indicating that TDREMOTE is ready to accept new remote commands from TD or TDRF. If you also want to exit TDREMOTE on the remote system at this point, press ⟨Ctrl⟩-⟨Break⟩ on that computer's keyboard. (Leave TDREMOTE running if you intend to repeat these steps and continue debugging this or another program.)

Note: Run RESET64 on the remote system to reset the interrupt 64h vector. A more complete TSR would have an "unload" command, which you could run at this time. Or, you can reboot to remove the TSR from memory.

Nonresident Remote Debugging

The previous instructions won't work with a TSR that's already in RAM before you start TD. In that case, follow these steps instead. (You can use the sample LOADTSR program or substitute your own TSR code.)

1. Load the TSR on the remote system. (Use TDRF to transfer the code file if necessary.) If you are using the sample TSR, execute LOADTSR from the remote system's DOS command line. Also run CALL64 to display the TSR's code segment address—you'll need that value in a moment. If you receive an error message from LOADTSR, run RESET64 or reboot, then try again.

2. Start TDREMOTE on the remote computer.

3. On the local keyboard, issue the command **tdstrip -s loadtsr** to copy the symbol table from LOADTSR.EXE to LOADTSR.TDS. (If you performed this step earlier, you'll receive the message "Program does not have a symbol table." In this case, ignore the message—you already created the necessary files. But at other times, you might have to reassemble (or recompile) the program and give the TDSTRIP command again.) As before, double the size of the .TDS file and round down to the nearest 1,000 bytes to determine how much memory TD will require to hold the symbol table. Start TD with the command **td -sm3 -r** (no file name) to begin a remote debugging session and reserve 3,000 bytes for the symbol table.

4. Use File:Symbol load (⟨Alt⟩-FS) to load the symbol table file LOAD-TSR.TDS. If you receive an error message, quit TD and increase the -sm value to reserve more space.

5. Use `File:Table relocate` (⟨**Alt**⟩-**FT**) to enter the TSR's code-segment address you noted earlier. Remember to enter this address in the correct format for the current language. For example, in assembly language, if the reported code-segment address is 3E85, enter **03e85h**.

6. Press ⟨**F3**⟩ to select `loadtsr` and open the `Module` window (if it's not open). Optionally press ⟨**F5**⟩ to zoom the view to full screen.

7. Set a breakpoint inside the TSR's resident code—at `sti` on line 35 if you're following along. Then, use `File:Resident` (⟨**Alt**⟩-**FR**) on the local keyboard to force TDREMOTE into the background, returning the DOS prompt on the remote system and temporarily deactivating TD on the local computer. Switch to the remote's keyboard and run CALL64 (or press your own TSR's hot keys).

8. You can now continue to debug the code as described under step 8 in the previous section. But this time, when you quit TD locally, it does not unload the TSR from the remote system's RAM. To do that, quit TDREMOTE on the remote and use the TSR's unload command or, for the sample listing, reboot.

Common TSR Bugs

Just about anything that can go wrong with nonresident programs can affect a TSR, of course, but the following bugs tend to show up with increased regularity in resident code. If your TSR is failing, check these possibilities first.

Failing to Preserve All Registers

Active TSRs must preserve all registers and flags. (Flag preservation is automatic for interrupt service routines that return via an `iret` instruction.) Passive TSRs may change registers as long as they will be activated only by an explicit `int` instruction in another program. When activated in this manner, a passive TSR operates as a resident subroutine—similar to the way DOS `int 21h` functions operate—and you may pass values back in registers and flags. In that case, a passive TSR must never be activated by an external event that might interrupt a program at an unpredictable time.

Mishandling Segment Registers

Never assume that segment registers ES, DS, or SS address any specific locations in memory. Only CS can be trusted—after all, it must address the current code segment that contains the resident code when that code is active. Many programmers use this fact to initialize DS to the same segment by executing the instructions:

```
push cs
pop  ds
```

That sets DS equal to CS, allowing variables to be located in the TSR's segment group. But this works only if data and code share the same segment. A large TSR may have separate data and code segments, and, in that case, you'll have to initialize DS with a MOV instruction such as:

```
mov  ds, TSR_DATA
```

Confusion over which data segment is current is another source of problems, particularly in cases where the transient loader has its own data apart from the resident portion's. You must be careful to address the correct segment at all times—use **ASSUME** directives to tell the assembler which is the current data segment. Read through LOADTSR.ASM in Listing 19.2 for examples that show how to manipulate DS and ES when dealing with multiple data segments.

Use TD to verify DS and ES values. If you aren't sure if the program is using the correct segment, insert a dummy string variable into the TSR's data segment:

```
dummy  db  "This is the data segment"
```

Then, after halting at a breakpoint in the TSR, and after stepping through the instructions that initialize DS (or ES), open a Dump window, press ⟨**Ctrl**⟩-**G**, and enter **ds:dummy** or **es:dummy**. If you see your test string, you know that DS is set correctly.

Conflict with a BIOS Routine

Active TSRs must never call a ROM BIOS routine that was interrupted by the event that triggered the TSR's code. Routines in the BIOS are not reentrant, which means they cannot be interrupted and restarted, mostly because they store values in variables at fixed addresses and, therefore, can use only one set of those variables at a time.

Because there are no mechanisms available to tell if a BIOS routine was interrupted, TSR programmers are forced to invent their own clever solutions. One such method examines the return address on the stack. If the segment address is high (0F000h, for example), then you know that a BIOS routine was interrupted. But this method isn't foolproof—some systems move BIOS routines into RAM to improve performance.

A better method is to insert hooks into each BIOS interrupt vector that a program uses. The hook intercepts calls to that vector, increments a counter, and calls or jumps to the original vector address to complete the BIOS function call. When the TSR receives its activation signal, it first checks whether any BIOS hook counts are nonzero. If so, then the BIOS was interrupted, and the

TSR must delay activation—usually accomplished by setting an internal flag that can be inspected on subsequent clock ticks. Only when all's quiet on the BIOS front does the TSR pop into action.

Strange lockups and other problems can be caused by failing to follow this rule, and because such bugs are difficult to repeat, there isn't much that TD can do to help you find them. The best solution is to include hooks for every BIOS routine that you call in the TSR and to be absolutely certain that none of those routines was interrupted by the TSR's activation event.

Conflict with a Nonreentrant DOS Routine

A TSR must also monitor DOS activity to be certain that no nonreentrant calls were interrupted. The best way to accomplish this (and maybe it's the only way) is to call the "undocumented" DOS interrupt 21h, function 34h, which returns in ES:BX the address of the *In-DOS* flag. DOS increments this flag on each call to interrupt 21h and then decrements the value on each return. The active TSR's transient loader should obtain and save the *In-DOS* flag address in the resident data segment.

When the TSR receives its activation signal, it should test the *In-DOS* flag by examining the byte at the address determined by the TSR's loader. If the flag is nonzero, then a DOS routine was interrupted, and the TSR must delay activation, usually by setting a flag that a clock-tick routine can test later on. Only when the *In-DOS* flag is 0 should the TSR awaken.

The fly in the ointment that causes a lot of trouble is that COMMAND.COM waits for a keypress via DOS function 01h. Because this sets the *In-DOS* flag, the TSR can never pop up from DOS. Programmers often solve this problem by tapping into interrupt 28h (DOS's "undocumented" idle interrupt), which DOS function 01h calls repeatedly while waiting for a keypress. If this interrupt is called, and if the *In-DOS* flag is set, the TSR may safely activate itself.

> Note: See "Failing to Deal With Critical Errors" later in this section for another note that concerns the *In-DOS* flag.

Interrupting a Hardware Interrupt

Serious bugs can occur when a TSR interrupts a hardware interrupt before that interrupt's routine can send an end-of-interrupt signal to the 8259A interrupt priority controller. Generally, the method for doing this is to set ax to 00001011b, execute out 20h, al, wait a couple of machine cycles, and then execute in al, 20h. This returns 0 in AL if no hardware interrupts are being serviced. If AL is not zero, then the TSR must delay activation until hardware interrupt processing stabilizes.

A hung system is often caused by this problem. Narrow the bug to as small a section of code as possible using TD's code-tracing commands and be sure that your interrupt routines do not prevent others from completing their jobs.

Miscalculating the Resident Portion Size

When terminating via DOS interrupt 21h, function 31h, you must calculate the size in paragraphs of the resident code, data, and stack and pass that value in DX. The usual way to do this is to load the PSP segment address into AX and subtract that value from the current CS register while the TSR's transient loader runs. (The PSP's segment address is in ES just before an .EXE-style TSR's transient portion runs.)

Be sure not to confuse this method of determining the resident portion's size with the older method of assigning to DX the offset to the first byte in the transient portion (in other words, the byte after the end of the resident code and data) and ending the program with interrupt 27h. This is especially dangerous because confusing the old and new methods might not surface as a bug if the value in DX causes DOS to reserve enough memory to hold the TSR. But later, if the TSR's size changes, the program may fail.

If you are struggling to discover why a TSR is crashing, determine the TSR's transient size manually (use TLINK's /m option to generate a .MAP file), set a breakpoint at the end of the TSR's loader just before exiting via function 31h, and compare the value in DX with the expected resident size in 16-byte paragraphs.

Loading an Unprotected Resident Data Segment

When using the GROUP directive to collect a TSR's resident code, data, and stack segments—especially when the TSR's transient loader shares one or more of those same segments, usually the stack—you must be careful to construct the program's source code to ensure that all resident segments are loaded into memory in the correct order. Consult a good assembly language reference or your assembler's manuals for details on how various GROUP parameters affect segment order.

The symptom of this problem is usually a serious crash, often caused by a data segment in the wrong position and, therefore, not protected when the transient loader ends via DOS function 31h. One way to check for this error is to create a segment map file with TLINK's /s option and inspect the resident segment addresses. For example, here's a portion of the map file for LOAD-TSR.ASM (Listing 19.2):

```
0000:0000 0033 C=TSRCODE S=TSR_CODE G=TSR_GROUP M=LOADTSR.ASM ACBP=28
0003:0004 004C C=TSRDATA S=TSR_DATA G=TSR_GROUP M=LOADTSR.ASM ACBP=48
0008:0000 0100 C=STACK S=TSR_STACK G=TSR_GROUP M=LOADTSR.ASM ACBP=54
0018:0000 00C2 C=CODE S=LOADER_CODE G=(none) M=LOADTSR.ASM ACBP=68
0025:0000 002E C=CODE S=COMMON_CODE G=(none) M=COMMON.ASM ACBP=68
0027:000E 0067 C=DATA S=LOADER_DATA G=(none) M=LOADTSR.ASM ACBP=48
```

Notice that the TSR_CODE, TSR_DATA, and TSR_STACK segments are correctly grouped and that the transient code (C = CODE) and data (C = DATA) segments follow the resident group.

PRINT.COM Conflict

Some TSR's use interrupt 2Fh as a means of identifying themselves and to determine whether that same TSR is already installed in memory. Using this trick can also cause a nasty bug if PRINT.COM is loaded before the TSR under DOS 2.x. In those DOS versions, PRINT.COM also uses interrupt 2Fh, causing a conflict. Try loading the TSR before PRINT.COM to see if the error disappears.

Hint: Because this requires loading the TSR from DOS, you'll have to use one of the methods for loading a symbol table to debug the resident code with TD.

Not Letting Interrupt 09h Finish

A common mistake in active TSRs is to monitor keyboard interrupt 09h and activate the TSR immediately upon recognizing one or more keystrokes. Doing this violates the general rule that all hardware interrupts should be allowed to finish before the TSR activates; therefore, a better method sets a flag, lets interrupt 09h finish normally, and then activates the TSR at a later time—usually on the next clock tick.

Not Letting Interrupt 08h Finish

Many TSR's include a clock-tick routine that hooks into interrupt 08h or installs an interrupt 1Ch timer-control handler, which is called by interrupt 08h about 18.2 times a second. Usually, the clock-tick routine monitors a flag that another routine sets—most often by the code that watches the keyboard or other device for the TSR's activation signal.

Problems arise when a TSR's clock-tick routine preempts normal interrupt 08h processing. Because that interrupt is responsible for a variety of system tasks—turning off disk drive motors, for example—it must finish before the TSR gains control. Also, interrupt 08h must be allowed to reset the 8259A interrupt controller, or future interrupt signals could be locked out, causing a hung system.

The usual solution is to `call` the original interrupt 08h handler in the TSR's own clock-tick routine. Then, after the original code returns, the TSR can safely begin. But, watch out for a second gotcha: the next timer interrupt will again call this same routine, which needs to determine if it has just interrupted itself. A second flag that indicates whether the TSR's clock-tick routine is currently running will handle this problem while allowing critical system functions to continue.

Failing to Deal With Critical Errors

Some of today's TSRs are more sophisticated than many stand-alone applications. Some TSRs read and write disk files, print graphics, and perform other tasks that require careful handling of DOS critical errors.

A common mistake is to ignore this subject and allow whatever critical-error handlers are now in effect to intercept disk and other device errors that may occur while the TSR runs. This is a dangerous practice, and a well-written TSR should install its own critical error handler (interrupt 24h), plus ⟨Ctrl⟩-⟨Break⟩ (interrupt 1Bh) and ⟨Ctrl⟩-C (interrupt 23h) interceptors. Of course, the TSR must restore the original handlers when finished. Writing and installing DOS critical-error handlers is too involved to discuss in detail here. Consult a good DOS reference (see Bibliography) that covers the subject.

A related problem involves DOS's switching of internal stacks to allow certain DOS routines to interrupt themselves. This process permits DOS's own critical error handlers to call DOS routines. But it also complicates the logic of checking whether a DOS routine is active by examining the *In-DOS* flag, which DOS zeros before executing interrupt 24h. While it may seem strange that DOS zeros *In-DOS* while a DOS routine is running, this is necessary because of the way some interrupt 24h handlers fail to return control to their callers. In that event, the *In-DOS* flag would never be reset, causing a hung system.

The fix to this tricky problem is to examine another flag, called the *critical error flag*. For DOS 3.1 and later versions, this 1-byte value is stored just above (at a lower address) than the *In-DOS* flag. In other DOS versions, a TSR's loader needs to search DOS for this byte. (Many DOS references and public domain TSRs explain how to accomplish this.)

Device Drivers—A Quick Review

There are two kinds of device drivers: those that are built into DOS and those that are stored externally in disk files, usually ending with the extension .SYS.

Built-in, or *intrinsic,* drivers need no special installation. The external kind are loaded at boot time by `DEVICE=` commands in the CONFIG.SYS configuration file in the disk's root directory.

Although programming device drivers is a whole new resident-code ball game, the steps to debug them with TD follow the same rules for debugging TSRs. For that reason, I won't include a sample driver here (even a do-nothing shell would take over 500 lines of assembly language code). See the Bibliography for references that describe how to program DOS device drivers.

Debugging Device Drivers

You can debug device drivers locally or remotely, but a remote link may be best. As their names suggest, device drivers control *devices*—and, therefore, they may affect the operation of the computer. Isolating the debugger (and your important files) from the device driver is often wise. It may also be easier to reinstall a modified driver by transferring it to the remote and rebooting than to reset your (probably overstuffed) development system.

Before debugging an installed device driver, try to get as many bugs out of the low-level subroutines by inserting them in small test programs, which you can debug using conventional methods. Device-driver debugging is rarely easy, and a little advance work will help prevent errors in the finished code.

To prepare a device driver for debugging, compile or assemble in the usual way but do not link the result. Instead, use TDSTRIP with the -s and -c options to copy the program's symbol table to a .TDS file and to convert the .EXE code file to .COM format. (You can rename this file's extension to .SYS, although that isn't necessary.) After those steps, insert a line such as DEVICE = C:\WORK\MYDEV.COM into CONFIG.SYS and reboot to install the device driver code.

Run the TDDEV utility to determine the driver's segment address. (You could also insert programming into the driver to report its address at boot time.)

With the .TDS and source-code files in the current directory, start TD with the -sm option to reserve space for loading the symbol table. Use a value about 1.5 times the size of the .TDS file. For example, if the .TDS file is 5,144 bytes long, type the command **td -sm8** to reserve 8K of symbol space. Do not specify a file name when you start the debugger.

Press ⟨**Esc**⟩ to clear TD's startup message, then use the `File:Symbol load` command to load the .TDS file prepared earlier. Use `File:Table relocate` to position the symbols at the segment address of the device driver as reported by TDDEV.

Set breakpoints in the code, open the `Module` view, and use other TD commands to prepare for debugging. When you're ready to begin a test run, use `File:Resident` to push TD into the background. The DOS prompt will reappear, and you can now use whatever commands are appropriate to activate the driver's code. When the device driver reaches a breakpoint, TD will intercept control and let you examine the current state of affairs.

Debugging Device Drivers in Remote Mode

With two computers, TD can run locally while the remote system installs and runs the driver code, which you can transfer from the local computer to the remote using TDRF. Except for this difference, the steps to debug a device driver are similar to those described in the previous section.

Compile normally, and then use TDSTRIP with -s and -c options to create a .TDS symbol table file and to convert the .EXE file to .COM format. Transfer and install the device driver code on the remote computer, and start TDREMOTE on that system. Back at the local keyboard, start TD with the command **td -sm8 -r** to reserve 8K for symbol space (or about 1.5 times the size of the .TDS file) and to engage remote-mode debugging. Adjust the value after -sm to reserve more or less space.

Use `File:Symbol load` and `File:Table relocate` as explained in the previous section to load the .TDS symbol table file and position it to the location of the driver in RAM. Set your breakpoints and choose `File:Resident` to push TDREMOTE into the background, returning the DOS prompt on the remote system. You can now give whatever commands are needed to test the device-driver code.

Note: When debugging in remote mode, the `File:Resident` command makes TDREMOTE go resident, not TD. On the local system, the debugger remains dormant until it intercepts a breakpoint from the remote.

Debugging Interrupt Service Routines

Most TSR's and some device drivers are implemented as interrupt service routines, and the steps outlined in the beginning of this chapter are similar for debugging any ISR.

If possible, incorporate the ISR code inside a shell program that you can run normally. You can then load the entire program into TD for debugging. In that case, you don't need to use any special commands to tell TD where to find the ISR's code.

But, if the ISR is installed permanently in RAM (acting in that case like a TSR), you can strip the symbol table from the code file using TDSTRIP, use the

-sm command to reserve space, and then load the symbols into the debugger with `File:Symbol load` and `File:Table relocate`.

In some cases, you may find it difficult if not impossible to debug hardware ISRs with TD. This is especially true of externally generated interrupts, for example, from an I/O port. You might be able to use TD to investigate portions of the code, but for best results, you'll probably need a hardware debugging board such as the *Periscope III* (see chapter 18).

Debugging "Exec-ed" Processes

Programs that run other programs via DOS "exec" function 4Bh (or a related C function or Pascal procedure) pose a special problem for debugging. After loading the parent program into the debugger and running, how do you tell TD where to find a child process called home by its parent?

In a sense, an "exec-ed" child process is a kind of temporary resident program, and you can use TD's `Resident` and symbol table commands to debug a child process as you do for TSRs and device drivers. But, there's a catch. Unlike other resident programs, a child process doesn't exist in memory until after the parent process calls the "exec" function. For that reason, TD can't set breakpoints in the child, which remains on disk when the parent is loaded into the debugger.

The answer is to run TD in the background and have the child process itself awaken the debugger. To do this, insert an `int 3` breakpoint in the "exec-ed" child. In Pascal, use an `inline( $CC );` instruction. In C, use `asm int 3;`. In assembly language, insert an `int 3` instruction.

Listings 19.5 (PARENT.PAS) and 19.6 (CHILD.PAS) demonstrate how to use this technique to prepare and debug "exec-ed" *Turbo Pascal* programs. The steps are similar for C and assembly language.

Listing 19.5.   PARENT.PAS.

```
 1:  {$M 2048, 0, 0}
 2:  program parent;
 3:  uses DOS;
 4:  var s : string[80];
 5:  begin
 6:     writeln( 'Inside parent' );
 7:     write( 'Enter argument: ' );
 8:     readln( s );
 9:     exec( 'child.exe', s );
10:     writeln( 'Back inside parent again' );
11:  end.
```

Listing 19.6. CHILD.PAS.

```
1:  {$M 2048, 0, 0}
2:  program child;
3:  begin
4:      inline( $CC );
5:      writeln( 'Inside child' );
6:      writeln( 'Argument = ', paramStr(1) );
7:      write( 'Press Enter...' );
8:      readln;
9:  end.
```

When compiling and linking, add debugging information to the child, but not to the parent. (If you need to debug the parent's statements, do that separately.) To compile and link the sample listings, use these two commands:

```
tpc parent
tpc -v child
```

Prepare a symbol table file for the child process, using TDSTRIP's -s option. In this case, enter the command **tdstrip -s child**. Use DIR to find CHILD.TDS's file size. Then, start TD with -sm, specifying about 2.5 times that size in 1,000-byte increments. For instance, enter the command **td -sm4** to reserve 4K. Do not supply a file name.

Note: Tests indicate that debugging child processes with the techniques described here requires more space for the symbol table than for TSRs or device drivers. You may have to experiment with different -sm values to find the correct value for your programs.

When TD's opening screen appears, press ⟨**Esc**⟩ to erase the startup message and then choose the `File:Resident` command (⟨**Alt**⟩-**FR**) to push TD into the background. The DOS prompt will reappear. If you run TDMEM at this point, you'll see where TD is stored in RAM as a TSR (unless you're running TD386).

Now, run the parent program. If you're following along, enter **parent** and press ⟨**Enter**⟩. Type a short string and press ⟨**Enter**⟩ to execute PARENT's `exec` statement and call the child. When the program reaches the `int 3` instruction in the child's code, TD intercepts the breakpoint and opens the `CPU` window.

So you can inspect the child's symbols and source code, use `File:Symbol load` (⟨**Alt**⟩-**FS**) to load the CHILD.TDS symbol table file into the memory you reserved earlier with -sm. (If you receive an error, press ⟨**Esc**⟩ and ⟨**Alt**⟩-**X** to quit TD, then restart the debugger, this time using a larger -sm value.)

You also have to tell TD the child's address so the debugger can match symbols with code and data in RAM. To do this, press ⟨**Alt**⟩-**FT** to choose `File:Table relocate`. Enter **cs** and press ⟨**Enter**⟩. (Note: Also press ⟨**Ctrl**⟩-**O** if `CPU` does not display the child's source code.) You should see one or more source-code lines mixed in with the assembly language disassembly in `CPU`.

Next, open a `Module` window, showing the child's statements. Assuming you have the source-code file available (CHILD.PAS in this example), press ⟨**F3**⟩ and select the module's name. Press ⟨**F5**⟩ to zoom to full screen. You can now set breakpoints, examine variables, and use other TD commands to inspect the child process.

When you're done debugging, if TD is active, press ⟨**Alt**⟩-**X** to quit. This restores conditions as they existed before running the parent program. Or, if the parent program ran to completion and the DOS prompt is displaying, press ⟨**Ctrl**⟩-⟨**Break**⟩ twice to return to TD. Then quit normally.

Note: Be sure to remove any inline `int 3` instructions before compiling the finished child process programs.

Summary

TD can now run in the background, simulating the way a hardware debugger hides behind the DOS scene so you load and debug TSRs and device drivers.

Other related commands let you load symbol tables stored in .TDS files (usually prepared by TDSTRIP) and tell TD the address of the code to which the symbols apply. Using these commands along with TD's resident abilities lets you debug TSRs and device drivers loaded into memory before starting TD.

You can debug TSRs locally or in remote mode using two computers as described in chapter 17. For best results, and to prevent disasters on your development system, it's usually a good idea to debug device drivers remotely.

TD's symbol table and resident commands are also useful for debugging interrupt service routines and "exec-ed" child processes.

Part Four

Data-Structure Guides

Chapter 20

C and C++ Data Structures

 TD'S INSPECTOR WINDOWS are the ultimate data-structure browsers. With inspectors, you can study variables of any types, from the simplest integers to those in a complex linked list.

This chapter and the next two show how to use TD inspectors and the `Watches` view to examine data structures in C, C++, Pascal, and assembly language. Use these chapters as references when you're debugging a program and need more information about how to inspect a real number, an array, or another kind of structure. (See chapters 4 and 5 for general information about using inspectors and the `Watches` view.)

Note: I used Turbo C 2.0 and Turbo C++ 1.0 to prepare the sample source code in this chapter.

Where Are My Variables?

Knowing where variables are often gives useful clues about why a program isn't behaving as expected. In C and C++, there are five basic categories for defining storage space for variables:

- *Static variables* retain their values between function calls. May be scoped globally to an entire program or locally to one or more functions or modules.

- *Automatic variables* are allocated temporary space during a function call. Variables are available only to the declaring function and are stored on the stack.

- *Register variables* behave as automatic variables but are stored in registers, usually SI and DI.

- *Function parameters* are identical to automatic variables but receive initial values from the function's caller. They are always passed by value in C and by value or by reference (address) in C++.

- *Pointer variables* usually address variables allocated in the heap but may point to data stored anywhere in memory.

Read the following notes for tips about using TD to inspect variables created by each of these allocation methods.

Static Variables

Static variables are defined outside any function (including `main()`) or with the keywords `static` and `extern`. Static variables retain their values between function calls, but their scope extends only to their declaring module or function. When declared `extern`, a variable has a global scope and refers to a fixed location that's allocated space elsewhere.

TD can inspect and watch static variables of both kinds. To avoid confusion when monitoring `static` variables, it's a good idea to assign them unique names. For example, if you define `int count` in `main()` and `static int count` in a function `f()`, the compiler allocates space for two distinct `count` variables at two different locations. But while debugging, it may not be clear which `count` value you're viewing.

When you can't change variable names to resolve this kind of conflict, use a pound sign (#) to specify the variable's scope. For example, to inspect `count` in function `f()`, enter **#f#count** as the variable name. To inspect the same variable in `main()`, enter **#main#count**. This trick lets you monitor a variable without having to switch to the module in which the variable is defined.

Automatic Variables

Automatic variables are stored on the stack by the function that declares them. Because that allocation occurs each time the function runs, automatic variables do not retain their values between function calls. Beginning C programmers often forget this and mistakenly assume they can reuse the value assigned to `int count` on subsequent calls to function `f()`. To do that, you would have to define the variable as `static`, reserving permanent storage for its value.

When inspecting an automatic variable, pay attention to the address line in the inspector window. The segment value should match the stack segment, which you can determine with `View:Registers`. If the segment values don't match, then the variable is not automatic. Perhaps it's defined to be `static`, or perhaps due to a typing error, the program refers to a global `count` instead of a local `cnt`.

Register Variables

Many C compilers store `int`-size automatic variables in registers SI and DI. These *register variables* behave as other automatic values—they don't retain their values between function calls, and they are scoped to their declaring function.

In an inspection window, TD replaces a register variable's address with the word `Register`. (See Figure 20.1 for two samples.) When you see this word, you know that the value is stored in a processor register, not on the stack with other automatic variables. Unfortunately, TD does not show you which register holds which value. But you can quickly find this out by opening `View:Registers`. If SI and DI hold the same value, change one of the two registers and observe which inspector also changes.

 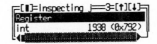

Figure 20.1. Inspecting two register variables.

Function Parameters

Arguments are passed to function parameters either directly by value or indirectly by address on the stack. C functions always pass parameters by value, but that value may be a pointer to another location where the actual value is stored. In C++, arguments can be passed by value or by reference (address).

Confusing the kind of parameter a function uses can lead to all kinds of bugs. For example, don't write code like this:

```
void g(int x, int *y)
{
   x = 10;
   y = 30;      /* ??? */
}
```

When function `g()` runs, the assignment to `y` is stored in the pointer's offset value, probably not the intended result. Future assignments to `*y` will then store values at that modified location, which may belong to another variable or even part of the program's code. The correct assignment is:

```
*y = 30;
```

Knowing where your variables are is a good way to prevent this sort of mistake. Use TD inspectors to confirm that your variables are where you expect them to be. As Figure 20.2 illustrates, a direct parameter's address will always be a simple value like `@8523:FFD6`, the segment part of which (hexadecimal `8523`) should match the stack segment register SS—a fact you can verify with `View:Registers`. An indirect parameter such as `int *y` has the two-part address `@8523:FFD8 : ds:0610 [_q]` where hexadecimal `8523:FFD8` is the address of the pointer variable, and `ds:0610` is the address where that pointer points. If TD recognizes the addressed value, it also displays the variable's name prefaced with an underbar in brackets.

 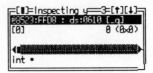

Figure 20.2.   Inspecting direct (left) and indirect (right) function parameters.

Get used to these formats. A quick glance at an inspector window will tell you whether your parameters are passed by value or by address—and that knowledge is often enough to locate and fix a bug that's caused by confusing the two conventions.

Pointer Variables

Later on in this chapter we'll take a closer look at C pointers and the bugs that can arise due to pointer abuse. But the key element to keep in mind while debugging is that a pointer is a two-faced critter: it exists somewhere in memory, and it addresses a variable that exists somewhere else.

As explained in the previous section, a pointer always has two parts: an address such as `@7411:FFD6` where the pointer is stored and the address where the pointer points. If that location is in a known segment, TD displays the appropriate segment register, for example, `@ds:0472`. This gives you a good way to check that variables are located where they should be.

> Hint: Don't assume that an address in the form `@ds:xxxx` references a global variable in the data segment. It might address a dynamic variable declared on the heap, which in some memory models shares the same segment space with the data segment and the stack.

When inspecting pointer values, the inspector window displays the value of the addressed item. Because pointers and arrays are virtually interchangeable in C, the value often shows up as an array index, for example, `[0] 100 (0x64)`. If you move the selector bar to that line and press ⟨**Enter**⟩, TD opens a second inspector window for the value addressed by the pointer.

Size of Variables

Every data type, and therefore every variable of any type, has a size equal to the number of bytes required to store that value in memory. To verify how much space a variable occupies, use `Data:Evaluate/modify` (press ⟨**Ctrl**⟩-**F4**) and enter **sizeof(v)** where *v* is the name of a variable.

For example, to find the size of a variable `float fp`, enter **sizeof(fp)** in the `Evaluate/modify` window's `Expression` area. When I did this, TD reported that `fp` was an `unsigned int 4 (0x4)`. This indicates that a variable of type `float` takes 4 bytes. The `unsigned int` refers to the data type of the `sizeof()` pseudo function, not to the data type of the inspected variable.

Take care when using `sizeof()` not to introduce unexpected side effects that will affect your debugging session. If the program declares a function `f()`, the expression **sizeof(f())** tells you the number of bytes returned by the function, but it also executes the function code.

Internal Variables

Most programs carry a lot of excess baggage including variables used internally by library runtime routines. To examine those variables, use `View:Variables` and scroll through the top pane of this two-pane window.

In many cases, TD knows the names but not the types and sizes of many library variables. For example, `????` is listed as the value for `DGROUP@`. To find the actual value, position the highlight bar over the variable name and press ⟨**Enter**⟩. Although this opens an inspector window for the variable, the window still doesn't show the value or size. But no matter; just press ⟨**Alt**⟩-**VD** to open a `Dump` window, which picks up the starting address from the inspector and shows you the value in RAM for this unknown item. If you try this, you'll see the word value that locates the beginning of the data-segment group. You can use the same trick to examine other internal system variables of unrecognized types.

Viewing Local Symbols

The bottom pane of the `View:Variables` window shows all the local symbols that are within the scope of the current function. Use this command for a quick peek at a function's data—it's much easier than opening inspector windows for all local symbols or adding them to `Watches` one by one. The window pane also shows argument values passed to function parameters.

> Hint: When single-stepping through a program's function calls, you may have to press ⟨F8⟩ to execute the function's startup code before the local symbols will come into view.

By the way, the bottom pane in `View:Variables` is useful for spotting bad assignments to indirect parameters, as in the earlier example where the statement `y = 30` incorrectly changes the pointer address value for a parameter declared as `int *y`. While single-stepping through a function's code, watch the `Variables` window for changes to similar indirect parameter *addresses,* which should remain constant under most circumstances. Although this takes time, any faulty assignments will be obvious.

Examining Basic Data Types

Not counting `void`, there are four basic C data types: `char`, `int`, `float`, and `enumeration`. Most program variables are declared to be one of these types, or one of their signed, unsigned, long, and short variations. Of course, TD can display all such variables, showing their names, data types, current values, and locations in memory.

You already learned many ways to view variables, but if you're reading this chapter out of order, here's a quick review. Most of the time, the easiest technique is to position the cursor on the variable's name in the `Module` window and press ⟨**Ctrl**⟩-**I**. This opens an inspector window that gives you the most extensive information possible about the variable's address, value, and type. You can also press ⟨**Ctrl**⟩-**W** to add the variable to the `Watches` window, which shows less detailed information but lets you view several variables at once. Or, use `View:Variables` to examine all of your program's global and local symbols. You can also enter a variable's name into the `Evaluate/modify` dialog box.

Char Types

Figure 20.3 shows three variables, `c` a plain `char`, `uc` an `unsigned char`, and `sc` a `signed char`. Notice that TD displays `char` and `signed char`, which are equivalent, as type `char`.

When displaying `char` variables, just below the variable's address, TD shows the data type plus three information fields: the value expressed as a character,

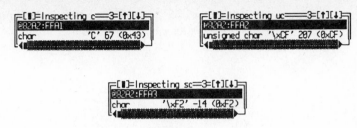

Figure 20.3. Inspecting C's char types.

the value in signed or unsigned decimal, and the value in unsigned hexadecimal (unless you changed the `Integer format` setting with `Options:Display options`). Standard ASCII characters are shown for common values; others are shown as *escaped* hexadecimal values such as '\xCF' and '\xF2'. The unsigned hexadecimal values are in standard C notation—for example, 0xCF for hex CF.

Int Types

Figure 20.4 shows inspector windows for the five integer types: `int`, `short int`, `long int`, `unsigned int`, and `unsigned long`. Following the address of each variable is the type and value in decimal and hexadecimal in parentheses.

A useful trick is to use an inspector window as a negative-to-positive value converter. Even if a variable's data type is unsigned, TD still allows assignments of negative values to that variable, providing a quick way to convert negative to unsigned positive decimal equivalents. For example, changing an `unsigned int` to **-432** displays **65104** in the inspector—the equivalent positive value in decimal.

Float Types

The three floating point (or *real*) data types in C are `float`, `double`, and `long double`. Figure 20.5 shows example inspector windows for each of these types

Figure 20.4. Inspecting C's integer types.

and also shows the two ways that TD displays floating-point values: in decimal (3.14159 and 0.01) and in scientific notation (1e + 21). In general, very large and small values are displayed in scientific notation while other values are shown in decimal.

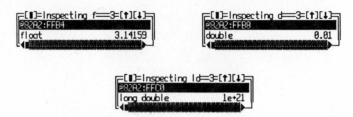

Figure 20.5.   Inspecting C's floating-point types.

When you enter new floating-point values—usually by opening an inspector window and typing the new value—TD may show a different value from the one you enter. For example, if you type **10e + 20** for a `long double`, the inspector window will show the value as **1e+21**, which, of course, is the same. Similarly, if you enter **1e − 2**, the inspector displays the result as **0.01**.

One of the most common errors is to expect perfect accuracy from floating-point calculations. Floating-point values are stored in fixed-width variables, and for that reason, some values are approximate. Don't use floating-point variables to count your chickens. You may get only half a bird.

> Note: TD faithfully emulates an 80x87 and can use a math coprocessor if your system has one to evaluate real-number expressions.

Enumeration Types

Enumeration types add clarity to C programs and, therefore, also serve as powerful weapons in the fight against bugs. A typical enumeration type is:

```
enum Boolean { NO, YES };
```

The new type `Boolean` is associated with two constant symbols, `NO` and `YES`. Internally, the compiler represents those symbols as `int` values: 0 for `NO` and 1 for `YES`. You can assign other values to enumerated constants, but usually, it's best to let the compiler make the assignments for you.

After defining an enumeration type, you can create variables in the usual way. For example, this declares a variable `choice` of type `Boolean` and sets the initial value to `YES`:

```
enum Boolean choice = YES;
```

Examining `choice` with a TD inspector window (see Figure 20.6) shows the address and data type as usual. It also shows the enumerated constant value (`YES`) plus the underlying `int` value (1). Being able to examine enumeration types this way is a useful debugging tool.

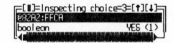

Figure 20.6.   Inspecting a C enumeration type.

Unfortunately, TD does not permit you to use constant identifiers in breakpoint expressions. For example, to set a breakpoint for when `choice` equals `YES`, you have to enter **choice == 1** using `Breakpoints:Expression true global`. Apparently, TD does not recognize enumerated constants as program symbols, only as translated values in inspector windows. It also does not let you enter constant names to change an enumeration's value. To set `choice` to `NO`, you have to enter **0**—you can't type **NO**.

Despite these restrictions, with a little extra programming, you can get TD to cough up all the enumerated symbols it associates with an enumeration data type. To do this, construct a small `for` loop in your code—something like this:

```
for (choice = 0; choice < 10; choice++)
    printf("%d\n", choice);
```

Even though `choice` is of type `Boolean`, I wrote the loop to cycle ten times to cover all the possible enumerated constants. For other enumeration types, you might loop 10, 20, or 100 times. The exact number isn't important.

Next, load the program into TD and set a code breakpoint (⟨**F2**⟩) on the `printf` statement. Open `View:Breakpoints`, highlight the breakpoint, and press ⟨**Ctrl**⟩-**S** to set options. Change `Action` to `Log` and set `Action expression` to **choice**. Press ⟨**Enter**⟩ to close the options window and press ⟨**F9**⟩. When the loop finishes, open the `Log` window (⟨**Alt**⟩-**VL**). You'll see all of the enumerated constants (plus others that you can ignore) showing their symbolic names and `int` values.

Constants

There are two kinds of constants in C: macros created by `#define` and stored variables that don't change during the course of a program run.

Defined macros are not variables. They are simply text that the compiler inserts in place of the macro's symbol. Once you compile the program, the macro symbols are no longer available, and for that reason, you can't inspect or watch them with TD.

However, TD recognizes constants defined with the `const` keyword. For example, you might create these constant values:

```
const int INTCONST = 1234;
const char CHARCONST = 'x';
const float FPCONST = 3.14159;
```

Figure 20.7 shows sample inspector windows for these three constants, sometimes also called *static variables*. While debugging, you can watch and inspect constants just as you can variables.

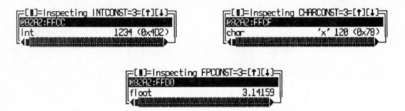

Figure 20.7. Inspecting C constants.

Hint: Unlike the compiler, TD allows you to change a constant's value. This is not a bug in the debugger—it's a feature that makes experimenting with new constant values possible without having to recompile the sources.

Examining Derived Data Types

The range of basic data types in C is sparse, but well-chosen. Together with the basic `int`, `char`, and other types, the language's *derived types*—arrays, strings, bit fields, structures, and unions—make it possible to build any data structure you can imagine.

Being able to peer into the dark corners of even the most complex data structures is essential for finding bugs that demolish your carefully constructed C castles. As the following sections explain, with TD's inspector windows, you can shine light onto arrays, strings, bit fields, and other structures.

Arrays

Figure 20.8 (left) shows an inspector window opened to an array of floating-point values defined as `float fp_array[10]`. The inspector displays the data type of that and similar arrays as `float [10]`. As in all inspector windows, the top line below the window's border shows the variable's address—the location of the first array element at index `[0]`. Below the address are some (or, for short arrays, all) of the items in the array, with the index values displayed in brackets at left and the array element values at right. Press the cursor or page movement keys to scroll this part of the window to see other array elements. At the bottom of the window (below the horizontal scroll bar), you see the data type and array range for the highlighted line above—`float [10]` when the address is highlighted, as it is in the figure, or `float` for an individual array element.

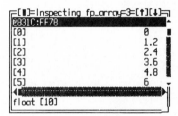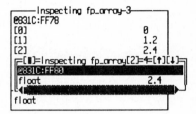

Figure 20.8. Inspecting an array.

When inspecting an array with dozens or more elements, it may be inconvenient to scroll to the values you need to see. In that case, press ⟨**Ctrl**⟩-**R** to select the inspector window's `Range` command and enter the starting index, a comma, and a number of array elements to view. For example, to display ten values starting with indexed entry `[20]`, enter **20,10**. You'll then see values for indexes `[20]` through `[29]` in the window.

Figure 20.8 (right) shows how to examine an individual element stored in an array. To create this image, I moved the selector bar to index entry `[2]` and pressed ⟨**Enter**⟩. This pops up a new inspector window for that array element. The window title `Inspecting fp_array[2]` tells you this is an element from an array and not a common floating-point variable. Also, the smaller inspector shows the address of the inspected element, useful knowledge for debugging programs that calculate array-element addresses.

> Hint: When viewing multiple inspector windows this way, press ⟨**Esc**⟩ to close only the topmost window. Press ⟨**F3**⟩ to close the topmost window plus all others.

Unlike inspectors, when adding arrays to `Watches`, you'll see only as many array elements in braces as can fit horizontally on screen. Although you can scroll left and right to view other elements, it's easier to view multiple array elements with inspectors.

But it's often useful to add a *single* array element to `Watches`. To do that, press ⟨**F6**⟩ to make `Watches` the current window and enter an array name with a bracketed index, for example, **fp_array[4]**. To switch from one array element to another, position the highlight bar on the array name (it can be an indexed element or the entire array) and press ⟨**Enter**⟩. This opens an `Edit watch expression` window with the name of the array ready for editing. (You can also press ⟨**Ctrl**⟩-**E** to do the same, but pressing ⟨**Enter**⟩ is easier.) Use the cursor movement keys to edit the array index value to display in `Watches`.

Arrays of Pointers

Pointers are covered in more detail later in this chapter. But arrays of pointers are so common in C programming, they deserve special mention here.

Figure 20.9 (left) shows an inspector window for an array of pointers to integer values. (In practice, this may not be a useful structure, but the principles apply to any array of pointers to other kinds of data types.) I defined the array as `int *ap[10]` and initialized it by allocating heap space to each array element. Because those elements are addressed by pointers, they show as addresses to the right of the indexed values in the inspector window. The segment portion of those addresses is listed as `ds:`, indicating in this case that the heap is inside the program's data segment.

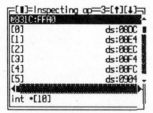 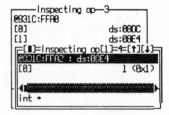

Figure 20.9. Inspecting an array of pointers.

To create the image to the right of Figure 20.9, I positioned the highlight bar on index entry [1] and pressed ⟨**Enter**⟩. This opened another inspector window for the array element—the pointer, not the value to which it points. You can tell this because the top line of the new inspector shows a double address, listing the location of the pointer (its position inside the array). Because the variable is a pointer, the inspector also shows the addressed location, `ds:08E4`. At that address is an integer value equal to 1. Notice how the inspector displays the pointer as though it were an array with a lone indexed position ([0]). Pointers and arrays are practically equivalent in C, and, therefore, TD displays array elements in arrays of pointers as though they addressed other arrays.

> Note: In Figure 20.9 (right), if you were to move the highlight bar to [0] and press ⟨**Enter**⟩, TD would open an inspector window for a simple `int` variable at `ds:08E4`. This is not necessary, however, because the inspector already shows the value at that location.

Strings

Character strings in C are implemented as arrays of `char`; therefore, you can use the same techniques for inspecting strings as you can for other arrays.

Figure 20.10 shows an inspector window opened to a string variable defined as `char *s`. Because this allocates space for a pointer (`s`), the inspector's address line shows both the location of that pointer plus the addressed location. To the extreme right, the address line also shows the first few characters in the string. Below that line are the individual array elements of type `char`, also showing the characters in the string.

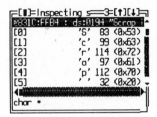

Figure 20.10.   Inspecting a C character string.

Because an inspector window lists string array elements vertically, it may be difficult to use this method to examine lengthy strings. For easier viewing, open the inspector to the string pointer as shown in Figure 20.10. Then, press **⟨Cursor Down⟩** to highlight the first character at index [0]. Press **⟨Alt⟩-VD** to open a `Dump` window to that address. This displays the string as a block of bytes, showing all of a string's characters in a group.

Note: If you press **⟨Alt⟩-VD** with the highlight bar on the inspector window's address line, you won't see the string's characters. You'll see the memory allocated to the string *pointer*—probably not what you want. Remember to highlight the first character in the string before opening the `Dump` view.

Bit Fields

Bit fields are highly system-dependent and, therefore, highly susceptible to catching bugs. Often, a bit-field structure is used to access peripheral registers or operating system switches, such as the DOS keyboard flag, as in this sample:

```
struct kb_flag {
    unsigned int right_shift  : 1;
    unsigned int left_shift   : 1;
    unsigned int ctl_shift    : 1;
```

```
  unsigned int alt_shift    : 1;
  unsigned int scroll_state : 1;
  unsigned int num_state    : 1;
  unsigned int caps_state   : 1;
  unsigned int ins_state    : 1;
};
```

Usually, programs address structures like `kb_flag` using a pointer variable, which you might declare this way:

```
struct kb_flag far *key_state;
```

Another reason that this and similar declarations are so bug-prone is that different compilers may allocate individual fields in the bit-field structure either from top to bottom or from bottom to top. Obviously, declaring fields in the wrong order is likely to cause problems—such as the ⟨Caps Lock⟩ light coming on when you press ⟨**Left Shift**⟩.

TD can help you locate such errors. As Figure 20.11 (left) shows, a bit-field structure in an inspector window looks very much like an array, but instead of index values, individual bit fields are listed to the left with the field names and sizes in bits separated by colons.

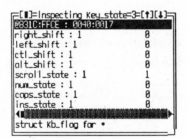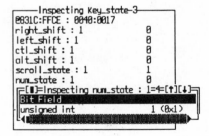

Figure 20.11. Inspecting a bit-field structure.

As with other multipart structures, you can highlight an individual field and press ⟨**Enter**⟩ to examine that bit (or bits) more closely. For example, to create the image in Figure 20.11 (right), I highlighted `num_state` and pressed ⟨**Enter**⟩ to pop up another `inspector`, which shows the value of that field as an `unsigned int`. If you use a lot of bit fields, you'll find this process to be very handy for extracting values from packed bit structures. It's a good way to confirm that your program's logic is extracting the right bits from the right places.

Figure 20.11 also illustrates a problem with TD that can sometimes cause headaches, especially when debugging programs that directly access resources through bit fields. In this case, `key_state` points to a byte that keeps the current status of ⟨Shift⟩ and various other keys such as ⟨Num Lock⟩ and ⟨Caps⟩. To initialize that pointer, you can execute the statement:

```
key_state = (struct kb_flag far *) MK_FP(0x0040, 0x0017);
```

If you then load the program into TD and open an inspector window for `key_state`, you may be surprised to discover that pressing the listed keys does not cause the expected changes in the bit-field values listed in the window. This is because your program and the debugger share the keyboard, and the current bit values won't show up in the inspector until the debugger releases control to your code or until it accesses the inspected register or variable.

For instance, examine the right side of Figure 20.11 closely. Notice that the value for `num_state` in the partially covered window is 0 but that the same value in the smaller foreground window is 1. This discrepancy arose because I pressed ⟨**Num Lock**⟩ after opening the inspector to `key_state`, then I opened the second inspector for the `num_state` bit field. This caused TD to reexamine the keyboard byte flag in memory and display the new value for the inspected field.

In similar circumstances, you may have to open or reopen an inspector window to be sure you are viewing the current bit-field values after those values are updated by events external to the debugger and your code. For common program variables, TD automatically updates inspected and watched values when they change. But for system-dependent items like the keyboard flags, an inspector operates more like a camera that takes a snapshot of memory at the time you open the window. TD does not update the "pictures" of those values when they change.

A common `struct` technique—unnamed bit fields—throws TD for a loop. Here's a typical example:

```
struct no_name {
    unsigned int x : 3;
    unsigned int   : 3;   /* unnamed bit field */
    unsigned int y : 2;
};
```

Two named bit fields x and y are separated by an unnamed 3-bit field. Apparently, *Turbo C* doesn't include information in the program's symbol table for unnamed bit fields, causing TD to miscalculate the location of any following fields. In this example, because TD is unaware of the unnamed field's existence, the debugger is unable to display field y's correct value in an inspector window. Unfortunately, there seems to be no easy work-around for this problem—except, that is, to use a `Dump` window to view `struct` variables and extract bit-field values yourself.

Structures

C structures can house variables of many different data types under a `struct`'s roof. Inspectors make it easy to examine all the bits and pieces that make up even the most complex multipart structures.

As an example, consider the `palettetype` structure from the *Borland Graphics Interface* (BGI) library supplied with *Turbo C.* This structure is declared as:

```
struct palettetype {
   unsigned char size;
   signed char colors[MAXCOLORS + 1];
};
```

A `palettetype` structure has two fields: a `size` and an array of `colors`. To define storage for variables of and pointers to `palettetype` structures, you can write:

```
struct palettetype color_palette;
struct palettetype *cp_ptr = &color_palette;
```

Here, `color_palette` is a variable of type `palettetype`, and `cp_ptr` is initialized as a pointer to that structure. Figure 20.12 shows inspector windows opened to these variables and to various elements in the multipart structures.

Figure 20.12. Inspecting a complex structure.

As you can see in the sample inspectors, TD shows all of a structure's fields, and it lets you highlight individual fields and press ⟨**Enter**⟩ to open additional inspector windows for those elements. In cases where a field is itself a derived type, you can open even more inspector windows to travel deeply into a structure's back roads.

Viewing complex structures in the `Watches` window is not as handy. Because this window shows data horizontally, watching an entire structure usually shows only the first field or two, and it requires you to scroll the window horizontally to see more of the structure's contents. For that reason, I prefer to inspect structures with inspectors.

But, you can add individual structure fields to `Watches`, similar to the way you can watch individual array elements. To do that, press ⟨**Ctrl**⟩-⟨**F7**⟩ (`Data:Add watch`), and enter the `struct`'s name, a period, and the field you want to examine, for example, **color—palette.size**. `Watches` will then show only the `size` field in the window.

Unions

Unions are structures of fields that are stored at the same location. A union lets you create variables that can hold more than one type of data in the same memory space, but only one variable at a time. For example, here's how to declare a union `fair_share` and variable `fp_val` with `float` and `char` array fields that share the same address, which you might do to "convert" a floating-point value to an array of bytes:

```
union fair_share {
   float fp_field;
   char fp_chars[ sizeof(float) ];
} fp_val;
```

Figure 20.13 (left) shows an inspector window opened to the `fp_val` union. Except for the `union` keyword at the bottom of the window, the inspector looks the same as it does when showing a common `struct`. To the right of the figure, another inspector is opened to the `fp_chars` field. Notice that the address of this field (`@831C:FFCA`) is identical to the address of the union, even though `fp_chars` is the second declared field. This fact plus the `union` keyword tell you this is a union where all fields have the same addresses, and not a common `struct`, where fields are displaced from one another. Because variables of `structs` and `unions` look very similar in TD inspectors, you need to look carefully in order to tell the two constructions apart.

As with other complex data types, inserting a union into `Watches` may be more confusing than helpful. Complex unions require you to scroll horizontally to view more than the first field or two. But you can watch individual fields, separated from their union identifiers with periods, for example, `fp_val.fp_field` and `fp_val.fp_chars`.

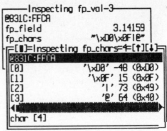

Figure 20.13.   Inspecting a union.

Pointers

Pointers get more than their fair share of blame for bugs in C programs. Or, maybe the stigma is deserved. Pointers can address variables of any type anywhere in memory. Most beginning C programmers find pointer concepts difficult to learn, and compared with other data types, pointer syntax, with its cryptic symbols `*`, `->`, and `&`, can be confusing to read and understand.

Following are several tips about using TD inspectors and other features to view pointers and the data they address.

Pointers and Arrays

When you open an inspector window to a pointer variable, TD displays both the address of that variable and the address to which the pointer points. Figure 20.14 (left) shows this for a pointer defined as `int *buffer`. The first line inside the window lists the two addresses, often with a segment register (`ds` in the figure). Sometimes, just inspecting the pointer's address values can find bugs caused by pointer variables that aim at the wrong targets.

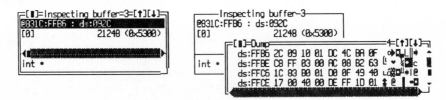

Figure 20.14.   Inspecting a pointer variable.

Figure 20.14 (right) shows what happened when I typed ⟨**Alt**⟩-**VD** with the address line highlighted as shown to the left. This opened a `Dump` window to the location where the pointer variable is stored, showing the pointer's byte values 2C 09. To follow this 16-bit pointer value to its destination, you could move the cursor to the first of those two bytes and press ⟨**Ctrl**⟩-**FO** (Follow:Offset to data). This will replace the Dump window's contents with the data at that location. Notice that the pointer's byte values in the Dump window are in byte-swapped order.

If this were a far 32-bit pointer, you could press ⟨**Ctrl**⟩-**FS** to select Follow:Segment:offset to data, replacing the data in the Dump view with the bytes at that location. Or, to do the same directly from the inspector, highlight the line that begins with index [0] and press ⟨**Alt**⟩-**VD**. Either of these methods shows the contents of memory addressed by a pointer variable.

Typed and Untyped Pointers

Pointers that address variables of known data types—int, char, struct, and so on—are called *typed pointers*. Other pointers that address a location in memory of unknown type are called *untyped* or *generic pointers*. In C's recent past, char * was the de facto generic pointer data type, leading to some confusion between that and a string pointer, both of which share the identical syntax. Today, void * is the new standard for declaring generic pointers.

Figure 20.15 (left) shows an inspector window opened to a void pointer defined as void *nothing. To the right is another inspector, which I opened by first pressing ⟨**Cursor Down**⟩ to highlight nothing's index [0] and then pressing ⟨**Enter**⟩. Because a generic pointer of type void * addresses nothing in particular, TD shows the data type and value for the addressed information as *** UNKNOWN ***.

Figure 20.15.   Inspecting a void pointer.

Many times, you'll know that void pointers actually address a specific data type or structure. To see that data in a more appropriate form, recast the pointer to the other type. First, open an inspector window for the void pointer as illustrated in Figure 20.15 (left). Then press ⟨**Ctrl**⟩-**N** to select the inspector's New expression command. Recast the pointer—for example, enter **(int *)nothing**—and the inspector window will show the pointer type as int *. It will also display the addressed data as type int.

NULL Pointers

Whether initialized or not, a pointer always points *somewhere*. But there is an exception to that rule. When equal to the constant NULL, equivalent to 0, a pointer addresses no specific location.

Unfortunately, TD doesn't display the word NULL as the value of a pointer that equals NULL. Instead, it displays the pointer's offset value as 0000. When you see 0000 to the right in the address line of an inspector window opened to any pointer, it tells you this is a NULL pointer.

Also be aware of a subtle difference between near and far pointers that equal NULL. For a near pointer, TD might display the address as ds:0000, which you can easily misinterpret as meaning a pointer to the first byte of the data segment. This is not the case. A near 16-bit pointer's segment value is assumed to be relative to a segment register, usually DS. That's why TD displays ds: as the pointer's segment. Even so, if the offset equals 0000, it's still a NULL pointer.

Contrasting that, TD fully displays a NULL far pointer as 0000:0000. Logically, both near and far NULL pointers are equivalent—they both address nothing in particular. But TD displays them differently.

Files

Typically, files in C are defined as FILE *stream. When you open an inspector window to a file variable, the results will be similar to those shown in Figure 20.16.

Figure 20.16.   Inspecting a FILE structure.

A FILE is a structure defined in the header file STDIO.H. Like all structures, a FILE variable has various fields that TD can display symbolically. For debugging, the fd (file descriptor), buffer, curp (current pointer), and token fields are most useful. The file descriptor is the DOS handle associated with this file. The buffer and curp are pointers to the stream's I/O buffer. And token should always equal the offset address of the FILE variable—it's used to verify that this is a valid FILE structure.

A useful trick is to set a breakpoint for any changes to the stream's buffer. This can halt a program every time it reads a new block of data from disk or when the code writes any data to the buffer through the stream. To set this kind of breakpoint, assuming the FILE variable is a pointer named stream, press ⟨**Alt**⟩-**B** to open the Breakpoints menu and choose the Changed memory global command. Enter **stream-⟩buffer, stream-⟩bsize** to monitor the I/O buffer for changes. Then, press ⟨**F9**⟩ to run.

Debugging Dynamic Structures

Dynamic data structures such as trees and lists are composed of variables (usually structs) that contain pointers to other variables, most often of the same data types. TD makes fast work of these *recursive data structures*, which can be tricky to debug.

Using inspector windows, it's possible to examine dynamic structures and to follow the links that join them in memory. For example, consider a tree of node structures, which you might define as:

```
struct item {
   char *data;
   struct item *left;
   struct item *right;
};
struct item *root;
```

The struct item contains three fields: a character pointer to the data for this node and two recursive pointers to other structures of this same type. The variable root addresses the base or root of the tree, formed by assigning left and right addresses after comparing new strings alphabetically with the data stored previously in one or more other nodes. (Most good C tutorials cover the algorithms for creating trees.)

To inspect a tree (or any other linked data structure), open an initial inspector window to the root structure (see Figure 20.17). Then, highlight one of the structure's pointers and press ⟨**Enter**⟩ to open another inspector to the addressed item that's hanging out on that branch of the tree. Keep repeating those steps until you see as much of the tree as you need.

When opening many inspector windows this way, depending on how much RAM is available, you may receive an out-of-memory error from TD. If this happens, press ⟨**Esc**⟩ to close some of the inspectors that you no longer need. After closing a few unused windows, you should have enough memory to continue viewing more of the tree.

Another way to conserve memory when inspecting linked nodes is to open an inspector window to the root pointer, highlight one of the structure's pointer fields (left or right in Figure 20.17), and press ⟨**Ctrl**⟩-**D** to choose the Descend command. This reuses the current inspector for the addressed data, which doesn't require TD to allocate additional memory for another inspector window.

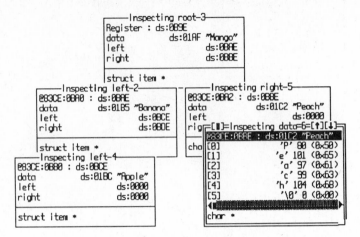

Figure 20.17.   Inspecting a tree.

Pseudo Variables

Turbo C defines several pseudo variables that let program statements refer directly to processor registers. For example, if you assign a value to variable _SI, the compiler generates a machine-code instruction that changes the SI register.

TD recognizes all *Turbo C* pseudo variables, and you can use them to set breakpoints and watches and to open inspector windows for processor registers. To see how this works, use the Data menu's Inspect command and enter **_AX** when prompted for the item to inspect. (You must type **AX** in uppercase.) Also open the Registers window and step through a few program statements—you'll see the value in the inspector updated to match AX's register value.

Apparently, to make life with pseudo variables simple, TD considers AX, ax, and _AX to all refer to the AX register, even though *Turbo C* recognizes only _AX. But, if your program declares a variable of the same name—ax or AX, for example—then to view the register, you must type **_AX** with the underbar.

Debugging C++ Objects

Objects in C++ encapsulate code and data, much the way structs can collect variables of different data types. A C++ object declaration, or *class,* usually includes one or more *instance variables* (for example, pointers and variables of various types) plus *methods* that carry out the class's tasks. Classes can inherit the properties of one or more other classes, and they can declare virtual methods that can change the behavior of existing code at runtime, a process known as *polymorphism.* As mentioned in earlier chapters, these concepts come under the heading of *object-oriented programming,* or OOP.

When debugging C++ programs that declare one or more classes, TD enables the `View:Hierarchy` command, which is useful for investigating class relationships, and to locate the source code for class methods. Also, inspector windows can display object classes and *instances* (variables) of those classes, making TD a powerful tool for debugging and browsing C++ objects.

Watching Objects

Because objects tend to be complex entities, viewing them in the `Watches` window is possible, but not usually convenient. `Watches` displays variables, including objects, all on one line, and for that reason, I prefer to use inspectors to look inside objects.

As with other kinds of structures, however, it's often useful to monitor individual object data fields in `Watches`. To do that, press ⟨**Alt**⟩-**DW** and enter an expression with an object instance's name, a period, and a field—for example, **myobject.mydata** or **mybike.topSpeed**.

> Note: You can add only object instances and fields in an instance, but not classes, to the `Watches` view.

Browsing Object Classes

Be sure that you understand the difference between a class and an instance. An object class is a template that programs can use to define instances (variables) of that class. Instances are stored in memory like other variables; classes aren't.

There are two ways to inspect object classes: in the `Hierarchy` view and in an inspector window. Opening the `Hierarchy` window displays object names sorted alphabetically at left and a tree of object relationships at right (see Figure 20.18).

The right side of the `Hierarchy` view is divided into two panes. The top pane lists class names along the left edge, attached by lines to descendants below and to the right. For example, in the figure, there are two "root" ancestors: `Vehicle` and `Boat`. Descended directly from `Vehicle` are `FourWheeler` and `TwoWheeler`. A single object, `Amphibious`, is descended from two other objects, `Boat` and `FourWheeler`, an example of *multiple inheritance.*

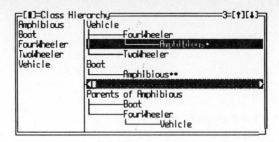

Figure 20.18.   Viewing C++ object relationships in the Hierarchy view.

Notice that **Amphibious** is followed by one or two asterisks. The primary class has two asterisks; each secondary class has one. When a class is marked this way, the **Hierarchy** view's lower right pane lists that object's parents, showing the complement of the information above. (If all objects have only single parents, this pane does not appear.) As Figure 20.18 shows, **Amphibious** lists its immediate parents as **Boat** and **FourWheeler** (it could have more than two parents). This window also lists an object's distant relatives, in this case, the single grandparent **Vehicle**.

The **Hierarchy** view is easy to use (see chapter 5 for more information). After selecting a class at left by typing part or all of its name or by using the cursor and page movement keys, press ⟨**Ctrl**⟩-**T** to move the cursor to the class tree pane, showing the class's position among its relatives. Or, press ⟨**Tab**⟩ to move from pane to pane. After highlighting a class name in any pane, press ⟨**Enter**⟩ to open an inspector window, listing the items declared in the class *plus* all items inherited from ancestor objects (see Figure 20.19).

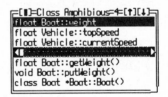

Figure 20.19.   Inspecting a C++ object class.

The top portion of a class inspector lists the object's declared and inherited fields. Because this is only a class, not an instance, fields do not have values, and you can't change them.

The bottom portion of a class inspector lists the methods available to instances of this class. Press ⟨**Tab**⟩ to move the cursor into this pane, select a method, and press ⟨**Enter**⟩ to open another inspector window, showing the method's address. Press ⟨**Enter**⟩ once again to hop to the method's source code in the **Module** view—a neat way to browse through all of a program's methods. (TD must be able to find the method's source-code file, or this tip won't work.)

> Note: When the word **Class** appears in an inspector's window title (see Figure 20.19), you are viewing an object class, not an instance.

Browsing Object Instances

Listing 20.1 is the sample *Turbo C++* program that I used to prepare the object class and instance figures in this section. To keep the listing short, the program is only a demonstration, and it doesn't perform any useful tasks. But if you want to experiment with TD's commands for viewing classes and instances, enter the text and compile from the DOS command line with the command **tcc -v vehicle.cpp**.

Listing 20.1. VEHICLE.CPP.

```
 1:  // vehicle.cpp for TC++ 1.0
 2:
 3:  #include <stdio.h>
 4:
 5:  // == Class declarations
 6:
 7:  // -- A Vehicle is an "abstract" class
 8:  class Vehicle {
 9:     float topSpeed;
10:     float currentSpeed;
11:  public:
12:     void accelerate(float amount);
13:     void decelerate(float amount);
14:     void stop();
15:     float getTopSpeed(void) { return topSpeed; }
16:     void putTopSpeed(float s) { topSpeed = s; }
17:     float getSpeed(void) { return currentSpeed; }
18:     void putSpeed(float s) { currentSpeed = s; }
19:     Vehicle() { topSpeed = currentSpeed = 0.0; }
20:     Vehicle(float maxSpeed);
21:     ~Vehicle() { stop(); }
22:  };
23:
24:  // -- A TwoWheeler is a Vehicle with a top speed of 35.0
25:  class TwoWheeler : public Vehicle {
26:  public:
27:     TwoWheeler() { putTopSpeed(35.0); }
28:  };
```

```
29:
30:  // -- A FourWheeler is a Vehicle with a top speed of 120.0
31:  class FourWheeler : public Vehicle {
32:  public:
33:      FourWheeler() { putTopSpeed(120.0); }
34:  };
35:
36:  // -- A Boat is a new class
37:  class Boat {
38:      float weight;   // Exceed this and she sinks
39:  public:
40:      float getWeight(void) { return weight; }
41:      void putWeight(float w) { weight = w; }
42:      Boat() { weight = 0.0; }
43:  };
44:
45:  // -- An amphibious vehicle is a boat with four wheels!
46:  class Amphibious : public Boat, FourWheeler {
47:  public:
48:      Amphibious() { putTopSpeed( 45.0 ); }
49:  };
50:
51:  // == Method implementations
52:
53:  void Vehicle::accelerate(float amount)
54:  {
55:     currentSpeed += amount;
56:     if (currentSpeed > topSpeed)
57:        putSpeed(topSpeed);
58:  }
59:
60:  void Vehicle::decelerate(float amount)
61:  {
62:     currentSpeed -= amount;
63:     if (currentSpeed < 0.0)
64:        putSpeed(0.0);
65:  }
66:
67:  void Vehicle::stop()
68:  {
69:     while (currentSpeed > 0.0)
70:        decelerate(1.0);
71:  }
72:
73:  Vehicle::Vehicle(float maxSpeed)
```

```
 74:  {
 75:      topSpeed = maxSpeed;
 76:      currentSpeed = 0.0;
 77:  }
 78:
 79:  main()
 80:  {
 81:      TwoWheeler mybike;    // Define test objects for each class
 82:      FourWheeler mycar;
 83:      Boat myboat;
 84:      Amphibious mytank;
 85:
 86:      myboat.putWeight(1200);      // Assign weights to myboat, mytan
 87:      mytank.putWeight(20000);
 88:
 89:      mybike.accelerate(2.0);        // Call a few object methods
 90:      /* myboat.putSpeed(46.5);*/    // Incorrect--no setSpeed metho
 91:      mytank.putSpeed(58.0);         // Okay--inherited from Vehicle
 92:      mytank.decelerate(20.0);
 93:      mytank.stop();
 94:
 95:      printf("mybike's top speed = %f\n", mybike.getTopSpeed());
 96:      printf("mycar's top speed = %f\n", mycar.getTopSpeed());
 97:      printf("myboat's weight  = %f\n", myboat.getWeight());
 98:      printf("mytank's top speed = %f\n", mytank.getTopSpeed());
 99:      printf("mytank's weight = %f\n", mytank.getWeight());
100:  }
```

After compiling, load the VEHICLE sample program into TD; press ⟨**F8**⟩ about five times to initialize all object instances. Then, press ⟨**Alt**⟩-**DI** and enter **mytank** to inspect that instance of the `Amphibious` class (see Figure 20.20).

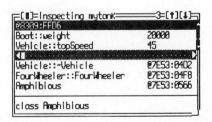

Figure 20.20. Inspecting a C++ object instance.

When it shows an object instance, the inspector window divides into three panes. Under the window title is the object's memory address. If this were a pointer to an object, the address would have two parts as it does for other pointers, showing the location of the pointer variable and the location of the addressed object. Under the address are the object's instance variables (or fields), in this case, `weight` and `topSpeed`. To the left of the double colons (`::`) are the object class names that declare these variables. As usual, values are shown at left in the window (**20000** and **45** here).

The middle pane of an instance inspector shows the object's method names with their declaring classes plus the address of each method's code. The bottom pane describes the currently highlighted item above.

After opening an instance inspector, press ⟨**Ctrl**⟩**-H** to show that object's class position in the `Hierarchy` view. You can also highlight a method name (after pressing ⟨**Tab**⟩ to move the cursor into the middle pane) and press ⟨**Enter**⟩ twice to see that method's source code. See chapter 4 for more information about using other local commands with inspector windows.

Summary

This chapter is a reference to inspecting C and C++ data structures. Use the information in this chapter as a guide for investigating variables in your programs.

The next two chapters describe how to inspect common data structures in Pascal and assembly language programs.

Chapter 21

Pascal Data Structures

U SE THIS CHAPTER as a guide to examining variables in *Turbo Pascal* programs with TD inspector and **Watches** windows. As in Chapter 20, this one begins with a review of where Pascal programs typically store variables. It then shows sample variables and lists tips for viewing simple, complex, and object-oriented data types.

> Note: I used *Turbo Pascal* 5.5 to prepare the sample code for this chapter. Except for the object-oriented information, most of the details should apply to versions 4.0 and 5.0 as well.

Where Are My Variables?

Pascal variables typically fall into one of three categories:

- *Global variables* stored in the data segment.
- *Local variables* and parameters stored in the stack.
- *Pointer variables* address data stored in the heap (usually).

The following notes describe these categories and list a few hints for using TD to examine variables stored in these memory locations.

Global Variables

Variables in the global data segment include all typed constants and those declared in the program's outermost **var** section. They are called *global* *variables* because they exist within the scope of the entire program. The compiler collects all global variables including those declared in unit interfaces into one memory segment, which can be as large as 64K. Register DS addresses this segment.

The location of a program's first global variable is not at ds:0000 as you might expect. This is because the `system` unit plus others that the program uses add their own globals to the data segment. So, don't assume that your variables will be stored at the beginning of the global data segment even when they are the "first" variables in your program text. Use an inspector window to determine the exact address of variables.

Local Variables and Parameters

Local variables include parameters and those declared in procedures and functions. Space for local variables is allocated on the stack. For that reason, local variables are *dynamic*—they exist only within the scope of activated routines. Any memory occupied by local variables that are no longer in scope is available for reuse. This is why, when examining local variables and parameters with TD, you may have to pause the debugger inside a procedure or function to view local variables.

When inspecting local variables with identical names, TD usually shows the value of the variable in scope. For example, if procedures A and B declare `count` variables, TD shows the value of `count` for whichever procedure happens to be active. This can be confusing if the program also declares a global variable of the same name. Use *dot notation* when inspecting or watching variables to resolve any such conflicts, prefacing the variable with the procedure, function, unit, or program name. For example, **a.count** refers to the `count` variable in procedure A, even if B is active.

Pointer Variables

Variables addressed by pointers typically exist in the heap, which usually occupies the amount of memory left after loading the program into RAM and setting up the data and stack segments. The "heap" is an appropriate name for this area, upon which programs might throw any sort of data structure.

Typed pointers in Pascal are bound to a specific data type. TD always knows the type of variable addressed by a pointer. If the pointer addresses an integer, the debugger shows the integer's value. If the pointer addresses a string, the debugger displays the string's characters.

Untyped pointers may point to a data structure of any type, or they may hold addresses for other purposes. For example, the `system` unit declares several `pointer` variables such as `saveInt00` for saving system interrupt vectors redirected by runtime routines.

Other untyped pointers may address data structures. In that case, use a type cast to tell TD the data type. For example, if an untyped pointer p actually addresses a real number, enter **real(p)** as the expression to view in a Watches or inspector window.

When inspecting pointer values, remember to type a caret (as in **p^**) to refer to the variable that the pointer addresses, usually located somewhere inside the heap. To examine the pointer itself, omit the caret.

It's possible but less common for pointers to address variables not in the heap. Turbo Pascal's ə symbol allows programs to assign the address of any variable to a pointer. If p addresses an integer, and num is a global integer variable, this assigns the address of num to p:

```
p := @num;
```

Because num is global, the variable is in the data segment. If num were a local variable or a parameter, its address would be in the stack. Normally, pointer variables are in the heap—but, as this example shows, that's not always the case. Use inspectors to verify that variables are where you think they are.

Size of Variables

You'll often need to know how many bytes a variable occupies. One way to do this is to call the sizeof function with the Evaluate/modify command. For example, to check how many bytes a Boolean variable named switch occupies, press ⟨Ctrl⟩-⟨F4⟩ and enter **sizeof(switch)**. The Result field in the Evaluate/modify window then shows 1 ($1) : WORD. This indicates that switch occupies 1 byte in memory. The first value is decimal; the second hexadecimal.

When using this method to determine a variable's size, don't let the WORD in the result fool you—that's just the data type of the sizeof function. It's not the type of the sized variable. If measure is type real, evaluating **sizeof(measure)** displays 6 ($6) : WORD, indicating that real variables occupy 6 bytes.

System Variables

When you drive a compiled Pascal program under TD, many system and unit variables come along for the ride. The debugger recognizes all identifiers declared in system and other units. It also recognizes standard procedure and function names such as new and odd.

Refer to the SYSTEM.DOC file supplied with *Turbo Pascal* for a list of these identifiers. Other .DOC files document interface sections for other units— valuable information to keep handy while debugging. For example, to locate the start of the heap after loading a program and pressing ⟨**F7**⟩ to execute any startup code, enter **heaporg** into the Evaluate/modify dialog box (⟨**Ctrl**⟩-⟨**F4**⟩). The heap's starting address will then appear in the window's Result box. Or, just open the Variables window (press ⟨**Alt**⟩-**VV**) and use the cursor and page movement keys to view all system and other variables.

Examining Simple Data Types

Most program variables are simple integers, real numbers, Boolean true and false values, and so on. Of course, TD can display all such variables, showing their names, data types, current values, and locations in memory. The following reference shows examples of each of these simple types and discusses associated debugging techniques.

As explained in other chapters, there are many ways to examine variables, but the easiest is to position the cursor on the variable's identifier and press ⟨**Ctrl**⟩-**I**, opening an inspector window to show the variable's value, data type, and address. Or, press ⟨**Ctrl**⟩-**W** to add a variable to Watches. You can also choose View:Variables to display all program variables in one window. Or, use the Data menu's Evaluate/modify command (⟨**Ctrl**⟩-⟨**F4**⟩) and enter a variable's name for inspection.

Boolean Types

Figure 21.1 shows an inspector window for a Boolean variable named switch. The value on the second line at far right is always true or false. Enter **true** or **false** to change the variable's value.

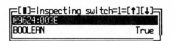

Figure 21.1.   Inspecting a Boolean variable.

In Pascal, the ordinal value of false is 0. True equals 1. Other ordinal values may cause bugs in code that expects Booleans to have no values outside this limited range. You might be able to trap this condition with a breakpoint expression like **byte(ord(switch)) > 1**, which will halt the program if switch's value is not true or false. This might also help detect uninitialized Boolean variables.

Char Types

Figure 21.2 shows a char (character) variable named initial in an inspector window. ASCII values ranging from 32 to 126 display as characters, for example

'A' and '&'. Values outside of this range display as decimal values preceded with a hatch mark like this: #220.

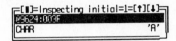

Figure 21.2.   Inspecting a char variable.

When entering `char` values, you can type standard ASCII characters in single quotes, or you can precede values with a hatch mark—for example, **'A'** or the equivalent **#65** (in hexadecimal, **#$**). To enter extended ASCII characters, you must use the second form, for example, typing **#220** or **#245**. You can also enter expressions such as **chr($41)**, useful for typing ASCII character values in hexadecimal.

Enumerated Types

Enumerated types are rarely declared directly as variables. Most of the time, a program creates an enumerated type identifier and then defines a variable of that type, as in these sample lines:

```
type
   RGBcolor = ( RED, BLUE, GREEN );
var
   color : RGBcolor;
```

Figure 21.3 shows how variable `color` of type `RGBcolor` normally appears in an inspector window. If the element name doesn't show up—in other words, if you see a value such as 1 but not the associated name (`GREEN` in this sample)—try pressing ⟨**F7**⟩ to execute the program's startup code. (Press ⟨**Ctrl**⟩-⟨**F2**⟩ first to reset TD if the program has terminated.)

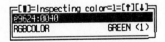

Figure 21.3.   Inspecting an enumerated variable.

To enter new enumerated values, you can specify an element by name—**RED**, **BLUE**, or **GREEN**—or you can use a type cast with the data type and element value in parentheses. For example, because the first element is always represented by 0, changing `color` to `RGBcolor(1)` is the same as setting it to **BLUE**, the second enumerated element.

Integer Types

Turbo Pascal recognizes five integer types: byte, integer, longint, shortint, and word. Figure 21.4 shows sample inspector windows for variables of each. In all cases, the variable name is in the top border, and the address is on the first line below followed by the data type and value in decimal and hexadecimal. Hexadecimal values are in parentheses and are preceded by a dollar sign. (This assumes you haven't changed TD's Integer format in the Display options dialog box, or with TDINST.)

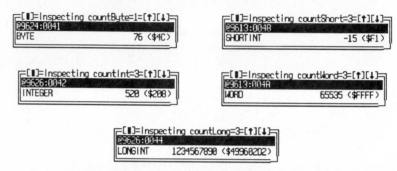

Figure 21.4.   Inspecting Turbo Pascal's integer types.

Byte parameters passed to procedures and functions occupy 2-byte words on the stack. When linking assembly language modules to Pascal programs, a common error is to assign a byte value to AH and then push AX onto the stack to pass the value to another subroutine. But this is not correct. The value should be stored in AL, the "lower" half of the 2-byte AX. This problem sometimes occurs when the code stores a byte in a temporary word variable and then loads that value into AX. If the original operation stores the byte in the wrong half of the variable, its value will be transferred into AH instead of AL. Inspecting variables and registers can clear this kind of fog in a hurry.

To confuse matters even more, the Stack pane in TD's CPU window shows stack entries as 2-byte words in byte-swapped order. For example, as Figure 21.5 shows, the highlighted value 0003 at ss:3FF6 is actually stored as the two bytes 03 and 00 at 9309:3FF6. For that reason, when inspecting integer arguments passed on the stack, it may be easier to view them in the Dump pane. To do this, press ⟨**Tab**⟩ to move the cursor to that pane, press ⟨**Ctrl**⟩**-G**, and enter **ss:sp**.

Data pane   Stack pane

```
9309:3FF6 03 00 02 00 01 00 00 00 ▼ ▌ ▯     ss:3FFA 0001
9309:3FFE 00 00 5E 0E 74 15 FF 46   ^▒tS F     ss:3FF8 0002
9309:4006 06 C4 76 02 26 8B 44 02 ←v▒&iD▒     ss:3FF6 0003
9309:400E 26 8B 1C 89 46 04 89 5E &ïL▄F♦ê^     ss:3FF4 003A
9309:4016 02 EB DB 8B 46 06 83 C4 ▌▓iF♦ô-     ss:3FF2▶3FFC
```

Figure 21.5.   The stack pane shows byte parameters as byte-swapped words.

One of the most common bugs involving integer variables is caused by the wrap-around effect that occurs when adding and subtracting values close to the maximum and minimum of a data type's allowed range. For example, the result of adding 1 to an integer variable equal to 32,767 is not 32,768, which is $8000 in hexadecimal, or −32,768 decimal. Likewise, adding 1 to the word value 65,535 equals 0, not 65,536 as you might expect.

Pascal does nothing to guard against mistakes caused by inadvertent wrap-arounds, which are easy to introduce into complex expressions that mix variables of different integer types. Use Evaluate/modify (⟨**Ctrl**⟩-⟨**F4**⟩) to test suspect expressions, breaking those expressions into pieces until you find what's wrong.

Often, a judicious type cast will fix a wrap-around problem by promoting smaller types to larger ones. For example, if a and b are word values and c is of type longInt, the expressions c := a + b may not give the same result as c := longInt(a) + b. Recasting a to a longInt prevents the wrap-around error because, in the other expression, the result of the addition is converted to longInt *after* adding the two integer values.

Another common error that crops up all the time when using unsigned byte and word values is to forget that unsigned values can never be negative. Loops like this one are bound to fail:

```
while w >= 0 do
begin
   something;
   w := w + 1
end;
```

If w is a word, the loop never ends because words are always greater or equal to 0. The symptom of this problem is usually a hung system. Use TD's code-tracing commands to find the bug by narrowing the problem to where the program stops.

Real Types

Except for type real, Turbo Pascal's real-number types follow IEEE conventions and are compatible with formats used by a hardware numeric data processor (NDP).

Bugs caused by real numbers frequently involve round-off errors, especially in business calculations where every penny counts. I find it helpful to remember that real numbers represent *measurements,* not *increments.* Integer data types are appropriate for counting the number of apples in a barrel. Real numbers are appropriate for measuring how much the barrel weighs. Bugs are certain to bore holes in programs that use a numeric data type for the wrong purpose.

Figure 21.6 shows sample inspector windows for each of *Turbo Pascal's* five real types: `comp`, `double`, `extended`, `real`, and `single`. Notice that very large and small values are shown in scientific notation, while midrange values are displayed in more common decimal form. When entering new values using the `Change` command in an inspector or `Watches` view, you can type digits in either format, but TD may display the result differently from what you enter. For example, if you type **65e9** for a variable of type `real`, TD displays the equivalent value **6.5e+10**. Of course, you can also enter decimal values such as **1.5** and **3.14159**.

Hint: When using the inspector and `Watches` local `Change` commands, remember that you can type expressions. For instance, suppose a program has a `real` variable named `inches`. You can inspect that variable and enter new test expressions such as **7/8** and **5 + 1/3**. TD will evaluate the expressions and store the decimal equivalents in the variable.

Subrange Types

Subranges specify an integer type's minimum and maximum range, helping to prevent bugs caused by statements that assign values outside of that range to variables. In *Turbo Pascal,* subranges are more useful when range checking is enabled with the {$R+} option. With that switch engaged, the compiler generates code to ensure that assignments to subrange variables are within limits. With range checking off, subranges are treated no differently than other integer types, except that out-of-range constant values during compilation will cause a compile-time error.

Figure 21.7 shows an inspector window open to a subrange type declared as `1..max`, using the constant `max` (not shown) equal to 100. Notice that the data type lists the range of values as `1..100`. TD does not pick up the use of the constant in forming the new type, a minor inconvenience. Subranges in the `Watches` view show up similarly.

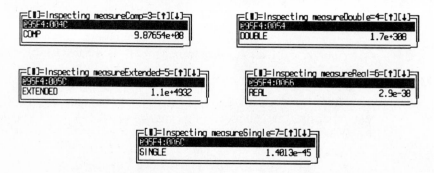

Figure 21.6.   Inspecting Turbo Pascal's real-number types.

If you suspect that your code is failing due to a range error, instead of recompiling with the {$R +} switch, set an `Expression true global` breakpoint for an expression such as **(n 〈 min) or (n 〉 max)**. The program will then halt if n is outside of the range `min .. max`.

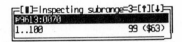

Figure 21.7. Inspecting a subrange data type.

Constants

Pascal constants are used directly by compiled code, they aren't stored in a data segment or on the heap. Even so, you can use TD to inspect constants—you just can't change their values.

The same is not true of *typed constants,* which are not really constants at all, but more like preinitialized global variables stored in the data segment with other globals. For this reason, I usually prefer to use the term *variable constant* instead of typed constant, but I'll defer to the common term here. TD allows you to inspect and change typed constants as though they were variables.

All constants are represented internally as values of specific data types, which, in some cases, might not be obvious. For example, this constant:

```
const    max = 100;
```

appears to declare a byte value `max` equal to 100. Internally, however, `max` is stored as a 32-bit `longInt`. To prove this, load a test program with the `const` declaration, position the cursor on `max`, and press 〈**Ctrl**〉**-I**, opening an inspector window to examine the constant type and value. As Figure 21.8 shows, `max` is stored internally as a `longint`, not a `byte`. TD helps to shine light on this and other similar hidden facts about internal storage details, which may affect the results of expressions.

Examining Complex Data Types

TD's ability to examine complex data types exceeds similar features in other debuggers. Of course, this is a valuable aid for debugging, but you don't have to

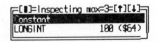

Figure 21.8. Inspecting a constant shows its internal data type and value.

wait for problems to appear to use TD to inspect data. Inspector windows make great browsers for verifying that data structures contain expected values, as demonstrated in the following sections on Pascal's complex data types.

Array Types

Figure 21.9 shows an inspector window opened to a variable `realArray` declared as:

```
var
    realArray : array[ 1 .. 20 ] of real;
```

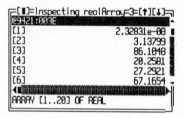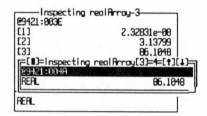

Figure 21.9.   Inspecting an array.

Positioning the cursor on `realArray` and pressing ⟨**Ctrl**⟩-**I** opens the inspector window shown at left in the figure. Like all such windows, the address locates the start of the variable in memory, in this case, the first byte of the array at 9421:003E. Below that are the indexes and values for individual array elements.

To see other values in large arrays, press the cursor and page movement keys to scroll the inspector window's contents. Or, use the `Range` command (press ⟨**Ctrl**⟩-**R**) and enter the index values of the array elements that you want to inspect—for example, **12,18**. Be careful not to exceed the size of the array. If you do, and if you then use a `Change` command to assign values to elements outside of the memory allocated to the array, you may overwrite another value or instruction in memory.

To the right of Figure 21.9, two overlapping inspector windows illustrate how to view individual array elements. To make this figure, I positioned the cursor on index value `[3]` and pressed ⟨**Enter**⟩. Notice that the smaller inspector window's title is `realArray[3]`, which tells you this value belongs to the array. The address in the window locates the array element in memory.

Of course, TD can also inspect multidimensional arrays. When debugging such structures, it's helpful to keep in mind that a multidimensional array is just a conceptual model for an array of other arrays. For example, if `multi` is declared as `array[1..10, 1..5] of integer`, this is just a handy way to describe a structure that consists of 10 five-integer arrays.

Inside inspector windows, TD displays multidimensional arrays in a way that mirrors that model. To investigate individual elements in the structure, highlight successive index values and keep pressing ⟨**Enter**⟩ until you get to the item you want to see.

Record Types

Pascal `record` variables store various fields, which may be of any type, including other records. As Figure 21.10 illustrates, using TD inspector windows makes it easy to step into a record and examine individual field values. The left of the figure shows an inspector window for a record declared as:

```
var
   collection : record
      r : real;
      s : string[20];
      c : longInt;
   end;
```

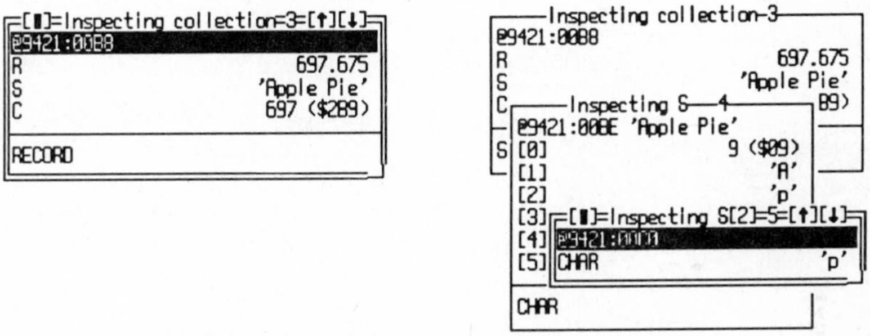

Figure 21.10. Inspecting a record variable.

As always, the address in the inspector window locates the first byte of the record in memory (see the left half of Figure 21.10). Individual fields are listed below the address. The right half of the figure shows three inspector windows, produced by positioning the selector bar first on `string` variable s, pressing ⟨**Enter**⟩, positioning the selector on [2], and pressing ⟨**Enter**⟩ again. This displays the data type and address of the second character of this record's string field. As you can see, it takes only a few simple keystrokes to dig deeply into any `record` structure, no matter how complex.

When inspecting record fields, TD follows the rules that apply to simple variables of those same types. `Integer` fields display like `integer` variables, `real` fields display like `real` variables, and so on. Refer to the appropriate section in this chapter for more information about these and other data types.

Problems with "With"

The `with` keyword in Pascal makes it easy to refer to record elements without having to type the record's identifier over and over. For example, to display the elements of the `collection` record from the previous section, you can write:

```
with collection do
   writeln( s, ' ', r, ' ', c );
```

Unfortunately, this kind of statement gives TD indigestion. If you attempt to watch or inspect the field names by positioning the cursor on `s`, `r`, or `c`, the debugger displays `Symbol not found` error messages, probably because TD can't look back and "see" the `with` statement, which tells the compiler that these symbols are fields in the `collection` record. There are two solutions to this problem:

- Inspect the full record name instead of individual fields. For example, press ⟨**Alt**⟩-**DI** and enter **collection**. Then, highlight a field in the inspector window and press ⟨**Enter**⟩ to inspect the value.
- Inspect or watch a qualified record and field name, separated by a period (called *dot notation*). To do this, press ⟨**Alt**⟩-**DI** to inspect (or ⟨**Alt**⟩-**DW** to watch) an expression such as **collection.r** or **collection.s**.

Set Types

`Sets` occupy from 1 to 32 bytes, with each bit representing the presence (1) or absence (0) of a corresponding element. TD displays sets using a form that closely mirrors their source-code declarations. For example, Figure 21.11 shows a sample inspector window for a set of characters assigned the set `['0'..'9']` and declared as:

```
var
   digits : set of char;
```

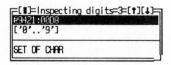

Figure 21.11.   Inspecting a set.

The set's elements are shown below the address. As the figure shows, `['0'..'9']` displays the range of values now in the set, in this case, the ten

ASCII digit characters 0 through 9. Use the `Change` command in an inspector or `Watches` window to enter new set values in this same format. When entering character sets, though, you have to type # for extended ASCII characters as in **[#128..#255]**.

> Changing a character set variable to an expression such as [#128..#255] erases the variable to the null set []. TD also fails to recognize set values such as [chr(65), chr(72)]. Even ['a', 'b', 'c'] produces a "Syntax error." Also, there seems to be no easy way to assign extended ASCII values to character set variables, not even by pressing ⟨Alt⟩ and digit keys on the numeric keypad. Perhaps a future TD release will do a better job at handling Pascal character sets.

To view the bytes in a set variable, open an inspector window and press ⟨**Alt**⟩-**VD**, displaying a `Dump` window positioned to the variable's address. When you need to inspect a set element's bit position, open both windows and either change the set value or type new byte values in the `Dump` view. This lets you experiment with bit patterns and view the resulting set (or enter sets and see the bit patterns), which might be useful for examining the source of a problem that you suspect is related to the way sets are stored in memory.

String Types

Strings in Pascal are specialized character arrays, where the first byte represents the number of characters stored in the string. Because this value is a byte, a string's maximum length is limited to 255 characters.

Bugs sometimes occur when programmers forget that a string variable's size and length can never be the same. A string variable's *size* in bytes is constant, while its *length* can vary from 0 to *(size − 1)* characters. Keeping these facts firmly in mind can prevent lots of problems.

Figure 21.12 shows an inspector window for a string variable named `title`. The format of this window is similar to other kinds of arrays, but with one difference. Element [0] shows the string's length in decimal and hexadecimal. The other elements show the characters in the string. Technically, the inspector

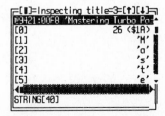

Figure 21.12. Inspecting a string variable.

shows the incorrect data type for the string's length byte, which Pascal considers to be of type `char`. But it's helpful to see this value in decimal anyway, so TD is justified in bending Pascal's rule in this case.

Despite this feature, however, to enter a *new* string length, you must preface the value with a # symbol, or TD will not allow the assignment. For example, to change the length of `title` from 26 to 34, position the selector bar on [0] and enter #34.

A common and very dangerous bug arises in procedures that declare variable string parameters of type `string`:

```
procedure message( var s : string );
begin
   s := 'Some message to return in s';
end;
```

That looks harmless enough, and it is, provided that variables passed to procedure `message` are long enough to hold the result. With Turbo Pascal's {$V-} string-length switch in effect, the following declarations and statement cause a major bug:

```
{$V-}
type
   string10 = string[10];
var
   shortString : string10;
{- insert message procedure here }
begin
   message( shortString );
end.
```

Variable `shortString` can hold up to ten characters, but the parameter to `message` is declared as a generic `string`, which can store up to 255 characters. Because the {$V-} switch turns off automatic string-length checks, `message` can overwrite other bytes in memory outside of the space allocated to `shortString`.

Note: See "String Length Problems" in chapter 12 for more information about dealing with this common bug.

Files

You can examine file variables using the same methods that work for other kinds of data. Even though you normally can't look at a file variable's details,

TD allows you to add a file variable to the `Watches` or an inspector window for any file, for example a variable defined as `myFile : FILE of Real` or `textFile : TEXT`. Examining `myFile`, `textFile`, and other file variables reveals their addresses, status (open or closed), name, and type. All such files are one of these three types:

- Text file
- Typed file
- Untyped file

To see still more details inside file variables, add the `Dos` unit to a program's `uses` statement. Then, press 〈**Alt**〉-**DI** or 〈**Alt**〉-**DW** and enter a type-cast expression such as **textRec(t)** or **fileRec(f)** where t is any text file and f is any typed or untyped file. Casting the variables to these `record` declarations lets TD display all normally hidden fields inside the file variables. See the DOS.DOC file on your Turbo Pascal diskettes and your reference manuals for information about each of these fields.

As you can see in Figure 21.13, which shows the contents of a `text` file named `textFile`, there's a lot more to a file variable than is usually apparent. The top of the figure shows the inspector window for the file variable. The bottom shows the inspector window open to the same variable but using the type-cast expression **textRec(textFile)**. The file is currently open to a disk file named DATA.1 and has a test line loaded into the output buffer. You could also open additional inspector windows to view even more details about individual fields. To see more of the buffer's contents, highlight the `BUFFER` field and press 〈**Enter**〉. Or, highlight the field and type 〈**Alt**〉-**VD** to open a `Dump` window, showing the buffer's contents as a block of bytes.

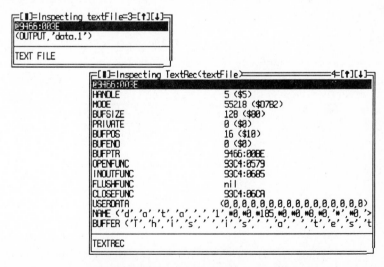

Figure 21.13. Inspecting a text file.

Figure 21.14 shows another example, this time for a typed file declared as a `file of rec` where `rec` is a simple three-field `record`. The top inspector window shows TD's normal view for file variables; the bottom shows the results of inspecting the type-cast expression **fileRec(typedFile)**, which reveals the hidden fields inside the file variable. Untyped files declared as type `file` have the same internal structure as typed files.

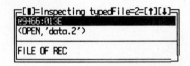

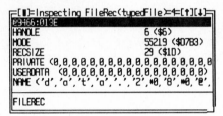

Figure 21.14.   Inspecting a typed file.

Debugging Dynamic Structures

Of all the bugs that can flutter into a program, those that involve pointer variables are often the most difficult to net. This is especially true of structures such as lists and trees, where multiple variables are linked by pointer fields that address other variables, all of the same types.

Such recursive data structures provide powerful ways to store and organize information in memory. By using inspector windows, its possible to step through individual records in a complex list or tree, using TD as a browser to locate data simply by following pointers—as easy as drawing a picture by connecting the dots. For example, consider these definitions:

```
type
   string20 = string[20];
   itemPointer = ^item;
   item = record
            data : string20;
            left, right : itemPointer
          end;
var
   root : itemPointer;
```

Variable `root` addresses an `item` record, which serves as the root of a tree—a special kind of ordered linked list. By opening an inspector window to `root`, all elements linked to the tree are available for inspection. Figure 21.15 illustrates several inspector windows that stem from `root` and show the contents of a sample tree. In this case it's a fruit tree with data values equal to the strings `'Mango'`, `'Banana'`, `'Apple'`, and `'Peach'`.

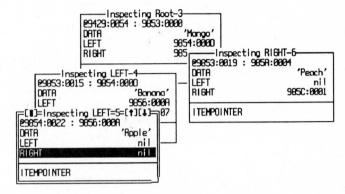

Figure 21.15.   Inspecting a tree's elements.

I constructed Figure 21.15 by first opening an inspector window to `root`. Then, I positioned the cursor on `LEFT` and `RIGHT` pointer fields and pressed ⟨**Enter**⟩ to open additional inspectors for items linked to those branches. Pointers marked `nil` represent the end of a branch.

Note: TD displays `nil` for pointers set to that value (represented internally as 0000:0000), but it does not prevent you from opening an inspector for the "data" at that location, even though, technically, a `nil` pointer doesn't address a valid memory location. For this reason, when inspecting linked lists and trees, it's up to you to know when to stop following pointers to new information.

Debugging Objects

The most complex kinds of inspectors are those that display the contents of object instances or types (also called *classes*). In *Turbo Pascal* 5.5, an object encapsulates both data fields (instance variables) and methods (procedures, functions, constructors, and destructors). Those methods may be static (directly addressable) or virtual (addressable via a lookup table).

While debugging any program that declares at least one object, you can press ⟨**Alt**⟩-**VH** to view a hierarchy of object relationships among all classes available to the program. Remember that this window shows only classes; it does not show object instances. See chapter 5 for more information about using this window as an object class browser—a great way to get the broad picture of an object-oriented program's organization.

Watching Objects

Because most objects tend to be extremely complex structures, I find that adding objects to Watches is rarely of much use. Instead, to examine an object's parts and pieces, I prefer to open an inspector window to an instance of that object's class or to the class declaration itself. However, at times, I'll specify expressions such as **list.count** or **list.root** to watch individual object fields in Watches—useful when I don't want to see all that an object contains.

Figure 21.16 shows an inspector window open to an object instance called namesFile. The top pane of the window lists data fields in the object, which you can inspect as you can other Pascal variables by highlighting entries and pressing ⟨**Enter**⟩. The bottom inspector pane lists the object's methods. Press ⟨**Tab**⟩ to move the cursor into this pane, highlight a method, and press ⟨**Enter**⟩ to open an inspector window listing that method's address and type. If you then press ⟨**Enter**⟩ a second time, TD will switch to the Module window and show you the method's source code. (If the source-code file isn't available to TD, it will open a CPU window instead.)

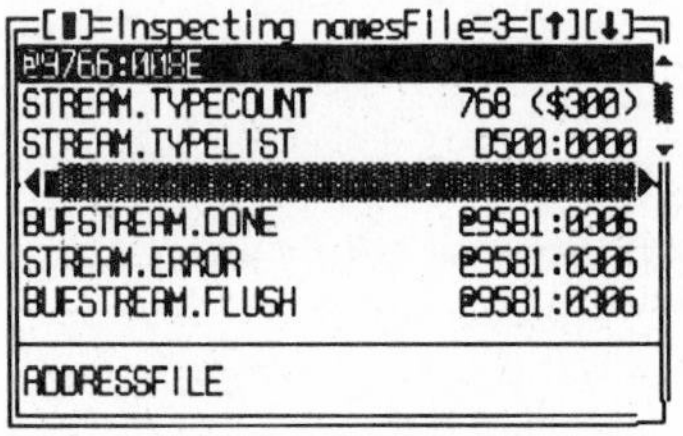

Figure 21.16.   Inspecting an object instance.

Classes vs Instances

Be sure to understand the difference between an object class and an object instance. A class is like a record declaration or another data type. Classes don't exist in memory; they're merely schematics for creating variables of those types. An instance, on the other hand, is a variable of an object class (like a variable of a record type). Like other variables, object instances may be stored in the data segment, on the stack, or in the heap.

Because only object instances have substance, when inspecting instances, you can view and change data fields stored in an object. But, when inspecting classes, those same fields don't exist anywhere—they merely show you what a variable of that class will contain when and if a program statement defines a variable of that type—or, to use the proper OOP buzzwords, when the program "instantiates the class."

Finding the VMT

Object types that define a constructor or that have one or more virtual methods have an associated *Virtual Method Table* (VMT) stored in the global data segment. Calls to virtual methods consult this table and, therefore, can be redirected at runtime to call replacement routines in descendant objects, a process known as *polymorphism.*

Object instances that require VMTs begin with a single 2-byte field that holds the offset value of the VMT address in the data segment. Normally, this field is invisible, but it might be useful to inspect it while debugging OOP code. To find the VMT, open an inspector to an object instance. Then, press ⟨**Alt**⟩-**VD** to view a dump of the bytes where the object is stored. The first two bytes are the VMT's offset in byte-swapped order. When I tried this on a test object, the Dump window displayed the two bytes 1A 00, indicating that the VMT is stored at DS:001A.

After doing this, you could press ⟨**Ctrl**⟩-**G** to Goto that address and view the bytes that make up the VMT. But there's a better way to view VMTs. First, add the following type definition to the main program module and recompile:

```
VMTptr = ^VMT;
VMT = record
   size : word;
   negSize : integer;
   methods : array[ 1 .. 1000 ] of procedure
end;
```

The VMT record describes the VMT's format, which begins with a word field equal to the size of an object instance of the class. The following integer field (negSize) is the negation of size and is used by Pascal to verify that the object has been initialized. For example, if size equals 27, then negSize should equal −27; otherwise, the object instance has not been initialized by a call to its constructor method. To check for this condition, recompile with the {$R+} option in effect, which inserts automatic runtime checks to halt the code if a virtual-method call is made to an uninitialized object. The option works by comparing the size and negSize fields in object instances before every call to a virtual method.

The third field in the VMT record is an array of 1000 procedure pointers. I used 1000 because it's unlikely that any object would declare more than that number of methods. The actual value isn't too important, however.

Figure 21.17 illustrates how to use the **VMT** record to inspect an object's VMT in the data segment. After obtaining the VMT's offset address from a **Dump** window as explained previously, press ⟨**Alt**⟩**-DI**. When prompted for an expression to inspect, enter something like **VMTptr(ds:$001A)**, replacing 001A with the address of the VMT that you want to see. The top of the figure shows the result. The **Constant** line displays the VMT's address. Below that are the **SIZE**, **NEGSIZE**, and **METHODS** fields. Notice that **SIZE** and **NEGSIZE** complement each other (26 and −26).

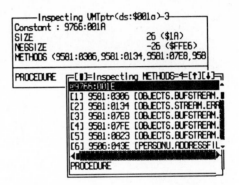

Figure 21.17.   Inspecting an object's VMT.

The bottom of Figure 21.17 shows the result of positioning the selector on the **METHODS** field and pressing ⟨**Enter**⟩ to open another inspector window. This lists all virtual methods stored in the table and identifies the methods by their full dot-notation names. (Press ⟨**F5**⟩ to zoom this window to full screen if the names are truncated as they are here.)

At this point, you can inspect individual methods. For example, Figure 21.18 shows what happened after I highlighted the sixth entry in **methods** (see Figure 21.17) and pressed ⟨**Enter**⟩. I then pressed ⟨**Cursor Down**⟩ to select the **[1]** field in the inspector and pressed ⟨**Enter**⟩ a second time to view this method. Pressing ⟨**Enter**⟩ once more would then take me to the method's source code, a useful technique for navigating from a VMT back to the source.

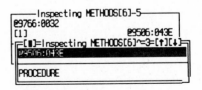

Figure 21.18.   Inspecting an object method by way of the object's VMT.

Summary

This chapter is a reference to inspecting Turbo Pascal data structures. Use the information in this chapter as a guide for investigating variables in your programs.

Chapter 20 describes how to inspect common C and C++ data structures. The next chapter explains how to inspect variables in assembly language programs.

Chapter 22

Assembly Language
Data Structures

ASSEMBLY LANGUAGE allows programmers great freedom, but it also demands great care. Bugs that are stopped at the gate by a Pascal or C compiler are waved through by the assembler, which does little to outlaw errors caused by out-of-bounds array indexes, mismatched data types, and other vices.

Of course, that freedom is also one of assembly language's main strengths. If you want to treat a structure as a collection of strings for one operation but as an array of binary words for another, that's fine with the assembler, and it might be useful for writing tight code that runs at top speed. But it also complicates debugging by shifting error prevention from the language to your shoulders.

This chapter explores TD's capability to examine assembly language data structures created with *Turbo Assembler* (TASM) or *Microsoft's Macro Assembler* (MASM). Use it as a source of tips for investigating data structures in your own programs.

Where Are My Variables?

One of the keys to successful assembly language programming (and debugging) is to know where your variables are at all times. Because assemblers loosely enforce data-type checking, careful control over the *location* of data in assembly language programming is more important than it is with high-level languages, which take over most data addressing details. For that reason, assembly language bugs are often location-dependent, and a good bit of your debugging efforts will be concentrated on examining the addresses and values in memory.

Entering Values

With `Options:Language` set to `Assembler` (or `Source` after loading an assembled and linked assembly language program), TD's default data-entry radix is hexadecimal, a fact that can't be changed. This means that, at most times, if you enter **10**, the debugger silently converts the value to 16 decimal. This can be handy, for example, when using the `Evaluate/modify` command as a hex-to-decimal converter. Just press ⟨**Ctrl**⟩-⟨**F4**⟩, enter **10**, and press ⟨**Enter**⟩. The `Result` window then shows `word 16 (10h)`.

Unfortunately, as you can see from this experiment, the result is in decimal followed by the equivalent hex value in parentheses—a small, but potentially confusing, detail. What's more, the default radix for most TASM and MASM programs is decimal, which further complicates debugging.

Of course, one thing nobody needs during debugging is more confusion! For that reason, it's probably best to add a trailing h to hex values, d for decimals, and b for binary values at all times.

> Note: Be especially wary of ambiguous values such as 0101b and 0110b. Are these hexadecimal values 101B and 110B, or are they binary values 0101 and 0110? The answer is, they are binary, even though TD's default radix is hex. In fact, the only way to enter such values in hex is to add a trailing h as in 101Bh and 110Bh. You must include the h to resolve the ambiguity of hexadecimal values that end with b.

Size of Variables

It's often helpful to check how many bytes a variable occupies. You may discover that you accidentally declared a byte with **db** when you intended to declare a word with **dw** or that you've used the wrong constant to declare an array with the **dup** directive.

Unfortunately, TD lacks a way to determine the size of assembly language variables directly. One way around the limitation is to change languages. To do this, press ⟨**Alt**⟩-**O** to open the `Options` menu, press ⟨**Enter**⟩, and press **P** to change the language to `Pascal` (press **C** for C). Press ⟨**Enter**⟩ again to accept the change, and then use the `Data` menu's `Evaluate/modify` command to enter an expression such as **sizeof(aByte)** or **sizeof(anArray)**. The result shows the size in bytes:

```
2 ($2) : WORD
```

The size of the variable is displayed first in decimal, then in hex preceded by a dollar sign—*Turbo Pascal*'s symbol for a hexadecimal value. (If you changed the language to C, you'd see **0x2** for the hexadecimal equivalent.) Ignore the **WORD**. That's the data type of the **sizeof** pseudo function, not of the inspected variable.

> Hint: After using this trick, be sure to reset the language to **Assembler** or **Source**.

Examining Simple Data Types

Simple data types are declared with one of the seven **Define-Memory** directives listed in Table 22.1. The following sections explain how to examine each of these fundamental assembly language data types with TD inspector windows.

Table 22.1. Simple assembly language data types.

Directive	Name	Size in Bytes
db	Define byte	1
dw	Define word	2
dd	Define doubleword	4
dp	Define pointer	6
df	Define far pointer	6
dq	Define quadword	8
dt	Define ten bytes	10

Byte (db) Variables

Figure 22.1 shows an inspector window open to assembly language's simplest data type, a single byte. The variable **aByte** was defined with this **db** directive:

```
aByte           db          61h       ; Byte or char in hex
```

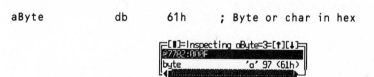

Figure 22.1. Inspecting a byte (db) variable.

TD normally displays all byte values in three ways: as an ASCII character, in decimal, and in hex (inside parentheses). The full 32-bit address is shown above the data type (**byte**).

Figure 22.2 shows a similar inspector window for a variable `aChar`, also defined with `db`, but initialized to the character value 'a' with the directive:

```
aChar           db      'a'      ; Same as aByte
```

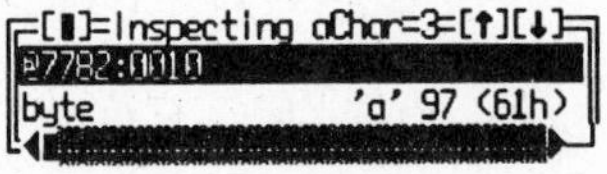

Figure 22.2. Inspecting a character (db) variable.

Because characters and bytes in assembly language are one and the same, except for the variables' names, there isn't any difference between the inspector windows in Figures 22.1 and 22.2. You can use the **Change** command (press **⟨Ctrl⟩-G**) to assign new standard ASCII characters to these variables, but to enter extended characters in the range of 128–255, you must enter the ASCII values in hex or decimal.

Word (dw) Variables

Variables defined with `dw` occupy 2 bytes, which are stored in byte swapped order with the most significant byte first. Figure 22.3 shows a sample inspector window for a variable `aWord` defined as:

```
aWord           dw      65535    ; A word in decimal
```

Figure 22.3. Inspecting a word (dw) variable.

There are two details to keep in mind when debugging `dw` variables. First, remember that there are no explicit signed and unsigned data types in assembly languages; therefore, legal word values may range from −32,768 to 65,535. Even so, the values from 32,768 to 65,535 are identical in binary to the values from −32,768 to −1, a common source of confusion.

The second detail to remember is that words are always stored in byte-swapped order. To verify this, press **⟨Alt⟩-VD** to open a **Dump** window after inspecting a word value such as 0FF55h. This will show you the physical byte order of the value as stored in memory—in this case, in the two bytes **55 FF**. Remember this detail also when using the **Dump** window's **Search** command (**⟨Ctrl⟩-S**). To find a specific word value, you can enter the full value as **1234h** or the individual bytes as **34h 12h**. Either argument will locate the same value in RAM, and at times, one form may be more convenient to use than the other.

Doubleword (dd) Variables

A doubleword takes 4 bytes, as illustrated by Figure 22.4, which shows a **dd** variable defined as:

```
aDoubleWord      dd        450000  ; A double word in decimal
```

Figure 22.4. Inspecting a doubleword (dd) variable.

Like word values, doublewords may be signed and unsigned and may range in decimal from −2,147,483,648 to 4,294,967,295. However, as with word values, negative doublewords duplicate in binary the positive values starting from 2,147,483,648. (TD allows you to enter negative doubleword values using the **Change** command in an inspector window or **Watches** view, but it displays only the positive equivalents.)

When examining doubleword values in **Dump** windows, remember that both of the two words and the two bytes in each word are stored in byte-swapped order. The doubleword value 12345678h appears in the window as the four hex bytes: **78 56 34 12**. As with **dw** word values, this is also important to remember when using the **Dump** window's **Search** command (**⟨Ctrl⟩-S**). To find a specific doubleword variable, you can enter the full value as **12345678h** or the individual bytes as **78h 56h 34h 12h**.

Pointer (df, dp) Variables

Both **df** (define far pointer) and **dp** (define pointer) give the same result, a 48-bit pointer, which TD displays as type **pword** (see Figure 22.5). Unlike most other inspector windows open to pointer variables, this one shows the variable's address in the first line, but not the location to which the pointer points. Instead, that value is displayed as the 6-byte hexadecimal figure to the right of the data type.

Figure 22.5. Inspecting a df or dp 48-bit pointer variable.

Most 8086 assembly language programs won't use **df** and **dp** directives. If you're trying to use them to define pointers, try **dd** (define doubleword) instead. Despite this directive's name, it's suitable for creating 32-bit integers and pointers composed of 16-bit segment and offset parts, as the next section explains.

Doubleword (dd) Pointers

When dd is used to create 32-bit, or *far,* pointers, TD displays the variables as type far ptr, where *type* might be byte, word, and so on. Figure 22.6 shows a sample of a variable declared as:

```
aPointer        dd        aByte   ; A "far" pointer
```

```
┌[■]=Inspecting aPointer═══════════3=[↑][↓]┐
│@7794:0017 : 7794:000F [#testexe#abyte]   │
│[0]                           'a' 97 <61h> │
│◄                                         ►│
├──────────────────────────────────────────┤
│byte far ptr                              │
└──────────────────────────────────────────┘
```

Figure 22.6.   Inspecting a 32-bit pointer (dd) variable.

As you can see in Figure 22.6, the inspector displays the address of aPointer followed by the addressed location. It also identifies the target's name and module, in this case, #testexe#abyte. Below this line is the value of the variable at that location, here 97, or in ASCII, the lowercase character 'a'. Notice that TD displays a single index [0] as though the variable addressed an array.

TD distinguishes between doubleword integer values and pointers created by dd directives. Inspectors show integer values in decimal and hexadecimal (see Figure 22.4). They show pointers as illustrated in Figure 22.6.

Quadword (dq) Variables

A quadword typically defines real (floating-point) numbers, as in this directive, which initializes aQuadWord to π:

```
aQuadWord       dq        3.14159 ; A real number
```

Unfortunately, as Figure 22.7 illustrates, TD displays quadwords in hexadecimal, even though dq is rarely used to define 8-byte integers. Also, TD does not allow you to enter new floating-point values for quadword variables using an inspector or Watches local Change commands.

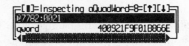

Figure 22.7.   Inspecting a quadword (dq) variable.

One way around these limitations is to switch languages to `Pascal` with the `Options` menu `Language` command. After doing that, open an inspector window to a quadword variable and press ⟨**Ctrl**⟩-**N**. Enter a type-cast expression such as **double(aQuadWord)**, replacing `aQuadWord` with your variable's identifier. This displays the `dq` value formatted as a real number, and it lets you use the `Change` command to enter new values and expressions like **2.5** or **1/7**. However, if you then change `Language` back to `Source` or `Assembler`, TD becomes confused about the variable's data type and erases the inspector window's contents.

Ten-Byte (dt) Variables

Variables defined with `dt` are usually in *Binary Coded Decimal* (BCD) format, stored as 4-bit hex digits in 10 bytes. This creates enough room for values that range from 1 to 20 digits, equal to integer values from 0 to a number with 20 9s. Figure 22.8 shows an inspector window for a 10-byte variable defined as:

```
aTenBytes       dt      81659247 ; A Binary Coded Decimal
```

Figure 22.8.   Inspecting a 10-byte (dt) variable.

For some unexplained reason, TD does not let you enter new values for `dt` variables using an inspector or `Watches` local `Change` commands. To get around this limitation, open the inspector and then press ⟨**Alt**⟩-**VD**, creating a `Dump` window showing the variable's bytes. You can then enter new BCD values, but in reverse byte order.

Memory-Addressing Modes

TD's `Data:Evaluate/modify` command is useful for experimenting with the first five of assembly language's seven addressing modes, listed in Table 22.2. Many bugs in assembly language programming are caused by misunderstanding (and misusing) these addressing modes.

Entering test expressions into the dialog's `Expression` input box lets you preview an addressing mode's results. For example, enter **aBuffer + si** to see the location and data addressed by that expression. You can also preface an expression with operators such as `byte`, `word`, `offset`, and `seg` to change the type of data addressed.

Table 22.2. Assembly language addressing modes.

Mode	Example
Direct	mov ax, [aByte]
Register-Indirect	mov ax, [byte ptr bx]
Base	mov ax, [aBuffer + bp]
Indexed	mov ax, [aBuffer + si]
Base-Indexed	mov ax, [aBuffer + bx + si]
I/O Port	in ax, dx
String	stosb

To experiment with I/O Port addressing, open the **CPU** window, press ⟨**Ctrl**⟩-**I**, and select an input or output command from the small pop-up menu. After that, specify the port number to read or write, using the registers pane to enter and inspect byte or word values.

There's no easy way to test string-addressing operations such as **stosb** and **lodsw**. But you can assemble short tests into an unused memory location (open **CPU** and start typing), or create test programs in the usual way, and load them into TD.

Note: Be careful when experimenting with I/O ports. Just reading a port address may activate devices or change a peripheral's configuration. Poking around aimlessly might have disastrous consequences.

Equates and Expressions

Errors frequently crop up in equated (**EQU**) expressions for a variety of reasons. Because equates are evaluated at assembly time, it's easy to use the wrong radix in a constant, or to type **SHL** when you meant to use **SHR**, and not notice the mistake until the program runs—and fails.

Because equated expressions evaluate to constants, their results are usually combined inside instructions or buried in other directives, making them difficult to inspect, even with TD. For example, suppose you declare these three constants:

```
C1      EQU     100
C2      EQU     C1 SHL 1
C3      EQU     C2 AND 0FF00h
```

The values are arbitrary, but they demonstrate a situation that occurs often in assembly language programming. Constant **C1** declares a simple value, which is manipulated twice: first through an intermediate constant `C2` and then through a third constant `C3` to produce a final value. None of these constants is stored in RAM, and none is available for inspection with TD, making errors in logic difficult to trace. TD reports "Symbol not found" if you try to inspect `C1`, `C2`, or `C3`.

One solution is to use the `Data` menu's `Evaluate/modify` command (⟨**Ctrl**⟩-⟨**F4**⟩) to enter test expressions. You can't use constant identifiers in expressions, but you can enter text such as **(100 shl 1) shr 2** to test `C3`'s result in the final code.

Hint: If you need to inspect various constants with TD, add temporary variables in the assembly language source code to hold the constant values. You can then inspect the variables with TD. Remove the temporary variables before you compile the finished code.

True and False Expressions

Table 22.3 lists comparison operators that are useful in `Evaluate/modify` commands for testing whether certain values and symbols are equal, not equal, less, and greater.

Table 22.3. Assembly language comparison operators.

Operator	Meaning
eq	Equal
ge	Greater than or equal
gt	Greater than
le	Less than or equal
lt	Less than
ne	Not equal

Don't try to use ⟨, ⟩, =, and ⟨⟩ in expressions—they aren't recognized by TD when `Language` is set to `Assembler`. Instead, use comparison expressions such as **aWord eq 100h** and **aByte le 8**, which produce results like these:

```
word -1 (FFFFh)
word 0 (0h)
```

Because there are no **TRUE** and **FALSE** symbols in assembly language, you have to memorize that −1 means "true" and 0 means "false." True to assembly language form, TD displays the decimal and hex results of comparisons, leaving the interpretation of those results to you. Likewise, to enter true and false values, you must enter their decimal, hex, or other equivalents.

> Note: See chapter 9 for more information about entering assembly language expressions.

Examining Complex Data Types

Assembly language's complex data types are severely limited and more difficult to use than similar structures in C and Pascal. It's your responsibility to cook up array indexes and field offsets—items that high-level languages hand to you on a platter. Of course, this also gives you the opportunity to customize algorithms for top performance.

TD inspectors are great for browsing through complex assembly language structures, and they also make good teachers. If you're a little unsure how to create a complex data type, run test programs in TD, use the `Evaluate/modify` command to examine expressions and variables, and patch in new instructions with the `CPU` view. Use the debugger to find out whether your source-code constructions create the structures you need.

The following sections describe ways to use TD to inspect arrays, strings, structures, and unions—four of the most common complex data structures in assembly language programming.

Arrays

The simplest kind of array in assembly language is a buffer of bytes, illustrated in Figure 22.9, created with the definition:

```
aBuffer        db      256 DUP (?) ; A byte buffer
```

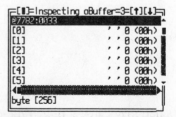

Figure 22.9.   Inspecting a byte array.

The **DUP** operator repeats a define-memory directive (**db** in this case) to allocate space for storing multibyte values. TD treats such arrays as collections of the base type, in this example, an array of bytes. It shows the address of the array in the first line of the inspector window, followed by each element's index in parentheses. The first index is always 0. The array's data type is shown at the bottom with the total number of elements in brackets. To see more array elements, press ⟨**F5**⟩ to zoom the window to full screen or scroll the window's contents with the cursor and page movement keys.

Figure 22.10 shows a second array, this time created with a **dw** directive:

```
aSeries        dw      512 DUP (0AAAAh,0BBBBh)
```

Notice how two initializing values, **0AAAAh** and **0BBBBh**, are stored in all array positions—a good debugging trick to remember. After a program finishes, use the **Dump** view or an inspector to examine the array contents. Any breaks in the repeating pattern will show you how much of the array was used.

To inspect an individual array element, highlight any indexed entry and press ⟨**Enter**⟩ or ⟨**Ctrl**⟩**-I**. This opens a second inspector for that element and also shows the element's address in the array. This can be useful for verifying whether a program calculates those same addresses correctly.

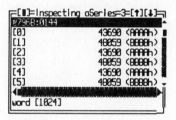

Figure 22.10. Inspecting a word array.

Strings

Strings and byte arrays are equivalent in assembly language, and both are defined with the **db** directive. Most often, a terminating character—either a dollar sign '$' or a zero byte—marks the end of the string. Figure 22.11 shows an inspector window open to a string defined as:

```
aString        db      "Practice Makes Perfect"
```

Each character in **aString** occupies 1 byte, but as defined here, the lack of a terminating value may cause a bug in the code. Most of the time, you'll define strings like these:

```
aString          db        "A better string", '$'
aString          db        "Even better", 0
```

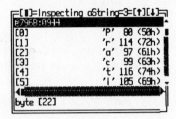

Figure 22.11.   Inspecting a string variable.

The first definition uses a dollar-sign terminator, probably for passing the string to DOS function 9 (print character string). The second conforms to C's string type, which ends with a null character equal to 0. Whichever format you use, if you forget the terminating character, the symptom is usually a lot of garbage letters and symbols on screen. If you see this, use TD to verify that string variables end with the correct byte values.

Another less commonly used string in assembly language programming begins with a byte value that represents the count of characters in the string. This *length-byte* design is the same as used in *Turbo Pascal* strings. The following section describes how to create this format with an assembly language struc keyword.

Structures

A struc (no ending t) in assembly language is like a Pascal record or a C struct (with an ending t). Inside a struc, you can insert *fields* of other simple types. You can then define a single variable to contain all the elements of your struc. For example, to declare an 80-character Pascal length-byte string type, you could write:

```
struc    PasString
 strLen  db     0
 chars   db     80 dup (?)
ends     PasString
```

Then, in the program's data segment, you can define a variable of type PasString with the line:

```
aPasString  PasString  <26,"Mastering Turbo Pascal 5.5">
```

Figure 22.12 shows how TD displays this structure in an inspector window. Each field name is shown below the address of the structure. After opening the inspector, you can move the highlight bar to any field and press ⟨**Enter**⟩ to inspect that field's value. This will also display the address of that element.

When assembling with TASM's **Ideal** mode, two or more structures may use the same names for field identifiers. When assembling with MASM or with TASM in **MASM** mode, field names must be unique. This can lead to confusion (and to a whopper of a bug) if you calculate field offsets using the wrong structure.

To examine individual fields in the **Watches** window, rather than inspecting the entire **struc**, use dot notation, limiting the amount of information shown on one line. For example, to monitor the string length byte, you can enter:

```
aPasString.strlen
```

> Note: TD correctly handles unnamed **struc** fields. For example, if **PasString**'s **strLen** field weren't named (in other words, if you simply declared it as **db 0**), an inspector window will still be able to show other named fields correctly, although the unnamed fields are hidden from view. Contrast this with the way TD fails to handle unnamed bit fields in C **struct**s (see chapter 20).

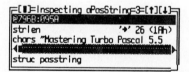

Figure 22.12. Inspecting a struc variable.

Unions

Unions are identical to **struc** data types, except they use the **union** directive, and most importantly, their fields overlay the same address in the structure. TD lets you inspect unions to see all values for all fields, regardless of which field is currently significant. This can be a great help in discovering errors (assigning values to the wrong field, for example) and for examining data in more than one way at once.

Using a sample from my book *Mastering Turbo Assembler,* a **struc** and a **union** demonstrate the idea:

```
struc   TwoBytes
 LoByte db    ?
 HiByte db    ?
ends    TwoBytes
```

```
union ByteWord
 asBytes TwoBytes <>
 asWord  dw      ?
ends  ByteWord
```

TwoBytes (a **struc**) declares two uninitialized byte fields. **ByteWord** (a **union**) declares one field as a **TwoBytes struc**, another as a plain word. This lets **ByteWord** variables function as double byte and word values, and it also lets TD display values in both of those ways.

After declaring the data types, the next step is to define a single variable of type **ByteWord**:

```
aByteWord        ByteWord        <,0FACEh>
```

Figure 22.13 demonstrates how TD skillfully displays the contents of this complex variable. The inspector window at top left shows the individual fields in **aByteWord** as two bytes (in ASCII) and as a single word value (in decimal and hex). Opening other inspector windows for these fields displays even more details about the separate byte and word values. To make the other two inspectors in the figure, I highlighted fields **asbytes** and **aswords** and pressed **⟨Enter⟩**. Notice that the inspectors show the same addresses for both fields, further proof that this is a **union** and not a common **struc**.

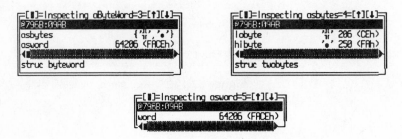

Figure 22.13. Inspecting a union variable and its fields.

Note: TD incorrectly displays a **union** as a **struc** (see top left window in Figure 22.13). Be aware of this problem—there isn't any way to tell the two data types apart in TD inspectors except by examining field addresses.

Records

Records in assembly language are not like records in a data base or in Pascal. An assembly language record is a collection of 8 or 16 bits packed into a byte or word, usually called *bit fields*. These are very useful devices for packing lots of information into tight spaces—and TD is a very useful tool for examining bit-field values. A quick look at a record in an inspector window instantly shows the values and positions of all defined fields.

An example demonstrates how to use TD to examine bit fields. First, declare a few constants:

```
MALE     EQU 0
FEMALE   EQU 1
YES      EQU 1
NO       EQU 0
```

Then, define a `RECORD` data type, listing the fields and their sizes in bits:

```
RECORD person sex:1,married:1,divorced:1,employed:1,children:4,age:7
```

The bits do not have to total exactly 8 or 16. Finally, create a variable of type `person` in a data segment:

```
aPerson  person  <FEMALE, NO, YES, YES, 3, 32>
```

You can then inspect `aPerson` or add it to the `Watches` view. Figure 22.14 shows how this looks in an inspector window opened to `aPerson` and another opened for the 4-bit field `children`.

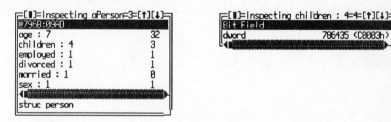

Figure 22.14. Inspecting a record's bit fields. (The value listed for the children bit field at right is not correct.)

As Figure 22.14 shows, each field in `aPerson` is listed in reverse declaration order. To check which bits are affected by modifications to individual bit fields, open a `Dump` window, press ⟨**Ctrl**⟩**-G**, and enter a record variable's name. This will show the byte or bytes assigned to the variable. Then, switch back to the inspector window and move the highlight bar to any field. (If you press ⟨**Enter**⟩ or ⟨**Ctrl**⟩**-I** at this time, another inspector opens for this field, as shown at right in Figure 22.14.) Next, type the new bit-field value and watch the `Dump` window. You'll see the byte value change. This test may be easier to perform if all fields are initially zero.

Note: As Figure 22.14 shows, TD displays individual bit fields as **dword** data types, but it does not list the correct values for extracted fields. Also, TD permits setting data breakpoints for bit-field identifiers, but those breakpoints do not work correctly. Perhaps these problems will be fixed in a later TD version. Until then, use the record's inspector (as shown at left in the figure) to view bit-field values and set breakpoints only for entire record variables, not selected fields.

Summary

This chapter is a reference to inspecting assembly language (MASM and TASM) data structures. Use the information in this chapter as a guide for investigating variables in your program.

Chapters 20 and 21 describe how to inspect common C, C + +, and Pascal data structures.

Bibliography

Companies and Products

Borland International, 1800 Green Hills Road, Scotts Valley, CA 95066, 408/438-5300, *Turbo Debugger and Tools 2.0* (includes *Turbo Debugger 2.0, Turbo Profiler 1.0, Turbo Assembler 2.0*); *Turbo C 2.0*; *Turbo C++ 1.0*; *Turbo Pascal 5.5.*

Compuserve Information Service, P. O. Box 20212, Columbus, OH 43220, 800/848-8199, *Compuserve.*

Intel Corporation, *iAPX 86/88, 186/188 User's Manual*; *80286 and 80287 Programmer's Reference Manual*; *80386 Programmer's Reference Manual*; *i486 Microprocessor Programmer's Reference Manual*, Box 58130, Santa Clara, CA 95052-8130, 800/548-4725.

Irata Systems, Inc., 2562 E Glade, Mesa, AZ 85204, 602/926-7969, *Irata Reset Switch.*

Microsoft Corporation, Box 97017, Redmond, WA 98073-9717, 206/882-8080, *Microsoft Macro Assembler 5.1, Microsoft C 5.1* and *6.0, Microsoft Windows 3.0*; *Microsoft Programmer's Library CD-ROM.*

Multisoft Corp., 15100 SW Koll Parkway, Beaverton, OR 97006, 800/274-5945, *PC-Kwik.*

Paradigm Systems, Inc., 3301 Country Club Road, Suite 2214, Endwell, NY 13760, 800/537-5043, 607/748-5966, *Locate.*

Periscope Company, Inc., 1197 Peachtree Street Plaza Level, Atlanta, GA 30361, 800/722-7006, *Periscope I, Periscope III.*

Phar Lap Software, Inc., 60 Aberdeen Avenue, Cambridge, MA 02138, 617/876-2972.

PKWare, Inc., 7545 N. Port Washington Rd., Glendale, WI 53217, 414/352-3670, *PkZIP*.

Purart, Inc., P. O. Box 189, Hampton Falls, NH, 603/772-9907, *Trapper*.

Qualitas, Inc., 7101 Wisconsin Ave. Suite 1386, Bethesda, MD, 20814, 301/907-6700, *386-Max*.

Quarterdeck Office Systems, 150 Pico Boulevard, Santa Monica, CA 90405, 213/392-9851, *Desqview*.

References

Duncan, Ray, *Advanced MS-DOS*, 1986, Microsoft Press, Redmond, WA.

Kernihan, Brian W. and Plauger, P. J., *The Elements of Programming Style*, 1978, McGraw-Hill, Reading MA.

Kerhihan, Brian W. and Ritchie, Dennis M., *The C Programming Language*, *2nd Ed.*, 1988, Prentice Hall, Englewood Cliffs, NJ.

Stroustrup, Bjarne, The *C++ Programming Language*, 1986, Addison-Wesley, Reading MA.

Swan, Tom, *Mastering Turbo Pascal 5.5*, 1989, Howard W. Sams, Carmel, IN.

Swan, Tom, *Mastering Turbo Assembler*, 1989, Howard W. Sams, Carmel, IN.

Ward, Robert, *Debugging C*, 1986, Que, Carmel, IN.

Index